SUNDAYS AND SEASONS

Sundays and Seasons

2009, Year B

Guide to Worship Planning

Related resources

Worship Planning Calendar, 2009, Year B (AFP 978-0-8066-7124-6)
Words for Worship, 2009, Year B (AFP 978-0-8066-7129-1)
Icon Three (AFP 978-0-8066-7020-1)

Acknowledgments

Annual materials

The Year of Mark: Elizabeth Struthers Malbon

Seasonal materials

Preparing for the Season: Stephen Crippen, Mary Mortimore Dossin, Joy McDonald-Coltvet, Steve Meysing, Clint Schnekloth
Celebrating the Season with Children: Lauren Wrightsman, Patricia Lundeen, Joy McDonald-Coltvet, Amanda Weitzel, Beth Olson
Seasonal Worship Texts: Rhoda Schuler, Paul Krampitz, Anne Edison-Albright, Ryan Mills, Blake Rohrer
Advent and Lent Preaching Series: Elsa Clark
Seasonal Rites: Carla Thompson Powell, Mark Molldrem, Valerie Hess, Roger Eigenfeld, Richard Bruxvoort-Colligan, Laurie Klein, Merlin Schlichting

Weekly materials

Introductions to the Day: Elaine Ramshaw, Craig Mueller
Introductions to the Readings: Kathryn Schifferdecker, Richard Carlson
Prayers of Intercession: Gwenn Bazajou, Jim Boline, Jim Drury, Paul Erickson, Jeffrey Louden, Anna Mercedes, Kristin Nygaard, Kevin Shock
Ideas and Images for the Day: Terry Bianchi, Mark Buchan, Eric Burtness, Roger Eigenfeld, Ann Hafften, Justin Lind-Ayres, Harry McDowell, Russell Meyer, Joel Nau, Christine Nessel, Monte Peterson, Linda Rose, John Saraka, Rebecca Schlatter, Dena Williams
Notes on Commemorations: The Church's Year, Renewing Worship, vol. 8 (Augsburg Fortress, 2004) pp. 12–41.

Music materials

Hymns for Worship: Cheryl Dieter
Psalmody: Augsburg Fortress staff
Choral: Zebulon Highben
Children's Choir: Carole Arenson
Keyboard/Instrumental: Arletta Anderson
Handbell: Donna Hanna
Praise Ensemble: Linda Holcombe, Craig Schweitzer
Global: Mary Preus

Development staff

Suzanne Burke, Norma Aamodt-Nelson, Carol Carver, Robert Buckley Farlee, Martin A. Seltz

Design

Art: Julie Lonneman
Book design: Laurie Ingram, Jessica Hillstrom

Editorial production

Jessica Hillstrom

Manufactured in Canada

1   2   3

978-0-8066-7123-9

Introduction

Advent

Christmas

Time after Epiphany

Lent

The Three Days

Easter

Time after Pentecost — Summer

Time after Pentecost — Autumn

Time after Pentecost — November

Index of Seasonal Rites

Lectionary Conversion Chart

Time after Pentecost, Year B, 2009

If today is . . .	. . . it falls within this date range.	The "lectionary" number assigned to this date range in Evangelical Lutheran Worship is . . .	. . . which is equivalent to "proper ____" in previous printed lectionaries.	In 2009, this Sunday is the "____ Sunday after Pentecost."
Sunday, June 14	Sunday between June 12 & 18 (if after Holy Trinity)	Lectionary 11	6	2nd
Sunday, June 21	Sunday between June 19 & 25 (if after Holy Trinity)	Lectionary 12	7	3rd
Sunday, June 28	Sunday between June 26 & July 2	Lectionary 13	8	4th
Sunday, July 5	Sunday between July 3 & 9	Lectionary 14	9	5th
Sunday, July 12	Sunday between July 10 & 16	Lectionary 15	10	6th
Sunday, July 19	Sunday between July 17 & 23	Lectionary 16	11	7th
Sunday, July 26	Sunday between July 24 & 30	Lectionary 17	12	8th
Sunday, August 2	Sunday between July 31 & Aug 6	Lectionary 18	13	9th
Sunday, August 9	Sunday between Aug 7 & 13	Lectionary 19	14	10th
Sunday, August 16	Sunday between Aug 14 & 20	Lectionary 20	15	11th
Sunday, August 23	Sunday between Aug 21 & 27	Lectionary 21	16	12th
Sunday, August 30	Sunday between Aug 28 & Sept 3	Lectionary 22	17	13th
Sunday, September 6	Sunday between Sept 4 & 10	Lectionary 23	18	14th
Sunday, September 13	Sunday between Sept 11 & 17	Lectionary 24	19	15th
Sunday, September 20	Sunday between Sept 18 & 24	Lectionary 25	20	16th
Sunday, September 27	Sunday between Sept 25 & Oct 1	Lectionary 26	21	17th
Sunday, October 4	Sunday between Oct 2 & 8	Lectionary 27	22	18th
Sunday, October 11	Sunday between Oct 9 & 15	Lectionary 28	23	19th
Sunday, October 18	Sunday between Oct 16 & 22	Lectionary 29	24	20th
Sunday, October 25	Sunday between Oct 23 & 29	Lectionary 30	25	21st
Sunday, November 1	Sunday between Oct 30 & Nov 5	Lectionary 31	26	22nd
Sunday, November 8	Sunday between Nov 6 & 12	Lectionary 32	27	23rd
Sunday, November 15	Sunday between Nov 13 & 19	Lectionary 33	28	24th
Christ the King, November 22	Sunday between Nov 20 & 26	Lectionary 34	29	Last

Lectionary Color Chart
Year B, 2009

Advent

Nov 30	First Sunday of Advent	Blue
Dec 7	Second Sunday of Advent	Blue
Dec 14	Third Sunday of Advent	Blue
Dec 21	Fourth Sunday of Advent	Blue

Christmas

Dec 24/25	Nativity of Our Lord	White
Dec 28	First Sunday of Christmas	White
Jan 4	Second Sunday of Christmas	White
Jan 6	Epiphany of Our Lord	White

Time after Epiphany

Jan 11	Baptism of Our Lord	White
Jan 18	Second Sunday after Epiphany	Green
Jan 25	Third Sunday after Epiphany	Green
Feb 1	Fourth Sunday after Epiphany	Green
Feb 8	Fifth Sunday after Epiphany	Green
Feb 15	Sixth Sunday after Epiphany	Green
Feb 22	Transfiguration of Our Lord	White

Lent

Feb 25	Ash Wednesday	Purple
Mar 1	First Sunday in Lent	Purple
Mar 8	Second Sunday in Lent	Purple
Mar 15	Third Sunday in Lent	Purple
Mar 22	Fourth Sunday in Lent	Purple
Mar 29	Fifth Sunday in Lent	Purple
Apr 5	Sunday of the Passion	Scarlet/Purple
Apr 6	Monday in Holy Week	Scarlet/Purple
Apr 7	Tuesday in Holy Week	Scarlet/Purple
Apr 8	Wednesday in Holy Week	Scarlet/Purple

Three Days

Apr 9	Maundy Thursday	Scarlet/White
Apr 10	Good Friday	None
Apr 11/12	Resurrection of Our Lord	White/Gold

Easter

Apr 19	Second Sunday of Easter	White
Apr 26	Third Sunday of Easter	White
May 3	Fourth Sunday of Easter	White
May 10	Fifth Sunday of Easter	White
May 17	Sixth Sunday of Easter	White
May 21	Ascension of Our Lord	White
May 24	Seventh Sunday of Easter	White

Time after Pentecost

May 31	Day of Pentecost	Red
June 7	The Holy Trinity	White
June 14	Lectionary 11	Green
June 21	Lectionary 12	Green
June 28	Lectionary 13	Green
July 5	Lectionary 14	Green
July 12	Lectionary 15	Green
July 19	Lectionary 16	Green
July 26	Lectionary 17	Green
Aug 2	Lectionary 18	Green
Aug 9	Lectionary 19	Green
Aug 16	Lectionary 20	Green
Aug 23	Lectionary 21	Green
Aug 30	Lectionary 22	Green
Sept 6	Lectionary 23	Green
Sept 13	Lectionary 24	Green
Sept 20	Lectionary 25	Green
Sept 27	Lectionary 26	Green
Oct 4	Lectionary 27	Green
Oct 11	Lectionary 28	Green
Oct 12	Day of Thanksgiving (Canada)	Green
Oct 18	Lectionary 29	Green
Oct 25	Reformation Sunday	Red
Oct 25	Lectionary 30	Green
Nov 1	All Saints Day	White
Nov 1	Lectionary 31	Green
Nov 8	Lectionary 32	Green
Nov 15	Lectionary 33	Green
Nov 22	Christ the King (Lect. 34)	White/Green
Nov 26	Day of Thanksgiving (USA)	Green

USER GUIDE

2009 Highlights
A Record Number of Contributors

This year's edition of *Sundays and Seasons* represents the work of 58 individual contributors. Pastors, associates in ministry, musicians, educators, artists, and laypeople from 27 states and Canada crafted prayers and other liturgical texts, contributed creative ideas for opening up the day's readings, compiled hymn suggestions and music listings, created images, and shared ideas for celebrating the seasons of the church year and the rhythms of congregational life with children, youth, and adults. Their work, offered out of various and varied contexts, is a gift to all worship planners and to the wider church. Contributors to this year's volume are listed on pp. 11–12. All of them deserve our thanks.

New Seasonal Rites

In response to user feedback, the majority of seasonal rites offered in the seasonal sections are new this year. You will find two options for recognizing and blessing graduates, a family Christmas Eve service outline, a commissioning and blessing of teachers, a new blessing of the animals service, a new order of blessing for a home (from the provisional *Evangelical Lutheran Worship* pastoral care volume), a gathering rite for All Saints Day, and much more. A complete index of seasonal rites contained in this volume appears on p. 7.

Evangelical Lutheran Worship

This year's edition continues to include the following content from *Evangelical Lutheran Worship*: the church year calendar of Sundays, lesser festivals, and commemorations; prayer of the day; psalm refrains; gospel acclamations; hymn suggestions; and references to service music and liturgies. The brief introductions to each day are drawn from *Indexes to Evangelical Lutheran Worship*.

Art

This year's edition continues to feature images by Cincinnati artist Julie Lonneman. Both black and white and colorized versions of these images for print and projection are available on the 2-CD set *Icon Three*, and for download at SundaysandSeasons.com. Julie's images will also be featured on the 2009 *Calendar of Word and Season*.

Other Helps

- The lectionary conversion chart for the time after Pentecost (p. 8) makes it easy to compare a day's Lectionary number (used in this volume), its Proper number (used in previous printed lectionaries), and its consecutively numbered Sunday after Pentecost in 2009.
- Reproduce the chart of each Sunday and festival's liturgical color (p. 9) for parish administrators, altar guilds, those who prepare worship folders, and those who attend to worship environment.
- New seasonal worship texts throughout the year.
- New worship series for Advent and Lent (pp. 23–24, 109–112).
- The music listings have been expanded to include a suggestion for each week's gospel acclamation and enhanced with additional information about praise ensemble music that is available online.
- "Ideas and Images for the Day" continues to offer an entry point to each Sunday and festival via the lectionary. A diverse collection of illustrative examples and suggestions amplify directions and themes in the texts and provide a springboard for worship planners of all kinds.
- "Preparing for the Season," a streamlined introduction to each season with attention to lectionary, music, and worship space, may be used for personal reflection or with a worship planning group. Reproduce it for educators, altar guilds, choirs, etc.

How can I get the most out of *Sundays and Seasons*?

- Read ahead. Know what is coming up.
- Know your "keys" (pp. 330–331). They will help you quickly decode the various music listings. Please note that OP stands for "out of print." Why do we occasionally list music if it is out of print? Primarily because many music planners may have that piece in the files, and can still consider it for use.
- Use the seasonal rites index (p. 7) and the worship helps in each seasonal section.

- Read through the list of resources on pp. 324–329. This list is refreshed and updated each year.
- Use *Sundays and Seasons* with a cross-functional team.
- Use the print volume in partnership with Sundaysand Seasons.com, our online worship planning tool. The online tool helps you create your weekly worship folder, and allows multiple worship planners to save information to a single location available anywhere, anytime, from any computer with Internet access. The print version is your indispensable desk reference and idea-generator. The online tool eases the weekly task of creating your worship folder.
- Submit your feedback (see "How can I help?" on p. 12).

Who can I thank for sharing their gifts via this resource?

Annual and Seasonal Materials

- Elsa L. Clark, pastor of St. Paul's Evangelical Lutheran, Drakes Mills, in Cambridge Springs, Pennsylvania (worship series for Advent and Lent)
- Richard Bruxvoort Colligan, minister of worship life at First Lutheran in Cedar Rapids, Iowa (Blessing of Graduates 2, Commissioning and Blessing of Teachers)
- Joy McDonald Coltvet, director of vocation and recruitment at the Lutheran School of Theology at Chicago (Preparing for Lent, Three Days; Celebrating with Children: Three Days, Easter)
- Stephen Crippen, Seattle, postulant for the Episcopal Church diaconate and private psychotherapist (Preparing for Advent, Christmas)
- Mary Mortimore Dossin, a writer and a member of Redeemer Lutheran in Plattsburgh, New York (Preparing for the Time after Epiphany, Summer)
- Anne Edison-Albright, an ordination-track student at Yale Divinity School (seasonal worship texts: Lent, Easter)
- Roger C. Eigenfeld, former senior pastor of St. Andrew's Lutheran in Mahtomedi, Minnesota (Blessing of Mothers, Fathers, and Graduates 1)
- Valerie E. Hess, author and coordinator of music ministries at Trinity Lutheran in Boulder, Colorado (Service for Saturday in Holy Week)
- Laurie Klein, free-lance writer, consulting editor of *Rock & Sling: A Journal of Literature, Art and Faith,* Deer Park, Washington (Blessing of Animals)
- Paul D. Krampitz, pastor of St. Andrew Evangelical Lutheran in Bristol, Connecticut (seasonal worship texts: Advent, Christmas, Time after Epiphany)
- Julie Lonneman, a free-lance illustrator living in Cincinnati, Ohio (art; more information in the back of the book)

- Patricia Lundeen, church musician in the Brainerd Lakes area of Minnesota (Celebrating with Children: Lent, Autumn)
- Elizabeth Struthers Malbon, professor of religious studies at Virginia Polytechnic Institute and State University (The Year of Mark)
- Steve Meysing, pastor of Holy Family Lutheran (ELCIC) in Yellowknife, Northwest Territories, Canada (Preparing for Easter, November)
- Ryan D. Mills, pastor of Our Redeemer Lutheran in Grand Prairie, Texas (seasonal worship texts: Summer)
- Mark J. Molldrem, pastor of First Evangelical Lutheran in Beaver Dam, Wisconsin (Lessons and Carols for Christmas, Volunteer Recognition)
- Beth A. Olson, an ELCA pastor, homemaker, and substitute teacher in Waverly, Iowa (Celebrating with Children: Time after Epiphany, November)
- Carla Thompson Powell, associate pastor of Ebenezer Lutheran in Chicago (Christmas Eve Family Service)
- Blake E. Rohrer, pastor at Midvale Community Lutheran in Madison, Wisconsin (seasonal worship texts: Autumn, November)
- Merlin Schlichting, pastor of St. Peter Lutheran in Dubuque, Iowa (All Saints Day gathering rite)
- Clint Schnekloth, pastor of East Koshkonong Lutheran in Cambridge, Wisconsin (Preparing for Autumn)
- Deaconess Rhoda Schuler, pro bono liturgist at Jehovah Lutheran in St. Paul, Minnesota (Advent wreath blessings)
- Amanda G. Weitzel, pastoral associate for middle school ministry at St. Philip the Deacon Lutheran in Plymouth, Minnesota (Celebrating with Children: Summer)
- Lauren J. Wrightsman, associate pastor of St. Andrew's Lutheran in Mahtomedi, Minnesota (Celebrating with Children: Advent, Christmas)

Day Materials

- Richard Carlson, professor of New Testament language, literature, and theology, Lutheran Theological Seminary at Gettysburg (New Testament reading introductions)
- Craig Mueller, pastor of Holy Trinity Lutheran in Chicago (introductions to the day)
- Elaine Ramshaw, a spiritual director who teaches pastoral care courses online from her home in Branford, Connecticut (introductions to the day)
- Kathryn Schifferdecker, assistant professor of Old Testament, Luther Seminary, St. Paul (Old Testament reading introductions)

Prayers of Intercession

- Gwenn A. Bazajou, pastor of New Hope Lutheran in Alvarado, Minnesota
- James E. Boline, pastor of St. Paul Lutheran in Santa Monica, California
- James Hugh Drury, pastor of historic Sitka Lutheran in Sitka, Alaska
- Paul D. Erickson, pastor of Augustana Lutheran in West St. Paul, Minnesota
- Jeffrey D. Louden, an ELCA pastor in Park City, Utah
- Anna Mercedes, instructor of theology and gender, College of Saint Benedict/Saint John's University, Collegeville, Minnesota
- Kristin Nygaard, staff member at Christ College, Valparaiso University, Indiana
- Kevin Shock, pastor of St. Mark Lutheran in Pleasant Gap, Pennsylvania

Ideas and Images for the Day

- Theresa Bianchi, chaplain at Elliot Hospital in Manchester, New Hampshire
- Mark Buchan, an ELCA pastor living in Columbia, South Carolina
- Eric Burtness, senior pastor of St. Matthew Lutheran in Beaverton, Oregon
- Roger C. Eigenfeld, former senior pastor of St. Andrew's Lutheran in Mahtomedi, Minnesota
- Ann Hafften, a free-lance writer, blogger, and activist for Middle East peace in Weatherford, Texas
- Justin Lind-Ayres, associate pastor of Good Shepherd Lutheran in Woodstock, Georgia
- Harry W. McDowell II, senior pastor of St. Paul's Lutheran in Ardmore, Pennsylvania
- Russell L. Meyer, Executive Director of the Florida Council of Churches
- Joel Nau, pastor, Lumen Episcopal/Lutheran Campus Ministry at the University of Utah in Salt Lake City
- Christine M. M. Nessel, wife, mom, and pastor of Salem Lutheran in Naugatuck, Connecticut
- Monte Peterson, a baker and lay minister in Hanover, New Hampshire
- Linda Rose, pastor of Emmanuel Lutheran in Shepherd, Montana
- John P. Saraka, pastor of Christ Ascension Lutheran in Philadelphia

- Rebecca L. Schlatter, associate pastor of Lutheran Church of the Good Shepherd in Reno, Nevada
- Dena Williams, pastor of King of Glory Lutheran in Arvada, Colorado

Hymn and Music Suggestions

- Arletta Anderson, associate in ministry and cantor at Queen Anne Lutheran in Seattle (keyboard/instrumental)
- Carole Lea Arenson, former director of music ministry at King of Glory Lutheran in Tempe, Arizona (children's choir)
- Cheryl Dieter, minister of worship and music at Trinity Lutheran in Valparaiso, Indiana (hymns)
- Donna Hanna, associate in ministry and associate minister of music at Christ Lutheran in Charlotte, North Carolina (handbell)
- Zebulon M. Highben, associate in ministry and choirmaster at Westwood Lutheran in St. Louis Park, Minnesota (choral)
- Linda R. Holcombe, Crossroads praise band leader at Christ Lutheran in Highlands Ranch, Colorado (praise ensemble)
- Mary Preus, director of music at Our Saviour's Lutheran and worship coordinator for the ecumenical Community of St. Martin in Minneapolis (global)
- Craig A. Schweitzer, music and worship minister at Good Shepherd Lutheran in Bismarck, North Dakota (praise ensemble)

How can I help?

The mission of *Sundays and Seasons* is to be useful to all who have responsibility for preparing the assembly's worship. In order to fulfill this mission, we need your feedback! What do you find most and least helpful, and what additional materials would you like to see covered in these pages? Interested in contributing to this resource? Let us know that, too. Thank you for your praise, encouragement, and suggestions for improvement over the past thirteen years. We will continue to work to meet your needs with the breadth of resources offered in each new edition of *Sundays and Seasons*.

—*Suzanne K. Burke, general editor*
burkes@augsburgfortress.org or 800.426.0115

THE YEAR OF MARK

The Gospel of Mark is not contemporary—it is ancient. Because readers continue to find Mark relevant, we sometimes forget that it was written in Greek, somewhere in the ancient Mediterranean world, around the year 70 of the Common Era. That was the year of the destruction of the Jewish temple in Jerusalem by the Romans, and many interpreters suggest that Mark's gospel was written in anticipation of or in response to that devastating event. Before this first-century text can speak to our world we must listen to its world. That world was an oral world—a world of anonymous storytellers and live audiences, not isolated authors and silent readers. I will follow ancient tradition in calling this gospel "Mark," but I will follow the lead of its teller in finding the story more important than the storyteller.

The Gospel of Mark is not the Gospel of Matthew—it is unique. Mark has dwelt in the shadow of Matthew for most of its life—since Augustine concluded in the fourth century that Mark must be a shortened version of Matthew. But since the eighteenth century most scholars have agreed that Matthew was more likely using Mark as a source. This makes Mark our oldest gospel, as far as we know the first document to combine stories of and about Jesus, from healings and teachings to his passion. Yet Mark still strikes some readers as incomplete. Lectionary readings in year B are sometimes drawn from other gospels because Mark has no "Christmas story"—neither shepherds (Luke) nor kings (Matthew). In addition, the "Easter story" in Mark (16:1-8) is stark—so challenging to hear that early interpreters made additions to it (16:9-20). Yet year B challenges us to read, hear, and preach Mark's gospel on its own terms, listening to the force of Mark's voice without harmonizing it with the other gospels.

The Gospel of Mark is not an objective account of the historical Jesus, and it is not a collection of theological affirmations about Jesus as the Christ. Mark is a gospel, good news of and about Jesus, told by the persuaded to be persuasive. And Mark is a story—a continuous narrative with settings, characters, plot, and rhetoric—a story with rich theological dimensions but in the form most frequent in the entire Bible—the story of God's people in conversation with God and those who speak for God. Here the challenge of year B is to keep this story going for a congregation through interruptions from other gospels and disjunctions in the lectionary readings from Mark. Mark's gospel is our shortest one, and its dramatic integrity invites—indeed demands—reading or hearing in one sitting at least once in year B. (See Elizabeth Struthers Malbon, *Hearing Mark: A Listener's Guide* [Trinity Press International, 2002].)

In this brief overview, perhaps one key term can serve to highlight both form and content central to Mark's gospel: juxtaposition. Mark's gospel is not known for smooth transitions but for dramatic contrasts in which settings jump from the synagogue to the sea, responses to Jesus shift between adulation and antagonism (with a good measure of misunderstanding), and actions follow actions "immediately" with few connections and little commentary. Narrative settings juxtapose Galilee, the scene of Jesus' deeds of power and strangely authoritative teaching, with Jerusalem, the scene of Jesus' passion; settings juxtapose the private and secular "house" with the public and religious "synagogue" and "temple." Character interaction juxtaposes three levels of conflict: the foundational but background cosmic struggle of God and Satan—and their respective representatives, Jesus and the demons and unclean spirits; the middle-ground conflict of authority between Jesus and the political, social, and religious establishment; and the often foregrounded human struggle for understanding between Jesus and his followers, both the twelve and a larger group of followers. The Markan storyteller employs the disciples as a rhetorical device to teach the audience what it means to follow this Jesus who proclaims and enacts the in-breaking of the rule (kingdom) of God.

The plot juxtaposes deeds of power and authoritative teaching that bring God's rule in the present age with service to the oppressed and suffering at the hands of the oppressors, deeds that challenge traditional understandings of power and authority. The Markan audience is challenged to hear these juxtapositions meaningfully: to consider the varied responses to Jesus in light of each other, to ponder Jesus' proclamation of God's rule in light of the status quo it challenges, to connect existentially the parables of the kingdom of the God and the passion of the Son of Humanity. Mark's gospel *is* a sermon, and it invites sermons to continue its trajectory of placing one event or teaching in juxtaposition with another to encourage thought and action. Mark's gospel offers no answers for passive readers but engages the audience in Jesus' struggle to understand and do the will of God and the disciples' struggle to understand and follow Jesus.

Mark's rhetoric is a rhetoric of juxtaposition. Sometimes juxtaposition involves two adjacent stories: by intercalation Mark places one story inside another for interpretive purposes; e.g., Jairus must have the faith of the woman who touches the hem of Jesus garment (5:22-24/25-34/35-43). Sometimes juxtaposition involves a cluster of stories: the conflict between Jesus and traditional religious leaders is presented in a concentric structure (2:1—3:6: healing legs/eating with the "wrong" people/eating instead of fasting/preparing food and eating on the wrong day/healing hand), highlighting the conflict of the "new" that cannot be contained by the "old" (2:21-22, at the center). (It is important to avoid the anachronistic—and even dangerous—reading of this conflict between the Jewish authorities and the Jewish Jesus as a conflict between "Judaism" and "Christianity"; rather, the juxtaposition portrays a prophetic conflict between practitioners and authorities that recurs in all religious and cultural traditions.)

Sometimes two passages at a distance are juxtaposed: the two longer speeches of the Markan Jesus stand out from the actions that surround them and are juxtaposed in content—the parables discourse of chapter 4 presenting the surprising blessings of God's rule in the present age and the eschatological discourse of chapter 13 revealing the challenges yet assurances of God in the transition to the age to come. The passion narrative exhibits a variety of juxtapositions in the form of irony: the juxtaposition of a surface meaning understood by the characters with a deeper meaning understood by the audience; think of the audience's understanding of the actions of the anointing woman (14:3-9), of Jesus' "I am" reply to the high priest (14:62), of the centurion's statement at the foot of the cross, "Truly this man was God's Son!" (15:39).

Sometimes a larger section of the narrative is woven together by repetition and juxtaposition. Mark 4:35—8:21 is punctuated by two parallel multiplication of loaves stories and three happenings on the sea—calming the sea, walking on the sea, and a climactic conversation on the sea about the loaves, focusing on the symbolic numbers 12 (Israel) and 7 (the nations). In the "way section" (8:22—10:52) Jesus predicts his passion and resurrection three times and teaches his disciples (and the Markan audience!) that the goal of the journey is to serve those with less power and authority than oneself, not to be served by others, to serve even at the risk of challenging those who hold power and authority in society. The "way section" is framed by two stories of healing of physical blindness that clearly image the difficulty of seeing and following a way that challenges the status quo. This "way section" serves as the transition between the two juxtaposed halves of Mark's gospel: 1-8, in Galilee, dominated by Jesus' powerful words and actions in inaugurating the rule of God, and 11-16, in Jerusalem, where the cost of participating in the rule of God, and thus challenging the rule of empire, is made manifest.

Thus juxtaposition is central to the gospel's theological affirmation of the paradox of the rule of God that has broken into history but does not dominate peoples; of the paradox of the ministry of Jesus as the Christ that manifests power in words and deeds but only as service, conquering only demonic forces and never human ones; and the paradox of the followers of Jesus, both within and beyond the narrative, who do not always understand but continue to struggle on the way of service rather than being served. Mark's gospel juxtaposes ways of understanding and acting with *exousia*, a Greek word that can be translated "power" or "authority." Mark's Jesus teaches with "authority" (1:27) and announces that his followers will see "the kingdom of God . . . come with power" (9:1), but not the authority of the traditional religious leaders of his day nor the power of the dominating political power of his day, the Roman Empire. To hear Mark's gospel, to preach Mark's gospel in this lectionary year B is to juxtapose this story of Jesus with our own stories as latter-day followers, rejoicing in the blessings of the rule of God in the present age but also living with the challenges of the transition to the new age, challenges that put us at odds with the status quo when we insist on serving rather than being served.

—*Elizabeth Struthers Malbon is Professor of Religious Studies at Virginia Polytechnic Institute and State University.*

ADVENT

Preparing for Advent

"All Earth Is Hopeful . . ."

"The time is fulfilled, and the kingdom of God has come near; repent, and believe in the good news" (Mark 1:15). Jesus, speaking for the first time in Mark's gospel, offers us this startling message.

The scholar Thomas Cahill, in his book *Desire of the Everlasting Hills*, translates this phrase: "The time has come: the kingdom of God draws near. Open your hearts and believe the good news." Cahill explains: "The 'Time' that has come is the time of the fulfillment of Jewish dreams, the time when God will show his special love for the Jews by breaking the bonds of their servitude and exalting them among the nations. It is the time they have been waiting for—waiting so long that they had almost ceased to believe that it could ever come to pass. . . . They are invited to shake off their worldly preoccupations and 'open [their] hearts.' The Greek imperative is *metanoeite*, which means literally 'change your minds'" (New York: Doubleday, 1999, p. 69).

Christians today, hearing these words, understand that Jesus is speaking not just to his Jewish contemporaries, but also to all who are willing to listen in our own place and time. But what an extraordinary thing for him to say! "The kingdom of God draws near." "Believe the good news." Really? Really?! No wonder the season of Advent offers as its climactic story the unexpected news of a pregnancy brought to a young girl, news from out of the blue, news wholly unexpected, and news not entirely welcome. I'm pregnant? Really? Really?!

Mary recovers, as we know, from her initial shock and goes on to sing her great song of rejoicing, the Magnificat, sung by many of us, her sisters and brothers in the faith, on the fourth Sunday of Advent in place of the appointed psalm. But that shock—receiving good, yet unsettling, news—that shock is also something we share with Mary. For this message of Jesus is not just glad tidings of hope for a weary and war-torn world; it also is a calling, an invitation to turn from our "worldly preoccupations" and "open our hearts." Something from us, then, is required. We're going to have to step up, get to work, prepare, watch, wait, turn, open, change.

And so we begin our journey once more around the great circle of the Christian year: Advent has come again.

Advent is a joyful season. It is a time of hope amid crisis, light in deep darkness, a growing sense of expectation, a growing trust in the promises of God. Advent offers an optimistic outlook: a way of looking at the world and our troubled human problems that may seem senseless at first. "Do not be afraid," the angel tells Mary. A nervous mother listens to the hopes of her heart. A prophet stirs people to action, encourages their expectation of a coming age of justice and peace. Wake up! The news will be good, even if, like the Judeans of Jesus' time, we have "almost ceased to believe that it could ever come to pass."

"Furrows, Be Glad. Though Earth Is Bare . . ."

Our worship during the season of Advent should be an expression of this tension: we are soberly watching, waiting, and preparing for God's coming reign of justice and peace; yet we are more and more hopeful, excited, even joyous as we see that reign come to pass in our own place and time.

The gathering and sending rites in the Sunday liturgy can speak to this tension by using joyful or stirring Advent music and proper prayers and texts, but choose them carefully, balancing them with silence, keeping things simple. The hymn of praise is not used, making its return on Christmas Eve in the angels' "Gloria!" all the more exciting. Consider lighting the Advent wreath before the liturgy begins, rather than weighing down the gathering rite with a lighting ceremony that could get complicated by the awkwardness of lighting an overhead wreath. The sending can be simpler still: you may omit the sending hymn and/or postlude, underscoring the solemnity of the season with a silent recessional. Or you could sing with minimal or no accompaniment, or with the simple accompaniment of handbells, particularly on well-known hymns and chants.

Like Lent, Advent is a season in which the rule "less is more" applies to environment and art. Hold to two or three colors: green (wreaths, garlands), white (candles), and deep blue (elegant fabrics on the altar and pulpit). As the season continues, parishioners may notice small additions you're making to the evergreen arrangements. Were those undecorated evergreen trees there last week? Resist the urge to light electric white lights until Christmas Eve, when the blaze of light will be most striking.

"Shine Your Future on This Place . . ."

Advent is a good season to support and develop the health and life of the congregation. This is a perfect time to encourage more activity in the area of arts and music. Some congregations find that during times of growth and renewal there are more people interested in participating in artistic events, and these events in turn contribute to further growth and renewal of the whole parish. You may have adults who want to work on an Advent play to be performed by adults and children alike, and you may have writers in your midst who would write a new work to perform! During a month of so many holiday concerts and events, you might need to be creative about when you hold music concerts or plays: short performances could be given after coffee hour on a Sunday, for example, or in the late morning on a Saturday.

In addition to the arts and music, you could further develop your parish's participation in other spiritual practices and activities that are new to them: you could hold an Advent Quiet Morning in which one or two members (or clergy and staff) intersperse long periods of silence and reflection with poetry readings or discussion about a timely issue (the meaning of Advent, how Jesus is portrayed in Mark's gospel, grief and hope in this time of year, etc.). Finish the morning with a simple lunch.

"Each Winter As the Year Grows Older . . ."

Children and adults alike enjoy keeping time during the season with a (tasteful) Advent calendar. Some parishes have made their own out of wood or other simple materials.

Rather than making an Advent calendar with doors for each day of Advent, you could make an "Incarnation Calendar" for weekly/seasonal parish use, with doors for each Sunday of Advent, Christmas Eve and Day, the Sundays after Christmas, and Epiphany. When constructing the calendar, think big: create a large and well-constructed shelf of compartments. Every Sunday, at coffee hour, the door for that day is opened. Behind each door, children would find coloring sheets or other art activities that help them more fully hear and understand the themes of the week and season. Adults would find handouts with table prayers, house blessings, and suggested activities for the week. And if you know a good visual artist, invite that person to decorate the doors to add more color and interest to the calendar and reflect (yet again) that day's readings. You could also invite children to create the art that is placed on the doors.

"He Comes, the Broken Heart to Bind . . ."

Through all your Advent activities, remain mindful of the deeper political implications of the "good news" announced by Jesus Christ. This is a season when a congregation would do well to reinvest in the ministries it offers to the surrounding community year-round. This is the season to hear most clearly the cry of the poor and to deepen and develop the parish's answer to that cry. Amid the crush of anxious Christmas commercialism, the simple tasks parishioners are already doing in behalf of their neighbors in need is a cause for celebration, a sign that God's intentions for humanity and the world are being realized right here, right now.

Celebrating Advent with Children

With Advent, we begin our celebrations and welcome a new year of Christ's presence among us. The Christian calendar is quite different from the worldly calendar or that of the school year, and it is important to help children and their families recognize the differences among the calendars. While many cultures are winding down the year and looking forward to the Christmas and New Year's celebrations, it is important to remind ourselves that as Christians we walk in the world but are not *of* the world. The celebration of Advent is a perfect way to bring these lessons home to children as our church year begins.

During these four weeks we hear the prophecies of old foretelling Christ's birth. We are encouraged, through the words of the Bible and the songs sung, to remember the words found in the Gospel of John 1:1-4, "In the beginning was the Word, and the Word was with God, and the Word was God. He was in the beginning with God. All things came into being through him, and without him not one thing came into being. What has come into being in him was life, and the life was the light of all people."

Enjoy this time of spiritual awakening as we are renewed by Christ's birth and hope for his coming among us!

Ideas for Advent

- Many churches follow the tradition in the season of Advent of lighting a candle on their Advent wreath. Have children and their families come forward during the gathering song, during the gospel reading, before the sermon, or at another place during worship to light the candle for the week.
- In addition to having the Advent candle lit, have a "Living Advent Nativity" at your church. The backdrop can be a simple empty manger. Each Sunday different children, dressed as the character, are added to the scene. When the Advent candle is lit, have children come forward as the following characters. Add a character to the nativity each Sunday:
  Advent 1: the angel—symbolizing the hope of creation in greeting the Savior.
  Advent 2: the shepherds—symbolizing our need for forgiveness.
  Advent 3: the magi—symbolizing our constant searching for the Savior.
  Advent 4: Mary—symbolizing our waiting in expectation for the Savior to come.
- Have children write "What I Wish for Christmas . . . ," focusing on the themes listed above for Advent 1–4. Invite a few children to read their wish lists in worship (practice ahead of time) or publish them in your Sunday bulletin week-by-week.
- Advent comes from the Latin word *adventus*, meaning to visit, come, or arrive. Children are, of course, excited about the arrival of their gifts—but Advent is a time of waiting for the gift of Jesus Christ. Wrap five boxes inside one another during this time. At each Advent service, have a child come forward to unwrap the gift. Each Sunday brings a new surprise to hang on the Christmas tree in your place of worship and a gift to be unwrapped at the next Sunday service. Some ideas:
  Advent 1: an angel
  Advent 2: a shepherd's crook or a lamb
  Advent 3: a star
  Advent 4: an empty manger, or an ornament depicting a pregnant Mary.
  If you carry this over into Christmas, a child can unwrap the last gift, Jesus Christ—either a small baby or a cross—on Christmas Eve or Day.
- Many visitors come to places of worship during Advent. Have the children write "Welcome" cards to visitors along with their artwork. Mail them to all visitors who come to you during the season of Advent along with your Christmas Eve/Day schedule.
- Encourage worshipers, especially the children, to wear blue to worship during Advent. Deep blue reflects the changing sky during this season and symbolizes hope.
- Host an Advent Fair at the beginning of Advent for all generations to come together to make and create Advent decorations for their home. Pair older families with younger ones. Suggestions: an Advent wreath for the home, ornaments following the Advent themes listed above, and Advent calendars.

Worship Helps for Advent

Advent Checklist

- Order candles and greens for the Advent wreath. Perhaps more than one wreath will be desired for your congregation if Sunday school students and other groups gather for worship during the season in locations other than the worship space.
- Arrange a day and time before the first Sunday of Advent (Nov. 30) to place the Advent wreath and any seasonal decorations. Plan a subsequent day and time to decorate for Christmas, and solicit volunteer help.
- Look ahead to the checklist on p. 43 as you plan for Christmas and the Epiphany of Our Lord.

Shape of the Communion Liturgy

- See the seasonal worship texts for Advent on pp. 20–21.
- Use the Kyrie. Omit the hymn of praise.
- Use the Nicene Creed.

- See the prayers of intercession for each Sunday of Advent.
- Use the proper preface for Advent (*Evangelical Lutheran Worship* Leaders Edition, p. 181).
- Thanksgiving at the table: see options in *Evangelical Lutheran Worship*, especially Prayer III (Pew Edition, p. 110; Leaders Edition, p. 196); *WOV*, Prayer A (Leaders Edition, p. 65).

Other Helps

- See the suggestions for music and worship space in the essay "Preparing for Advent," pp. 16–17.
- See the Advent wreath blessings on p. 22.
- See the Advent worship series in the seasonal rites section (pp. 23–24).

SEASONAL WORSHIP TEXTS FOR ADVENT

Confession and Forgiveness

All may make the sign of the cross, the sign that is marked at baptism, as the presiding minister begins.

Blessed be the holy Trinity, ☩ one God,
who is the light and life of all the ages.
Amen.

Trusting in Jesus Christ,
who came to share our humanity
and bring light to this broken world,
let us come before God without fear to make our confession.

Silence is kept for reflection.

Comforting God,
**we confess before you and in the presence of one another
that we are sinners who fail to live as you desire.
So often we place our trust in ourselves and not in you.
We do not love each other as you have commanded.
Because of us, your whole creation suffers.
For the sake of your Son, Jesus Christ, forgive us.
In your boundless patience and mercy,
lead us to live by faith in your promise.**
Amen.

God's love for us is greater than all our sins.
God promises full pardon and complete forgiveness
to all who turn from sin
and place their trust in Christ, the light of the world.
Hear and believe the good news that all your sins are forgiven.
With God nothing is impossible.
Amen.

Greeting

Grace and peace be with you in the name of the Triune God,
who was, who is, and who is to come.
And also with you.

Offering Prayer

God of faithfulness,
we bring before you the precious gifts of your creation,
and with them our very lives.
Teach us patience and hope as we care for those in need
and prepare for your Son's advent into our hearts.
Amen.

Invitation to Communion

Come, the table is ready.
These are God's gifts for God's people.

Prayer after Communion

God for whom we wait,
we give you thanks for this meal of life
that you have set before us.
May our sharing of this heavenly food,
in which you are present even now,
nourish our faith, strengthen us for service,
and deepen our hunger for the coming of your reign
on earth as in heaven.
Amen.

Sending of Communion

Compassionate God,
you sent forth prophets
to bring good news to the oppressed,
to bind up the brokenhearted,
to proclaim release to the prisoners,
and to comfort all who mourn.
Bless those who go forth from this assembly
bearing your word and sacrament.
Nourish and strengthen all who share in this communion,
that this foretaste of your coming
will bring hope and comfort,
in the name of Jesus Christ our Lord.
Amen.

Blessing

God our Father fill you with the light of divine love.
Amen.
Jesus, our Emmanuel, bring you assurance
he will come again.
Amen.
The Holy Spirit lead you until the dawning of the new day.
Amen.
Almighty God, Father, ✛ Son, and Holy Spirit,
bless you now and forever.
Amen.

Dismissal

Go in peace. Christ is with you.
Thanks be to God.

SEASONAL RITES FOR ADVENT

Blessing of the Advent Wreath
First Sunday of Advent

Holy are you, God of power and glory;
you promised to make your mighty presence known
among the nations,
and to strengthen your people to the end,
when Christ will come in clouds to gather his people.
As we light this candle,
open our eyes to see the sin
that separates us from you and from one another,
and restore us again, that we may be blameless
on the day of our Lord Jesus Christ.
Stir up your might and come to save us.
Reveal your face to us, and give us life. Amen.

Light one candle.

Second Sunday of Advent

Holy are you, God of righteousness and peace;
you promised to wait with patience
for all to come to repentance,
and to send your prophet to cry in the wilderness
to prepare the way of the Lord.
As we light these candles,
open our ears to hear you speak tenderly to your people;
open our hearts to welcome you as a shepherd
who gently leads the flock.
Comfort us, O God, and forgive the sin of your people.
**Reveal your glory to us,
and speak to us your word of peace. Amen.**

Light two candles.

Third Sunday of Advent

Holy are you, God of the brokenhearted and oppressed;
you promised to send your chosen one
who gives a garland instead of ashes to those who mourn;
who brings down the powerful and lifts the lowly.
As we light these candles,
open our lips to testify to the true light
coming into the world who enlightens everyone.
Restore our fortunes, O Lord, like streams in the desert.
**Reveal your truth to us,
and fill our mouths with shouts of joy
that declare the great things you have done for us.
Amen.**

Light three candles.

Fourth Sunday of Advent

Holy are you, God of steadfast love and faithfulness;
you promised to make a covenant with your chosen ones,
and to establish the throne of your servant David forever.
As we light these candles,
open our hearts to the mystery of the incarnation
revealed to your servant Mary,
and plant your word in us that it may grow and prosper.
Show us your favor, O Rock of our salvation.
**Reveal your love to us, and strengthen us
for service in your name. Amen.**

Light four candles.

Blessing of the Christmas Tree

See page 46.

Christ Is Coming—Prepare!
An Advent Worship Series

Advent is a time of anticipation. For there to be anticipation there must be something or someone coming. Anticipation doesn't take place in a vacuum, though. We don't just feel or think anticipation; we live it. In other words, when we anticipate a coming, we prepare. During this Advent we live in anticipation of the final coming of Christ by pleading, preparing, proclaiming, and participating in his coming.

This four-week series is based on the Revised Common Lectionary readings for Advent, year B (see pp. 27, 30, 33, and 36 for reading citations). It may be used for Sunday worship or for a midweek gathering during Advent.

The series might be briefly introduced the week before Advent begins, on Christ the King Sunday (Nov. 23), by pointing out that the one who is coming is not Santa Claus or some casual visitor, but Jesus Christ, the King of kings.

Advent 1: Plead for the Coming

Whether an exile in Babylon, a convert in a pagan culture, or a disciple concerned with the end of the world, God's people plead for God to end their human suffering. In our sin and human limitation we long to be with God.

In the reading from Isaiah we hear of Israel's temporality and sin, and how the prophet begged for restoration. In the psalm, the people plead for God's anger to abate and for restoration of relationship with God. In 1 Corinthians we are assured that by God's grace we will be given all we need to endure until we are restored to full fellowship with Christ. The gospel speaks of the impossibility of knowing when Christ's coming will take place, and reminds us of the need to be alert. Taken together, the preacher could remind people that no matter what their situation today, a greater day is coming, and they need to be ready.

Some ideas for involving the congregation:
- Create a calendar of prayer concerns that highlight reasons we long for Christ's coming (for example, sickness, war, poverty, broken relationships).

- Give the children Advent calendars and explain their meaning and purpose.
- Make a "To Do" list to help people get ready for Christ's coming at Christmas and beyond. These could be daily, weekly, or unspecified-time tasks such as praying for those without a church home, putting money aside for a special offering, or inviting someone to Christmas Eve worship.
- Print reflection questions on one of the day's readings or this week's theme in the bulletin.

Advent 2: Prepare for the Coming

The word *prepare* is stated or implied in all three of the readings for this day. Isaiah calls for the way to be prepared for God, who will lead the people from exile. Second Peter warns believers that they need to be prepared for the second coming at all times, because no one knows when the Lord will return. In the gospel, we see how John the Baptist helped the people prepare through repentance and baptism. Even the psalm implies preparation, as the psalmist expresses a desire to hear God's word of salvation.

Some ideas for involving the congregation:
- For a children's message show a first-aid kit and explain its use, then bring out a kit for being prepared for Christ's coming: a cross to remind us of our sins and God's forgiveness, a band bracelet (like people wear for their favorite cause) to remind us that we belong to Jesus, a Bible for instruction on wound care, etc.
- Have Sunday school children decorate bookmarks with the word PREPARE and the gospel reading citation, and distribute them to worshipers for use in their Bibles at home.
- Print reflection questions on one of the day's readings or this week's theme in the bulletin.

Advent 3: Proclaim the Coming

Simply reading today's texts stirs up the spirit. Isaiah urges us to recount all that God has done and announce the good news to all who need to hear it. This urging is echoed in Mary's song of praise (the alternate psalmody from Luke 1), also called the Magnificat. New Testament people are exhorted to rejoice and pray constantly, thus obeying God's will in Christ. Then, with prophetic passion, John the Baptist proclaims in the gospel that the Messiah has come. It hardly seems necessary to preach after these readings. By themselves they should be enough to make people get to their feet singing God's praise and moving out into the world to share the good news. So why are they still in their seats? Maybe the day's sermon should ask them.

Some ideas for involving the congregation:

- For a children's message, give the children signs that say JESUS IS COMING. Lead them in a procession around the church as everyone sings "Hark, the glad sound!" (ELW 239, LBW 35) or "He came down" (ELW 253, TFF 37).
- Hang a banner (could be a sheet or tablecloth) with the same message outside your church.
- Print business card-sized announcements of Christ's coming along with your church's name and its Christmas worship schedule. Give several to each member, with instructions to leave a card where someone in the community will find it (on the table after a meal out, on a community bulletin board, as a bookmark in a popular book at the library, etc.).
- Print reflection questions on one of the day's readings or this week's theme in the bulletin.

Advent 4: Participate in the Coming

Today's texts show that faith is participatory. The covenant between God and the people of Israel provided a framework for doing God's will, a means of participation. The reading from Romans declares that even the Gentiles were invited to participate in the event of Jesus' coming. The gospel reveals that God invites participation from the lowliest and most unsuspecting of people—a young girl in a little-known town. A sermon could explore the ways that God invites us to participate in Christ's coming at Christmas and beyond.

Some ideas for involving the congregation:

- For a children's message, talk about the gospel reading and how God might ask the children to participate in celebrating Jesus' coming. Then distribute materials for making a simple angel that can be hung on a Christmas tree or placed somewhere it will remind the children that they too are invited to participate in celebrating the coming of Christ.
- Invite people to meditate on how they may be called to participate in Christ's coming.
- Angels in the Bible are messengers of God. Ask people to identify who in their lives has been a messenger of God, and then to write a thank-you note to this person (even if the person is no longer alive).
- Mary is the unexpected bearer of God's gift of Jesus. This week give a small gift to someone who would least expect it from you.

Lessons and Carols for Advent
(Based on the O Antiphons)

The O Antiphons are a set of medieval refrains originally used before and after the singing of the Magnificat. They were in use already in the eighth century. Each invokes the Messiah under a different title derived from the Old Testament. This title is then amplified and followed by an appeal to "come" and save us in a particular way. Around the twelfth century, they were collected into a Latin verse hymn, which was later translated by John Mason Neale, finally becoming the beloved Advent hymn "O come, O come, Emmanuel" (ELW 257, LBW 34). (The version in Evangelical Lutheran Worship restores two original stanzas that were omitted in the LBW version.) These antiphons form the structure of this service. They are pointed for chanting, or they may be spoken. The corresponding stanza of "O come, O come, Emmanuel" is sung after each antiphon.

Gathering Song

Hark, the glad sound!   ELW 239, LBW 35
Fling wide the door   ELW 259, LBW 32
Wait for the Lord   ELW 262

Dialogue

Blessed is the king who comes in the name of the Lord.
Peace in heaven, and glory in the highest heaven!
I will hear what the Lord God has to say—
a voice that speaks for peace.
Peace for all faithful people
and those who turn to him in their hearts.
God's help is near for those who fear him,
that his glory may dwell in our land.
Blessed is the king who comes in the name of the Lord.
Peace in heaven, and glory in the highest heaven!

Opening Prayer

The Lord be with you.
And also with you.
Let us pray.
Gracious God, through the ages you have sent your promise to your people in many ways, through many voices. But in these last days, your Son has come to bring it among us in person. Through your Spirit, prepare our hearts to recognize him in his many forms, and to receive him as our Lord and Savior.
Amen.

Lessons and Carols

Antiphon

O Wisdom,
proceeding from the mouth of the Most High,
pervading and permeating all creation,
mightily order- ˡ ing all things:
    Come and teach us the ˡ way of prudence.
Hymn stanza: O come, O Wisdom   ELW 257, st. 2
Lesson: Isaiah 40:3-5
Carol: Comfort, comfort now my people   ELW 256, LBW 29

Antiphon

O Adonai and ruler of the house of Israel,
who appeared to Moses in the burning bush
and gave him the ˡ Law on Sinai:
    Come with an outstretched arm ˡ and redeem us.
Hymn stanza: O come, O Lord of might   ELW 257, st. 3;
LBW 34, st. 2
Lesson: Exodus 6:2-7a
Carol: Come, thou long-expected Jesus   ELW 254, LBW 30

Antiphon

O Root of Jesse,
standing as an ensign before the peoples,
before whom all kings are mute,
to whom the nations ⎸ will do homage:
   Come quickly to de- ⎸ liver us.
Hymn stanza: O come, O Branch of Jesse   ELW 257, st. 4;
   LBW 34, st. 3
Lesson: Isaiah 11:1-10
Carol: Lo, how a rose e'er blooming   ELW 272, LBW 58

Antiphon

O Key of David and scepter of the house of Israel,
you open and no one can close,
you close and no ⎸ one can open:
   Come and rescue the prisoners
   who are in darkness and the shad- ⎸ ow of death.
Hymn stanza: O come, O Key of David   ELW 257, st. 5;
   LBW 34, st. 5
Lesson: Isaiah 42:5-9
Carol: O Lord, how shall I meet you   ELW 241, LBW 23

Antiphon

O Dayspring,
splendor of light ⎸ everlasting:
   Come and enlighten those who sit in darkness
   and in the shad- ⎸ ow of death.
Hymn stanza: O come, O Dayspring   ELW 257, st. 6;
   LBW 34, st. 4
Lesson: Luke 1:68-79
Carol: As the dark awaits the dawn   ELW 261

Antiphon

O King of the nations, the ruler they long for,
the cornerstone unit- ⎸ ing all people:
   Come and save us all,
   whom you formed ⎸ out of clay.
Hymn stanza: O come, O King of nations   ELW 257, st. 7
Lesson: Isaiah 35:4-7a
Carol: Savior of the nations, come   ELW 263, LBW 28

Antiphon

O Emmanuel, our king and our lawgiver,
the anointed of the nations ⎸ and their Savior:
   Come and save us, ⎸ Lord our God.
Hymn stanza: O come, O come, Emmanuel   ELW 257, st. 1;
   LBW 34, st. 1
Lesson: Isaiah 7:14
Carol: Awake! Awake, and greet the new morn   ELW 242,
   WOV 633

Responsive Prayer

Our world stumbles blindly toward chaos—
come and be our Wisdom.
What we imagine to be strength is really weakness—
come and be our mighty Lord.
We yearn for a standard to look up to—
come and be our Root of Jesse.
We languish in prisons of mind and spirit—
come and be our Key of David.
The darkness grows thick around us—
come and be our Light of day.
We are scattered, lacking a sure leader—
come and be our King of peace.
We need to know that God is with us—
**come and be our Emmanuel, that we may rejoice in you.
Amen.**

Lord's Prayer

Blessing and Dismissal

Let us bless the Lord.
Thanks be to God.
In our Savior Christ, God is with us.
Almighty God, Father, ✚ Son, and Holy Spirit,
bless you now and forever.
Amen.

Sending Song

Rejoice, rejoice believers   ELW 244, LBW 25
People, look east   ELW 248, WOV 626

November 30, 2008
First Sunday of Advent

Stir up your power, and come! The psalmist's plea in Psalm 80:2 has become familiar to us in the Advent prayers. Isaiah wants God to rip the heavens open. Both cry out for an apparently distant, angry God to show up, to save, to restore. When we hear Jesus describing the coming of the Son of Man with stars falling from heaven, it can sound dire and horrible, not like anything we would ever hope for. But when we really look at the suffering of people God loves, we can share the hope that God would tear open the heavens and come.

The observance of the festival of Andrew, apostle, is transferred this year to December 1.

Prayer of the Day

Stir up your power, Lord Christ, and come. By your merciful protection awaken us to the threatening dangers of our sins, and keep us blameless until the coming of your new day, for you live and reign with the Father and the Holy Spirit, one God, now and forever.

Gospel Acclamation

Alleluia. Show us your steadfast | love, O LORD,*
and grant us | your salvation. *Alleluia.* (Ps. 85:7)

Readings and Psalm

Isaiah 64:1-9

This lament comes from a people who have had their hopes shattered. The visions of a rebuilt Jerusalem and a renewed people of God, spoken of in Isaiah 40–55, have not been realized. Instead, the people experience ruin, conflict, and famine. This lament calls God to account—to be the God who has brought deliverance in the past.

Psalm 80:1-7, 17-19

Let your face shine upon us, and we shall be saved. (Ps. 80:7)

1 Corinthians 1:3-9

As the Christians in Corinth await the advent of Jesus, Paul reminds them how the Lord has already enriched them through spiritual gifts and will continue to strengthen them until the coming day of the Lord.

Mark 13:24-37

In today's reading, Jesus encourages his followers to look forward to the day when he returns in power and glory to end all suffering.

Color   Blue

CD-ROM Images

Icon Three: Advent1_B
Icon Two: Advent1_B
Icon: 067

Prayers of Intercession

In hope and expectation, let us pray for restoration and peace, light and life.
A brief silence.
Come down, O God, and give life to the nations of the world, that where there is strife and warfare, your peace will prevail, and where there is hatred and mistrust, your presence will restore. Stir up your power, O God;
stir up your power and come.
Come down, O God, and give life to your church. Let the light of your holy word awaken your people to deeds of love and mercy, that all may know you are near.
Stir up your power, O God;
stir up your power and come.
Come down, O God, and give life to creation. May your handiwork in the heavens and the earth proclaim your glory even as we your creatures care for all that you have made.
Stir up your power, O God;
stir up your power and come.
Come down, O God, and give life to those who live in fear. For those whose strength is fading, who cannot sleep, and who struggle with chronic pain, draw near with your healing light. Stir up your power, O God;
stir up your power and come.
Come down, O God, and give life to the ministries of this congregation. Keep us alert to the needs of the community beyond these walls, that with thankful hearts we would be strengthened to serve anyone in any need.
Stir up your power, O God;
stir up your power and come.

Here other intercessions may be offered.

Come down, O God, and give life to all who grieve. Comfort those whose sorrows are deep, and reveal yourself to them through the care of friends and neighbors, that with *(Andrew your apostle and)* all the saints we may all be gathered at your table of eternal grace.
Stir up your power, O God;
stir up your power and come.
You are with us, O God, and our spirits rejoice in your goodness, through Jesus Christ, our Savior.
Amen.

Ideas and Images for the Day

Advent is a time when we look again and anew at how our lives today are tied to both the past and the future of God's presence with God's people. We are drawn, in a heightened way, into the meaning of God's coming to us and being present with us. This image of a God who draws near is at once terrifying and delightful, humbling and hopeful. In Isaiah, we cry to God to rend the heavens and come; the psalmist calls on God to restore our fortunes; the community in Corinth waits for Christ to be revealed; and Mark's "little apocalypse" helps us understand the birth pangs of the world around us. We are drawn into God's presence in baptism, freed from sin and death by being joined to the death and resurrection of our Lord Jesus Christ.

1. In the final scene of the film *She's Having a Baby* (Paramount, 1988), Kristen (Elizabeth McGovern) is giving birth to their first child, while the father, Jefferson (Kevin Bacon), waits anxiously in the hospital waiting room. There have been complications during the pregnancy, which adds tension to the birth by fusing it with the possibility of death. It is a time of remembrance, reflection, prayer, a time of connection between the anxiety of the present moment and the hope of what will be. How might we connect our cycles of life to this season of Advent and see in God's presence and coming God in the midst of our birth and death?

2. When you drive cross-country you may run into all types of weather. It is not uncommon to move from clear blue skies to a torrential downpour in moments. The heavens seem torn open. In these times of heavy rain, one's focus becomes sharper, you grip the wheel a little tighter, you look to the skies to see if you will drive out of the danger soon. Advent can be a time when we reflect upon the heavens opening up before us. We are filled with the presence of God, which can be both terrifying and nourishing. The rains that cause our tensions also cause us to grip our faith tighter and are the rains that feed new growth.

3. Martin Luther said, "Our Lord has written the promise of resurrection, not in books alone, but in every leaf in springtime." The fig tree of Mark's gospel helps us to see that in the new life of the branches of the tree we also remember that the end time is near. The seasons are brought together. In the tender branches and sprouting leaves we see the rugged cross. In the approaching infant Jesus we see the new life of the world, found in the life, death, and resurrection of Christ.

Hymns for Worship
Gathering
Awake! Awake, and greet the new morn   ELW 242, WOV 633
God the sculptor of the mountains   ELW 736
Each winter as the year grows older   ELW 252, WOV 628

Hymn of the Day
Lo! he comes with clouds descending   ELW 435, LBW 27   *HELMSLEY*
Wake, awake, for night is flying ELW 436, LBW 31   *WACHET AUF*
The King shall come   ELW 260, LBW 33   *CONSOLATION*

Communion
My Lord, what a morning   ELW 438, WOV 627
As the dark awaits the dawn   ELW 261

Sending
Hark! a thrilling voice is sounding!   ELW 246, LBW 37
O Lord, how shall I meet you   ELW 241, LBW 23

Additional Hymns and Songs
We light the Advent candles (sts. 1, 2)   LS 9
O Savior, rend the heavens wide   LBW 38
Stay awake, be ready   LS 1
The night will soon be ending   LSB 337

Music for the Day
Psalmody and Acclamations
Ferguson, John. *Gospel Acclamations for Advent–Transfiguration.* AFP 9780800620363.
Psalter for Worship Year B, Evangelical Lutheran Worship Edition. AFP 9780806683839.
Wold, Wayne L. "Psalm 80" from *Psalm Settings for the Church Year.* AFP 9780800678562.

Choral

Bach, J. S. "Savior of the Nations, Come" from *Bach for All Seasons*. SATB, org. AFP 9780800658540.

☐ Christiansen, F. Melius. "Wake, Awake." SATB, div. AFP 9780800645069. *The Augsburg Choirbook*. AFP 9780800656782.

Davis, Taylor. "Come, Thou Long-Expected Jesus." SAB, pno. CG A1078.

Sedio, Mark. "Christ Comes among Us." SATB, org, assembly, opt tpt. AFP 9780800678326.

Spurlock, William D. "Come, Thou Long-Expected Jesus." SATB, pno, fl, cl. AFP 9780800678135.

Children's Choir

Maeker, Nancy. "First Sunday in Advent (B) Proclamation." UE. Narr, perc. AFP 9786000118440. OP

Ramseth, Betty Ann. "Praise God. Praise Him" from *Take a Hymn*. UE. U, Orff, perc. AFP 9786000106461. OP

Sleeth, Natalie. "Light One Candle" from *Sunday Songbook*. LE. U, kybd. HIN HMB102.

Smith, G. Alan. "Antiphonal Hosanna." UE. Antiphonal trbl, pno. HOP F973.

Keyboard / Instrumental

Diemer, Emma Lou. "Wachet auf" from *Augsburg Organ Library: Advent*. Org. AFP 9780800658953.

Frahm, Frederick. "Consolation" from *Faith Alive: Hymn Improvisations for Organ*, vol. 2. Org/kybd. AFP 9780800678784.

Johnson, David N. "Consolation" from *Augsburg Organ Library: Advent*. Org. AFP 9780800658953.

Raabe, Nancy M. "Helmsley" from *Day of Arising*. Pno. AFP 9780800637460.

Wold, Wayne L. "Wachet auf" from *Light One Candle*. Org. AFP 9780800655747.

Handbell

Hanna, Donna, arr. "Savior of the Nations, Come." 5-6 oct hb/hc, L2. GIA G-6342.

Larson, Lloyd, arr. "Wake, Awake, for Night Is Flying." 3-5 oct, L4. AFP 9780800655105.

McKlveen, Paul A., arr. "O Come, O Come, Emmanuel." 3-5 oct, L2. CPH 97-6549.

Praise Ensemble

■ Foote, Billy James/Charles Silvester Horne. "Sing to The King" from WT. WT/Sixsteps Music.

Hanson, Handt/Paul Murakami. "I Wonder If He Knew" from *Spirit Calls . . . Rejoice!* CC 0933173385.

■ Mark, Robin. "Days of Elijah" from www.musicnotes.com. INT.

■ Smith, Martin. "Did You Feel the Mountains Tremble?" from *Delirious? Deeper The d:finitive Worship Experience*. WT 3474011995.

☐ denotes choral suggestions that relate to the hymn of the day.
■ denotes songs that are available on iTunes®.

Global

Berthier, Jacques. "Two Pieces for Advent." SATB, cant, kybd, gtr. GIA G-5577.

Erickson, Richard. "Light One Candle to Watch for Messiah." SAB, org. AFP 9780800657512.

Monday, December 1

Andrew, Apostle (transferred)

Andrew was the first of the Twelve. He is known as a fisherman who left his net to follow Jesus. As a part of his calling, he brought other people, including Simon Peter, to meet Jesus. The Byzantine church honors Andrew as its patron and points out that because he was the first of Jesus' followers, he was, in the words of John Chrysostom, "the Peter before Peter." Together with Philip, Andrew leads a number of Greeks to speak with Jesus, and it is Andrew who shows Jesus a boy with five barley loaves and two fish. Andrew is said to have died on a cross saltire, an X-shaped cross.

Wednesday, December 3

Francis Xavier, missionary to Asia, 1552

Francis Xavier (SAYV-yehr) was born in the Basque region of northern Spain. Francis's native Basque language is unrelated to any other, and Francis admitted that learning languages was difficult for him. Despite this obstacle he became a missionary to India, Southeast Asia, Japan, and the Philippines. At each point he learned the local language and wrote catechisms for the instruction of new converts. Another obstacle Francis overcame to accomplish his mission work was a propensity to seasickness. All his travels to the Far East were by boat. Together with Ignatius Loyola and five others, Francis formed the Society of Jesus (Jesuits). Francis spoke out against the Spanish and Portuguese colonists when he discovered their oppression of the indigenous people to whom he was sent as a missionary.

Thursday, December 4

John of Damascus, theologian and hymnwriter, c. 749

Born to a wealthy family in Damascus and well educated, John left a career in finance and government to become a monk in an abbey near Jerusalem. He wrote many hymns as well as theological works. Foremost among the latter is a work called *The Fount of Wisdom*, which touches on philosophy, heresy, and the orthodox faith. This summary of patristic theology remained influential for centuries.

Saturday, December 6

Nicholas, Bishop of Myra, c. 342

Though Nicholas is one of the church's most beloved saints, little is known about his life. In the fourth century he was a bishop in what is now Turkey. Legends that surround Nicholas tell of his love for God and neighbor, especially the poor. One famous story tells of Nicholas secretly giving bags of gold to the three daughters of a father who was going to sell them into prostitution because he could not provide dowries for them. Nicholas has become a symbol of anonymous gift giving.

December 7, 2008
Second Sunday of Advent

John called people to repent, to clear the decks, to completely reorder their lives so that nothing would get in the way of the Lord's coming. The reading from Isaiah gives the context for this radical call: the assurance of forgiveness that encourages us to repent; the promise that the coming one will be gentle with the little ones. Isaiah calls us all to be heralds with John, to lift up our voices fearlessly and say, "See, your God is coming!" We say it to one another in worship, in order to say it with our lives in a world in need of justice and peace.

Today the church commemorates Ambrose, Bishop of Milan, to whom the text of the Advent hymn "Savior of the nations, come" is attributed.

Prayer of the Day

Stir up our hearts, Lord God, to prepare the way of your only Son. By his coming strengthen us to serve you with purified lives; through Jesus Christ, our Savior and Lord, who lives and reigns with you and the Holy Spirit, one God, now and forever.

Gospel Acclamation

Alleluia. Prepare the way ǀ of the Lord.* All flesh shall see the salva- ǀ tion of God. *Alleluia.* (Luke 3:4, 6)

Readings and Psalm

Isaiah 40:1-11

In grand, flowing, poetic lines, the prophet announces that the exile of God's people in Babylon is over. The Lord will deliver Israel and will care for her as a shepherd cares for his sheep. This word can be trusted, because the only enduring reality in life is the word of the Lord.

Psalm 85:1-2, 8-13

Righteousness shall prepare a pathway for God. (Ps. 85:13)

2 Peter 3:8-15a

This short letter deals with pressing concerns regarding the final advent of Jesus, especially concerns that could arise over its apparent delay. The author of the letter calls on Christians to anticipate the promised coming of the Lord through conduct dedicated to God.

Mark 1:1-8

The Gospel of Mark does not begin with a story of Jesus' birth but with the voice of one crying out in the wilderness: Prepare the way of the Lord.

Color   Blue

CD-ROM Images

Icon Three: Advent2_B
Icon Two: Advent2_B
Icon: 068

Prayers of Intercession

In hope and expectation, let us pray for restoration and peace, light and life.
A brief silence.
Prepare the way for your people of every language, tribe, and nation, O God, and comfort them with compassionate leaders whose hearts are set on your ways of truth, righteousness, and justice. Stir up your power, O God;
stir up your power and come.

Prepare the way for your church, O God. Like John the Baptizer, may it fearlessly yet humbly announce the coming of your Son, who promises to feed his flock like a shepherd. Stir up your power, O God;
stir up your power and come.
Prepare the way for all creation, O God, that every element be infused with your care through our concern for all that you have made. Stir up your power, O God;
stir up your power and come.
Prepare the way for the weak and elderly, O God, and through us be their tender strength and comforting courage. Let them know that they are not forgotten.
Stir up your power, O God;
stir up your power and come.
Prepare the way for this assembly, O God, that we would lift up our voice in strength and faithfully speak your word of favor, pardon, and peace for all people.
Stir up your power, O God;
stir up your power and come.
Here other intercessions may be offered.
Prepare the way for the communion of saints to be realized more fully among us, O God, that with (*Ambrose and*) all our beloved dead, we might be united with one voice to sing your praises in heaven and on earth.
Stir up your power, O God;
stir up your power and come.
You are with us, O God, and our spirits rejoice in your goodness, through Jesus Christ, our Savior.
Amen.

Ideas and Images for the Day

John the Baptist calls us to repentance. We are drawn to the call to repentance with comfort, patience, the meeting of love and faithfulness, righteousness and peace. The very one for whom John is unworthy to untie a sandal becomes the one who stoops low and washes feet. It is God who is patient and kind, slow to anger, and abounding in steadfast love. This Sunday draws us into repentance and forgiveness and empowers us to comfort others with the good news of Jesus. Like the voice in Isaiah, "Comfort, comfort," this becomes our call as the community: to love our neighbor as Christ has loved us.

1. Ballet, baseball, and many other activities have appropriate stances or forms that are needed to execute the beauty of the event. One shift of a foot to the right or left can cause an imbalance that throws off an entire routine or game. The "form" or "stance" of Advent is repentance, seeking the patient forgiveness of God. What stances throw off our balance? What does the form of repentance look like in your life and in the life of the community?

2. It is customary in many communities to bring meals to the grieving. When we have trouble putting our connections to others into words and struggle to find ways to speak a word of comfort, sometimes we are able to offer connection and comfort without words. In Isaiah, comfort comes in tender speaking that freed the people. Even when words fail us, the Spirit of God speaks on our behalf. That word is spoken in baptism, in the word proclaimed, and at the table in the midst of the grieving community. It is the food laid out for us when we cannot speak.

3. Creating scrapbooks and photo albums has taken on a new life in the era of fix-it-up reality shows. There is something to the role of collecting and recollecting your memories, holding onto the things you cherish, even if they can no longer be with you physically. The psalmist invites us to remember not just as individuals, but to join the community in remembering what God has done for the people. In this season of repentance and eager expectation, let us also hold up the collective memories of our communities and remember how God has had an impact on our lives.

4. John the Baptist's appearance in today's gospel provides an opportunity to reflect on the image and power of water in scripture. In baptism we remember God moving over the waters at creation, delivering Noah and his family, cradling Moses to safety, leading the Israelites from slavery to freedom, pouring out of the rock, claiming us as daughters and sons, and renewing our lives with forgiveness, love, and grace. Use a form of thanksgiving for baptism today (for example, *Evangelical Lutheran Worship*, p. 97).

Hymns for Worship
Gathering

Lord our God, with praise we come   ELW 730, LBW 244
Come, thou long-expected Jesus   ELW 254, LBW 30

Hymn of the Day

On Jordan's bank the Baptist's cry   ELW 249,
    LBW 36   *PUER NOBIS*
There's a voice in the wilderness   ELW 255   *ASCENSION*
Hark! A thrilling voice is sounding   ELW 246   *MERTON*
    LBW 37   *FREUEN WIR UNS ALL IN EIN*

Communion

Comfort, comfort now my people   ELW 256, LBW 29
Wait for the Lord   ELW 262

Sending

Prepare the royal highway   ELW 264, LBW 26
Hark! a thrilling voice is sounding!   ELW 246, LBW 37

Additional Hymns and Songs

We light the Advent candles (sts. 1, 3)   LS 9
Like a shepherd   GC 332
Herald, sound the note of judgment   LBW 556
What is the crying at Jordan?   H82 69
Wild and lone the prophet's voice   HG 18
Prepare the way of the Lord   GC 330
Psalm 85   GS 20

Music for the Day
Psalmody and Acclamations

Ferguson, John. *Gospel Acclamations for Advent–Transfiguration.* AFP 9780800620363.

Mummert, Mark. "Psalm 85" from *Psalm Settings for the Church Year.* AFP 9780800678562.

Psalter for Worship Year B, Evangelical Lutheran Worship Edition. AFP 9780806683839.

Choral

Berthier, Jacques. "Two Songs for Advent." SATB, assembly, kybd, insts. GIA G-5577.

◻ Gjeilo, Ola. "Hark! A Herald Voice Is Calling." SATB, div. WAL WW1352.

Helman, Michael. "Comfort, Comfort Now My People." SATB, kybd. AFP 9780800678166.

Miller, Aaron David. "Rejoice! Rejoice!" 2 pt mxd, pno. AFP 9780800678555.

Pote, Allen. "Prepare the Royal Highway." SATB, kybd, fl, tamb. HIN HMC-914.

Proulx, Richard. "His Name Is John." 2 pt mxd, hb. AFP 9780800656385. OP

Children's Choir

Ahner, Sally. "Light One Candle: Christ Is Coming" from *LifeSongs.* LE. U, hb, Orff, pno. AFP 9780806642710.

Bach, J. S. "Prepare Thyself, Zion." UE. U, kybd, C inst, opt cello/bsn. MSM 50-0415.

Exner, Max V. "Give Me Oil in My Lamp." UE. U/2 pt, pno, opt narr. CG A59.

Helgen, John. "Keep Your Lamps." UE. U/2 pt, pno, perc. AFP 9780800677497.

Keyboard / Instrumental

Cool, Jayne Southwick. "Merton" from *Piano Plus: Advent/Christmas.* Pno, C/B-flat inst. AFP 9780800638542.

Culli, Benjamin. "Freuen wir uns all in ein" from *A Voice Is Sounding.* Org. CPH 97-7012U1.

Dahl, David P. "Puer nobis" from *Hymn Interpretations for Organ.* Org. AFP 9780800658243.

Maynard, Lynette. "Puer nobis" from *Songs for All Seasons*, vol. 2. Pno. AFP 9780800677862.

Handbell

Dobrinski, Cynthia, arr. "O Come, O Come, Emmanuel." 3-5 oct, L2+. AG 1399.

Organ, Anne Krentz. "Three Advent Settings." 3 oct, L2. AFP 9780800674915.

Roberts, Philip L., arr. "Puer nobis" from *Hymns for Handbells*, vol. 2. 3-5 oct. GIA G-5899.

Praise Ensemble

■ Frager, Russell. "Holy Spirit Rain Down" from *Praise & Worship Songbook* 15. INT 17736.

Hanson, Handt. "Waterlife." ELW 457, W&P 145.

■ Hemingway, Beki/arr. Jonathan Rundman. "O Come, O Come, Emmanuel" from www.jonathanrundman.com.

■ Walker, Tommy. "Prepare Ye the Way" from www.tommywalker.net/songs. MAR.

Global

Hopson, Hal H. "If You Believe and I Believe." SATB, kybd, opt fl. AFP 9780800674588.

Keesecker, Thomas. "All Earth Is Hopeful." SATB, kybd, fl. AFP 9780800657413.

Sunday, December 7

Ambrose, Bishop of Milan, c. 397

Ambrose was a governor of northern Italy and a catechumen when he was elected bishop of Milan. He was baptized, ordained, and consecrated a bishop all on the same day. While bishop he gave away his wealth and lived in simplicity. He was a famous preacher and is largely responsible for the conversion of Augustine. He is also well known for writing hymns. On one occasion, Ambrose led people in a hymn he wrote while the church in which they were secluded was threatened by attack from Gothic soldiers. The soldiers turned away, unwilling to attack a congregation that was singing a hymn.

◻ denotes choral suggestions that relate to the hymn of the day.
■ denotes songs that are available on iTunes®.

Saturday, December 13
Lucy, martyr, 304

Lucy was a young Christian of Sicily who was martyred during the persecutions under Emperor Diocletian. Apparently she had decided to devote her life to God and her possessions to the poor. Beyond that, however, little is known

for certain about Lucy. However, her celebration became particularly important in Sweden and Norway, perhaps because the feast of Lucia (the name means "light") originally fell on the shortest day of the year. A tradition arose of a girl in the household, wearing a crown of candles, bringing saffron rolls to her family early in the morning on the day of Lucia.

December 14, 2008
Third Sunday of Advent

"Rejoice always," begins the reading from First Thessalonians. Isaiah and the psalmist make clear that God is turning our mourning into laughter and shouts of joy. "All God's children got a robe," go the words of the spiritual. It is not so much a stately, formal, pressed outfit as it is a set of party clothes, clothes that make us feel happy just to put on. We receive that robe in baptism, and in worship we gather for a foretaste of God's party.

Today the church commemorates John of the Cross, a Carmelite monk and a contemporary of Teresa of Ávila.

Prayer of the Day

Stir up the wills of your faithful people, Lord God, and open our ears to the words of your prophets, that, anointed by your Spirit, we may testify to your light; through Jesus Christ, our Savior and Lord, who lives and reigns with you and the Holy Spirit, one God, now and forever.

Gospel Acclamation

Alleluia. I am sending my messen- | ger before you,* who will prepare your | way before you. *Alleluia.* (Matt. 11:10)

Readings and Psalm
Isaiah 61:1-4, 8-11

Though the people had returned to Jerusalem from exile in Babylon, they continued to face hardship and oppression. In the language of the jubilee year described in Leviticus 25, the prophet, moved by the spirit of the Lord, announces deliverance for those who are oppressed and comfort for those who mourn.

Psalm 126

The LORD has done great things for us. (Ps. 126:3)

or Luke 1:46b-55

You, Lord, have lifted up the lowly. (Luke 1:52)

I Thessalonians 5:16-24

Paul concludes his letter to the Thessalonians by encouraging them to live lives of continual joy, prayer, and thanksgiving. The closing blessing is grounded in the hope of Christ's coming.

John 1:6-8, 19-28

John's gospel describes Jesus as the "light of the world." John the Baptist is presented as a witness to Jesus, one who directs attention away from himself to Christ, the true light.

Color   Blue

CD-ROM Images
Icon Three: Advent3_B
Icon Two: Advent3_B
Icon: 069

Prayers of Intercession

In hope and expectation, let us pray for restoration and peace, light and life.
A brief silence.
We rejoice in you, God of liberty, for you promise to give wisdom to the leaders of the nations. Guide those whose courage falters in times of crisis, that they may govern with

compassion. Stir up your power, O God;
stir up your power and come.
We rejoice in you, God of release, for you have anointed the church with your Spirit and given us glad tidings of comfort and joy to proclaim to all who are imprisoned by doubt and fear. Stir up your power, O God;
stir up your power and come.
We rejoice in you, God of wondrous deeds, for your hands have created us and all that exists. Anoint our hands to be extensions of yours in caring for the earth and all its creatures. Stir up your power, O God;
stir up your power and come.
We rejoice in you, God of justice, for in you there is good news for the oppressed. Use our voices to name and our arms to embrace those who are burdened by discrimination or exclusion. Stir up your power, O God;
stir up your power and come.
We rejoice in you, God of gladness, for you have given us this community of faith, where we sing the story of your love and faithfulness and bless your holy name.
Stir up your power, O God;
stir up your power and come.
Here other intercessions may be offered.
We rejoice in you, God of holiness, for you have made us one with (*John of the Cross and*) all the faithful departed who in life held fast to your goodness and in death sing your praises in heaven. Stir up your power, O God;
stir up your power and come.
You are with us, O God, and our spirits rejoice in your goodness, through Jesus Christ, our Savior.
Amen.

Ideas and Images for the Day

There is increasing pressure in our culture as we move closer to Christmas to be ready for this celebration. Shopping lists, decorations, meal preparations, and getting the house ready for visitors all point us in the direction of readying ourselves for the arrival of others. By now we are flooded with the images of this season. Our scripture this week invites us to continue this preparation by filling ourselves with the good news of God's presence with us, and the rejoicing that follows the preparation. We are pointed with Isaiah, Paul, and John to prepare not just for ourselves but, more importantly, for others who will come. God's arrival and presence is for the entire creation. Isaiah 61 describes the purpose of the one who will arrive after John. When this one arrives, our lives will be entirely reordered around this mender of the brokenhearted, this bearer of good news to the oppressed, this one who proclaims liberty to the captives. Like John, we decrease as Christ increases, and the connecting music for all of us is Mary's song of rejoicing and the psalmist's theme of reversal and restoration where tears are replaced with joy.

1. A New Orleans jazz funeral captures the movement of this day. Represented in this rite is the somber movement to the gravesite and the exuberant return from it. Playing solemn music, the band walks to the grave in measured steps joining the grief of the mourners. But, like Mary's song, this somberness is replaced by a jauntiness of spirit as the mourners depart from the gravesite. A metamorphosis takes place when we can celebrate even in the midst of death. For more on the tradition of New Orleans jazz funerals, see *Rejoice When You Die: The New Orleans Jazz Funerals*, Louisiana State University Press, 1988 (photographs by Leo Touchet). Images of New Orleans jazz funerals by artist Barbara Zuber are included in both *Evangelical Lutheran Worship* (p. 271) and *This Far by Faith* (p. 113).

2. Explore the theme of mistaken identity in these films: *The Wrong Man* (Warner Bros., 1956), *Galaxy Quest* (DreamWorks, 1999), and *Monty Python's Life of Brian* (Independent Artists, 1979). In the last example, as in today's gospel reading, John the Baptist is mistaken for the Messiah.

3. Explore the work of organizations such as Habitat for Humanity in your area and the impact of rebuilding houses and lives. Link this work to the words of Isaiah 61:4: "They shall build up the ancient ruins, . . . they shall repair the ruined cities."

4. We are called to be like John, simultaneously the proclaimers of the good news and the hearers of it. This may be a good week to explore the Lutheran understanding of *simul justus et peccator*. We are both justified saint and sinner.

Hymns for Worship
Gathering

Come now, O Prince of peace   ELW 247
Come, thou long-expected Jesus   ELW 254, LBW 30
Lost in the night   ELW 243, LBW 394

Hymn of the Day

There's a voice in the wilderness   ELW 255   *ASCENSION*
On Jordan's bank the Baptist's cry   ELW 249,
   LBW 36   *PUER NOBIS*
Hark! A thrilling voice is sounding   ELW 246   *MERTON*
   LBW 37   *FREUEN WIR UNS ALL IN EIN*

Communion

Christ, Be Our Light   ELW 715
O Lord, how shall I meet you   ELW 241, LBW 23
We come to the hungry feast   ELW 479, WOV 766

Sending

Hark, the glad sound!   ELW 239, LBW 35
I want to walk as a child of the light   ELW 815, WOV 649
O Splendor of God's glory bright   ELW 559, LBW 271

Additional Hymns and Songs

We light the Advent candles (sts. 1, 4)   LS 9
Are you the coming one   HG 71
Come to be our hope, O Jesus   RWSB 240
Sweet coming for which we long   OBS 79
Blest be the King whose coming   H82 74

Music for the Day
Psalmody and Acclamations

Ferguson, John. *Gospel Acclamations for Advent–Transfiguration.*
   AFP 9780800620363.
Psalter for Worship Year B, Evangelical Lutheran Worship Edition.
   AFP 9780806683839.
Roberts, William Bradley. "Psalm 126" from *Psalm Settings for the
   Church Year.* AFP 9780800678562.

Choral

Gibbons, Orlando. "This Is the Record of John." SAATB, tenor solo.
   OXF TCM 42R 352084-2.
▫ Monteverdi, Claudio. "On Jordan's Bank the Baptist's Cry." SAB,
   cont, inst. GIA G-2834.
Organ, Anne Krentz. "Come, My Light." 2 pt mxd, pno. AFP
   9780800675813.
Proulx, Richard. "His Name Is John." 2 pt mxd, hb. AFP
   9780800656385. OP

Children's Choir

Anderson, Norma. "I Have a Secret." LE. U, pno, glock/hb. CG
   A576.
Cool, Jayne Southwick. "Lumen Christi." UE. U, kybd. CG A1098.
Helgen, John/Karla Singer. "Something Special." LE. U, pno. AFP
   9780800675325.
Page, Anna Laura. "The World's True Light." U, kybd, opt fl. AFP
   9780800678395.
Ramseth, Betty Ann. "Come, Thou Long Expected Jesus" from *Take
   a Hymn.* UE. U, Orff, drm. AFP 9786000106461. OP

Keyboard / Instrumental

Archer, Malcolm. "Merton" from *Augsburg Organ Library: Advent.*
   Org. AFP 9780800658953.
Benson, Robert A. "Ascension" from *A Lovely Rose.* Org. AFP
   9780800675714.
Magness, Phil. "Freuen wir uns all in ein" from *Hymns for the Contemporary Ensemble*, vol. 1. Kybd, gtr, C/B-flat/E-flat inst. CPH
   97-7058U1.
Miller, Aaron David. "Puer nobis" from *Piano Plus: Advent/Christ-
   mas.* Pno, C/B-flat inst. AFP 9780800638542.

▫ denotes choral suggestions that relate to the hymn of the day.
■ denotes songs that are available on iTunes®.

Handbell

Biggs, Susan, arr. "Come, Thou Long-Expected Jesus." 3 oct, L2.
   AFP 9780800659875.
Lohr, Alan, arr. "O Come, O Come, Emmanuel." 3-5 oct, L4. AG
   35146.
Muschick, John, arr. "Every Valley." 4-6 oct, L3. BP HB136.

Praise Ensemble

■ Anderson, Tai/Brad Avery/David Carr/Mark D. Lee/Johnny Mac
   Powell. "All The Heavens" from www.musicnotes.com. BMG
   Music, Inc.
Olson, Larry. "Messiah" from *Dakota Road Music Keyboard/Guitar
   Edition* 1.5. Dakota Road Music. www.dakotaroadmusic.com.
■ Smith, Henry. "Give Thanks." W&P 41.
Tallman, James. "What a Mighty Word God Gives." W&P 155.

Global

Bell, John L. "He Will Come." SATB, kybd, cl. GIA G-5486.
Benson, Robert A. "My Lord, What a Morning." SATB, pno. AFP
   9780800623876.

Sunday, December 14
John of the Cross, renewer of the church, 1591

John was a monk of the Carmelite religious order who met
Teresa of Ávila when she was working to reform the Carmelite Order and return it to a stricter observance of its
rules. He followed Teresa's lead and encouraged others to
follow her reform. He was imprisoned when he encountered
opposition to the reform. His writings, like Teresa's, reflect
a deep interest in mystical thought and meditation. In one
of John's poems, "The Spiritual Canticle," he cried, "Oh,
that my griefs would end! Come, grant me thy fruition full
and free!"

Saturday, December 20
Katharina von Bora Luther,
renewer of the church, 1552

Born to an impoverished nobleman, Katharina (Katie) was
five when her mother died and she was sent to live in a convent. She later took vows as a nun, but at about age twenty-
four she and several other nuns who were influenced by
the writings of Martin Luther left the convent. Six children
were born to Katie and Martin. Though initially Luther felt
little affection for Katie, she proved herself a gifted household manager and became a trusted partner. She was so
influential that Luther took to calling her "my lord Katie."

December 21, 2008
Fourth Sunday of Advent

God keeps the promise made to David, to give him an everlasting throne. The angel tells Mary that God will give David's throne to her son Jesus. She is perplexed by Gabriel's greeting and by the news of her coming pregnancy, but she is able still to say, "Count me in." We who know that Jesus is called king only as he is executed still find it a mystery hard to fathom, but with Mary today we hear the news of what God is up to and say, "Count us in."

Prayer of the Day

Stir up your power, Lord Christ, and come. With your abundant grace and might, free us from the sin that would obstruct your mercy, that willingly we may bear your redeeming love to all the world, for you live and reign with the Father and the Holy Spirit, one God, now and forever.

Gospel Acclamation

Alleluia. Here I am, the servant | of the Lord;* let it be with me according | to your word. *Alleluia.* (Luke 1:38)

Readings and Psalm

2 Samuel 7:1-11, 16

Instead of David building a house (temple) for the Lord, the Lord promises to establish David's house (dynasty) forever. Centuries later, after the Babylonian exile, no king sat on the throne. Even then, however, the people of Israel remembered this promise and continued to hope for a king, the messiah, the Lord's anointed.

Luke 1:46b-55

You, Lord, have lifted up the lowly. (Luke 1:52)

or **Psalm 89:1-4, 19-26**

Your love, O LORD, forever will I sing. (Ps. 89:1)

Romans 16:25-27

Paul closes his letter to the Romans by praising God because in the proclamation of the gospel of Jesus Christ God has revealed the promised, divine plan of salvation for all humanity. Paul proclaims this gospel of Christ in order to bring about the obedience of faith among all nations.

Luke 1:26-38

In this annunciation, Luke makes clear that God comes with good news for ordinary people (Mary) from little-known places (Nazareth). This king will not be born to royalty in a palace, but to common folk in a stall. Here Luke highlights the role of the Spirit, a special emphasis in his gospel.

Color   Blue

CD-ROM Images

Icon Three: Advent4_B
Icon Two: Advent4_B
Icon: 070

Prayers of Intercession

In hope and expectation, let us pray for restoration and peace, light and life.
A brief silence.
Come, Emmanuel, and lead warring nations to lay down their weapons. Come and bring peace where there is violence and unrest. Stir up your power, O God;
stir up your power and come.
Come, Emmanuel, and show the church your ways of unity amid the things that threaten to divide it. Come and strengthen your holy church in the proclamation of Jesus Christ. Stir up your power, O God;
stir up your power and come.
Come, Emmanuel, and teach humanity your creative ways of caring for the earth, sea, air, and all their creatures, that all creation will be whole and well to the praise of your glory. Stir up your power, O God;
stir up your power and come.
Come, Emmanuel, and heal the brokenhearted, that those who are without loved ones or resources will know that you

are near and promise to supply their need.
Stir up your power, O God;
stir up your power and come.
Come, Emmanuel, and enliven the worship of this assembly
as we celebrate the joy of the holy days ahead through the
gifts of musicians, artists, decorators, poets, and all who
proclaim your advent among us. Stir up your power, O God;
stir up your power and come.
Here other intercessions may be offered.
Come, Emmanuel, and comfort us as we remember and give
thanks for all those who have departed this life and now
rejoice in your eternal presence (*especially*). Stir up your
power, O God;
stir up your power and come.
You are with us, O God, and our spirits rejoice in your
goodness, through Jesus Christ, our Savior.
Amen.

Ideas and Images for the Day

In the biblical tradition of births, God can create life in
places and people that seem unlikely or even impossible.
The grace and favor that rests upon God's children enables
us to join the call of Mary to be bearers of the good news
and servants of God. We hold onto the mystery and wonder
of God's presence among us, while also clinging to the God
who is present in the flesh in Christ. With David and Mary
we are given an answer to the question of where God will
dwell. God will make a home among mortals. Whether in
a tent or carried by a virgin, the mystery of God's presence
comes to us and is with us, housed in our presence. God's
incarnation continues to be alive for the sake of the world's
salvation.

1. Gabriel's announcement to Mary invites us to tie the
   incarnation of God to images of motherhood and birth.
   These images include the giving of life, the bearing of
   hope, and the carrying of new beginnings.

2. Nathan and Gabriel play prominent roles in today's
   texts as messengers of God to the servants of God. They
   serve as reminders that God's presence was, is, and will
   be with the people of God. They also serve as the voice
   of God in the face of our brokenness. How does the
   good news of God both confront us and comfort us?

3. We meditate this Sunday on the miracle that God
   would become human to draw near to us. We are
   drawn in this meditation with Mary to ask, "How can
   this be?" How can this happen to us and for us?

4. Mary, like John the Baptist, gives way to the light of
   Christ being born into the world. Like John's words last

week ("I am not the Messiah"), Mary's words, "Here
am I, the servant of the Lord; let it be with me according to your word," witness to her discipleship. Mary,
like the other disciples, follows the way of the cross.

5. Word and sacrament are joined in the announcement
   of Jesus' birth: the baby that rests nestled in the bosom
   of the mother is the life that rests in the cradle of the
   font. The breath that moves in and out of this tiny
   infant is the breath of life that springs from the words
   of scripture creating life. The infant laid in a manger
   that provides food for those in need becomes the food
   set out for the hungry world.

Hymns for Worship
Gathering
Come and fill our hearts   ELW 528
Signs and wonders   ELW 672
Creator of the stars of night   ELW 245

Hymn of the Day
The angel Gabriel from heaven came   ELW 265,
   WOV 632   *GABRIEL'S MESSAGE*
All earth is hopeful   ELW 266, WOV 629, TFF 47
   TODA LA TIERRA
O come, O come, Emmanuel   ELW 257, LBW 34
   VENI, EMMANUEL

Communion
Come now, O Prince of peace   ELW 247
As the dark awaits the dawn   ELW 261
Let all together praise our God   ELW 287, LBW 47

Sending
Joy to the world   ELW 267, LBW 39
Savior of the nations, come   ELW 263, LBW 28

Additional Hymns and Songs
We light the Advent candles (sts. 1, 5)   LS 9
A stable lamp is lighted   LBW 74
When to Mary, the Word   HG 144
Get ready!   LS 12
When all the world was cursed   LSB 346

Music for the Day
Psalmody and Acclamations
Ferguson, John. *Gospel Acclamations for Advent–Transfiguration.*
   AFP 9780800620363.
Pavlechko, Thomas. "Psalm 89" from *Psalm Settings for the Church
   Year.* AFP 9780800678562.
Psalter for Worship Year B, Evangelical Lutheran Worship Edition.
   AFP 9780806683839.

Choral

Distler, Hugo. "Lo, How a Rose E'er Blooming" from *Chantry Choirbook*. SATB. AFP 9780800657772.

▫ Keesecker, Thomas. "All Earth Is Hopeful." U/SA/SSA, kybd, fl. AFP 9780800657413.

Lovelace, Austin C. "The Comings of the Lord." SAB, kybd. CPH 98-3210.

▫ Nelson, Ronald A. "The Angel Gabriel." SAB, kybd. AMSI 736.

Rogers, Sharon Elery. "Rosa Mystica." SATB, kybd. AFP 9780800678173.

Children's Choir

Keesecker, Thomas. "All Earth Is Hopeful." UE. 2/3 pt, pno. AFP 9780800657413.

Patterson, Mark. "Light One Candle" from *Young Children Sing*. LE. U, kybd, opt hc/resonator bells/glock. AFP 9780800676803.

Patterson, Mark. "With One Heart." UE. U, kybd, opt fl. CG A804.

Sleeth, Natalie. "O Come, O Come Immanuel." UE. 2 pt, kybd. CG A273.

Keyboard / Instrumental

Cherwien, David. "Toda la tierra" from *O God Beyond All Praising*. Org. AFP 9780800657246.

Ferguson, John. "Veni, Emmanuel" from *An Advent Triptych*. Org. MSM 10-008.

Manz, Paul. "Gabriel's Message" from *Augsburg Organ Library: Advent*. Org. AFP 9780800658953.

Organ, Anne Krentz. "Toda la tierra" from *Piano Plus: Advent/ Christmas*. Pno, C/B-flat inst. AFP 9780800638542.

Handbell

Afdahl, Lee J., arr. "Prepare the Royal Highway." 3-5 oct, L2. AFP 9780800655778.

Honoré, Jeffrey, arr. "The King of Glory." 3-5 oct, L3. CPH 97-6528. OP

McChesney, Kevin. "Angel Glory." 3 oct, L3. AFP 9780800653958. OP

Praise Ensemble

■ Brown, Brenton/Brian Doerksen. "Lord, Reign in Me" from *Come, Now Is the Time to Worship Songbook*. VIN VMB9367.

■ Eaton, Chris/Amy Grant. "Breath of Heaven" from www.music notes.com. *Age to Age*, Bug Music.

■ Hearn, Naida. "Jesus, Name Above All Names" from *Best of the Best, The Other Songbook 2*. FEL 1891062034.

■ Morgan, Reuben. "Touching Heaven, Changing Earth" from www.praisecharts.com. Hillsong Publishing/INT.

Global

Bread for the Journey. "Come to Be Our Hope, O Jesus" from *Global Songs 2*. U, kybd, gtr. AFP 9780800656744.

Cooney, Rory. "Canticle of the Turning." SAB/U, kybd, gtr. GIA G-3407.

CHRISTMAS

Preparing for Christmas

"Once in Royal David's City . . ."

Where? Royal David's city . . . Bethlehem . . . hmmm . . . Bethlehem?! Not Jerusalem? Not Alexandria? Not Athens? Not Rome?

In the unlikeliest of places, in the unlikeliest of families, in what probably was a back room of a family home, to parents who were dealing with all the inconveniences of life on the road, an extraordinary birth took place. On Christmas night we celebrate unlikely glad tidings, unbelievably good news.

Yet we can't go back in time, and don't pretend to. We know how the story ends. We don't rehearse the story as if it's happening now, at least literally. But we do proclaim good tidings in the here and now: we do sing that Christ was "born to raise each child of earth, born to give us second birth" (ELW 270). So that birth long ago, which was good news for that generation's children of earth, is also about us, intended for us. And we proclaim something more: "For lo!" we sing, "The days are hastening on, by prophets seen of old, when with the ever-circling years shall come the time foretold, when peace shall over all the earth its ancient splendors fling, and all the world give back the song which now the angels sing" (ELW 282). So the birth we celebrate at Christmas has to do with the future of human life on earth, the future peace that will finally be flung all over the world. This holy night, then, captures past, present, and future, and proclaims the good news of God's grace that transcends all times, all places.

Steven Pinker, a professor of psychology at Harvard, wrote an article titled "A History of Violence: We're Getting Nicer Every Day." He cites considerable evidence that "violence has been in decline over long stretches of history, and today we are probably living in the most peaceful moment of our species' time on earth" (*The New Republic*, March 19, 2007). This idea is hard to believe, knowing as we do the terrible acts of genocide that seem to have covered most of the twentieth century in blood, and the wars of today that continue to claim so many thousands of lives. It's hard to believe, knowing as we do how flawed and furious human beings can be, and often are. Yet research does show that violence of all kinds, from something relatively small like cruelty to animals to continent-wide acts of genocide, is on the decline. There are more people in the world today than at any time in history, so the numbers of those killed by violence is staggering, yet as a percentage of the population, we are, as Pinker says, "getting kinder and gentler."

What we celebrate at Christmas isn't a statistical reduction in oppression, violence, or injustice—although that's always welcome news—but our conviction that God in Christ is at work in the world, and in us, to accomplish those and other things. What is the good news? For the Hebrew prophets and Christian gospels tell us that while God's grace is offered for the spiritual salvation of all who believe, God also intends to "fill the hungry with good things" (Luke 1:53a), to "bind up the brokenhearted" (Isa. 61:1b), and to "cause righteousness and praise to spring up before all the nations" (Isa. 61:11b, from the Old Testament reading for the first Sunday of Christmas). And on Christmas night we encounter this vivid image: "For all the boots of the tramping warriors and all the garments rolled in blood shall be burned as fuel for the fire" (Isa. 9:5). They won't be needed, then, these artifacts of war, these blood-soaked signs of age-old human violence. God has given us a new birth of peace, a new dawn of justice. Glory to God in the highest, indeed!

"Here Let All, Great and Small, Kneel in Awe and Wonder . . ."

"Glory to God in the highest," we sing. That's quite a song: let's sing it well. It's essential that the Christmas liturgies be planned well, rehearsed well, led well, and experienced by regular members and visitors alike as delightful feasts, glorious celebrations. A parish doesn't have to be wealthy to do this. Small congregations, like large ones, need only focus on what they already do well, and develop it. If you have a good singing congregation, carefully plan hymns—and stanzas within hymns—that are mostly familiar and offer opportunities for soloists, harmony singing, and creative instrumentation. If your strength lies in your worship space (and even if it doesn't), be sure that everything is clean, that greens are refreshed, and that the entrance appears well-lit and inviting. Warmly welcome everyone—including those who are often called "Christmas and Easter Christians." They are guests, all of them, and thus should be received as Christ. As you plan, consider two things: how do we evoke awe and wonder in our Christmas liturgies and how do we focus on what we do best and do it well? This is the season when the parish and its celebrations should gleam.

"For His Bed a Cattle Stall . . ."

Central to the awe and wonder of Christmas is the simplicity of it all: the quiet, ordinary beauty of candlelight, unaccompanied song, silence, the darkness of Christmas night, the pale winter light of Christmas dawn. Experiment with unaccompanied song, if you haven't already, using the most well-known tunes (like "Silent night, holy night!" ELW 281). People love candles, as you know. Experiment with candles throughout the room (but be careful!) in unexpected places. Allow more time than you might have done in the past for the congregation to hold their own candles, contemplating in silence the wonder of Christmas night. Train readers carefully to ensure that all readings are read clearly, accurately, and with an understated (not melodramatic) enthusiasm. Allow the liturgies to speak for themselves: try to minimize spoken instructions and announcements when possible. In the weeks before Christmas, encourage regular parishioners to be on the lookout for Christmas visitors, and welcome them. Don't forget, though, that some visitors may not want much help and would rather simply experience the liturgy and let the congregation carry them in worship. There's nothing wrong with that. Be careful not to work so hard that you undermine the grace and beauty of the liturgy.

"Brightest and Best of the Stars of the Morning . . ."

Be sure your worship space continues to gleam on the day of Epiphany. Like the second Sunday of Easter, Epiphany can be something of a letdown: people are back at school, back at work; winter has fully arrived (in most northern climates), and it's easy for all the energy and light of Christmas to slip away. No one is better able to stop that from happening than children: now is the time for them to (quite literally) shine. Stars, banners, ribbons: encourage children to add their artistic talent to entryways, corridors, and the worship space itself. The Christmas greens may be faded and gone, so replace them with fresh flowers or seasonal greens from your region. Celebrate the music and customs of the season: sing "We three kings" in the parish hall around an Epiphany cake—a white or coconut cake in which is hidden a ring, a cross, and perhaps other small objects. Whoever finds the ring must make next year's cake; whoever finds the cross must pray for the congregation all year; and so on. There aren't hard-and-fast rules about these things. Be sure to have fun, and invent your own prizes.

Celebrating Christmas with Children

As we celebrate Christ's coming among us, we reflect on our need to invite him again and again into our lives. During this season when many of us find all of our senses engaged and heightened, there are many opportunities to recognize and reflect on the amazing promises of God given to us in the Christ child. Celebrating the Word made flesh in Jesus, we still long for Christ to live among us and with us. Christmas and Epiphany are times in which we pray Christ will come again and again to dwell with us, lead us, and guide us. By the power of the Holy Spirit we learn from this Word and witness, along with the people of old, to the meaning of Christ's birth for all of creation.

Ideas for Christmas Eve/Day

- At worship on either of these days, have a child come forward at each reading with an ornament that express-es the words of the text visually. Hang the ornament on a cross or tree.
- Many churches have Christmas services especially designed for children and their families. During the offering have families or individuals write their names on a nativity star and come forward to hang it on a tree in the front of the worship space. You may use a large cookie cutter as your template. Cut the stars out beforehand and distribute to worshipers as they arrive. Provide red ribbons for them to attach to the cutout or have this prepared before worship.
- Provide each family or individual with a votive candle as they arrive for worship. At a designated time dur-ing the service, invite families or individuals to light their candles from the Christ candle or another candle provided for this purpose. Set the lit votives on the altar or other appropriate locations as a testimony to all who gather together as the family of God. Sing "Silent night" (ELW 281, LBW 65) or "Love has come" (ELW 292) by candlelight.

Ideas for the Sundays of Christmas

The readings for these Sundays encourage all of us to praise the Lord in all that we do. As we celebrate Christ's birth, may we not keep silent, but may our voices speak out pro-claiming God's glory and might!

- Christmas 1: Have children join in a special chorus of praise. Provide children with homemade maracas (seeds placed in two cups taped together). Ask the children to listen for the word "praise" as Psalm 148 is sung. When they hear the word, have them shake their "praises."
- Christmas 2 (if celebrated as Epiphany of Our Lord): The word *epiphany* means to show or make known. Children are visual learners. You may wish to begin the worship service in darkness and gradually bring up the lights at different points in the service, or light a candle for each part of worship: Gathering, Word, Meal, and Sending. Older children could be invited to light the candles. The growing light reflects the themes of Epiphany, which falls on Tuesday, January 6.
- The gifts of the magi: Even though many churches interweave the story of the magi with the Christmas story, make this a special day by having the children unwrap the gifts of the magi: gold, frankincense, and myrrh. Gold symbolizes a gift for a king; incense, a gift for a priest; and myrrh, a gift for one who will die. Have samples of each for the children to hold or smell.
- Provide all of the children with paper crowns at the beginning of worship. As the Epiphany gospel from Matthew is introduced, have them come forward. At the conclusion of the gospel reading, provide the children with cutout stars and send them back into the assembly, reminding them that they too are light-bearers in Jesus' name.
- In many countries it is the custom on the eve of Epiph-any (Twelfth Night) to have children dress as kings and, following a large star, go door-to-door in their neigh-borhoods, singing "We three kings of orient are" (WOV 646). Plan a congregational caroling and ask each household visited to provide something for a local food shelf. You may wish to provide a paper cutout star with your church's worship times on them to each house-hold, along with a "Thank you for your gift" written on the other side.

Worship Helps for Christmas
(includes Epiphany of Our Lord)

Christmas Checklist

- Prepare materials for Christmas flower/poinsettia sponsorship.
- Order greens, tree(s), and Christmas flowers.
- Locate any decorations that are in storage from previous years for the Christmas tree, the crèche, the chancel, and other interior or exterior areas. Repair or replace decorations as needed.
- If handheld candles are used by worshipers on Christmas Eve, determine how many candles and holders can be used from previous seasons and how many new candles and holders will be needed.
- Publicize Christmas services in local newspapers and in other media.
- Order special bulletin covers if needed for services on Christmas Eve, Christmas Day, and Epiphany.
- Design service folders for Christmas worship that guests will be able to follow easily, including specific instructions for communion distribution.
- Determine communion-distribution procedure for services with large numbers of communicants, and make sure sufficient communion elements and communion-ware are available. Rehearse communion assistants if necessary.
- Make arrangements for adequate seating, along with additional worship books and service folders for larger assemblies on Christmas Eve.
- Determine whether Epiphany decorations are needed.
- Consider using incense on Epiphany of Our Lord; purchase incense (and quick-lighting charcoal) if it will be used. See "other helps" for instructions on using incense.
- Arrange for removal of Christmas decorations following January 6.
- Look ahead to the checklist on p. 71 as you plan for the time after Epiphany.

Shape of the Communion Liturgy

- See the seasonal worship texts for Christmas on pp. 44–45.
- See the seasonal worship texts for the Time after Epiphany for use on the Epiphany of Our Lord (pp. 72–73).
- Use the hymn of praise ("Glory to God"). In addition to the form in the communion setting, see options in the service music section of *Evangelical Lutheran Worship*, #162–164.
- Use the Nicene Creed.
- See the prayers of intercession for each Sunday, Christmas Eve, Christmas Day, and Epiphany.
- Use the proper preface for Christmas (*Evangelical Lutheran Worship* Leaders Edition, p. 182); use the proper preface for Epiphany of Our Lord on January 6 (Leaders Edition, p. 183).
- Thanksgiving at the table: see options in *Evangelical Lutheran Worship*, especially Prayer III (Pew Edition, p. 110; Leaders Edition, p. 196); *WOV*, Prayer B (Leaders Edition, p. 66).

Other Helps

- See the suggestions for music and worship space in the essay "Preparing for Christmas," pp. 40–41.
- See the blessing of the nativity scene and the Proclamation of the Birth of Christ on p. 46–47.
- For instructions on using incense, consult *Altar Guild and Sacristy Handbook* (p. 81).

SEASONAL WORSHIP TEXTS FOR CHRISTMAS

Confession and Forgiveness

All may make the sign of the cross, the sign that is marked at
baptism, as the presiding minister begins.
Blessed be the holy Trinity, ✛ one God,
who is the light and life of all the ages.
Amen.

Trusting in Jesus Christ,
who came to share our humanity
and bring light to this broken world,
let us come before God without fear to make our confession.

Silence is kept for reflection.

Comforting God,
we confess before you and in the presence of one another
that we are sinners who fail to live as you desire.
So often we place our trust in ourselves and not in you.
We do not love each other as you have commanded.
Because of us, your whole creation suffers.
For the sake of your Son, Jesus Christ, forgive us.
In your boundless patience and mercy,
lead us to live by faith in your promise.
Amen.

God's love for us is greater than all our sins.
God promises full pardon and complete forgiveness
to all who turn from sin
and place their trust in Christ, the light of the world.
Hear and believe the good news
that all your sins are forgiven.
With God nothing is impossible.
Amen.

Greeting

The grace and peace of Jesus Christ,
the Word made flesh, be with you all.
And also with you.

Offering Prayer

Loving God,
you sent your only Son to live among us,
bringing us your grace and truth.
As we prepare to receive the gift
of Christ's presence once again,
all we have to offer is what you have given us.
Receive all that we have and all that we are
to your glory and for your service,
in the name of Jesus Christ, our Savior and Lord.
Amen.

Invitation to Communion

Come, all is ready.
Eat and drink the good news that is Christ Jesus,
the Word made flesh.

Prayer after Communion

God of all creation,
you have set before us our inheritance of salvation,
which you have prepared in the presence of all peoples.
You have filled us with your goodness and peace.
Use us that all might be satisfied with your abundance;
through your only Son, Jesus Christ our Lord.
Amen.

Sending of Communion

Compassionate God,
you sent forth prophets
to bring good news to the oppressed,
to bind up the brokenhearted,
to proclaim release to the prisoners,
and to comfort all who mourn.
Bless those who go forth from this assembly
bearing your word and sacrament.
Nourish and strengthen all who share in this communion,
that this foretaste of your coming will bring hope and comfort,
in the name of Jesus Christ our Lord.
Amen.

Blessing

May the good news that is Jesus, the Messiah,
bring you great joy each day.
Almighty God, Father, + Son, and Holy Spirit,
bless you now and forever.
Amen.

Dismissal

Go in peace. Share the good news.
Thanks be to God.

SEASONAL RITES FOR CHRISTMAS

Blessing of the Christmas Tree

This reading and blessing may be used when the tree is first lit, perhaps as part of a parish decorating party.

Psalm 96:11-13

Let the heavens rejoice, and let the earth be glad;
let the sea thunder and all that is in it;
let the field be joyful and all that is therein.
Then shall all the trees of the wood shout for joy
at your coming, O LORD,
for you come to judge the earth.
You will judge the world with righteousness
and the peoples with your truth.

Blessing

Be praised, O God, for the blessings around us
that point to you.
Be praised, O God, for the signs of this holy season
that awaken in us wonder.
Praise for the steadfast green of this tree,
like your love, enduring all seasons.
Praise for the light that illumines our darkness,
like Christ, who brings light to the world.
Join our voices with those of the tree and of all creation,
who sing at your coming:
Glory to God in the highest,
and peace to God's people on earth.
Amen.

Blessing of the Nativity Scene 1

At a Christmas service with young children present, they may be invited to gather around the nativity scene. The blessing may be used in the following way.

Reading

Luke 2:1-14

Children's Talk

Blessing

Blessed are you, O Lord our God, ruler of the universe.
With Mary and Joseph, with the angels and shepherds,
and with the animals in the stable
we gather around your Son, born for us.
Bless us, and fill us with joy and wonder
as we look upon this manger scene.
May Jesus be born in our lives,
that we might share his love with all the world,
for he is our light and our salvation.
Blessed be God forever.

Song

Away in a manger ELW 277, 278; WOV 644; LBW 67
The children may sing stanza 1 and return to their seats during stanzas 2 and 3.

Blessing of the Nativity Scene 2

This blessing may be used when figures are added to the nativity scene throughout the days of Christmas and on the day of Epiphany.

Bless us, O God, bless us who gather around this stable.
As we celebrate Christ's birth into the world,
may we receive the Christ child into our hearts
with gratitude and song.
Amen.

Proclamation of the Birth of Christ

The services on Christmas Eve may begin with the proclamation of the birth of Christ, taken from the ancient martyrology. The proclamation should be understood as the announcement of the incarnation within human history rather than a literal counting of years. The proclamation may be read or sung on one note by a leader standing at the entrance to the church. Following the proclamation, the gathering song is begun.

Many ages after God created the heavens and the earth,
     when man and woman were formed
          in God's own image;
long after the great flood, when God set the rainbow
     in the clouds as a sign of the covenant;

twenty-one centuries from the time of Abraham and Sarah;
thirteen centuries after Moses led God's people to freedom;
eleven centuries from the time of Ruth and the judges;
a thousand years from the anointing of David as king;
in the sixty-fifth week as Daniel's prophecy takes note;
in the one hundred and ninety-fourth Olympiad;
the seven hundred and fifty-second year
     from the founding of the city of Rome;
the forty-second year of the reign of Octavian Augustus;
in the sixth age of the world,
     all earth being at peace,
Jesus Christ, eternal God, Son of the eternal Father,
     willing to hallow the world by his coming in mercy,
          was born of the virgin Mary in Bethlehem of Judea.
Today is the birth of our Lord Jesus Christ,
     God made flesh.

Christmas Eve Family Service

The following order is especially appropriate for a service at which many children will be present.

Welcome

Gathering Song

O come, all ye faithful   ELW 283, LBW 45
Children may be invited to carry and wave pennants or ribbons of gold, white, and silver in a procession during the gathering song.

Prayer of the Day

Readings and Psalm

Isaiah 9:2-7
Psalm 96
Titus 2:11-14

Welcoming the Gospel

Angels we have heard on high, sts. 1 and 2   ELW 289, LBW 71
Invite children to ring bells each time "Gloria in excelsis Deo" is sung. Bells may be brought from home or provided as children enter the worship space.

Gospel: Luke 2:1-20

The gospel may be proclaimed using two or more readers. A call and response between the reader and the assembly is placed throughout the gospel reading. Each time the reader announces To us is born a Savior, *the assembly responds:*
Jesus Christ our Lord.

Our Christmas Eve story comes from the Gospel of Luke.

In those days a decree went out from Emperor Augustus that all the world should be registered. This was the first registration and was taken while Quirinius was governor of Syria. All went to their own towns to be registered. To us is born a Savior.
Jesus Christ our Lord.

Joseph also went from the town of Nazareth in Galilee to Judea, to the city of David called Bethlehem, because he was descended from the house and family of David. He went to be registered with Mary, to whom he was engaged and who was expecting a child. To us is born a Savior.
Jesus Christ our Lord.

While they were there, the time came for her to deliver her child. And she gave birth to her firstborn son and wrapped him in bands of cloth, and laid him in a manger, because there was no place for them in the inn. To us is born a Savior.
Jesus Christ our Lord.

In that region there were shepherds living in the fields, keeping watch over their flock by night. Then an angel of the Lord stood before them, and the glory of the Lord shone around them, and they were terrified. To us is born a Savior.
Jesus Christ our Lord.

But the angel said to them, "Do not be afraid; for see—I am bringing you good news of great joy for all the people: to you is born this day in the city of David a Savior, who is the Messiah, the Lord. This will be a sign for you: you will find a child wrapped in bands of cloth and lying in a manger." To us is born a Savior.
Jesus Christ our Lord.

And suddenly there was with the angel a multitude of the heavenly host, praising God and saying, "Glory to God in the highest heaven, and on earth peace among those whom he favors!" To us is born a Savior.
Jesus Christ our Lord.

When the angels had left them and gone into heaven, the shepherds said to one another, "Let us go now to Bethlehem and see this thing that has taken place, which the Lord has made known to us." So they went with haste and found Mary and Joseph, and the child lying in the manger. To us is born a Savior.
Jesus Christ our Lord.

When they saw this, they made known what had been told them about this child; and all who heard it were amazed at what the shepherds told them. But Mary treasured all these words and pondered them in her heart. To us is born a Savior. **Jesus Christ our Lord.**

The shepherds returned, glorifying and praising God for all they had heard and seen, as it had been told them. To us is born a Savior.
Jesus Christ our Lord.

Celebrating the Gospel

Angels we have heard on high, st. 3   ELW 289, LBW 71
Bells may be rung again.

Children's Message

Hymn of the Day

If the congregation's practice includes a nativity scene or manger, the children may be invited to gather at that place during the singing.
Away in a manger   ELW 277/278, LBW 67
O little town of Bethlehem   ELW 279, LBW 41
Your little ones, dear Lord   ELW 286, LBW 52

Prayers of Intercession

A service with communion continues with the peace. A service without communion concludes with the peace, the Lord's Prayer, blessing, sending song, and dismissal.

Sending Song

Silent night, holy night!   ELW 281, LBW 65
Jesus, what a wonderful child   ELW 297, TFF 51
Go tell it on the mountain   ELW 290, TFF 52, LBW 70

Lessons and Carols for Christmas

This service may be used during the twelve days of Christmas.

Gathering Song

Joy to the world   ELW 267, LBW 39
Angels we have heard on high   ELW 289, LBW 71
It came upon the midnight clear   ELW 282, LBW 54

Dialogue

Jesus, the bright Morning Star, shines light in the world.
By day and night he shines for all to see.
Jesus was born in the midst of injustice and poverty
that the world may see the justice and richness of God.
God so loved the world that God sent Jesus,
so that all who believe in him may not perish but have eternal life.
Jesus is the light of the world.
Jesus is the light of our lives.
Sing to God a new song!
A song of hope, joy, and peace around the world.

Opening Prayer

The Lord be with you.
And also with you.
Let us pray. Gracious God of heaven and earth,
you have thrown a lifeline to us in our darkness—
a beam of light that shines through Jesus.
Though born in a manger, he is the firstborn of all creation.
Though crucified on a cross, he is the Lord of life.
Fill us with the wonder and joy of his presence in the world and in our hearts.
Amen.

Lessons and Carols

First Reading: Genesis 1:1-5, 14-18
Midnight stars make bright the skies   ELW 280
I wonder as I wander   WOV 642, TFF 50
'Twas in the moon of wintertime   ELW 284, LBW 72

Second Reading: Micah 5:2-5a

    O little town of Bethlehem   ELW 279, LBW 41

    Once in royal David's city   ELW 269, WOV 643

    Let our gladness have no end   ELW 291, LBW 57

Third Reading: Luke 1:26-35, 38

    The angel Gabriel from heaven came   ELW 265, WOV 632

    Lo, how a rose e'er blooming   ELW 272, LBW 58

    Cold December flies away   ELW 299, LBW 53

Fourth Reading: Matthew 1:18-25

    Jesus, what a wonderful child   ELW 297, TFF 51

    Peace came to earth   ELW 285, WOV 641

    That boy-child of Mary   ELW 293, TFF 54

Fifth Reading: Luke 2:8-20

    All my heart again rejoices   ELW 273

    On Christmas night   ELW 274

    Angels, from the realms of glory   ELW 275, LBW 50

Sixth Reading: Matthew 2:1-11

    In the bleak midwinter   ELW 294

    Your little ones, dear Lord   ELW 286, LBW 52

    What child is this   ELW 296, LBW 40

Seventh Reading: John 1:1-14

    Of the Father's love begotten   ELW 295, LBW 42

    Let all together praise our God   ELW 287, LBW 47

    Love has come   ELW 292

Responsive Prayer

It is you, loving God, who lights our path with truth.

Your Word, Jesus, is truth.

In his light, draw all to the manger

to gather in wonder with the shepherds.

In his light, draw all to the manger

to kneel in reverence with the wise ones.

In his light, draw all to the manger

to sing for joy with the angels.

In the brightness of his life

cast away the darkness of injustice, poverty,

and hunger in the world.

It is you, loving God, who meets us on our way.

In the light of Jesus, show the world the way of life.

Amen.

Lord's Prayer

Blessing

Praise God, from whom all blessings flow!

Praise God, all creatures here below!

You are the shepherds telling the story.

We tell it in the streets and across the land.

You are the wise ones worshiping with thanksgiving.

We worship with gifts of song and service,

talents and treasures.

You are the angels announcing peace.

We live with joy and go now in peace.

Almighty God, Father, ✛ Son, and Holy Spirit,

bless you now and forever.

Amen.

Sending Song

Good Christian friends, rejoice   ELW 288, LBW 55

Angels we have heard on high   ELW 289, LBW 71

Jesus, what a wonderful child   ELW 297, TFF 51

December 24, 2008

Nativity of Our Lord
Christmas Eve

On a long winter evening we gather to proclaim the coming of the light. Isaiah announces that the people who walked in darkness have seen a great light. Paul reminds us that the grace of God has appeared, bringing salvation to all. In the familiar account of Christ's birth, the evening sky is bright with the heavenly host singing, "Glory to God in the highest." Amid our broken world we proclaim that the prince of peace is born among us. God comes to us in human flesh—in Christ's body and blood—so that we may be bearers of divine light to all the world.

I
Particularly appropriate for Christmas Eve

Prayer of the Day

Almighty God, you made this holy night shine with the brightness of the true Light. Grant that here on earth we may walk in the light of Jesus' presence and in the last day wake to the brightness of his glory; through your Son, Jesus Christ our Lord, who lives and reigns with you and the Holy Spirit, one God, now and forever.

Gospel Acclamation

Alleluia. I am bringing you good news of great joy for | all the people:* to you is born this day in the city of David a Savior, who is the Messi- | ah, the Lord. *Alleluia.*
(Luke 2:10-11)

Readings and Psalm
Isaiah 9:2-7

This poem promises deliverance from Assyrian oppression, a hope based on the birth of a royal child with a name full of promise. While Judah's king will practice justice and righteousness, the real basis for faith lies in God's passion for the people: The zeal of the Lord of hosts will do this!

Psalm 96

Let the heavens rejoice and the earth be glad. (Ps. 96:11)

Titus 2:11-14

The appearance of God's grace in Jesus Christ brings salvation for all humanity. Consequently, in the present we live wisely and justly while also anticipating the hope of our Savior's final appearance.

Luke 2:1-14 [15-20]

God's greatest gift comes as a baby in a manger. Angels announce the "good news of great joy" and proclaim God's blessing of peace.

Color   White

CD-ROM Images

Icon Three: ChristmasI_Eve01_ABC, ChristmasI_Eve02_ABC
Icon Two: ChristmasI_Eve02_ABC
Icon: 132, 133, 134

Prayers of Intercession

Rejoicing that the grace of God has been revealed in the birth of Jesus Christ, the light of the world, let us pray for the church, those in need, and all of God's creation.
A brief silence.
God of grace, bless your church that it may faithfully proclaim the good news of Jesus' birth and declare his glory among the nations. Gracious God,
hear our prayer.
God of glory, the heavens are glad and the earth rejoices on this holy night. The seas roar and the forests sing for joy. Move us to respond in loving care for all of creation. Gracious God,
hear our prayer.
God of counsel and might, grant your wisdom to all world leaders, that they may serve in the name of justice and righteousness and all may live in peace. Gracious God,
hear our prayer.

God of light, illumine the lives of all who walk in the darkness of oppression, homelessness, poverty, or sickness (*especially*). Lift the yoke of their burden and give them rest from their weariness. Gracious God,
hear our prayer.
God of welcome, lead this congregation to receive with love all who enter our doors, especially those for whom the world has no room. Gracious God,
hear our prayer.
Here other intercessions may be offered.
God of life, we give you thanks for all the saints who have gone before us and now sing a new song with you. Keep us faithful until that last day when we join them in the brightness of your glory. Gracious God,
hear our prayer.
Into your hands, gracious God, we commend all for whom we pray, trusting in your mercy; through Jesus Christ, our Savior.
Amen.

Ideas and Images for the Day

The birth of Jesus is an overcoming as light trumps darkness, hope overcomes despair, assurance vanquishes fear, and wholeness overcomes brokenness. Christmas is a time of overturning as God becomes "God with us" and invades human and earthly time and space, where the mighty are knocked off their high horses and the lowly are raised up to become regal attendants for the boy who would be king. Overturning the expected and accepted, Jesus is born through Mary, a teenager with an unexpected pregnancy, not an expected royal lineage. The new King of kings and Lord of lords was attended by shepherds, marginal folks, not the usual royal court. These themes of *overcoming* and *overturning* set the focus for the *overwhelming* miracle of this night.

1. Isaiah tells us, "The people who walked in darkness have seen a great light; those who lived in a land of deep darkness—on them light has shined." In Luke, the sky was blazingly bright as the angel announced the birth to the shepherds. In setting the theme of overcoming and overturning becoming the overwhelming, the sermon might begin by focusing on light arising from darkness. The overcoming image is picked up in the other Christmas gospel: "In him was life, and the life was the light of all people. The light shines in the darkness, and the darkness did not overcome it" (John 1:5).

2. Henry Wadsworth Longfellow's poem "I Heard the Bells on Christmas Day" is familiar to many. Some stanzas are often omitted, however, because of their reference to the Civil War, in which the poet's son Charles received crippling wounds. After stanzas of lament, the concluding verses make this confident statement: "Then pealed the bells more loud and deep: / 'God is not dead; nor doth he sleep! / The wrong shall fail, / the right prevail, / with peace on earth, goodwill to men!'" Read the entire poem at www.cyberhymnal.org/htm/i/h/iheardtb.htm or at www.wikipedia.org.

3. Coventry Cathedral in England is an architectural proclamation of hope arising from despair. The new cathedral looms over the ruins of the old one, which was bombed and destroyed during World War II. After the bombing, the faithful of Coventry entered what remained of their church and carved the words "Father Forgive" in the remaining wall behind the altar. From that experience the congregation of Coventry resolved to be a leading witness in social outreach to their industrial community and to worldwide ecumenism and understanding among nations.

Hymns for Worship
Gathering
O come, O come, Emmanuel   ELW 257, LBW 34
On Christmas night   ELW 274
Once in royal David's city   ELW 269, WOV 643

Hymn of the Day
Hark! The herald angels sing!   ELW 270, LBW 60
  MENDELSSOHN
Peace came to earth   ELW 285, WOV 641   SCHNEIDER
From heaven above   ELW 268, LBW 51   VOM HIMMEL HOCH

Communion
Away in a manger   ELW 277, 278, LBW 67, WOV 644
Midnight stars make bright the skies   ELW 280
I am so glad each Christmas Eve   ELW 271, LBW 69
Jesus, what a wonderful child   ELW 297

Sending
Angels we have heard on high   ELW 289, LBW 71
Go tell it on the mountain   ELW 290, LBW 70
Joy to the world   ELW 267, LBW 39

Additional Hymns and Songs
While shepherds watched their flocks   RWSB 118
See amid the winter's snow   RWSB 119
The virgin Mary had a baby boy   TFF 53

Music for the Day
Psalmody and Acclamations

Ferguson, John. *Gospel Acclamations for Advent–Transfiguration.* AFP 9780800620363.

Psalter for Worship Year B, Evangelical Lutheran Worship Edition. AFP 9780806683839.

Shute, Linda Cable. "Psalm 96" from *Psalm Settings for the Church Year.* AFP 9780800678562.

Choral

▫ Bach, J. S. "From Heaven Above to Earth I Come" from *Bach for All Seasons.* SATB, org. AFP 9780800658540.

▫ Burkhardt, Michael. "Hark! The Herald Angels Sing." SATB, children's choir, assembly, org, br, hb. CG A900.

Miller, William. "Sussex Carol." SATB, kybd, hb. AFP 9780800678180.

Schalk, Carl F. "Before the Marvel of This Night" from *Augsburg Easy Choirbook*, vol. 1. 2 pt mxd, org. AFP 9780800676025.

Smith, Michael W./Wayne Kirkpatrick/arr. Lloyd Larson. "All Is Well." SATB, pno, opt insts. HOP C5351.

Children's Choir

Arenson, Carole Lea. "Bring a Torch, Jeannette, Isabella." LE. U, kybd, opt hb/synth. KJO 6257.

Christopherson, Dorothy/Tom Christopherson. "The Virgin Mary Had a Baby Boy." UE. U, kybd, bng, perc. CPH 98-3094.

Lucío, Evy. "La Nana (Lullaby)." UE. 2 pt, solo, opt pno. KJO ED6282.

Sleeth, Natalie. "Were You There on That Christmas Night?" UE. U/2 pt, pno, opt gtr. HOP CF190.

Keyboard / Instrumental

Blair, Dallas. "Mendelssohn" from *Hymn Introductions and Descants for Trumpet and Organ*, set 3. Org, tpt. MSM 20-141.

Pelz, Walter L. "Vom Himmel hoch" from *Augsburg Organ Library: Christmas.* Org. AFP 9780800659356.

Raney, Joel. "Mendelssohn" from *Christmas for 4-Hand Piano.* Pno. HOP 8194.

Zachau, Friedrich Wilhelm. "Vom Himmel hoch" from *Song of the Gospel*, vol. 1. Org. CPH 97-7202U1.

Handbell

Dobrinski, Cynthia, arr. "Lo, How a Rose E'er Blooming." 3-5 oct, L3. AG 1685.

Moklebust, Cathy, arr. "People Look East." 3-5 oct, L2. AFP 9780800656669.

Waldrop, Tammy. "Glorious Christmas Glorias." 3-5 oct, L3. Ring Out Press 3209.

Praise Ensemble

■ Cash, Ed/Chris Tomlin. "Angels We Have Heard on High" from praisecharts.com. EMI Christian Music Publishing.

Deibler, Jeromy, arr. "The First Noel" from *WOW Christmas Songbook* (Orange). WM 080689442285.

■ Fieldes, Mia. "O Rejoice" from www.praisecharts.com. Hillsong Publishing/INT.

LeBlanc, Lenny. "Come and See." W&P 29.

Global

Bedford, Michael. " 'Twas in the Moon of Wintertime." U/2 pt, fl, kybd, perc. AFP 9780800674311.

Collins, Dori Erwin. "Hasten Now, O Shepherds/Vamos, Pastorcitos." U, desc, pno, fl, gtr, perc. AFP 9780800655808.

▫ denotes choral suggestions that relate to the hymn of the day.
■ denotes songs that are available on iTunes®.

December 25, 2008
Nativity of Our Lord
Christmas Day

On this Christmas morning the people of God gather to celebrate the birth of the Word made flesh, Christ our Lord. Luke recounts the familiar story of shepherds and angels; John's gospel tells of the Word that dwells among us, full of grace and truth. The meaning of Christmas is made clear: the light shines in the darkness. It is in the liturgy that we encounter the Word made flesh—in the people of God gathered together as the body of Christ, and in the meal around the holy table. We go forth to be bearers of light as we proclaim this good news to all the ends of the earth.

II
Particularly appropriate for Christmas Day

Prayer of the Day

All-powerful and unseen God, the coming of your light into our world has brightened weary hearts with peace. Call us out of darkness, and empower us to proclaim the birth of your Son, Jesus Christ, our Savior and Lord, who lives and reigns with you and the Holy Spirit, one God, now and forever.

Gospel Acclamation

Alleluia. A holy day has dawned upon us. Come, you nations, and a- | dore the Lord.* For today a great light has come up- | on the earth. *Alleluia.*

Readings and Psalm
Isaiah 62:6-12

The prophet invites the people to give God no rest until God reestablishes Jerusalem. In turn, they will receive names full of promise: Holy People, the Redeemed of the Lord, a City Not Forsaken.

Psalm 97

Light dawns for the righteous, and joy for the honest of heart. (Ps. 97:11)

Titus 3:4-7

God saves us not because of what we do. Rather, God is a God of mercy and salvation who graciously cleanses us in baptism and renews our lives through the Holy Spirit.

Luke 2:[1-7] 8-20

The world's deep night is shattered by the light of God's new day. The glory of God is revealed to poor shepherds, who share the good news with others.

III
Particularly appropriate for Christmas Day

Prayer of the Day

Almighty God, you gave us your only Son to take on our human nature and to illumine the world with your light. By your grace adopt us as your children and enlighten us with your Spirit, through Jesus Christ, our Redeemer and Lord, who lives and reigns with you and the Holy Spirit, one God, now and forever.

Gospel Acclamation

Alleluia. I am bringing you good news of great joy for | all the people:* to you is born this day in the city of David a Savior, who is the Messi- | ah, the Lord. *Alleluia.*
(Luke 2:10-11)
or
Alleluia. A holy day has dawned upon us. Come, you nations, and a- | dore the Lord.* For today a great light has come up- | on the earth. *Alleluia.*

Readings and Psalm
Isaiah 52:7-10

A messenger races home to Jerusalem with the marvelous words: "Your God reigns!" In comforting the people, God proves to be the best brother or sister (redeemer) they have ever known. Everyone will witness the victory (salvation) of God.

Psalm 98

All the ends of the earth have seen the victory of our God. (Ps. 98:3)

Hebrews 1:1-4 [5-12]

This letter opens with a lofty declaration of Jesus' preeminent status as the Son through whom God created the world and through whom our sins are cleansed. God speaks to us now through the Son, who is exalted even above the angels.

John 1:1-14

The prologue to the Gospel of John describes Jesus as the Word of God made flesh, the one who reveals God to be "full of grace and truth."

Color   White

CD-ROM Images

Icon Three: ChristmasII_Day01_ABC, ChristmasII_Day02_ABC, ChristmasIII_Day01_ABC, ChristmasIII_Day02_ABC
Icon Two: Sun2afterChristmas02_ABC, ChristmasII_Day02_ABC, ChristmasII_Day03_ABC
Icon: 005, 132, 133, 134

Prayers of Intercession

Rejoicing that the grace of God has been revealed in the birth of Jesus Christ, the light of the world, let us pray for the church, those in need, and all of God's creation.
A brief silence.
O God, through water and your word you called us out of darkness and gave us the power to become children of God. Lead all the baptized to be bearers of light to the world. Gracious God,
hear our prayer.
O God, in the beginning all things came into being through your word. Empower us to be good stewards of all that you have created. Gracious God,
hear our prayer.
O God, you judge the world with righteousness and the peoples with equity. Make the leaders of all nations messengers of peace. Gracious God,
hear our prayer.
O God, Jesus Christ became flesh and lived among us. Send your living presence to all who are depressed, alone, or sick in this holy season (*especially*), that they may know your love. Gracious God,
hear our prayer.
O God, your Son came to bring life and light. Guide this congregation to be a source of hope and warmth for all in this community and in the world. Gracious God,
hear our prayer.

Here other intercessions may be offered.
O God, we give thanks for all who have testified to the light of Jesus Christ, especially the evangelists and martyrs. Keep us in this light until we come into your holy courts. Gracious God,
hear our prayer.
Into your hands, gracious God, we commend all for whom we pray, trusting in your mercy; through Jesus Christ, our Savior.
Amen.

Ideas and Images for the Day

Today's readings are glorious and highlight in a poetic (rather than narrative) form the mysterious coming of Christ, the Word of God. The poetry is particularly fitting, as poets know the weight and importance of words, and these readings give us a chance to direct attention to Jesus as the Word. This Word not only created the world but sustains it, and is the very expression of God. It is interesting that many religions don't use words for God, understanding that words, at best, can only approximate. Our faithful Christmas proclamation is that Jesus, as the Word, is no approximation. Jesus is God with us.

1. Hebrews 1:3 describes Jesus in this way: "He is . . . the exact imprint of God's very being." *Imprint* has a number of meanings and usages in our language, most of which have fruitful theological tie-ins. From the publisher's information on the title page of a book to the way an animal identifies with its mother, many of these meanings signify not just a replica but a claim of belonging.

2. We can physically see the literal weight that words have with this simple demonstration, which might be used in a children's sermon: Weigh a piece of paper on a sensitive scale, write on it with a lead pencil (or have a child write on it), then weigh it again. It is surprising that the weight indeed changes.

3. In addition to many beloved Christmas carols, *Evangelical Lutheran Worship* includes other hymns that would be appropriate on this day. "He comes to us as one unknown" (ELW 737) speaks of the many ways Jesus comes to us, the many ways God speaks to us. "Word of God, come down on earth" (ELW 510) speaks specifically of Jesus as the Word of God and of the Word's role in creation and salvation.

4. *The Message*, a contemporary version of the New Testament, renders John 1:14 this way: "The Word became flesh and blood, and moved into the neighborhood" (Eugene Peterson, *The Message*, Colorado Springs: NavPress Publishing Group, 2002). Talk about the ways your church community can mimic Jesus' incarnational ministry by fully "moving into the neighborhood." What are the specific needs your immediate neighbors have? How can your church be a good neighbor to the surrounding area?

Hymns for Worship
Gathering

O come, all ye faithful   ELW 283, LBW 45

Angels, from the realms of glory   ELW 275, LBW 50

Hymn of the Day

Of the Father's love begotten   ELW 295, LBW 42   DIVINUM MYSTERIUM

Let our gladness have no end   ELW 291, LBW 57   NARODIL SE KRISTUS PÁN

Let all together praise our God   ELW 287, LBW 47   LOBT GOTT, IHR CHRISTEN

Communion

Jesus, what a wonderful child   ELW 297

That boy-child of Mary   ELW 293

Let all mortal flesh keep silence   ELW 490, LBW 198

Sending

Good Christian friends, rejoice   ELW 288, LBW 55

Love has come   ELW 292

Additional Hymns and Songs

Break forth, O beauteous heavenly light   RWSB 111

Let our gladness banish sadness   LSB 371

Holy Child within the manger   WOV 638

Jesus, the Light of the World   TFF 59

Music for the Day
Psalmody and Acclamations

Anderson, Mark. "Psalm 98" from *Psalm Settings for the Church Year*. AFP 9780800678562.

Ferguson, John. Gospel *Acclamations for Advent–Transfiguration*. AFP 9780800620363.

Psalter for Worship Year B, Evangelical Lutheran Worship Edition. AFP 9780806683839.

Roberts, William Bradley. "Psalm 97" from *Psalm Settings for the Church Year*. AFP 9780800678562.

Choral

Batastini, Robert J. "Gaudete." SATB, hb, fc, drm. GIA G-3056.

Ellingboe, Bradley. "In the Bleak Midwinter." 2 pt mxd/SAB/SATB, pno. KJO 8947.

Nelson, Ronald A. "The Prince of Peace." SATB. CPH 98-3145.

Praetorius, Michael. "To Us Is Born Emmanuel" from *Chantry Choirbook*. SATB. AFP 9780800657772.

Children's Choir

Bailey, Lynn Shaw/Becki Slagle Mayo. "Arise, Shine, Jesus Has Come!" LE. U, opt narr, pno, opt hb. CG A997.

Jacobsen, Roger. "Go See, the King Is Born!" UE. 2 pt, pno, opt fl, fc. Sacred Music Press AD2011.

Maeker, Nancy. "Christmas, a Proclamation for the Church Year." UE. U/2 pt, Orff, narr. AFP 11-3504. OP

Rutter, John. "Angels' Carol." UE. 2 pt, pno, opt hp. HIN HMC-986.

Shields, Valerie. "Arise Now, You Shepherds." UE. 2 pt, fl, pno. MSM 50-1453.

Sleeth, Natalie. "Sing Noel" from *Sunday Songbook*. LE. U/2 pt, kybd. HIN HMB102.

Keyboard / Instrumental

Eggert, John. "Lobt Gott, ihr Christen" from *Creative Hymn Accompaniments for Organ*, vol. 2. Org. CPH 97-6851U1.

Manz, Paul. "Lobt Gott, ihr Christen" from *Improvisations for the Christmas Season*, set 3. Org. MSM 10-102.

Maynard, Lynette. "Divinum mysterium" from *Sing We Now of Christmas*. Pno. AFP 9780800677619.

Sedio, Mark. "Narodil se Kristus Pán" from *Let It Rip! at the Piano*, vol. 2. Pno. AFP 9780800675806.

Handbell

Helman, Michael, arr. "What Child Is This?" 3-5 oct hb/hc, L3. AG 351612.

Moklebust, Cathy, arr. "Still, Still, Still." 2-3 oct hb/hc, L1+. CG B210.

Morris, Hart, arr. "Joy to the World." 3-5 oct, L3. CPH 97-7083.

Praise Ensemble

Baloche, Paul. "Offering" (Christmas version) from www.leadworship.com or www.praisecharts.com. INT.

■ Christensen, Chris. "Go" from www.ccli.com. INT.

■ Tomlin, Chris, arr. "Angels We Have Heard on High" from *WOW Christmas Songbook* (Green). WM 080689498282.

Global

Haugen, Marty. "He Came Down." SATB, children, solo, pno, gtr, perc. GIA G-3808.

Shute, Linda Cable. "The Magi Who to Bethlehem Did Go." SATB, kybd, perc. AFP 9780800658366.

■ denotes songs that are available on iTunes®.

Friday, December 26

Stephen, Deacon and Martyr

Stephen was a deacon and the first martyr of the church. He was one of those seven upon whom the apostles laid hands after they had been chosen to serve widows and others in need. Later, Stephen's preaching angered the temple authorities, and they ordered him to be put to death by stoning. The Christmas song "Good King Wenceslas" takes place on the feast of Stephen. The king sees a peasant gathering wood near the forest and sends his page to invite the peasant to a feast. The song, with its theme of charity to the poor, can be a way to remember Stephen, who cared for widows and those in need.

Saturday, December 27

John, Apostle and Evangelist

John, the son of Zebedee, was a fisherman and one of the Twelve. John, his brother James, and Peter were the three who witnessed the light of the Transfiguration. John and James once made known their desire to hold positions of power in the kingdom of God. Jesus' response showed them that service to others was the sign of God's reign in the world. Tradition has attributed authorship of the gospel and the three epistles bearing his name to the apostle John. John is a saint for Christmas through his proclamation that the Word became flesh and lived among us, that the light of God shines in the darkness, and that we are called to love one another as Christ has loved us.

December 28, 2008
First Sunday of Christmas

In the psalm all the natural world praises God, including all humanity, male and female, young and old. The voices of Simeon and 84-year-old Anna join the chorus today, recognizing what God is doing in Jesus. Simeon's song is often sung after communion, for we have seen God's salvation in the assembled community and have held Jesus in our hands in the bread. Then, like the prophet Anna, we speak of Jesus to all who look for the healing of the world.

The observance of the Holy Innocents, the remembrance of the children of Bethlehem who were victims of King Herod's quest for power, is transferred this year to December 29.

Prayer of the Day

Almighty God, you wonderfully created the dignity of human nature and yet more wonderfully restored it. In your mercy, let us share the divine life of the one who came to share our humanity, Jesus Christ, your Son, our Lord, who lives and reigns with you and the Holy Spirit, one God, now and forever.

Gospel Acclamation

Alleluia. Let the peace of Christ rule ! in your hearts,* and let the word of Christ dwell ! in you richly. *Alleluia.*
(Col. 3:15, 16)

Readings and Psalm

Isaiah 61:10—62:3

To the people who returned to Jerusalem after the exile, the prophet proclaims that the Lord's salvation will fully come to pass. Jerusalem will become a shining light to the nations and righteousness and praise will spring up as surely as the earth puts forth vegetation.

Psalm 148

The splendor of the LORD is over earth and heaven.
(Ps. 148:13)

Galatians 4:4-7

Paul seeks to show the Galatians that the purpose of Christ's birth was to liberate us from the law's condemnation so that we would be fully adopted into God's family as sons and daughters.

Luke 2:22-40

Luke's narrative continues with stories that emphasize Jesus' connection to Judaism. His family is devout in its obser-vance of the law, and Jesus himself is recognized as one who will bring glory to Israel.

Color   White

CD-ROM Images

Icon Three: Sun1ofChristmas_B
Icon Two: Sun1afterChristmas_B
Icon: 071

Prayers of Intercession

Rejoicing that the grace of God has been revealed in the birth of Jesus Christ, the light of the world, let us pray for the church, those in need, and all of God's creation.
A brief silence.
Let us pray for the ministry of the church, that the Holy Spirit would continue to raise up and guide devout servants like Simeon and Anna. Gracious God,
hear our prayer.
Let us give thanks for the sun and moon, fire, snow, and frost, and pray for those who do rescue and repair work in harsh weather, that they may be kept safe. Gracious God,
hear our prayer.
Let us pray for relief workers, agencies that provide aid throughout the world, and all who work to restore the dig-nity of human life, that all people may know their worth in you. Gracious God,
hear our prayer.
Let us pray for the fearful, the sick, and all who cry out to you (*especially*), that they may know you as their loving Abba. Gracious God,
hear our prayer.
Let us pray for this assembly, that we might be advocates for victims of violence and neglect, especially children.

Gracious God,
hear our prayer.
Here other intercessions may be offered.
Let us give thanks for all who have died in you *(especially the infant martyrs of Bethlehem).* Keep us faithful until the day comes when we join them and all the saints. Gracious God,
hear our prayer.
Into your hands, loving God, we commend all for whom we pray, trusting in your mercy; through Jesus Christ, our Savior.
Amen.

Ideas and Images for the Day

Adoration and telling are the focus of today's reading about Simeon and Anna, who are overwhelmed with joy at the sight of the Christ child. Today we meet two elders who lived the words "O, come, let us adore him." The Holy Spirit promised Simeon he would not die before seeing the "Lord's Messiah." Simeon had journeyed from Jerusalem to the temple. Eighty-four-year-old Anna—a prophet, a widow—had been there all the time since the death of her husband. It is not unusual for Luke to lift up those overlooked by societal customs or those on whom society looked down.

1. The Isaiah reading sets the focus on rejoicing and telling. The prophet is so overwhelmed with the promise of salvation that he cannot contain himself with the good news. Similarly, Simeon rejoices and tells that this child will be both "a light for revelation to the Gentiles and for glory to your people Israel" (Luke 2:32). Simeon had a dream of seeing the Christ child, and once he did, he had a vision of the future. Anna too rejoices and tells about the child "to all who were looking for the redemption of Jerusalem" (Luke 2:38). A theme of rejoicing and telling could be a focus of the sermon. In the words of the hymn, "Go tell it on the mountain, over the hills and everywhere."

2. We sing the Song of Simeon after communion (Luke 2:29-32). Compare the three "songs" that surround Christmas and the Christ child. They are consecutive, one starting where another ends. Mary sings of her son's work as the Messiah, pulling down the high and lifting up the lowly, and saving Israel "according to the promise he made to our ancestors, to Abraham and to his descendants forever" (Luke 1:46-55). Zechariah sings of the triumph of Israel (Luke 1:68-79), and Simeon announces hope for the Gentiles.

3. The opening verse of the gospel indicates the holy family's desire to adhere to the prevailing religious law (Lev. 12:2-8; Exod. 13:2, 12). Here, the rite of purification serves two purposes. It underscores that Jesus was fully human, often a stumbling block for early Christians. And it declares Jesus' purpose to fulfill the law. The second reading is helpful here: "God sent his Son, born of a woman, born under the law, in order to redeem those who were under the law" (Gal. 4:4-5).

4. Jesus was taken for the rite of purification. Rituals of birth are significant even today: choosing a name, announcing the pregnancy, the first "presentation" in church, the baptism. For more information on the Jewish rite of purification see www.jewishencyclopedia.com and *The Jewish Lifecycle* by Ivan Marcus (Seattle: University of Washington Press, 2004).

Hymns for Worship
Gathering
Let all together praise our God   ELW 287, LBW 47
Love has come   ELW 292
Good Christian friends, rejoice   ELW 288, LBW 55

Hymn of the Day
In his temple now behold him   ELW 417, LBW 184
REGENT SQUARE
O Lord, now let your servant   ELW 313, LBW 339
KUORTANE
Lo, how a rose e'er blooming   ELW 272, LBW 58
ES IST EIN ROS

Communion
Peace came to earth   ELW 285, WOV 641
Your little ones, dear Lord   ELW 286, LBW 52

Sending
O Lord, now let your servant   ELW 313, LBW 339 *or* ELW 200–203
Cold December flies away   ELW 299, LBW 53
Lord, dismiss us with your blessing   ELW 545, LBW 259

Additional Hymns and Songs
See Mary setting out at dawn   HG 121
Our Father, by whose name   ELW 640, LBW 357
O rejoice, ye Christians, loudly   LSB 897
O Zion, open wide thy gates   H82 257

Music for the Day
Psalmody and Acclamations
Ferguson, John. *Gospel Acclamations for Advent–Transfiguration.* AFP 9780800620363.
Mummert, Mark. "Psalm 148" from *Psalm Settings for the Church Year.* AFP 9780800678562.
Psalter for Worship Year B, Evangelical Lutheran Worship Edition. AFP 9780806683839.

Choral

Edwards, Malcolm V. "Hymn of the Poor." SA, pno. Alliance Music Publications 0462.

Ferguson, John. "Unto Us Is Born God's Son." SATB, org. AFP 9780800652395.

Scholz, Robert. "Nunc Dimittis." SSATB, kybd, opt orch. AFP 9786000001216.

Sedio, Mark. "The Coventry Carol." 2 pt mxd, org. SEL 405-234.

Children's Choir

Bailey, Lynn Shaw/Becki Slagle Mayo. "Oh, Come, Little Children." UE. U/2 pt, pno, opt fc, wood blocks, drm/conga, hb/hc. CG A1099.

Burroughs, Bob. "Once in Royal David's City." LE. U, kybd, opt hb. CG A526.

Lau, Robert. "Little One, Holy One." UE. 2 pt, pno. LOR E222.

Rotermund, Donald. "Carol of the Angels and Shepherds." UE. U/2 pt, glock, xyl, tri, fc, gtr/cello. CPH 98-2318.

Keyboard / Instrumental

Blair, Dallas. "Regent Square" from *Hymn Introductions and Descants for Trumpet and Organ*, set 3. Org, tpt. MSM 20-141.

Brahms, Johannes. "Es ist ein Ros." Org. Various ed.

Cherwien, David. "Kuortane" from *Organ Plus One*. Org, C/B-flat inst. AFP 9780800656188.

Moore, David W. "Es ist ein Ros" from *Piano Plus: Advent/Christmas*. Pno, C/B-flat inst. AFP 9780800638542.

Handbell

Krug, Jason, arr. "Il Est Ne." 3-5 oct, L3-. BP HB286.

Morris, Hart, arr. "God Rest You Merry, Gentlemen." 3-5 oct, opt perc, L3. AG 35230.

Sternowski, Cathy, arr. "Awake, Awake and Greet the New Morn." 3 oct hb/hc, L3+. GIA G-7085.

Praise Ensemble

■ Doerksen, Brian. "Come, Now Is the Time to Worship" from www.praisecharts.com. VIN.

■ Richards, Noel/Tricia Richards. "All Heaven Declares" from *More Songs for Praise & Worship 2*. WM 080689314186.

■ Zschech, Darlene. "Glory to the King" from www.praisecharts.com. Hillsong Publishing/INT.

■ Zschech, Darlene. "Shout to the Lord." ELW 821, W&P 124.

Global

Sosa, Pablo. "Gloria/Glory." SATB, assembly, pno, gtr. GIA G-7010.

Stevens, Ronald L. "What'cha Gonna Call the Pretty Little Baby." SATB. GIA G-6058.

■ denotes songs that are available on iTunes®.

Monday, December 29

The Holy Innocents, Martyrs (transferred)

The infant martyrs commemorated on this day were the children of Bethlehem, two years old and younger, who were killed by Herod, who worried that his reign was threatened by the birth of a new king. Augustine called these innocents "buds, killed by the frost of persecution the moment they showed themselves." Those linked to Jesus through their youth and innocence encounter the same hostility Jesus encounters later in his ministry.

Remembering all innocent victims and taking up the words of the prayer of the day, which ask God to "frustrate the designs of evil tyrants and establish your rule of justice, love, and peace," can mark this commemoration.

Thursday, January 1

Name of Jesus

The observance of the octave (eighth day) of Christmas has roots in the sixth century. Until the recent past, Lutheran calendars called this day "The Circumcision and Name of Jesus." The emphasis on circumcision is the older emphasis. Every Jewish boy was circumcised and formally named on the eighth day of his life. Already in his youth, Jesus bears the mark of a covenant that he makes new through the shedding of his blood, now and on the cross. That covenant, like Jesus' name, is a gift that marks the children of God. Baptized into Christ, the church begins a new year in Jesus' name.

Friday, January 2

Johann Konrad Wilhelm Loehe, renewer of the church, 1872

Loehe was a pastor in nineteenth-century Germany. From the small town of Neuendettelsau, he sent pastors to North America, Australia, New Guinea, Brazil, and the Ukraine. His work for a clear confessional basis within the Bavarian church sometimes led to conflict with the ecclesiastical bureaucracy. Loehe's chief concern was that a parish find its life in the eucharist, and from that source evangelism and social ministries would flow. Many Lutheran congregations in Michigan, Ohio, and Iowa were either founded or influenced by missionaries sent by Loehe. The chapel at Wartburg Theological Seminary is named in his honor. Loehe's vision to see the eucharist at the center of parish life can lead us to think about ways that the incarnate presence of Christ in holy communion sends us out into a life of ministry and mission.

January 4, 2009
Second Sunday of Christmas

Within the gospel reading's profound words lies the simple message that God is revealed in a human person. Though we may try to understand how the Word existed with God from the beginning of time, the wonder we celebrate at Christmas is that the Word continues to dwell among us. Christ comes among us in the gathered assembly, the scriptures, the waters of new birth, and the bread and the wine. Through these ordinary gifts we receive the fullness of God's grace and truth.

Prayer of the Day

Almighty God, you have filled all the earth with the light of your incarnate Word. By your grace empower us to reflect your light in all that we do, through Jesus Christ, our Savior and Lord, who lives and reigns with you and the Holy Spirit, one God, now and forever.

or

O God our redeemer, you created light that we might live, and you illumine our world with your beloved Son. By your Spirit comfort us in all darkness, and turn us toward the light of Jesus Christ our Savior, who lives and reigns with you and the Holy Spirit, one God, now and forever.

Gospel Acclamation

Alleluia. All the ends ⎮ of the earth* have seen the victory ⎮ of our God. *Alleluia.* (Ps. 98:3)

Readings and Psalm

Jeremiah 31:7-14

God promises to bring Israel back to its land from the most remote parts of exile. In Zion Israel will rejoice over God's gift of food and livestock. Young women will express their joy in dancing; God will give gladness instead of sorrow.

or **Sirach 24:1-12**

The figure of Wisdom played a major role in early discussions about the person and work of Christ. Wisdom is the divine word, coming from the mouth of God, and ruling over all of creation. Wisdom, created at the beginning of time, made her dwelling place in Jerusalem among God's people.

Psalm 147:12-20

Worship the Lord, O Jerusalem; praise your God, O Zion. (Ps. 147:12)

or **Wisdom 10:15-21**

We sing, O Lord, to your holy name. (Wis. 10:20)

Ephesians 1:3-14

In Jesus, all of God's plans and purposes have been made known as heaven and earth are united in Christ. Through Jesus, we have been chosen as God's children and have been promised eternal salvation.

John 1:[1-9] 10-18

John begins his gospel with this prologue: a hymn to the Word through whom all things were created. This Word became flesh and brought grace and truth to the world.

Color   White

CD-ROM Images

Icon Three: Sun2ofChristmas01_ABC, Sun2ofChristmas02_ABC, Sun2ofChristmas03_ABC
Icon Two: Sun2afterChristmas01_ABC, Sun2afterChristmas02_ABC, Sun2afterChristmas03_ABC
Icon: 005, 007, 132, 136

Prayers of Intercession

Rejoicing that the grace of God has been revealed in the birth of Jesus Christ, the light of the world, let us pray for the church, those in need, and all of God's creation.
A brief silence.
You have given your church grace upon grace. Bless its mission to proclaim your salvation to the farthest parts of the earth. Gracious God,
hear our prayer.
You have filled us with the finest wheat. Move us to share from our bounty that others may be satisfied. Gracious God,
hear our prayer.

You have made all nations one in you. Grant your wisdom and insight to those who lead, and give all countries peace within their borders and with other nations. Gracious God,
hear our prayer.

You hear the needs of all. Send your healing Spirit to the blind, the lame, and the sick (*especially*), that they may know your consolation. Gracious God,
hear our prayer.

You have marked your children with the seal of the promised Holy Spirit and have adopted us as your own. Empower us to claim our inheritance as children of God in service to others. Gracious God,
hear our prayer.

Here other intercessions may be offered.

You promise comfort for all who grieve and turn their mourning into joy. We give you thanks for all who have died in Christ (*especially*), and we wait in anticipation for the day when you gather all things in heaven and on earth in you. Gracious God,
hear our prayer.

Into your hands, gracious God, we commend all for whom we pray, trusting in your mercy; through Jesus Christ our Savior.
Amen.

Ideas and Images for the Day

As we hear the soaring symphony of John's prologue, we are transported from angels and shepherds and the first family to a cosmic explosion that inaugurated a new era, a new kingdom. Rather than a quiet, silent night with a birth in a stable, John's nativity story is more like a rushing meteor plummeting toward and smashing into the earth. Christmas, he tells us, is God's purposeful invasion of our time, God's decisive and determined action to become flesh and live among us. John moves us beyond the baby to the Creator of all! In this version of the story, nothing could stop God.

1. It is no mistake that the symbol of this gospel writer is the eagle. John's Christmas story begins in the vaulted heavens but does not end there. Not only did the Word create life and light from heavenly splendor, but the Eagle suddenly dives toward the ground. Mission Control, the Eagle has landed, but not in the gentle glide of our present-day space shuttles. In this symphony the violins give way to the sudden thud of the bass drum. Heaven crashes to earth with startling news: the Word became flesh and lived among us. "Now all the vault of heaven resounds" (ELW 367) might be a good hymn choice today.

2. Themes such as invasion, cosmic explosion, and decisive action would be good sermon images. The hymn "You are holy" (ELW 525) could be used as the "Holy, holy, holy" at the great thanksgiving, particularly because of the line "Let the cosmos praise you, Lord!"

3. A quote from Symeon, abbot at Constantinople and mystic (949–1022): "For this unique being that appears, shines forth, is radiantly splendid, is participating in, is communicating, is everything good. . . . He is light and peace and joy, life, food and drink, clothing, a robe, a tent and a divine dwelling. He is the east, the resurrection, repose and a bath, fire, water, river, source of life and a flowing stream, bread and wine, the new delight of believers, the banquet, the pleasure which we enjoy in a mystical way, sun, indeed, without any setting, star always shining, lamp that burns inside the dwelling of the soul" (quoted in Gail Ramshaw, *Richer Fare for the Christian People*, New York: Pueblo Publishing Co., 1990, pp. 12–13).

4. The Jewish people have a long litany they recite at Passover: *Dayenu! It would have been enough.* Recounting salvation history, *Dayenu* proclaims the mighty acts of God in saving them. It begins, "If He had brought us out from Egypt, and had not carried out judgments against them—Dayenu, it would have been enough!" See http://en.wikipedia.org/wiki/Dayenu for the complete litany. The sermon could tie in God's invasion of our time and space with all of salvation history: It *should* have been enough, but it wasn't. God *had* to come!

Hymns for Worship
Gathering
What child is this   ELW 296, LBW 40
Angels, from the realms of glory   ELW 275, LBW 50
Hark! The herald angels sing   ELW 270, LBW 60

Hymn of the Day
Of the Father's love begotten   ELW 295, LBW 42
    DIVINUM MYSTERIUM
Let our gladness have no end   ELW 291, LBW 57
    NARODIL SE KRISTUS PÁN
Word of God, come down on earth   ELW 510,
    WOV 716   LIEBSTER JESU, WIR SIND HIER

Communion
O Splendor of God's glory bright   ELW 559, LBW 271
Let all mortal flesh keep silence   ELW 490, LBW 198

Sending

O come, all ye faithful   ELW 283, LBW 45
Jesus, what a wonderful child   ELW 297

Additional Hymns and Songs

Holy Child within the manger   WOV 638
Word of God, when all was silent   HG 82
Emmanuel   W&P 35, TFF 45
There Was the Word   DH 55

Music for the Day
Psalmody and Acclamations

Ferguson, John. *Gospel Acclamations for Advent–Transfiguration.* AFP 9780800620363.

Pavlechko, Thomas. "Wisdom 10" from *Psalm Settings for the Church Year.* AFP 9780800678562.

Psalter for Worship Year B, Evangelical Lutheran Worship Edition. AFP 9780806683839.

Woehr, Roland. "Psalm 147" from *Psalm Settings for the Church Year.* AFP 9780800678562.

Choral

Bouman, Paul. "God Is Light." SATB, org. AFP 9780800653255.

Hassler, Hans Leo. "God Now Dwells Among Us." SAB/TBB, kybd. MFS MF129.

Hovland, Egil. "The Glory of the Father." SATB. WAL W2973.

Mendelssohn, Felix. "There Shall a Star Come Out of Jacob" from *Chantry Choirbook.* SATB, org. AFP 9780800657772.

Children's Choir

Leaf, Robert. "Children's Voices Joyfully Sing." UE. 2 pt, org. Celebrations Unlimited 229.

Sherman, Arnold B. "He Is Born." UE. 2 pt, kybd, opt hb. HOP RS7727.

Shields, Valerie. "Polish Lullaby Carol." UE. 2 pt, desc, pno, fl. PLY XM525.

Keyboard / Instrumental

Frahm, Frederick. "Liebster Jesu, wir sind hier" from *Augsburg Organ Library: Epiphany.* Org. AFP 9780800659349.

Held, Wilbur. "Divinum mysterium" from *Augsburg Organ Library: Christmas.* Org. AFP 9780800659356.

Leavitt, John. "Narodil se Kristus Pán" from *Hymn Preludes for the Church Year.* Org. AFP 9780800650322. OP

Organ, Anne Krentz. "Divinum mysterium" from *Let It Rip! at the Piano*, vol. 1. Pno. AFP 9780800659066.

Handbell

Dobrinski, Cynthia, arr. "Infant Holy, Infant Lowly." 3-5 oct, opt fl, L2+. AG 1703.

McChesney, Kevin, arr. "Sussex Carol." 3-4 oct, L1+. CG B133.

Rogers, Sharon Elery. "Two German Chorales for Christmas." 2-3 oct, L1+. GIA G-7084.

Praise Ensemble

■ Allen, Blaine. "Little Baby Jesus" from www.ccli.com. HOP.

■ Brown, Scott W./Jeff Nelson. "Grace Alone" from *More Songs for Praise & Worship 2.* WM 080689314186.

■ Millard, Bart/Pete Kipley. "Word of God Speak" from *Word of God, Speak: 25 Modern Praise Favorites.* WM 080689481284.

■ Smith, Michael W. "Agnus Dei" from WT. Milene Music.

Global

Hesla, Bret. "Sing We All on This Day" from *Justice, Like a Base of Stone.* U, kybd. AFP 9780800623562.

Sosa, Pablo. "El cielo canta alegría/Heaven Is Singing for Joy." SATB, kybd, gtr, perc. GIA G-7014.

■ denotes songs that are available on iTunes®.

January 6, 2009
Epiphany of Our Lord

Epiphany means "manifestation." On this day we celebrate the revelation of Christ to the Gentiles—that is, to all nations. Some Christian traditions celebrate three great epiphanies on this day: the magi's adoration of the Christ child, Jesus' baptism in the Jordan River, and his first miracle, in which he changes water into wine. The word and sacraments are for us the great epiphany of God's grace and mercy. We go forth to witness to the light that shines brightly in our midst.

Prayer of the Day

O God, on this day you revealed your Son to the nations by the leading of a star. Lead us now by faith to know your presence in our lives, and bring us at last to the full vision of your glory, through your Son, Jesus Christ our Lord, who lives and reigns with you and the Holy Spirit, one God, now and forever.

or

Almighty and ever-living God, you revealed the incarnation of your Son by the brilliant shining of a star. Shine the light of your justice always in our hearts and over all lands, and accept our lives as the treasure we offer in your praise and for your service, through Jesus Christ, our Savior and Lord, who lives and reigns with you and the Holy Spirit, one God, now and forever.

or

Everlasting God, the radiance of all faithful people, you brought the nations to the brightness of your rising. Fill the world with your glory, and show yourself to all the world through him who is the true light and the bright morning star, your Son, Jesus Christ, our Savior and Lord, who lives and reigns with you and the Holy Spirit, one God, now and forever.

Gospel Acclamation

Alleluia. We have observed his star ' at its rising,* and have come to ' worship him. *Alleluia.* (Matt. 2:2)

Readings and Psalm

Isaiah 60:1-6

Jerusalem is assured that nations will make a pilgrimage to her, because the light of God's presence is in her midst. The bountiful food of the sea and the profits of international trade will come streaming to Jerusalem and thereby declare God's praise.

Psalm 72:1-7, 10-14

All kings shall bow down before him. (Ps. 72:11)

Ephesians 3:1-12

What had been hidden from previous generations is now made known through the gospel ministry of Paul and others. In Christ both Jews and Gentiles participate in the richness of God's promised salvation.

Matthew 2:1-12

God's promise shines bright in the night as magi follow a star to honor a new king. Strangers from a faraway land, they welcome the long-awaited messiah of Israel.

Color   White

CD-ROM Images

Icon Three: EpiphanyDay01_ABC, EpiphanyDay02_ABC, EpiphanyDay03_ABC
Icon Two: 1EpiphanyDay01_ABC, 1EpiphanyDay02_ABC
Icon: 008, 137

Prayers of Intercession

Rejoicing that the grace of God has been revealed in the birth of Jesus Christ, the light of the world, let us pray for the church, those in need, and all of God's creation.
A brief silence.
God of light, raise up your church as a light for the world, defending the cause of the poor and giving deliverance to the needy. Gracious God,
hear our prayer.
God of glory, shower the earth with your grace, that the mountains and the hills yield prosperity for all of creation. Gracious God,
hear our prayer.

God of light, bring all nations to the brightness of your dawn, that righteousness may flourish and peace abound. Gracious God,
hear our prayer.
God of glory, reveal your great love to those who are oppressed, weak, or sick *(especially)*, that they may know they are precious in your sight. Gracious God,
hear our prayer.
God of light, make known to us the mystery of Christ, that we may recognize our own calling to serve others. Gracious God,
hear our prayer.
Here other intercessions may be offered.
God of glory, receive our thanks for all the apostles, prophets, and saints who are our fellow heirs in your grace. As you guided them through their earthly journey, so guide and support us until we join them in your eternal rest. Gracious God,
hear our prayer.
Into your hands, gracious God, we commend all for whom we pray, trusting in your mercy; through Jesus Christ our Savior.
Amen.

Ideas and Images for the Day

A star is born on Christmas Day. Not a star as in star athlete or a Hollywood star, but a beacon, an ensign, a beckoning light that would draw all people to himself; an irresistible, magnetic, superstar who would become the "light of life." Today, Epiphany, marks the seeming end of our Christmas journey. The readings for the time after Epiphany, however, continue the journey as they focus on God's revelation in Jesus Christ.

1. Folklore, legend, tales, stories, dance, and music have all contributed to enhancing the biblical story of the Epiphany. Why? Perhaps because the day is so mystical, filled with the unexpected: twists and turns, mysterious visitors who probably traveled a year (not twelve days) to greet the Christ child. It is a day of surprises and strange gifts.

2. How is Jesus made known to us? Ambrose, Bishop of Milan (339–397), answers this way: "Can anyone say that the Lord is made known to us by signs of little import, when the magi come and adore him, the angels serve him, and the martyrs confess him? He comes forth from a womb, but he shines like lightning from above; he lies in an earthly resting place, but round about him is the brightness of heaven. The espoused

has brought forth; but a virgin has conceived. A wife has conceived, but a virgin has given birth" (Gail Ramshaw, *Richer Fare for the Christian People*, New York: Pueblo Publishing Co., 1990, p. 13).

3. Herbert O'Driscoll writes of our fascination with the magi and how they fit into the Christmas story. "The magi fascinate us also because they do not fit into this tiny stage of hill village and humble stable. Their sophistication clashes with this simplicity, their obvious power sits uneasily beside the vulnerability of child and family. They are urban in a rural world, affluent in the midst of poverty, cosmopolitan amid the provincial" ("Kingly Presence," *The Christian Century*, December 27, 2003, p. 18).

4. "The day you gave us, Lord, has ended" (ELW 569) picks up the theme of light as it proclaims that the light of Jesus is never dimmed nor is the church's proclamation of that light. As the sun sets on one continent, it rises on another. "The sun, here having set, is waking your children under western skies, and hour by hour, as day is breaking, fresh hymns of thankful praise arise."

Hymns for Worship
Gathering
Bright and glorious is the sky   ELW 301, LBW 75
Angels, from the realms of glory   ELW 275, LBW 50
Hail to the Lord's anointed   ELW 311, LBW 87

Hymn of the Day
As with gladness men of old   ELW 302, LBW 82   DIX
Brightest and best of the stars   ELW 303, LBW 84
   MORNING STAR
Bright and glorious is the sky   ELW 301, LBW 75
   DEJLIG ER DEN HIMMEL BLÅ

Communion
The first Noel   ELW 300, LBW 56
What child is this   ELW 296, LBW 40

Sending
Rise, shine, you people!   ELW 665, LBW 393
Arise, your light has come!   ELW 314, WOV 652
Shine, Jesus, Shine   ELW 671, WOV 651

Additional Hymns and Songs
The magi who to Bethlehem did go   RWSB 122, LLC 317
We three kings of Orient are   WOV 646
Alleluia   W&P 6

Music for the Day
Psalmody and Acclamations

Ferguson, John. *Gospel Acclamations for Advent–Transfiguration.* AFP 9780800620363.

Mummert, Mark. "Psalm 72" from *Psalm Settings for the Church Year.* AFP 9780800678562.

Psalter for Worship Year B, Evangelical Lutheran Worship Edition. AFP 9780806683839.

Choral

Hirten, John Karl. "For Glory Dawns Upon You" from *The Augsburg Choirbook.* 2 pt mxd, kybd. AFP 9780800656782.

Langlois, Kristina. "I Want to Walk as a Child of the Light." SAB, assembly, org, opt tpt. AFP 9780800678197.

Nelson, Ronald A. "What Can We Bring?" SAB, kybd. HIN HMC-1706.

Thompson, Randall. "Arise, Shine" from *Twelve Canticles.* SATB. ECS 4104.

Children's Choir

Christopherson, Dorothy. "The Night of the Star." UE. U/2 pt, pno, fl, perc. AFP 9780800657543. OP

Gullickson, Karen Nelson. "See the Star." UE. 2 pt, pno. AFP 9786000118532. OP

Lowe, Helenclaire. "Tell Me, Who Is This Tiny Little Baby." UE. U, pno. CG A466.

Walker, David S. "Rise Up, Shepherd, and Follow." UE. U, solo, Orff, opt gtr/autoharp. CPH 98-2141.

Keyboard / Instrumental

Dahl, David P. "Morning Star" from *A Scandanavian Suite for Organ.* Org. AFP 9780800678432.

Henkelmann, Brian. "Dejlig er den Himmel bla" from *Chorale Preludes for the Liturgical Year*, vol. 1. Kybd, fl. CPH 97-7227.

Oquin, Wayne. "Dix" from *All Things New.* Pno. CPH 97-7205U1.

Wold, Wayne L. "Morning Star" from *God With Us.* Org. AFP 9780800658212.

Handbell

Behnke, John A. "Dance Africana" (Dix). 3-5 oct, opt perc, L2. CPH 97-6745.

Larson, Lloyd. "Beautiful Savior." 3-4 oct, L2. AFP 9780800653965.

Tucker, Sondra K., arr. "I Want to Walk as a Child of the Light." 3-5 oct, L3. AFP 9780800658861.

Praise Ensemble

- Agnew, Todd. "God With Us/We Three Kings" from www.ccli.com. Ardent/Koala Music.
- Cull, Bob. "Open Our Eyes" from *Maranatha Greenbook.* MAR 738597141690.
- Green, Melody. "There Is a Redeemer." W&P 140.
- Zschech, Darlene. "It Is You" from www.praisecharts.com. Hillsong Publishing/INT.

Global

Hassell, Michael. "This Little Light of Mine." SATB, pno. AFP 9780800657536.

Sosa, Pablo/Bread for the Journey. "El cielo canta alegría/Heaven Is Singing for Joy" from *Pave the Way: Global Songs 3.* U, kybd, gtr, perc. AFP 9780800676896.

■ denotes songs that are available on iTunes®.

TIME AFTER EPIPHANY

Preparing for the Time after Epiphany

Lectionary

What did the magi ponder on their long journey home? Did they consider their astonishment at finding the king they were seeking not in Herod's palace, their first stop, but as a baby in a humble house in the little town of Bethlehem? How were they different when they arrived home? Christmas is all about disruption: lives are never the same after an encounter with the Christ child. God catapults people out of the comfortable places of their lives into a journey whose end they cannot know.

The time after Epiphany demonstrates many different ways to respond to God's call. The baptism of repentance described in Acts causes people to immediately speak in tongues and prophesy. Samuel's response, after he realizes that it is God calling him in the night and not Eli, is also immediate: "Speak, Lord, for your servant is listening." He went on to rule wisely and well for many years. Nathanael marvels at Jesus' deep knowledge of him and responds with a firm statement that Jesus is indeed the Son of God. When Jesus calls the first disciples, the fishermen leave their boats and follow him instantly.

On the other hand, Jonah is a fine example of how God also calls flawed and uncooperative people to carry out God's purposes. When God called Jonah to prophesy to the people of Nineveh, Jonah fled in the opposite direction. But it's not easy to escape God, and after three days in the belly of a fish, Jonah, still reluctant, dragged himself to Nineveh to do what God had asked.

And who but God would have thought to call Saul, that violent persecutor of the followers of Jesus, to be a key figure in the spread of God's word to the Gentiles? Prominent though often overlooked in this event was Ananias, whose response to God's call echoes that of Samuel, Mary, and so many others: "Here I am, Lord." When he hears the task God has designed for him, he reminds God that Saul is a murderous fanatic, sworn to kill Ananias and his kind. God reassures him, and Ananias obeys. Ananias's service to God was not as flashy or as celebrated as Paul's, but its example of obedience, trust, and love is one that many can follow.

When Naaman, army commander and ingrate, was told by Elisha to wash seven times in the Jordan to cure his leprosy, Naaman shouted angrily that he wanted the gift of healing to be bigger, flashier, and different. In scripture and in our own lives, God's gifts don't always come in the desired form. A suffering Savior, rather than a triumphant Messiah, was not what everyone expected or wanted—then or now.

The time after Epiphany ends with the transfiguration. The clear message of this event is that neither Jesus nor his followers can stay on a mountaintop, removed from the mess, suffering, and evil of human life. The surprise the wise men experienced at the beginning of Jesus' earthly life continues at its end.

Space and Music

"How odd is God!" an old pastor used to say. In the time after Epiphany, while the world sighs with relief that the hectic holiday season is over and trudges back into daily routine, God's children set forth renewed in their vision of the Christ child and refreshed by the reminder of their own baptism, transformed by water and the word.

Even though the time after Epiphany is a so-called "green season," a time of relative calm between Epiphany and Lent, it's also a good time for congregational activities that illuminate the Epiphany by proclaiming the manifestation of the incarnation in all the cultures and nations of the world. Choral performances on Sunday afternoons could feature music from other lands, or an art show (even a small one, featuring a local artist) could celebrate the cultural diversity in the neighborhoods next door. If your congregation is active in the political affairs of your community, this is a good season to join community events like a Martin Luther King Jr. Day observance. Is someone in your church volunteering for Lutheran World Relief? Mission work? Bring their ministry into the worship space artistically, if you can, whether it's art they've received in their travels or music they've learned. Accompany this with *Evangelical Lutheran Worship* music from around the world. Keep the energy going, keep the parish lively, keep the stars shining.

There are many stories of Jesus' healing in this season, and the church, too, is called to be a healing presence in the world. Jesus calls the disciples, teaches with authority, casts out unclean spirits, heals, and prays. It's a good time to display evidence of the congregation's and the wider church's ministries in the world—and to invite people to join or contribute to these ministries. Take the poinsettias or other Christmas flowers to the homebound or those in hospitals and nursing homes. Put the basket for food-shelf donations in a prominent spot and distribute, again, a list of appropriate foods with which to fill it. Bulletin inserts, brief temple talks, videos, banners, or poster displays will inform new members and remind longer-term members of the work of the church and of opportunities to serve. Perhaps some space in the church newsletter could be devoted to brief articles by members about their personal, individual ministries, which often go unheralded. For example, the woman who devotes herself to making a quilt for each child in the homeless families that come through the Interfaith Hospitality Network could hang some of the quilts in the worship space. Soliciting suggestions for new ministries would also be appropriate.

One must be careful, of course, not to fall into the seductive "works righteousness" frame of mind that sees people earning God's favor by their good deeds. The situation is exactly the opposite: loving actions grow out of a response to God's grace.

Appropriate words to print at the bottom of the worship folder or to paint or post above the outside door are: "The worship is over. The service begins." Service does not consist in racking up points with God by exhausting participation on dozens of committees and projects. Another wise old pastor said often that service in God's kingdom should be fun, a joyful response to God's love that prompts love for the people sharing the neighborhood and the planet.

"Let there be light," God proclaimed, and the newly created world was never again the same. The power of God's word is also demonstrated in Jesus' baptism by John. His public ministry was launched, and the tired, old, sin-sick world was never the same.

What is sung on Sunday rings in people's minds all week and seeps into their souls. A 90-year-old woman told her writing group about leaving her husband and making the long drive by herself to her sister's home in Florida—two things not many women did in those days. For hundreds of miles she sang at the top of her voice the many wonderful hymns about God's power and protection. They got her through.

Hymns sung on Sunday and at other times can "get God's people through." Martin Luther believed strongly in the role of hymns in faith formation. The powerful words of God that permeate this season can permeate lives as well.

Verbs are the engines of the sentence; they're where the action is. The verbs that punctuate this season demonstrate how God works with God's people, changing them so that they too are never again the same. Powerful imperatives such as *transform*, *renew*, *call*, *reveal*, *protect*, *restore*,

transfigure, *illumine*, *immerse*, and *strengthen* echo the pleas of the people for God's action in their lives. God has acted in the lives of the many witnesses, missionaries, teachers, renewers of the church and of society, and martyrs who are commemorated in this season.

In *Evangelical Lutheran Worship*, the Time after Epiphany section, new in this edition, has 18 hymns. Three hymns that may be new to Lutherans are well-suited to the themes described above. "Come, beloved of the Maker" (#306) is a lovely prayer that for those who "behold the First-born One," God will "bear us into light at last." "Light shone in darkness" (#307) picks up the "illumine" imperative at three points in time: the world's creation, Christ's resurrection, and the "global transformation" still to come. "Jesus on the mountain peak" (#317) renders the full glory of Jesus' transfiguration. Understandably, Peter and the other witnesses wanted to prolong this moment!

Some of the other sections in *Evangelical Lutheran Worship*, including three new ones*, contain hymns appropriate to the season: Vocation/Ministry*, Grace/Faith*, Confession/Forgiveness, Healing*, Commitment/Discipleship, and Witness.

Most Christians don't experience the drama of Paul's conversion. With the great majority, God works through the means of spiritual sustenance that Jesus himself made use of: the Holy Spirit that comes in baptism, study of scripture, worship, fellowship, service, and prayer. Another component of spiritual sustenance is the eucharist. Hymns that celebrate these means of grace through which God works are good ones for this season. Some fruitful sources in *Evangelical Lutheran Worship* are Pentecost/Holy Spirit, Holy Baptism, Word of God, Gathering, Praise and Thanksgiving, Community in Christ, Stewardship, Prayer, and Holy Communion.

Transfiguration Sunday

Finally, one more mountaintop experience to bring the incarnational cycle to a close: Transfiguration Sunday. *Alleluia* is sung for the last time before Lent. Choirs can perform a larger work, or simply offer bright descants to transfiguration hymns. This is the time of Carnival, so cookies, decorations, the fats and delights of the season—they're all here! All this sparkle, all this celebration, offers one more reminder of God's glorious grace, promised in Advent, revealed at Christmas, and carried to the ends of the world at the Epiphany. For one last time, let us shout our song of alleluia!

Celebrating the Time after Epiphany with Children

A scan of the gospels for this season reveals that the time after Epiphany begins and ends with a theme of identity. At Jesus' baptism, and again at his transfiguration, he is identified as God's Son, the Beloved.

During these weeks, Jesus is revealed as host, storyteller, and listener. The fourth, fifth, and sixth Sundays after Epiphany portray Jesus as healer, offering a natural connection to make with children, who often have an innate sense of compassion.

Jesus also becomes known to us through his gifts of invitation, encouragement, and compassion. Each of these identities of Jesus flows from his main identity as the beloved Son of God. Children share that same identity in baptism. During the time after Epiphany, invite and encourage the children of your congregation to become aware of the blessing of their baptismal identity, using either of the first two ideas listed below.

Ideas for the Time after Epiphany

- Make children name tags that say " _____ is a beloved child of God." Fill in their names or have them write their own names. Give each child name tags to share with worshipers. The children may stand at the doors before or after worship to give out the name tags to worshipers. This would be especially fitting for the Baptism of Our Lord or Transfiguration Sunday.

- On the Baptism of Our Lord, have a child pour water into the baptismal font during thanksgiving for baptism or while the prayer of the day is spoken. Invite the children to come forward to dip their fingers in the water. Instruct them to share a blessing with at least two other people, by saying "God loves you" while tracing the sign of the cross on the other person's forehead. If coming forward takes too much time, invite the children to turn to the people around them and trace the sign of the cross on peoples' foreheads, telling them, "God loves you." Alternately, teach children to make the sign of the cross with the verse "My head, my heart, my left, my right."

- Invite the children to lead prayers in worship. Work with them ahead of time to write their prayers and practice using a microphone.

- Gather the knitters in your congregation and ask them to teach interested children how to knit bandages for Global Health Ministries (directions at www.ghm.org/). Bless the bandages during a worship service.

- Host a healing service crafted for children. You may wish to address life issues from a child's point of view: death, bullying, divorce, and the ups and downs of friendship.

- Teach children the refrains to healing songs, and invite them to lead the assembly in singing these songs. Try "Healer of our every ill" (ELW 612, WOV 738), "There is a balm in Gilead" (ELW 614, WOV 737, TFF 185), or "I'm so glad Jesus lifted me" (ELW 860, WOV 673, TFF 191).

- Is there a nursing home in your area? Have children decorate posters using the theme Jesus the Healer. Display their posters in the gathering space for a few Sundays before the posters are delivered.

- Create a Children, Cookies, and Cards Crew, where the children come together to decorate cookies. Children could also craft cards for delivery to those in need. Accompany the children when they deliver the cards and cookies. Pray for the "CCC Crew" and their work during worship.

- Have a Compassionate Kids Challenge to collect items for Lutheran World Relief or other charities. Does the women's shelter need pillows? Does the school need extra supplies for those who can't afford them? Consider a grade-by-grade challenge. Invite the children to bring these offerings forward to place in tubs or baskets during the congregational offering.

- Flashlight Tag is a great game for the time after Epiphany. Everyone needs a flashlight. You're "caught" when someone's light beam touches yours. The person who is caught tells the group about someone who has taught them about Jesus. Sing "This little light of mine" (ELW 677, TFF 65) for an extra connection.

Worship Helps for the Time after Epiphany

Time after Epiphany Checklist

- See p. 43 for helps related to celebrating the Epiphany of Our Lord on January 6.
- If the Baptism of Our Lord (Jan. 11) will be observed as a baptismal festival, publicize the festival for the congregation and arrange for baptismal preparation sessions with parents, sponsors, and candidates. When the day arrives, set out the following:
  - towel (baptismal napkin) for each person baptized
  - baptismal candle for each person baptized
  - shell (if used)
  - oil for anointing (also a lemon wedge and a towel for removing oil from the presiding minister's hands)
  - baptismal garment for each person baptized (if used)
  - fresh water in a ewer (pitcher) or the font
- If a form of baptismal remembrance is used, evergreen branches for sprinkling may be desired.
- If the Alleluia will be symbolically buried or bid farewell on the festival of the Transfiguration, make the appropriate arrangements (for example, prepare for the burial of an Alleluia banner).
- Look ahead to the checklist on p. 107 as you plan for Lent.

Shape of the Communion Liturgy

- See the seasonal worship texts for the Time after Epiphany on pp. 72–73.
- On the festivals of the Baptism of Our Lord and Transfiguration, consider using thanksgiving for baptism instead of confession and forgiveness during the gathering portion of the service. Thanksgiving for baptism may be led at the baptismal font. A form is provided in *Evangelical Lutheran Worship* (Pew Edition, p. 97; Leaders Edition, p. 169).

- Use the Kyrie on the festivals of the Baptism of Our Lord and Transfiguration; omit it on the "green" Sundays after Epiphany.
- Use the hymn of praise ("Glory to God").
- Use the Nicene Creed for festival Sundays in this season; use the Apostles' Creed for the "green" Sundays after Epiphany.
- See the prayers of intercession for each Sunday.
- Use the proper preface for Baptism of Our Lord, Transfiguration, or Sundays as appropriate (*Evangelical Lutheran Worship* Leaders Edition, pp. 183, 184, 180).
- Thanksgiving at the table: see options in *Evangelical Lutheran Worship*, especially Prayer I for Sundays after Epiphany (Pew Edition, pp. 108–109; Leaders Edition, pp. 194–195); and *WOV*, Prayer C (Leaders Edition, p. 67).

Other Helps

- See the suggestions for music and worship space in the essay "Preparing for the Time after Epiphany," pp. 68–69.
- The Week of Prayer for Christian Unity is January 18–25. Resources for observing this week of prayer may be obtained from the Graymoor Ecumenical and Inter-religious Institute, 475 Riverside Dr., Room 1960, New York, NY 10115; e-mail: lmnygeii@aol.com; phone: 212/870-2330; or at www.geii.org. Resources on the Web site include a brief history of the Week of Prayer for Christian Unity, an ecumenical celebration of the word of God, music suggestions, bulletin announcements, and more.

SEASONAL WORSHIP TEXTS FOR THE TIME AFTER EPIPHANY

Confession and Forgiveness

All may make the sign of the cross, the sign that is marked at baptism, as the presiding minister begins.
In the name of the Father, and of the ✠ Son,
and of the Holy Spirit.
Amen.

Gathered by the Holy Spirit, let us confess our sin.

Silence is kept for reflection.

Holy One who makes all things new,
we confess that we have sinned against you
and one another.
We have wounded the whole creation
by the things we have done
and the things we have failed to do.
In your infinite compassion,
set us free from sin and death
and lead us to the new life
that you have prepared for us.
Amen.

Through the death and resurrection of Christ,
and by the power of the Holy Spirit
washed over us in baptism,
we have been freed from sin and death.
Hear again this good news: God forgives all your sins.
You are free to live the abundant life that is ours in Christ.
Amen.

Greeting

The people who walked in darkness have seen a great light.
The grace of our Lord Jesus Christ, the love of God,
and the communion of the Holy Spirit be with you all.
And also with you.

Offering Prayer

God of abundance,
all that we have is yours.
Receive these gifts and all who gather at your table,
for the sake of the one who gave himself for us,
Jesus Christ our Lord.
Amen.

Invitation to Communion

Come to the banquet, for all is now ready.

Prayer after Communion

God, from whom are all things and in whom we exist,
we give you thanks that in this meal
you have fed us with the presence of Christ.
Use us as beacons of light and bearers of Christ's love
for the sake of the whole world.
In Jesus' name we pray.
Amen.

Sending of Communion

Loving God,
by the light of a star you led the magi
bearing treasure to your Son.
By the power of your Holy Spirit,
lead those who go forth from this assembly
bearing these gifts of word and sacrament.
Be present with all who receive these gifts,
that they may know the healing power
of your light and your peace.
Amen.

Blessing

May the love of Jesus Christ, the light of the world,
fill your hearts and illumine your path.

Almighty God, Father, ✝ Son, and Holy Spirit,
bless you now and forever.
Amen.

Dismissal

Go in peace. Share the good news.
Thanks be to God.

SEASONAL RITES FOR THE TIME AFTER EPIPHANY

Blessing for a Home

From Evangelical Lutheran Worship Pastoral Care: Readings, Prayers, and Occasional Services (final draft, February 2008).

Blessing for a Home is a celebration of vocation in the deepest and broadest sense. We bless and thank God for the gift of a home while engaging and honoring the ways people practice their faith in their life at home: chores and hobbies, cooking and eating, ways of relaxing, relationships within the household and beyond it, caring for our bodies, connecting with the creation.

Blessing for a Home is commonly used when people move into a new residence. Besides the geographical moves that households make, other examples include moving into a nursing home or a dormitory room. The service may also be used to mark a change in the membership of a household: for example, an elderly parent moves in with younger relatives; a foster child comes into the home; a single-parent household is formed after a divorce. In some traditions, a blessing for a home is an annual observance—for example, during the time after Epiphany.

This order is meant to provide a pattern to follow, not an exact script. The basic pattern involves moving around the home and stopping at various places for scripture and prayer. Those planning for this rite may feel free to choose from the options here, rearrange them as makes best sense in the context, and add other stopping places as desired (selecting an appropriate scripture passage and crafting a suitable prayer).

Symbols may be used to mark the journey. Remembrances of baptism, such as carrying a candle from place to place or sprinkling water at each stopping place, recall that the life of the baptized is lived within these places. Carrying a cross from place to place, perhaps a cross that will hang on one of the walls, is a reminder that those who live here are called to follow in the way of the cross also in their daily lives.

Leadership may be shared among members of the household, friends and relatives, and the pastor or others from the faith community.

Gathering

When all have gathered in a convenient place, the leader begins.

In the name of the Father, and of the ☩ Son,
and of the Holy Spirit.
Amen.

or

Blessed be the holy Trinity, ☩ one God,
who spreads forth the heavens like a tent,
who shelters our lives,
who comes to make a home with us.
Amen.

Peace to this *house/dwelling/room* and to all who enter here.

Friends in Christ: Today we bless God and we seek God's blessing as we gather to give thanks for this dwelling and to pray for *those* who make it *their* home.

A reading from Proverbs: By wisdom a house is built, and through understanding it is established; through knowledge its rooms are filled with rare and beautiful treasures. (Prov. 24:3-4)

or

A reading from Isaiah: Be glad and rejoice forever in what I am creating, says the Lord; for I am about to create Jerusalem as joy, and its people as a delight. They shall build houses and inhabit them; they shall plant vineyards and eat their fruit. (Isa. 65:18, 21)

or

A reading from Matthew: Jesus said, Everyone who hears these words of mine and acts on them will be like a wise householder who built a house on rock. (Matt. 7:24)

A candle may be lighted, and these words may be spoken.
Jesus said, I am the light of the world. Whoever follows me will have the light of life.

The people may move around the home, stopping in various places to read scripture and to pray. Or, the people may stay in one place and the leaders may move to various places.

Welcome and Community

Entering and leaving, such as the outside doors

A reading from the Psalms: The Lord will watch over your going out and your coming in, from this time forth and forevermore. (Ps. 121:8)

Let us pray. O God, watch over _name/s_ in all _their_ going out and _their_ coming in; keep all evil away from _their_ door; and let _them_ share the hospitality of this home with all who visit, that those who enter here may know your love and peace. In Jesus' name we pray.
Amen.

Welcoming guests, such as a chair for a visitor

A reading from Romans: Welcome one another, therefore, just as Christ has welcomed you, for the glory of God. (Rom. 15: 7)
_or_
A reading from Acts: The Lord opened Lydia's heart to listen eagerly to what was said by Paul. When she and her household were baptized, she urged us, saying, "If you have judged me to be faithful to the Lord, come and stay at my house." And she prevailed upon us. (Acts 16:14-15)

Let us pray. O God, bless all who visit this home; may they find here warmth and peace. Bless also _name/s_, who _welcome_ others into _their_ home, as you blessed Sarah and Abraham when they entertained angels unawares. In Jesus' name we pray.
Amen.

Sharing of conversation and communal activities, such as a living room

A reading from Acts: Then Paul went upstairs, and after he had broken bread and eaten, he continued to converse with them until dawn; then he left. (Acts 20:11)
_or_
A reading from Ecclesiastes: So I commend enjoyment, for there is nothing better for people under the sun than to eat, and drink, and enjoy themselves, for this will go with them in their toil through the days of life that God gives them under the sun. (Eccles. 8:15)

Let us pray. O God, you set apart time for rest and enjoyment of the world you made. Bless those who gather here for fellowship and recreation, that they may be renewed and refreshed. In Jesus' name we pray.
Amen.

Household Work

Studying and communicating with others, such as a computer station

A reading from Proverbs: To get wisdom is to love oneself; to keep understanding is to prosper. (Prov. 19:8)
_or_
A reading from Proverbs: Like cold water to a thirsty soul, so is good news from a far country. (Prov. 25:25)

Let us pray. O God, you are the teacher who leads us to all truth. Grant that _those_ who _study_ and _learn_ in this place may use knowledge to heal and help your world. Draw us together through our technology for every good purpose. In Jesus' name we pray.
Amen.

Making or repairing things, such as a sewing area or workbench

A reading from the Psalms: May the graciousness of the Lord our God be upon us; prosper the work of our hands; prosper our handiwork. (Ps. 90:17)

Let us pray. O God, you are the source of our creativity. You fashioned our minds to imagine and our hands to shape new things. Prosper the work that is done in this place. In Jesus' name we pray.
Amen.

Preparing meals, such as a kitchen

A reading from Joel: I am sending you grain, wine, and oil, and you will be satisfied. Be glad and rejoice in the Lord your God. (Joel 2:19, 23)
_or_
A reading from John: When they had gone ashore, they saw a charcoal fire there, with fish on it, and bread. Jesus said to them, "Come and have breakfast." (John 21:9, 12)

Let us pray. O God, you fill the hungry with good things. Send your blessing on *those* who *prepare* food here, and make us all ever thankful for daily bread. In Jesus' name we pray.
Amen.

Caring for Ourselves

The gift of food, such as at a dining table

A reading from the Psalms: The eyes of all wait upon you, O Lord, and you give them their food in due season. You open wide your hand and satisfy the desire of every living thing. (Ps. 145:15-16)

Let us pray. Blessed are you, Creator of heaven and earth, for you give us food and drink to sustain our lives and make our hearts glad. Make us grateful for all your mercies, and mindful of the needs of others. In Jesus' name we pray.
Amen.

The gift of clothing, such as near a laundry area

A reading from Exodus: So Moses went down from the mountain to the people. He consecrated the people, and they washed their clothes. (Exod. 19:14)

Let us pray. O God, you are our clothing, wrapping us in love. We bless you for the gift of clothing, and we pray that *all who live here/ name* may be clothed and blanketed in safety. In Jesus' name we pray.
Amen.

The gift of caring for the body, such as near a bathroom or an exercise area

A reading from the Psalms: You yourself created my inmost parts; you knit me together in my mother's womb. I will thank you because I am marvelously made; your works are wonderful, and I know it well. (Ps. 139:13-14)

Let us pray. O God, through the waters of baptism you raise us up and make us alive together with Christ. Let the waters of this room refresh and renew *all who use them/ name* in each new day. In Jesus' name we pray.
Amen.

or

Let us pray. O God, you revealed yourself in human flesh, making holy what is ordinary and earthly. Bless us as we care for our ordinary, marvelous bodies. In Jesus' name we pray.
Amen.

The gift of rest, such as in a bedroom

A reading from the Psalms: In peace, I will lie down and sleep; for you alone, O Lord, make me rest secure. (Ps. 4:8)

Let us pray. Guide us waking, O Lord, and guard us sleeping, that awake we may watch with Christ, and asleep we may rest in peace.
Amen.

A couple's room

A reading from the letter to the Colossians: Above all, clothe yourselves in love, which binds everything together in perfect harmony. And let the peace of Christ rule in your hearts, to which indeed you were called in the one body. And be thankful. (Col. 3:14-15)

Let us pray. O God, let your love be a seal upon the hearts of *name* and *name,* a mantle about their shoulders, and a crown upon their foreheads. Bless them in their companionship and in their rest, in their sleeping and in their waking. In Jesus' name we pray.
Amen.

or

Let us pray. O God, bless *name* and *name* in their waking and in their sleeping, and let them find in one another comfort, respect, and delight. In Jesus' name we pray.
Amen.

A child's room

A reading from the Psalms: I will dwell in your house forever, O God; I will take refuge under the cover of your wings. (Ps. 61:4)

or

A reading from the Psalms: The Lord watches over you; God will not fall asleep. (Ps. 121:5, 3)

Let us pray. O God, hold _name_ in your unfailing love. May _she/he_ dream peacefully and grow in health and strength. Bring _her/him_ in safety to each new day. In Jesus' name we pray.
Amen.

A teenager's room

A reading from Jeremiah: "I will satisfy the weary, and all who are faint I will replenish," says the Lord. Thereupon I awoke and looked, and my sleep was pleasant to me. (Jer. 31:25-26)
_or_
A reading from the Psalms: It is in vain to rise so early and go to bed so late. You, Lord, give sleep to your beloved. (Ps. 127:2)

Let us pray. O God, may _name_ find here rest and respite, privacy and connection, challenge and enjoyment. And in all these things, may _she/he_ hear you calling _her/him_ by name. In Jesus' name we pray.
Amen.

Caring for Creation
Where a pet sleeps or animals are kept

A reading from the Psalms: Your righteousness is like the strong mountains, your justice like the great deep; you save humankind and animals, O Lord. (Ps. 36:6)
_or_
A reading from the Psalms: Praise the Lord from the earth, you sea monsters and all deeps, wild beasts and all cattle, creeping things and flying birds, young men and maidens, old and young together. (Ps. 148:7, 10, 12)

Let us pray. O God, we thank you for bringing [pet's name] to _name/s_ to be _their_ companion and friend. May they be blessings one to another. In Jesus' name we pray.
Amen.
or (at, for example, an aquarium)
Let us pray. O God, how manifold are your works! In wisdom you have made them all. Give _name/s_ the wisdom to care for _these creatures_ and to delight in _them_. In Jesus' name we pray.
Amen.

A garden or outdoor space

A reading from Job: Ask the animals, and they will teach you; the birds of the air, and they will tell you; ask the plants of the earth, and they will teach you; and the fish of the sea will declare to you. Who among all these does not know that the hand of the Lord has done this? In God's hand is the life of every living thing and the breath of every human being. (Job 12:7-10)
_or_
A reading from Jeremiah: They shall be radiant over the goodness of the Lord, over the grain, the wine, and the oil; their life shall become like a watered garden, and they shall never languish again. (Jer. 31:12)

Let us pray. O God, we praise you for the green plants that make the oxygen we breathe and for the animals that breathe it with us. Sustain us all together in this place by your Spirit. In Jesus' name we pray.
Amen.

After the readings and prayers (and the procession), the group may continue with a meal or other activities.
_or_
The order may be concluded with Affirmation of Christian Vocation (Evangelical Lutheran Worship, p. 84).
_or_
The Lord's Prayer may be prayed by all.

Notes on the Service
Hymns that may be appropriate and useful include the following.
I bind unto myself today   ELW 450
All Are Welcome   ELW 641, sts 1, 4, 5
Now thank we all our God   ELW 839/840

During the procession, or after each area's prayer
Ubi caritas et amor   ELW 642

At a table where meals are shared
Draw us in the Spirit's tether   ELW 470, sts 1, 3
Another sung grace that the household knows

In a bedroom
>God, who made the earth and heaven   ELW 564
>All praise to thee, my God, this night   ELW 565

In a young child's bedroom
>Now rest beneath night's shadow   ELW 568, st 2
>Thy holy wings   ELW 613
>Away in a manger   ELW 277/278, st 3

In a garden or outdoor space
>Lord, your hands have formed   ELW 554
>For the fruit of all creation   ELW 679
>Oh, that I had a thousand voices   ELW 833, sts 1, 3, 5
>Beautiful Savior   ELW 838

In places where a pet sleeps or animals are kept
>Oh, that I had a thousand voices   ELW 833, sts 1, 4, 5
>All things bright and beautiful   WOV 767

The tradition of Epiphany home blessings involves writing an inscription over the lintel of the main door to the outside. The traditional inscription is in the form: "20 + C M B + 09", where the "2009" is the year the inscription is made, and the initials stand for either the Latin blessing "Christe, mansionem benedicat," which means "Christ, bless this house," or the legendary names of the magi (Caspar, Melchior, and Balthasar). This tradition can be adapted for any blessing for a home. The inscription can be written with chalk over the door (colored chalk on a white surface).

Ecumenical Service during the Week of Prayer for Christian Unity

This service is especially appropriate between January 18 and 25. See p. 71 for additional resources for observing the Week of Prayer for Christian Unity.

Confession and Forgiveness

We gather as the people of God
to offer our repentance and praise,
to pray for the unity of the church
and the renewal of our common life.
Trusting in God's mercy and compassion,
let us ask for the forgiveness of our sins.

Silence for reflection and self-examination.

Lord Jesus, you came to reconcile us
to one another and to the Father:
Lord, have mercy on us.
Lord, have mercy on us.
Lord Jesus, you heal the wounds
of pride and intolerance.
Christ, have mercy on us.
Christ, have mercy on us.
Lord Jesus, you pardon the sinner
and welcome the repentant.
Lord, have mercy on us.
Lord, have mercy on us.
May almighty God grant us pardon and peace,
strengthen us in faith,
and make us witnesses to Christ's love.
Amen.

Hymn of Praise

Prayer of the Day

God our Father, your Son Jesus prayed that his followers might be one. Make all Christians one with him as he is one with you, so that in peace and concord we may carry to the world the message of your love, through Jesus Christ, our Savior and Lord.
Amen.

Readings and Psalm

Isaiah 2:2-4
Psalm 133
Ephesians 4:1-6
John 17:15-23

Sermon

Hymn of the Day

Thanksgiving for Baptism

The people remain standing after the hymn as the ministers gather at the font. After the prayer, the people may be sprinkled with water from the font. Or at the conclusion of the service they may be invited to dip their hands in the font and trace the sign of the cross over themselves.

The Lord be with you.
And also with you.
Let us give thanks to the Lord our God.
It is right to give our thanks and praise.
Holy God and mighty Lord, we give you thanks,
for you nourish and sustain us and all living things
with the gift of water.
In the beginning your Spirit moved over the waters,
and you created heaven and earth.
By the waters of the flood you saved Noah and his family.
You led Israel through the sea out of slavery
into the promised land.
In the waters of the Jordan
your Son was baptized by John and anointed with the Spirit.
By the baptism of his death and resurrection
your Son set us free from sin and death
and opened the way to everlasting life.

We give you thanks, O God,
that you have given us new life in the water of baptism.
Buried with Christ in his death,
you raise us to share in his resurrection
by the power of the Holy Spirit.
May all who have passed through the water of baptism
continue in the risen life of our Savior.
To you be all honor and glory, now and forever.
Amen.

Confession of Faith

There is one Lord, one faith, and one baptism.
United in Christ, let us confess the faith we hold in common.
The people profess the Apostles' Creed.

Prayers

At the conclusion, the people pray the Lord's Prayer.

Greeting of Peace

The Lord Jesus prayed for the unity of his disciples.
We look for the day when the church will shine forth
in unity at his holy supper.
The peace of Christ be with you always.
And also with you.
The ministers and the assembly may greet one another with a gesture of Christ's peace.

Blessing and Dismissal

Sending Hymn

January 11, 2009
Baptism of Our Lord
Lectionary 1

Our re-creation in baptism is an image of the Genesis creation, where the Spirit/wind moved over the waters. Both Mark's gospel and the story in Acts make clear that it is the Spirit's movement that distinguishes Jesus' baptism from John's. The Spirit has come upon us as upon Jesus and the Ephesians, calling us God's beloved children and setting us on Jesus' mission to re-create the world in the image of God's vision of justice and peace.

Prayer of the Day

Holy God, creator of light and giver of goodness, your voice moves over the waters. Immerse us in your grace, and transform us by your Spirit, that we may follow after your Son, Jesus Christ, our Savior and Lord, who lives and reigns with you and the Holy Spirit, one God, now and forever.

Gospel Acclamation

Alleluia. A voice from heaven said, "This is my Son,
the Beloved,* with whom I am well pleased." *Alleluia.*
(Matt. 3:17)

Readings and Psalm

Genesis 1:1-5

Out of chaos, God brings order. Out of the primeval darkness, God brings light. This familiar story was good news for the Israelites, who experienced much chaos in their history. It remains good news for any person living in the chaos and darkness of despair. God created and continues to create new life.

Psalm 29

The voice of the Lord is upon the waters. (Ps. 29:3)

Acts 19:1-7

In Ephesus, Paul encounters people who had received John's baptism of repentance but had never heard of the Holy Spirit or of baptism in the name of Jesus. After Paul baptized them, the Holy Spirit came upon them and empowered them with gifts of the Spirit.

Mark 1:4-11

Mark's gospel reports the story of Jesus' baptism with some irony: the one on whom the Spirit descends is himself the one who will baptize others with the Holy Spirit.

Color White

CD-ROM Images

Icon Three: BaptismLord02_Lect1_ABC
Icon Two: BaptismLord02_ABC
Icon: 009, 138

Prayers of Intercession

Living in the light of Christ, who reveals both our need and God's abundant love, let us pray for the church, those in need, and all of God's creation.
A brief silence.
Heavenly Father, you poured out the Holy Spirit on your beloved Son in his baptism. Renew all who are baptized into Christ, that the fruits of your Spirit may flourish.
Hear us, O God.
Your mercy is great.
You pour out water on your children to cleanse them. Provide clean water for your people to drink and bathe safely, and lead us to use our resources responsibly. Hear us, O God.
Your mercy is great.
The message of your love transcends human language. Create in the peoples of all nations a loving spirit, that our acts of love may proclaim your goodness when words fail us. Hear us, O God.
Your mercy is great.
You send messengers to prepare the coming of your reign. Send us to help those who are ailing from doubt, fear, depression, and sickness (*especially*). Fill those in need with the hope of salvation. Hear us, O God.
Your mercy is great.
You have welcomed us as your beloved children. Make our congregation a place of welcome for the stranger, a place where your gospel is clearly spoken in word and action. Hear us, O God.

Your mercy is great.

Here other intercessions may be offered.

As we give thanks for all who have been washed in your grace, shower us with your Holy Spirit until the day when we will be united with Christ and all the saints in your heavenly reign. Hear us, O God.

Your mercy is great.

Into your hands, gracious God, we commend all for whom we pray, trusting in your mercy; through Jesus Christ, our Savior.

Amen.

Ideas and Images for the Day

John the Baptizer enters the scene as one who works outside the established channels and is therefore a threat to the established religion. That the people throng to John reveals their hunger for renewal and change in the systems of the day. How can one not be full of wonder as the wilderness prophet exclaims, "The one who is more powerful than I is coming after me. . . . I have baptized you with water; but he will baptize you with the Holy Spirit" (Mark 1:7-8)?

As Jesus is baptized by John, God not only tears open the heavens but also tears through our expectations. When the heavens break apart, we expect a divine unleashing, much like Elijah at the cave (1 Kings 19:11-13). But what Jesus encounters is a still, small voice, the life-giving Spirit descending like a peaceable dove. Just as God was not in the fire, earthquake, and storm, but in the small voice of the Spirit, so God is not to be found in overwhelming structures of power and privilege but in the peaceful kingdom proclaimed and lived out in Jesus.

1. In *The Bridge to Terabithia* (Disney, 2007), the characters Jessie and Leslie cross a river to enter the mythical realm of Terabithia. Baptism, like the river in the film, is a liminal place where God's grace enters on the margins to create life amid a culture bordered by death.

2. The Epiphany or baptismal icon in the Orthodox tradition has a wealth of symbols that offer a rich interpretation of Jesus' baptism, foreshadowing the temptations in the wilderness, the cross, and the resurrection. View the icon and commentary at www.orthodoxonline.com/icons.htm.

3. In "The God Who Is For Us" (*The Witness*, January 3, 2006; www.thewitness.org), author Jeff Krantz explores further peacemaking perspectives on the readings for today. Find the article at www.thewitness.org/article.php?id=1001.

4. In the song "God Is a River" (*Midwinter*, 2005), Peter Mayer challenges listeners to expand images of God by offering metaphors of water and a river. Listen to this and other songs at http://petermayer.net/music/.

5. The Rev. Barbara K. Lundblad, in her sermon "Torn Apart Forever" (www.day1.net, January 12, 2003, in the Sermon Library) calls our attention to Mark's use of the Greek verb *schizo* to describe the tearing apart of the heavens, in contrast to Matthew's and Luke's choice of *anoignumi*, to open. She remarks that when something is torn it is not so easily repaired, but "the torn place is where God comes through, the place that never again closes as neatly as before."

Hymns for Worship
Gathering

Songs of thankfulness and praise   ELW 310, LBW 90
O living Breath of God   ELW 407

Hymn of the Day

Christ, when for us you were baptized   ELW 304
   LOBT GOTT, IHR CHRISTEN
When Jesus came to Jordan   ELW 305, WOV 647
   KING'S LYNN
Crashing waters at creation   ELW 455   *STUTTGART*

Communion

Oh, love, how deep   ELW 322, LBW 88
Baptized and Set Free   ELW 453
Wade in the water   ELW 459

Sending

God, whose almighty word   ELW 673, LBW 400
Go, make disciples   ELW 540
Go, my children, with my blessing   ELW 453, WOV 721

Additional Hymns and Songs

Song over the Waters   RWSB 160
Mark how the Lamb of God's self-offering   HG 141, LSB 600
Christ, your footprints through the desert   HG 138
King of kings   W&P 80
Waterlife   ELW 457, W&P 145

Music for the Day
Psalmody and Acclamations

Ferguson, John. *Gospel Acclamations for Advent–Transfiguration.* AFP 9780800620363.

Mummert, Mark. "Psalm 29" from *Psalm Settings for the Church Year.* AFP 9780800678562.

Psalter for Worship Year B, Evangelical Lutheran Worship Edition. AFP 9780806683839.

Choral

Biery, James. "The Waters of Life." SATB, org. AFP 9780800657680. *The Augsburg Choirbook*. AFP 9780800656782.

Foley, John B. "Come to the Water." SATB, assembly, pno, inst. OCP 9489.

Hayes, Mark. "I'm Going on a Journey" from *Augsburg Easy Choirbook*, vol 1. U/2 pt mxd, pno, opt fl. AFP 9780800676025.

Pinkham, Daniel. "For the Gift of Water." SATB, opt org. ECS 5204.

Children's Choir

Bertalot, John. "When Jesus Christ Came Down to Earth." UE. U, kybd. CG A909.

Christopherson, Dorothy. "As the Water Sings." LE. U, kybd, 2 cl, tuba/bass. AFP 9780800652531. OP

Hopson, Hal H. "God Said Yes and It Was So." LE. U, kybd. HOP JR218.

Kemp, Helen. "God's Great Lights." UE. U/2 pt, pno, narr, opt ch, opt assembly. CPH 98-3072.

Keyboard / Instrumental

Buxtehude, Dietrich. "Lobt Gott, ihr Christen." Org. Various ed.

Fruhauf, Ennis. "King's Lynn" from *Augsburg Organ Library: Epiphany*. Org. AFP 9780800659349.

Harbach, Barbara. "Wade in the Water" from *Come Join the Dance: Folk Tunes and Spirituals for Organ*. Org. AFP 9780800678760.

McCarthy, David. "Stuttgart" from *Augsburg Organ Library: Baptism and Communion*. Org. AFP 9780800623555.

Moore, Bob. "The Lord Will Bless Us with Peace (Psalm 29)" from *Miniatures for Solo Instrument and Piano*. Pno, C inst. GIA G-5374.

Handbell

Linker, Janet/Jane McFadden. "Morning Has Broken." 5 oct, opt org, L2. AFP 9780800654320.

McChesney, Kevin. "Come, Thou Fount of Every Blessing." 3-5 oct, L2+. JEF MJHS9186.

Moklebust, Cathy. "Let All Things Now Living." 3-5 oct, L3. CG B170.

Praise Ensemble

Hanson, Handt. "Waterlife." ELW 457, W&P 145.

■ Harrah, Walt. "The Lord Is My Light" from *Maranatha Greenbook*. MAR 738597141690.

■ Paris, Twila. "We Will Glorify" from WT. Singspiration Music/ BBM.

■ Park, Andy. "The River Is Here" from www.praisecharts.com. Mercy/VIN.

Global

Hayes, Mark. "I'm Going on a Journey." U/2 pt, pno, fl. AFP 9780800675523.

Helman, Michael. "Jesus, We Want to Meet." U, hb, perc. AFP 9780800655884.

■ denotes songs that are available on iTunes®.

Thursday, January 15

Martin Luther King Jr., renewer of society, martyr, 1968

Martin Luther King Jr. is remembered as an American prophet of justice among races and nations, a Christian whose faith undergirded his advocacy of vigorous yet nonviolent action for racial equality. A pastor of churches in Montgomery, Alabama, and Atlanta, Georgia, his witness was taken to the streets in such other places as Birmingham, Alabama, where he was arrested and jailed while protesting against segregation. He preached nonviolence and demanded that love be returned for hate. Awarded the Nobel Peace Prize in 1964, he was killed by an assassin on April 4, 1968. Though most commemorations are held on the date of the person's death, many churches hold commemorations near Dr. King's birth date of January 15, in conjunction with the American civil holiday honoring him. An alternate date for the commemoration is his death date, April 4.

Saturday, January 17

Antony of Egypt, renewer of the church, c. 356

Antony was born in Qemen-al-Arous, Upper Egypt, and was one of the earliest Egyptian desert fathers. Born to Christian parents from whom he inherited a large estate, he took personally Jesus' message to sell all that you have, give to the poor, and follow Christ. After making arrangements to provide for the care of his sister, he gave away his inheritance and became a hermit. Later, he became the head of a group of monks that lived in a cluster of huts and devoted themselves to communal prayer, worship, and manual labor under Antony's direction. The money they earned from their work was distributed as alms. Antony and his monks also preached and counseled those who sought them out. Antony and the desert fathers serve as a reminder that certain times and circumstances call Christians to stand apart from the surrounding culture and renounce the world in service to Christ.

Pachomius, renewer of the church, 346

Another of the desert fathers, Pachomius (puh-KOME-ee-us) was born in Egypt about 290. He became a Christian during his service as a soldier. In 320 he went to live as a hermit in Upper Egypt, where other hermits lived nearby. Pachomius organized them into a religious community in which the members prayed together and held their goods in common. His rule for monasteries influenced both Eastern and Western monasticism through the Rule of Basil and the Rule of Benedict, respectively.

January 18, 2009
Second Sunday after Epiphany
Lectionary 2

All the baptized have a calling in God's world. God calls not just the clergy but also the youngest child, like Samuel. The story of the calling of Nathanael plays with the idea of place. Nathanael initially dismisses Jesus because he comes from Nazareth. But where we come from isn't important; it's where—or rather whom—we come to. Jesus refers to the story of the vision of Jacob, who called the place of his vision "the house of God, and . . . the gate of heaven" (Gen. 28:17). Jesus says he himself is the place where Nathanael will meet God.

The Week of Prayer for Christian Unity begins today. The observance of the festival of the Confession of Peter is transferred this year to January 19.

Prayer of the Day

Thanks be to you, Lord Jesus Christ, most merciful redeemer, for the countless blessings and benefits you give. May we know you more clearly, love you more dearly, and follow you more nearly, day by day praising you, with the Father and the Holy Spirit, one God, now and forever.

Gospel Acclamation

Alleluia. We have found ⌐ the Messiah:* Jesus Christ, who brings us ⌐ grace and truth. *Alleluia.* (John 1:41, 17)

Readings and Psalm

1 Samuel 3:1-10 [11-20]

At a time when visions are rare and unexpected, the Lord comes to Samuel and calls him to speak the divine word. Though just a boy, Samuel responds to God obediently, as Eli the priest has taught him to respond. This marks the beginning of Samuel's prophetic ministry.

Psalm 139:1-6, 13-18

You have searched me out and known me. (Ps. 139:1)

1 Corinthians 6:12-20

Paul is helping the Corinthians understand that God has claimed the entirety of their lives through the death of Christ. Hence Christian relationships and conduct, including areas of human sexuality, are to reflect the reality that we belong to Christ and that the Holy Spirit lives within us.

John 1:43-51

In John's gospel, Jesus' ministry begins with the call of disciples, who then bring others to Jesus. Philip's friend Nathanael moves from skepticism to faith when he accepts the invitation to "Come and see."

Color Green

CD-ROM Images

Icon Three: Epiphany2_Lect2_B
Icon Two: Epiphany2_Sun2_B
Icon: 074

Prayers of Intercession

Living in the light of Christ, who reveals both our need and God's abundant love, let us pray for the church, those in need, and all of God's creation.
A brief silence.
Compassionate God, you call to people of all ages and places. Open our ears to your voice, and give us the will and wisdom to follow you. Hear us, O God.
Your mercy is great.
You know all of your creatures before they are even born. Bless pregnant and nursing mothers of every species. Give health and strength to the young for whom they care. Hear us, O God.
Your mercy is great.
You raise up workers for peace and justice. Guard those who are called to work for justice among nations, ethnic groups, families, and individuals, so that your peace may prevail. Hear us, O God.
Your mercy is great.

You know that which troubles all people. Stay near those who face trials in life due to unemployment, discord, grief, and illness (*especially*). Bring them relief from their struggles. Hear us, O God.
Your mercy is great.
You grant unity by your Spirit. Inspire the many traditions in the Christian church to find ways for us all to bear witness to Christ together, that all people may see visible signs of unity within your church. Hear us, O God.
Your mercy is great.
Here other intercessions may be offered.
As we remember all who have confessed their faith in you (*especially the apostle Peter*), strengthen us to trust in your promises and to confidently confess our faith with the church of every time and place. Hear us, O God.
Your mercy is great.
Into your hands, gracious God, we commend all for whom we pray, trusting in your mercy; through Jesus Christ, our Savior.
Amen.

Ideas and Images for the Day

Today's readings lead us into an awareness that the living God wants to have a vital relationship with us. Taken together, these texts create a tapestry that reveals our God to be a seeking God who desires to lead, guide, influence, and encourage us. But for us to hear what God has to say, we need to first listen for God's voice—to become aware, once again, that God is constantly communicating with us every second, every moment, of our lives. God is a lover who wants nothing more than the very best for the beloved. Like Nathanael we may find ourselves dumbfounded that God is this interested in our welfare, but for the believer who stops a moment and says, "Speak, Lord, for your servant is listening," amazing and exciting adventures await.

1. In his song "Here I Am, Lord" (ELW 574, WOV 752, TFF 230) author and composer Daniel L. Schutte paints a picture of the Lord as an incredibly powerful and, at the same time, very sensitive and tender God. God is the "Lord of sea and sky" yet hears the cries of the people. The Lord is the one who "made the stars of night" and still is compassionate enough to bear the people's pain. Take a good look at this hymn, filled with vivid images of a God in touch with our concerns and needs.

2. In 1519, Martin Luther had his "tower experience," where the previously imagined God of vengeance reveals himself to Luther as a just and merciful God who justifies us by faith. Luther reads Romans 1:17 and is struck by the phrase "The one who is righteous will live by faith." Luther writes, "All at once I

felt that I had been born again and entered into paradise itself through open gates. Immediately I saw the whole of Scripture in a different light." Read more at *Modern History Sourcebook: Martin Luther: The Tower Experience, 1519,* www.fordham.edu/halsall/mod/1519luther-tower.html.

3. We sometimes make our relationship with God more complicated than it need be. It could just be that when it comes to life and God we need to keep in mind the KISS principle: "Keep It Simple, Stupid." God loves us—we love God! How much simpler could it be than that?

4. In his Large Catechism, Luther calls upon us to become serious about our understanding of who God is. He sees the Apostles' Creed as a definition of the Trinity and urges us to look at this creed in greater depth. Look especially at the Third Article, which deals with the Holy Spirit, and see how it is God's own self, through the Holy Spirit, who calls, gathers, and enlightens the whole Christian church. Were it not for the Spirit we would know nothing of Christ and his love for us. See Robert Kolb and Timothy J. Wengert, eds., *The Book of Concord* (Minneapolis: Fortress Press, 2000), especially paragraph 63, p. 439.

5. Consider the role prayer plays in the dialogue that takes place between God and the believer. Dietrich Bonhoeffer's *Letters and Papers from Prison* (various editions) and Roger Hazelton's *God's Way with Man: Variations on the Theme of Providence* (Nashville: Abingdon, 1956) offer good insights into the power of this dynamic relationship.

Hymns for Worship
Gathering
Listen, God is calling   ELW 513, WOV 712
God is here!   ELW 526, WOV 719
Lord, speak to us, that we may speak   ELW 676, LBW 403

Hymn of the Day
Here I Am, Lord   ELW 574, WOV 752, TFF 230
   HERE I AM, LORD
Will you come and follow me   ELW 798   KELVINGROVE
The Son of God, our Christ   ELW 584, LBW 434
   SURSUM CORDA

Communion
Take, oh, take me as I am   ELW 814
Around you, O Lord Jesus   ELW 468, LBW 496
He comes to us as one unknown   ELW 737, WOV 768

Sending

Send me, Jesus   ELW 549

Let us talents and tongues employ   ELW 674, WOV 754

Additional Hymns and Songs

We need no ladder now   HG 135

Come and see   W&P 29

Come and See   DH 56

Whom shall I send?   UMH 582

Music for the Day
Psalmody and Acclamations

Ferguson, John. Gospel *Acclamations for Advent–Transfiguration*. AFP 9780800620363.

Haugen, Marty. "Psalm 139" from *Psalm Settings for the Church Year*. AFP 9780800678562.

Psalter for Worship Year B, Evangelical Lutheran Worship Edition. AFP 9780806683839.

Choral

▫ Bell, John L. "The Summons (Will You Come and Follow Me)." 2 pt mxd/SA, assembly, pno, fl, opt gtr. GIA G-5410.

Cherwien, David. "Signs and Wonders." 2 pt, org, fl. AFP 9780800678319.

How, Martin. "Day by Day." SAB/SSA, org. GIA G-4178.

Keesecker, Thomas. "That All May Be One." SATB, pno, opt inst, assembly. AFP 9780800678739.

Nelson, Ronald A. "O Lord, Thou Hast Searched Me and Known Me." SATB, org, opt vln. AUR AE65.

▫ Schutte, Daniel L./arr. Ovid Young. "Here I Am, Lord." SATB, kybd. AFP 9780800656058.

Children's Choir

Dietterich, Philip P. "Come One, Come All, Come Follow." LE. U, opt antiphonal, kybd. CG A553.

Exner, Max V. "Samuel Lay Down." UE. U, narr, kybd, opt fc/tri. AFP 9780800646738. OP

Potter, Kenney. "Where Shall I Go From Your Spirit?" UE. 2 pt, kybd. CG A916.

Keyboard / Instrumental

Berg, Georg. "Voluntary." Pno, ob. GIA G-2906.

Burkhardt, Michael. "Kelvingrove" from *Festive Hymn Settings*, set 7. Org. MSM 10-730.

Linker, Janet. "Here I Am, Lord." Org, pno, fl, ob. CPH 97-6803U1.

Miller, Aaron David. "Kelvingrove" from *Organ Preludes on Folk Songs*. Org. AFP 9780800677572.

Handbell

Dobrinski, Cynthia. "He Leadeth Me." 3-5 oct, L3. HOP 1461.

Hopson, Hal H. "The Gift of Love." 3-5 oct, L1. AG 1419.

Larson, Lloyd. "Simple Gifts." 3 oct, L2. BP MBEH297.

Praise Ensemble

■ Engle, Joel. "Salt and Light" from www.ccli.com. INT.

■ Hughes, Tim. "Here I Am to Worship" from www.praisecharts.com. Thankyou Music.

■ Redman, Matt and Beth. "Blessed Be Your Name" from www.praisecharts.com.

■ Zschech, Darlene. "The Potter's Hand" from *Best of the Best, The Other Songbook 2*. FEL 1891062034.

Global

Emmerson, Roger, "Cantate Brasilia!" SATB/SAB/SSA, pno, perc. HAL 08711354.

Sedio, Mark. "Each New Day/Al despuntar en la loma el dia." SATB, kybd, opt C inst, gtr, rhythm. AFP 9780800658281.

Monday, January 19
Confession of Peter (transferred)

The Week of Prayer for Christian Unity is accompanied by two commemorations, the Confession of Peter (a relatively recent addition to the calendar) and the older Conversion of Paul. Both are remembered together on June 29, but these two days give us an opportunity to focus on key events in each of their lives. Today we remember that Peter was led by God's grace to acknowledge Jesus as "the Christ, the Son of the living God" (Matt. 16:16).

This confession is the common confession that unites us with Peter and with all Christians of every time and place. During the time after Epiphany, with its emphasis on mission, consider an ecumenical worship service with neighboring congregations to embody the unity we share in our confession of Christ, a unity granted us in our one baptism, a unity we yearn to embody more fully. The hymn "We all are one in mission" (ELW 576, WOV 755) could be sung at this service.

Monday, January 19
Henry, Bishop of Uppsala, martyr, 1156

Henry, an Englishman, became bishop of Uppsala, Sweden, in 1152 and is regarded as the patron of Finland. He traveled to Finland with the king of Sweden on a mission trip and remained there to organize the church. He was murdered in Finland by a man he had rebuked and who was disciplined

▫ denotes choral suggestions that relate to the hymn of the day.

■ denotes songs that are available on iTunes®.

by the church. Henry's burial place became a center of pilgrimage. His popularity as a saint is strong in both Sweden and Finland.

Today is an appropriate day to celebrate the Finnish presence in the Lutheran church. Consider singing "Arise, my soul, arise!" (ELW 827), which uses a Finnish folk tune. During the time after Epiphany we celebrate the light of Christ revealed to the nations, and martyrs such as Henry continue to reveal that light through their witness to faith.

Wednesday, January 21

Agnes, martyr, c. 304

Agnes was a girl of about thirteen living in Rome, who had chosen a life of service to Christ as a virgin, despite the Roman emperor Diocletian's ruling that outlawed all Christian activity. The details of her martyrdom are not clear, but she gave witness to her faith and was put to death as a result, most likely by the sword. Since her death, the church has honored her as one of the chief martyrs of her time.

January 25, 2009
Third Sunday after Epiphany
Lectionary 3

Stories of the call to discipleship continue as the time after Epiphany plays out the implications of our baptismal calling to show Christ to the world. Jesus begins proclaiming the good news and calling people to repentance right after John the Baptist is arrested for preaching in a similar way. Knowing that John was later executed, we see at the very outset the cost of discipleship. Still, the two sets of fisherman brothers leave everything they have known and worked for all their lives to follow Jesus and fish for people.

The Week of Prayer for Christian Unity ends today. The observance of the festival of the Conversion of Paul is transferred this year to January 26.

Prayer of the Day

Almighty God, by grace alone you call us and accept us in your service. Strengthen us by your Spirit, and make us worthy of your call, through Jesus Christ, our Savior and Lord.

Gospel Acclamation

Alleluia. The time is fulfilled, and the kingdom of God | has come near;* repent, and believe in | the good news. *Alleluia.* (Mark 1:15)

Readings and Psalm
Jonah 3:1-5, 10

The book of Jonah is a comedy starring a reluctant prophet who is given a one-sentence message: Nineveh will be destroyed in forty days. Much to Jonah's dismay, the people of Nineveh repent. The point of the story is to get the reader to wrestle with the question "On whom should God have mercy?"

Psalm 62:5-12

God alone is my rock and my salvation. (Ps. 62:6)

1 Corinthians 7:29-31

Paul does not disapprove of marriage or other human social institutions. He does, however, want Christians to live in the present in fervent anticipation of God's future, which even now has dawned through the death and resurrection of Jesus Christ.

Mark 1:14-20

Before Jesus calls his first disciples, he proclaims a message that becomes known as "the gospel" or good news from God. God is ready to rule our lives. Those who realize this will respond with repentance and faith.

Color   Green

CD-ROM Images

Icon Three: Epiphany3_Lect3_B

Icon Two: Epiphany3_Sun3_B

Icon: 075

Prayers of Intercession

Living in the light of Christ, who reveals both our need and God's abundant love, let us pray for the church, those in need, and all of God's creation.

A brief silence.

God of new life, renew your church when we are paralyzed by sin and evil. Breathe your word into us, showing us your will, so that we may live according to your purpose. Hear us, O God.

Your mercy is great.

Strengthen those who sow seeds, raise livestock, and catch fish. Bless them in their labor for the sake of all who depend on them for food. Hear us, O God.

Your mercy is great.

Give all governments the wisdom to serve the least of those who are in their care. Assist all public servants (*especially those who have recently taken office*) to seek justice in their work. Hear us, O God.

Your mercy is great.

Bring healing to the lives of people who are in distress. Comfort those who hurt, relieve those who worry, restore those who are sick (*especially*). Make them whole again. Hear us, O God.

Your mercy is great.

Bind people together by your Holy Spirit. Be present in relationships between family members, loved ones, and friends, that each may find joy in the blessing of others. Hear us, O God.

Your mercy is great.

Here other intercessions may be offered.

As we remember the lives of all the saints (*especially the apostle Paul*), make us into your willing servants, who will one day rejoice with all the inhabitants of your heavenly reign. Hear us, O God.

Your mercy is great.

Into your hands, gracious God, we commend all for whom we pray, trusting in your mercy; through Jesus Christ, our Savior.

Amen.

Ideas and Images for the Day

Is the Christian faith only one generation away from extinction? Yes, the Holy Spirit calls, gathers, and enlightens the whole Christian church, but Christ has also made us trustees and custodians of the faith, with the responsibility of raising the next generation in faith. The texts for today share a common theme of "going forth" with God's good news. For Jonah it took a bit of convincing, but when he went and did as the Lord commanded his words changed the heart of a nation. And that's the challenge Jesus places before ordinary people like Simon and Andrew and James. One by one he calls them to "Come and follow me!" It's an invitation Jesus extends to us and one he is asking us to share with whoever will hear.

1. At the 1997 Churchwide Assembly the ELCA adopted seven "Initiatives for a New Century." Centered on the call to discipleship and in response to our Lord's command to make disciples of all nations, the ELCA has prepared a Web site with an abundance of information, ideas, and suggestions that can be of help to pastors, associates in ministry, and congregational leaders. Take a look at http://elca.org/christianeducation/disci pleship/calltodiscipleship.html.

2. No treatment of discipleship is complete without a look at Dietrich Bonhoeffer's *The Cost of Discipleship* (New York: Macmillan, 1963). Take special note of the chapter "The Call to Discipleship."

3. The dynamic film *Sophie Scholl: The Final Days* has been released on DVD (Zeitgeist Films, 2006; German with English subtitles). It's the story of a group of university students in Hitler's Germany who as members of the White Rose take it upon themselves to print and distribute leaflets outlining the atrocities taking place in their country. That decision led to their capture, interrogation, and execution. This film is a powerful depiction of courage, conviction, faith, and the lengths to which discipleship might go.

4. Evangelism is a word that needs action to bring it to life. How active is your congregation in bringing someone new to worship? How willing are you to tell others about how meaningful your congregation is to you? We are all called to be evangelists—in the business of making invitations to friends without a church home.

Hymns for Worship

Gathering

When pain of the world surrounds us   ELW 704

This little light of mine   ELW 677

Let us ever walk with Jesus   ELW 802, LBW 487

Hymn of the Day

Jesus calls us; o'er the tumult   ELW 696, LBW 494   *GALILEE*

You have come down to the lakeshore   ELW 817, WOV 784, TFF 154   *PESCADOR DE HOMBRES*

Come, follow me, the Savior spake   ELW 799, LBW 455   *MACHS MIT MIR, GOTT*

Communion

I love to tell the story   ELW 661, LBW 390

Light shone in darkness   ELW 307

God extends an invitation   ELW 486

Sending

I want to walk as a child of the light   ELW 815, WOV 649

Go, make disciples   ELW 540

Come, beloved of the Maker   ELW 306

Additional Hymns and Songs

You walk along our shoreline   HG 35, NCH 504

Rest in God alone   DH 37

Music for the Day
Psalmody and Acclamations

Ferguson, John. *Gospel Acclamations for Advent–Transfiguration.* AFP 9780800620363.

Psalter for Worship Year B, Evangelical Lutheran Worship Edition. AFP 9780806683839.

Shute, Linda Cable. "Psalm 62" from *Psalm Settings for the Church Year.* AFP 9780800678562.

Choral

Ellingboe, Bradley. "There's a Wideness in God's Mercy." SATB, kybd. AFP 9780800676544.

Erickson, Richard. "I Want to Walk as a Child of the Light." SATB, org. AFP 9780800658397.

Hobby, Robert A. "Strengthen for Service." 2 pt, org, opt assembly. AFP 9780800678265.

Martinson, Joel. "We All Are One in Mission" from *Augsburg Easy Choirbook*, vol. 2. 2 pt mxd, org. AFP 9780800677510.

Sedio, Mark. "Light Shone in Darkness." SATB, pno. AFP 9780800678302.

Thomas, André. "Walk in the Light." SATB, pno. CG A1063

Children's Choir

Pote, Allen. "Listening for the Call." UE. U/2 pt, pno, opt tpt. CG A1094.

Sleeth, Natalie. "God Is Like a Rock." LE. U, kybd. CG A395.

Sleeth, Natalie. "The Kingdom of the Lord." UE. 2 pt, pno/org/hpd, opt fl. AMSI 301.

Keyboard / Instrumental

Albrecht, Timothy. "Galilee" from *Grace Notes XI for Organ*. Org. AFP 9780800676735.

Carlson, J. Bert. "Galilee" from *Let It Rip! at the Piano*, vol. 2. Pno. AFP 9780800675806.

Hildebrand, Kevin. "Machs mit mir, Gott" from *Sonus Novus*, vol. 5. Org. CPH 97-7085.

Sedio, Mark. "Pescador de hombres" from *A Global Piano Tour*. Pno. AFP 9780800658199.

Handbell

Helman, Michael. "Variations on 'Gather Us In'." 3-5 oct, L4. AFP 9780800674922.

Larson, Lloyd. "I Want Jesus to Walk with Me." 3-5 oct, L2. BP HB296.

Tucker, Sondra K. "Make Me a Channel of Your Peace." 3-5 oct, L3. AFP 9780800659868.

Praise Ensemble

- Getty, Keith/Stuart Townend. "In Christ Alone" from *More Songs for Praise & Worship 3*. WM 080689318184.

- Gonzales, Nic/Jason Ingram. "Shine" from www.musicnotes.com. Wordspring Music.

- Redman, Matt/Martin Smith. "All over the World" from WT. Thankyou Music\Curious? Music UK.

- Zschech, Darlene. "All Things Are Possible" from *WOW Worship Green Songbook*. INT 000768195567.

Global

Dargie, Dave. "Sizohamba naye/We will go with God" from *Global Songs 2*. SATB. AFP 9780800656744.

Sedio, Mark. "Take My Life, That I May Be/Toma, oh Dios, mi voluntad." SATB, pno, fl, opt gtr. AFP 9780800658298.

Monday, January 26
Conversion of Paul (transferred)

At the end of the Week of Prayer for Christian Unity the church remembers how a man of Tarsus named Saul, a former persecutor of the early Christian church, was led by God's grace to become one of its chief preachers. The risen Christ appeared to Paul on the road to Damascus and called him to proclaim the gospel. The narratives describing Paul's conversion in the Acts of the Apostles, Galatians, and 1 Corinthians inspire this commemoration, which was first celebrated among the Christians of Gaul.

The entire Week of Prayer for Christian Unity gives us a chance to consider our calling in light of Paul's words in Galatians that all are one in Christ.

■ denotes songs that are available on iTunes®.

Monday, January 26

Timothy, Titus, and Silas, missionaries

On the two days following the usual date for the Conversion of Paul, his companions are remembered. Timothy, Titus, and Silas were missionary coworkers with Paul. Timothy accompanied Paul on his second missionary journey and was commissioned by Paul to go to Ephesus, where he served as bishop and overseer of the church. Titus was a traveling companion of Paul, accompanied him on the trip to the council of Jerusalem, and became the first bishop of Crete. Silas traveled with Paul through Asia Minor and Greece and was imprisoned with him at Philippi, where they were delivered by an earthquake.

This festival invites the church to remember Christian leaders, bishops, pastors, and teachers—both men and women—who have been influential in the lives of individual members as gospel signs of the light of Epiphany.

Tuesday, January 27

Lydia, Dorcas, and Phoebe, witnesses to the faith

On this day the church remembers three women who were companions in Paul's ministry. Lydia was Paul's first convert at Philippi in Macedonia. She was a merchant of purple-dyed goods, and because purple dye was extremely expensive, it is likely that Lydia was a woman of some wealth. Lydia and her household were baptized by Paul, and for a time her home was a base for Paul's missionary work. Dorcas is remembered for her charitable works, particularly making clothing for needy widows. Phoebe was a diakonos, a deaconess in the church at Cenchreae, near Corinth. Paul praises her as one who, through her service, looked after many people.

Today provides an opportunity for congregations to reflect on the ministry of women, ordained and lay, wealthy and poor, who have given of themselves in service to the church and to the ministry of the gospel in their congregations.

Wednesday, January 28

Thomas Aquinas, teacher, 1274

Thomas Aquinas was a brilliant and creative theologian of the thirteenth century. He was first and foremost a student of the Bible and profoundly concerned with the theological formation of the church's ordained ministers. As a member of the Order of Preachers (Dominicans), he worked to correlate scripture with the philosophy of Aristotle, which was having a renaissance in Aquinas's day. Some students of Aristotle's philosophy found in it an alternative to Christianity. But Aquinas immersed himself in the thought of Aristotle and worked to explain Christian beliefs in the philosophical culture of the day. The worship cultural studies done in the 1990s by the Lutheran World Federation resonate with Aquinas's method.

February 1, 2009
Fourth Sunday after Epiphany
Lectionary 4

In Deuteronomy God promises to raise up a prophet like Moses, who will speak for God; in Psalm 111 God shows the people the power of God's works. For the church these are ways of pointing to the unique authority people sensed in Jesus' actions and words. We encounter that authority in God's word, around which we gather, the word that trumps any lesser spirit that would claim power over us, freeing us to follow Jesus.

Prayer of the Day

Compassionate God, you gather the whole universe into your radiant presence and continually reveal your Son as our Savior. Bring wholeness to all that is broken and speak truth to us in our confusion, that all creation will see and know your Son, Jesus Christ, our Savior and Lord.

Gospel Acclamation

Alleluia. The people who sat in darkness have seen ˡ a great light;* for those who sat in the shadow of death ˡ light has dawned. *Alleluia.* (Matt. 4:16)

Readings and Psalm
Deuteronomy 18:15-20

Today's reading is part of a longer discourse in Deuteronomy, an updating of the law for the Israelite community as the people wait to enter the promised land. Here Moses assures the people that God will continue to guide them through prophets who will proclaim the divine word.

Psalm 111

The fear of the LORD is the beginning of wisdom. (Ps. 111:10)

1 Corinthians 8:1-13

Paul is concerned about how some Corinthian Christians use their freedom in Christ as license to engage in non-Christian behavior that sets a damaging example to other, impressionable, believers. Christians have a responsibility to each other that their behavior does not cause a sister or brother to sin.

Mark 1:21-28

The story has barely begun, and already the battle is joined. Jesus sides with humanity against every force that would bring death and disease. These forces recognize Jesus and know what his power means for them. This, however, is only the first fight. The war will go on much longer.

Color   Green

CD-ROM Images

Icon Three: Epiphany4_Lect4_B
Icon Two: Epiphany4_Sun4_B
Icon: 076

Prayers of Intercession

Living in the light of Christ, who reveals both our need and God's abundant love, let us pray for the church, those in need, and all of God's creation.

A brief silence.

Almighty God, you dwell among your assembled people. Help us to welcome the stranger into our midst with graciousness, and give us words to proclaim the good news of salvation. Hear us, O God.
Your mercy is great.

By your word creation came into being. Speak to us by your Spirit when creation is groaning for rescue and relief, that we may commit ourselves to thoughtful care of all you have made. Hear us, O God.
Your mercy is great.

You have authority over all the rulers of the world. Help all people to put their trust in you, even as they support and honor their earthly rulers. Hear us, O God.
Your mercy is great.

You answer those who cry out to you. Care for all those who live with mental illness and those who are sick or hospitalized (*especially*). Speak compassion and healing into their lives. Hear us, O God.

Your mercy is great.

You desire peace among peoples. Promote conversation and acceptance among brothers and sisters of different faiths. Lead us to share what we hold in common and to understand and accept our differences. Hear us, O God.

Your mercy is great.

Here other intercessions may be offered.

Remembering the prophets, disciples, and saints who came before us, we pray your blessing on saints who live among us, that their commitment may be an example for us and that we may remain faithful to Christ. Hear us, O God.

Your mercy is great.

Into your hands, gracious God, we commend all for whom we pray, trusting in your mercy; through Jesus Christ, our Savior.

Amen.

Ideas and Images for the Day

We have all dealt with authority figures in our life. Some we see as nothing more than paper tigers who have an inflated view of themselves but with no real authority to get anything done. In our texts for today the writers all point to the person the Lord will send who will have undisputed authority to speak for God. That person, as we see in the Gospel of Mark, is Jesus. Those who encountered Jesus were sometimes quite surprised by his ability to take old teachings and make them come alive with new relevancy. Real authority is able to cut through the red tape and get things done. And Jesus, through his authority over sin, death, and the power of the devil, has done exactly that. He has swept away every impediment that was in the way and has given us the gift of forgiveness, wholeness, and the promise of everlasting life with him.

1. Christians believe in the power of the word: the written word, which is scripture; the spoken word, which is proclamation of the gospel; and the Word made flesh, Jesus Christ himself. John gives perfect testimony to the power and presence of the Word when he writes: "In the beginning was the Word, and the Word was with God, and the Word was God. He was in the beginning with God. All things came into being through him, and without him not one thing came into being. What has come into being in him was life, and the life was the light of all people. The light shines in the darkness, and the darkness did not overcome it" (John 1:1-5). Consider delving into what it means that "all things came into being through him and without him not one thing came into being."

2. In his doctrine of the two kingdoms, Luther speaks of the power of the secular (state) and the power of the spirit (church). He speaks of the healthy tension that should exist between these two kingdoms, recognizing that each has a different kind of authority that needs to be expressed for proper checks and balances to take place. What is the proper role for the church to play in today's society? What should the state's role be?

3. Invite your people to take a personal inventory of how much control they have knowingly and willingly given to Christ over their lives. Is their Sunday world much different from their Monday world? If Christ had total authority over their lives, what might their lives look like? What would change? What would stay the same? What kind of believer might they become?

Hymns for Worship
Gathering

Oh, for a thousand tongues to sing   ELW 886, LBW 559
Hail to the Lord's anointed   ELW 311, LBW 87
You are holy   ELW 525

Hymn of the Day

Songs of thankfulness and praise   ELW 310, LBW 90   *SALZBURG*
Rise, shine, you people!   ELW 665, LBW 393   *WOJTKIEWIECZ*
There is a balm in Gilead   ELW 614, WOV 737, TFF 185   *BALM IN GILEAD*

Communion

I'm so glad Jesus lifted me   ELW 860
Healer of our every ill   ELW 612, WOV 738
You Are Mine   ELW 581

Sending

The Lord now sends us forth   ELW 538
We all are one in mission   ELW 576, WOV 755
We Are Called   ELW 720

Additional Hymns and Songs

Silence! Frenzied, unclean spirit   HG 152
Thy word   TFF 132, W&P 144
Thy word   W&P 143
Satan, we're going to tear your kingdom down   TFF 207

Music for the Day
Psalmody and Acclamations

Ferguson, John. *Gospel Acclamations for Advent–Transfiguration.* AFP 9780800620363.

Long, Larry. "Psalm 111" from *Psalm Settings for the Church Year.* AFP 9780800678562.

Psalter for Worship Year B, Evangelical Lutheran Worship Edition. AFP 9780806683839.

Choral

Bach, J. S. "Bring Low Our Ancient Adam" from *Bach for All Seasons.* SATB, kybd. AFP 9780800658540.

❑ Fleming, Larry L. "There Is a Balm in Gilead." TTBB. MSM 50-5809.

Pote, Allen. "I Will Give Thanks." SATB, pno, opt 2 tpt. AFP 9780800652906.

❑ Wood, Dale. "Rise, Shine!" SATB, org. AFP 9780800655921. *The Augsburg Choirbook.* AFP 9780800656782.

Children's Choir

Pote, Allen. "I Will Greatly Rejoice." UE. U/2 pt, pno. BRD 0767393058.

Ramseth, Betty Ann. "Make Us to Be." UE. U, Orff, autoharp, fc, wood blocks, fl. AFP 11-0349. OP

Sleeth, Natalie. "The Holy Book" from *Sunday Songbook.* LE. U, kybd. HIN HMB102.

Keyboard / Instrumental

Carlson, J. Bert. "Balm in Gilead" from *Let It Rip! at the Piano*, vol. 1. Pno. AFP 9780800659066.

Cherwien, David. "Wojtkiewiecz" from *Augsburg Organ Library: Epiphany.* Org. AFP 9780800659349.

Hobby, Robert A. "Salzburg" from *Three Epiphany Preludes*, vol. 1. Org. MSM 10-208.

Raabe, Nancy M. "Balm in Gilead" from *Grace and Peace.* Pno. AFP 9780800677602.

Handbell

McKlveen, Paul A. "The Blessing." 3-5 oct, L2-. LAK HB95039.

Moklebust, Cathy. "Rejoice and Be Glad." 3-5 oct, L3. CG CGB117.

Prins, Matthew. "Fantasie on 'There Is a Balm in Gilead'." 4-5 oct, L3+. GIA G-6597.

Praise Ensemble

■ Ash, Jeremy/Matt Bronleewe/Rebecca St. James. "Lamb of God" from wt. Up in the Mix Music/Bibbitsong Music/Songs of Windswept Pacific/Songs from the Farm/Project 76.

■ Del Hierro, Jude. "More Love, More Power" from *Breakforth Worship Songbook.* New Creation Ministries. www.new-creation.net.

■ Morgan, Reuben. "I Give You My Heart" from *Best of the Best, The Other Songbook 2.* FEL 1891062034.

■ Redman, Matt. "Beautiful News" from www.praisecharts.com. Thankyou Music.

❑ denotes choral suggestions that relate to the hymn of the day.
■ denotes songs that are available on iTunes®.

Global

Matsikenyiri, Patrick/Bread for the Journey. "Nzamuranza" from *Pave the Way: Global Songs 3.* SATB, perc. AFP 9780800676896.

Traditional Russian. "Almighty God, O Hear My Prayer" from *Global Praise 2.* SATB. Cokesbury 1890569224.

Monday, February 2
Presentation of Our Lord

Forty days after the birth of Christ we mark the day Mary and Joseph presented him in the temple in accordance with Jewish law. There a prophet named Anna began to speak of the redemption of Israel when she saw the young child. Simeon also greeted Mary and Joseph. He responded to the presence of the consolation of Israel in this child with the words of the Nunc dimittis. His song described Jesus as a "light for the nations."

Because of the link between Jesus as the light for the nations, and because an old reading for this festival contains a line from the prophet Zephaniah, "I will search Jerusalem with candles," the day is also known as Candlemas, a day when candles are blessed for the coming year. If no service is planned to celebrate this day in the congregation, be sure to read the story about the presentation when congregational groups meet, and include a setting of the Song of Simeon.

Tuesday, February 3
Ansgar, Bishop of Hamburg, missionary to Denmark and Sweden, 865

A traditional emphasis during the weeks after Epiphany has been the mission of the church. Ansgar is a monk who led a mission to Denmark and later to Sweden, where he built the first church. His work ran into difficulties with the rulers of the day, and he was forced to withdraw into Germany, where he served as bishop in Hamburg. Despite his difficulties in Sweden, he persisted in his mission work and later helped consecrate Gothbert as the first bishop of Sweden. Ansgar had a deep love for the poor. He would wash their feet and serve them food provided by the parish.

Ansgar is particularly honored by Scandinavian Lutherans. The Church of Sweden honors him as an apostle. His persistence in mission and his care for the poor invite congregations to reflect on their own ministry of bearing the light of Christ during the time after Epiphany.

Thursday, February 5

The Martyrs of Japan, 1597

In the sixteenth century, Jesuit missionaries, followed by Franciscans, introduced the Christian faith in Japan. But a promising beginning to those missions—perhaps as many as 300,000 Christians by the end of the sixteenth century—met complications from competition between the missionary groups, political difficulty between Spain and Portugal, and factions within the government of Japan. Christianity was suppressed. By 1630, Christianity was driven underground. Today we commemorate the first martyrs of Japan, twenty-six missionaries and converts who were killed by crucifixion. Two hundred and fifty years later, when Christian missionaries returned to Japan, they found a community of Japanese Christians that had survived underground. The Martyrs of Japan are a somber reminder of the cost of Christianity and discipleship. Their witness invites us to pray for the church's own witness to the gospel and encourages us to trust that the church is sustained in times of persecution.

February 8, 2009
Fifth Sunday after Epiphany
Lectionary 5

In Isaiah it is the one God who sits above the earth and numbers the stars—it is that God who strengthens the powerless. So in Jesus' healing work we see the hand of the creator God, lifting up the sick woman to health and service (diakonia). Like Simon's mother-in-law, we are lifted up to health and diakonia. Following Jesus, we strengthen the powerless; like Jesus, we seek to renew our own strength in quiet times of prayer.

Prayer of the Day

Everlasting God, you give strength to the weak and power to the faint. Make us agents of your healing and wholeness, that your good news may be made known to the ends of your creation, through Jesus Christ, our Savior and Lord.

Gospel Acclamation

Alleluia. The servant of God took | our infirmities* and bore | our diseases. *Alleluia.* (Matt. 8:17)

Readings and Psalm

Isaiah 40:21-31

The Judeans in exile have a good reason to be hopeful: the one who will bring them to freedom is the God who created the world, the God who subdues the rulers of the earth and gives strength to those who are weary.

Psalm 147:1-11, 20c

The LORD heals the brokenhearted. (Ps. 147:3)

I Corinthians 9:16-23

God entrusted Paul with the responsibility of bringing the gospel to diverse people. Hence the focus of Paul's ministry is not his own rights or privileges as an apostle but the privilege of serving God by freely sharing the good news of Christ with others.

Mark 1:29-39

Everywhere Jesus goes, many people expect him to set them free from oppression. Everywhere he goes, he heals them and sets them free. Disease, devils, and death are running for their lives. The forces that diminish human life are rendered powerless by Jesus.

Color   Green

CD-ROM Images

Icon Three: Epiphany5_Lect5_B
Icon Two: Epiphany5_Sun5_B
Icon: 077

Prayers of Intercession

Living in the light of Christ, who reveals both our need and God's abundant love, let us pray for the church, those in need, and all of God's creation.

A brief silence.

Everlasting God, place in the mouths of your disciples the good news of salvation in Christ. Keep us steadfast in proclamation, yet able to speak in many ways, so that all may know you. Hear us, O God.

Your mercy is great.

Provide relief to all creatures that have been affected by harsh weather. By your creative power, renew the land and cleanse the water, so that signs of life may return to devastated places. Hear us, O God.

Your mercy is great.

Provide shelter for those without homes. Grant protection to those who live on the street, and provide safety for all refugees. Guide organizations that reach out to displaced people. Hear us, O God.

Your mercy is great.

Bind the wounds of the injured and make whole those who have broken bodies and hearts (*especially*). Let those in need see compassion and healing in the wounds of Christ. Hear us, O God.

Your mercy is great.

Grant respite to firefighters, police officers, paramedics, and all who respond to emergencies. Give them rest, so that they may serve with strength and courage when help is needed. Hear us, O God.

Your mercy is great.

Here other intercessions may be offered.

As we give thanks for the diversity of saints who have gone before us, unite us as we journey together and keep us faithful to the end. Hear us, O God.

Your mercy is great.

Into your hands, gracious God, we commend all for whom we pray, trusting in your mercy; through Jesus Christ, our Savior.

Amen.

Ideas and Images for the Day

Today we get a picture of Jesus "back when" he was merely a local celebrity. But unlike yesterday's commercials by today's superstars, we already see in Jesus' early days the fullness of his ministry: healing, undoing the forces of the demonic, and proclaiming the good news of the kingdom of God. Even though we do not have an inaugural address as in Luke's gospel, we see early on the core thrust of Jesus' mission: "The Spirit of the Lord is upon me, because he has anointed me to bring good news to the poor. He has sent me to proclaim release to the captives and recovery of sight to the blind, to let the oppressed go free, to proclaim the year of the Lord's favor" (Luke 4:18-19; see also Isa. 61:1-2; 58:6).

It will take the rest of the story, and the continuing story of the church, to understand just *how* this anointed one will fulfill his task to bring about true hope for hurting humankind. But for now, there is all the excitement of something new coming into being, a sense of anticipation where all this might lead, and where it might lead *us*.

1. In J.R.R. Tolkien's *The Return of the King*, the future king, Aragorn, becomes known to the people first for his power to heal. Although characters in the story try to defeat personified evil in Lord Sauron by responding to violence with violence (providing visually stunning sequences in director Peter Jackson's film version [New Line, 2003]), these tactics ultimately fail. Evil is undone by a surprise. How is the story of Jesus a similar "eucatastrophe" (Tolkien's word for a surprising, fortunate, reversal) against all that would harm us?

2. What are we modern or postmodern people to make of demons? A helpful discussion is found in *Journeying Into God: Seven Early Monastic Lives* (Minneapolis: Fortress, 1996, pp. 9–12), where Tim Vivian describes the role of the demons in early monastic literature as that of distraction, whose purpose is to draw us away from God. Might they also represent the forces of victimization that exclude and scapegoat certain people? (See Robert Hamerton-Kelly, *The Gospel and the Sacred*, Minneapolis: Fortress, 1994, p. 75.) How do we engage in language about liberation from demons that resonates with our contemporary experiences?

3. Henri Nouwen, in the *Wounded Healer* (New York: Doubleday, 1972), reminds readers that those who would follow the crucified and risen one also acknowledge their own wounds so as to be of service to another. His parable from the Talmud of Rabbi Yoshua ben Levi and his encounter with the wounded messiah (pp. 81, 94–95) provide thought-provoking insights into ways we can both see Christ in the wounded and despairing, as well as share hope for God's new creation.

4. Peter's mother-in-law receives healing that leads to service. Educator Parker Palmer relates his journey out of depression and into a vocation of service in his poem "Harrowing" (*Let Your Life Speak*, San Francisco: Jossey-Bass, 2000, p. 72). What "greening seasons" are you or your congregation anticipating in your journey into deeper service?

Hymns for Worship
Gathering
Praise the One who breaks the darkness   ELW 843
God, whose almighty word   ELW 673, LBW 400
Creating God, your fingers trace   ELW 684, WOV 757

Hymn of the Day
Praise to the Lord, the Almighty   ELW 858/859,
LBW 543   LOBE DEN HERREN
Rise, shine, you people!   ELW 665, LBW 393
WOJTKIEWIECZ
Praise the One who breaks the darkness   ELW 843
NETTLETON

Communion
Thy holy wings   ELW 613, WOV 741
In the singing   ELW 466
We sing to you, O God   ELW 671

Sending
God be with you till we meet again   ELW 536
The Lord now sends us forth   ELW 538
Rise, shine, you people!   ELW 665, LBW 393

Additional Hymns and Songs
May the God of all healing   ELW 220
Have you not known?   CPH 98-2807
On Eagle's Wings   ELW 787, WOV 779
May you run and not be weary   W&P 97
Heal me, O Lord   TFF 189

Music for the Day
Psalmody and Acclamations
Ferguson, John. *Gospel Acclamations for Advent–Transfiguration.*
AFP 9780800620363.
Psalter for Worship Year B, Evangelical Lutheran Worship Edition.
AFP 9780806683839.
Woehr, Roland. "Psalm 147" from *Psalm Settings for the Church Year.*
AFP 9780800678562.

Choral
Aune, Elaine. "Heal Me, Hands of Christ." SATB, kybd. AFP
9780800676193.
▫ Christiansen, F. Melius. "Praise to the Lord." SATB, div. AFP
9780800645045.
Jennings, Kenneth. "The Lord Is the Everlasting God (II)." SATB,
div. MFS MF2137.
Keesecker, Thomas. "That All May Be One." SATB, pno, cant, opt
assembly, fl. AFP 9780800678739.
Schelat, David. "Praise the Lord, God's Glories Show." SAB, conga
drm. OXF 9780193865518.

Children's Choir
Horman, John D. "Small Deeds." UE. U, opt desc, pno. CG A562.
Patterson, Mark. "Lord, We Are Your People." UE. U/2 pt, pno, opt
hb/hc. CG A1104.
Whitaker, Paul. "Sing a Little Song." LE. U, opt desc, pno. BP 1081.

Keyboard / Instrumental
Albrecht, Mark. "Nettleton" from *Three for Piano and Sax.* Pno, alto
sax/C inst. AFP 9780800657970.
Burkhardt, Michael. "Wojtkiewiecz" from *Five Hymn Accompaniments for Brass Quartet and Organ*, set 5. Org, br qrt. MSM
20-848.
Micheelsen, Hans Friedrich. "Lobe den Herren" from *Augsburg
Organ Library: November.* Org. AFP 9780800658960.
Oquin, Wayne. "Lobe den Herren" from *All Things New.* Pno. CPH
97-7205U1.

Handbell
Ingram, Bill, arr. "Come, Thou Fount of Every Blessing." 2-5 oct, L2.
Ring Out Press 3221.
Moklebust, Cathy. "Praise to the Lord, the Almighty." 4-5 oct, L3.
AFP 9780800658908. Full Score: AFP 9780800659332.
Starks, Howard. "Praise to the Lord, the Almighty." 3-6 oct, L3.
Ringing Word 8130.

Praise Ensemble
■ King, Fran/Wes King. "I Believe" from www.musicnotes.com. BMG
Music Publishing, Inc.
■ Smith, Martin. "Shout to the North" from *I Could Sing of Your Love
Forever 2.* WT 0000809251.
■ Tomlin, Chris/Ed Cash/Jesse Reeves. "How Great Is Our God" from
www.praisecharts.com.
■ Zschech, Darlene. "My Hope" from www.praisecharts.com. Hillsong Publishing/INT.

Global
Bread for the Journey. "Hamba Nathi/Come, Walk With Us" from
Global Songs 2. SATB. AFP 9780800656744.
Graves, Avis D. "Guide My Feet." SATB, pno. GIA G-5952.

Saturday, February 14

Cyril, monk, 869; Methodius, bishop, 885; missionaries to the Slavs
These two brothers from a noble family in Thessalonika in northeastern Greece were priests and missionaries. After some early initial missionary work by Cyril among the Arabs, the brothers retired to a monastery. They were later sent to work among the Slavs, the missionary work for

▫ denotes choral suggestions that relate to the hymn of the day.
■ denotes songs that are available on iTunes®.

which they are most known. Because Slavonic had no written form at the time, the brothers established a written language with the Greek alphabet as its basis. They translated the scriptures and the liturgy using this Cyrillic alphabet.

The Czechs, Serbs, Croats, Slovaks, and Bulgars regard the brothers as the founders of Slavic literature. The brothers' work in preaching and worshiping in the language of the people is honored by Christians in both East and West.

February 15, 2009
Sixth Sunday after Epiphany
Lectionary 6

The leper is confident in Jesus' power to heal. Naaman, on the other hand, is comically hard to convince that he can be healed by such an unlikely foreigner as Elisha, who directs him to wash in such a sorry excuse for a river as the Jordan. Jesus' healing power is here among us in the ordinary water of the font, in the ordinary bread, in the ordinary people who make up the body of Christ. We would be well-advised to take the advice of the least powerful among us (like the servant girl in Naaman's household) if we want to find the one who will heal us.

Prayer of the Day

Almighty and ever-living God, with mercy you look upon our weaknesses. Stretch out your wondrous hand to protect us from danger and restore us to health, through Jesus Christ, our Savior and Lord.

Gospel Acclamation

Alleluia. The word about Jesus | spread abroad;* the power of the Lord was with | him to heal. *Alleluia.* (Luke 4:15, 17)

Readings and Psalm

2 Kings 5:1-14

Elisha tells Naaman, a Syrian general, to immerse himself in the Jordan River to be cleansed of his leprosy. Initially refusing to do this humble act, Naaman eventually obeys and is healed, revealing not the magic of the water but the power of Israel's God.

Psalm 30

My God, I cried out to you, and you restored me to health. (Ps. 30:2)

1 Corinthians 9:24-27

Using the athletic imagery of a runner and a boxer, Paul illustrates to the Corinthians how Christians have a focus committed to the ministry of the gospel, so that their victorious goal is not individual glory but eternal life for all.

Mark 1:40-45

Jesus cures a leper and asks him to tell no one but a priest, in accordance with Levitical law. Though Jesus performs miracles, his identity as Messiah will not be understood until the cross.

Color   Green

CD-ROM Images

Icon Three: Epiphany6_Lect6_B
Icon Two: Epiphany6_Sun6_B
Icon: 078

Prayers of Intercession

Living in the light of Christ, who reveals both our need and God's abundant love, let us pray for the church, those in need, and all of God's creation.
A brief silence.
God of hope, give your church the courage to live faithfully. Fill us with hope that outlasts any suffering, and faith that draws all people together in the name of Christ.
Hear us, O God.
Your mercy is great.
Reveal the goodness of your creation to all people, and help us to be good stewards of your precious gifts of land, water, and air and of the people and animals that depend on them.

Hear us, O God.

Your mercy is great.

Heal the wounds of hatred and mistrust that exist between people of different nations, religions, and ethnic backgrounds. Raise up leaders who will hear the cries of their people for peace and justice. Hear us, O God.

Your mercy is great.

Share your abundant love with families who care for and support one another, that they may find all they need in you. Keep them free from strife, and strengthen their bonds with each new day. Hear us, O God.

Your mercy is great.

Comfort and heal your children who are suffering (*especially*). Restore them to health by the help of others, and encourage us all to show mercy to people in need. Hear us, O God.

Your mercy is great.

Here other intercessions may be offered.

We give you thanks for the faithful ones who have gone before us. Use their lives to teach us how to live in hope and to work for justice as we serve one another. Hear us, O God.

Your mercy is great.

Into your hands, gracious God, we commend all for whom we pray, trusting in your mercy; through Jesus Christ, our Savior.

Amen.

Ideas and Images for the Day

Leprosy, or Hansen's disease, has a long history of fear and violence. John Tayman's book *The Colony* (New York: Scribner, 2006) details the horrific expulsion of the disease's victims to the "natural prison" of Kalawao on the Hawaiian island of Molokai. Tayman also tells the story of Father Damien de Veuster, whose calm and fearless presence among the people was healing, even though he eventually contracted the illness.

Father Damien's model was Jesus, who today crosses the boundaries of fear of contagion to touch and heal a man suffering a skin disease (leprosy in the Bible refers to a host of skin ailments). Although Jesus gives the man clear instructions to follow Mosaic law and not tell anyone, he, like the Aramean Naaman (2 Kings 5:1-19) cannot keep from living the good news. Now cleansed, the man tells the story "freely," with the result that Jesus can no longer go out in public. The message of God's healing love in Jesus, which passes over fear-driven boundaries, is contagious!

1. If we were to be honest with ourselves, we would recognize a temptation to follow our own internal "social map." How does Jesus challenge that map? What

boundaries sustained by fear is he challenging you or your congregation to traverse for the gospel's sake?

2. For more on the story of Father Damien and the Kalawao Colony on Molokai, listen to Terry Gross's interview with John Tayman broadcast on her Fresh Air radio show: www.npr.org/templates/story/story.php?storyId=5183996. The interview also relates how residents of the colony created their own social map regarding newcomers from the outside by the use of gestures.

3. The Rev. Dan Clendenin shares his own insider-outsider stories in his entry for this week's texts on his Web site Journey with Jesus: www.journeywithjesus.net/Essays/20060206JJ.shtml. The page includes several images of Naaman washing in the Jordan River.

4. The movie *Chocolat* (Miramax, 2000) tells the story of a small French village fearful of outsiders. When Vianne, an exotic chocolatier, comes to town, she is treated in a fashion similar to the man with leprosy in today's reading. And when a band of river drifters comes to town, it is more than some, especially the village's mayor, can bear. The people of the village soon learn, however, that the newcomers bring surprising gifts that revitalize their community.

Hymns for Worship
Gathering

Come, ye disconsolate   ELW 607
Oh, for a thousand tongues to sing   ELW 886, LBW 559
When morning gilds the skies   ELW 853, LBW 545, 546

Hymn of the Day

Healer of our every ill   ELW 612, WOV 738
    HEALER OF OUR EVERY ILL
O Christ, the healer, we have come   ELW 610, LBW 360
    DISTRESS
We come to you for healing, Lord   ELW 617   *MARTYRDOM*

Communion

Healer of boundless compassion   ELW 219
Come, let us eat   ELW 491, LBW 214
Here is bread   ELW 483

Sending

Go, my children, with my blessing   ELW 543, WOV 721
Guide me ever, great Redeemer   ELW 618, LBW 343

Additional Hymns and Songs

We give God thanks for those who knew   HG 128

May you run and not be weary   W&P 97

Mourning into dancing   W&P 99

I've just come from the fountain   TFF 111, WOV 696

Come, let us join our friends above   UMH 709

Music for the Day
Psalmody and Acclamations

Ferguson, John. *Gospel Acclamations for Advent–Transfiguration.* AFP 9780800620363.

Haugen, Marty. "Psalm 30" from *Psalm Settings for the Church Year.* AFP 9780800678562.

Psalter for Worship Year B, Evangelical Lutheran Worship Edition. AFP 9780806683839.

Choral

Cherwien, David. "Healing River." SATB, pno. AFP 9780800675882.

Gardner, John. "Fight the Good Fight." SATB, kybd. OXF 9780193531406.

Schütz, Heinrich. "Praise to the Lord, God." 2 pt mxd/SA, kybd. MCF DMC-8090.

Whitehill, Erik. "Wade in the Water" from *Wade in the Water.* SAB, solos, pno. AFP 9780800678616.

Children's Choir

Bedford, Michael. "I Will Love the Lord." UE. U/2 pt, kybd. CG A419.

Patterson, Mark. "My God Is with Me" from *Young Children Sing.* LE. U, kybd. AFP 9780800676803.

Ramseth, Betty Ann/Melinda Ramseth Hoiland. "If You But Trust in God to Guide You" from *Take a Hymn.* UE. U, kybd, fl. AFP 9786000106461. OP

Keyboard / Instrumental

Carlson, J. Bert. "Martyrdom" from *Let It Rip! at the Piano*, vol. 1. Pno. AFP 9780800659066.

Eggert, John. "Distress" from *Creative Hymn Accompaniments for Organ*, vol. 2. Org. CPH 97-6851U1.

Honoré, Jeffrey. "Healer of Our Every Ill" from *Augsburg Organ Library: Lent.* Org. AFP 9780800658977.

Langlois, Kristina. "Martyrdom" from *Miniatures and Interpretations for Organ.* Org. AFP 9780800623548.

Handbell

Hanna, Donna. "If You But Trust in God to Guide You." 3-5 oct, L2. GIA G-6166.

McKlveen, Paul A. "Faith." 3-5 oct, L2. JEF MJHS9396.

Sherman, Arnold B. "Grazioso." 3-5 oct, L2+. RR HB0042.

Praise Ensemble

■ Bryson, Jim/Nathan Cochran/Barry Graul/Bart Millard/Mike Scheuchzer/Robby Shaffer. "Hold Fast" from www.musicnotes .com. Simpleville Music\Wet as a Fish Music.

■ Evans, Darrell. "Trading My Sorrows" from *WOW Worship Green Songbook.* INT 000768195567.

■ Greenwell, Dorothy Dora/Aaron Shust. "My Savior, My God" from www.praisecharts.com. Bridge Building Music, Inc.

■ Smith, Martin. "I Could Sing of Your Love Forever" from *I Could Sing of Your Love Forever 2.* WT 0000809251.

Global

Hesla, Bret. "Shower Your Spirit Upon Us All" from *Justice, Like a Base of Stone.* SATB, cant. AFP 9780800623562.

Trinkley, Bruce. "Wade in the Water." SATB, pno. AFP 9780800657.

Wednesday, February 18

Martin Luther, renewer of the church, 1546

For those in the habit of remembering the work of Martin Luther on Reformation Day, this commemoration may seem out of place. But it is a custom to remember saints on the day of their death, their "heavenly birthday." On this day Luther died at the age of 62. For a time, he was an Augustinian monk, but it is his work as a biblical scholar, translator of the Bible, reformer of the liturgy, theologian, educator, and father of German vernacular literature that holds him in our remembrance. In Luther's own judgment, the greatest of all of his works was his catechism, written to instruct people in the basics of faith. And it was his baptism that sustained him in his trials as a reformer.

If a congregation has catechumens who will be baptized at the Easter Vigil, they might receive the catechism during the Enrollment of Candidates on the first Sunday in Lent. If there are no catechumens, a congregation might study the catechism during Lent to renew its own baptismal faith.

■ denotes songs that are available on iTunes®.

February 22, 2009
Transfiguration of Our Lord
Last Sunday after Epiphany

The Sundays after Epiphany began with Jesus' baptism and end with three disciples' vision of his transfiguration. In Mark's story of Jesus' baptism, apparently only Jesus sees the Spirit descending and hears the words from heaven. But now Jesus' three closest friends hear the same words naming him God's beloved son. As believers, Paul writes, we are enabled to see the God-light in Jesus' face, because the same God who created light in the first place has shone in our hearts to give us that vision. The light of God's glory in Jesus has enlightened us through baptism and shines in us also for others to see.

Prayer of the Day

Almighty God, the resplendent light of your truth shines from the mountaintop into our hearts. Transfigure us by your beloved Son, and illumine the world with your image, through Jesus Christ, our Savior and Lord, who lives and reigns with you and the Holy Spirit, one God, now and forever.

Gospel Acclamation

Alleluia. This is my | Son, my Chosen,* lis- | ten to him! *Alleluia.* (Luke 9:35)

Readings and Psalm

2 Kings 2:1-12

Today's reading centers on the transfer of power and authority from the prophet Elijah to Elisha. Their travels, which retrace the path of Joshua back to Moab (the place where Moses died) and the parting of the waters, demonstrate that Elisha and Elijah are legitimate successors of the great prophet Moses.

Psalm 50:1-6

Out of Zion, perfect in beauty, God shines forth in glory. (Ps. 50:2)

2 Corinthians 4:3-6

The spotlight of Christian ministry is not on the people who carry out ministry but on the Lord Jesus Christ. Just as God made light shine out of darkness at creation, God makes the light of Jesus Christ shine in our lives through Christian ministry.

Mark 9:2-9

Mark's gospel presents the transfiguration as a preview of what would become apparent to Jesus' followers after he rose from the dead. Confused disciples are given a vision of God's glory manifest in the beloved Son.

Color   White

CD-ROM Images

Icon Three: Transfiguration02_ABC, Transfiguration03_ABC
Icon Two: Transfiguration02_ABC, Transfiguration03_ABC
Icon: 017, 146

Prayers of Intercession

Living in the light of Christ, who reveals both our need and God's abundant love, let us pray for the church, those in need, and all of God's creation.
A brief silence.
Holy God, you reveal all things through your Son. Shine Christ's light into your church. Change us by your mercy, and lead us forth to share life-changing mercy with others. Hear us, O God.
Your mercy is great.
You make your creation awe-inspiring and beautiful. Show us your glory in every living thing, so that we may treat all of creation with humility and deep respect. Hear us, O God.
Your mercy is great.
You have unveiled your salvation in Christ. Draw out all people who are in bondage to sin, shining your light in their lives and redeeming all nations. Hear us, O God.
Your mercy is great.
Your healing touch makes people whole. Soothe the pain of people living with illness, grief, hopelessness, and confusion (*especially*). Comfort your suffering children.

Hear us, O God.
Your mercy is great.

In one another you give us faithful companions. Build up deep friendships among coworkers, students, and neighbors, that we may support one another in our earthly journey. Hear us, O God.
Your mercy is great.

Here other intercessions may be offered.

Remembering those who now dwell fully in the light of Christ, we look for that day when we will see the glory of God in the face of Jesus. Hear us, O God.
Your mercy is great.

Into your hands, gracious God, we commend all for whom we pray, trusting in your mercy; through Jesus Christ, our Savior.
Amen.

Ideas and Images for the Day

At the transfiguration of Jesus, we, as audience, have been groomed by Mark for a typical theophany scene: mountaintop experience, bright lights, appearances of heroes long since gone (Elijah and Moses, representing prophecy and the law). No wonder Peter wants to erect a memorial to create a sacred site. Even the holy voice adds to the shock and awe of the sequence: "This is my Son, the Beloved; listen to him!"

But in a grand reversal that rivals the best of Hollywood, the glory is given only to highlight what appears to be the reverse: the humiliation and rejection of the cross. Jesus' passion prediction underscores the cross that is glory—but only in Easter retrospection. Listening to Jesus becomes more difficult when circumstances lead him to a new mountain, Golgotha, the mount of the skull.

1. The Orthodox icon of the transfiguration, in its many forms, gives a visual interpretation of the gospels' accounts. Notice the sandal falling off the foot of the disciple, a reference to the third chapter of Exodus and the "holy ground" on which they stand (or fall). View the icon and commentary online at www.orthodoxonline.com/icons.htm.

2. Listening is an acquired skill that seems all the more difficult in our media-saturated world. Mary Oliver's poem "The Summer Day" models mindful listening for us. The poem concludes with a haunting question for all who seek to listen to Jesus: "Tell me, what is it you plan to do / with your one wild and precious life?" (*New and Selected Poems*, Boston: Beacon Press, 1992, p. 94).

3. The animated film *Monsters, Inc.* (Disney Pixar, 2001) is a fantastical story about monsters who scare children but actually live in fear of them. The realization that joy, not fear, is truly powerful leads to a surprising transformation of Monsters, Inc. and Monstropolis. Likewise, how do our texts for today foreshadow the "fear not" of Jesus' resurrection?

4. The transfiguration of Jesus also foreshadows the transformation of Peter and the disciples following the resurrection. Literature offers many such conversion stories: for example, the transformation of Raskolnikov in the last few pages of Dostoyesky's *Crime and Punishment*. While in prison for murder and theft, the character moves from self-pity and guilt to a new vision for life, thanks to the love and presence of Sonya (Wisdom). In most stories like this one, the great transformation only occurs after a series of little ones. How do these mini-mountaintop experiences shape our hope for God's new vision when we come down from them?

Hymns for Worship
Gathering

Shine, Jesus, shine   ELW 671, WOV 651
Come, beloved of the Maker   ELW 306
O Morning Star, how fair and bright!   ELW 308, LBW 76

Hymn of the Day

Jesus on the mountain peak   ELW 317   *BETHOLD*
    WOV 653   *ST. ALBINUS*
Oh, wondrous image, vision fair   ELW 316, LBW 80
    DEO GRACIAS
How good, Lord, to be here!   ELW 315, LBW 89   *POTSDAM*

Communion

Christ, Be Our Light   ELW 715
Beautiful Savior   ELW 838, LBW 518
All of us go down to the dust   ELW 223

Sending

Alleluia, song of gladness   ELW 318, WOV 654
In thee is gladness   ELW 867, LBW 552
We are marching in the light   ELW 866, WOV 650

Additional Hymns and Songs

Swiftly pass the clouds of glory   LSB 416
Transform us as you, transfigured   HG 149
Come to the mountain   W&P 32
Swing low, sweet chariot   TFF 171
Eternal light, shine in my heart   H82 465, 466

Music for the Day
Psalmody and Acclamations

Ferguson, John. *Gospel Acclamations for Advent–Transfiguration*. AFP 9780800620363.

Organ, Anne Krentz. "Psalm 50" from *Psalm Settings for the Church Year*. AFP 9780800678562.

Psalter for Worship Year B, Evangelical Lutheran Worship Edition. AFP 9780806683839.

Choral

Balakireff, M. A. "Send Out Thy Light." SATB. MSM 50-6035.

Forsberg, Charles. "Fairest Lord Jesus." SATB, pno. AFP 9780800656966.

Pooler, Marie. "Be Thou My Vision" from *Augsburg Easy Choirbook*, vol. 1. U, desc, kybd. AFP 9780800676025.

Walker, Gwyneth. "Dazzling as the Sun." SATB, div, org. ECS 6513.

Children's Choir

Helgen, John. "Beautiful Savior." UE. U/2 pt, kybd. AFP 9780800638368.

Hughes, Pamela L. "Come to the Mountain" from *LifeSongs*. LE. U, pno. AFP 9780806642710.

Sleeth, Natalie. "Laudamus Te." UE. 2 pt, kybd. HIN HMC681.

Keyboard / Instrumental

Guse, Berkley. "Potsdam" from *Organ Music for the Seasons*, vol. 2. Org. AFP 9780800658779.

Manz, Paul. "Deo gracias" from *Improvisations on Great Hymns of Faith*. Org. MSM 10-839.

Organ, Anne Krentz. "Deo gracias" from *Let It Rip! at the Piano*, vol. 1. Pno. AFP 9780800659066.

Rotermund, Donald. "Potsdam" from *Seven Hymn Preludes*, set 1. Org. CPH 97-6138U1.

Handbell

Dobrinski, Cynthia. "Rondo Passacaglia." 4-5 oct, L1. AG 1237.

Helman, Michael. "On Eagle's Wings." 3-5 oct, L2-. CPH 97-6429.

Moklebust, Cathy. "Rejoice and Be Glad!" 3 oct, L3. CG B117.

Praise Ensemble

■ Cash, Ed/Jesse Reeves/Chris Tomlin. "How Great Is Our God" from WT. WT/Sixsteps Music/Alletrop Music.

■ Kendrick, Graham. "Shine, Jesus, Shine." ELW 671, W&P 123.

■ Mullins, Rich. "Awesome God" from *Breakforth Worship Songbook*. New Creation Ministries. www.new-creation.net.

■ Smith, Deborah D./Michael W. Smith. "Shine on Us" from WT. Milene Music/Deer Valley Music.

Global

Johnson, Ralph/Bread for the Journey. "African Processional" from *Global Songs, Local Voices*. SATB, cant. AFP 9780806650227.

Hopson, Hal H. "We Are Singing, For the Lord Is Our Light/Siya–hamba." 2 pt mxd, kybd. HOP C5330.

Monday, February 23
Polycarp, Bishop of Smyrna, martyr, 156

Polycarp was Bishop of Smyrna and a link between the apostolic age and the church at the end of the second century. He is said to have been known by John, the author of Revelation. In turn he was known by Iranaeus, bishop of Lyons in France, and Ignatius of Antioch. At the age of eighty-six he was martyred for his faith. When urged to save his life and renounce his faith, Polycarp replied, "Eighty-six years I have served him, and he never did me any wrong. How can I blaspheme my king who saved me?" The magistrate who made the offer was reluctant to kill a gentle old man, but he had no choice. Polycarp was burned at the stake, his death a testimony to the cost of renouncing temptation.

■ denotes songs that are available on iTunes®.

LENT

Preparing for Lent

Lent: A Journey

Lent is a journey, and that means taking risks. Experienced travelers have tips to share for making the trip go as smoothly as possible, but most people who have been on a journey know that things can go wrong. Buses break down. Planes are delayed. Storms interfere. Luggage gets lost. All these variables mean releasing some of the control we have over our lives. We are at the mercy of pilots, wind and weather, other workers. However, in spite of—or maybe because of—all the ways a journey can throw us off balance, travelers have the opportunity to see, taste, hear, smell, feel, experience, even *be* something new.

Personal and Communal

Lent is often experienced as a season of reflection, looking inward, soul-searching. It's a season for looking intently toward Jesus, the author of our faith, and longing to know him better. It's a season of community, because in many congregations people are coming together twice as often as normal and may come for extra time—to share a simple supper, a bowl of soup, to help with a cleaning or service project, to get to know one another's stories more deeply than they've known them before. This community-building aspect of Lent can be so powerful that people are a little sad when Lent is done, because the commitment to come together for a season has been so powerful. This is a season where in simplicity there is great strength.

Many Waters

Lent begins with ashes but it is not only a dry season—the waters of baptism flow through it. Lent is a time when many congregations use confession and forgiveness weekly; leading this order from the font highlights the connection to baptism. Another option, especially if your congregation typically uses confession and forgiveness, is to use thanksgiving for baptism throughout the seasons of Lent and Easter. This provides a focus on God, the fountain of living water during the wilderness journey. Because of a focus on baptism, God's gracious gift, the baptismal font is a central symbol during Lent. Depending on the size of the baptismal font, you might place a single large shell with purple tones beside the bowl, or place reflective stones directly in the font, immersed in the baptismal water and appropriate to the size of the baptizing space. You could also draw attention to the font by placing simple green arrangements beside it. Save bright flowers for Easter.

Trust, Truth, Transparency

A continual theme of trust moves through the lectionary during this season. Isaiah reassures people, "The LORD will guide you continually, and satisfy your needs in parched places, and make your bones strong; and you shall be like a watered garden, like a spring of water, whose waters never fail" (Isa. 58:11). In stories from Genesis, Exodus, and Numbers, we encounter God's covenant with creation—learning once again the greatness of God and God's vision for how people ought to live together. Finally, Jeremiah points toward a time when the covenant will be manifest—when everyone will know God, and God's promise will be written on their hearts.

New Testament readings throughout the season reinforce these themes and take them a step further. Recalling the story of Abraham and Sarah, who were promised to bear a child though their bodies were too old, the apostle Paul teaches us that there is reason for hope and faith in spite of the evidence, and that there can be reconciliation not only between God and humanity, but among all people in our diverse human community. "For by grace you have been saved through faith, and this is not your own doing; it is the gift of God—not the result of works, so that no one may boast. For we are what he has made us, created in Christ Jesus for good works, which God prepared beforehand to be our way of life" (Eph. 2:8-10).

A third theme woven through the lectionary during Lent is truth—who God is, who we are—and truthful expression of a wide array of complex emotions such as anger, jealousy, loyalty, deep grief, and love. A transparency in these texts encourages us to communicate and live in open and honest ways. Being honest with ourselves and others is important in every aspect of life, including the way we practice spiritual disciplines, the way we live each day, and the way we die.

Loving Life and Losing It

In Lenten readings from both Mark and John, we hear Jesus express an important truth about life and the ability to face death. In the gospel for the second week of Lent, Jesus says, "For those who want to save their life will lose it, and those who lose their life for my sake, and for the sake of the gospel, will save it" (Mark 8:35). Jesus describes his body as a temple that will be destroyed and raised up, then as the serpent in the wilderness that is "raised up" to bring eternal life. Finally, in the fifth week of Lent, Jesus says, "Those who love their life lose it, and those who hate their life in this world will keep it for eternal life" (John 12:25). In these words, Jesus confronts the deeply human will to live, and the deeply human fear of death. Because Jesus allows himself to be killed and is raised from the dead, death itself no longer needs to be feared. Because of this gift, it's our choice to go on in life, realistic about what we face, but also fearless.

Purple Lenten Spring

The color palette of this season includes deep purple, indigo, plum. Care should be taken so that the sanctuary features only a few focal points: the font, the cross, the table. This does not mean that the changing season outside should be ignored. What is happening in your climate during these months? Even if you don't have a dramatic climate change in your region from February to April, do subtle changes appear through the budding and blossoming of various kinds of plants? How might the space inside reflect the gradually changing creation outside? Gather plants with branches, then buds, then flowers, or something else that will reflect the journey into Lenten spring in your area. In some regions, forsythia is a good choice of branches that begin bare, bud, and bloom in the weeks of Lent. Place these native plants around the baptismal font.

Turn Around

If your congregation has moveable furniture, it is important to arrange the furniture differently for Lent. This can symbolize the turning that we are invited to do as we repent and see ourselves more clearly. An arrangement in which people face one another may initially be jarring but can become meaningful in this season of truth-telling and reconciliation. If your congregation does not have moveable furniture, worshipers can still have the experience of turning. Invite people to face the baptismal font for the thanksgiving for baptism or confession and forgiveness; invite worshipers to turn toward one another, across a middle aisle, for the prayers of intercession. Creatively make a choice around space and movement that will lift up the themes of the season in your space and context.

Prayer Journey

If your building and/or grounds allow for it, you may want to create a labyrinth as a place to pray during this season. A labyrinth is a walking space in which there is only one way in and one way out—different from a maze in that you cannot get lost—but the way turns and bends, and you simply walk until you reach the center. In the center, there is sacred ground to pray, meditate, and release all things to God. Then, in time, you come out. Large labyrinth tarps can be purchased, but they may also be created outside using stones to mark the borders. They can be placed inside by creating a pattern with string on the floor. Small labyrinths can be traced with a finger or pencil. Use this prayer tool as you walk together on the spiritual journey of Lent.

Choosing the Music for Sundays

Lent is a good season to try a new musical setting of the liturgy. It is a long enough season to really learn and become comfortable with unfamiliar music. People may be willing to try something new as a Lenten discipline, even if it isn't their first choice. Depending on your context and what would be different and meaningful for your congregation, you might try Setting Two or Setting Eight in *Evangelical Lutheran Worship*. If your congregation regularly changes the music with the seasons, or if you belong to a bilingual parish, or if you just love a challenge, you might try Setting Seven, which is presented in both English and Spanish. One smaller change (if you don't change all the liturgical music) could be the use of the song "Vuelva al Señor, tu Dios" (Turn back to the Lord, your God) as the gospel acclamation (ELW, p. 179).

Wednesday Evenings

Through the years, many congregations have used *Holden Evening Prayer* on Wednesday evenings in the season of Lent. However, this evening prayer service was not designed to be combined with holy communion. In response to the desire that the meal not simply be tacked on to vespers, Marty Haugen and Susan Briehl have created another beautiful and singable setting that congregations might consider for Lent this year: *Unfailing Light: An Evening Setting of Holy Communion* (GIA, 2004). This setting includes an alternate gathering rite that is especially appropriate for Lent, described in detail in the introduction.

Celebrating Lent with Children

The Lenten season affects the rhythm of Sunday worship, and the season will feel different to children. You may wish to provide instructions for the change in your worship bulletin. For example: "The canticle of praise is omitted during Lent because . . ." Changes in worship and the appearance of the worship space are intriguing and provide opportunities for deepened understanding of what it means to practice our faith in the context of the liturgical year.

Ideas for Lent

Ash Wednesday

- Drama, ritual, and sensory experiences engage even the youngest child. Include all children in these times of worship and the experiential learning that is possible.
- At this service, children feel the sign of the cross traced on their foreheads, and see the black cross on others; all are marked, no matter what age. Encourage a conversation about this visual reminder of the connection of repentance and forgiveness.

The Sundays in Lent: "Covenant" stories

- Read the introductions to each Sunday in Lent on pp. 116, 119, 122, 125, and 128 for background on the covenants God makes in the Hebrew scriptures. Then develop and distribute a "covenant" worship handout for each Sunday. Include the Bible verse, a brief summary, key words, and a picture of a related symbol for children to color (Lent 1: Gen. 9:8-17; Lent 2: Gen. 17:1-7, 15-16; Lent 3: Exod. 20:1-17; Lent 4: Num. 21:4-9; Lent 5: Jer. 31:31-34).
- Encourage time for family devotions during Lent, using the readings for each Sunday. *What Wondrous Love: Devotions for the Home: Lent, Holy Week, Easter* (Augsburg Fortress, 1997; ISBN 9780806629834) is a wonderful resource.
- Place a bare tree branch in a bucket or clay pot filled with sand in the gathering space. The shape of pretzels is a symbol of prayer. Attach prayer requests printed on slips of paper to pretzels, and hang the pretzels with purple ribbon on the branches. Include prayer requests for family and local concerns, and general prayers (see *Evangelical Lutheran Worship*, pp. 72–87).
- Make an Acts of Love sign-up sheet available. Families covenant to do an act of love during the time of Lent by signing their names to the list. The activities accomplished and the family experiences can be a "table talk" at your church's Wednesday evening Lenten suppers.

Additional suggestions for worship

- Lent 1: Make the connection between baptism and the Noah story by using the thanksgiving for baptism or thanksgiving at the font (*Evangelical Lutheran Worship*, pp. 97, 230).
- Lent 2: Have children distribute cutouts of stars as everyone enters worship. During worship, have everyone write their name on a star and collect it as a special offering. Hang the stars in a prominent place for the coming Sundays of Lent to remind us that we are part of the promise given to Abraham and Sarah.
- Lent 3: Distribute paper and crayons to the children as they enter worship. Read Psalm 19:1 and ask the children to imagine how the heavens declare the glory of God. Display their artwork in the gathering space.
- Lent 4: Teach the sign language for the words *God, love, world, Jesus, Son, us, me,* and *give* (www.commtechlab.msu.edu/sites/aslweb/browser.htm). Sign "God loves world," "God loves Jesus," "God loves us," "God loves me," and "God (so) loved the world (that to) us (a) Son (was) given."
- Lent 5: Make the connection between Psalm 51 and its use on Ash Wednesday.
- Passion/Palm: Encourage children to participate in worship leadership. Provide instrumental music for the palm parade, play the refrain of "All glory, laud, and honor" (ELW 344) on instruments, ask young gymnasts or dancers to join the processional, use ribbons or streamers in addition to palms. Have a child or children's choir serve as cantor, or help with the random ringing of handbells as the procession begins.

Worship Helps for Lent

Lent Checklist

- Review the liturgies for Ash Wednesday and the Sunday of the Passion provided in *Evangelical Lutheran Worship* (Pew Edition, pp. 247–257; Leaders Edition, pp. 611–627).
- Arrange to simplify the worship environment during Lent.
- Burn palms from the previous Passion Sunday or obtain ashes from a church supplier for use on Ash Wednesday (Feb. 25).
- If midweek services will be held during Lent, determine the style, content, and leadership. Order bulletin covers if needed.
- If a healing service will be held during Lent, consider using the order provided in *Evangelical Lutheran Worship* (Pew Edition, pp. 276–278; Leaders Edition, pp. 660–665).
- Order worship participation leaflets if used for the Ash Wednesday liturgy or Passion Sunday procession with palms liturgy.
- Order palm branches for Passion Sunday. Additional palm branches or plants might be used as part of the worship environment that day. If long, individual palm fronds are used, they will need to be separated ahead of time.
- Determine how and where the procession with palms will take place on Passion Sunday. Prepare signs or recruit volunteers to help direct people. Determine how those with physical disabilities will participate in the procession or be seated ahead of time.
- Schedule a rehearsal of readers in preparation for the passion reading on Passion Sunday.
- Reserve leftover palm branches to be burned for ashes next Ash Wednesday.
- Look ahead to the worship helps and task lists on pp. 141–145 as you plan for worship during the Three Days.

Shape of the Communion Liturgy

- See the seasonal worship texts for Lent on p. 108.
- Use a Kyrie or Trisagion ("Holy God"). In addition to the form in the communion setting, see options in the service music section of *Evangelical Lutheran Worship*, #151–161.
- Omit the hymn of praise.
- Use the Apostles' Creed.
- See the prayers of intercession for Ash Wednesday and each Sunday.
- Use the preface for Lent or Passion Sunday, as appropriate (*Evangelical Lutheran Worship* Leaders Edition, pp. 185, 186).
- Thanksgiving at the table: see options in Evangelical Lutheran Worship, especially Prayer IV (Pew Edition, p. 111; Leaders Edition, p. 197); *WOV*, Prayer D (Leaders Edition, p. 68).

Other Helps

- See the suggestions for music and worship space in the essay "Preparing for Lent," pp. 104–105.
- See the midweek Lenten worship series in the seasonal rites section (pp. 111–112).
- See *Evangelical Lutheran Worship* (Pew Edition, pp. 232–233; Leaders Edition, pp. 30, 592) or *Welcome to Christ: Lutheran Rites for the Catechumenate* (pp. 18–34) for resources for preparing candidates for baptism at Easter.

SEASONAL WORSHIP TEXTS FOR LENT

Confession and Forgiveness

All may make the sign of the cross, the sign that is marked at baptism, as the presiding minister begins.

Trusting in the word of life given in baptism,
we are gathered in the name of the Father,
and of the + Son, and of the Holy Spirit.
Amen.

Let us return to God with all our hearts,
confessing our sins and our need for healing.

Silence is kept for reflection.

Gracious God,
you know the depths of our sins against you,
each other, and your whole creation;
have mercy on us.
We pray for forgiveness we cannot earn
and renewal we do not merit,
given only through your Son,
Jesus Christ our Lord.
Amen.

God knows and loves us completely, just as we are.
Through water and word, Spirit and saving Son,
we are cleansed from sin,
joined with the communion of saints,
and brought to new and abundant life.
In the name of + Jesus Christ, your sins are forgiven.
Live in newness of life.
Amen.

Greeting

Now is the acceptable time, now is the day of salvation.
May the grace of God, through Christ our salvation,
be with you all.
And also with you.

Offering Prayer

Merciful God,
we cry out for the hope and healing you offer.
Guide us continually to your service.

Make us your hands to feed the hungry
and prepare us to receive the bread of life,
Jesus Christ, your Son, our Savior.
Amen.

Invitation to Communion

Let us lift up the bread of life and cup of salvation
and call on the name of the Lord.

Prayer after Communion

Generous God,
you have fed and renewed us in your holy meal.
Send us into the world you love.
Through our fasting and devotion
draw us to you and to our neighbors,
that we may break bonds of injustice,
feed the hungry,
and set the oppressed free.
In Jesus' name we pray.
Amen.

Sending of Communion

Compassionate God,
bless those whose ministry brings us into communion
with the brothers and sisters whose presence we miss.
Embolden these ministers to share your word,
our prayers, and the healing meal of life
through the body and blood, life and death of your Son,
Jesus Christ our Lord.
Amen.

Blessing

As we die and rise with Christ in baptism,
may we also live and serve like Christ.

Almighty God, Father, + Son, and Holy Spirit,
bless you now and forever.
Amen.

Dismissal

Go in peace. Remember the poor.
Thanks be to God.

SEASONAL RITES FOR LENT

Midweek Prayer during Lent

This flexible order of evening prayer may be celebrated as a midweek service during Lent. The readings and psalms are drawn from the daily lectionary as presented in Evangelical Lutheran Worship (Pew Edition, pp. 1134–1135). The foundational premise of this set of daily readings is their relationship to the Sunday lectionary. The readings are chosen so that the days leading up to Sunday (Thursday through Saturday) prepare for the Sunday readings. The days flowing out from Sunday (Monday through Wednesday) reflect upon the Sunday readings. The Old Testament readings and psalms suggested in this midweek order are the Wednesday readings following each Sunday in Lent.

Opening

The assembly stands. A large, lighted candle may be carried to its place.

The following dialogue may accompany or follow the procession. It may be spoken or sung to the tone given in Evangelical Lutheran Worship, p. 309, the assembly echoing the leader.

Behold, now is the accept- ˡ able time;
now is the day ˡ of salvation.
Turn us again, O God of ˡ our salvation,
that the light of your face may ˡ shine on us.
May your justice shine ˡ like the sun;
and may the poor be ˡ lifted up.

Hymn of Light

A hymn of praise to Christ the light may be sung. See Evangelical Lutheran Worship #229–231, 560–563.

Thanksgiving for Light

A form is provided in Evangelical Lutheran Worship, pp. 310–311.

Psalmody

The psalmody begins with Psalm 141, a song of forgiveness and protection; Psalm 121; or another psalm appropriate for evening. For musical settings of Psalm 141 see Evangelical Lutheran Worship, pp. 312–313 and #232–233.

Week of Lent 1: Psalm 77
Prayer for God to remember us
Week of Lent 2: Psalm 105:1-11, 37-45
God promises life to Abraham
Week of Lent 3: Psalm 84
How lovely is God's dwelling place
Week of Lent 4: Psalm 107:1-16
God gives food and light
Week of Lent 5: Psalm 119:9-16
I treasure your promise in my heart

Song

Possibilities for assembly song related to the readings for each of the Wednesdays of Lent follow.

Week of Lent 1
I want Jesus to walk with me   ELW 325, TFF 66, WOV 660
If you but trust in God to guide you   ELW 769, LBW 453
Week of Lent 2
How firm a foundation   ELW 796, LBW 507
O God, my faithful God   ELW 806, LBW 504
Week of Lent 3
Canticle of the Turning   ELW 723, W&P 26
Built on a rock   ELW 652, LBW 365
Week of Lent 4
Salvation unto us has come   ELW 590, LBW 297
O God of mercy, God of light   ELW 714, LBW 425
Week of Lent 5
Restore in us, O God   ELW 328, WOV 662
You are mine   ELW 581, W&P 158

Reading

Week of Lent 1: Proverbs 30:1-9
Plea to be safe from temptation
Week of Lent 2: Jeremiah 30:12-22
God will restore Israel
Week of Lent 3: Ezra 6:1-16
King Darius orders the temple rebuilt
Week of Lent 4: Isaiah 60:15-22
God is our light
Week of Lent 5: Haggai 2:1-9, 20-23
God promises future blessings

The reading of scripture is followed by silence for reflection. Other forms of reflection may also follow, such as brief commentary, teaching, or personal witness; nonbiblical readings; interpretation through music or other art forms; or guided conversation among those present.

The reflection may conclude with a scriptural dialogue.
Long ago God spoke to our ancestors in many and various ways by the prophets,
but in these last days God has spoken to us by the Son.

Gospel Canticle

For musical versions of the gospel canticle for evening, the song of Mary, see Evangelical Lutheran Worship, pp. 314–315 and #234–235; 251, 573, 723, 882.

Prayers

A form is provided in Evangelical Lutheran Worship, pp. 316–318.

Blessing

Let us bless the Lord.
Thanks be to God.
The peace of God, which surpasses all understanding, keep our hearts and minds in Christ Jesus.
Amen.

The greeting of peace may be shared by all.

Stones: A Midweek Lenten Series

Overview

This six-part worship series can be used for Lenten midweek services or for weekend services not based on the Revised Common Lectionary.

Two options for scripture readings and preaching themes are presented within this series. Option 1 offers texts and themes focused on stones; Option 2 offers an exploration of the Ten Commandments. Presented on the next page are series ideas, rituals, music, and questions suitable for either preaching theme.

Weekly Preaching Themes and Readings

Using only the first reading listed for each week following Ash Wednesday would provide more time for worshipers to meditate. Additional readings are provided in brackets for those who desire them.

Option 1: Stones

Week 1: Ash Wednesday / Stones of the covenant

Readings: Deuteronomy 5:1-22; 2 Corinthians 3:1-3; Matthew 21:42-46

Week 2: God's law engraved on stone and on human hearts

Readings: Exodus 34:1-10 [Romans 2:12-16; Matthew 5:17-20]

Week 3: A millstone as metaphor for punishment of sin

Readings: Matthew 18:6-9 [2 Thessalonians 1:6-10]

Week 4: Jesus is a stumbling stone for unbelievers and the rock of salvation for believers

Readings: Romans 9:30-33 [Isaiah 12:1-6; 1 Corinthians 10:1-4]

Week 5: Jesus the living stone upon which the church is founded

Readings: 1 Peter 2:1-10 [Matthew 3:7-12]

Week 6: Jesus, the foundation stone for life

Readings: Matthew 7:24-29 [Deuteronomy 8:1-10; Ephesians 3:14-21]

Option 2: Ten Commandments: From Tablets of Stone

Week 1: Ash Wednesday / What is sin?

Readings: Exodus 20:1-20, Romans 2:12-16; Matthew 5:17-20 *or* Matthew 22:34-40

Week 2: First Commandment

Readings: Exodus 20:1-6 [Isaiah 43:10-13; Matthew 22:34-40]

Week 3: Second and Third Commandments

Readings: Exodus 20:7-11 [Isaiah 2:5-11; James 3:1-10; Matthew 5:33-37; Genesis 2:1-4a]

Week 4: Fourth and Fifth Commandments

Readings: Exodus 20:12-13 [Romans 12:9-21; Matthew 5:43-48]

Week 5: Sixth and Seventh Commandments

Readings: Exodus 20:14-15 [Ephesians 5:1-8; Matthew 15:10-20]

Week 6: Eighth, Ninth, and Tenth Commandments

Readings: Exodus 20:16-17 [Zechariah 8:15b-17; Ephesians 4:25-32; Mark 12:28-34]

Series Ideas

Using stones as an aid to prayer and meditation

On Ash Wednesday and each week thereafter, each worshiper is given a rough, natural stone. It is important that the stones be rough, because they will be used to represent the person's sins. The size of the stones will be dependent on factors such as the size of the congregation and how you plan to use them toward the end of Lent.

Each week, stones could be distributed just before the sermon or time for meditation, with the suggestion that worshipers hold the stones through the time of meditation or preaching. Proclamation each week would center on a scripture reading and theme related to stones (Option 1) or to one or more of the Ten Commandments (Option 2). Preaching might best take the form of a short meditation followed by a period of silence in which to reflect on the stone and its meaning.

Worshipers may be encouraged to use the stones as a focal point for prayer and meditation each day during Lent.

Concluding ritual using stones

Ask worshipers to bring all their stones to the last midweek service. Have extras for anyone who forgets or has missed previous weeks. Include a time for silent meditation on one's sins after the sermon. As the silence concludes, invite worshipers to leave their stones at a specially prepared place in the church. Assembly song may accompany this action.

Possibilities for the stones

- Have someone construct a cross-shaped wooden box large enough to accommodate all the stones. Worshipers deposit their stones in the box. Sometime in the week following the service, move the box outside to a place where the cross can be seen, then fill the box with concrete. When dry, the wooden frame can be dismantled and the cross left as a reminder that we lay our sins on Jesus.
- Place a large wooden cross (six feet or more) with a stand into a barrel. Worshipers place their stones in the barrel. A variation might be to dig a deep hole and bury the stones to represent our sins being buried with Jesus.
- Outline a large cross on a piece of heavy, clear plastic (to protect the floor) and lay it in a prominent place. Worshipers place their rocks inside the outline. Depending on its location, this could be left in place until Easter morning.
- If the weather and the church's physical plant allow, prepare a place outdoors for a cross-centered garden. Worshipers leave their stones at the prepared site at the end of the service. Just before Easter and/or throughout the Easter season, flowering plants could be planted in the garden, symbolizing the resurrection and forgiveness of our sins.

Assembly song suggestions

God loved the world   ELW 323, LBW 292
Jesus is a rock in a weary land   ELW 333
Alas! And did my savior bleed   ELW 337, TFF 71, LBW 98
Beneath the cross of Jesus   ELW 338, LBW 107
Jesus, remember me   ELW 616, WOV 740, W&P 78
In the cross of Christ I glory   ELW 324, LBW 104
Now behold the Lamb   ELW 341, TFF 128
Lamb of God   ELW 336

Questions for discussion or reflection

If your congregation shares a meal before its midweek service, each table could have a table tent with discussion questions around that day's theme. Encourage those at the table to spend a few minutes sharing their thoughts. Some possible questions:

- How does a stone speak to me of sin?
- What are some stumbling blocks (stones) in the path of my faith journey?
- How do I deal with obstacles to my faith?
- What does it feel like to be stoned, and how may we sometimes throw stones at others?
- How do I deal with my sins? Do I face them head on, avoid thinking about them, make excuses, etc.?
- What is my understanding of the scope of the commandment(s) featured this week?

February 25, 2009
Ash Wednesday

Lent begins with a solemn call to fasting and repentance as we begin our journey to the baptismal waters of Easter. As we hear in today's readings, now is the acceptable time to return to the Lord. During Lent the people of God will reflect on the meaning of their baptism into Christ's death and resurrection. The sign of ashes suggests our human mortality and frailty. What seems like an ending is really an invitation to make each day a new beginning, in which we are washed in God's mercy and forgiveness. With the cross on our brow, we long for the spiritual renewal that flows from the springtime Easter feast to come.

Today the church commemorates the deaconess Elizabeth Fedde.

Prayer of the Day

Almighty and ever-living God, you hate nothing you have made, and you forgive the sins of all who are penitent. Create in us new and honest hearts, so that, truly repenting of our sins, we may receive from you, the God of all mercy, full pardon and forgiveness through your Son, Jesus Christ, our Savior and Lord, who lives and reigns with you and the Holy Spirit, one God, now and forever.

or

Gracious God, out of your love and mercy you breathed into dust the breath of life, creating us to serve you and our neighbors. Call forth our prayers and acts of kindness, and strengthen us to face our mortality with confidence in the mercy of your Son, Jesus Christ, our Savior and Lord, who lives and reigns with you and the Holy Spirit, one God, now and forever.

Gospel Acclamation

Return to the ǀ LORD, your God,* who is gracious and merciful, slow to anger, and abounding in ǀ steadfast love. (Joel 2:13)

Readings and Psalm

Joel 2:1-2, 12-17

Because of the coming Day of the Lord, the prophet Joel calls the people to a community lament. The repentant community reminds God of his gracious character and asks God to spare the people, lest the nations doubt God's power to save.

or Isaiah 58:1-12

Shortly after the return of Israel from exile in Babylon, the people were troubled by the ineffectiveness of their fasts. God reminds them that outward observance is no substitute for genuine fasting that results in acts of justice, such as feeding the hungry, sheltering the homeless, and clothing the naked. Sincere repentance will lead to a dramatic improvement of their condition.

Psalm 51:1-17

Have mercy on me, O God, according to your steadfast love. (Ps. 51:1)

2 Corinthians 5:20b—6:10

The ministry of the gospel endures many challenges and hardships. Through this ministry, God's reconciling activity in the death of Christ reaches into the depths of our lives to bring us into a right relationship with God. In this way, God accepts us into the reality of divine salvation.

Matthew 6:1-6, 16-21

In the Sermon on the Mount, Jesus commends almsgiving, prayer, and fasting, but emphasizes that spiritual devotion must not be done for show.

Color   Purple

CD-ROM Images

Icon Three: AshWednesday01_ABC, AshWednesday02_ABC, AshWednesday03_ABC
Icon Two: AshWednesday01_ABC, AshWednesday02_ABC, AshWednesday03_ABC
Icon: 018, 082, 147, 257

Prayers of Intercession

Led by Christ in our journey of repentance and moved by his compassion, let us pray for the church, those in need, and all of God's creation.

A brief silence.

Holy God, you gather your people in solemn assembly. Grant us grace, so that we may observe a holy Lent through fasting, prayer, and works of love. Lord, in your mercy, **hear our prayer.**

You give bountifully to your creatures. Provide for all animals whose winter rations are dwindling, and prepare the earth for renewal in coming weeks. Lord, in your mercy, **hear our prayer.**

You move your people to cry out for justice. Bring to light all the ways in which we oppress others. Turn us from our complacency, and move us to work on behalf of the oppressed. Lord, in your mercy, **hear our prayer.**

You lift up the poor. Care for all who know poverty of any kind: of health, of daily needs, of spirit (*especially*). Pour your abundant mercy upon them. Lord, in your mercy, **hear our prayer.**

You turn people from their sin to live for you alone. Renew us in the covenant of baptism, that we might live in hope of a creation reconciled and restored. Lord, in your mercy, **hear our prayer.**

Here other intercessions may be offered.

As we remember saints who have gone before us (*especially Elizabeth Fedde, deaconess*), guide us in our journey and open our lives to the cleansing and renewing power of your abundant forgiveness. Lord, in your mercy, **hear our prayer.**

Into your hands, gracious God, we commend all for whom we pray, trusting in your mercy; through Jesus Christ, our Savior.

Amen.

Ideas and Images for the Day

Some traditions may see Lent as hard work, but these Ash Wednesday texts remind us that the season is primarily "heart work." Jesus speaks of spiritual practices—helping the needy, praying, fasting—and contrasts the motivations of being seen and rewarded by others with having "treasure in heaven." Through such spiritual practices, especially during the Lenten season, the heart is called home to God ("return to me with all your heart," Joel writes) when we take a good, hard look at what lurks within our own "secret" hearts. Ultimately, God accomplishes "heart work" more profound than any we could achieve ourselves: creating "clean hearts," mending the broken-hearted, and turning our hearts toward the needs of others.

1. Heart disease is epidemic in both men and women. Web sites of the American Heart Association (www.americanheart.org) and the ELCA (www.elca.org/ health) offer suggestions for keeping physical hearts healthy. What connections might we find there in caring for our hearts spiritually? For example, might we consider "losing the weight" of resentment and guilt, or fasting from foods high in cholesterol?

2. Paulo Coelho's novel *The Alchemist* (HarperSanFrancisco, 1994) and Mark Allan Powell's biblical study *Giving to God: The Bible's Good News about Living a Generous Life* (Wm. B. Eerdmans, 2006) help flesh out meanings of "treasure in heaven." In his book, subtitled "A Story about Following Your Dream," Coelho writes, "It was his heart that would tell him where his treasure was hidden. 'Where your treasure is, there also will be your heart,' the alchemist had told him" (pp. 167–168). Powell, in his book on stewardship, argues that the way we use our earthly treasures can lead our hearts where they need to go.

3. "Jesus lives in your heart" has been a staple of Sunday school teaching and the grown-up faith of many. Connecting an inward faith with outward practice is a concern for public life, regardless of political affiliation. With regard to poverty and world events, Jim Wallis (www.sojourners.com) has called people—sometimes controversially—to a faith that is not merely *private* or *public* but which has deeply *personal* roots.

4. Several hymns and songs in *Evangelical Lutheran Worship* work well as prayers for the heart-work of Lent: "Spirit of God, descend upon my heart" (800), "Be thou my vision" (793), "Change my heart, O God" (801), and "Lord, let my heart be good soil" (512).

5. Heart-work deepens an understanding of reconciliation. How might our practice of confession and reconciliation strengthen our motivations for faith and service, and sustain the heartfelt ministry to which Isaiah and Paul call us?

Hymns for Worship
Gathering

None (Psalm 51 is recommended)

Hymn of the Day

Restore in us, O God   ELW 328   *BAYLOR*
  WOV 662   *CATECHUMEN*
Lord Jesus, think on me   ELW 599, LBW 309   *SOUTHWELL*
Our Father, we have wandered   ELW 606, WOV 733
  HERZLICH TUT MICH VERLANGEN

Communion

Just as I am, without one plea   ELW 592, LBW 296
Change my heart, O God   ELW 801
Once we sang and danced   ELW 701

Sending

Eternal Lord of love, behold your church   ELW 321
On my heart imprint your image   ELW 811, LBW 102

Additional Hymns and Songs

Again we keep the solemn fast   HG 158
Return to God   GC 410
Where your treasure is   GC 647
Remember You Are Dust   GC 391
Dust and ashes   GC 392
Create in me a clean heart   W&P 35

Music for the Day
Psalmody and Acclamations

Cherwien, David. "Psalm 51" from *Psalm Settings for the Church Year.* AFP 9780800678562.
Miller, Aaron David. *Gospel Acclamations for Lent–Holy Trinity.* AFP 9780800635589.
Psalter for Worship Year B, Evangelical Lutheran Worship Edition. AFP 9780806683839.

Choral

▫ Beck, John Ness. "Prayer to Jesus" (Southwell). SATB, opt assembly, pno. BP 1197.
Brahms, Johannes. "O World So Vain" from *Chantry Choirbook.* SATB. AFP 9780800657772.
Schalk, Carl F. "Have Mercy on Me, O God." SATB. AFP 9780800657840.
Scott, K. Lee. "Out of the Depths I Cry to Thee." 2 pt mxd, kybd. AFP 9780800647322. *Augsburg Easy Choirbook*, vol. 1. AFP 9780800676025.

Children's Choir

Berthier, Jacques. "Jesus, Remember Me" from *LifeSongs.* LE. U, pno. AFP 9780806642710.
Gallina, Jill. "Let Us Break Bread Together." UE. 2 pt, kybd. GS EA5114.
Sleeth, Natalie. "Prayer." UE. U/2 pt, kybd, opt trbl inst. CG A565.

Keyboard / Instrumental

Brahms, Johannes. "Herzlich tut mich verlangen." Org. Various ed.
Gehring, Philip. "Deep Blue" from *Five Hymn Preludes for Organ.* Org. AFP 9780800678777.
Lasky, David. "Southwell" from *All Glory, Laud, and Honor.* Org. AFP 9780800637484.
Organ, Anne Krentz. "Southwell" from *Woven Together*, vol. 2. Pno, C/B-flat inst. AFP 9780800677664.
Sowash, Bradley. "Eventide" from *Great English Hymns.* Pno. AFP 9780800678791.

Handbell

Gramann, Fred, arr. "Fantasy on 'King's Weston'." 3-6 oct, L3+. AG 1671.
Page, Anna Laura. "What Wondrous Love Is This." 3-5 oct hb/hc, L3. CG B244.
Semmann, Barbara. "O Sacred Head Now Wounded." 4 oct, L1+. National Music Publications HB203.

Praise Ensemble

■ Jernigan, Dennis L. "You Are My All in All" from *Breakforth Worship Songbook.* New Creation Ministries. www.new-creation.net.
■ Park, Andy. "In the Secret" from *Best of the Best, The Other Songbook 2.* FEL 1891062034.
■ Redman, Matt. "The Heart of Worship" from www.praisecharts.com. Thankyou Music.
■ Smith, Martin. "Lord, You Have My Heart" from WT. Thankyou Music.

Global

Hesla, Bret. "Mercy, We Abide in You" from *Justice, Like a Base of Stone.* SATB, cant. AFP 9780800623562.
Hopson, Hal H. "O God in Heaven." SATB. HOP MA501.

Wednesday, February 25
Elizabeth Fedde, deaconess, 1921

Fedde was born in Norway and trained as a deaconess. In 1882, at the age of 32, she was asked to come to New York to minister to the poor and to Norwegian seamen. Her influence was wide-ranging, and she established the Deaconess House in Brooklyn and the Deaconess House and Hospital of the Lutheran Free Church in Minneapolis. She returned home to Norway in 1895 and died there.

▫ denotes choral suggestions that relate to the hymn of the day.
■ denotes songs that are available on iTunes®.

March 1, 2009
First Sunday in Lent

On Ash Wednesday the church began its journey toward baptismal immersion in the death and resurrection of Christ. This year, the Sundays in Lent lead us to focus on five covenants God makes in the Hebrew Scriptures and to use them as lenses through which to view baptism. First Peter connects the way God saved Noah's family in the flood with the way God saves us through the water of baptism. The baptismal covenant is made with us individually, but the new life we are given in baptism is for the sake of the whole world.

Today the church commemorates the hymnwriter George Herbert, who died in 1633.

Prayer of the Day

Holy God, heavenly Father, in the waters of the flood you saved the chosen, and in the wilderness of temptation you protected your Son from sin. Renew us in the gift of baptism. May your holy angels be with us, that the wicked foe may have no power over us, through Jesus Christ, our Savior and Lord, who lives and reigns with you and the Holy Spirit, one God, now and forever.

Gospel Acclamation

One does not live by [|] bread alone,* but by every word that comes from the [|] mouth of God. (Matt. 4:4)

Readings and Psalm

Genesis 9:8-17

Today's reading is the conclusion to the flood story. Because of human sin, the Lord destroys the earth by flood, saving only Noah, his family, and the animals on the ark. Yet divine destruction gives way to divine commitment. As in the first creation, God blesses humanity and establishes a covenant with all creatures.

Psalm 25:1-10

Your paths, O LORD, are steadfast love and faithfulness. (Ps. 25:10)

1 Peter 3:18-22

As God acted through Christ's suffering and death to bring us to God, so God acts through baptism to save us from a sinful existence. This spiritual cleansing marks our new life in Christ.

Mark 1:9-15

The Spirit that comes upon Jesus at his baptism sustains him when he is tested by Satan so that he might proclaim the good news of God's reign.

Color   Purple

CD-ROM Images

Icon Three: Lent1_B
Icon Two: Lent1_B
Icon: 083

Prayers of Intercession

Led by Christ in our journey of repentance and moved by his compassion, let us pray for the church, those in need, and all of God's creation.

A brief silence.

Almighty God, remember the covenant you have established with your people. Preserve us by your mercy, and lead us to live mercifully with others. Lord, in your mercy,
hear our prayer.

Pour out the gift of water for all of your creation. Provide clean water for those who lack it, curb the use of those who waste it, and guide the efforts of those who seek to conserve it. Lord, in your mercy,
hear our prayer.

Extend your gift of renewal to all nations. Where leaders exert overwhelming power and where militaries exert unjust might, deliver your sheltering peace to people who live in fear. Lord, in your mercy,
hear our prayer.

Deliver your gift of healing to all who suffer. Make well those who are ill, and those who struggle with brokenness whole *(especially)*. Renew them with your promises.

Lord, in your mercy,
hear our prayer.

Here other intercessions may be offered.

Giving thanks for the gifts of all the saints *(especially George Herbert)*, may our faith be enlivened by their music, visual arts, and written words. Lord, in your mercy,
hear our prayer.

Into your hands, gracious God, we commend all for whom we pray, trusting in your mercy; through Jesus Christ, our Savior.
Amen.

Ideas and Images for the Day

In the Old Testament, covenants were a common expression of relationship between God and God's people. This was a way for the people to commit to serving God and for God to commit to upholding them. The "bow in the clouds" was a sign of God's covenant with Noah and his family and every living creature. What's unusual about this covenant agreement is that it's one-sided. It's all God's action, with no expectation other than to live under God's blessing. Whenever they see the bow in the clouds they are to remember God's promise to protect them from the devastation of the flood. Christians are drowned in the floodwaters of baptism and raised up with the promise of new life as God's children. In baptism we receive a sign of God's unfailing commitment and love for us. It is not a bow in the clouds but the sign of Christ's cross marked on our foreheads. As we begin the season of Lent, we receive this sign of God's promise in the form of ashes on our forehead. As we approach the Easter Vigil, we will again see this sign as the cross is traced on the foreheads of the newly baptized.

1. "He saw the heavens torn apart" (Mark 1:10). There is a lot of talk about global warming and the dire predictions that the ozone layer is thinning to the point of being torn apart. There is an understandable fear of catastrophe. In contrast, the phrase that describes the heavens being torn apart, with the Holy Spirit descending like a dove through the tear, suggests a more uplifting theme of God being present in the tear. On Good Friday the temple curtain is torn in two as Jesus dies (Mark 15:38). The result of this tearing is the opening up of the way of salvation for all who believe.

2. Realtors often advise those selling their homes to have the aroma of freshly baked cookies wafting through the house. When buyers enter the house, the smell draws them in and makes them feel at home. The hope is that the buyers will feel so at home that they'll buy the house. The smells of warm baked cookies, Mom's apple pie, or hot chicken soup make us think "home." We seek such comforts when the stresses of life bombard our senses. When life's troubles overwhelm us, God's promises comfort us with the promise of God's abiding presence and healing touch. The cross and the rainbow are visual images reminding us of this promise.

3. Remember your baptism! During Lent it is appropriate to remember the gift of baptism by placing the open water-filled baptismal font at the entrance to the chancel area or at the entrance to the sanctuary. Invite worshipers to dip their fingers into the water and make the sign of the cross as a reminder of their baptism.

Hymns for Worship
Gathering

Wash, O God, our sons and daughters   ELW 445, WOV 697
Oh, love, how deep   ELW 322, LBW 88
I'm going on a journey   ELW 446

Hymn of the Day

O Lord, throughout these forty days   ELW 319
    CONSOLATION   LBW 99   *CAITHNESS*
If God my Lord be for me   ELW 788, LBW 454
    IST GOTT FÜR MICH
Lord of our life   ELW 766, LBW 366   *ISTE CONFESSOR*

Communion

I want Jesus to walk with me   ELW 325
Thy holy wings   ELW 613, WOV 741
Lead me, guide me   ELW 768

Sending

Guide me ever, great Redeemer   ELW 618, LBW 343
Bless now, O God, the journey   ELW 326

Additional Hymns and Songs

Mark how the Lamb of God's self-offering   HG 141, NCH 167
Yield not to temptation   TFF 195

Music for the Day
Psalmody and Acclamations

Miller, Aaron David. *Gospel Acclamations for Lent–Holy Trinity.* AFP 9780800635589.

Psalter for Worship Year B, Evangelical Lutheran Worship Edition. AFP 9780806683839.

Shute, Linda Cable. "Psalm 25" from *Psalm Settings for the Church Year.* AFP 9780800678562.

Choral

Bach, J. S. "Lord Jesus Christ, God's Only Son" from *Bach for All Seasons.* U, kybd. AFP 9780800658540.

Byrd, William. "Lord, Hear My Prayer." SAB. Choral Public Domain Library. www.cpdl.org.

Organ, Anne Krentz. "Bless Now, O God, the Journey." 2 pt mxd, kybd. AFP 9780800678951.

◻ Pelz, Walter L. "O Lord, throughout These Forty Days." SAB, kybd, opt C inst. AFP 9780800637538.

Pinkham, Daniel. "For the Gift of Water." SATB, opt org. ECS 5204.

Children's Choir

Patterson, Mark. "Show Me Thy Ways" from *ChildrenSing: Seven Anthems for Elementary Age Singers*. UE. 2 pt, pno. AFP 9780800677695.

Ramseth, Betty Ann. "The Breath of God Is Moving." UE. 2 pt, kybd. AFP 9786000119157. OP

Ziegenhals, Harriet. "Tapestry." LE. U, pno. CG A533.

Keyboard / Instrumental

Burkhardt, Michael. "Consolation" from *Five Advent Hymn Improvisations*, set 1. Org. MSM 10-004.

Frahm, Frederick. "Ist Gott für mich" from *Faith Alive*. Org. AFP 9780800675738.

Hassell, Michael. "Woodworth" from *Jazz Old Time Favorites*. Pno. AFP 9780800678814.

Moore, Bob. "Prelude II" from *Four Preludes*. Pno, fl/vln/ob, cello/bsn. GIA G-4790.

Rotermund, Donald. "Iste confessor" from *Introductions, Interludes, and Codas on Traditional Hymns*. Org. MSM 10-535.

Handbell

Helman, Michael. "Fantasy." 3-5 oct hb/hc, L4-. AG 5117.

Sherman, Arnold B. "He Never Said a Mumbalin' Word." 3-5 oct, L3. AG 1844.

Zabel, Albert Heinrich. "Adagio in G Minor." 5 oct, L3. Shawnee Press HP5395. OP

Praise Ensemble

■ Butler, Terry. "Cry of My Heart" from *Best of the Best, The Other Songbook 2*. FEL 1891062034.

■ Maher, Matt. "40 Days" from www.ccli.com. www.Spiritandsong.com.

■ Ruis, David. "Sweet Mercies" from www.praisecharts.com. Mercy/VIN.

■ Zschech, Darlene. "The Potter's Hand" from *Best of the Best, The Other Songbook 2*. FEL 1891062034.

Global

Bell, John L. "Come and Let Us Worship God." SATB. GIA G-5160.

Gunderson, Jerry. "We Come to the Hungry Feast." SAB, pno, 1/2/3 C inst, opt assembly. AFP 9780800658717.

Sunday, March 1

George Herbert, hymnwriter, 1633

As a student at Trinity College, Cambridge, England, George Herbert excelled in languages and music. He went to college with the intention of becoming a priest, but his scholarship attracted the attention of King James I. Herbert served in parliament for two years. After the death of King James and at the urging of a friend, Herbert's interest in ordained ministry was renewed. He was ordained a priest in 1630 and served the little parish of St. Andrew Bremerton until his death. He was noted for unfailing care for his parishioners, bringing the sacraments to them when they were ill, and providing food and clothing for those in need. Herbert is best remembered, however, as a writer of poems and hymns such as "Come, my way, my truth, my life" (ELW 816).

Monday, March 2

John Wesley, 1791; Charles Wesley, 1788; renewers of the church

The Wesleys were leaders of a revival in the Church of England. Their spiritual discipline of frequent communion, fasting, and advocacy for the poor earned them the name "Methodists." The Wesleys were missionries in the American colony of Georgia for a time, but returned to England discouraged. Following a conversion experience while reading Luther's *Preface to the Epistle to the Romans*, John was perhaps the greatest force in eighteenth-century revival. The brothers' desire was that the Methodist Societies would be a movement for renewal in the Church of England, but after their deaths the societies developed a separate status.

Charles wrote more than 600 hymns, including several that are especially appropriate for Lent: "Christ, whose glory fills the skies" and "Love divine, all loves excelling."

Saturday, March 7

Perpetua and Felicity and companions, martyrs at Carthage, 202

In the year 202 the emperor Septimius Severus forbade conversions to Christianity. Perpetua, a noblewoman, Felicity, a slave, and other companions were all catechumens at Carthage in North Africa. They were imprisoned and sentenced to death. Perpetua's father, who was not a Christian, visited her in prison and begged her to lay aside her Christian convictions in order to spare her life and spare the family from scorn. Perpetua responded and told her father, "We know that we are not placed in our own power but in that of God."

During the weeks of Lent, congregations that do not have catechumens can pray for those who do as they approach their own death and rebirth in the waters of baptism at the Easter Vigil, and are clothed with the new life of Christ.

March 8, 2009
Second Sunday in Lent

The second covenant in this year's Lenten readings is the one made with Abraham and Sarah: God's promise to make them the ancestors of many, with whom God will remain in everlasting covenant. Paul says this promise comes to all who share Abraham's faith in the God who brings life into being where there was no life. We receive this baptismal promise of resurrection life in faith. Sarah and Abraham receive new names as a sign of the covenant, and we too get new identities in baptism, as we put on Christ.

Prayer of the Day

O God, by the passion of your blessed Son you made an instrument of shameful death to be for us the means of life. Grant us so to glory in the cross of Christ that we may gladly suffer shame and loss for the sake of your Son, Jesus Christ our Savior and Lord, who lives and reigns with you and the Holy Spirit, one God, now and forever.

Gospel Acclamation

May I never boast of anything except the cross of our Lord [|] Jesus Christ,* by which the world is crucified to me, and I [|] to the world. (Gal. 6:14)

Readings and Psalm
Genesis 17:1-7, 15-16

As with Noah, God makes an everlasting covenant with Abraham and Sarah. God promises this old couple that they will be the ancestors of nations, though they have no child together. God will miraculously bring forth new life from Sarah's old womb. The name changes emphasize the firmness of God's promise.

Psalm 22:23-31

All the ends of the earth shall remember and turn to the Lord. (Ps. 22:27)

Romans 4:13-25

Paul presents Abraham as the example for how a person comes into a right relationship with God not through works of the law but through faith. Though Abraham and Sarah were far too old for bearing children, Abraham trusted that God would accomplish what God had promised to accomplish.

Mark 8:31-38

After Peter confesses his belief that Jesus is the Messiah, Jesus tells his disciples for the first time what is to come. Peter's response indicates that he does not yet understand the way of the cross that Jesus will travel.

Color   Purple

CD-ROM Images

Icon Three: Lent2_B
Icon Two: Lent2_B
Icon: 084

Prayers of Intercession

Led by Christ in our journey of repentance and moved by his compassion, let us pray for the church, those in need, and all of God's creation.

A brief silence.

God of salvation, we pray for the members of the body of Christ. Send your Spirit to those who struggle with faith, and let the faith of the church carry them in difficult times. Lord, in your mercy,

hear our prayer.

We pray for all parts of the earth where seasons are beginning to change. Reveal the wonder of life in this transition, and give us knowledge and determination to care for the earth with reverence. Lord, in your mercy,

hear our prayer.

We pray for all families, clans, tribes, and nations. Make them mindful of others affected by their deliberations and decisions, that peace and justice may benefit all people. Lord, in your mercy,

hear our prayer.

We pray for those who struggle with survival because of illness or need *(especially)*. Bless them with your presence and through the caring of those who attend to them.
Lord, in your mercy,
hear our prayer.
We pray for children everywhere. Raise them up in your care, especially those who do not have parents or have neglectful parents. Show them holy, parental love.
Lord, in your mercy,
hear our prayer.
Here other intercessions may be offered.
Remembering those who have died in faith and the goodness you have shown all generations before us, we pray that we may remain faithful, trusting the promises you have made. Lord, in your mercy,
hear our prayer.
Into your hands, gracious God, we commend all for whom we pray, trusting in your mercy; through Jesus Christ, our Savior.
Amen.

Ideas and Images for the Day

In calling us back to the basics, Lent reminds us of what really counts: following Jesus. This Sunday we are encouraged to understand and tell the truth about discipleship, both its costs—losing one's life—*and* its promises—receiving one's life back. In this gospel from Mark, discipleship means "getting behind" Jesus, even in the midst of pressure to save one's own life and preserve one's habits. It means believing in God's promises—even ones that seem far-fetched—and living as if they are true. It may mean giving something up for Lent, but even beyond that it means giving up *anything* that prevents us from receiving the eternal, abundant life that Jesus longs to give us and would die for us to have.

1. When Jesus openly reveals his fate to his disciples, Peter "rebukes" Jesus. In *The Lord of the Rings* (J.R.R. Tolkien, HarperCollins, 1995; see also the film trilogy: New Line Cinema, 2001, 2002, and 2003), Frodo accepts his fateful task of bearing the ring to its destruction, and he speaks openly about the journey's dangers. Even while bemoaning Frodo's fate at times, his companion, Sam, accompanies Frodo on the journey with a devotion that provides an interesting comparison with Peter's erratic discipleship.

2. For early Christians, persecution and pressure worked to prevent them from practicing their faith. In that environment, one could hardly practice one's faith by accident—it had to be intentional. Today, other public and private pressures (particularly the busy-ness of work and activities) can push one's faith to the margins. Like the early Christians, we also must look at what we are willing to sacrifice in order to follow Jesus intentionally.

3. In Jesus' words to Peter, "Get behind me," Mark uses a Greek preposition that appears mainly when Jesus calls people to follow "behind" him. Peter is called to get behind Jesus, to follow him, instead of setting his mind on human things. In our lives and in our churches, what kinds of human or divine things (ministries, causes, people, activities) do we tend to "get behind"?

4. Worship not only *invites* us to "set our minds on divine things" but can also *help* us do so. By modeling ways of speaking and listening to God in word, song, and silence, worship can teach people to "seek first the kingdom of God" (Matt. 6:33). On Sundays, we learn ways to set our minds on God during the rest of the week.

5. In God's eyes, what counts? Jesus tells us that the life he gives is what really counts, rather than "gaining the whole world." Paul tells us that Abraham's faith counted; it was "reckoned to him as righteousness." How might this shed light on our own human ways of counting and keeping score?

Hymns for Worship
Gathering
The God of Abraham praise (esp. sts. 1–4)   ELW 831, LBW 544
How firm a foundation   ELW 796, LBW 507
He comes to us as one unknown   ELW 737, WOV 768

Hymn of the Day
Let us ever walk with Jesus   ELW 802, LBW 487   *LASSET UNS MIT JESU ZIEHEN*
My faith looks up to thee   ELW 759, LBW 479   *OLIVET*
Take up your cross, the Savior said   ELW 667   *BOURBON* LBW 398   *NUN LASST UNS DEN LEIB BEGRABEN*

Communion
He comes to us as one unknown   ELW 737, WOV 768
Around you, O Lord Jesus   ELW 468, LBW 496

Sending
In the cross of Christ I glory   ELW 324, LBW 104
How clear is our vocation, Lord   ELW 580

Additional Hymns and Songs

Guide my feet   TFF 153
Make our church one joyful choir   HG 1
Step by Step   W&P 132
We will glorify   W&P 154, TFF 281

Music for the Day
Psalmody and Acclamations

Miller, Aaron David. *Gospel Acclamations for Lent–Holy Trinity.*
AFP 9780800635589.

Mummert, Mark. "Psalm 22" from *Psalm Settings for the Church
Year.* AFP 9780800678562.

Psalter for Worship Year B, Evangelical Lutheran Worship Edition.
AFP 9780806683839.

Choral

Billingham, Richard. "I Want Jesus to Walk with Me." SATB, pno.
AFP 9780800638719.

Bruckner, Anton. "God So Loved the World." SATB. GIA G-1438.

Ferguson, John. "When I Survey the Wondrous Cross" from *St. John
Passion.* SATB, assembly, org. AFP 9780800658588.

Frahm, Frederick. "The Road to Damascus." SATB, kybd. AFP
9780800678975.

☐ Manz, Paul. "Let Us Ever Walk with Jesus." U, org. CPH 98-2423.

Miller, Aaron David. "I Want Jesus to Walk with Me." U, opt desc,
kybd. AFP 9780800678418.

Children's Choir

Cox, Joe. "We Are Climbing Jacob's Ladder." LE. U, kybd. CG A604.

Jothen, Michael. "We Are Children of Our God." UE. U/2 pt, kybd,
fl/vln, opt hb, opt assembly. CG A731.

Sleeth, Natalie. "Go Now in Peace" from *Sunday Songbook.* UE. 3 pt,
kybd, opt Orff. HIN HMB102.

Keyboard / Instrumental

Cherwien, David. "Lasset uns mit Jesu ziehen" from *Organ Plus,* vol.
2. Org, inst. AFP 9780800678548.

Gieschen, Thomas. "Lasset uns mit Jesu ziehen" from *Augsburg
Organ Library: Autumn.* Org. AFP 9780800675790.

Hampton, Keith. "Olivet" from *Let It Rip! at the Piano,* vol. 2. Pno.
AFP 9780800675806.

Lind, Richard. "Third Mode Melody" from *Piano Impressions for
Worship.* Pno. AFP 9780800678807.

Osterland, Karl. "Olivet" from *Augsburg Organ Library: Lent.* Org.
AFP 9780800658977.

Handbell

Helman, Michael. "Kum-Ba-Ya." 3-5 oct hb/hc, L3. AG 35124.

Linker, Janet/Jane McFadden. "Great Is Thy Faithfulness." 3-5 oct,
org, L3. AG 910.

Sherman, Arnold B. "Beneath the Cross of Jesus." 3-5 oct, L2. LOR
052L.

☐ denotes choral suggestions that relate to the hymn of the day.
■ denotes songs that are available on iTunes®.

Praise Ensemble

■ Byrd, Marc/Steve Hindalong/Bebo Norman. "Yes I Will" from
musicnotes.com. Meaux Mercy/New Spring/Never Say Never
Songs/Appstreet Music.

■ Coelho, Terry. "Father, I Adore You." W&P 37.

■ Doerksen, Brian. "Come, Now Is the Time to Worship" from *Come,
Now Is the Time to Worship.* VIN VMB9367.

■ Morgan, Reuben. "What the Lord Has Done in Me" from www
.praisecharts.com. Hillsong Publishing/INT.

Global

Bell, John. "While the Earth Remains." SATB. GIA G-5160.

Hopson, Hal H. "When We Are Living/Pues si vivimos" SATB,
kybd. AFP 9780800658304.

Tuesday, March 10

Harriet Tubman, 1913; Sojourner Truth, 1883; renewers of society

Harriet Tubman was born into slavery in Maryland and
remained a slave until about age 30 when, fearing she would
be sold and moved farther south, she escaped with the help
of the Underground Railroad. After that, she helped about
300 others to escape until slavery was abolished. After the
Civil War, her home in Auburn, New York, became a center
for women's rights and served the aged and poor.

Sojourner Truth, too, was born a slave, in New York
state. Her birth name was Isabella. After slavery was abolished in New York in 1827, she was freed and, while working
as a housekeeper, became deeply involved in Christianity.
A number of years later, she discerned a call to become a
preacher. Taking the name Sojourner Truth, she set out on
an evangelistic journey, where people found her testimony
to be deeply moving. In later life, she also became a popular
speaker against slavery and for women's rights.

Thursday, March 12

Gregory the Great, Bishop of Rome, 604

Gregory was born into a politically influential family. At one
time he held political office and at another time he lived as a
monk, all before he was elected to the papacy. Gregory's work
was extensive. He influenced public worship through the
establishment of a lectionary and prayers to correlate with the
readings. He established a school to train church musicians.
Gregorian chant is named in his honor. He wrote a treatise
underscoring what is required of a parish pastor serving a
congregation. He sent missionaries to preach to the Anglo-
Saxons who had invaded England. And at one time he organized grain distribution during a shortage of food in Rome.

March 15, 2009
Third Sunday in Lent

The third covenant in this year's Lenten readings is the central one of Israel's history: the gift of the law to those God freed from slavery. The ten commandments are one of the chief parts of Luther's catechism, a core piece of baptismal instruction. They begin with the statement that because God alone has freed us from the powers that oppressed us, we are to let nothing else claim first place in our lives. When Jesus throws the merchants out of the temple, he is defending the worship of God alone and rejecting the ways commerce and profit-making can become our gods.

Prayer of the Day

Holy God, through your Son you have called us to live faithfully and act courageously. Keep us steadfast in your covenant of grace, and teach us the wisdom that comes only through Jesus Christ, our Savior and Lord, who lives and reigns with you and the Holy Spirit, one God, now and forever.

Gospel Acclamation

We proclaim Christ **|** crucified,* the power of God and the wis- **|** dom of God. (1 Cor. 1:23, 24)

Readings and Psalm

Exodus 20:1-17

After escaping from slavery, the Israelites come to Mount Sinai, where God teaches them how to live in community. The ten commandments proclaim that God alone is worthy of worship. Flowing from God, the life of the community flourishes when based on honesty, trust, fidelity, and respect for life, family, and property.

Psalm 19

The commandment of the LORD gives light to the eyes. (Ps. 19:8)

1 Corinthians 1:18-25

The word of the cross is pure foolishness and nonsense to the world because it claims that God is mostly revealed in weakness, humiliation, and death. But through such divine foolishness and weakness, God is working to save us. The center of Paul's preaching is Christ crucified.

John 2:13-22

Jesus attacks the commercialization of religion by driving merchants out of the temple. When challenged, he responds mysteriously, with the first prediction of his own death and resurrection. In the midst of a seemingly stable religious center, Jesus suggests that the center itself has changed.

Color   Purple

CD-ROM Images

Icon Three: Lent3_B
Icon Two: Lent3_B
Icon: 085

Prayers of Intercession

Led by Christ in our journey of repentance and moved by his compassion, let us pray for the church, those in need, and all of God's creation.

A brief silence.

Righteous God, you raise up leaders in every time and place. Guide those who lead your church, that your gospel of love may be clearly proclaimed throughout the world. Lord, in your mercy,
hear our prayer.

Your law orders everything in the universe. As you show faithfulness in providing light from the sun and water from the atmosphere, make us careful stewards, that all of creation may thrive. Lord, in your mercy,
hear our prayer.

Your wisdom and strength are greater than our comprehension. Grant leaders of nations the understanding and strength to rule justly, teaching them to rely on your wisdom. Lord, in your mercy,
hear our prayer.

Your care for the lowly is made known in your commandments. Lift up those who do not know mercy or peace because of injustice, conflict, or sickness (*especially*).

Lord, in your mercy,
hear our prayer.
You desire that we show mercy to others, just as you show mercy to us. Strengthen us as we gather to share your word and sacraments, that we may live lives of mercy and justice. Lord, in your mercy,
hear our prayer.
Here other intercessions may be offered.
As we give thanks for the lives of those who have lived your commandments in faith, grant us strength also to journey faithfully, that we might know the joy that comes with life in your covenant. Lord, in your mercy,
hear our prayer.
Into your hands, gracious God, we commend all for whom we pray, trusting in your mercy; through Jesus Christ, our Savior.
Amen.

Ideas and Images for the Day

In this reading from John's gospel, Jesus overturns more than the tables of the money changers. He confronts an entire religious system of temple sacrifices and offerings. He sets new boundaries around the meaning of "God's house," just as the ten commandments had set boundaries around the lives of God's people. God's house is not a marketplace. The place to find God present was no longer the temple but Jesus' own body. Thus Jesus overturns the whole system— and not only that, says Paul in 1 Corinthians. Through the "weakness" and "foolishness" of his death on the cross, Jesus overturns everything the world considers sensible and wise.

1. This gospel story, and indeed the whole Lenten season, teaches us where to seek God: in the cross of Christ, where the "temple" of Jesus' body is destroyed, only to be raised up again in three days. And yet, many look for God in the wrong places. If Johnny Lee's song "Lookin' for Love" (*Greatest Hits*, 1980) has it right, this is a widespread human problem: we are looking "in all the wrong places" —and we're "blessed" when we finally find or are found by the one we seek.

2. In our time, images of "zeal" and righteous anger suggest power and control. For example, the musical *Les Misérables* (Mandalay Entertainment, 1998; based on the novel by Victor Hugo) tells the story of Inspector Javert, a police officer obsessed for years with recapturing Jean Valjean, an upright man imprisoned for stealing a loaf of bread. Javert searches zealously, with no rest possible until Valjean would again be behind bars. In John's gospel, how might the demonstration of Jesus' righteousness have looked different from Javert's and others' zeal?

3. Human beings are always tempted to place more trust in tried-and-true systems than in Jesus. In politics, such an "overturning," a dramatic change from one system to another, is sometimes termed a regime change. What regime changes might Jesus effect in our lives or communities?

4. "No Trespassing" signs mark boundaries. In one version of the Lord's Prayer, we ask forgiveness for our "trespasses." It can be helpful to understand God's commandments as boundaries around our behavior. For example, what boundaries are necessary in our lives to observe the Sabbath, honor our parents, or avoid coveting?

5. *Patch Adams* (Universal Studios, 1998) tells the story of a would-be doctor who confronts the "wisdom" of the established medical system with the "foolishness" of humor and personal connection with patients. Based on a true story, the movie suggests that sometimes foolishness can be more effective than accepted human wisdom.

Hymns for Worship
Gathering
God the sculptor of the mountains   ELW 736
When I survey the wondrous cross   ELW 803, LBW 482
Your Heart, O God, Is Grieved   ELW 602, LBW 96

Hymn of the Day
All my hope on God is founded   ELW 757, WOV 782
    MICHAEL
Holy God, holy and glorious   ELW 637   *NELSON*
Lord Christ, when first you came to earth   ELW 727,
    LBW 421   *MIT FREUDEN ZART*

Communion
I am the Bread of life   ELW 485, WOV 702
Alas! And did my Savior bleed   ELW 337, LBW 98
Oh, that the Lord would guide my ways   ELW 772, LBW 480

Sending
Lord Christ, when first you came to earth   ELW 727, LBW 421
Restore in us, O God   ELW 328, WOV 662

Additional Hymns and Songs
You strode within the temple, Lord   HG 78
Thy word   TFF 132, W&P 144
Thy word   W&P 143
Come and taste   W&P 30

Music for the Day
Psalmody and Acclamations

Haugen, Marty. "Psalm 19" from *Psalm Settings for the Church Year*. AFP 9780800678562.

Miller, Aaron David. *Gospel Acclamations for Lent–Holy Trinity*. AFP 9780800635589.

Psalter for Worship Year B, Evangelical Lutheran Worship Edition. AFP 9780806683839.

Choral

Christiansen, Paul J. "Wondrous Love." SATB. AFP 9780800652661. *The Augsburg Choirbook*. AFP 9780800656782.

▫ Farlee, Robert Buckley. "Holy God." SATB, kybd. AFP 9780800675202.

Haydn, F. J. "The Heavens Are Telling the Glory of God." SATB, 3 solos, pno. LG 51147.

Meyer, Daniel C. "You Will I Love." SAB, pno. GIA G-4146.

Children's Choir

Carter, John. "The Good Lord Made It All." UE. 2 pt, pno, fl. BP 1124.

Christopherson, Dorothy. "The Lord Is My Light." LE. U, pno, fc, opt choreography. AFP 9780800647476. OP

Miller, Aaron David. "I Want Jesus to Walk with Me." U, kybd, opt desc. AFP 9780800678418.

Sleeth, Natalie. "If You Love Me" from *Laudamus*. UE. 2/3 pt, kybd. HIN HMB126.

Keyboard / Instrumental

Burkhardt, Michael. "Michael" from *Five Hymn Accompaniments for Brass Quartet and Organ*, set 4. Org, br qrt. MSM 20-845.

Callahan, Charles. "Michael" from *Two English Voluntaries for Organ*. Org. CPH 97-6174U1.

Ferguson, John. "Mit Freuden zart" from *Three Psalm Preludes*. Org. AFP 9780800656843.

Sedio, Mark. "Michael" from *Organ Tapestries*, vol. 1. Org. CPH 97-6812U1.

Handbell

Page, Anna Laura. "Brother James' Air." 3-5 oct hb/hc, fl, L3. ALF 19650.

Sherman, Arnold B. "Prayer." 3-4 oct, L3. LOR 20-1147L.

Sherman, Arnold B. "What Wondrous Love Is This." 4-5 oct, L2+. RR HB0020B.

Praise Ensemble

■ Barnett, Maria. "Breathe" from *WOW Worship Green Songbook*. INT 000768195567. Also from www.praisecharts.com. Mercy/VIN.

■ Morgan, Reuben/Darlene Zschech. "At the Cross" from www.praisecharts.com. Hillsong Publishing/INT.

■ Tomlin, Chris. "Famous One" from www.praisecharts.com.

▫ denotes choral suggestions that relate to the hymn of the day.
■ denotes songs that are available on iTunes®.

Global

Perera, Homero/Bread for the Journey. "Tenemos esperanza/In Hope We Celebrate" from *Pave the Way: Global Songs 3*. U, pno, perc. AFP 9780800676896.

Henke, Christopher. "When the Storms of Life Are Raging." SATB, sop solo. AFP 9780800678258.

Tuesday, March 17
Patrick, bishop, missionary to Ireland, 461

At sixteen, Patrick was kidnapped by Irish pirates and sold into slavery in Ireland. He himself admitted that up to this point he cared little for God. He escaped after six years, returned to his family in southwest Britain, and began to prepare for ordained ministry. He later returned to Ireland, this time to serve as a bishop and missionary. He made his base in the north of Ireland and from there made many missionary journeys with much success. In his autobiography he denounced the slave trade, perhaps from his own experience as a slave. Patrick's famous baptismal hymn to the Trinity, "I bind unto myself today" (ELW 450), can be used as a meditation on Lent's call to return to our baptism.

Thursday, March 19
Joseph, Guardian of Jesus

The gospels are silent about much of Joseph's life. We know that he was a carpenter or builder by trade. The Gospel of Luke shows him acting in accordance with both civil and religious law by returning to Bethlehem for the census and by presenting the child Jesus in the temple on the fortieth day after his birth. The Gospel of Matthew tells of Joseph's trust in God, who led him through visionary dreams. Because Joseph is not mentioned after the story of a young Jesus teaching in the temple, it is assumed that he died before Jesus reached adulthood.

Saturday, March 21
Thomas Cranmer, Bishop of Canterbury, martyr, 1556

Cranmer was serving as bishop of Taunton in England when he was chosen by King Henry VIII to become archbishop of Canterbury, largely because Cranmer would agree to the king's divorce. Cranmer's lasting achievement is contributing to and overseeing the creation of the *Book of Common Prayer*, which in revised form remains the worship book of the Anglican Communion. He was burned at the stake under Queen Mary for his support of the Protestant Reformation.

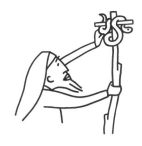

March 22, 2009
Fourth Sunday in Lent

The fourth of the Old Testament promises providing a baptismal lens this Lent is the promise God makes to Moses: those who look on the bronze serpent will live. In today's gospel Jesus says he will be lifted up on the cross like the serpent, so that those who look to him in faith will live. When we receive the sign of the cross in baptism, that cross becomes the sign we can look to in faith, for healing, for restored relationship to God, for hope when we are dying.

Today the church commemorates Jonathan Edwards, a teacher and missionary to American Indians, who died in 1758.

Prayer of the Day

O God, rich in mercy, by the humiliation of your Son you lifted up this fallen world and rescued us from the hopelessness of death. Lead us into your light, that all our deeds may reflect your love, through Jesus Christ, our Savior and Lord, who lives and reigns with you and the Holy Spirit, one God, now and forever.

Gospel Acclamation

God so loved the world that he gave his | only Son,* so that everyone who believes in him should not perish, but have e- | ternal life. (John 3:16)

Readings and Psalm

Numbers 21:4-9

Though God provides food and water for the Israelites in the wilderness, they whine and grumble. They forget about the salvation they experienced in the exodus. God punishes them for their sin, but when they repent God also provides a means of healing: a bronze serpent lifted up on a pole.

Psalm 107:1-3, 17-22

You deliver your people from their distress. (Ps. 107:19)

Ephesians 2:1-10

While we were dead in our sinfulness, God acted to make us alive as a gift of grace in Christ Jesus. We are saved not by what we do but by grace through faith. Thus our good works are really a reflection of God's grace at work in our lives.

John 3:14-21

To explain the salvation of God to the religious leader, Nicodemus, Jesus refers to the scripture passage quoted in today's first reading. Just as those who looked upon the bronze serpent were healed, so people will be saved when they behold Christ lifted up on the cross.

Color   Purple

CD-ROM Images

Icon Three: Lent4_B
Icon Two: Lent4_B
Icon: 086

Prayers of Intercession

Led by Christ in our journey of repentance and moved by his compassion, let us pray for the church, those in need, and all of God's creation.

A brief silence.

God of abundant grace, send forth messengers into the world proclaiming salvation in Jesus Christ. Make us bearers of the light of Christ in our homes, schools, and places of employment. Lord, in your mercy,

hear our prayer.

Refresh the earth with satisfying water and seed-carrying animals and wind. Bring forth life from the earth in this season, that our hope in new life would be revived. Lord, in your mercy,

hear our prayer.

Encourage nations to work together for the sake of all people. Break down barriers that prejudice has built up, and restore the dignity of every living thing. Lord, in your mercy,

hear our prayer.

Provide respite and healing for all who suffer (*especially*). Cure all people by your expansive love, and restore wholeness of body, mind, and spirit to every human being. Lord, in your mercy,

hear our prayer.

Turn our hearts to praise as we are forgiven, healed, and freed from every evil that binds us. Shine your light upon us, that nothing about our life in you would be hidden. Lord, in your mercy,
hear our prayer.
Here other intercessions may be offered.
Giving thanks for all witnesses, teachers, and missionaries (*especially Jonathan Edwards*), we pray that our lives would bear Christ's salvation to all who await good news from you. Lord, in your mercy,
hear our prayer.
Into your hands, gracious God, we commend all for whom we pray, trusting in your mercy; through Jesus Christ, our Savior.
Amen.

Ideas and Images for the Day

On this fourth Sunday of the Lenten journey, the biblical imagery keeps moving us forward to the cross, where Jesus will be "lifted up" in humiliation and exaltation. Just like Moses' bronze serpent lifted up in the wilderness, this one lifted up will bring healing and salvation to all who look on him and believe. Within John's understanding of belief as relationship with Jesus, talk of judgment is descriptive rather than prescriptive. Rejecting a relationship with Jesus does not call down judgment—separation from him *is* the judgment. Through Jesus, God offers the world eternal life, which describes a *quality* of life with Jesus, more than a *quantity* of time. This life, consisting of a never-ending relationship with Jesus, brings light out of darkness and healing through the cross.

1. Christ's judgment (see also John 5:27-30) is never separate from God's love for the world, which Jesus incarnates. Theologian Frederick Buechner writes, "The one who judges us most finally will be the one who loves us most fully. . . . Christ's love so wishes our joy that it is ruthless against everything in us that diminishes our joy" (*Wishful Thinking: A Seeker's ABC*, HarperCollins, 1993, p. 58). In Christ's judgment, law and gospel come together.

2. Both Numbers and John speak of "looking on" the one who is lifted up. Lutheran tradition has emphasized that "faith comes from what is heard" (Rom. 10:17), valuing the ears more than the eyes in worship and community life. In today's more visually oriented culture, the cross is used outside the church both as faith statement and, often, fashion statement. How might it be healing to "look on" a cross in everyday life, in addition to *hearing* about it in church?

3. The word for lifted up can also mean exalted—Jesus' humiliation on the cross is, in fact, his exaltation. In John Irving's novel *A Prayer for Owen Meany* (Ballantine Books, 1989), humiliation and exaltation come together in the title character, whose humiliating tiny size and voice belie the exalted purpose he's convinced God has for him. In the first chapter, we discover that Owen's tiny body is frequently "lifted up," literally, and passed around by the Sunday school children.

4. The battle between light and darkness has long fascinated artists of all kinds. In the film version of *The Phantom of the Opera* (Warner Bros., 2004), darkness carries a mystical attraction along with its danger, when singer Christine is torn between her fiancé Raoul and the dark Phantom who has tutored her in "the music of the night."

5. In the communion liturgy, the elements of bread and wine are lifted up for all to look on. We are reminded that this is a sacrament of healing for us, who not only look upon it, but also partake in it.

Hymns for Worship

Gathering

Jesus, keep me near the cross   ELW 335
Lamb of God   ELW 336

Hymn of the Day

God loved the world   ELW 323   *ROCKINGHAM OLD*
   LBW 292   *DIE HELLE SONN LEUCHT*
Amazing grace, how sweet the sound   ELW 779, LBW 448
   NEW BRITAIN
Salvation unto us has come   ELW 590, LBW 297
   ES IST DAS HEIL

Communion

That priceless grace   ELW 591
I am the Bread of life   ELW 485, WOV 702
Lord Jesus, you shall be my song   ELW 808

Sending

Lift high the cross   ELW 660, LBW 377
There in God's garden   ELW 342, WOV 668

Additional Hymns and Songs

Alone and filled with fear   HG 143
For by grace   W&P 38
You are my hiding place   W&P 160

Music for the Day
Psalmody and Acclamations

Miller, Aaron David. *Gospel Acclamations for Lent–Holy Trinity.* AFP 9780800635589.

Psalter for Worship Year B, Evangelical Lutheran Worship Edition. AFP 9780806683839.

Wold, Wayne L. "Psalm 107" from *Psalm Settings for the Church Year.* AFP 9780800678562.

Choral

Cherwien, David. "My Song Is Love Unknown." SAB, opt assembly, org, fl. AFP 9780800655488.

Chilcott, Bob. "God So Loved the World." SATB, sop solo. OXF 9780193432765.

Giamanco, Anthony. "Take Up Your Cross." 2 pt mxd, kybd. AFP 9780800678968.

Johnson, Ralph M. "As Moses Lifted Up." U, org, fl. CG A550.

□ McCutchen, Keith. "Amazing Grace." SATB, div, pno. EAR S-200.

Pelz, Walter L. "Love and Mercy." SATB, kybd. AFP 9780800638696.

Children's Choir

Eggert, John. "Is There Anybody Here." LE. U, solo, opt desc, pno. AFP 9780800651992. OP

Fyock, Joan A. "Three Psalm Settings." UE. U/2 pt, kybd. HOP JR216.

Ramseth, Betty Ann. "God Is Love." UE. U/2 pt, Orff, fl. CG A568.

Keyboard / Instrumental

Farlee, Robert Buckley. "Rockingham Old" from *Augsburg Organ Library: Lent.* Org. AFP 9780800658977.

Harbach, Barbara. "New Britain" from *Come Join the Dance: Folk Tunes and Spirituals for Organ.* Org. AFP 9780800678760.

Hurd, David. "New Britain" from *Hymn Intonation, Harmonization, and Free Prelude Series*, vol. XIII. Org. SEL 160-733.

Kallman, Daniel. "New Britain" from *Three Hymns for Two Violins and Piano.* Pno, 2 vln. MSM 20-971.

Raabe, Nancy M. "Rockingham Old" from *Grace and Peace.* Pno. AFP 9780800677602.

Handbell

Wood, D. Ann, arr. "Amazing, Wondrous!" 2 oct hb/hc, L2. GIA G-6016.

Larson, Lloyd. "Beautiful Savior." 3-4 oct, L2. AFP 9780800653965.

Sherman, Arnold B. "Jesus Loves Me." 3-6 oct, L3. AG 1734.

Praise Ensemble

■ Bullock, Geoff. "The Power of Your Love" from www.musicnotes .com. WM/MAR.

■ Foote, Billy James. "You Are My King (Amazing Love)" from *WOW Worship Green Songbook.* INT 000768195567. Also from WT.

■ Springer, Chris/Darrell Evans. "Redeemer, Savior, Friend" from *Best of the Best, The Other Songbook 2.* FEL 1891062034.

□ denotes choral suggestions that relate to the hymn of the day.
■ denotes songs that are available on iTunes®.

Global

Ellingboe, Bradley. "How Can I Keep From Singing?" SATB, pno, C inst. KJO 8884

Ylvisaker, John. "Drawn to the Light." U, pno, gtr. ELW 593.

Sunday, March 22
Jonathan Edwards, teacher, missionary to American Indians, 1758

Edwards was a minister in Connecticut and described as the greatest of the New England Puritan preachers. One of Edwards's most notable sermons found its way into contemporary anthologies of literature. In this sermon, "Sinners in the Hands of an Angry God," he spoke at length about hell. However, throughout the rest of his works and his preaching he had more to say about God's love than God's wrath. His personal experience of conversion came when he felt overwhelmed with a sense of God's majesty and grandeur, rather than a fear of hell. Edwards served a Puritan congregation, where he believed that only those who had been fully converted ought to receive communion; his congregation thought otherwise. Edwards left that congregation and carried out mission work among the Housatonic Indians of Massachusetts. He became president of the College of New Jersey, later to be known as Princeton University.

Tuesday, March 24
Oscar Arnulfo Romero, Bishop of El Salvador, martyr, 1980

Romero is remembered for his advocacy on behalf of the poor in El Salvador, though it was not a characteristic of his early priesthood. After being appointed as bishop, he preached against the political repression in his country. He and other priests and church workers were considered traitors for their bold stand for justice, especially defending the rights of the poor. After several years of threats to his life, Romero was assassinated while presiding at the eucharist. During the 1980s thousands died in El Salvador during political unrest. Romero is remembered as a martyr who gave his life on behalf of the powerless in his country.

Wednesday, March 25

Annunciation of Our Lord

Nine months before Christmas we celebrate the annunciation. In Luke the angel Gabriel announces to Mary that she will give birth to the Son of God, and she responds, "Here am I, the servant of the Lord." Ancient scholars believed that March 25 was also the day on which creation began and was the date of Jesus' death on the cross. Thus, from the sixth to eighth centuries, March 25 was observed as New Year's Day in much of Christian Europe.

Mary's openness to the will of God is an example of faithful discipleship and leads us to consider the work of God in our own lives. To honor this day, consider singing "The angel Gabriel" or a setting of the Magnificat, such as the paraphrase "My soul proclaims your greatness."

March 29, 2009
Fifth Sunday in Lent

God promises Jeremiah that a "new covenant" will be made in the future: a covenant that will allow all the people to know God by heart. The church sees this promise fulfilled in Christ, who draws all people to himself when he is lifted up on the cross. Our baptismal covenant draws us to God's heart through Christ and draws God's light and truth into our hearts. We see God's heart most clearly in the way Jesus shares human suffering, in an agony both the John and Hebrews readings describe.

Today the church commemorates Hans Nielsen Hauge, a renewer of the church, who died in 1824.

Prayer of the Day

O God, with steadfast love you draw us to yourself, and in mercy you receive our prayers. Strengthen us to bring forth the fruits of the Spirit, that through life and death we may live in your Son, Jesus Christ, our Savior and Lord, who lives and reigns with you and the Holy Spirit, one God, now and forever.

Gospel Acclamation

Unless a grain of wheat falls into the earth and dies, it remains a | single grain;* but if it dies, it | bears much fruit. (John 12:24)

Readings and Psalm

Jeremiah 31:31-34

The Judeans in Babylon blamed their exile on their ancestors, who had broken the covenant established at Sinai. Here the prophet looks to a day when God will make a new covenant with the people. There will be no need to teach the law, because God will write it on their hearts.

Psalm 51:1-12

Create in me a clean heart, O God. (Ps. 51:10)

or Psalm 119:9-16

I treasure your promise in my heart. (Ps. 119:11)

Hebrews 5:5-10

Using priestly imagery and references to the Old Testament, the author explains how Christ lived in trusting obedience to God, and so God has made Christ the source of our eternal salvation.

John 12:20-33

Jesus entered Jerusalem for the last time to celebrate the Passover festival. Here Jesus' words about seeds planted in the ground turn the disaster of his death into the promise of a harvest in which everyone will be gathered.

Color   Purple

CD-ROM Images

Icon Three: Lent5_B
Icon Two: Lent5_B
Icon: 087

Prayers of Intercession

Led by Christ in our journey of repentance and moved by his compassion, let us pray for the church, those in need, and all of God's creation.

A brief silence.

Living God, you make your word known to your people. Let us see your Word made flesh, Jesus Christ, in one another, that in our communities we might find the solace and strength that comes from your Word. Lord, in your mercy, **hear our prayer.**

You bring forth grain from the earth and fruit from the vine. Fill us with your bounty, and teach us to equitably distribute that which you provide. Lord, in your mercy, **hear our prayer.**

You know the suffering of all people. Draw near to those whose lives are in danger and to those for whom death approaches. Show them compassion and grant them hope in salvation. Lord, in your mercy, **hear our prayer.**

You bless humankind with community. Send bearers of your peace to all who are in need (*especially*). Put your words in their mouths, that they might deliver comfort and hope. Lord, in your mercy, **hear our prayer.**

Your Spirit incites us to go and spread good news. Grant a share of your Spirit to laypersons who tell of salvation in Christ (*as did Hans Nielsen Hauge, renewer of the church*), that gatherings of the faithful might sprout in far-reaching corners of the earth. Lord, in your mercy, **hear our prayer.**

Here other intercessions may be offered.

Remembering the lives of all who have been drawn to Christ in death, we pray for the faith to see Christ, the source of salvation, that our lives would be conformed to his. Lord, in your mercy, **hear our prayer.**

Into your hands, gracious God, we commend all for whom we pray, trusting in your mercy; through Jesus Christ, our Savior. **Amen.**

Ideas and Images for the Day

Many interpret this gospel reading to focus on the inclusive nature of the gospel—it was Greeks who came to see Jesus and to whom, presumably, this was addressed. This inclusivity is both right and good, for Jesus declares himself to be the Son of Man—not the Son of David or of Abraham—but an even broader expression of his full and total humanity. But this full humanity is more than belonging to every race of people on earth, although he does. Jesus also belongs to every *experience* of people's life on earth. He goes on to speak about his impending death and sacrifice, and it is clear that his full humanity includes suffering and loss, just as ours does. Suffering is an inescapable part of the human lot, and even Jesus wasn't exempt.

1. In the movie *Simon Birch* (Hollywood Pictures, 1998), Simon at the end of the film has a clear sense of his calling, along with knowing that it might cost him his life. This sense of call is not unlike what Jesus feels, and Simon's dedication is not unlike what we ourselves are called to.

2. Two hymns in particular speak of the commitment required in today's reading—the willingness to die to self and to count all gain as loss: "When I survey the wondrous cross" (ELW 803, TFF 79) and "Take my life, that I may be" (ELW 583/685).

3. For many people Lent is a time of giving things up, of learning to die to self and practice what Jesus says in John 12:24-26. Most often, this is applied individually. Consider what this might mean on a congregational level. Is it possible that sometimes we should be more willing to "die" to our desires for familiar worship and our favorite liturgical setting, or to talk only with our old friends during the coffee hour? Are we doing everything we can to be welcoming and accessible to outsiders, who don't know the jargon or how to follow the liturgy? How often do people—especially outsiders—come into our churches and say, "We wish to see Jesus"?

Hymns for Worship

Gathering

Eternal Lord of love, behold your church   ELW 321
Christ, the life of all the living   ELW 339, LBW 97

Hymn of the Day

Christ, the life of all the living   ELW 339, LBW 97
   JESU, MEINES LEBENS LEBEN
A Lamb goes uncomplaining forth   ELW 340, LBW 105
   AN WASSERFLÜSSEN BABYLON
Restore in us, O God   ELW 328   *BAYLOR*
   WOV 662   *CATECHUMEN*

Communion

Seed that in earth is dying   ELW 330
We raise our hands to you, O Lord   ELW 690
Let us break bread together   ELW 471, LBW 212

Sending

Now We Remain   ELW 500
As we gather at your table   ELW 522
In the cross of Christ I glory   ELW 324, LBW 104

Additional Hymns and Songs

Give me a clean heart   RWSB 199

Deep within   GC 419

Be merciful, O Lord   GC 39

Step by Step   W&P 132

Music for the Day

Psalmody and Acclamations

Cherwien, David. "Psalm 51" from *Psalm Settings for the Church Year*. AFP 9780800678562.

Miller, Aaron David. *Gospel Acclamations for Lent–Holy Trinity*. AFP 9780800635589.

Psalter for Worship Year B, Evangelical Lutheran Worship Edition. AFP 9780806683839.

Choral

Christiansen, F. Melius. "Lamb of God." SATB. AFP 9780800652593. *The Augsburg Choirbook*. AFP 9780800656782.

▫ Distler, Hugo. "A Lamb Goes Uncomplaining Forth" from *Chantry Choirbook*. SATB. AFP 9780800657772.

Ellingboe, Bradley. "Seed That in Earth Is Dying." SAB, kybd. AFP 9780800638849.

Farlee, Robert Buckley. "Rich in Promise." SAB, kybd. AFP 9780800638856.

Nelson, Ronald A. "Create in Me a Clean Heart." SATB. KJO 8808.

Whitehill, Erik. "Now the Green Blade Rises" from *Wade in the Water*. SAB, kybd. AFP 9780800678616.

Children's Choir

Hoiland, Melissa Ramseth. "Lord, Whose Love in Humble Service" from *Take a Hymn*. UE. U, autoharp/gtr, rec/fl. AFP 9786000106461. OP

Marshall, Jane. "God Speaks: 4. Words of Faith." UE. 2 pt, assembly, kybd. CG A538.

McClune, Ellen/A. Steven Taranto. "Let Us Go to the House of the Lord." LE. U, opt solo, pno. CG A872.

Keyboard / Instrumental

Kickstat, Paul. "An Wasserflüssen Babylon" from *Eight Lenten Chorales for Manuals*. Org. MSM 10-307.

Organ, Anne Krentz. "Jesu, meines Lebens Leben" from *Christ, Mighty Savior*. Pno. AFP 9780800656805.

Peeters, Flor. "Jesu, meines Lebens Leben" from *Augsburg Organ Library: Lent*. Org. AFP 9780800658977.

Sedio, Mark. "An Wasserflüssen Babylon" from *Music for the Paschal Season*. Org. AFP 9780800656232.

Handbell

Hascall, Nancy. "Gethsemane." 3-5 oct hb/hc, L3. BP HB122.

Helman, Michael. "Meditations of the Heart." 3-6 oct, L4-. BP HB253.

Kerr, J. Wayne. "Liebster Jesu." 3-4 oct, fl/C inst, L2+. CG B131.

Praise Ensemble

■ Adkins, Donna. "Glorify Thy Name." W&P 42.

■ Baloche, Paul/Lenny LeBlanc. "Above All" from www.praisecharts.com. INT/LenSongs Publishing.

■ Engle, Joel. "Living Sacrifice" from www.ccli.com. SPIN Three-Sixty Music/Music Services.

■ Strasser, David (Beaker). "Step by Step" from www.praisecharts.com. W&P 132.

Global

Haas, David. "Song of the Body of Christ." SAB, cant, assembly, kybd, gtr, perc. GIA G-3360.

Peña, Donna. "For Living, for Dying." SATB, cant, pno, gtr. GIA G-5071.

Sunday, March 29

Hans Nielsen Hauge, renewer of the church, 1824

Hans Nielsen Hauge was a layperson who began preaching about "the living faith" in Norway and Denmark after a mystical experience that he believed called him to share the assurance of salvation with others. At the time, itinerant preaching and religious gatherings held without the supervision of a pastor were illegal, and Hauge was arrested several times. He also faced great personal suffering: his first wife died and three of his four children died in infancy.

Tuesday, March 31

John Donne, poet, 1631

This priest of the Church of England is commemorated for his poetry and spiritual writing. Most of his poetry was written before his ordination and is sacred and secular, intellectual and sensuous. He saw in his wife, Anne—their marriage resulted in his imprisonment—glimpses of the glory of God and a human revelation of divine love. In 1615 he was ordained and seven years later he was named dean of St. Paul's Cathedral in London. By that time his reputation as a preacher was firmly in place. In his poem "Good Friday, 1613. Riding Westward," he speaks of Jesus' death on the cross: "Who sees God's face, that is self life, must die; What a death were it then to see God die?"

▫ denotes choral suggestions that relate to the hymn of the day.

■ denotes songs that are available on iTunes®.

Saturday, April 4

Benedict the African, confessor, 1589

Born a slave on the island of Sicily, Benedict first lived as a hermit and labored as a plowman after he was freed. When the bishop of Rome ordered all hermits to attach themselves to a religious community, Benedict joined the Franciscans, where he served as a cook. Although he was illiterate, his fame as a confessor brought many visitors to the humble and holy cook, and he was eventually named superior of the community. A patron saint of African Americans, Benedict is remembered for his patience and understanding when confronted with racial prejudice and taunts.

Use the story of Benedict's ministry as a confessor to revisit Martin Luther's notion of the spiritual importance of mutual consolation.

April 5, 2009
Sunday of the Passion
Palm Sunday

The first and second readings and psalm are the same this Sunday every year: Christ emptying himself of divine power and protection, willingly becoming vulnerable to those who struck him and put him to death. With Christ we lament his suffering and all human suffering, but expect God's final vindication. Mark's passion story begins with an unnamed woman anointing his head, perhaps to proclaim him Messiah, and Jesus saying she has anointed him beforehand for burial. Mark's Easter story will begin with women going to anoint Jesus for burial, only to find that he has been raised, God's living Anointed One.

Prayer of the Day

Everlasting God, in your endless love for the human race you sent our Lord Jesus Christ to take on our nature and to suffer death on the cross. In your mercy enable us to share in his obedience to your will and in the glorious victory of his resurrection, who lives and reigns with you and the Holy Spirit, one God, now and forever.

or

Sovereign God, you have established your rule in the human heart through the servanthood of Jesus Christ. By your Spirit, keep us in the joyful procession of those who with their tongues confess Jesus as Lord and with their lives praise him as Savior, who lives and reigns with you and the Holy Spirit, one God, now and forever.

or

O God of mercy and might, in the mystery of the passion of your Son you offer your infinite life to the world. Gather us around the cross of Christ, and preserve us until the resurrection, through Jesus Christ, our Savior and Lord, who lives and reigns with you and the Holy Spirit, one God, now and forever.

Gospel Acclamation

Christ humbled himself and became obedient to the point of death—even death | on a cross.* Therefore God also highly exalted him and gave him the name that is above | every name. (Phil. 2:8-9)

Readings and Psalm

Procession with Palms: Mark 11:1-11 *or* John 12:12-16
Isaiah 50:4-9a

The image of the servant of the Lord is one of the notable motifs in the book of Isaiah. Today's reading describes the mission of the servant, whom early Christians associated with Jesus. Like Jesus, the servant does not strike back at his detractors but trusts in God's steadfast love.

Psalm 31:9-16

Into your hands, O LORD, I commend my spirit. (Ps. 31:5)

Philippians 2:5-11

Christ did not act to attain status and glory but was obedient to God even to the point of death. Following Christ's example, we do not seek personal status or glory but care for others as God cared for us in Christ's death.

Mark 14:1—15:47 or Mark 15:1-39 [40-47]

The passion story in Mark's gospel presents Jesus as one who dies abandoned by all. He shows himself to be the true Son of God by giving his life for those who have forsaken him.

Color   Scarlet or Purple

CD-ROM Images

Icon Three: Passion_Palm01_ABC, Passion_Palm02_ABC
Icon Two: Passion_Palm01_ABC, Passion_Palm02_ABC
Icon: 024, 088, 153, 259

Prayers of Intercession

Led by Christ in our journey of repentance and moved by his compassion, let us pray for the church, those in need, and all of God's creation.

A brief silence.

Merciful God, we pray for your holy church. Put in us the same mind that was in Christ Jesus, and teach us to regard one another with humility and love, that you may be glorified before all people. Lord, in your mercy,

hear our prayer.

We pray for all animals that work for the benefit of humans. Grant them ample rest from their labors, and guide their owners to treat them as gifts from the Creator.
Lord, in your mercy,

hear our prayer.

We pray for all people who serve their nations as elected officials, employees of government, or members of the armed forces. Guide their service and keep them safe from harm. Lord, in your mercy,

hear our prayer.

We pray for those who look for hope from you, O God (*especially*). Grant them hope in their despair, fulfillment in their longing, and healing in their illnesses.
Lord, in your mercy,

hear our prayer.

We pray for those who are unjustly imprisoned, for victims of torture, for those who mourn for missing or executed family members. Ease their pain, and give them hope for new life. Lord, in your mercy,

hear our prayer.

Here other intercessions may be offered.

Remembering the saints who have died in Christ, we pray that the hope you give in Christ's death and resurrection would cover all of creation and bring renewal to every life. Lord, in your mercy,

hear our prayer.

Into your hands, gracious God, we commend all for whom we pray, trusting in your mercy; through Jesus Christ, our Savior.

Amen.

Ideas and Images for the Day

Palm Sunday is all about making an entrance. We wave palm branches and sing "Hosanna." Some congregations have big processions in their neighborhoods and through their church buildings. But this Sunday is not just about entrances; today is also the Sunday of the Passion, when we tell the story of what happens after Jesus gets to Jerusalem. There is more to this story. Jesus didn't just go to Jerusalem. Jesus was arrested, tortured, crucified, and buried in Jerusalem. For this reason the focus of today's readings is not on entrance but *emptying*. Jesus "emptied himself . . . and became obedient to the point of death—even death on a cross" (Phil. 2:7-8). We do not just enter Holy Week on this Sunday; we are drawn into it.

1. This is a Sunday of changing moods. We begin with triumph, move into despair, and end with hope. Pay attention to the use of lighting in your worship space and how it might fit the mood of what is taking place. During the reading of the passion narrative, consider dimming the lights and then turning them off completely when Jesus cries out, "My God, my God, why have you forsaken me?"

2. In the 1960s, television's Dick Van Dyke never entered his living room without tripping over a misplaced ottoman. In the 1980s, whenever Norm walked into Cheers, the bar that was his second—maybe first—home, all the other patrons would shout out his name, and he would reply with a one-liner. Throughout the 1990s, Jerry Seinfeld's eccentric neighbor, Kramer, never simply came through the door; it would fly open with him attached to it. Jesus' entrance into Jerusalem pulls us into a different kind of story that is neither comedy nor tragedy, but one of new life.

3. Have children carrying palms lead your procession today. The children might be invited to drop palm branches as they enter the space. (Do not encourage this, however, if the combination of larger branches and a slippery floor could create a potential hazard for those with mobility concerns.) Provide extra palms for children to take home after worship.

4. "Eloi, Eloi, lema sabachthani?" From the cross Jesus speaks the beginning words of the twenty-second psalm. This psalm begins with desperation but ends with words of praise for all that God has done and will do for future generations. Psalm 22 is the appointed psalm for Good Friday, later this week.

5. Many people cannot attend worship services during the coming week. Some don't drive at night, and others have obligations they cannot set aside. For this reason the passion narrative read as today's gospel becomes their Holy Week experience.

Hymns for Worship
Gathering

All glory, laud, and honor   ELW 344, LBW 108
Ride on, ride on in majesty!   ELW 346, LBW 121
Prepare the royal highway   ELW 264, LBW 26

Hymn of the Day

My song is love unknown   ELW 343, WOV 661
LOVE UNKNOWN   LBW 94   RHOSYMEDRE
O sacred head, now wounded   ELW 351/352, LBW 116/117   HERZLICH TUT MICH VERLANGEN
Jesus, I will ponder now   ELW 345, LBW 115
JESU KREUZ, LEIDEN UND PEIN

Communion

At the name of Jesus   ELW 416, LBW 179
Were you there   ELW 353, LBW 92

Sending

On my heart imprint your image   ELW 811, LBW 102
Go to dark Gethsemane   ELW 347, LBW 109
Ride on, ride on in majesty!   ELW 346, LBW 121

Additional Hymns and Songs

Filled with excitement   RWSB 140, LS 49
Ride on, Jesus, ride   GC 424
Sanna, sannanina   GS2 13
Pave the Way with Branches   GS3 34

Music for the Day
Psalmody and Acclamations

Miller, Aaron David. *Gospel Acclamations for Lent–Holy Trinity.* AFP 9780800635589.
Psalter for Worship Year B, Evangelical Lutheran Worship Edition. AFP 9780806683839.
Sedio, Mark. "Psalm 31" from *Psalm Settings for the Church Year.* AFP 9780800678562.

Choral

Grundahl, Nancy. "Sing Hosanna! Sannanina!" SATB, opt perc. AFP 9780800638726.
Jennings, Carolyn. "Hosanna! Ride On." SATB, children's choir, kybd, hb/Orff. MSM 50-3054.
▫ Leaf, Robert. "O Sacred Head, Now Wounded." SATB, org, cl. AFP 9780800652739.

▫ Shute, Linda Cable. "What Language Shall I Borrow." SATB, org. AFP 9780800657055.
Willan, Healey. "Behold the Lamb of God." SATB/2 pt mxd, org. CPH 98-1509.

Children's Choir

Christopherson, Dorothy. "There Was a Man." UE. U/2 pt, pno, ob. AFP 9780800657048. OP
Lovelace, Austin C. "Who Comes Riding?" UE. U/2 pt, kybd. CG A247.
Patterson, Mark. "Praise the Lord" from *ChildrenSing with Instruments.* LE. U, pno, tri, drm. AFP 9780800620349.
Ramseth, Betty Ann. "Gather at the Gate." UE. U, SATB, opt assembly, org, fl, narr. AFP 9786000101312. OP

Keyboard / Instrumental

Below, Robert. "Jesu Kreuz, Leiden und Pein" from *Augsburg Organ Library: Lent.* Org. AFP 9780800658977.
Busarow, Donald. "Herzlich tut mich verlangen" from *Come with Songs of Gladness.* Org, C/B-flat inst. CPH 97-7158U1.
Hovhaness, Alan. "Prayer of Saint Gregory." Org/pno, tpt. Peer Music Classical 8016042407.
Vaughan Williams, Ralph. "Rhosymedre" from *Augsburg Organ Library: Lent.* Org. AFP 9780800658977.

Handbell

Childers, Brian. "Meditation on 'Passion Chorale'." 3-5 oct, L4+. GIA G-6933.
Moklebust, Cathy. "My Song Is Love Unknown." 3-5 oct, L3. CG B203.
Parrish, Mary Kay. "Hosanna, Loud Hosanna." 3-5 oct, perc, L2. CG B442. Full Score: CG B441.

Praise Ensemble

■ Atwell, Steve/Mark Blackburn/Jerry Davison. "These Thousand Hills" from ccli.com. Broken Songs.
■ Baloche, Paul/Lenny LeBlanc. "Above All" from *iWorship Songbook 1.* INT 23366.
■ Olson, Larry. "Weeping over Jerusalem" from *Dakota Road Music Keyboard/Guitar Edition 1.5.* Dakota Road Music .dakotaroadmusic.com.
■ Redman, Matt. "Once Again" from Best of the Best, The Other Songbook 2. FEL 1891062034.

Global

Grundahl, Nancy. "Sing Hosanna! Sannanina!" SATB, perc. AFP 9780800638726.
Hesla, Bret. "Pave the Way with Branches" from *Pave the Way: Global Songs 3* SATB, perc. AFP 9780800676896.

▫ denotes choral suggestions that relate to the hymn of the day.
■ denotes songs that are available on iTunes®.

April 6, 2009
Monday in Holy Week

During Holy Week some communities gather each day to meditate on Jesus' final days before his death on the cross. Today's gospel commemorates the anointing of Jesus by Mary, a foreshadowing of his death and burial. Isaiah speaks of the suffering servant who is a light for the nations and who faithfully brings forth justice. For Christians, Jesus' suffering is the path to resurrection and new life. We eagerly await the celebration of the great Three Days later this week.

Today the church commemorates sixteenth-century artists Albrecht Dürer, Matthias Grünewald, and Lucas Cranach.

Prayer of the Day

O God, your Son chose the path that led to pain before joy and to the cross before glory. Plant his cross in our hearts, so that in its power and love we may come at last to joy and glory, through Jesus Christ, our Savior and Lord, who lives and reigns with you and the Holy Spirit, one God, now and forever.

Gospel Acclamation

May I never boast of | anything* except the cross of our Lord | Jesus Christ. (Gal. 6:14)

Readings and Psalm
Isaiah 42:1-9

God's servant Israel is endowed with the Spirit in order to bring justice to the nations. The servant will not exercise authority boisterously or with violence, nor will weariness ever keep it from fulfilling its task. God's old promises have been fulfilled; the new assignment of the servant is to bring light to the nations.

Psalm 36:5-11

All people take refuge under the shadow of your wings. (Ps. 36:7)

Hebrews 9:11-15

Prior to Christ, forgiveness was mediated through animal sacrifice. Christ came as the great high priest to establish a new covenant. Through his blood we are liberated from our sins and promised eternal life.

John 12:1-11

A few days after raising Lazarus from the dead, Jesus visits the man's home. Lazarus's sister Mary is criticized when she anoints the feet of Jesus with costly perfume.

Color Scarlet *or* Purple

Monday, April 6

Albrecht Dürer, 1528;
Matthias Grünewald, 1529;
Lucas Cranach, 1553; artists

These great artists revealed through their work the mystery of salvation and the wonder of creation. Dürer's (DYOO-rer) work reflected the apocalyptic spirit of his time, when famine, plague, and social and religious upheaval were common. He was sympathetic to the reform work of Luther but remained Roman Catholic. At his death, Luther wrote to a friend, "Affection bids us mourn for one who was the best."

Grünewald (GREE-neh-vahld) was born Mathis Neithardt, and is sometimes referred to as "Master Mathis" or "Mathis the Painter" (Mathis der Maler); the name Grünewald was applied to him after his death. His paintings are known for their dramatic forms, vivid colors, and depiction of light. Several religious works are included in his small surviving corpus, the most famous being the Isenheim Altarpiece.

Lucas Cranach (KRAH-nakh) the Elder was born in southern Germany and studied in Vienna, but then moved to Wittenberg, where he spent most of his career as a court painter to the Saxon electors. His work includes many fine religious examples and several portraits of Martin Luther, although he also painted secular subjects. Besides being one of the greatest German painters of his time, Cranach was also widely known for his woodcuts, some of which illustrated the first German printing of the New Testament.

April 7, 2009
Tuesday in Holy Week

As the great Three Days draw near, some communities gather each day of Holy Week for worship. Paul proclaims Christ cruci-fied as the wisdom and power of God. Jesus speaks of the grain of wheat that falls into the earth and dies in order that it may bear fruit. We die with Christ in baptism that we may be raised with him to new life. We will celebrate this great mystery of death and resurrection at the Easter Vigil later this week.

Prayer of the Day

Lord Jesus, you have called us to follow you. Grant that our love may not grow cold in your service, and that we may not fail or deny you in the time of trial, for you live and reign with the Father and the Holy Spirit, one God, now and for-ever.

Gospel Acclamation

May I never boast of [|] anything* except the cross of our Lord [|] Jesus Christ. (Gal. 6:14)

Readings and Psalm
Isaiah 49:1-7

Here the servant Israel speaks for herself and acknowledges herself as God's secret weapon. Called like Jeremiah and John the Baptist before her birth, the servant is not only to restore Israel itself, but the servant's ultimate assignment is to bring news of God's victory to the ends of the earth. God in faithfulness has chosen Israel for this task.

Psalm 71:1-14

From my mother's womb you have been my strength. (Ps. 71:6)

I Corinthians 1:18-31

To the world, the word of the cross is silly, because it claims God's power is most fully revealed in complete, utter weak-ness. For those who are being saved, however, the word of the cross unveils God's true wisdom, power, and source of true life.

John 12:20-36

Knowing that his hour has come, Jesus announces that his death will be an exaltation. God's name will be glorified when his death draws people to new life.

Color   Scarlet *or* Purple

April 8, 2009
Wednesday in Holy Week

This day was formerly called "Spy Wednesday," an allusion to the gospel accounts in which Judas is identified as the betrayer of Jesus. As Jesus endured the suffering of the cross, we are called to run the race of life with perseverance, confident of the joy to come. In the Three Days, which begin tomorrow evening, we will journey with Christ from darkness to light, from captivity to freedom, from death to life.

Prayer of the Day

Almighty God, your Son our Savior suffered at human hands and endured the shame of the cross. Grant that we may walk in the way of his cross and find it the way of life and peace, through Jesus Christ, our Savior and Lord, who lives and reigns with you and the Holy Spirit, one God, now and forever.

Gospel Acclamation

May I never boast of [|] anything* except the cross of our Lord [|] Jesus Christ. (Gal. 6:14)

Readings and Psalm
Isaiah 50:4-9a

The servant of the Lord expresses absolute confidence in his final vindication, despite the fact that he has been struck and spit upon. This characteristic of the servant played an important role in the early church for understanding the suffering, death, and resurrection of Jesus.

Psalm 70

Be pleased, O God, to deliver me. (Ps. 70:1)

Hebrews 12:1-3

In the way of the cross, Jesus has blazed the trail for our salvation. With faithful perseverance, we follow in his foot-steps.

John 13:21-32

At the last supper, Jesus identifies Judas Iscariot as the one who will betray him, and sends him on his way.

Color   Scarlet *or* Purple

THE THREE DAYS

Preparing for the Three Days

In a Japanese tea ceremony, every movement is scripted. There is as proper way for guests to take off their shoes as they enter. There is a ritual for how guests admire the room, the art, the tea bowl, and the tea itself—before, during, and after drinking the tea. The host also has a whole script of movement as she performs all the details of serving tea to her guest. Because of the time and care taken to communicate and soak in every detail, both host and guest leave having experienced new awareness, awakening, gratitude, peace, even delight.

The Three Days are this kind of threshold experience. As the assembly gathers for these three days of worship, many of the movements are highly scripted. There is an order to these days and important roles for both host and guests. On Thursday, we take off our shoes. We tell the truth and are forgiven. We share a meal. We watch carefully as illusions are stripped away. We wait and watch. On Friday, we recall the trial, torture, suffering, and crucifixion of Jesus. We give thanks for God's continuing presence in pain, grief, and death. We pray for the whole world. We adore and bless the one who powerfully triumphs over death. On Saturday, we hear how God creates and saves God's people, carrying them through the waters, breathing life into dry bones. We baptize and remember our own baptisms. We sing "Alleluia" and rejoice in Christ's resurrection.

When time and care are taken to communicate and soak in every detail, we have the opportunity to leave this three-day liturgy with new awareness, awakening faith, gratitude, peace, even delight. In short, God changes us.

Taking Worship Outdoors

Make sure that at least parts of the Three Days are celebrated outside, weather permitting. The most obvious moment is the beginning of the Vigil, when the assembly gathers, lights a new fire, and proceeds through the doorway into the darkened church. Depending on your climate and your assembly's needs, you might also consider a "progressive worship" in which you move from place to place for the Vigil readings as well. Be sure that in advertising your worship, you clearly communicate with outdoor signs that indicate where you will be so that people know where to gather and where to find you if they arrive slightly late. This is a way to practice hospitality not only to those who are on the "inside" of the church body but also to those who are crossing a threshold, checking to see whether our doors are really open, wondering if they want to come in.

Maundy Thursday

On Maundy Thursday, we read from Exodus the instructions for the first Passover meal. Then, in the Gospel of John, we hear of Jesus' actions before his last Passover meal—how Jesus loved his disciples to the end and showed them, by washing their feet, how they should love one another. Jesus acknowledges that this is incredibly uncomfortable for them. "Do you know what I have done to you?" Jesus asks (John 13:12b). But even more uncomfortable than allowing Jesus to wash our feet, we are told to wash one another's feet.

Washing Feet

Footwashing is one of the primary liturgical actions of this night, and the setting of worship should reflect that. A pitcher, bowl, and plenty of towels should be visible in the front from the beginning of worship—a symbol of Jesus' action and invitation to us.

Footwashing is a complicated liturgical act that requires a lot of careful planning. Encourage worshipers to step out of their comfort zones and come forward to be washed, but do not be concerned if some choose not to come forward. If space allows, create two or three stations to expedite the process, which may encourage more people to come forward. Consider inviting all who come forward to wash the feet of their neighbor: each person first washes the feet of the person in front of him or her, and then sits down while the next person washes his or her feet. Carefully plan the washing space to allow a place for the one being washed to sit comfortably. Pour clean water from a pitcher over the feet into a bowl, rather than submerging multiple feet in one bowl, to avoid spreading germs. Dry each person's feet with a clean towel. These towels can then be washed and used from year to year.

Good Friday

After the many visual images and movements of worship that are a part of Maundy Thursday, Good Friday features only the cross. A large, simple cross is perhaps most effective. Other than this one visual image, the worship space is sparse and empty. It is filled only with silence, preaching, prayer, and song. Songs that people know by heart or songs that are simple and easily learned are best on this night.

Sing the Spirituals

You might also consider the power of using African American spirituals as the only music on this day. There are numerous choices in *Evangelical Lutheran Worship*: "They crucified my Lord" (#350), "Were you there" (#353), "Calvary" (#354), "There is a balm in Gilead" (#614), "This little light of mine" (#677), "Give Me Jesus" (#770), "I want Jesus to walk with me (#325), and "Jesus is a rock in a weary land" (#333). They are meant to be learned by hearing, so they are accessible even to those who can't read yet. Even children can be the ones to teach them to the congregation, if they are taught to sing them with great reverence and respect. Make sure that the teachers of spirituals learn the appropriate tempos and the significance of these songs, as powerful words of witness and songs of faith in the face of suffering.

Vigil of Easter

This is a wonderful night to involve many people with many different skills in the planning and leadership of worship. Tonight, you need fire-builders and tenders, actors and storytellers, designers, musicians, singers, readers, communion assistants, ushers, and so on. It's a great night to invite the whole church into fullest participation. Plan ahead so that no one's gifts are left behind.

In choosing which scriptures to bring to life, consider more than the time the service will take. Consider the stories people need to experience so that the Holy Spirit can call, strengthen, enlighten, and sanctify them. Do not just read the word. Proclaim it through word and gesture, dramatizing it. If your congregation is filled with gifted actors, use them on this night. If someone has the gift of memorizing scripture and communicating it with passion, invite them to use their gift. If a group wants to communicate the story in a multimedia way, try it out. This is a night where variety and passionate communication invite all to put away their watches, if only for a night, and have a timeless experience of worship.

The first celebration of the resurrection of Jesus Christ is another dramatic moment. Celebrative music begins, colorful spring flowers are brought in, there is light and alleluias and a sense of excitement—but this move to Easter is not a race. People do not have to move especially fast to communicate the joy and wonder of moving from death to life.

Dry Bones Dance

One of the Vigil stories not to miss is the vision of Ezekiel 37, the valley of the dry bones. If you have children, youth, or adults in your congregation interested in dance or movement, gather these people in the weeks ahead to create a multisensory experience of the story of the dry bones. This can work with a group of 5–10 people. In addition to the dancers, you will need a narrator and musician(s). Each of the dancers wears black or white, and as the narrator begins the story, they are lying on the floor as "heaps" of bones. (You can intersperse actual animal bones if you have these—if you do not, consider making a request to the congregation; you may be surprised at what emerges!) As the story progresses, the people begin to "come to life," moving a hand or a foot, gradually moving more and more. When God's breath comes into them, they stand. In rehearsals, each dancer will design a movement that the others will follow. So the rest of the dance is a rehearsed "follow the leader," with each one taking a turn as leader. The reader should pause between verses 10 and 11 for the dance to progress. At the end of the scripture, before the music comes to an end, the people dance into a circle, join hands, and raise their hands and faces, in praise of God, who breathes life into dry bones.

The story of the dry bones need not be the only story told by a group. You might assign every reading to a group or family to "tell" in the most creative way they can imagine. Encouraging creativity can make for memorable biblical stories. Certain members of your congregation might be delighted to oversee the making of a great bonfire for the story of creation. Perhaps there's a Sunday school class whose members would love to convey the story of the Exodus. The more children of all ages who are involved, the more people who will be there to enrich the experience.

A Rich Feast

The Easter Vigil begins the season of Easter, so the first communion of Easter should be festive. Use your best vessels, bake fresh bread, and pour good wine at this joyful feast. Then, after the service, encourage everyone to break their Lenten fast at a late-night reception with rich desserts, sweet breads, juices, cider, and sparkling wine. Alleluia, indeed!

Celebrating the Three Days with Children

For children, these three days can be the best days of worship of the church year. They are filled with memorable and unique symbols and actions informing us that worship is not just sitting and listening, but *doing*. The Three Days offer opportunities to fully include children in the church community.

As you first enter Lent, announce to the congregation that everyone—including children—will need to be involved in some way in these tremendous days. People will be needed to wash feet, strip the altar, participate in the procession of the cross, assist guests and visitors with candles, proclaim or enact scripture, sing, and lead—the possibilities are nearly endless. Form teams that include people who are experienced and inexperienced, young and old, and make sure that everyone plays a part.

During these days, think about how you can give some simple instructions throughout worship so that everyone, including young children and those new to faith, can fully participate. Don't assume that everyone has experienced the power of the Three Days before.

Ideas for the Three Days
Thursday

- Maundy Thursday has four prominent events in which the word is proclaimed: confession and forgiveness with laying on of hands; footwashing; meal; and in many congregations, stripping of the altar.
- Walk alongside the children as they fully participate in these movements of worship. Children need to know that they are loved and forgiven. It is powerful to feel gentle hands on the head and water on the feet—and powerful for both parents and children to witness God's forgiveness of the other, especially if it has been a challenge to make it to worship that evening.

Friday

- If your congregation reads the passion narrative from John's gospel on Good Friday, ask older children to prepare significant parts. Practice for these, and any other roles, so that the child-leaders are confident, convey emotions, and are loud enough to be clearly understood by everyone in the assembly. For more information about this way of sharing scripture, see the article "Let anyone with ears to hear listen!" by Heather B.P. Wallace (*The Lutheran*, May 2007, available online at www.thelutheran.org).
- Create a large cross and invite the children to write on it, with permanent markers, some sins that they witness, and their hopes and prayers for God's healing in the world.

Saturday

- Show children the art on page 266 of *Evangelical Lutheran Worship*. On the island of Java in Indonesia, it's said that if you put a stick into the ground, it begins to sprout and grow. How are the cross and the tree of life related? How might the cross in your sanctuary or the processional cross be artistically transformed into the tree of life on this night? Songs reinforcing this image: "Tree of life and awesome mystery" (ELW 334) and "There in God's garden" (ELW 342, WOV 668).
- The use of fire in worship brings out the child in many of us. Take care so that even small children can participate in the service of light safely.
- If your space allows, make this a progressive worship service, in which you move from one space to another. For added interest, invite youth to build a temporary tomb over the sanctuary entry, so that you go through the tomb as you journey to the baptismal font or to the meal portion of the service.
- Invite children to gather close to the baptismal font so they can see and hear what's going on. They can also be the first to be sprinkled in the remembrance of baptism or invited to dip their fingers in the water and make the sign of the cross on each other's foreheads.
- Portions of this weekend may evoke these questions from children: Why do we do this? What's going on? Before explaining the worship practices, ask the child, "What do you think?" to learn how the worship message is being conveyed to the youngest worshipers.

Worship Helps for the Three Days

In General

Overview

- Review the liturgies for the Three Days in *Evangelical Lutheran Worship* (Pew Edition pp. 247–270; Leaders Edition, pp. 611–653).
- Read *The Three-Day Feast: Maundy Thursday, Good Friday, Easter*, by Gail Ramshaw (Worship Matters series, Augsburg Fortress, 2004).
- Read the other essays in this seasonal section for suggestions for this year's celebration.

Plan Ahead

- Gather planning, implementation, and hospitality teams.
- Develop timelines with intermediate deadlines.
- Develop lists of participants, identify recruiters and coordinators (for example, someone to invite and rehearse the readers, someone to spearhead production of the worship folders, someone to coordinate hospitality needs), and obtain commitment of all participants to predetermined rehearsal times.
- Develop lists of all the tools and elements required, who is responsible for gathering them, and where they will be placed.
- Develop environment and art plans. How must the environment be prepared and shift from day to day? When will the Easter Day environment be executed if there is a Saturday night Vigil? Make separate lists for the liturgy preparers and the seasonal decorators.
- Remember that Lenten and Palm Sunday services will have their own demands. Don't expect to have extra time then.
- Look ahead to the checklist on p. 171 as you plan for the Easter season.

Task List

- Order worship participation leaflets if used for the Maundy Thursday, Good Friday, or Easter Vigil liturgies.
- Order bulletin covers for Holy Week liturgies.
- Publicize Holy Week and Easter services in local newspapers and in other media.
- Arrange for a thorough cleaning of the worship space sometime between the Maundy Thursday liturgy and the Easter Vigil.
- Determine whether additional handheld candles are needed for the Easter Vigil.
- Purchase a new paschal candle.
- Prepare extra communion elements and communionware needed for large numbers of communicants during Holy Week and Easter.

Participants

- Arrange rehearsals for all the liturgies of the Three Days. These liturgies are unique, so all worship leaders, even those who have been involved in previous years, need to prepare for their roles.
- It is helpful to prepare printed materials for worship leaders for the Three Days. Consider placing all the texts and musical resources needed by worship leaders into three-ring binders (ceremonial binders in liturgical colors are available from Augsburg Fortress). Highlight speaking parts and instructions for each worship leader in individual copies.
- Be sure that altar guild members are well equipped and informed about their tasks for these busy days.

To Think About

Be intentional about demonstrating the unity of the Three Days. Consider:

- a single worship folder containing all three liturgies;
- silencing bells or chimes from the beginning of the Maundy Thursday liturgy until the hymn of praise at the Easter Vigil (or the first celebration of Easter);
- gathering and sending rites that suggest the worship of the Three Days continues as we take occasional breaks to attend to the necessary tasks of life;
- selective use of silence or prelude/postlude as "couplers" to link the days together;
- instruction and articles during Lent to help the assembly understand the unity of these days;
- scheduling the Three Days liturgies at the times thought of as the primary services in your local setting, and schedule other Holy Week rites familiar to the congregation in other time slots (for example, Tenebrae, Tre-ore).

Maundy Thursday

Overview

- The *Evangelical Lutheran Worship* Maundy Thursday service places the sermon in the more familiar place following the readings, rather than at the beginning of the service. The footwashing embodies servant leadership and may function as an experiential sermon.
- If this is the first absolution of sin since before Ash Wednesday, it could be heightened with music or a hymn response. For the individual laying on of hands, invite the assembly to the font, kneeler, or communion rail, using the communion distribution pattern familiar to the assembly, if appropriate.
- If used in its fullness, Maundy Thursday rites will have the assembly moving three times during the service: for absolution, footwashing, and communion. Be sure the rites are well choreographed and aisles are clear.
- Use the preface for Maundy Thursday (*Evangelical Lutheran Worship* Leaders Edition, p. 186).
- Thanksgiving at the table: see options in *Evangelical Lutheran Worship*, especially Prayer IV (Pew Edition, p. 111; Leaders Edition, p. 197); WOV, Prayers II and D (Leaders Edition, pp. 58–60, 68).
- After communion the worship space is stripped of its adornments. A psalm may be read or sung by a single voice or choir.
- No post-communion canticle, blessing, or dismissal on Maundy Thursday.

Plan Ahead

- Footwashing is countercultural. Teaching and writing in advance will open the assembly to the experience. Encourage easy-to-remove footwear for those who plan to participate.
- Prepare the assembly to receive absolution this day if it has been withheld during Lent.

Task List

- Prepare a place to kneel for individual laying on of hands.
- Prepare for footwashing with one or more sets of basins and pitchers of warm water, inexpensive (try the automotive section of a big-box store) or rented towels for all, and aprons and hand sanitizer for leaders. Two chairs (with arms) per station allow for one person to remove shoes/socks while the minister attends to another.
- Prepare a pad to kneel on if there will be many feet to wash.
- Will there be anything unique to this celebration of the institution of the Lord's supper? Real bread? First communion recipients?
- Choreograph and rehearse the stripping of the altar; include the altar guild and communicate any special needs.

Participants

- Some assemblies invite a representative group to have their feet washed, sometimes twelve, sometimes the congregation council. Other assemblies provide for the whole assembly to come to have their feet washed.
- Acolytes or assisting ministers attend water vessels, hand out towels, assist with steps, etc. Ministers of word and service, deacons, deaconesses, diaconal ministers, and associates in ministry might join presiding ministers as washers of feet.
- Volunteers to recruit and rehearse: assisting minister, footwashers and assistants for each station, those who will strip the altar and worship space, lighting technician.

Good Friday

Overview

- As the single, united service of the Three Days continues, Good Friday begins with a minimal gathering rite—simply the prayer of the day.
- The passion according to John is the centerpiece of the proclamation of the word.
- The bidding prayer serves as the prayers of intercession. This prayer is among the church's most ancient and invites quiet reflection between bids, which are invitations to prayer.
- The procession of the cross offers opportunity for creativity and demands sensitivity to the prayer practices of the local assembly. A single cross may be carried through the assembly. Once the cross is in place, worshipers may be invited to make individual signs of adoration. The concrete actions by the assembly or individual will vary widely. Accompanied by hymns of adoration or a simple Taizé-like musical refrain, most worshipers will feel comfortable walking to the cross as if to communion. Some may quietly pray, some may kneel at kneelers or a communion rail, some may bow, touch, or even kiss the cross.

- The assembly may be offered small votive candles to place around the cross as a sign of their adoration. This physical activity of adoration is one in which worshipers of all ages can participate. Hospitality ministers or acolytes may be positioned to assist with candles or navigating chancel steps.
- The *Evangelical Lutheran Worship* Good Friday service introduces the option for using the solemn reproaches. The reproaches are said or sung following the procession and before or during the adoration of the cross. Alternatively, a hymn may conclude the assembly's prayer on Good Friday.
- No communion, blessing, or dismissal on Good Friday.
- The Three Days service continues on Holy Saturday with the Vigil of Easter.

Plan Ahead

- Determine how the passion will be proclaimed. Possibilities include:
  - a single reader, a pair of readers, or up to seven readers simply reading in succession;
  - a reader's theater group or a more elaborate dramatic interpretation;
  - a published dramatized version with congregational participation;
  - a musical interpretation of St. John's Passion;
  - accompanying the reading with projected media art.
- The cross used in procession may be the assembly's processional cross, a piece of congregational art, a rough wood cross, the remnant of the Christmas tree, or a cross created specifically for this celebration. Find a cross that serves well but does not compete with or further dilute the symbol by introducing too many crosses into the environment. The cross may be carried by the presiding minister, assisting minister, acolytes, or even passed overhead by the entire assembly.

Task List

- Select passion to be proclaimed.
- Select cross for procession and adoration.
- Select music for the solemn reproaches (if used).

Participants

- Recruit and rehearse assisting minister, all readers, musicians, procession and adoration leaders, and assistants.

Vigil of Easter

Getting Started

The Vigil is new for our congregation

- Experience one. Attend an Easter Vigil locally with your worship committee and other key leaders. You might even encourage the whole congregation to join you.
- Join with another congregation to plan a joint Easter Vigil, perhaps with a full-communion partner.

We're ready to plan our own Vigil

- Start small and simple. Don't plan to do all the options, proclaim all the readings, or use too many of the ideas you have gathered until your assembly grasps the essentials: new fire, salvation history, baptism, and first communion of Easter.
- Host a potluck meal or prepared dinner prior to the Vigil. Introduce what is to come, so everyone is prepared and comfortable.

Plan Ahead

- Begin early to find and prepare a candidate for holy baptism. If there is no candidate for baptism, plan to celebrate baptismal renewal with the whole assembly.
- Begin early to enlist all the participants and "stage managers" needed for each portion of the liturgy, or each location if it is to move through several spaces.
- Involve the musicians early in the planning process.
- Be family friendly; provide childcare, escape hatches, activities that appeal to all ages.
- Be honest in announcements about how long the Easter Vigil may last: one hour (an unrealistic expectation for all but the simplest celebrations or an abbreviated service); 90 minutes (a good realistic expectation for a simple celebration); two hours (not longer unless your assembly has thoroughly embraced the Easter Vigil).
- Plan adequate rehearsal times—perhaps a different time for each portion of the service. The two Saturday mornings before Easter work well. Blocking and choreography will need to be rehearsed. Lighting levels should be predetermined and operators trained (ideally when it is dark outside), acolytes familiarized with their responsibilities, and readers rehearsed and given guidance. Address logistics such as where the paschal candle/stand will be for each portion of the service and who will move it each time. Several able-bodied assistants may be needed to handle fires, heavy objects, water vessels, etc.

- Decide how light will be provided for assisting ministers and readers. Determine what level of light is needed so all members of the assembly can participate during this liturgy.
- Consider your environment. It is effective to hold the Easter Vigil in at least two locations (outdoors and in the worship space); three locations (outdoors, baptismal font, nave); or as a "stational" liturgy of four different locations—one for each of the four parts of the liturgy: outdoors for the new fire/gathering; in a chapel or fellowship hall for the word; around the font for baptism; and in the nave or around the altar-table for the meal.
- How will the worship space be decorated? Will anyone see it before gathering there for holy communion?
- Plan a way to introduce the elements of the celebration to the assembly prior to gathering rite. Welcome the assembly in a way that makes them comfortable. Give permission to take breaks.
- Plan a celebration for after the Vigil—a pie potluck, a feast of rich desserts, champagne and chocolate-covered strawberries, an Easter breakfast, or a lamb dinner!

Overview: Gathering/New Fire

- Plan your Vigil to begin no earlier than sunset.
- Prepare a brazier for the new fire—a fire pit already in use, or a large, inexpensive, portable fireplace from a big-box store. Use cat litter, sand, or gravel to protect the metal from being deformed by heat.
- Lighting the new fire in front of a gathered assembly can challenge any presider's elegance. A better solution may be to have the fire burning as the assembly arrives at sunset, in a location they must pass on their way into the building.
- Think through the particular challenges of assembly participation when it is dark. If printed materials are used for the gathering rite, be sure that they can be easily held along with a lighted candle.
- Deliver the fire from the brazier to the paschal candle with a small taper.
- The paschal candle may be incised during the rite with symbols of the resurrection and the current year of grace, or a plain or previously decorated candle may be used.
- Design a processional route into the church building that is accessible, has few or no stairs (it will be dark), and allows the assembly to form a circle around the worship space for the Easter proclamation. Invite those unable to stand for long periods to be seated.

- Walk through the service one night after dark or during the actual hour you plan to hold the Vigil to be sure of lighting and safety.
- Have a bad-weather plan for the gathering rite.
- After the Easter proclamation the assembly may move into their seats and extinguish their candles for the readings. Alternatively, the readings could be proclaimed in the dark with the assembly holding candles for some or all of the word portion of the Vigil. Make advance plans for worship leaders and readers to be able to see the texts they will be proclaiming.

Overview: Word

- The readings appointed for the Vigil in *Evangelical Lutheran Worship* are in some cases slightly different from those in *Lutheran Book of Worship*. The placement of the New Testament readings too has changed slightly. While previously the New Testament reading and gospel were proclaimed after the baptism and before the meal, in *Evangelical Lutheran Worship* they (and the sermon) follow immediately after the Old Testament readings. This revised pattern unifies the stories of God's saving activity, reaching its zenith in the Easter gospel.
- Selecting the number of Vigil readings will be a critical decision. As many as twelve are traditional—for a Vigil that truly lasts through the night. A minimum of four readings are proclaimed: creation (Genesis), deliverance at the Red Sea (Exodus), salvation freely offered to all (Isaiah), and deliverance from the fiery furnace (Daniel). A greater number of stories may be read if there is little or no elaboration, or if the assembly is familiar with the Vigil pattern. Fewer readings with greater attention to their telling or musical responses is another approach. Minimally, silence and a prayer follow each reading.
- Readings may be proclaimed by one reader, a reader's theater group, as a paraphrase or dramatic interpretation, with sound or visual effects or images, or even set to music. A variety of treatments add interest. Consider opportunities for the assembly to participate in the readings. Musical responses to the readings might include psalms and canticles or hymns celebrating God's saving work. Plan for a balanced use of voices, male and female, old and young.
- The alleluia returns. It might return with a festive fanfare, a gospel procession, or in a familiar melody.

Overview: Baptism

- The Litany of the Saints (ELW 237), a setting of the Kyrie, or a hymn may be sung as candidates for baptism, sponsors, and parents gather with the ministers at the font.
- Celebrate baptism in its fullness, using abundant water. The thanksgiving over the water summarizes God's saving activity, just remembered in the readings. Use abundant fragrant oil, a large baptismal candle, and an ample baptismal garment. Sprinkle the assembly with water.
- If there are no candidates for baptism, affirmation of baptism may be celebrated. See the order for affirmation of baptism in *Evangelical Lutheran Worship* (Pew Edition, pp. 234–237; Leaders Edition, pp. 596–600). The assembly may mark themselves or one another in remembrance of their membership in God's saving activity. Consider "You belong to Christ" (ELW 212, 213) or "You have put on Christ" (WOV 694) as an ostinato for the assembly to sing while marking each other with the sign of the cross.

Overview: Meal

- The celebration of the meal at the Easter Vigil may be festive or subdued, saving the trumpets for sunrise, depending on local tradition. In introducing the Vigil, some congregations adjourn after the baptisms and celebrate the meal at sunrise.
- Use the preface for Easter at the Easter Vigil and on Easter Day (*Evangelical Lutheran Worship* Leaders Edition, p. 187).

- Thanksgiving at the table: see options in *Evangelical Lutheran Worship*, especially Prayer IV (Pew Edition, p. 111; Leaders Edition, p. 197); WOV, Prayers II and E (Leaders Edition, pp. 58–60, 69).
- Plan a reception to follow the Easter Vigil.

Task List

- Prepare water and fire extinguishers for use in an emergency in all locations.
- Secure rhythm instruments, wind chimes, or rain sticks to accompany the Vigil readings.
- Have a party to thank all the participants in your Three Days celebration.

Participants

- Gathering/New fire: ushers, lighting technicians, fire starter, Easter proclamation singer, assisting minister, processional corps for banners/kites/wind chimes/candles/torches, paschal candle stand mover.
- Word: readers, readings coordinator, assistant and technician, chancel dressers.
- Baptism: acolyte, baptismal candle and garment presenter, congregational welcomer.
- Meal: communion ministers, altar guild.
- Hospitality: rich dessert makers, coffee makers, setup and clean-up crews.
- Later: overnight environment changers, cleaners.

SEASONAL WORSHIP TEXTS FOR THE THREE DAYS

MAUNDY THURSDAY

Confession and Forgiveness

Most merciful God,
**we confess that we are captive to sin
and cannot free ourselves.
We have sinned against you in thought, word, and deed,
by what we have done and by what we have left undone.
We have not loved you with our whole heart;
we have not loved our neighbors as ourselves.
For the sake of your Son, Jesus Christ, have mercy on us.
Forgive us, renew us, and lead us,
so that we may delight in your will and walk in your ways,
to the glory of your holy name. Amen.**

God, who is rich in mercy, loved us
even when we were dead in sin,
and made us alive together with Christ.
By grace you have been saved.
In the name of ✝ Jesus Christ, your sins are forgiven.
Almighty God strengthen you
with power through the Holy Spirit,
that Christ may live in your hearts through faith.
Amen.

Greeting

The grace of our Lord Jesus Christ,
the love of God,
and the communion of the Holy Spirit
be with you all.
And also with you.

Offering Prayer

Merciful God,
we cry out for the hope and healing you offer.
Guide us continually to your service.
Make us your hands to feed the hungry
and prepare us to receive the bread of life,
Jesus Christ, your Son, our Savior.
Amen.

Invitation to Communion

Let us lift up the bread of life and cup of salvation
and call on the name of the Lord.

Prayer after Communion

Generous God,
you have fed and renewed us in your holy meal.
Send us into the world you love.
Through our fasting and devotion
draw us to you and to our neighbors,
that we may break bonds of injustice,
feed the hungry,
and set the oppressed free.
In Jesus' name we pray.
Amen.

VIGIL OF EASTER

Greeting

The grace of our Lord Jesus Christ, the love of God,
and the communion of the Holy Spirit be with you all.
And also with you.

Sisters and brothers in Christ, on this most holy night
when our Savior Jesus Christ passed from death to life,
we gather with the church throughout the world
in vigil and prayer. This is the passover of Jesus Christ.
Through light and the word, through water and oil,
bread and wine, we proclaim Christ's death and resurrection,
share Christ's triumph over sin and death,
and await Christ's coming again in glory.

Invitation to Communion

The Lord swallows up death forever
and makes a feast of rich food and wine.
Eat, drink, the gift is for you.

Prayer after Communion

Good Shepherd,
lead us from the fulfillment and joy of this meal
to bring joy and fulfillment to others.
Guide us on paths of justice.
Teach us to live for you as servants to one another.
Enfold us in your abiding love.
We give thanks in the name of the risen Christ.
Amen.

Blessing

Children by the grace of God,
one in Christ,
and inspired by the Holy Spirit,
rejoice in the resurrection
and live in hope, peace, and joy.

Almighty God,
Father, ☩ Son, and Holy Spirit,
bless you now and forever.
Amen.

Dismissal

Go in peace. Share the good news.
Thanks be to God. Alleluia, alleluia!

SEASONAL RITES FOR THE THREE DAYS

Good Friday Service of Light and Darkness

This service is designed for congregations that celebrate Tenebrae, yet would like to move toward the Good Friday liturgy as presented in Evangelical Lutheran Worship (Pew Edition, pp. 262–265; Leaders Edition, pp. 634–642).

Tenebrae (Latin for "darkness") was the name given to the medieval predawn morning prayer celebrated by monks during the last three days in Holy Week. In recent centuries, this monastic liturgy—despite its early-morning light imagery—was transferred to Wednesday evening in Holy Week. In the monastic practice, it was a service of prayers and readings from scripture. As the light began to dawn, the candles used for reading were gradually extinguished, so that at the end of the service, the rising sun provided the necessary light for reading and singing.

In the service presented here, the extinguishing of candles has been placed within the reading of the Passion according to John, the ancient gospel narrative for Good Friday. With this form, eight candles are used. Following each section, one candle is extinguished.

The Johannine passion account is appointed for Good Friday because the synoptic passion accounts are read in successive years on the Sunday of the Passion. John's passion account sees Jesus' death as his glorification. Rather than mourning the dying or dead Jesus on Good Friday, the cross is acclaimed as the sign of the world's redemption. The procession of the cross and adoration of the crucified Christ become the primary symbolic action of this day. We offer honor and reverence to the one who, lifted up from the earth, draws all people to himself. This service does not end in darkness and sadness, as if the assembly were reenacting the death of Christ. Rather, the liturgy ends with Christ exalted on the cross, an image from John's gospel.

Pastoral preaching and teaching will help to place this service appropriately within the Three Days. The procession of the cross has an important connection to the procession of the paschal candle in the Easter Vigil. More importantly, all three days celebrate the mystery of Jesus' dying and rising. We do not wait until Easter Sunday to see what will happen. Already on Good Friday, the church celebrates the Lord's death and resurrection as the central event of our salvation.

Gathering

All gather in silence. The assembly stands when the ministers stand.

Prayer of the Day

Reading

Isaiah 52:13—53:12

Psalm or Hymn

The Passion According to John

John 18:1-11

First candle may be extinguished.
Hymn: Jesus, I will ponder now   ELW 345, LBW 115

John 18:12-27

Second candle may be extinguished.
Hymn: O sacred head, now wounded, sts. 1–2   ELW 351/352, LBW 116/117

John 18:28-40

Third candle may be extinguished.
Hymn: O sacred head, now wounded, sts. 3–4   ELW 351/352, LBW 116/117

John 19:1-7

Fourth candle may be extinguished.
Hymn: Ah, holy Jesus, sts. 1–2   ELW 349, LBW 123

John 19:8-16a

Fifth candle may be extinguished.
Hymn: Ah, holy Jesus, sts. 3–5   ELW 349, LBW 123

John 19:16b-22

Sixth candle may be extinguished.
Hymn: Calvary, sts. 1–2   ELW 354, TFF 85

John 19:23-30

Seventh candle may be extinguished.
Hymn: Calvary   ELW 354, sts. 3–4; TFF 85, sts. 3–5

John 19:31-42

Eighth candle may be extinguished.

Hymn: Were you there   ELW 353, TFF 81, LBW 92

Meditation

Silence for reflection follows.

Bidding Prayer

See *Evangelical Lutheran Worship* Leaders Edition, pp. 636–638.

The assembly kneels or sits.

Procession of the Cross

A large cross is carried in procession through the church and placed before the assembly. The assembly stands and faces the cross as it is brought forward.

The following dialogue is sung on a tone three times, the assembly echoing the leader, at the beginning, midpoint, and end of the procession.

Behold, the life-giving cross, on which was hung the Savior of ˡ the whole world.

Oh, come, let us ˡ worship him.

The assembly may be seated. Hymns expressing adoration of the crucified Christ may be sung. During this time, or at the end of the service, worshipers may come to the large cross to make a sign of reverence. Reverencing the cross may include actions such as pausing before the cross, bowing, kneeling before it for prayer, or touching it.

Hymns

Holy God, holy and glorious   ELW 637

What wondrous love is this   ELW 666, LBW 385

On my heart imprint your image   ELW 811, LBW 102

After a brief silence, the minister continues.

We adore you, O Christ, ˡ and we bless you.

By your holy cross you have re- ˡ deemed the world.

All stand and sing, proclaiming the triumph of the cross. "Sing, my tongue" (ELW 355/356, LBW 118) and "There in God's garden" (ELW 342, WOV 668) are especially appropriate.

All depart in silence.

Service for Saturday in Holy Week

This order may be used for services other than the Vigil of Easter.

Gathering Song

Prayer of the Day

O God, Creator of heaven and earth: Grant that, as the crucified body of your dear Son was laid in the tomb and rested on this holy Sabbath, so we may await with him the coming of the third day, and rise with him to newness of life; who now lives and reigns with you and the Holy Spirit, one God, forever and ever.
Amen.

Readings and Psalm

Job 14:1-14
or Lamentations 3:1-9, 19-24
Psalm 31:1-4
1 Peter 4:1-8
Matthew 27: 57-66
or John 19:38-42

The reading of scripture is followed by silence for reflection. Other forms of reflection may also follow, such as brief commentary, teaching, or personal witness; nonbiblical readings; interpretation through music or other art forms; or guided conversation among those present.

The reflection may conclude with the following dialogue.
In the midst of life we are in death;
from whom can we seek help?
From you alone, O Lord,
who by our sins are justly angered.

**Holy God, holy and mighty,
holy and merciful Savior,
deliver us not into the bitterness of eternal death.**

Lord, you know the secrets of our hearts;
shut not your ears to our prayers,
but spare us, O Lord.

**Holy God, holy and mighty,
holy and merciful Savior,
deliver us not into the bitterness of eternal death.**

O worthy and eternal Judge,
do not let the pains of death
turn us away from you at our last hour.

**Holy God, holy and mighty,
holy and merciful Savior,
deliver us not into the bitterness of eternal death.**

Lord's Prayer

Sending Song

Sending

May the God of hope fill us
with all joy and peace in believing
through the power of the Holy Spirit.
Amen.

Suggested Hymns

Sing, my tongue   ELW 356
How long, O God   ELW 698
In deepest night   ELW 699
Once we sang and danced   ELW 701
O Christ the same   ELW 760
What God ordains is good indeed   ELW 776
Shepherd me, O God   ELW 780
Grant peace, we pray, in mercy, Lord   ELW 784
On Eagle's Wings   ELW 787
Will you come and follow me   ELW 798

Notes on the Service

- This brief service of scripture, song, and reflection may be held on the morning of Saturday in Holy Week.
- This service might be scheduled at a time convenient for those coming to prepare for the Easter Vigil or for Easter Sunday.
- In a culture where stopping and waiting is almost unheard of, a brief time of reflection on what it was like for the disciples to wait through the long sabbath following the death and burial of Jesus may be instructive.

- In his introduction to Ezekiel in *The Renovaré Spiritual Formation Bible*, Edwin Searcy writes: "Whenever the church finds itself living between the terror of Good Friday's horrible ending and the wonder of Easter Sunday's impossible homecoming, it recognizes what it is to be a people exiled on a long Holy Saturday between denial and the truth, between despair and hope" (HarperCollins, p. 1178).

The prayer of the day and dialogue are from *The Book of Common Prayer*, pp. 283, 492.

April 9, 2009
Maundy Thursday

With nightfall our Lenten observance comes to an end, and we gather with Christians around the world to celebrate the Three Days of Jesus' death and resurrection. At the heart of the Maundy Thursday liturgy is Jesus' commandment to love one another. As Jesus washed the feet of his disciples, we are called to follow his example as we humbly care for one another, especially the poor and the unloved. At the Lord's table we remember Jesus' sacrifice of his life, even as we are called to offer ourselves in love for the life of the world.

Today the church commemorates the theologian Dietrich Bonhoeffer, who was executed on this day in 1945.

Prayer of the Day

Holy God, source of all love, on the night of his betrayal, Jesus gave us a new commandment, to love one another as he loves us. Write this commandment in our hearts, and give us the will to serve others as he was the servant of all, your Son, Jesus Christ, our Savior and Lord, who lives and reigns with you and the Holy Spirit, one God, now and forever.

or

Eternal God, in the sharing of a meal your Son established a new covenant for all people, and in the washing of feet he showed us the dignity of service. Grant that by the power of your Holy Spirit these signs of our life in faith may speak again to our hearts, feed our spirits, and refresh our bodies, through Jesus Christ, our Savior and Lord, who lives and reigns with you and the Holy Spirit, one God, now and forever.

Gospel Acclamation

I give you a | new commandment,* that you love one another just as I | have loved you. (John 13:34)

Readings and Psalm

Exodus 12:1-4 [5-10] 11-14

Israel remembered its deliverance from slavery in Egypt by celebrating the festival of Passover. This festival featured the Passover lamb, whose blood was used as a sign to protect God's people from the threat of death. The early church described the Lord's supper using imagery from the Passover, especially in portraying Jesus as the lamb who delivers God's people from sin and death.

Psalm 116:1-2, 12-19

I will lift the cup of salvation and call on the name of the LORD. (Ps. 116:13)

I Corinthians 11:23-26

In the bread and cup of the Lord's supper, we experience intimate fellowship with Christ and with one another, because it involves his body given for us and the new covenant in his blood. Faithful participation in this meal is a living proclamation of Christ's death until he comes in the future.

John 13:1-17, 31b-35

The story of the last supper in John's gospel recalls a remarkable event not mentioned elsewhere: Jesus performs the duty of a slave, washing the feet of his disciples and urging them to do the same for one another.

Color Scarlet *or* White

CD-ROM Images

Icon Three: 1MaundyThursday01_ABC, 1MaundyThursday 02_ABC, 1MaundyThursday03_ABC
Icon Two: 1MaundyThursday01_ABC, 1MaundyThursday 02_ABC
Icon: 025, 089, 154, 243, 261, 274

Prayers of Intercession

With a holy mandate to love one another as Christ has loved us, let us pray for the needs of the world, the church, and all creation so beloved of God.

A brief silence.

Source of all love, as your beloved Son Jesus has given the whole world an example of how to love one another, so now let this love be made known in word and deed to the uttermost ends of the earth. Hear us, O God.
Your mercy is great.

Source of all mercy, as your church enters into these holy days marking the mysteries of our salvation, make them for us a time of renewed faith and deepened love for one another and for all you have made. Hear us, O God.
Your mercy is great.
Source of all life, as Jesus washed the feet of his disciples in a sign of humble service, so let us serve the needs of future generations through our care for your creation.
Hear us, O God.
Your mercy is great.
Source of all compassion, as many this night have no bread to eat nor a place to call home, so grant us your vision to see Christ in all persons, and give us the will to serve all in any need. Hear us, O God.
Your mercy is great.
Source of all goodness, as you have called us into the community where your word is faithfully preached and your sacraments freely celebrated, draw us closer to your heart as we learn to serve. Hear us, O God.
Your mercy is great.
Here other intercessions may be offered.
Source of all holiness, as your word reminds us that the death of your faithful ones is precious in your sight, we give thanks for (*Dietrich Bonhoeffer and*) all our beloved who are now at rest in you. Hear us, O God.
Your mercy is great.
Immerse us in your grace and lead us into service, for the sake of the one whose command is to love one another as we have been loved, Jesus Christ our Lord.
Amen.

Ideas and Images for the Day

John 13 explicitly links the festival of the Passover with Jesus' tableside actions mere hours before his crucifixion. The narrative function of this Passover setting necessarily recalls the events of the exodus—a story of liberation and freedom offered and given by God, who knows the suffering of God's own people. As a continuation of the exodus story, Jesus' words and actions exemplify God's liberating love now offered through the body and blood of the one who intimately knows us and our suffering. Through the washing of feet, the breaking of bread, and wine outpoured, the living, breathing, serving body of Christ frees us to love one another as we have been loved. And so begins the Three Days and the giving of Love's broken body.

1. To bring John's gospel narrative to life, include a footwashing ritual in the service. Though there is much to commend in the symbolic action of the clergy washing the feet of the laity, try other examples of servitude, role-reversal, and intergenerational activity. For example, have the church council wash the feet of the youth group, the youth group the feet of elders in the congregation, and the elders the feet of young children.

2. In regard to the ritual practices of Maundy Thursday, liturgical scholar Gail Ramshaw writes: "In our worship it is not that we are performing a historical passion play, replicating the movements of Jesus. Rather, we are being the church" (*The Three-Day Feast: Maundy Thursday, Good Friday, Easter*, Augsburg Fortress, 2004, p. 38). In other words, we are not a reenacting church groping after memories of how it was in days past or Jesus' time; rather, we are an enacting church enlivened by the Spirit and empowered to proclaim Christ alive and at work among us and through us.

3. Maundy Thursday provides an opportunity to revisit the congregation's standing invitation to the table. How does the congregation's invitation—spoken or written—communicate the universality of Jesus' own hospitality? Who is welcome at your table to partake in the body and blood of Christ? What words or actions are used to extend this welcome? Apply these questions to the doors of the congregation: Who is welcome to cross the threshold into the assembly, and how would one know? How might these questions spill over into the evangelizing strategy of your congregation?

4. Returning to the issue of welcome and invitation in the previous idea, arrange for a Maundy Thursday study for the children of the congregation. (A good group may be those kids and their families preparing for their first communion experience.) As you discuss the full welcome of Jesus, have them write their own invitations to holy communion. As part of the Maundy Thursday communion liturgy, allow the kids to invite the congregation to the table with their welcome statements.

Hymns for Worship
Laying On of Hands
Take, oh, take me as I am   ELW 814
Blessed be God, who forgives   ELW 221
Great God, your love has called us   ELW 358, WOV 666
Healer of our every ill   ELW 612, WOV 738

Footwashing
Jesu, Jesu, fill us with your love   ELW 708, WOV 765
Where charity and love prevail   ELW 359, LBW 126
Ubi caritas et amor   ELW 642, WOV 665

Hymn of the Day
Where charity and love prevail   ELW 359, LBW 126
TWENTY-FOURTH   TFF 84   *MARTYRDOM*

Love consecrates the humblest act   ELW 360, LBW 122
TWENTY-FOURTH
Great God, your love has called us   ELW 358, WOV 666
RYBURN

Communion

Lord, who the night you were betrayed   ELW 463, LBW 206
Lamb of God, pure and sinless   ELW 357, LBW 111
Go to dark Gethsemane   ELW 347, LBW 109

Sending

None

Additional Hymns and Songs

Lord, help us walk your servant way   HG 150
A new commandment   WOV 664
Make me a servant   W&P 96
No Greater Love   GC 607
It happened on that fateful night   LBW 127

Music for the Day
Psalmody and Acclamations

Miller, Aaron David. *Gospel Acclamations for Lent–Holy Trinity.* AFP 9780800635589.
Mummert, Mark. "Psalm 116" from *Psalm Settings for the Church Year.* AFP 9780800678562.
Psalter for Worship Year B, Evangelical Lutheran Worship Edition. AFP 9780806683839.

Choral

Hopson, Hal H. "Love One Another." U/SA, kybd. CG A741.
Music, David W. "O Lord, Have Mercy on Me." SATB, org. AFP 9780800638689.
Organ, Anne Krentz. "Love One Another." SATB. AFP 9780800659646.
Sateren, Leland B. "Go to Dark Gethsemane." SATB. AMSI AM-2026.

Children's Choir

Carter, John. "Lamb of God." UE. 3 pt, kybd. HOP A631.
Eggert, John. "Is There Anybody Here." LE. U, solo, opt desc, pno. AFP 9780800651992. OP
Ramseth, Betty Ann. "The Lord Will Keep You." LE. U, kybd, fl. CG A333.

Keyboard / Instrumental

Behnke, John A. "Ryburn" from *Five Preludes of Praise*, set 4. Org. CPH 97-7039U1.
Callahan, Charles. "Twenty-Fourth" from *Rhapsody on American Folk Hymns.* Org, 2 fl. MSM 20-870.
Eggert, John. "Twenty-Fourth" from *Creative Hymn Accompaniments for Organ*, vol. 2. Org. CPH 97-6851U1.

Farlee, Robert Buckley. "Martyrdom" from *Augsburg Organ Library: Lent.* Org. AFP 9780800658977.

Handbell

Nelson, Susan T. "Elegy." 2 oct, opt sop sax/C/B-flat inst, solo ringer, pno, L2. AFP 9780800654344.
Payne, William. "Elegy." 4-5 oct, L4. AG 1277.
Roberts, Philip L. "O Waly, Waly" from *Hymns for Handbells*, vol. 3. 2-5 oct, L2. GIA G-6660.

Praise Ensemble

Gillard, Richard. "Worthy the Lamb" from www.ccli.com. West Wind Music.
Peterson, Hans. "Communion Response" from *Dakota Road Music Keyboard/Guitar Edition 1.5.* Dakota Road Music. www.dakotaroadmusic.com.
■ Scott, Kathryn. "Hungry" from *More Songs for Praise & Worship 3.* WM 080689452871.
■ Willard, Kelly. "Make Me a Servant" from *Best of the Best, The Other Songbook 2.* FEL 1891062034.

Global

Farlee, Robert Buckley. "When Twilight Comes." 2 pt mxd, pno. AFP 9780800675578.
Loh, I-to. "The Church Is Like a Table" from *Global Praise 2.* U, kybd. General Board of Global Ministries, GBGMusik 1890569224. http://new.gbgm-umc.org/resources/globalpraise/music/.

Thursday, April 9
Dietrich Bonhoeffer, theologian, 1945

Bonhoeffer (BON-heh-fer) was a German theologian who, at the age of 25, became a lecturer in systematic theology at the University of Berlin. In 1933, and with Hitler's rise to power, Bonhoeffer became a leading spokesman for the Confessing Church, a resistance movement against the Nazis. He was arrested in 1943. He was linked to a failed attempt on Hitler's life and sent to Buchenwald, then to Schönberg prison. After leading a worship service on April 8, 1945, at Schönberg prison, he was taken away to be hanged the next day. His last words as he left were, "This is the end, but for me the beginning of life."

A hymn written by Bonhoeffer shortly before his death includes the line "By gracious powers so wonderfully sheltered, and confidently waiting come what may, we know that God is with us night and morning, and never fails to greet us each new day" (ELW 626, WOV 736). Bonhoeffer's courage is a bold witness to the paschal mystery of Christ's dying and rising.

■ denotes songs that are available on iTunes®.

April 10, 2009
Good Friday

At the heart of the Good Friday liturgy is the passion according to John, which proclaims Jesus as a triumphant king who reigns from the cross. The ancient title for this day—the triumph of the cross—reminds us that the church gathers not to mourn this day but to celebrate Christ's life-giving passion and to find strength and hope in the tree of life. In the ancient bidding prayer we offer petitions for all the world for whom Christ died. Today's liturgy culminates in the Easter Vigil tomorrow evening.

Today the church commemorates Mikael Agricola, Bishop of Turku.

Prayer of the Day

Almighty God, look with loving mercy on your family, for whom our Lord Jesus Christ was willing to be betrayed, to be given over to the hands of sinners, and to suffer death on the cross; who now lives and reigns with you and the Holy Spirit, one God, forever and ever.

or

Merciful God, your Son was lifted up on the cross to draw all people to himself. Grant that we who have been born out of his wounded side may at all times find mercy in him, Jesus Christ, our Savior and Lord, who lives and reigns with you and the Holy Spirit, one God, now and forever.

Gospel Acclamation

Look to Jesus, who for the sake of the joy that was set before him endured the cross, disregard- ᴵ ing its shame,* and has taken his seat at the right hand of the ᴵ throne of God. (Heb. 12:2)

Readings and Psalm
Isaiah 52:13—53:12

The fourth servant poem promises ultimate vindication for the servant, who made his life an offering for sin. The early church saw in the servant's pouring himself out to death and being numbered with the transgressors important keys for understanding the death of Jesus.

Psalm 22

My God, my God, why have you forsaken me? (Ps. 22:1)

Hebrews 10:16-25

In the death of Jesus, forgiveness of sins is worked and access to God is established. Hence, when we gather together for worship and when we love others we experience anew the benefits of Jesus' death.

or Hebrews 4:14-16; 5:7-9

In his death Jesus functions as great high priest who experiences temptation and suffering in order that we would receive mercy and find grace, because he is the source of true salvation.

John 18:1—19:42

On Good Friday, the story of Jesus' passion—from his arrest to his burial—is read in its entirety from the Gospel of John.

Color   None

CD-ROM Images

Icon Three: 2GoodFriday01_ABC, 2GoodFriday02_ABC, 2GoodFriday03_ABC, 2GoodFriday04_ABC, 2GoodFriday05_ABC
Icon Two: 2GoodFriday01_ABC, 2GoodFriday02_ABC, 2GoodFriday03_ABC, 2GoodFriday04_ABC, 2GoodFriday05_ABC
Icon: 026, 027, 090, 091, 092, 093, 155

Prayers of Intercession

On Good Friday, the church's ancient Bidding Prayer is said or sung. See Evangelical Lutheran Worship *Leaders Edition, pp. 636–638.*

Ideas and Images for the Day

"Who has believed what we have heard?" (Isa. 53:1). Over and over again in John's gospel Jesus tells his disciples, "I am." When Jesus is arrested and then crucified, the disciples' belief in what they heard Jesus tell them is shattered. Who do we believe Jesus *is* on the cross? The last "I am" that Jesus speaks before dying is "I am thirsty." His was a real physical thirst, but it was also a thirst for what was to come in the resurrection. The thirst we feel on Good Friday is quenched by belief in the resurrection. Just as Jesus' thirst is not metaphorical, ours also is real and physical. What happens on this day is meant to quench the world's thirst.

1. We are already dehydrated by the time we feel thirsty. Being spiritually thirsty means we haven't been drinking enough from the waters of our baptism. The second stanza of "I heard the voice of Jesus say" (ELW 332) says "I came to Jesus, and I drank of that life-giving stream; my thirst was quenched, my soul revived, and now I live in him." What place does your church's baptismal font play in the worship for this day? How can it be a sign of hope?

2. In 2007 scientists found the underground remnants of a lake in Sudan's Darfur region, an area where more than 200,000 people have died from a civil war. This discovery is hope for a land where lack of water has caused great devastation. Historically there is an obvious connection between the supply of natural resources and the level of tension in the human community. For more on the story of the discovery in Darfur go to http://dsc.discovery.com/news/2007/07/18/sudan_pla. html?category=earth.

3. The documentary *Thirst* (PBS, 2004) asks: Is water part of a shared "commons," a human right for all people? Or is it a commodity to be bought, sold, and traded in a global marketplace? For more information on the movie and book (published by Jossey-Bass) go to www.thirstthemovie.org/index.html.

4. The words, "I thirst" had special meaning for Mother Teresa of Calcutta. The aim of her work was to satisfy the thirst of Christ from the cross. She called this "love in action." The work that Jesus did on the cross frees us from the bonds of sin, but it does not free us from the responsibility of putting our love into action. To see "I Thirst," a video of Mother Teresa talking about her ministry, go to www.youtube.com/watch?v=EXOM b-3Lgww.

Hymns for Worship
Gathering
None

Hymn of the Day
O sacred head, now wounded   ELW 351/352, LBW 116/117
    HERZLICH TUT MICH VERLANGEN
Ah, holy Jesus   ELW 349, LBW 123   *HERZLIEBSTER JESU*
Were you there   ELW 353, LBW 92, TFF 81
    WERE YOU THERE

Communion
None

Sending
There in God's garden   ELW 342, WOV 668
Sing, my tongue   ELW 355/356, LBW 118
What wondrous love is this   ELW 666, LBW 385

Additional Hymns and Songs
Behold the wood   GC 437
O crucified Redeemer   UMH 425
Jesus, remember me   ELW 616, WOV 740
They crucified my Lord   ELW 350, TFF 80

Music for the Day
Psalmody and Acclamations
Miller, Aaron David. *Gospel Acclamations for Lent–Holy Trinity.* AFP 9780800635589.
Mummert, Mark. "Psalm 22" from *Psalm Settings for the Church Year.* AFP 9780800678562.
Psalter for Worship Year B, Evangelical Lutheran Worship Edition. AFP 9780806683839.

Choral
◻ Bach, J. S. "O Sacred Head, Now Wounded" from *Bach for All Seasons.* SATB. AFP 9780800658540.
Goss, John. "God So Loved the World." SATB, opt org. AMC AE539.
◻ Jennings, Carolyn. "Ah, Holy Jesus." SA, vc. AFP 9780800645151.
Plater, Ormande. "The Passion Gospels (RCL)." Solo vcs, choir, assembly. Church Publishing 9780898695595 (PDF).
Simikic, Lisa Milena. "Svajti Boze/Holy God." SATB, div. Santa Barbara Music Publishers 467.

Children's Choir
African American spiritual. "Were You There" from *LifeSongs.* LE. U, pno. AFP 9780806642710.
Hoiland, Melissa Ramseth. "Lord, Whose Love in Humble Service" from *Take a Hymn.* UE. U, autoharp/gtr, rec/fl. AFP 9786000106461. OP
Sleeth, Natalie. "Bought with a Price." UE. 2 pt, kybd. HIN HMC542.

Keyboard / Instrumental
Held, Wilbur. "Hezliebster Jesu" from *A Suite of Passion Hymn Settings.* Org. CPH 97-4843U1.
Lind, Richard. "Herzliebster Jesu" from *Piano Impressions for Worship.* Pno. AFP 9780800678807.
Miller, Aaron David. "Herzliebster Jesu" from *Triptych for Lent and Easter.* Org. AFP 9780800659455.

◻ denotes choral suggestions that relate to the hymn of the day.
■ denotes songs that are available on iTunes®.

Peterson, Lynn L. "Were You There" from *Spiritual Sounds for Trombone and Organ*. Org, tbn. CPH 97-6887U1.

Young, Jeremy. "Were You There" from *At the Foot of the Cross*. Pno. AFP 9780800655396.

Handbell

Dobrinski, Cynthia, arr. "Were You There." 3-5 oct, L2. AG 1551.

Gramann, Fred. "Prelude on 'Herzliebster Jesu'." 4-7 oct, L5. LOR AG 47002.

Sherman, Arnold B. "O Sacred Head Now Wounded." 3-5 oct, L2. AG 1732.

Praise Ensemble

Olson, Larry/Karol Baer. "Take Up Your Cross" from *Work of the People*, vol. 1.5. Dakota Road Music. www.dakotaroadmusic.com.

■ Paris, Twila. "Lamb of God" from www.musicnotes.com. Straightway Music/Mountain Spring Music. ELW 336.

■ Reeves, Jesse/Chris Tomlin/J. D. Walt/Isaac Watts. "The Wonderful Cross" from www.praisecharts.com. WT/Sixsteps Music.

Global

Hesla, Bret. "Stand in Awe" from *Justice, Like a Base of Stone*. SATB, cant. AFP 9780800623562.

Sosa, Pablo. "Este Momento en Punto/This is the moment." SATB, assembly, pno, gtr. GIA G-7019.

Friday, April 10

Mikael Agricola, Bishop of Turku, 1557

Agricola was consecrated as the bishop of Turku in 1554, without papal approval. As a result, he began a reform of the Finnish church along Lutheran lines. He translated the New Testament, the prayerbook, hymns, and the mass into Finnish, and through this work set the rules of orthography that are the basis of modern Finnish spelling. His thoroughgoing work is particularly remarkable in that he accomplished it in only three years. He died suddenly on a return trip from negotiating a treaty with the Russians.

April 11, 2009
Resurrection of Our Lord
Vigil of Easter

This is the night! This is our Passover with Christ from darkness to light, from bondage to freedom, from death to life. Tonight is the heart of our celebration of the Three Days and the pinnacle of the church's year. The resurrection of Christ is proclaimed in word and sign, and we gather around a pillar of fire, hear ancient stories of our faith, welcome new sisters and brothers at the font, and share the food and drink of the promised land. Raised with Christ, we go forth into the world, aflame with the good news of the resurrection.

Prayer of the Day

Eternal giver of life and light, this holy night shines with the radiance of the risen Christ. Renew your church with the Spirit given us in baptism, that we may worship you in sincerity and truth and may shine as a light in the world, through your Son, Jesus Christ our Lord, who lives and reigns with you and the Holy Spirit, one God, now and forever.

or

O God, you are the creator of the world, the liberator of your people, and the wisdom of the earth. By the resurrection of your Son free us from our fears, restore us in your image, and ignite us with your light, through Jesus Christ, our Savior and Lord, who lives and reigns with you and the Holy Spirit, one God, now and forever.

Gospel Acclamation

Alleluia. Let us sing to the Lord, who has I triumphed gloriously;* our strength and our might, who has become I our salvation. *Alleluia.* (Exod. 15:1, 2)

Vigil Readings and Responses

1 **Genesis 1:1—2:4a**

Creation

Response: Psalm 136:1-9, 23-26

God's mercy endures forever. (Ps. 136:1)

2 **Genesis 7:1-5, 11-18; 8:6-18; 9:8-13**

Flood

Response: Psalm 46

The LORD of hosts is with us; the God of Jacob is our stronghold. (Ps. 46:7)

3 **Genesis 22:1-18**

Testing of Abraham

Response: Psalm 16

You will show me the path of life. (Ps. 16:11)

4 **Exodus 14:10-31; 15:20-21**

Deliverance at the Red Sea

Response: Exodus 15:1b-13, 17-18

I will sing to the LORD, who has triumphed gloriously. (Exod. 15:1)

5 **Isaiah 55:1-11**

Salvation freely offered to all

Response: Isaiah 12:2-6

With joy you will draw water from the wells of salvation. (Isa. 12:3)

6 **Proverbs 8:1-8, 19-21; 9:4b-6 *or* Baruch 3:9-15, 32—4:4**

The wisdom of God

Response: Psalm 19

The statutes of the LORD are just and rejoice the heart. (Ps. 19:8)

7 **Ezekiel 36:24-28**

A new heart and a new spirit

Response: Psalms 42 and 43

I thirst for God, for the living God. (Ps. 42:2)

8 **Ezekiel 37:1-14**

Valley of the dry bones

Response: Psalm 143

Revive me, O LORD, for your name's sake. (Ps. 143:11)

9 Zephaniah 3:14-20

The gathering of God's people
Response: Psalm 98
Lift up your voice, rejoice and sing. (Ps. 98:4)

10 Jonah 1:1—2:1

The deliverance of Jonah
Response: Jonah 2:2-3 [4-6] 7-9
Deliverance belongs to the LORD. (Jonah 2:9)

11 Isaiah 61:1-4, 9-11

Clothed in the garments of salvation
Response: Deuteronomy 32:1-4, 7, 36a, 43a
*Great is our God, the Rock, whose ways are just.
(Deut. 32:3-4)*

12 Daniel 3:1-29

Deliverance from the fiery furnace
Response: Song of the Three 35–65
Praise and magnify the Lord forever. (Song of Thr. 35)

New Testament Reading and Gospel
Romans 6:3-11

We were incorporated into the death of Jesus Christ in
baptism and so were liberated from the dominion of sin.
We also anticipate that we will be incorporated into the
resurrection of Christ and so will be liberated from the hold
death has over our mortal bodies.

John 20:1-18

John's Gospel describes the confusion and excitement of
the first Easter: the stone is moved, disciples race back and
forth, and angels speak to a weeping woman. Then, Jesus
himself appears.

Color   White *or* Gold

CD-ROM Images
Icon Three: 3EasterVigil01_Creation_ABC, 3EasterVigil02_
Flood_ABC, 3EasterVigil03_RedSea_ABC, 3EasterVigil
04_DryBones_ABC, 3EasterVigil05_Jonah_ABC, 3Easter
Vigil06_Daniel_ABC, 3EasterVigil07_John_ABC
Icon Two: 3EasterVigil01_ABC, 3EasterVigil02_ABC,
3EasterVigil03_ABC
Icon: 156, 157, 243, 263

Prayers of Intercession

With the fire of Easter in our hearts, the story of salvation
in our ears, the waters of baptism on our brow, and the
bread and cup of the risen Christ to nourish us, let us pray
for new life in the world, in the church, and among us now.
A brief silence.

God of new life, on this most holy night the fire of your love
for the world burns brightly. By the power of Jesus' resurrection from the dead, guide the nations of the world that
wars may cease and needless human suffering be alleviated.
Lord, in your mercy,
hear our prayer.

God of new life, on this most holy night your church has
heard again of your marvelous deeds, which have won salvation for the world. Empower your church to boldly proclaim Jesus' death and resurrection in all times and places.
Lord, in your mercy,
hear our prayer.

God of new life, on this most holy night the moon and stars
shine in the heavens, declaring your glory. Preserve our
planet by your mercy, and enable us to care for the creatures
that dwell on the earth, in the sky, and beneath the seas.
Lord, in your mercy,
hear our prayer.

God of new life, on this most holy night the darkness is
oppressive to those who wander homeless, to those who suffer from addictions, depression, or illness. Illumine them
with resurrection's hope, for in you even the darkness is as
the light. Lord, in your mercy,
hear our prayer.

God of new life, on this most holy night we give you thanks
for the gift of holy baptism and for all in this place who seek
to grow in its graces. Enrich those who teach the faith and
those among us who are being nurtured and shaped by your
grace. Lord, in your mercy,
hear our prayer.

Here other intercessions may be offered.

God of new life, on this most holy night you hold us in communion with all who are united with Christ in life and in
death (*especially*). Keep us ever mindful of our fellowship
with your saints of every time and place.
Lord, in your mercy,
hear our prayer.

Hear our prayers, God of new life, for the sake of Jesus,
crucified and risen, our Savior and Lord.
Amen.

Ideas and Images for the Day

The Vigil of Easter is, in a word, dramatic. The drama of
salvation history unfolds around us and within us as we,
like Mary Magdalene, Peter, and the enigmatic beloved
disciple, hurry to the empty tomb of Jesus. Each step we
take in the footrace to the risen Christ, we traverse the ter-
rain of God's abiding promise, illumined by the one who
proclaimed to be the light of world. With the Christ-light as
our guide, we move from creation to exodus, from Ezekiel's
boney valley to Daniel's fiery furnace, from holy font to
sacred meal. Stride for stride, our feet follow the imprints of

the faithful who have made this journey in every time and place. Tonight, our pilgrim-path leads us again, as if for the first time, to its dramatic fulfillment—Easter alleluias!

1. The Vigil is laden with texts. Aside from the Romans and John passages, up to twelve readings punctuate the drama of salvation history. Interspersed between these readings are psalms and other Old Testament responses (see p. 269 in *Evangelical Lutheran Worship* for the complete list). Consider some of the following options to dramatize the readings:
   - Use an inordinate number of instruments to spice up the readings: a bass drum to keep the beat of creation; a rain-stick to capture the feel of the flood; a tambourine during the crossing of the Red Sea; a xylophone to highlight the valley of dry bones; maracas to create fire for Daniel's furnace. End each reading with a loud cymbal clash or gong.
   - Enlist prose and poems to assist in telling the biblical narrative in colorful ways. Replace the creation account with James Weldon Johnson's poem "The Creation" (www.gale.com/free_resources/poets/poems/creation. htm); echo Paul's words in Romans with Susan Palo Cherwien's poem "Baptism" (in *Crossings: Meditations for Worship*, St. Louis: MorningStar Music Publishers, 2003); or pick a favorite Vigil scripture passage contemporized in Eugene Peterson's *The Message* (Colorado Springs: NavPress, 2003).
   - To incorporate dramatic action into the scripture responses following each of the twelve readings, enlist the help of liturgical dancers. As the worship moves through the drama of salvation history, stage the movement through dance.

2. The Vigil is a wonderful time to live out ecumenical partnerships. What might the worship service look like when held with another congregation in your neighborhood? If possible, have the joint assembly physically walk from one church to the other during the worship as a way to give life to the exodus story.

3. Norman Maclean's profound story "A River Runs Through It" is part memoir and part allegory. Near the end of the story, Norman encounters his father, a Presbyterian minister, sitting on the bank of the river reading his Greek New Testament. His father says, "In the part I was reading it says the Word was in the beginning, and that's right. I used to think water was first, but if you listen carefully you will hear that the words

are underneath the water" (*A River Runs Through It and Other Stories*, Chicago: The University of Chicago Press, 1976, p. 95).

Hymns for Worship
Gathering

For suggestions related to the vigil readings, see Indexes to Evangelical Lutheran Worship.

Hymn of the Day

We know that Christ is raised   ELW 449, LBW 189
   ENGELBERG
Christ Jesus lay in death's strong bands   ELW 370, LBW
   134   CHRIST LAG IN TODESBANDEN
Christ is arisen   ELW 372, LBW 136   CHRIST IST ERSTANDEN

Communion

Signs and wonders   ELW 672
At the Lamb's high feast   ELW 362, LBW 210
With high delight let us unite   ELW 368, LBW 140

Sending

This joyful Eastertide   ELW 391, WOV 676
We know that Christ is raised   ELW 449, LBW 189
Come, you faithful, raise the strain   ELW 363, LBW 132

Additional Hymns and Songs

They crucified my Savior   TFF 90
I'm going on a journey   ELW 446, TFF 115
Wade in the water   ELW 459, TFF 114
Welcome Table   RWSB 172, TFF 263

Music for the Day
Around the Light of Christ

Batastini, Robert. "Exsultet" (Easter Proclamation). U chant. GIA G-2351.
Easter Proclamation, *Evangelical Lutheran Worship*. www.augsburg fortress.org/worship/evangelicallutheranworship.
"Rejoice Now, All Heavenly Choirs" from *Music for the Vigil of Easter*. Cant, cong. AFP 9780806605791.
Tamblyn, Bill. "Lumen Christi." Presider, cant, SATB, org, perc. OCP 7235CC.
"The Exsultet." TP.

Around the Readings

Responses to all readings are included in *Psalter for Worship Year C*, Evangelical Lutheran Worship Edition. AFP 9780806653051.
Trapp, Lynn. "Responses for the Triduum." Cant, cong, kybd, opt solo/C inst. MSM 80-305.

Reading I

Carmona, Paul. "A Canticle of Creation." U/cant, desc, org, tpt. OCP 9973.

Erickson, Richard, arr. "When Long Before Time." SATB, org, fl. AFP 9780800656768.

Hopson, Hal H. "O Praise the Lord Who Made All Beauty." U, kybd. CG A143.

Smith, Alan." God's Love Is Forever!" from PS, vol. 2.

Reading 4

Barker, Michael. "Miriam's Song." U, kybd, opt tamb. CG A740.

Daw, Carl P., Jr. "Metrical Canticles 25 and 26" from *To Sing God's Praise*. Cong, kybd. HOP 921.

Gibbons, John. "Canticle of Moses" from *Psalm Songs 2*. AFP 9780800657710.

Reading 5

DeLong, Richard. "Seek Ye the Lord" from *Five Sacred Songs*. Solo, kybd. ECS 4759.

Lindh, Jody W. "Behold, God Is My Salvation." U/2 pt, org. CPH 98-3193.

Rusbridge, Barbara. "Sing a Song to the Lord" from *Psalm Songs 1*. AFP 9780800657703.

Surely it is God who saves me. WOV 635.

Reading 12

Daw, Carl P., Jr. "Metrical Canticles 13 and 14" from *To Sing God's Praise*. Cong, kybd. HOP 921.

Proulx, Richard. "Song of the Three Children." U/2 pt, cant, cong, perc, org. GIA G-1863.

Ray, Robert. "He Never Failed Me Yet." SATB, bar solo, kybd. HAL 4478014.

Around the Font

Cooney, Rory/arr. Gary Daigle. "Glory to God/Sprinkling Rite." Choir, cong, gtr, kybd, fl. GIA G-4020.

Farlee, Robert Buckley. "O Blessed Spring." SATB, ob, vln/cl, org, opt cong. AFP 9780800654245.

Harbor, Rawn. "Blessed Be God, the Source of All Life." ELW 209.

Hobby, Robert A. "You Belong to Christ." ELW 212.

Keesecker, Thomas. "Washed Anew." SAB/SATB, kybd, opt 2 oct hb, opt cong, vln/cl. APF 9786000001353.

Litany of the Saints. ELW 237.

Palmer, Nicholas. "Cleanse Us, O Lord: Sprinkling Rite." Cant, SATB, cong, gtr, org, opt inst. GIA G-4064.

Springs of water, bless the Lord. ELW 214.

Taylor-Howell, Susan. "You Have Put on Christ." U/3 pt, opt Orff inst. CG A325.

Trapp, Lynn. "Music for the Rite of Sprinkling." SATB, org. MSM 80-901.

Choral

Ferguson, John. "Let All Mortal Flesh Keep Silence." SATB, hb. AFP 9780800646684.

❑ Grundahl, Nancy. "Medieval Easter Chant" (Christ ist erstanden). SATB, hrn/other inst. AFP 9780800678036.

Jennings, Kenneth. "All You Works of the Lord, Bless the Lord." SATB, div, org. AFP 9780800645311. *The Augsburg Choirbook*. AFP 9780800656782.

❑ Schein, Johann Hermann. "Christ Lay in Death's Dark Tomb." SAB, cont. BRB.

Children's Choir

Nagy, Russell. "Day Is Dawning." UE. U/2 pt, kybd, opt hb. BP 1326.

Sleeth, Natalie. "Bought with a Price." UE. 2 pt, kybd. HIN HMC542.

Sleeth, Natalie. "This Is the Day" from *Sunday Songbook*. LE. U, kybd. HIN HMB102.

Keyboard / Instrumental

Cherwien, David. "Engelberg" from *Gotta Toccata*. Org. AFP 9780800658755.

Leupold, Anton Wilhelm. "Christ ist erstanden" from *Augsburg Organ Library: Easter*. Org. AFP 9780800659363.

Sedio, Mark. "Engelberg" from *How Blessed This Place*. Org. AFP 9780800658038.

Uhl, Daniel. "Christ lag in Todesbanden" from *Easter Suite for Trumpet, Organ, and Optional Timpani*. Org, tpt/C/B-flat inst, opt timp. AFP 9780800655419.

Handbell

Afdahl, Lee J. "And All Shall Clap Their Hands" (Isaiah 55:12). 3-5 oct, L3. AFP 9780800675059.

Afdahl, Lee J. "For As the Rain Comes Down" (Isaiah 55:10). 3-5 oct hb/hc, fc, rain sticks, L3. AFP 9780800658151.

Lamb, Linda R. "We Know that Christ Is Raised" (When in Our Music God Is Glorified). 3-5 oct hb/hc, L3. Ring Out Press 3261.

Praise Ensemble

■ Nystrom, Martin J. "As the Deer" from *Breakforth Worship Songbook*. New Creation Ministries. www.new-creation.net.

■ Tomlin, Chris/Jesse Reeves/Lawrence Tuttiett/Louie Giglio/Matt Redman. "Be Glorified" from www.praisecharts.com.

Global

"Alelouya!" from *Global Songs 3: Pave the Way*. AFP 9780800676896.

Makeever, Ray. "Brighter Than the Sun" from DH.

❑ denotes choral suggestions that relate to the hymn of the day.
■ denotes songs that are available on iTunes®.

April 12, 2009
Resurrection of Our Lord
Easter Day

This year may be the one in which John's resurrection account is likely to be chosen over Mark's, perhaps because Mark's gospel ends so abruptly, with astonishment and fear rather than joyful proclamation. Yet Mark may speak to our experience more directly than the other gospels. Corinthians and Acts fill out the story by telling of appearances of the risen Christ. Peter says we "ate and drank with him after he rose from the dead." And so do we, in a foretaste of the mountaintop feast where death will be no more.

Prayer of the Day

O God, you gave your only Son to suffer death on the cross for our redemption, and by his glorious resurrection you delivered us from the power of death. Make us die every day to sin, that we may live with him forever in the joy of the resurrection, through your Son, Jesus Christ our Lord, who lives and reigns with you and the Holy Spirit, one God, now and forever.

or

God of mercy, we no longer look for Jesus among the dead, for he is alive and has become the Lord of life. Increase in our minds and hearts the risen life we share with Christ, and help us to grow as your people toward the fullness of eternal life with you, through Jesus Christ, our Savior and Lord, who lives and reigns with you and the Holy Spirit, one God, now and forever.

Gospel Acclamation

Alleluia. Christ, our paschal lamb, | has been sacrificed.* Therefore, let us | keep the feast. *Alleluia.* (1 Cor. 5:7, 8)

Readings and Psalm
Acts 10:34-43

Peter crosses the immense religious and social boundary that separates Jews from Gentiles in order to proclaim the good news of Jesus' life, death, and resurrection, so that God's forgiveness in Jesus' name would reach out to the Gentiles just as it had to Jews.

or Isaiah 25:6-9

More than 700 years before Christ, the prophet Isaiah proclaims the good news of God's salvation and calls all people to rejoice! The Lord will make a rich feast for God's people.

The Lord will wipe the tears from their eyes. And most importantly, the Lord will destroy death itself.

Psalm 118:1-2, 14-24

This is the day that the LORD has made; let us rejoice and be glad in it. (Ps. 118:24)

1 Corinthians 15:1-11

The core of the Christian faith and Paul's preaching is the death and resurrection of Jesus Christ. As the crucified and risen Christ appeared to the earliest of his followers, so we experience the presence of the risen Lord in the preaching of this faith.

or Acts 10:34-43

See above.

Mark 16:1-8

The resurrection of Jesus is announced, and the response is one of terror and amazement.

or John 20:1-18

This morning began with confusion: the stone was moved and the tomb was empty. Disciples arrive, then angels, and finally Jesus himself. Out of the confusion, hope emerges, and a weeping woman becomes the first to confess her faith in the risen Lord.

Color   White *or* Gold

CD-ROM Images

Icon Three: EasterDay_B

Icon Two: EasterDay01_ABC, EasterDay02_ABC, EasterDay03_ABC

Icon: 028, 158, 159

Prayers of Intercession

Rejoicing in God's marvelous works of new life, let us pray for renewal in the world, in the church, and in every living creature.

A brief silence.

For the world, created and beloved of God, that nations in tumult of war and under siege of natural disaster would be renewed in peace and with compassionate relief. Lord, in your mercy,

hear our prayer.

For the church, redeemed and anointed by God, that united in the death and resurrection of Jesus, it would be renewed in its resolve to proclaim with one voice your limitless love for the world. Lord, in your mercy,

hear our prayer.

For the creation, fashioned and nurtured by God, that in this season of planting and blooming the earth would be renewed by your gracious rains and gentle warmth. Lord, in your mercy,

hear our prayer.

For the needy, held and uplifted in God, that all who are oppressed by illness, prejudice, grief, or neglect would be renewed by the promise of your mercy's impartiality. Lord, in your mercy,

hear our prayer.

In thanksgiving for this assembly, called and sent by God, that on this day of rejoicing we become what we receive: Christ's very body, broken and blessed for newness of life in all the world. Lord, in your mercy,

hear our prayer.

Here other intercessions may be offered.

In thanksgiving for the faithful departed, sanctified and kept by God (*especially*), that the memory of their witness and your goodness through them would renew our courage and commitment in life and service. Lord, in your mercy,

hear our prayer.

To you, O God of newness and renewal, we lift up all for whom we pray, through the one whom you lifted up from death and the grave, Jesus Christ our risen Lord.

Amen.

Ideas and Images for the Day

Easter! What a glorious and confident day in the life of a Christian! And yet it didn't start that way. "And they said nothing to anyone, for they were afraid" (Mark 16:8). Easter started in the midst of great fear and trembling. An entire Easter experience could be built around the antithesis of the first day of the week. "And they said nothing to anyone" is in direct opposition to the angel's urging to "go, tell his disciples." Yes, Jesus died, but here is the rest of the story, which is quite different from what came before it! Jesus died, but yes, he is raised; alleluia! The story does not end there; in fact, we complete the story when we tell its conclusion as it becomes alive in our lives.

1. Here's a possible three-point outline for an Easter Sunday sermon. First, because of Easter our past can be forgiven. There is no condemnation for those in Christ Jesus. Use the clean slate of an Etch A Sketch® to illustrate this point. Second, because of Easter our present can be managed. Life is not out of control, nor are we powerless over our circumstances. Third, because of Easter our future is secure. Our future is in God's hands when Jesus is Lord of our lives.

2. Jesus wants our whole life, not just a portion of it. William Booth, founder of the Salvation Army, was asked about the tremendous success of the Salvation Army. He said, "I will tell you the secret: God has had all that there was of me. There have been men with greater brains than I, even with greater opportunities, but from the day I got the poor of London on my heart and caught a vision of what Jesus Christ could do with me and them, on that day I made up my mind that God should have all of William Booth there was. And if there is anything of power in the Salvation Army, it is because God has had all the adoration of my heart, all the power of my will, and all the influence of my life." To put it in common evangelical language, if you don't trust Jesus in all, you don't really trust him at all.

3. Many people consider the words of Easter to be an idle tale, and they don't believe them. Almost every year in the weeks leading up to Easter, newspapers and magazines publish stories about belief in the resurrection. These articles often provide fertile ground for preaching in terms of contrasting the general opinion of Jesus with the eyes of faith.

Hymns for Worship
Gathering

Now all the vault of heaven resounds   ELW 367, LBW 143
Jesus Christ is risen today   ELW 365, LBW 151
This joyful Eastertide   ELW 391, WOV 676

Hymn of the Day

The strife is o'er, the battle done   ELW 366, LBW 135
  VICTORY
The day of resurrection!   ELW 361   *ELLACOMBE*   LBW 141
  HERZLICH TUT MICH ERFREUEN
Awake, my heart, with gladness   ELW 378, LBW 129
  AUF, AUF, MEIN HERZ

Communion

Now the green blade rises   ELW 379, LBW 148

At the Lamb's high feast we sing   ELW 362, LBW 210

I know that my Redeemer lives!   ELW 619, LBW 352

Sending

Christ has arisen, alleluia   ELW 364, WOV 678

Hail thee, festival day! (Easter)   ELW 394, LBW 142

Christ is risen! Alleluia!   ELW 382, LBW 131

Additional Hymns and Songs

Low in the grave he lay   TFF 94

Earth, earth, awake!   GC 441

These things did Thomas count as real   LSB 472

I will enter his gates   TFF 291

Alleluia, alleluia! Hearts to heaven   LSB 477

Music for the Day
Psalmody and Acclamations

Miller, Aaron David. *Gospel Acclamations for Lent–Holy Trinity.* AFP 9780800635589.

Mummert, Mark. "Psalm 118" from *Psalm Settings for the Church Year.* AFP 9780800678562.

Psalter for Worship Year B, Evangelical Lutheran Worship Edition. AFP 9780806683839.

Choral

Breedlove, Jennifer Kerr. "Early Easter Morning." 2 pt mxd/SA, kybd, opt hb. GIA G-5894.

□ Crüger, Johann. "Awake, My Heart, with Gladness" from *Chantry Choirbook.* SATB, 2 C inst. AFP 9780800657772.

Handel, G. F. "Hallelujah, Amen." SATB, kybd. GS 9835/various editions.

Helman, Michael. "This Is the Day." SAB, org. AFP 9780800638740.

Manuel, Ralph. "Alleluia." SATB, div. HIN HMC-927.

Pavlechko, Thomas. "Christ Is Risen! Shout Hosanna!" SATB, org, br. AFP 9780800638757.

Schwoebel, David. "Christ Is Risen! Alleluia!" SATB, org, br qt. AFP 9780800638733.

Spurlock, William D. "Good Christian Friends, Rejoice and Sing!" SAB, pno. AFP 9780800678944.

Children's Choir

Horman, John D. "Mary Told the Good News." UE. 2 pt, kybd, opt hb, Orff. ABP 072255.

Jennings, Carolyn. "Christ the Lord Is Risen Today." UE. U, Orff, fl. CG A566.

Jothen, Michael. "On This Day." UE. U/2 pt, kybd, fl. CG A267.

Sleeth, Natalie. "This Is the Day" from *Sunday Songbook.* LE. U, kybd. HIN HMB102.

Keyboard / Instrumental

Frahm, Frederick. "Auf, auf, mein Herz" from *Let It Rip! at the Piano*, vol. 2. Pno. AFP 9780800675806.

Lind, Richard. "Auf, auf, mein Herz" from *Piano Impressions for Worship.* Pno. AFP 9780800678807.

Lovinfosse, Dennis. "Victory" from *A New Liturgical Year.* Org. AFP 9780800656713.

Manz, Paul. "Auf, auf, mein Herz" from *Improvisations for the Easter Season.* Org. MSM 10-402.

Mayo, Becki Slagle. "Ellacombe" from *Journey Through the Seasons.* Pno. AFP 9780800676940.

Handbell

McChesney, Kevin. "Come Ye Faithful, Raise the Strain." 3-5 oct hb/hc, L5. CPH 97-6744.

Morris, Hart. "Canticle of Creation." 3-5 oct, opt perc, L4. RR HB0023.

Zabel, Alfred Heinrich. "The Strife Is O'er." 3-5 oct, L3. AFP 9780800658069.

Praise Ensemble

■ Baloche, Paul/Don Moen. "Arise" from www.leadworship.com.

DeShazo, Lynn/Gary Sadler. "For the Lord Is Good" from *Outrageous Joy.* INT 000768140567.

■ Houston, Joel. "Salvation Is Here" from www.praisecharts.com. Hillsong Publishing/INT.

■ Maher, Matt. "Resurrection Day" from www.musicnotes.com. Thankyou Music.

Global

Campbell, Derek. "He Is Not Here." SATB, cant, kybd, gtr. GIA G-5187.

Roberts, Leon C. "This Is the Day." SATB, kybd, gtr. GIA G-4600.

□ denotes choral suggestions that relate to the hymn of the day.
■ denotes songs that are available on iTunes®.

164

April 12, 2009
Resurrection of Our Lord
Easter Evening

Isaiah proclaims the great feast to come, when God will swallow up death forever. Paul invites us to celebrate the paschal feast with the unleavened bread of sincerity and truth. The Easter evening gospel tells of the risen Christ being made known to the disciples in the breaking of the bread. Our hearts burn within us as the hope of the resurrection is proclaimed in our midst, and as Jesus appears to us at the holy table.

Prayer of the Day

O God, whose blessed Son made himself known to his disciples in the breaking of bread, open the eyes of our faith, that we may behold him in all his redeeming work, Jesus Christ, our Savior and Lord, who lives and reigns with you and the Holy Spirit, one God, now and forever.

Gospel Acclamation

Alleluia. Our hearts | burn within us* while you open to | us the scriptures. *Alleluia.* (Luke 24:32)

Readings and Psalm
Isaiah 25:6-9

The prophet portrays a wonderful victory banquet at which death, which in ancient Canaan was depicted as a monster swallowing everyone up, will be swallowed up forever. The prophet urges celebration of this victory, which is salvation.

Psalm 114

Tremble, O earth, at the presence of the LORD. (Ps. 114:7)

I Corinthians 5:6b-8

In preparation to celebrate Passover, God's people cleaned out all the old leaven from their homes. Paul draws on this practice to portray Christ as our Passover lamb whose sacrifice means that we now clean out the old leaven of malice and wickedness from our lives and replace it with sincerity and truth.

Luke 24:13-49

On the day of his resurrection, Jesus joins two disciples on the road to Emmaus and makes himself known to them in the breaking of bread.

Color   White *or* Gold

CD-ROM Images

Icon Three: Easter3_A
Icon Two: Easter3_A
Icon: 030

Easter

Preparing for Easter

Lectionary

This year's Easter readings are direct. Here is the witness of our faith—salvation through Jesus Christ. Here is our purpose as a church—to share the story of Jesus Christ with the world, and to make disciples. The Easter lectionary takes us on the journey of faith and discipleship: We have seen the risen Lord! Now we understand the scriptures and believe Jesus really *is* the Messiah! So, what do we do now?

The Readings

Matthew, Mark, and Luke record the events of Jesus' ministry, and John explores further the meaning of what Jesus said and did. The readings help us look back and see with new eyes of faith. In John 15 we discover God's plan for Easter people: abide in and stay close to Christ; bear fruit by loving others as Christ loved you; testify, by the power of the Holy Spirit, to the risen Lord.

The plan for sharing good news begins with fearful disciples locked behind closed doors. Jesus appears to his disciples with purpose and power saying, "As the Father has sent me, so I send you" and "Receive the Holy Spirit" (John 20:22). Seeing Jesus and the fulfilled scriptures, the disciples are to preach repentance and forgiveness to all, starting right there in Jerusalem. The Good Shepherd continues to walk ahead of his sheep, calling them forward as shepherds who also will give their lives to bring other sheep into Jesus' fold. Gathered to Christ the vine, they draw their strength from "the true vine" and are pruned to produce more fruit that glorifies the Father. Growing in Christ, the disciples are not just servants with limited knowledge of God's desire, but friends chosen to fully know and do God's will. Knowing God's plan and their part in it, the disciples are sent out, protected and united with Jesus' prayer and God's word of truth. The Spirit of truth will testify to the disciples, and the disciples will testify to the world after Pentecost.

The actual sharing of the good news is recorded in Acts. A community united in purpose and trust gathered around the apostles' testimony to the resurrection. In the temple they witnessed to ordinary Jewish people, and thousands converted. Before the religious leaders they testified to the power of the risen Jesus. Philip is called to leave town and witness to a Jew from a foreign country; a new believer is baptized. Peter is called to a distant land to witness to a gentile, the powerful Roman soldier Cornelius; a household of friends and family believes and is baptized. The Holy Spirit arrives, Christ is proclaimed, and three thousand are converted. From the least to the greatest, from family to foreigners, the good news is shared and received with joy.

For living and witnessing in the world, 1 John gives guidance for discerning and living the true faith. The way of the world is darkness, lies, hatred, and sin; the way of Christ is light, truth, love, and righteousness. All other messages must be tested against these truths.

Easter season preaching can prepare the assembly for weeklong witnessing. Gospel and epistle readings recall the story of our faith from its earliest beginnings, and reveal to us how God intends us to be witnesses in the world. The book of Acts models a steady progression from witnessing at home with familiar situations and people to a larger world of unknowns. How are our fears similar to those of the first disciples? How can we overcome the hindrances in our witness today? With Peter, we may struggle to hear and accept God calling us beyond the familiar. Easter preaching can teach and prepare those called to witness on home's familiar ground, and those called to leave the familiar behind. Acts reminds us that both are necessary.

Worship

Liturgy

Easter is a season of sustained joy and rejoicing in the gift of salvation. Using the Kyrie during Easter recalls what the apostles' preaching in Acts demonstrated—joy can be more full when remembering what has been left behind to follow the risen Christ. With prominent images of Christ's victory over death, any of *Evangelical Lutheran Worship*'s settings of "This is the feast" makes a worthy hymn of praise for these weeks. Alternatively, some congregations like to sing one of the settings of "Glory to God" as a hymn of praise and then sing a setting of "This is the feast" as a communion hymn. The lilting Celtic Alleluia (ELW 174) can be expanded for Easter with a cantor singing the verses from the Accompaniment Edition.

For Pentecost, Web sites such as www.biblegateway.com can help create a multilingual reading of Acts 2:1-21 with phrases and verses to be spoken in languages of the student and adult worshipers.

Music

For many Lutherans, singing best expresses our joy and rejoicing during worship. Luther noted how music and singing make us cheerful, free us from cares, and when threatened by sadness help us "sing the devil down." A congregation of any size can sing joyful songs in the Easter season. A joyful offering song or hymn of praise can be drawn from Easter sections and indexes of our worship books each week.

Besides congregational singing of familiar favorites, ensembles or soloists interested in specific styles of music can introduce a new song of joy, then invite the people to join in. Youth and adult musicians can supplement or collaborate with the church musician. Over these seven weeks a variety of joyful music could come from seven centuries, seven cultures, or seven different styles of music—spirituals, Caribbean, German chorales, Latin American, chant, African, revival songs, classic English hymnody, contemporary praise songs and hymns, Southern harmonies, gospel music—all of which are found in *Evangelical Lutheran Worship*.

Congregations with more musical resources can look to the nearly three dozen cantatas Bach composed for this season. Utilizing a small or large number of singers and instrumentalists, a joyful excerpt or movement could be an offertory or prelude. Bach's eight-movement *Easter Oratorio* (BWV 4), echoed in the hymn "Christ Jesus lay in death's strong bands" (ELW 370), could be presented over the eight weeks of Easter to Pentecost, or as a complete work as a gift to the community. Free, downloadable public-domain choral music can be found on the Internet.

When the Thirty Years' War devastated music resources, Heinrich Schütz composed music for use during Eastertide for churches with fewer resources. Consider featuring the work of this lesser-known composer of joyous music.

Seeds of Change

As planting season arrives, you could include a blessing of seeds and soil as part of your Eastertide celebration. Broad farm fields and tiny urban garden plots are both fine places to gather for prayer and song. You may be able to tie your congregation's blessing into larger community efforts or events that work to restore urban green space, address environmental problems, or provide food to the hungry.

Space
Joy

In the tradition of John's gospel, joy and rejoicing come from knowing our salvation through Jesus Christ. *Joy* and *rejoicing* are not just Christmas words! While joy in Christ's victory over death and our salvation are part of *every* Sunday's celebration of the resurrection, this is a season of particular and contagious joy. Banners both simple and elaborate can declare "joy" and "rejoice" in bright, bold colors inside and outside the church. The Easter color of gold can express the supreme value of Christ and his redeeming work. If the cross was draped in Lenten colors, consider draping it with white and gold for the season.

A Resurrection Garden

A cross surrounded with flowers on Easter day can become a seasonal "garden" for joyful meditation and prayer when flowers continue to surround it throughout the season. Encourage use of this resurrection garden by providing chairs, kneelers or pillows, and devotional materials. Find a bright, pleasant location with easy access and a reasonable noise level, inside or outside.

Where fresh flowers are easily available, using aromatic flowers throughout this season can sustain the visual feast first shown by Easter lilies. Where the selection is more limited, consider the flora that mark the new life each spring—pussy willows, a branch with tender green shoots emerging, lily of the valley, or crocus. Floral fabrics, colorful vases, and flowerpots can also add color and joy.

Life in the Vine

Other ideas are inspired by the rich imagery of John 15:5: "I am the vine, you are the branches. Those who abide me and I in them bear much fruit. . . ." From Southerners already enjoying their growing season to the midnight-sun gardeners waiting for late-spring planting frenzies, God gives us a new season of growing. We remember our place and our role—God is the vinegrower, Jesus is the true vine, we are the fruit-bearing branches. A banner or dried grape vines can grace the worship space or entry. Leaves or clusters of fruit on the vine can bear the names of those who made Christ known to us, and the people with whom we share our faith—family, Sunday school students, friends, and neighbors.

Seeing Jesus

With the question "Where is Jesus now?" at the center, a wall of human faces can be assembled. Pictures from mission trips, family photographs, the community, many cultures and nations can be displayed to keep us attentive to Christ's presence in the world. A mirror among the face pictures can remind us of Luther's encouragement to be a "little Christ" to our neighbor.

Celebrating Easter with Children

Alleluia! Christ is risen! Christ is risen indeed! Alleluia!

A common theme found throughout this season of the church year is Jesus appearing along the road and way of life. Jesus meets weary travelers along the road to Emmaus, shows himself to Thomas, and instructs his disciples how to walk in his path after his ascension. This season also bears witness to how the early apostles, namely, Peter, Stephen, and Philip, boldly spoke about their experiences. This season, ask children to look for Jesus in their everyday life.

During this time of new life and resurrection, we look for the movement of the Holy Spirit in and among us. Consider allowing the children opportunities to lead in worship. When the children lead us, it is easier to embrace something we haven't tried before and experience delight in doing things that the child in each of us longs to do.

Ideas for Easter

- Make copies of the word *Alleluia* in rainbow colors and different fonts. Each Sunday "find" the word behind a significant object or place in the worship space (the cross, the altar, the baptismal font, the place where the readings are proclaimed, the middle of the assembly). Talk about how we can now sing "Alleluia" because of Jesus' actions in each of these places.
- Using recycled magazine pages, make butterflies to adorn the doors and entryways of the church building through the whole season. A pattern and photo can be found at www.bluebonnetvillage.com/foldbfly.htm.
- Provide a time in worship (perhaps in the prayers of intercession each week of Easter) for children to share and give thanks for a time they saw Jesus at work in the past week. The entire community may be surprised by how looking actively for these encounters helps us to see Jesus in our everyday life.

Ideas for the Day of Pentecost

- Rent a helium tank and gather people of all ages to inflate and decorate the entire worship space with red balloons. Place balloons throughout the worship space so that as people move, the balloons will react to their movement. During worship, as children invariably play with the balloons and as they move on their own with the breath of the people, all get to experience the breath and movement of God. *Recommendations:* Use 8-to-12-foot-long ribbon or string to attach the balloon to the weight. A bag of big washers from a hardware store can be used as weights and, if gathered at the end of worship, can be used year after year. At the end of the worship services, ask volunteers to stand by the doors and tie the strings of single balloons around the wrists of the children, to send the bright red balloons home without fear of losing them.
- Global Music Spirit Sundays. If your congregation is not already in the practice of singing songs from Christians throughout the world, today is a great day to do so. At Pentecost we emphasize the ability of God's Spirit to help us understand across language barriers, so it's a perfect day to try a song in another language. Teach children or youth the songs, then invite them to teach the rest of the assembly. If your congregation enjoys this break from their usual favorites, you might consider having Spirit Sundays periodically throughout the year. A few suggestions: "Njoo kwetu, Roho mwema" (ELW 401, WOV 687, TFF 103), "Veni Sancte Spiritus" (ELW 406, WOV 686), and "Soplo de Dios viviente" (ELW 407, LLC 368).
- For children who prefer not to sing, invite other kinds of active participation, such as drumming or other rhythm instruments—it's impossible to do it wrong with an egg shaker!
- Invite worshipers in the weeks before Pentecost to give red geraniums with specific prayers for how the Holy Spirit might call, gather, enlighten, and sanctify the community of faith. These prayers can be shared aloud by children in the prayers of intercession on Pentecost. After Pentecost worship, invite the assembly—especially children—to be a part of a planting party. Then transplant the geraniums into a garden plot outside the building for a reminder of the Spirit's presence throughout the summer. A group of people working and laughing together outside the building is also a witness to neighbors that something is going on here today!

Worship Helps for Easter

Easter Checklist

- Prepare materials for Easter flower sponsorship and order flowers.
- Publicize Holy Week and Easter services in local newspapers and in other media.
- Order extra bulletin covers for additional worshipers on Easter Day.
- Design service folders for Easter worship that guests will be able to follow easily, including specific instructions for communion distribution.
- Determine communion-distribution procedure for services with large numbers of communicants and make sure sufficient communion elements and communionware are available.
- Make arrangements for adequate seating, along with additional worship books and service folders for larger assemblies on Easter Day.
- Publicize Pentecost services, helping the congregation understand the importance of the festival.
- Determine ways to emphasize the Day of Pentecost, such as using red flowers, inviting people to wear red, or using a diversity of languages in scripture readings, prayers, or music for the day. (Some churches order red geraniums to be planted around the church grounds or given away following Pentecost services.)
- If Pentecost is to be observed as a baptismal festival, see the suggestions for the Baptism of Our Lord in the Time after Epiphany checklist, p. 71.
- On Pentecost, seven votive candles in red glass holders may be lighted and placed on or near the altar to recall the gifts of the Spirit.
- Look ahead to the checklist on p. 209 as you plan for the time after Pentecost.

Shape of the Communion Liturgy

- See the seasonal worship texts for Easter on pp. 172–173.
- As an alternative to confession and forgiveness, use thanksgiving for baptism. A form is provided in *Evangelical Lutheran Worship* (Pew Edition, p. 97; Leaders Edition, p. 169). Thanksgiving for baptism may be led at the font.
- Use the Kyrie.
- Use the hymn of praise ("This is the feast").
- Use the Nicene Creed.
- See the prayers of intercession for each Sunday and Ascension Day.
- Use the preface for Easter, Ascension, or Pentecost, as appropriate (*Evangelical Lutheran Worship* Leaders Edition, pp. 187, 188, and 189).
- Thanksgiving at the table: see options in *Evangelical Lutheran Worship*, especially Prayer IV (Pew Edition, p. 111; Leaders Edition, p. 197); *WOV*, Prayers E and F (Leaders Edition, pp. 69–70).

Other Helps

- See the suggestions for music and worship space in the essay "Preparing for Easter," pp. 168–169.
- Consider observing the Day of Pentecost (May 31) as a baptismal festival.
- If your congregation celebrates affirmation of baptism (confirmation) during this season, review the rite in *Evangelical Lutheran Worship* (Pew Edition, pp. 234–237; Leaders Edition, pp. 596–600).
- A blessing of graduates may be desired during this season. See the seasonal rites section for two possible forms (pp. 174–176).

SEASONAL WORSHIP TEXTS FOR EASTER

Confession and Forgiveness

All may make the sign of the cross, the sign that is marked at baptism, as the presiding minister begins.

Trusting in the word of life given in baptism,
we are gathered in the name of the Father,
and of the ✚ Son, and of the Holy Spirit.
Amen.

If we say we have no sin,
we deceive ourselves, and the truth is not in us.
If we confess our sins,
God who is faithful and just will forgive our sins
and cleanse us from all unrighteousness.

Silence is kept for reflection and self-examination.

Loving God,
we fear, we doubt, we do not trust you;
we do not love our neighbors as ourselves;
we sin against you in thought, word, and deed.
We pray for your mercy, forgiveness, and grace.
We hope in the gift of your Spirit
and we rejoice in the resurrection promise
of Jesus Christ, our living Savior.
Amen.

God, who is rich in mercy,
loved us even when we were dead in sin,
and made us alive together with Christ.
By grace you have been saved.
In the name of ✚ Jesus Christ, crucified and risen,
your sins are forgiven.
Almighty God strengthen you with power
through the Holy Spirit,
that Christ may live in your hearts through faith.
Amen.

Greeting

Alleluia! Christ is risen.
Christ is risen indeed. Alleluia!
The grace of our Lord Jesus Christ, the love of God,
and the communion of the Holy Spirit be with you all.
And also with you.

Offering Prayer

Everlasting God,
the whole universe sings a new song of praise:
the rivers clap their hands, the hills ring out for joy.
As you have raised us to new life in Christ,
give us voices ready to cry out for justice
and proclaim resurrection joy wherever your Spirit leads us.
In Jesus' name we boldly pray.
Amen.

Invitation to Communion

This is the feast of victory for our God!

Prayer after Communion

Good Shepherd,
lead us from the fulfillment and joy of this meal
to bring joy and fulfillment to others.
Guide us on paths of justice.
Teach us to live for you as servants to one another.
Enfold us in your abiding love.
We give thanks in the name of the risen Christ.
Amen.

Sending of Communion

Healing God,
bless the ministers who through word and sacrament
connect our community of faith
with brothers and sisters who are not here today.
Be with them in their care and service,
and sustain us all with the promise of your abiding presence.
Unified in your gracious love we pray.
Amen.

Blessing

Children by the grace of God,
one in Christ,
and inspired by the Holy Spirit,
rejoice in the resurrection
and live in hope, peace, and joy.

Almighty God,
Father, ✝ Son, and Holy Spirit,
bless you now and forever.
Amen.

Dismissal

Go in peace. Share the good news.
Thanks be to God. Alleluia, alleluia!

SEASONAL RITES FOR EASTER

Blessing of Graduates I

The following order may be used within the congregation's primary service or within a special baccalaureate service as a way to mark the important rite of passage associated with graduation. It may be used with as much flexibility as necessary or desired.

The leader may address the assembly with these or similar words.

Dear friends: Life presents us with various significant milestones that set the stage for the next phase in our earthly journey. Graduation from high school is one of these milestones. Today we wish to honor those who are moving through this special time of accomplishment, transition, and change, and to show them that we, their community of faith, stand with them and support them as fellow believers in Jesus Christ.

Graduates may be introduced by a leader or may introduce themselves.

The leader addresses the graduates and the assembly.

At this time of celebration and transition, hear these words from holy scripture.

One or more of the following or another brief scripture reading is proclaimed.

Psalm 71:1, 3, 5
Proverbs 16:9
Jeremiah 29:11-14a
Matthew 17:20

The leader continues with these or similar words:

Dear graduates: At this special time in your life we are eager to show you how delighted we are that you have reached this milestone in your life. As fellow members of this community of faith we rejoice with you and want you to know of our pride and excitement as you move from this accomplishment into the next phase of your life. We also want you to know that wherever you go and whatever you do, you are going forward with our prayers for God's continued guidance, power, protection, and strength.

The leader or other members of the congregation may speak additional words of blessing and encouragement at this time.

Parents and guardians may join the graduates. Families may join hands as the leader prays for God's blessing with these or similar words.

O Lord Jesus Christ, when you welcomed the children your invitation included each one of us. Your guiding hand has continually been upon these young men and women. You have sustained them. You have shared in their laughter and wiped away their tears. In times of confusion you have offered direction. In times of sorrow you have offered hope. In times of doubt your Holy Spirit has lifted them up. Grant, O Savior, to each of these graduates the knowledge of your continued presence as they go forth into the future. Bless them and keep them. Guide their steps. Hold them in the hollow of your hand.
Amen.

The leader addresses the assembly.

Members and friends of *name of congregation*, will you promise to keep these graduates and their families in your thoughts and prayers as they go forth into the future?
We will.

Will you, as fellow believers in Jesus Christ, promise to help these young men and women as need and opportunity arise?
We will.

Parents and guardians may place a hand on the shoulder or head of their child as they pray for God's blessing with these or similar words, assisted by the leader.

May the Lord bless you and keep you.

May the Lord watch over you and keep you safe.

May the Lord guide your every step.

May you always know of our unending love for you.

Amen.

Notes

- While the order is intended primarily for use with those graduating from high school, it may be adapted for use with those graduating from other institutions.
- Graduates may be introduced by the leader or by other members of the congregation such as mentors, youth leaders, or teachers.
- Graduates may be invited to share their post-graduation plans with the congregation.
- Additional words of blessing and encouragement may be offered by members of the congregation who have been important in the lives of the graduates.

Blessing of Graduates 2

This order may follow the sermon or an address to the graduates.

The leader may address the graduates with these or similar words.

We are delighted to honor you as you graduate from high school. We are proud of you! It is our privilege to affirm you as members of this congregation. You have completed an important phase of your lives and you are entering another.

The graduates stand. The leader addresses the graduates.

I ask you to affirm your commitment to a life of faith in the body of Christ.

Graduates, as you celebrate your achievements and prepare for your new endeavors, do you thank God for the many ways your faith has been your strength and guide?

Response: **With God's help I do.**

As you consider the next steps of your journey of life, do you acknowledge God going with you, before you, behind you, below you, above you, and within you?

Response: **With God's help I do.**

As you make choices about your new endeavors, do you promise to remain connected to the church, offering your gifts to the world as part of the body of Christ and receiving the support of a family of faith?

Response: **With God's help I do.**

The assembly stands. The leader addresses the assembly with these or similar words.

People of *name of congregation*, listen: Do you claim these graduates as brothers and sisters in Christ, called to ministry according to their talents?

In God's love, we claim them.

As their home congregation, do you promise to support them, take an interest in their future, be with them in their celebration and sadness, and welcome them whenever they return to *name of congregation*?

In God's love, we support them.

Do you promise to faithfully pray for these brothers and sisters, placing their futures into God's loving hands as they make their choices?
In God's love, we pray for them.

Let us pray.
Gracious God, you bless your servants with many achievements. We give thanks especially today for the milestones that these graduates have attained. As they begin new phases of their lives, may they know your love in all the experiences they have.

Bless the parents of these students, who have raised their children and nourished them in Christian faith. Give them strength in your holy presence, and give them many joyful reunions with their sons and daughters, those who are leaving home to go far away, and those staying close by. In Jesus' name we pray.
Amen.

The leader addresses the graduates and the assembly.
Go out into the world in peace;
be of good courage;
hold fast to what is good;
return no one evil for evil;
strengthen the fainthearted;
support the weak;
help the suffering;
honor all people;
love and serve God,
rejoicing in the power of the Holy Spirit.
Amen.

Blessing of Mothers

Gracious God,
in love you have given us the gift of mothers.
Grant to each of them your power and grace.
Strengthen them in their mothering
with tenderness and understanding,
with compassion and joy.
Endow them with wisdom and knowledge
so that they might teach their children
how to live and how to love;
how to seek and pursue that which is right and true;
how to turn away from all that is hurtful and wrong.
Deepen their own faith
so that they might instill in their children a love for you
that will sustain and keep them their whole life long.
We ask this in Jesus' name.
Amen.

Volunteer Recognition Litany

The following litany may be adapted as needed to reflect the congregation's volunteer ministries.

The body of Christ is made up of many members.
Not all have the same function.
We are blessed with many members who care for the functioning of the body of Christ at *name of congregation*.
We thank God for them.

They give of their time and talents.
Without their efforts and gifts we could not be all God calls us to be.
Paul writes of the Macedonian Christians who wanted to share in ministry: "They gave themselves first to the Lord and, by the will of God, to us." (2 Cor. 8:5)
Ministry flows from a commitment to serve the Lord.
By the will of God our volunteers are committed to the Lord and to us. God has worked mightily through them to bless us.
We thank God for them.

Our volunteers put flesh and bone on our call to be the body of Christ in the world.
They add muscle to our calling to be Christ to one another.
Sunday school and vacation Bible school teachers, confirmation and youth leaders, mentors and nursery helpers;
musicians, readers, assisting ministers, ushers, leaders of prayer, communion assistants, acolytes;
mission-project organizers, stewardship coordinators, offering counters, special event planners;
quilters, gardeners, artists, bakers, cooks;
prayer chain participants, visitors to the hospitalized and homebound, those who prepare funeral lunches;
ministers of hospitality of every kind;
cleaners, bulletin assemblers, envelope stuffers, office helpers, and so many more:
We thank God for you!

The doxology may be sung by all or spoken in dialogue.
Praise God, from whom all blessings flow.
Praise God, all creatures here below.
Praise God above, you heavenly host.
Praise Father, Son, and Holy Ghost. Amen.

Blessing of Fields and Gardens

Let us bless God, the creator of all things. God has given us the earth to cultivate, so that we might receive the bounty of its fruits. Just as the rain falls from heaven and waters the earth, bringing forth vegetation, so God's word will flourish and will not return empty.

Reading

Genesis 1:1, 11-12, 29-31

Prayer

Almighty God, we thank you for making the earth fruitful, so that it might produce what is needed for life.
Bless those who work in the fields;
give us seasonable weather;
and grant that we may all share the fruits of the earth, rejoicing in your goodness;
through Jesus Christ our Lord.
Amen.

Hymn

We plow the fields and scatter   ELW 680/681, LLC 492, LBW 362
Praise and thanksgiving   ELW 689, LBW 409
For the fruit of all creation   ELW 679, WOV 760, LBW 563

April 19, 2009
Second Sunday of Easter

The Easter season is a week of weeks, seven Sundays when we play in the mystery of Christ's presence, mostly through the glorious Gospel of John. Today we gather with the disciples on the first Easter, and Jesus breathes the Spirit on us. With Thomas we ask for a sign, and Jesus offers us his wounded self in the broken bread. From frightened individuals we are transformed into a community of open doors, peace, forgiveness, and material sharing such that no one among us is in need.

Today the church commemorates Olavus Petri and Laurentius Petri, two sixteenth-century renewers of the church.

Prayer of the Day

Almighty God, with joy we celebrate the day of our Lord's resurrection. By the grace of Christ among us, enable us to show the power of the resurrection in all that we say and do, through Jesus Christ, our Savior and Lord, who lives and reigns with you and the Holy Spirit, one God, now and forever.

Gospel Acclamation

Alleluia. Blessed are those who | have not seen* and yet have come | to believe. *Alleluia.* (John 20:29)

Readings and Psalm

Acts 4:32-35

While the apostles testified to others about the resurrection of Jesus, the early Christian community shared what they owned or sold their possessions to help their fellow believers who were in need.

Psalm 133

How good and pleasant it is to live together in unity. (Ps. 133:1)

1 John 1:1—2:2

The opening of this letter serves as a reality check. The reality of God is light, but our confessed reality has been sin. God cleanses us from our sinful reality through Christ's death so that we live in fellowship with Christ and walk in God's light.

John 20:19-31

The story of Easter continues as the risen Lord appears to his disciples. His words to Thomas offer a blessing to all who entrust themselves in faith to the risen Lord.

Color White

CD-ROM Images

Icon Three: Easter2_01_ABC, Easter2_02_ABC, Easter2_03_ABC

Icon Two: Easter2_01_ABC, Easter2_02_ABC

Icon: 029, 160

Prayers of Intercession

Transformed by the life-giving power of the empty tomb, let us pray for the church, the world, and all those in need.
A brief silence.

Blessed by God's continued love and presence among us, let us pray for the church to be the wounded hands of Christ to all who doubt or disbelieve. Hear us, O God.
Your mercy is great.

Blessed by a universe rich with wonder and vitality, let us pray for a common dedication to the well-being of all living creatures. Hear us, O God.
Your mercy is great.

Blessed by the bonds of community for mutual care and support, let us pray for safe neighborhoods, adequate housing, and sufficient food for all people. Hear us, O God.
Your mercy is great.

Blessed by peace and comfort in the midst of fear and confusion, let us pray for those facing the loss of a loved one, a job, or good health (*especially*). Hear us, O God.
Your mercy is great.

Blessed by firm tradition and ever-evolving transformation, let us give thanks (*for the courage and foresight of Olavus and Laurentius Petri, whom we commemorate today, and*) for all who work for renewal in this congregation. Hear us, O God.
Your mercy is great.

Here other intercessions may be offered.

Blessed by the timeless promise of the resurrection, let us give thanks for (*names and all*) the faithful departed, that at the last we may be united with them in the one true fellowship of Christ. Hear us, O God.
Your mercy is great.
Hear our prayers, gracious God, and grant all that we need to live as your Spirit-filled people, in the name of the risen Christ.
Amen.

Ideas and Images for the Day

Doubt is sometimes confused with unbelief, but doubt and unbelief are very different. To doubt is to question the truth or reality of something. Unbelief is the stubborn refusal to believe in something. Doubt is choosing *what to believe*. Unbelief is choosing *not to believe*. Doubt is *I can't*. Unbelief is *I won't*. Because we are human and are limited in what we can know, some degree of doubt is acceptable. Antidotes to doubt might include writing out your doubts, praying through them, or talking them through with trusted friends. Doubt is not an enemy of faith. Today might be a good day to contrast doubt with unbelief, and to invite people to a confident faith in Jesus as their risen Lord.

1. We often say that seeing is believing. Jesus says that those who have not seen and yet believe are blessed. An Easter faith says that believing is seeing the presence of God in our lives. An Easter faith sermon might include the five points that faith is believing when I don't see it, obeying when I don't understand it, persisting when I don't feel like it, thanking God before I receive it, and trusting even if I don't receive it.

2. Today a preacher might emphasize that an Easter faith is not about a place but about a people. It is not about a program but rather a power. It is not about a pastor but about a person whose name is Jesus and who has a claim on your life. What can you "do" with an Easter faith?

3. The disciples locked themselves in because they were afraid. Locking themselves in is a powerful image. How do we lock ourselves in and refuse to get out of our "skins" because we are too ashamed, too young, too old, too worried about what others think, or too (fill in the blank)? When we lock ourselves in, we also lock the world out. Consider examples or images today that express ways in which we invite the outside world into our world of faith, and images that demonstrate how our faith transforms our world.

4. Text, audio, and video of a 2004 reflection by ELCA Presiding Bishop Mark Hanson on this gospel text is available in the archives of *30 Good Minutes*, a weekly ecumenical and interfaith program on WTTW 11 (PBS) in Chicago. The reflection, "Fleeing or Engaging the World," is at www.csec.org/csec/sermon/Hanson_4714.htm.

Hymns for Worship
Gathering

Come, you faithful, raise the strain   ELW 363, LBW 132
Thine is the glory   ELW 376, LBW 145
Jesus lives, my sure defense   ELW 621, LBW 340

Hymn of the Day

O sons and daughters, let us sing   ELW 386, LBW 139
    O FILII ET FILIAE
Alleluia! Christ is arisen   ELW 375   SANTO DOMINGO
We walk by faith   ELW 635   SHANTI
    WOV 675   DUNLAP'S CREEK

Communion

We have seen the Lord   ELW 869
The peace of the Lord   ELW 646
Peace, to soothe our bitter woes   ELW 381, LBW 338

Sending

Be not afraid   ELW 388
The risen Christ   ELW 390
Come, you faithful, raise the strain   ELW 363, LBW 132

Additional Hymns and Songs

Come and see   LS 61
In the bulb there is a flower   LS 56, MBW 797, VU 703
Open our eyes, Lord   TFF 98, W&P 113
Come and see   W&P 29
We've a story to tell the nations   MBW 621
Hamba nathi (Come, walk with us)   GS2 6

Music for the Day
Psalmody and Acclamations

Miller, Aaron David. *Gospel Acclamations for Lent–Holy Trinity.* AFP 9780800635589.
Organ, Anne Krentz. "Psalm 133" from *Psalm Settings for the Church Year.* AFP 9780800678562.
Psalter for Worship Year B, Evangelical Lutheran Worship Edition. AFP 9780806683839.

Choral

Bach, Johann Ludwig/arr. Michael Burkhardt. "Rejoice, Praises Render." U, kybd/cont, opt inst. CG A902.

Bouman, Paul. "God Is Light." SATB, org. AFP 9780800653255.

Christiansen, Paul J. "Easter Morning." SATB. AFP 9780800645571. *The Augsburg Choirbook.* AFP 9780800656782.

◻ Ferguson, John. "O Sons and Daughters." SATB, hb, tamb. GIA G-4547.

Schelat, David. "Surprising Light." 2 pt mxd, org/kybd, fc. AFP 9780800638771.

Children's Choir

Patterson, Mark. "Alleluia, Christ Is Risen" from *ChildrenSing: Seven Anthems for Elementary Age Singers.* UE. U, pno. AFP 9780800677695.

Ramseth, Betty Ann. "Make Times Forgiven." UE. U/2 pt, kybd, fl. CG A289. OP

Smith, G. Alan. "Antiphonal Alleluia!" UE. Antiphonal trbl, kybd. HOP F983.

Keyboard / Instrumental

Biery, James. "Dunlap's Creek" from *We Walk by Faith.* Org. MSM 10-526.

Held, Wilbur. "O filii et filiae" from *Augsburg Organ Library: Easter.* Org. AFP 9780800659363.

Henkelmann, Brian. "O filii et filiae" from *Chorale Preludes for the Liturgical Year,* vol. 1. Kybd, fl. CPH 97-7227.

Uhl, Daniel. "Dunlap's Creek" from *Easter Suite for Trumpet, Organ, and Optional Timpani.* Org, tpt/C/B-flat inst, opt timp. AFP 9780800655419.

Handbell

Dobrinski, Cynthia, arr. "Good Christians All, Rejoice." 3-5 oct, L3. AG 1900.

Joy, Michael. "Dorian Dance." 3-6 oct, L4+. JEF MJHS9365.

Stephenson, Valerie N. "O Sons and Daughters, Let Us Sing!" 3-5 oct, opt 3 oct hc, L3. GIA G-6150.

Praise Ensemble

▪ Carswell, Eddie/Michael O'Brien. "Psalm 40" from www.praise charts.com. Sheltering Tree Music/INT/J.I.T.H. Music Publishing.

▪ Davis, Holland. "Let it Rise" from *iWorship Songbook 1.* INT 23366.

▪ Falson, Chris. "I Walk by Faith" from *WOW Worship Orange 2000 Songbook.* INT 17236.

Morgan, Reuben. "My Redeemer Lives" from www.praisecharts.com. Hillsong Publishing/INT.

Global

Burkhardt, Michael. "Nimemwona Bwana/We Have Seen the Lord" from *Part-Singing: Global Style.* U/2/3 pt. MSM 50-9811A.

Farlee, Robert Buckley. "Christ Is Living/Cristo Vive." SATB, org, gtr, perc, opt assembly. AFP 9780800658830.

Sunday, April 19

Olavus Petri, priest, 1552; Laurentius Petri, Bishop of Uppsala, 1573; renewers of the church

These two brothers are commemorated for their introduction of the Lutheran movement to the Church of Sweden after studying at the University of Wittenberg. They returned home and, through the support of King Gustavus Vasa, began their work. Olavus published a catechism, hymnal, and a Swedish version of the mass. He resisted attempts by the king to gain royal control of the church. Laurentius was a professor at the university in Uppsala. When the king wanted to abolish the ministry of bishops, Laurentius persuaded him otherwise. The historic episcopate continues in Sweden to this day. Together the brothers published a complete Bible in Swedish and a revised liturgy in 1541.

This week the Church of Sweden can be remembered in prayer. The hymns "How Great Thou Art" (ELW 856) and "Thy holy wings" (ELW 613) use Swedish folk tunes and can be sung to commemorate the contributions of the Petris and the Swedish church to our worship life.

Tuesday, April 21

Anselm, Bishop of Canterbury, 1109

This eleventh- and twelfth-century Benedictine monk stands out as one of the greatest theologians between Augustine and Thomas Aquinas. He is counted among the medieval mystics who emphasized the maternal aspects of God. Of Jesus Anselm says, "In sickness you nurse us and with pure milk you feed us." Anselm is perhaps best known for his "satisfaction" theory of atonement. He argued that human rebellion against God demands a payment, but because humanity is fallen it is incapable of making that satisfaction. But God takes on human nature in Jesus Christ to make the perfect payment for sin.

◻ denotes choral suggestions that relate to the hymn of the day.

▪ denotes songs that are available on iTunes®.

Thursday, April 23

Toyohiko Kagawa, renewer of society, 1960

Toyohiko Kagawa (toy-oh-hee-koh ka-ga-wa) was born in 1888 in Kobe, Japan. Orphaned early, he was disowned by his remaining extended family when he became a Christian. Kagawa wrote, spoke, and worked at length on ways to employ Christian principles in the ordering of society. His vocation to help the poor led him to live among them. He established schools, hospitals, and churches. He also worked for peace and established the Anti-War League. He was arrested for his efforts to reconcile Japan and China after the Japanese attack of 1940.

In celebration of his witness, recognize those people in your parish who work on behalf of the poor and oppressed and who, through their work, reveal the peace of Christ that is a gift of the resurrection.

Saturday, April 25

Mark, Evangelist

Though Mark himself was not an apostle, it is likely that he was a member of one of the early Christian communities. It is possible that he is the John Mark of Acts 12 whose mother owned the house where the apostles gathered. The gospel attributed to him is brief and direct. It is considered by many to be the earliest gospel. Tradition has it that Mark went to preach in Alexandria, Egypt, became the first bishop there, and was martyred.

Mark's story of the resurrection ends with women at the tomb who say nothing to anyone because of their fear. Though their witness faltered, the good news of the resurrection, the good news of these fifty days, reaches out to include us.

April 26, 2009
Third Sunday of Easter

The gospel for the third Sunday of Easter is always one in which the risen Christ shares food with the disciples, meals that are the Easter template for the meal we share each Lord's day. In today's gospel, Jesus both shares the disciples' food and shows them the meaning of his suffering, death, and resurrection through the scriptures: the two main elements of our Sunday worship.

Prayer of the Day

Holy and righteous God, you are the author of life, and you adopt us to be your children. Fill us with your words of life, that we may live as witnesses to the resurrection of your Son, Jesus Christ, our Savior and Lord, who lives and reigns with you and the Holy Spirit, one God, now and forever.

Gospel Acclamation

Alleluia. Our hearts | burn within us* while you open to | us the scriptures. *Alleluia*. (Luke 24:32)

Readings and Psalm

Acts 3:12-19

After healing a crippled man, Peter preaches to the people how God's promises to Israel have been fulfilled in Jesus. Through the proclamation of Christ's death and resurrection, God is offering them forgiveness and restoration in Jesus' name.

Psalm 4

The LORD does wonders for the faithful. (Ps. 4:3)

1 John 3:1-7

God has loved us in order to make us children of God. Though we do not yet know the full details of our future existence, we trust that God will reveal it just as God revealed Jesus to take away our sins.

Luke 24:36b-48

In this account of an appearance after his resurrection, Jesus opens the minds of the disciples to understand him as Messiah. Jesus convinces them that he has been raised and sends them on a mission to proclaim the message of repentance and forgiveness.

Color White

CD-ROM Images

Icon Three: Easter3_B

Icon Two: Easter3_B

Icon: 094

Prayers of Intercession

Transformed by the life-giving power of the empty tomb, let us pray for the church, the world, and all those in need.

A brief silence.

Sent forth as witnesses to the resurrection, let us pray for the church to boldly proclaim the message of repentance and forgiveness to all nations. Hear us, O God.

Your mercy is great.

Sent forth as stewards of creation, let us pray for the wise and mindful use of the earth's resources. Hear us, O God.

Your mercy is great.

Sent forth as peacemakers in a world of conflict, let us pray for all who work for cooperation and reconciliation among nations, communities, and within families. Hear us, O God.

Your mercy is great.

Sent forth as healers and caretakers, let us pray for capable minds and compassionate hearts in attending to all who are in pain, who suffer, or are afraid (*especially*). Hear us, O God.

Your mercy is great.

Sent forth as children of God to teach and guide, let us pray for the youth and education ministries of this congregation. Hear us, O God.

Your mercy is great.

Here other intercessions may be offered.

Sent forth to love and serve, let us give thanks for those who have faithfully carried out Christ's mission (*especially*), that at the end we may be clothed with them with power from on high. Hear us, O God.

Your mercy is great.

Hear our prayers, gracious God, and grant all that we need to live as your Spirit-filled people, in the name of the risen Christ.

Amen.

Ideas and Images for the Day

In this year of Mark, we borrow from Luke's account for this Sunday's gospel. It repeats the disciples' feelings of fear and uncertainty, which is especially useful for anyone who didn't hear the gospel for the second Sunday of Easter. Again Jesus shows his wounds and shares a meal with his disciples. Peace is shared among them—and something more. For the first time, Jesus opens their minds to understand the scriptures. For the first time, the disciples' confusion with the law, the prophets, and the psalms is replaced by a clarity that comes only through the light of the Messiah's suffering, death, and resurrection. Indeed, what Jesus tells them is that his followers can understand scripture properly only with the knowledge of Easter and the events leading to it. It must have been a word of grace to a group so frequently confused or mistaken about his meaning. We too can have our hearts and minds opened through our senses of sight, smell, touch, feel, and the taste of the bread and wine of holy communion. Jesus is risen. Jesus is real.

1. This week's gospel reading gives us better insight into the emotional state of the other disciples while taking the heat off Thomas. In Luke, too, these disciples were "startled," "terrified," and "disbelieving." Doubts and wonderings arose in their hearts as well. They too required physical proof. Though they did not place their fingers in the marks of the nails, Jesus did have to eat food to prove that he was real and not simply an apparition.

2. The community that follows Jesus is charged with giving testimony to his saving work—and that work is to be visible in the world. In the gospel Jesus himself says, "Look at me, touch me" and eats in the disciples' presence. We live in an increasingly visual culture, where the biblical and Reformation admonishments to *listen* feel hollow to many who base their lives on the evidence of what they see.

3. Today's gospel is nothing less than an invitation into a new world order. The disciples (and we) are invited, called, and welcomed into a new creation, and it will be their (and our) task to share this invitation with the rest of the world, beginning always with the Easter story.

Hymns for Worship

Gathering

The day of resurrection!   ELW 361, LBW 141

Alleluia! Jesus is risen!   ELW 377, WOV 674

The trumpets sound, the angels sing   ELW 531

Hymn of the Day

We who once were dead   ELW 495, LBW 207
MIDDEN IN DE DOOD

We walk by faith   ELW 635   *SHANTI*
    WOV 675   *DUNLAP'S CREEK*

As we gather at your table   ELW 522   *IN BABILONE*

Communion

Bread of life, our host and meal   ELW 464

Around you, O Lord Jesus   ELW 468, LBW 496

Draw us in the Spirit's tether   ELW 470, WOV 703

Sending

By your hand you feed your people   ELW 469
Christ is risen! Shout hosanna!   ELW 383, WOV 672

Additional Hymns and Songs

Stay with us   WOV 743
We rejoice in the grace of God   W&P 151
Make me a servant   W&P 96
On the road to Emmaus   BC 253

Music for the Day
Psalmody and Acclamations

Farlee, Robert Buckley. "Psalm 4" from *Psalm Settings for the Church Year.* AFP 9780800678562.

Miller, Aaron David. *Gospel Acclamations for Lent–Holy Trinity.* AFP 9780800635589.

Psalter for Worship Year B, Evangelical Lutheran Worship Edition. AFP 9780806683839.

Choral

▫ Helman, Michael. "We Walk by Faith." SATB, pno, opt hb, fl. AFP 9780800659752.

Mendelssohn, Felix. "See What Love." SATB, kybd. AFP 9780800645618.

Meyer, Erik. "This Is the Threefold Truth." SATB, org. AFP 9780800638795.

▫ Scott, K. Lee. "As We Gather at Your Table." SAB, kybd. AFP 9780800678081. *Augsburg Easy Choirbook*, vol. 2. AFP 9780800677510.

Sleeth, Natalie. "Christ Is Arisen, Indeed!" SAB, children's choir, kybd. HOP C5223.

Children's Choir

Christopherson, Dorothy. "There Was a Man." UE. U/2 pt, pno, ob. AFP 9780800657048. OP

Sleeth, Natalie. "This Is the Day" from *Sunday Songbook*. LE. U, kybd. HIN HMB102.

Ziegenhals, Harriet. "Now Let the Heavens Be Joyful." UE. U/3 pt, kybd, opt fl/vln. HOP JR220.

Keyboard / Instrumental

Kosche, Kenneth T. "Midden in de Dood" from *Augsburg Organ Library: Baptism and Communion*. Org. AFP 9780800623555.

Manz, Paul. "Midden in de Dood" from *Nine Hymn Improvisations*. Org. MSM 10-875.

Sedio, Mark. "In Babilone" from *Let It Rip! at the Piano*, vol. 2. Pno. AFP 9780800675806.

Wold, Wayne L. "In Babilone" from *Hymn Intonation, Harmonization, and Free Prelude Series*, vol. XIV. Org. SEL 160-734.

Handbell

Gramann, Fred. "Festive Praises." 4-5 oct, L6-. LOR AG45043.
Hanna, Donna. "Capriccio in A Minor." 3-5 oct, L2+. GIA G-6343.
Moklebust, Cathy. "Meditation on 'Beautiful Savior'." 3-5 oct, L3. CG B175.

Praise Ensemble

Byrd, Marc/Steve Hindalong. "Sing Alleluia" from www.musicnotes.com. New Spring Publishing, Inc./Never Say Never Songs/Meaux Mercy/Blue Raft Music.

■ Morgan, Reuben. "God So Loved" from www.praisecharts.com. Hillsong Publishing/INT.

■ Nelson, Marc. "I Believe in Jesus" from *Breakforth Worship Songbook*. New Creation Ministries. www.new-creation.net.

■ Smith, Leonard. "Our God Reigns" from *Songs for Praise & Worship*. WM 738597141690.

Global

Haugen, Marty. "Sim Shalom." 2 pt, kybd, gtr. GIA G-7106.
Parker, Alice. "Song of Peace/V'Chit' Tu." SATB. AFP 9780800675684.

Wednesday, April 29
Catherine of Siena, theologian, 1380

Catherine of Siena was a member of the Order of Preachers (Dominicans), and among Roman Catholics she was the first woman to receive the title Doctor of the Church. She was a contemplative and is known for her mystical visions of Jesus. This gift of mysticism apparently extended back into her childhood, much to the dismay of her parents, who wanted her to be like other children. Catherine was a humanitarian who worked to alleviate the suffering of the poor and imprisoned. She was also a renewer of church and society and advised both popes and any persons who told her their problems.

Catherine's contemplative life was linked to her concern for the poor and suffering. She is a reminder that prayer and activism belong together.

Friday, May 1
Philip and James, Apostles

Philip was one of the first disciples of Jesus, who after following Jesus invited Nathanael to "come and see." According to tradition, Philip preached in Asia Minor and died as a martyr in Phrygia. James, the son of Alphaeus, is called "the Less" (meaning "short" or "younger") to distinguish him from another apostle named James, commemorated July 25.

▫ denotes choral suggestions that relate to the hymn of the day.
■ denotes songs that are available on iTunes®.

Philip and James are commemorated together because the remains of these two saints were placed in the Church of the Apostles in Rome on this day in 561.

Their invitation to "come and see" is at the heart of the church's ongoing welcome to the Christian life. During these fifty days of Easter, how can your community invite others to come and see the new life of Christ?

Saturday, May 2
Athanasius, Bishop of Alexandria, 373

Athanasius (ath-an-AY-shus) attended the Council of Nicaea in 325 as a deacon and secretary to the bishop of Alexandria. At the council, and when he himself served as bishop of

Alexandria, he defended the full divinity of Christ against the Arian position held by emperors, magistrates, and theologians. Because of his defense of the divinity of Christ, he was considered a troublemaker and was banished from Alexandria on five occasions. As bishop, one of his paschal letters to surrounding bishops gives a list for books that should be considered canonical scripture. He lists the twenty-seven New Testament books that are recognized today.

Athanasius is an appropriate saint for Easter. His name means "deathless one," though he himself lived in threat of death because of his theological stand. We are made in God's likeness, Athanasius affirmed. By the resurrection we are remade in the likeness of the Son who conquered death.

May 3, 2009
Fourth Sunday of Easter

The image of the Good Shepherd shows us how the risen Christ brings us to life. It is the relationship between the shepherd and the sheep, one of mutual knowledge and love, that gives the shepherd authority. The shepherd's willingness to lay down his life for the sheep shows his love. First John illustrates what it means to lay down our lives for one another by the example of sharing our wealth with any sister or brother in need.

Prayer of the Day

O Lord Christ, good shepherd of the sheep, you seek the lost and guide us into your fold. Feed us, and we shall be satisfied; heal us, and we shall be whole. Make us one with you, for you live and reign with the Father and the Holy Spirit, one God, now and forever.

Gospel Acclamation

Alleluia. Jesus says, I am | the good shepherd.* I know my own and my | own know me. *Alleluia.* (John 10:14)

Readings and Psalm
Acts 4:5-12

Peter and John had been arrested the previous day because they were proclaiming the news of the resurrection to the people. In today's reading, Peter is filled with the Holy Spirit so that he is able to proclaim salvation in Jesus' name to the religious authorities.

Psalm 23

The LORD is my shepherd; I shall not be in want. (Ps. 23:1)

1 John 3:16-24

Jesus' death on our behalf is the clearest demonstration of divine love. This is the very love we share with others, not just through our words but especially through our deeds. In sharing such love we fulfill God's commandments.

John 10:11-18

In language that recalls the twenty-third psalm, Jesus describes himself as the shepherd who cares for his sheep. He is willing to die for them, and he is able to overcome death for them.

Color   White

CD-ROM Images

Icon Three: Easter4_B

Icon Two: Easter4_B

Icon: 095

Prayers of Intercession

Transformed by the life-giving power of the empty tomb, let us pray for the church, the world, and all those in need.

A brief silence.

Led by the Good Shepherd who gathers and guides all people, let us pray for missionaries throughout the world as they seek to bring new followers into the fold of the church. Hear us, O God.

Your mercy is great.

Led to quiet places of rest and renewal, let us pray for the protection and preservation of wilderness and sanctuary, parks and reserves. Hear us, O God.

Your mercy is great.

Led to a table of plenty where everyone is welcome, let us pray for international relief agencies, soup kitchens, and food pantries, and for all who are fed by them. Hear us, O God.

Your mercy is great.

Led through dark places and difficult circumstances, let us pray for the lost, the discouraged, and for all who are ill or in need of care and tending (*especially*). Hear us, O God.

Your mercy is great.

Led to the life-giving waters of baptism, let us pray for the newly baptized as they grow in wisdom and understanding. Hear us, O God.

Your mercy is great.

Here other intercessions may be offered.

Led at the last to our eternal home, let us soothe the dying, comfort all who mourn, and give thanks for the faithful departed (*especially*), that we may be gathered with them to dwell in the house of the Lord forever. Hear us, O God.

Your mercy is great.

Hear our prayers, gracious God, and grant all that we need to live as your Spirit-filled people, in the name of the risen Christ.

Amen.

Ideas and Images for the Day

Good Shepherd Sunday conjures up pastoral images of a smiling and gentle Jesus under a tree, with a beautiful, clean little lamb on his lap, or of Jesus walking with children with a lamb over his shoulders. Those are beautiful and safe images, but incomplete and out of context. The truth Jesus tells (John 10:1) is in response to the blindness of the Pharisees (9:40-41). John 10 is set within the immediate context of conflict with the Pharisees over Jesus' healing on the sabbath of a man born blind. Jesus compares the Pharisees' shepherding of the Jews to the wolves and hired hands that come only to steal, kill, and destroy. In contrast, Jesus, the good shepherd, came that all may have life and have it abundantly.

1. This is a day of contrasts. We live in the valley of the shadow of death, yet we fear no evil (Ps. 23). We live in a time of chaos and confusion, yet our texts speak of confidence and conviction. And, of course, the good shepherd stands in direct contrast to the wolf and hired hand. Lift up these contrasts today. It may be helpful to note that the verses immediately following today's gospel reading present yet another study in contrasts: the Jews who have heard Jesus' words about the good shepherd are divided about whether Jesus is raving mad or a healer from God (10:19-21). Jesus, the good shepherd, leads his sheep through conflict to safety. A final affirmation of this shepherd's calling is Jesus' threefold question and command to Peter at the end of the gospel (John 21:15-17).

2. "I have a dream," said Martin Luther King Jr., "that my four little children will one day live in a nation where they will not be judged by the color of their skin but by the content of their character." Jesus had a similar dream, in which he challenged his followers to live out his own dreams and values, often in contrast to cultural values. Today's gospel text, beyond the safe and comforting image of Jesus as shepherd, also offers us a more challenging image of a shepherd whose priorities are in direct contrast with the religious and government authorities.

3. Philip Yancey, in his book *The Jesus I Never Knew* (Zondervan, 2002), notes that most movies and images of Jesus portray him as a flat character with a monotone voice, a placid demeanor, and a dull personality. Yancey suggests that Jesus must have been much more joyful and engaging than many of our Sunday school images. People liked being around him, eating with him, and following him. Consider the good shepherd image from this perspective today.

Hymns for Worship
Gathering

Good Christian friends, rejoice and sing!   ELW 385, LBW 144

Lord, who the night you were betrayed   ELW 463, LBW 206

That Easter day with joy was bright   ELW 384, LBW 154

Hymn of the Day

At the Lamb's high feast we sing   ELW 362, LBW 210
SONNE DER GERECHTIGKEIT

With high delight let us unite   ELW 368, LBW 140
MIT FREUDEN ZART

Christ the Lord is risen today; alleluia!   ELW 369, LBW 128
LLANFAIR

Communion

You satisfy the hungry heart   ELW 484, WOV 711

Praise the Lord, rise up rejoicing   ELW 544, LBW 196

Savior, like a shepherd lead us   ELW 789

Sending

Christ the Lord is risen today; Alleluia!   ELW 369, LBW 128

God be with you till we meet again   ELW 536

Additional Hymns and Songs

Our Paschal Lamb, that sets us free   WOV 679

I will sing, I will sing   W&P 73

Join we all in one accord   MBW 525

Jesus, name above all names   W&P 77

Spirit Song   W&P 130

Music for the Day
Psalmody and Acclamations

Farlee, Robert Buckley. "Psalm 23" from *Psalm Settings for the Church Year*. AFP 9780800678562.

Miller, Aaron David. *Gospel Acclamations for Lent–Holy Trinity*. AFP 9780800635589.

Psalter for Worship Year B, Evangelical Lutheran Worship Edition. AFP 9780806683839.

Choral

Cool, Jayne Southwick. "I Am Jesus' Little Lamb." 2 pt mxd/SA, kybd, fl, narr. AFP 9780800676216.

Dexter, Noel. "The Lord Is My Shepherd." SATB, pno, perc. AFP 9780800638832.

Haugen, Marty. "Shepherd Me, O God." SATB/2 pt mxd, assembly, kybd, gtr, opt inst. GIA G-2950.

Leavitt, Paul. "The Lord Is My Shepherd." SATB. AFP 9780800678821.

Schütz, Heinrich. "O Lord, I Trust Your Shepherd Care" from *Chantry Choirbook*. SATB, org. AFP 9780800657772.

Thomson, Virgil. "My Shepherd Will Supply My Need." SATB. HWG GCMR02046.

Children's Choir

Carter, John. "The Shepherd Psalm." UE. 2 pt, kybd. HOP A555.

Patterson, Mark. "My God Is with Me" from *Young ChildrenSing*. LE. U, kybd. AFP 9780800676803.

Sleeth, Natalie. "A Little Love." UE. 2 pt, kybd. HIN HMC340.

Keyboard / Instrumental

Bender, Jan. "Sonne der Gerechtigkeit" from *Augsburg Organ Library: Easter*. Org. AFP 9780800659363.

Blair, Dallas. "Sonne der Gerechtigkeit" from *Hymn Introductions and Descants for Trumpet and Organ*, set 1. Org, tpt. MSM 20-400.

Kimball, James D. "Llanfair" from *Five Hymn Preludes*, set 2. Org. MSM 10-862.

Organ, Anne Krentz. "Sonne der Gerechtigkeit" from *Let It Rip! at the Piano*, vol. 1. Pno. AFP 9780800659066.

Handbell

Larson, Lloyd. "Come, Christians, Join to Sing." 3-5 oct, L3-. BP HB160.

McKechnie, D. Linda. "When Morning Gilds the Skies." 3-5 oct. AG 1528.

Tucker, Sondra K. "Christ the Lord Is Risen Again." 3-5 oct, opt fl/ob, tamb, L3+. AG 2350.

Praise Ensemble

■ Bullock, Geoff. "Have Faith in God" from www.ccli.com. WM/MAR.

■ Carpenter, Kelly. "Draw Me Close" from *Best of the Best, The Other Songbook 2*. FEL 1891062034.

■ Paris, Twila. "Hold Me Close" from www.praisecharts.com. INT/Mountain Spring Music.

■ Walker, Tommy. "He Knows My Name" from *WOW Worship Green Songbook*. INT 000768195567.

Global

Chichewa chorus. "Njo, Njo, Njo/Jump with Joy" from *Global Praise 2*. SATB. General Board of Global Ministries, GBGMusik 1890569224. http://new.gbgm-umc.org/resources/global praise/music/.

Halley, Paul. "Hold to God's Unchangin' Hand." SATB, pno, bass, perc. Pelagos PEL2028 www.pelagosmusic.com.

■ denotes songs that are available on iTunes®.

Monday, May 4

Monica, mother of Augustine, 387

Monica was married to a pagan husband who was ill-tempered and unfaithful. She rejoiced greatly when both her husband and his mother became Christian. But it is because she is the mother of Augustine that she is best known. Monica had been a disciple of Ambrose, and eventually Augustine came under his influence. Almost everything we know about Monica comes from Augustine's *Confessions*, his autobiography. She died far from her home, but said to her son, "Do not fret because I am buried far from our home in Africa. Nothing is far from God, and I have no fear that God will not know where to find me, when Christ comes to raise me to life at the end of the world." Her dying wish was that her son remember her at the altar of the Lord, wherever he was.

Monica's life bore witness to the vital role that parents play in the faith formation of their children. Consider how the church supports parents in that task.

Friday, May 8

Julian of Norwich, renewer of the church, c. 1416

Julian (or Juliana) was most likely a Benedictine nun living in an isolated cell attached to the Carrow Priory in Norwich (NOR-rich), England. Definite facts about her life are sparse. However, when she was about thirty years old, she reported visions that she later compiled into a book, *Sixteen Revelations of Divine Love*, a classic of medieval mysticism. The visions declared that love was the meaning of religious experience, provided by Christ who is love, for the purpose of love. A prayer of Julian is on page 87 of *Evangelical Lutheran Worship*.

Saturday, May 9

Nicolaus Ludwig von Zinzendorf, renewer of the church, hymnwriter, 1760

Count Zinzendorf was born into an aristocratic family and after the death of his father was raised by his Pietistic grandmother. This influence was a lasting one, and he moved away from what he felt was an overly intellectual Lutheranism. When he was twenty-two, a group of Moravians asked permission to live on his lands. He agreed, and they established a settlement they called Herrnhut, or "the Lord's watch." Eventually worldwide Moravian missions emanated from this community. Zinzendorf participated in these missions and is also remembered for writing hymns characteristic of his Pietistic faith (see ELW 624).

May 10, 2009
Fifth Sunday of Easter

This Sunday's image of how the risen Christ shares his life with us is the image of the vine. Christ the vine and we the branches are alive in each other, in the mystery of mutual abiding that we read of in the gospel and the first letter of John. Baptism makes us a part of Christ's living and life-giving self and makes us alive with Christ's life. As the vine brings food to the branches, Christ feeds us at his table. We are sent out to bear fruit for the life of the world.

Prayer of the Day

O God, you give us your Son as the vine apart from whom we cannot live. Nourish our life in his resurrection, that we may bear the fruit of love and know the fullness of your joy, through Jesus Christ, our Savior and Lord, who lives and reigns with you and the Holy Spirit, one God, now and forever.

Gospel Acclamation

Alleluia. I am the vine, you [|] are the branches.* Those who abide in me and I in them [|] bear much fruit. *Alleluia.* (John 15:5)

Readings and Psalm

Acts 8:26-40

Led by the Spirit, Philip encounters an Ethiopian official who is returning to his African home after having been to Jerusalem to worship. Philip uses their encounter to proclaim the gospel to him. Upon coming to faith in Jesus, the Ethiopian is baptized by Philip.

Psalm 22:25-31

All the ends of the earth shall remember and turn to the LORD. (Ps. 22:27)

1 John 4:7-21

We love God and others because God first loved us. We cannot say we love God, whom we have not seen, while hating fellow Christians, whom we regularly see. Love toward God is to be matched by love toward others because the essence of God is love.

John 15:1-8

On the night of his arrest, Jesus taught his disciples about the relationship they would have with him. Those who abide in his word and love would bear fruit, for apart from him, they could do nothing.

Color   White

CD-ROM Images

Icon Three: Easter5_B
Icon Two: Easter5_B
Icon: 096

Prayers of Intercession

Transformed by the life-giving power of the empty tomb, let us pray for the church, the world, and all those in need.
A brief silence.
Nourished by the body and blood of the resurrected Christ, let us pray that the church may reach out in love and service to all who are hungry and thirsty. Hear us, O God.
Your mercy is great.
Nourished by the abundance of creation, let us pray for plentiful rains, fertile soil, and safety for all who plant and harvest our food. Hear us, O God.
Your mercy is great.
Nourished by the freedoms of voice and vote, let us pray for just leaders and representative governments to administer fairly and equitably for all. Hear us, O God.
Your mercy is great.
Nourished by a kind word and a gentle touch, let us pray for all who are suffering in body or spirit (*especially*).
Hear us, O God.
Your mercy is great.

Nourished by the love of our mothers and of all who give motherly care, let us pray for strong bonds and tender affections in families and friendships. Hear us, O God.

Your mercy is great.

Here other intercessions may be offered.

Nourished by the fruitful lives of the saints both here and departed (*especially*), let us pray for that day when we will abide with them in Christ, joined in one great congregation. Hear us, O God.

Your mercy is great.

Hear our prayers, gracious God, and grant all that we need to live as your Spirit-filled people, in the name of the risen Christ.

Amen.

Ideas and Images for the Day

The seven "I am" sayings of Jesus in John's gospel all build up to this final one: I am the true vine. It might not seem impressive to us, but to Jesus' disciples this saying had profound meaning. Throughout the Old Testament Israel is portrayed as a vine or vineyard. The image of a vine would have meant Israel to the disciples, just as an eagle means the United States to many Americans. When Jesus says, "I am the true vine," it is not a nation, but a person, in whom we put our trust as we live out the mystery of this mutual abiding. Jesus, the vine, gives life to all those who are connected to him.

1. The Greek word for abiding (*meno*) is used eleven times in the gospel text this week and next. *Meno* carries the various meanings of *remain*, *stay*, *dwell*, *endure*, and *live*. If possible, project or hang a picture of a grown vine showing branches that are interwoven, interdependent, and even indistinguishable from one another. Let this vine provide a visual image of abiding, of the connectedness of the Christian community to Christ, and of the Christian's own *meno*-ing with Jesus the vine.

2. The question of the Ethiopian eunuch in today's first reading, "What is to prevent me from being baptized?" (Acts 8:36), and the emphasis in the gospel on Jesus being the true vine provides an opportunity to proclaim again today the centrality of baptism to a Christian's life of abiding faith. If you have a baptism today, even better.

3. The *Star Wars* movies have made the concept of "the Force" part of popular culture. Compare and contrast the concept of the Force with the concept of abiding as presented in today's second reading and gospel.

4. Bruce Wilkinson has based three Bible studies in his *Secrets of the Vine* series on this text from John 15. First, if your life consistently bears no fruit, God will intervene to discipline you. Second, if your life bears some fruit, God will intervene to prune you. Third, if your life bears a lot of fruit, God will invite you to abide more deeply with God's own self (*Secrets of the Vine: Breaking through to Abundance*, Sisters, Oregon: Multnomah Press, 2001).

Hymns for Worship
Gathering

Alleluia! Jesus is risen!   ELW 377, WOV 674
There in God's garden   ELW 342, WOV 668

Hymn of the Day

O blessed spring   ELW 447, WOV 695   *BERGLUND*
Alleluia! Jesus is risen!   ELW 377, WOV 674, TFF 91   *EARTH AND ALL STARS*
Like the murmur of the dove's song   ELW 403, WOV 685   *BRIDEGROOM*

Communion

Like the murmur of the dove's song   ELW 403, WOV 685
We raise our hands to you, O Lord   ELW 690
Thine the amen   ELW 826, WOV 801

Sending

We know that Christ is raised   ELW 449, LBW 189
Now all the vault of heaven resounds   ELW 367, LBW 143

Additional Hymns and Songs

Amid the world's bleak wilderness   LBW 378
I heard an old, old story   TFF 97
The branch that bends with clustered fruit   HG 25
I've just come from the fountain   TFF 111, WOV 696
Lord, let my heart be good soil   ELW 512, WOV 713

Music for the Day
Psalmody and Acclamations

Miller, Aaron David. *Gospel Acclamations for Lent–Holy Trinity.* AFP 9780800635589.

Mummert, Mark. "Psalm 22" from *Psalm Settings for the Church Year.* AFP 9780800678562.

Psalter for Worship Year B, Evangelical Lutheran Worship Edition. AFP 9780806683839.

Choral

Ashdown, Franklin D. "As the Branch Is to the Vine." SATB, opt assembly, org. SMP 10/3071S.

Benson, Robert A. "Let All the World in Every Corner Sing." SATB, org. AFP 9780800638825.

▫ Farlee, Robert Buckley. "O Blessed Spring." SATB, opt assembly, org, ob/vln/cl. AFP 9780800654245. *The Augsburg Choirbook*. AFP 9780800656782.

Ferguson, John. "Christ the Lord Is Risen Today!" SATB, drm, picc. AFP 9780800646363.

Norris, Brad. "An Easter Song of Praise." SATB, org. AFP 9780800678937.

Wagner, Douglas E. "For Love Shall Be Our Song." U, kybd, opt fl. CG A389.

Children's Choir

Brighton, James. "Tune My Heart." UE. U, pno, opt fl. CG A1101.

Jothen, Michael. "I Will Give Thanks." LE. U, pno, opt fl. BP 1101.

Schram, Ruth Elaine. "Now All the Vault of Heaven Resounds." 2 pt, kybd, opt C inst. AFP 9780800678388.

Sleeth, Natalie. "Everywhere I Go." UE. U/2 pt, pno, opt fl. CG A171.

Keyboard / Instrumental

Burkhardt, Michael. "Earth and All Stars" from *Praise and Thanksgiving Hymn Improvisations*, vol. 2. Org. MSM 10-752.

Cherwien, David. "Berglund" from *Organ Plus One*. Org, C/B-flat inst. AFP 9780800656188.

Dahl, David P. "Bridegroom" from *Hymn Interpretations for Organ*. Org. AFP 9780800658243.

Organ, Anne Krentz. "Berglund" from *On Eagle's Wings: Piano Reflections*. Pno. AFP 9780800655525.

Handbell

Behnke. John A. "O Waly, Waly." 2-3 oct, opt fl, L3. AFP 9780800657406.

Organ, Anne Krentz, arr. "Earth and All Stars and Alleluia! Jesus Is Risen." 3 oct hb/hc, L2. AFP 9780800658083.

Wagner, Douglas E. "Christ the Lord Is Risen Today." 3-5 oct, L2. AG 1189.

Praise Ensemble

■ Barnett, Maria. "Breathe" from *WOW Worship Green Songbook*. INT 000768195567.

■ Cash, Ed/Matt Redman/Chris Tomlin. "How Can I Keep from Singing" from WT. WT/Sixsteps Music/Alletrop Music/Thankyou Music.

■ Doerksen, Brian. "Come, Now Is the Time to Worship" from *I Could Sing of Your Love Forever 2*. WT 0000809251.

■ Fitts, Bob. "Amen" from www.ccli.com. INT.

Global

Hayes, Mark. "Welcome Table." SATB, kybd. AFP 9780800676032.

Helgen, John. "You Are Holy." SATB, kybd, perc. AFP 9780800676452.

Thursday, May 14

Matthias, Apostle

After Christ's ascension, the apostles met in Jerusalem to choose a replacement for Judas. Matthias was chosen over Joseph Justus by the casting of lots. Little is known about Matthias, and little is reported about him in the account of his election in Acts 1:15-26. Matthias traveled among the disciples from the time of Jesus' baptism until his ascension. His task, after he was enrolled among the eleven remaining disciples, was to bear witness to the resurrection.

Matthias was formerly commemorated on February 24, though the reason for that date is not known. More recently the Roman Catholic Church moved the celebration to May 14, so that it falls after the celebration of Jesus' resurrection, when Matthias was chosen as an apostle.

▫ denotes choral suggestions that relate to the hymn of the day.
■ denotes songs that are available on iTunes®.

190

May 17, 2009
Sixth Sunday of Easter

This Sunday's image of the life the risen Christ shares with us is the image of friendship. We are called to serve others as Jesus came to serve; but for John's gospel, the image of servanthood is too hierarchical, too distant, to capture the essence of life with Christ. Friendship captures the love, the joy, the deep mutuality of the relationship into which Christ invites us. The Greeks believed that true friends are willing to die for each other. This is the mutual love of Christian community commanded by Christ and enabled by the Spirit.

Prayer of the Day

O God, you have prepared for those who love you joys beyond understanding. Pour into our hearts such love for you that, loving you above all things, we may obtain your promises, which exceed all we can desire; through Jesus Christ, your Son and our Lord, who lives and reigns with you and the Holy Spirit, one God, now and forever.

Gospel Acclamation

Alleluia. Those who love me will keep my word, and my Fa-
I ther will love them,* and we will come to them and make our I home with them. *Alleluia.* (John 14:23)

Readings and Psalm

Acts 10:44-48

While Peter shares the good news of Jesus with a Gentile soldier and his family, the Holy Spirit comes upon them. Recognizing that the Spirit works inclusively in the lives of both Jews and Gentiles, Peter commands that these Gentiles also be baptized in the name of Jesus Christ.

Psalm 98

Shout with joy to the LORD, all you lands. (Ps. 98:4)

1 John 5:1-6

God's children believe that Jesus is the Messiah and love God by keeping God's commandments. Thus the world is conquered not through military might but through love and faith.

John 15:9-17

On the night of his arrest, Jesus delivers a final testimony to his disciples to help them in the days ahead. Here, he repeats the most important of all his commands, that they love one another.

Color White

CD-ROM Images

Icon Three: Easter6_B
Icon Two: Easter6_B
Icon: 097

Prayers of Intercession

Transformed by the life-giving power of the empty tomb, let us pray for the church, the world, and all those in need.
A brief silence.
Called to a love that exceeds our understanding or desire, let us pray for the church to embody Christ's perfect love in an imperfect world. Hear us, O God.
Your mercy is great.
Called to a love that requires difficult choices and decisions, let us pray for self-discipline and forethought to live within the limits of creation's resources. Hear us, O God.
Your mercy is great.
Called to a love that yearns for peace and reconciliation, let us pray for tolerance and respect between peoples of different cultures and creeds. Hear us, O God.
Your mercy is great.
Called to a love that reaches out to the vulnerable and the fearful, let us pray for the very young, the very old, those in distress, and those who are ill (*especially*). Hear us, O God.
Your mercy is great.
Called to a love that bears fruit in action and service, let us pray for the right use of gifts in this congregation to welcome the stranger, to feed the hungry, and to visit the homebound (*especially*). Hear us, O God.
Your mercy is great.
Here other intercessions may be offered.

Called to a love that transcends time and place, let us give thanks for all the saints who have served the church in faithfulness (*especially*), that at the last we will join with them in the perfect love and joy of heaven. Hear us, O God. **Your mercy is great.**

Hear our prayers, gracious God, and grant all that we need to live as your Spirit-filled people, in the name of the risen Christ. **Amen.**

Ideas and Images for the Day

What is a friend? Is she someone with whom you spend time, play, and share sleepovers as children? Is he someone with whom you can race bikes, or just share the fun and rush of life? "Show me your friends and I'll show you your future," some say. When we baptize infants and young children we ask their parents to continue in the covenant God made with them. We are asking them to choose Jesus as their friend. When couples say "I do," we ask them to choose Jesus as their friend. Jesus, our friend, gathers with us this day, supports and encourages us, and rekindles the gifts of God within us.

1. Being a "friend of God" needs to be carefully articulated so that we are not preaching Jesus as your buddy. An Easter faith is not a feeling, sensation, emotion, or impression. An Easter faith is not a formula with guaranteed results. Rather, an Easter faith is a friendship with Jesus Christ as Lord of your life. It is not a bunch of rules, nor an agenda, but a *relationship*: "I have called you friends, because I have made known to you everything that I have heard from my Father" (John 15:15).

2. A sermon today might be built around the acronym ASAP. How do we become friends of God? Not just As Soon As Possible but also in these ways: Acknowledge God's sovereignty. Seek to do God's will. Accept personal responsibility and accountability. Place Jesus first.

3. *Joy* is a "high level" word that we don't typically use in everyday conversation, because joy describes something from beyond. We may enjoy something, but joy is a borderline transcendent feeling that doesn't distinguish between the spiritual and the physical. Jesus wishes for his joy to be *in us* and to be complete. Joy can be seen in the eyes and felt in the heart. Joy is rare, but when it is experienced it is deeply treasured.

4. If your worship space has a screen, project images of joy and friendship during the gospel reading. Or, during the offering, project a show of joyful images accompanied by a live or recorded performance of "Joyful, joyful we adore thee" (ELW 836) or J.S. Bach's "Jesu, Joy of Man's Desiring."

Hymns for Worship
Gathering
Goodness is stronger than evil   ELW 721
O God beyond all praising   ELW 880
What wondrous love is this   ELW 666, LBW 385

Hymn of the Day
Great God, your love has called us   ELW 358, WOV 666
  RYBURN
Where true charity and love abide   ELW 653   UBI CARITAS
Christ is risen! Shout hosanna!   ELW 383   TURNBULL

Communion
Draw us in the Spirit's tether   ELW 470, WOV 703
Jesus loves me!   ELW 595
Blest be the tie that binds   ELW 656, LBW 370

Sending
We Are Called   ELW 720
O Christ, your heart, compassionate   ELW 722
Joyful, joyful we adore thee   ELW 836, LBW 551

Additional Hymns and Songs
A new commandment   WOV 664
No Greater Love   GC 607
The call is clear and simple   GC 604
Called together and united   MBW 624

Music for the Day
Psalmody and Acclamations
Anderson, Mark. "Psalm 98" from *Psalm Settings for the Church Year.* AFP 9780800678562.

Miller, Aaron David. *Gospel Acclamations for Lent–Holy Trinity.* AFP 9780800635589.

Psalter for Worship Year B, Evangelical Lutheran Worship Edition. AFP 9780806683839.

Choral
▫ Duruflé, Maurice. "Ubi Caritas." SATB, div. DUR 50561414.

Harris, William Henry. "This Joyful Eastertide." SATB, org. NOV 29.0151.

Haugen, Marty/arr. Jeremy J. Bankson. "Soli Deo Gloria." SATB, org, assembly, opt br qt, timp. AFP 9780800678852.

Hobby, Robert A. "Now All the Vault of Heaven Resounds/Ye Watchers and Ye Holy Ones." SAB, assembly, org, opt 2 tpt, opt hb. AFP 9780800658656.

Nelson, Ronald A. "If You Love One Another." U/SA, kybd. SEL 422-841.

▫ denotes choral suggestions that relate to the hymn of the day.
■ denotes songs that are available on iTunes®.

Children's Choir

Benson, Robert A. "What Shall We Give to God?" U, kybd, opt desc/C inst. AFP 9780800678333.

Hruby, Dolores M. "Celebrate This Happy, Holy Day." LE. U, kybd, opt C inst. CG A587.

Sleeth, Natalie. "Sing the Lord's Song." UE. 3 pt, kybd, hb. HIN HMC625.

Wilson, Mark. "Come as a Child." UE. 2 pt, pno. HIN HMC427.

Keyboard / Instrumental

Farlee, Robert Buckley. "Ryburn" from *Let It Rip! at the Piano*, vol. 2. Pno. AFP 9780800675806.

Haan, Raymond H. "Ubi caritas" from *Pilgrimage*. Org. AFP 9780800677527.

Hamilton, Gregory. "Ryburn" from *Give Praise to the Risen Lord*. Pno. AFP 9780800623487.

Lasky, David. "Ubi caritas" from *Augsburg Organ Library: Baptism and Communion*. Org. AFP 9780800623555.

Handbell

McMichael, Catherine. "Contemplation on 'Ubi Caritas'." 3-6 oct, opt 3 oct hc, L3+. AG 36036.

Moklebust, Cathy. "A Time to Rejoice." 3-5 oct, 2 fl, L3+. CG B342.

Rogers, Sharon Elery. "Easter Medley." 3-5 oct, L3+. JEF MJHS9266.

Praise Ensemble

- Brown, Brenton/Brian Doerksen. "Hallelujah (Your Love Is Amazing)" from www.praisecharts.com. VIN.

- Carpenter, Kelly. "Draw Me Close" from *Best of the Best, The Other Songbook 2*. FEL 1891062034.

- Muchow, Rich. "All About Love" from www.ccli.com. Encouraging Music.

- Zschech, Darlene. "Shout to the Lord" from *Shout to the Lord 2000 Songbook*. Hosanna! Music 14247. ELW 821, W&P 124.

Global

Hesla, Bret. "Shout Unto God" from *Justice, Like a Base of Stone*. SATB, cant, gtr. AFP 9780800623562.

Loperena, William/Bread for the Journey. "Le lo le lo lay lo" from *Pave the Way, Global Songs 3*. Cant, assembly, pno, gtr, perc. AFP 9780800676896.

Monday, May 18

Erik, King of Sweden, Martyr, 1160

Erik, long considered the patron saint of Sweden, ruled from 1150 to 1160. He is honored for efforts to bring peace to the nearby pagan kingdoms and for his crusades to spread the Christian faith in Scandinavia. He established a protected Christian mission in Finland that was led by Henry of Uppsala. As king, Erik was noted for his desire to establish fair laws and courts and for his concern for the poor and sick. Erik was killed by a Danish army that approached him at worship on the day after the Ascension. He is reported to have said, "Let us at least finish the sacrifice. The rest of the feast I shall keep elsewhere." As he left worship he was killed.

The commemoration of Erik could be the beginning of a discussion on the relationship between civil rule and the place of faith in the public sphere.

May 21, 2009
Ascension of Our Lord

In today's gospel the risen Christ ascends into heaven and his followers are assured that the Spirit will empower them to be witnesses throughout the earth. The disciples were told to not gaze up into heaven to look for Jesus; we find his presence among us as we proclaim the word and share the Easter feast. We too long for the Spirit to enliven our faith and invigorate our mission.

Today the church commemorates Helena, the mother of Constantine.

Prayer of the Day

Almighty God, your only Son was taken into the heavens and in your presence intercedes for us. Receive us and our prayers for all the world, and in the end bring everything into your glory, through Jesus Christ, our Sovereign and Lord, who lives and reigns with you and the Holy Spirit, one God, now and forever.

or

Almighty God, your blessed Son, our Savior Jesus Christ, ascended far above all heavens that he might fill all things. Mercifully give us faith to trust that, as he promised, he abides with us on earth to the end of time, who lives and reigns with you and the Holy Spirit, one God, now and forever.

Gospel Acclamation

Alleluia. Go and make disciples of all nations, | says the Lord;* I am with you always, to the end | of the age. *Alleluia.* (Matt. 28:19, 20)

Readings and Psalm

Acts 1:1-11

Before he is lifted into heaven, Jesus promises that the missionary work of the disciples will spread out from Jerusalem to all the world. His words provide an outline of the book of Acts.

Psalm 47

God has gone up with a shout. (Ps. 47:5)

or Psalm 93

Ever since the world began, your throne has been established. (Ps. 93:2)

Ephesians 1:15-23

The risen and exalted Christ reigns over the entire universe. The author of Ephesians prays that we would be given the wisdom to comprehend this and display it through love toward others.

Luke 24:44-53

On the day of his ascension, Jesus leaves his disciples with a commission, a blessing, and a promise of the Holy Spirit.

Color   White

CD-ROM Images

Icon Three: Ascension01_ABC, Ascension02_ABC, Ascension03_ABC
Icon Two: Ascension01_ABC, Ascension02_ABC
Icon: 034, 165

Prayers of Intercession

Transformed by the life-giving power of the empty tomb, let us pray for the church, the world, and all those in need.
A brief silence.

Ascended Christ, present to all who are gathered in your name, open our hearts and minds to know and understand the promises and joys of your heavenly reign.
Hear us, O God.
Your mercy is great.

Ascended Christ, present in the continuous birth and renewal of creation, wash over all that is fallen with the cleansing and life-giving waters of your Spirit.
Hear us, O God.
Your mercy is great.

Ascended Christ, present in the midst of all who cry out for mercy, raise up leaders who care more for justice than power, more for compassion than self-interest.

Hear us, O God.
Your mercy is great.
Ascended Christ, present for those in need of your care and healing, lay your hands on the fearful, the brokenhearted, and all who are sick (*especially*) and anoint them with your saving grace. Hear us, O God.
Your mercy is great.
Ascended Christ, present in the ministries of this congregation, send us forth (*like Helena, mother of Constantine,*) to serve the poor in love and faithfulness. Hear us, O God.
Your mercy is great.
Here other intercessions may be offered.
Ascended Christ, present in ages past and ages yet to come, join us with all your saints (*especially*), that we may be gathered together in the presence of your eternal throne. Hear us, O God.
Your mercy is great.
Hear our prayers, gracious God, and grant all that we need to live as your Spirit-filled people, in the name of the risen Christ.
Amen.

Ideas and Images for the Day

We know we are not alone; this is a promise of our faith. Jesus built a community that grew from a ragtag bunch of men and women into the whole church. For this to happen Jesus had to ascend to the Father, and the Spirit had to descend to us. Jesus' ascension brings about joy, worship, and blessing: the disciples returned to Jerusalem and were continually in the temple giving thanks to God. Every time we gather as a church we reenact this moment of joy and hope. Church is the place where we are most reminded of the gift of community that Christ made possible for us. And each time we are sent from the places where we gather, we do so with the purpose of spreading joy.

1. "Where did it go?" is a game we play with toddlers by hiding a favorite toy and seeing if they can find it. It is a milestone in their development when they recognize that even when something is gone from their sight, it still exists. Even though the disciples can't see Jesus anymore, they have reached a milestone in their faith: they know that Jesus is still with them. Likewise, even though we cannot see Jesus, we know that he is present in our lives.

2. Our communities of faith include more than the members of our individual congregations. Just because we can't see our brothers and sisters in Christ who live across the world doesn't mean they aren't part of our communities. The Companion Synods Program estab-lishes relationships between the sixty-five synods of the Evangelical Lutheran Church in America and its international companion churches around the world. Where is your sister synod? How does your congregation reach out to *this* part of its community? What about the ecumenical community in your area? Read more about the Companion Synods Program (including churches seeking a companion synod relationship) at www.elca.org/companionsynod/.

3. The angels who appear to the disciples after the ascension ask why they are looking up. The disciples weren't meant to stay stagnant, but to look forward and around them. Where is your congregation's focus? Is it in reaching out to others or does it stare up into empty space?

4. Does your font have water in it, or does it stay dry unless there is going to be a baptism? Baptism connects us to one another and to God as a community. Make a point of putting water in your font every time the community gathers. Pour it in during a thanksgiving for baptism or during the ritual of confession and forgiveness. Consider gathering the assembly around the font at the sending portion of this service. Remember the gift of baptism by making a sign of the cross on one another's foreheads with water from the font before the dismissal.

Hymns for Worship
Gathering

Rejoice, for Christ is king!   ELW 430, LBW 171
Crown him with many crowns   ELW 855, LBW 170

Hymn of the Day

Alleluia! Sing to Jesus   ELW 392, LBW 158   HYFRYDOL
A hymn of glory let us sing!   ELW 393, LBW 157
   LASST UNS ERFREUEN
O Christ, our hope   ELW 604, LBW 300
   LOBT GOTT, IHR CHRISTEN

Communion

Blessing, Honor, and Glory   ELW 433
The head that once was crowned   ELW 432, LBW 173

Sending

Hail thee, festival day! (Ascension)   ELW 394, LBW 142
Christ is alive! Let Christians sing   ELW 389, LBW 363
O Christ, our hope   ELW 604, LBW 300

Additional Hymns and Songs

Go to the world!   GC 469

Rejoice in the mission   W&P 120

Christ high-ascended, now in glory seated   LSB 840

For all the world   MBW 629

We praise thee, O God   TFF 100

Music for the Day
Psalmody and Acclamations

Colligan, Richard Bruxvoort. "Psalm 47" from *Psalm Settings for the Church Year*. AFP 9780800678562.

Miller, Aaron David. *Gospel Acclamations for Lent–Holy Trinity.* AFP 9780800635589.

Psalter for Worship Year B, Evangelical Lutheran Worship Edition. AFP 9780806683839.

Choral

Finzi, Gerald. "God Is Gone Up." SATB, div, org. B&H M-060-03028-4.

Fleming, Larry L. "Lord of the Dance." SATB. AFP 9780800655358.

◻ Pelz, Walter L. "Alleluia! Sing to Jesus." SATB, assembly, org, br, timp, opt hb. CPH 98-3185.

Roberts, William Bradley. "In All These You Welcomed Me." U, org, opt ob/other inst. AFP 9786000001209. *Augsburg Easy Choirbook*, vol. 2. AFP 9780800677510.

Children's Choir

Bedford, Michael. "Let All the Peoples Praise You, O God." UE. 2 pt, pno, fl. CG A933.

Ferguson, John. "Jesus, My Lord and God." UE. U/2 pt, org. AFP 9780800646196.

Leaf, Robert. "To the Glory of Our King." LE. U, pno/org. CG A173.

Keyboard / Instrumental

Bach, J. S. "Lobt Gott, Ihr Christen" from *Fourteen Chorale Preludes for Organ or Harpsichord*. Org/hpd. CPH 97-5130U1.

Blair, Dallas. "Lasst uns erfreuen" from *Hymn Introductions and Descants for Trumpet and Organ*, set 2. Org, tpt. MSM 20-702.

Ferguson, John. "Hyfrydol" from *Festival Hymns*, set III. Org, br qrt. GIA G-4124.

Manz, Paul. "Hyfrydol" from *Improvisations on Great Hymns of Faith*. Org. MSM 10-839.

Handbell

Hanna, Donna. "Prelude on 'Hyfrydol'." 3-5 oct, L2+. GIA G-7210.

Honoré, Jeffrey. "On Eagle's Wings." 3-5 oct, L2+. CPH 97-6429.

Moklebust, Cathy. "Lift High the Cross." 3-5 oct, org, opt br, L2. CG B193.

Praise Ensemble

■ Beeching, Vicky/Ed Cash. "Join the Song" from www.musicnotes.com. Thankyou Music/Alletrop Music.

■ Mullins, Rich. "Awesome God" from *Breakforth Worship Songbook*. New Creation Ministries. www.new-creation.net.

■ Ruis, David. "You're Worthy of My Praise" from www.praisecharts.com. MAR/Shade Tree Music.

■ Tomlin, Chris. "How Great Is Our God" from www.praisecharts.com.

Global

Hawkins, Walter. "I'm Goin' Up a Yonder." SATB, pno. HAL 48004366.

Toolan, Suzanne. "I Am the Bread of Life." SATB, cant, kybd, gtr. GIA G-5032.

Thursday, May 21

Helena, mother of Constantine, 330

Wife of the co-regent of the West, Helena (or Helen) was mother of Constantine, who later became the Roman emperor. After he was converted to Christianity, he influenced her also to become Christian. From that point she lived an exemplary life of faith, particularly through acts of generosity toward the poor. She is also remembered for traveling through Palestine and building churches on the sites she believed to be where Jesus was born, where he was buried, and from which he ascended.

◻ denotes choral suggestions that relate to the hymn of the day.
■ denotes songs that are available on iTunes®.

196

May 24, 2009
Seventh Sunday of Easter

The gospel for Easter's seventh Sunday is always taken from the long prayer Jesus prays for his followers in John's gospel on the night before his death, and always includes Jesus' desire that his followers will be one as he and the Father are one. This oneness is not mere doctrinal agreement or institutional unity, but mutual abiding, interpenetrating life, mutual love and joy. This oneness is the work of the Spirit whom we have received but also await. Come, Holy Spirit!

Today the church commemorates the scientists Nicolaus Copernicus and Leonhard Euler.

Prayer of the Day

Gracious and glorious God, you have chosen us as your own, and by the powerful name of Christ you protect us from evil. By your Spirit transform us and your beloved world, that we may find our joy in your Son, Jesus Christ, our Savior and Lord, who lives and reigns with you and the Holy Spirit, one God, now and forever.

Gospel Acclamation

Alleluia. I will not leave you orphaned, | says the Lord.*
I am com- | ing to you. *Alleluia*. (John 14:18)

Readings and Psalm

Acts 1:15-17, 21-26

In the days between Jesus' ascension and Pentecost, Peter oversees the process whereby one of the members of the community of believers is chosen to be the twelfth apostle, in order to fill the vacancy created by Judas' treachery and death.

Psalm 1

The LORD knows the way of the righteous. (Ps. 1:6)

1 John 5:9-13

God has borne witness to the gift of eternal life in Jesus Christ. Whoever believes in the Son of God believes in the witness of God and has the promise of eternal life.

John 17:6-19

In this reading the church hears Jesus' words on the night before his death. This gospel reports the words of Jesus' prayer, a prayer for his disciples and for all who would believe in him through their words.

Color   White

CD-ROM Images

Icon Three: Easter7_B
Icon Two: Easter7_02_ABC
Icon: 035

Prayers of Intercession

Transformed by the life-giving power of the empty tomb, let us pray for the church, the world, and all those in need.
A brief silence.
Sent to represent Christ in the world, let us pray for the church to be light in a world of darkness, hope in an age of despair. Hear us, O God.
Your mercy is great.
Sent to be fruitful in obeying God's word, let us pray for reforestation efforts that seek to reclaim desolate and barren lands. Hear us, O God.
Your mercy is great.
Sent to work for peace and justice for all people, let us pray for the safety and well-bring of all who serve in the military (*especially*), remembering all who have given their lives in service for the good of the nation (*especially*).
Hear us, O God.
Your mercy is great.
Sent to bring compassion and encouragement to all who are hurting, let us pray for the mentally ill, those bound by addiction, and all who are troubled in body or spirit (*especially*). Hear us, O God.
Your mercy is great.
Sent to use our gifts for the betterment of the world, let us pray for scientists and scholars who (*like Nicolaus Copernicus and Leonhard Euler*) ponder life's mysteries and search for new solutions and possibilities. Hear us, O God.
Your mercy is great.

Here other intercessions may be offered.

Sent to live a new life in Christ, let us pray for the dying and those who mourn (*especially*), rejoicing that at the end we will be united with them and all the faithful in the great and heavenly feast. Hear us, O God.

Your mercy is great.

Hear our prayers, gracious God, and grant all that we need to live as your Spirit-filled people, in the name of the risen Christ.

Amen.

Ideas and Images for the Day

"Holy Father, protect them in your name that you have given me, so that they may be one, as we are one" (John 17:11b). As we hear the prayer of Jesus for his disciples and, by inference, the church, we hear him looking toward his return to the Father (celebrated three days ago on Ascension Day). We hear Jesus looking forward to the church's presence and activity in the world. Yet he says his disciples are not of the world. The world seems under the power of the "evil one." By contrast, the disciples are under the power of God's love. Unified under Jesus' influence, they are protected from the power of evil.

1. Male emperor penguins incubate their eggs while the females travel to the ocean for food. The males crowd together in a mass of oneness, taking turns standing on the periphery of the circle to provide a barrier against the weather and keeping those on interior warm. This oneness serves as protection from the ferocious winter storms and cold that surround them for months. This unity also makes it possible to achieve their common goal of bringing to birth a future generation. The church exhibits this kind of unity when it acts as Christ's presence in the world.

2. What does it mean to have Christ's joy in us? Sing "Joyful, joyful, we adore thee" (ELW 836, LBW 551) as a corporate expression of the joy Christ has made complete in each of us.

3. Pilate makes an age-old question famous when he asks Jesus "What is truth?" (John 18:38). As Christians we are sanctified in the truth of Christ. This truth is more than the moral lesson taught to kids about telling the truth. It is the essence of God. Like a potter's clay, we are molded and shaped into God's truth through sanctification.

4. The church's mission is to be sent out from the comfort and support of the community into a world hungry for knowing God's truth. The faith community serves as a stable presence to keep us supported in our journey. Rock climbing is a popular sport today. A key technique of staying safe is being "on belay." This term is used to describe how one person supports another climber through the use of ropes and clips that keep the climber from falling too far if their feet should slip. The person on belay either sits on top of the wall while the climber descends, releasing rope as needed; or, if several climbers are climbing a steep mountain, they will use a system of ropes and clips and take turns being on belay.

Hymns for Worship

Gathering

Christ is made the sure foundation   ELW 645, WOV 747
Come now, O Prince of peace   ELW 247
Like the murmur of the dove's song   ELW 403, WOV 685

Hymn of the Day

Lord, who the night you were betrayed   ELW 463, LBW 206   SONG 1
Son of God, eternal Savior   ELW 655, LBW 364   IN BABILONE
I come with joy   ELW 482   DOVE OF PEACE

Communion

Blest be the tie that binds   ELW 656, LBW 370
We are all one in Christ   ELW 643
One bread, one body   ELW 496, WOV 710

Sending

We all are one in mission   ELW 576, WOV 755
Christ is the king!   ELW 662, LBW 386

Additional Hymns and Songs

How lovely on the mountains   TFF 99
Sing hallelujah, praise the Lord   MBW 543
For all the world   HG 34
You Are Mine   ELW 581, W&P 158

Music for the Day

Psalmody and Acclamations

Miller, Aaron David. *Gospel Acclamations for Lent–Holy Trinity.* AFP 9780800635589.

Psalter for Worship Year B, Evangelical Lutheran Worship Edition. AFP 9780806683839.

Wold, Wayne L. "Psalm 1" from *Psalm Settings for the Church Year.* AFP 9780800678562.

Choral

Ferguson, John. "Jesus, My Lord and God." U, org. AFP 9780800646196.

Handel, G. F. "All My Spirit Longs to Savor" from *Chantry Choir-book*. SATB, kybd. AFP 9780800657772.

Helgen, John. "I Come with Joy." 2 pt mxd, org. AFP 9780800677145.

Keesecker, Thomas. "That All May Be One." SATB, pno, opt int, assembly. AFP 9780800678739.

Children's Choir

Artman, Ruth. "Prayer of the Norwegian Child." UE. 2 pt, pno, opt fl, hb. HAL 08596454.

Lindh, Jody W. "Praise the Lord Who Reigns Above." UE. U, pno, opt hb, tamb, 2 xyl. CG A583.

Patterson, Mark. "I Will Give My Heart to the Lord" from *Young Children Sing*. LE. U, kybd, opt hc/glock. AFP 9780800676803.

Keyboard / Instrumental

Adams, Robert Train. "Dove of Peace" from *I Come with Joy*. Pno. AFP 9780800678494.

Helman, Michael. "Trumpet Tune on 'Mit Freuden zart'" from *Trumpet Tunes on Hymns*. Org. AFP 9780800678753.

Manz, Paul O. "Prelude on 'In Babilone'." Org. MSM 10-874.

Miller, Aaron David/Mark Sedio. "Dove of Peace" from *Pull Out the Stops*, vol. 2. Org. AFP 9780800677688.

Weber, Paul D. "Song 1" from *Hymn Preludes for Holy Communion*, vol. III. Org. CPH 97-5488.

Handbell

Leavitt, John. "A Joyful Flourish." 3 oct, L2. CPH 97-6867.

Praise Ensemble

- Denning, Troy/John G. Waller. "The Blessing" from www.greatworshipsongs.com. New Spring/John Waller Publishing/Troy Denning.
- Strasser, David (Beaker). "Step by Step" from www.praisecharts.com. W&P 132.
- Tomlin, Chris. "Forever" from WT. WT/Sixsteps Music.
- Zschech, Darlene. "All Things Are Possible" from *WOW Worship Green Songbook*. INT 000768195567.

Global

Hassell, Michael. "Mayenziwe/Your Will Be Done." SATB, kybd. AFP 9780800676254.

Hopson, Hal H. "Halle, Halle, Halle." SAB, perc. HOP C5038.

Sunday, May 24
Nicolaus Copernicus, 1543; Leonhard Euler, 1783; scientists

Remembering scientists such as Copernicus and Euler offers an opportunity to ponder the mysteries of the universe and the grandeur of God's creation. Copernicus is an example of a renaissance person. He formally studied astronomy, math-

■ denotes songs that are available on iTunes®.

ematics, Greek, Plato, law, medicine, and canon law. He also had interests in theology, poetry, and the natural and social sciences. Copernicus is chiefly remembered for his work as an astronomer and his idea that the sun, not the earth, is the center of the solar system.

Euler (OY-ler) is regarded as one of the founders of the science of pure mathematics and made important contributions to mechanics, hydrodynamics, astronomy, optics, and acoustics.

Include Psalm 8 as a devotion for parish meetings today. It praises God for the wonder of creation and at the same time ponders the mystery of God's care for all people and is a fitting commemoration for the work of Copernicus and Euler.

Wednesday, May 27
John Calvin, renewer of the church, 1564

John Calvin began his studies in theology at the University of Paris when he was fourteen. In his mid-twenties he experienced a conversion that led him to embrace the views of the Reformation. His theological ideas are systematically laid out in his *Institutes of the Christian Religion*. He is also well known for his commentaries on scripture. He was a preacher in Geneva, was banished once, and then later returned to reform the city with a rigid, theocratic discipline.

Calvin is considered the father of the Reformed churches. Hold up the ecumenical agreement the Evangelical Lutheran Church in America shares with churches of the Reformed tradition as an example of the unity we share in Christ.

Friday, May 29
Jiří Tranovský, hymnwriter, 1637

Jiří Tranovský (YEAR-zhee truh-NOF-skee) is considered the "Luther of the Slavs" and the father of Slovak hymnody. Trained at the University of Wittenberg in the early seventeenth century, Tranovský was ordained in 1616 and spent his life preaching and teaching in Prague, Silesia, and finally Slovakia. He produced a translation of the Augsburg Confession and published his hymn collection *Cithara Sanctorum* (Lyre of the Saints), the foundation of Slovak Lutheran hymnody.

Use the commemoration to pray for the Slovak church and to give thanks for the gifts of church musicians. Use Tranovský's "Your Heart, O God, Is Grieved" (ELW 602) as a sung confession and forgiveness at parish gatherings today.

May 30, 2009
Vigil of Pentecost

At this liturgy we gather in vigilant prayer as the disciples did in the days preceding Pentecost. Our world waits for an end to war and violence. The whole creation waits for an end to suffering. With undying hope we pray for the crowning gift of Easter—the Spirit of the risen Christ among us.

Prayer of the Day

Almighty and ever-living God, you fulfilled the promise of Easter by sending the gift of your Holy Spirit. Look upon your people gathered in prayer, open to receive the Spirit's flame. May it come to rest in our hearts and heal the divisions of word and tongue, that with one voice and one song we may praise your name in joy and thanksgiving; through Jesus Christ, our Savior and Lord, who lives and reigns with you and the Holy Spirit, one God, now and forever.

Gospel Acclamation

Alleluia. Come, Holy Spirit, fill the hearts ⎸ of your faithful,* and kindle in us the fire ⎸ of your love. *Alleluia.*

Readings and Psalm

Exodus 19:1-9

At Sinai God assured Israel that they were God's prized possession and commissioned them to serve as mediating priests for the nations. God's word spoken to Moses is the basis of the people's trust.

or Acts 2:1-11

Believers are filled with the Spirit to tell God's deeds.

Psalm 33:12-22

The LORD is our helper and our shield. (Ps. 33:20)

or Psalm 130

There is forgiveness with you. (Ps. 130:4)

Romans 8:14-17, 22-27

The Holy Spirit has made us God's children who eagerly await the glorious future God has prepared for all of creation. Although we cannot fully see what God has in store for us and creation, we eagerly anticipate it in hope. Even when we are unable to pray, the same Spirit prays for us.

John 7:37-39

Jesus describes the Holy Spirit as living water, quenching the thirst of all who come to him and filling the hearts of believers till they overflow.

Color   Red

CD-ROM Images

Icon Three: Pentecost_Vigil_ABC
Icon Two: Pentecost_Vigil_ABC
Icon: 036

May 31, 2009
Day of Pentecost

On the fiftieth day of Easter we celebrate the Spirit, through whom and in whom the people of God are created and re-created. Pentecost is sometimes called the church's birthday, but might more appropriately be called its baptism day, since the gift of the Spirit is the fullness of baptism. Ezekiel's vision shows the Spirit resurrecting and re-creating not just individuals but a whole people. Romans makes it clear that God is in the process of re-creating the entire cosmos; yet the Spirit is also at work in the most intimate and personal way, praying in us "with sighs too deep for words" when we do not know how to pray.

The observance of the festival of the Visit of Mary to Elizabeth is transferred this year to June 1.

Prayer of the Day

Mighty God, you breathe life into our bones, and your Spirit brings truth to the world. Send us this Spirit, transform us by your truth, and give us language to proclaim your gospel, through Jesus Christ, our Savior and Lord, who lives and reigns with you and the Holy Spirit, one God, now and forever.

Gospel Acclamation

Alleluia. Come, Holy Spirit, fill the hearts | of your faithful,* and kindle in us the fire | of your love. *Alleluia.*

Readings and Psalm

Acts 2:1-21

Originally Pentecost was a Jewish thanksgiving-type festival celebrated seven weeks after Passover. On this particular Pentecost, however, the Holy Spirit is poured out upon the entire community of believers just as Jesus had promised and the scriptures had prophesied. Empowered by the Spirit, the entire community bears witness to God's activity in multiple languages.

or Ezekiel 37:1-14

The Hebrew word *ruach* means spirit, wind, or breath. This reading plays on the different meanings of the word. Just as the dry bones in Ezekiel's vision are given new life, flesh, and breath (or spirit), so God will give the exiles his spirit and will bring them home to the land of Israel.

Psalm 104:24-34, 35b

Send forth your Spirit and renew the face of the earth. (Ps. 104:30)

Romans 8:22-27

By pouring the Holy Spirit into our hearts, God gives us the promised first fruit of eternal life so that we await God's future in hope. In the meantime, the Spirit also intercedes for us by carrying the prayers of our weak human hearts to God.

or Acts 2:1-21

See above.

John 15:26-27; 16:4b-15

When speaking to his disciples before his death, Jesus referred to the Holy Spirit as "the Helper" and described the difference the Spirit would make in their lives and in the world.

Color   Red

CD-ROM Images

Icon Three: PentecostDay01_ABC, PentecostDay02_ABC, PentecostDay03_ABC
Icon Two: PentecostDay01_ABC, PentecostDay02_ABC, PentecostDay03_ABC
Icon: 037, 098, 167

Prayers of Intercession

Transformed by the life-giving power of the empty tomb, let us pray for the church, the world, and all those in need.
A brief silence.
Breath of God, with a mighty rush your church was set alight by holy fire. Kindle in our hearts the blaze of your love, that we may proclaim your saving grace to all the world. Hear us, O God.
Your mercy is great.

Breath of God, every living thing depends on you for life and sustenance. Open your hand and fill us with good things that delight and satisfy. Hear us, O God.
Your mercy is great.
Breath of God, we are a people divided by color, nationality, and creed. Draw us together in our common humanity to work for peace and justice for all. Hear us, O God.
Your mercy is great.
Breath of God, in our weakness we know not how to pray. Intercede for us, bringing hope and healing to the anxious, the sorrowful, and those who are suffering or ill (*especially*). Hear us, O God.
Your mercy is great.
Breath of God, we need the visions of the young and the dreams of the old. Guide the ministries of this congregation that we (*like Mary and Elizabeth*) may bear the good news of Christ to others. Hear us, O God.
Your mercy is great.
Here other intercessions may be offered.
Breath of God, in hope we wait for that which we cannot see. Unite us with your blessed saints (*especially*) as we welcome the coming of the Lord's great and glorious day. Hear us, O God.
Your mercy is great.
Hear our prayers, gracious God, and grant all that we need to live as your Spirit-filled people, in the name of the risen Christ.
Amen.

Ideas and Images for the Day

Amid this "Farewell Discourse" in John's gospel, Jesus promises the arrival of the Spirit who, as a person of the Trinity, will speak truth. The manifestation of this promise is captured in the Acts reading with the whirling of winds, flickering of flames, and a cacophony of clatter, all of which point to the presence of the truth-Spirit. Admittedly, extraordinary acts and unbelievable signs are an odd way to communicate truth. After all, how do we believe the unbelievable? Enter the Spirit of truth! For, as Paul wrote, "the Spirit helps us in our weakness" (Rom. 8:26). It is the Spirit, our God-sent Advocate, who will lead and guide us into all truth, that is, "everyone who calls on the name of the Lord shall be saved" (Acts 2:21).

1. The Day of Pentecost is too often lost in the pages of our secular calendars and planners. As the academic and program years come to an end in May or June, the festival of Pentecost is often a casualty of fatigue. Commit the congregation to claiming Pentecost as a feast date on par with Christmas or Easter: schedule choirs to sing, plan for a baptism, invite a brass ensemble to play, arrange a large procession led by the children, order dozens of flame-colored flowers to dress the worship space, celebrate the eucharist, wear red, and pray again and again, "Come, Holy Spirit, come!"

2. Fire is a wonderful image and metaphor to use to teach children about the Holy Spirit. Prior to Pentecost, hold Pentecost planning sessions with the kids. Teach them about the properties of fire, likening them to the ultimate truth of the Spirit: the burning and spreading of God's love. Create Pentecost candleholders together out of glass jars, tissue paper, glue, and glaze. Use them to adorn the worship space for the festival.

3. Because "spirit" is a feminine noun in Hebrew, consider replacing masculine pronouns referring to the Holy Spirit with feminine pronouns in worship today. Be intentional about explaining today's replacement; print a rationale in the bulletin, reference it in the sermon, or incorporate the explanation into the gathering rite. Following worship, hold an informal discussion to allow people to share their experiences of the change.

4. To create the "cacophony of clatter" experienced in the Acts passage, secretly enlist the help of a dozen foreign language readers. Insert John 3:16 into the Acts reading following the fourth verse as a summary of the Pentecost proclamation. At the moment when the lector reads John 3:16 in English, the dozen or so readers burst into John 3:16 in other languages. The surprise of this Pentecost-like event might just create a taste of the bewilderment and astonishment experienced on that first Pentecost.

Hymns for Worship
Gathering

Holy Spirit, ever dwelling   ELW 582, LBW 523
Gracious Spirit, heed our pleading   ELW 401, WOV 687
O Holy Spirit, root of life   ELW 399, WOV 688

Hymn of the Day

O Spirit of life   ELW 405, WOV 680   *O HEILIGER GEIST*
O living Breath of God   ELW 407   *VÅRVINDAR FRISKA*
Eternal Spirit of the living Christ   ELW 402, LBW 441
   ADORO TE DEVOTE

Communion

O Spirit of life   ELW 405, WOV 680
Spirit of gentleness   ELW 396, WOV 684

Sending

God of tempest, God of whirlwind   ELW 400
Hail thee, festival day! (Pentecost)   ELW 394, LBW 142

Additional Hymns and Songs

Holy Spirit, rain down   RWSB 152
Send down the fire   RWSB 153
Fire of God, undying flame   RWSB 154
Send Us Your Spirit   GC 476
We are one   GC 482
Valley Psalm to the Holy Spirit   GS 15

Music for the Day
Psalmody and Acclamations

Miller, Aaron David. *Gospel Acclamations for Lent–Holy Trinity.* AFP 9780800635589.

Mummert, Mark. "Psalm 104" from *Psalm Settings for the Church Year.* AFP 9780800678562.

Psalter for Worship Year B, Evangelical Lutheran Worship Edition. AFP 9780806683839.

Choral

Bach, J. S. "Come, Holy Ghost, God and Lord" from *Bach for All Seasons.* SATB. AFP 9780800658540.

Benson, Robert A. "Fresh Fire." SATB, org. AFP 9780800678913.

Gearhart, Livingston. "Dry Bones." SATB, opt pno, opt perc, opt bass. SHW A0064.

Hogan, Moses. "I'm Gonna Sing 'Til the Spirit Moves in My Heart." SATB, div. HAL 8740284.

◻ Scott, K. Lee. "Gracious Spirit, Dwell with Me" (Adore te devote). 2 pt mxd, org. AFP 9780800646134. *The Augsburg Choirbook.* AFP 9780800656782. *Augsburg Easy Choirbook*, vol. 1. AFP 9780800676025.

Children's Choir

Hurford, Peter. "Litany to the Holy Spirit." UE. U, kybd. OXF 81037.

Patterson, Mark. "Spirit, Come Down" from *ChildrenSing with Instruments.* UE. U/2 pt, pno, C inst. AFP 9780800620349.

Ramseth, Betty Ann. "Spirit Boundless." UE. U, kybd, fl, fc. AFP 9780800645170. OP

Keyboard / Instrumental

Callahan, Charles. "Adoro te devote" from Sonus Novus, vol. 4. Org. CPH 97-7080U1.

Hildebrand, Kevin. "Adoro te devote" from Sonus Novus, vol. 5. Org. CPH 97-7085U1.

Mann, Adrian. "O Heiliger Geist" from *Arise and Rejoice!* Kybd, C/B-flat inst. AFP 9780800674960.

Organ, Anne Krentz. "Adoro te devote" from *Christ, Mighty Savior.* Pno. AFP 9780800656805.

Handbell

Moklebust, Cathy. "Come, Holy Spirit." 3-5 oct, L2+. AMSI HB-21.

Noland, Robert. "Spirit of Joy." 3-5 oct, opt fl, L2+. FLA HP5335.

Tucker, Sondra K. "Crosswind." 3-5 oct, L4-5. AFP 9780800659882.

Praise Ensemble

∎ Fragar, Russell. "Church on Fire" from www.praisecharts.com. Hillsong Publishing/INT.

∎ Fragar, Russell. "Holy Spirit, Rain Down" from www.praisecharts.com. Hillsong Publishing/INT.

∎ Hughes, Tim. "Here I Am to Worship" from *More Songs for Praise & Worship 3.* WM 080689452871.

∎ Zschech, Darlene. "The Potter's Hand" from *Best of the Best, The Other Songbook 2.* FEL 1891062034.

Global

Harling, Per. "Holy, Holy, Holy" from *Global Praise 2.* SATB, assembly, pno, gtr. General Board of Global Ministries, GBGMusik 1890569224. http://new.gbgm-umc.org/resources/global praise/music/.

Helgen, John. "Brighter Than the Sun." SATB, pno. AFP 9780800659158.

Monday, June 1

Visit of Mary to Elizabeth (transferred)

Sometime after the Annunciation, Mary visited her cousin Elizabeth. Elizabeth greeted Mary with the words "Blessed are you among women," and Mary responded with her famous song, the Magnificat. Luke's gospel tells that even John the Baptist rejoiced and leapt in his mother's womb when Elizabeth heard Mary's greeting. On this festival two women are seen: one, too old to have a child, bears the last prophet of the old covenant, and the other, still quite young, bears the incarnate Word and the new covenant.

In what ways does the church bear the good news of Christ to others and remain faithful to God's call?

Monday, June 1

Justin, martyr at Rome, c. 165

Justin was born of pagan parents. At Ephesus he was moved by stories of early Christian martyrs and came under the influence of an elderly Christian man he met there. Justin described his conversion by saying, "Straightway a flame was kindled in my soul and a love of the prophets and those who are friends of Christ possessed me." Justin was a teacher of philosophy and engaged in debates about the truth of Christian faith. He was arrested and jailed for practicing an unauthorized religion. He refused to renounce his faith, and he and six of his students, one a woman, were beheaded. Justin's description of early Christian worship around the year 150 is the foundation of the church's pattern of worship, East and West. His description of it is in *With One*

◻ denotes choral suggestions that relate to the hymn of the day.
∎ denotes songs that are available on iTunes®.

Voice (p. 6) and helps reveal the deep roots our contemporary order for holy communion has in the ancient worship of the church.

Wednesday, June 3

The Martyrs of Uganda, 1886

Christianity had been introduced to Uganda after 1877, but was made available primarily to those in the court of King Mutesa. His successor, King Mwanga, was angered by these Christian members of the court whose first allegiance was not to him but to Christ. On June 3, 1886, thirty-two young men were burned to death for refusing to renounce Christianity. Other martyrs followed. But many were impressed by the confident manner in which these Christians went to their deaths, and the persecution led to a much stronger Christian presence in the country.

John XXIII, Bishop of Rome, 1963

In his ministry as a bishop of Venice, John was loved by his people. He visited parishes and established new ones. He had warm affection for the working class—he himself was the child of Italian peasants—and he worked at developing social-action ministries. At age seventy-seven he was elected bishop of Rome. Despite the expectation that he would be a transitional pope, he had great energy and spirit. He convened the Second Vatican Council to open the windows of the church and "let in the fresh air of the modern world." The council brought about great changes in Roman Catholic worship, changes that have influenced Lutherans and many other Protestant churches as well.

Friday, June 5

Boniface, Bishop of Mainz, missionary to Germany, martyr, 754

Boniface (his name means "good deeds") was born Wynfrith in Devonshire, England. He was a Benedictine monk who at the age of thirty was called to missionary work among the Vandal tribes in Germany. His first missionary attempt was unsuccessful, but he returned two years later and was able to plant the gospel in an area filled with superstitious and violent practices. He led large numbers of Benedictine monks and nuns in establishing churches, schools, and seminaries. Boniface was also a reformer. He persuaded two rulers to call synods to put an end to the practice of selling church offices to the highest bidder. Boniface was preparing a group for confirmation on the eve of Pentecost when he and they were killed by a band of pagans.

Time after Pentecost
Summer

Preparing for Summer

Lectionary

The time after Pentecost, like summer, is a long, gentle season of growth, and images of the natural world abound in the prayers and the gospel readings. It's no wonder the liturgical color is green. On Trinity Sunday, the only festival that celebrates a doctrine rather than an event, God is addressed in the prayer of the day as "Author of creation, eternal Word of salvation, life-giving Spirit of wisdom." Many of the verbs in the prayers and gospel readings are gentle ones related to life in the physical world: *shelter, graft, nurture, pilot, preserve, instruct, shepherd, feed, protect, comfort, defend, heal, transform, shape, shine, turn.*

Jesus tells parables of the growing seed and of the mustard seed; he stills the storm; he heals people, even some who merely touch the hem of his garment. He feeds people when they're hungry and reveals that "the bread that I will give for the life of the world is my flesh" (John 6:51). At this point, many of his followers complain, don't understand, and turn back. The growing blindness of the disciples becomes apparent as James and John argue over who will sit at his right hand and left hand when he comes into his kingdom (Mark 10:35-40).

Somehow this blindness increases even though the disciples have had the profound privilege of spending three or more years with Jesus: times of challenging work, deep prayer, and close fellowship. They talked together; together they witnessed miracles of healing, shared food, and changed hearts. They laughed and cried together. For those so fortunate as to know him intimately, Jesus became a teacher, a healer, an advocate, a friend. Maybe their incomprehension and denial came because of this close association. They wanted Jesus to stay around, up close and personal. Away with all this talk about suffering and death!

Karl, a gentle, faithful pastor for thirty-three years, also followed the path of suffering. He had few signs of worldly success: no crowds, publications, or promotions to larger churches and higher salaries. He was, like many pastors who work in relative obscurity, quietly faithful at the everyday tasks of preaching, celebrating communion, preparing youngsters for confirmation. Jesus didn't choose flashy, brilliant, successful, impressive people to do his work. He worked, and continues to work, quietly and with humble things: a baby born in the muck and stink of a stable; a few fishermen; water, wine, bread. And Jesus worked—as he works with parishioners and faithful pastors everywhere—through Karl's quiet witness of word, sacrament, and life, year after year. When debilitating and eventually mortal illness came, Karl never lost his faith that the God whose suffering brought unending life to his people intends good for all, even in their suffering.

Space

In the time after Pentecost, the celebration of God's provision for our physical needs and the beauty of God's creation can transform the worship space. As much as is practical, let the outdoors in: open the windows, open the door. Hold coffee hour outside when feasible. Replace heavy banners with simple hangings of light, brightly colored cloth that can blow in the breeze, a reminder of the blowing of the Spirit through the gathering of God's people. People could sign up to decorate the worship space with flowers and produce from their gardens. Bouquets of wildflowers offer a pleasing change from the usual formal arrangements. These can often be found at farmers' markets, if other sources aren't readily available.

This is a popular time of year for vacation trips. Consider clearing off a cluttered bulletin board—not a bad idea in any case—or put up a big sheet of paper or poster board in an area where people gather. Ask people to post pictures and postcards and perhaps little notes about their travels: this will brighten the coffee-hour space and encourage fellowship.

If possible, your congregation may want to cultivate some of their property to plant a garden, the produce of which would go to the local food shelf. The initial tilling of the soil is a good project for a youth group. Later on in the growing season, others can participate, demonstrating care for neighbors and good stewardship of property and energy.

Many congregations have a one- or two-week vacation Bible school during the summer. Instead of relegating the children entirely to the church hall or basement or lawn, consider bringing them into the nave for some of their activities. In many cases, half or more of the children attending do not belong to the congregation, and some may never have been inside a church. Welcome them into the worship space and let their crafts and decorations adorn altar, nave, and narthex for a while. Parents could be invited to a Sunday worship service in which the children participate, followed by a picnic hosted by the congregation. The idea is not to snag new members, though that may happen, but to make the church a place that the families will remember as welcoming and joyful.

The best adornment of the worship space is smiles, handshakes, and eye contact on the part of the congregation. Visitors are likely to stop in while traveling or visiting. Make them feel noticed and welcomed, even in the parking lot, though the likelihood of their becoming members is small. Hospitality to strangers is a supreme virtue in scripture, and in no place should it be demonstrated more than in God's house.

Music

During the time after Pentecost, we proclaim gospel readings in which Jesus does his work in the world, demonstrating what God's kingdom is like: a place of stunning strangeness that turns all ideas of power and glory upside down. A place where a poor widow's mite is valued more than the vast riches of the wealthy. A place where children are welcomed and the rich and learned are humbled. A place where the greatest of all is the servant of all. A place where one who has power over wind and sea willingly empties himself of that power to embark on a path that will lead him to death on a cross.

A certain playfulness enters many people's lives during the summer, and the music of the season can reflect that playfulness. Introduce new hymns from *Evangelical Lutheran Worship* that celebrate the unexpected nature of God and God's kingdom. Have fun with these. Consider the surprises, contradictions, and paradoxes in Jesus' ministry and in God's kingdom. Part of the playfulness and surprise could come in using hymns out of context. Among the new hymn sections in *Evangelical Lutheran Worship* is "Justice, Peace," and many of the hymns that celebrate the oddity of God's kingdom are in this section. Some examples: "Jesu, Jesu, fill us with your love," st. 1 (#708); "Christ, Be Our Light," st. 5 (#715); "In a lowly manger born," st. 1 (#718); "O Christ, your heart, compassionate," st. 4 (#722); "Canticle of the Turning," st. 3 (#723); "All who love and serve your city," st. 3 (#724); "When the poor ones," st. 1 and refrain (#725); and "Blest are they," st. 1 (#728).

Celebrating Summer with Children

Summer can be a challenging time for children in worship. Many congregations suspend Sunday church school over the summer, so it is even more important to make worship kid-friendly. Summer is also a time when families are traveling—and when people who have moved into your community begin to look for a new church family. You may have more visitors and fewer of your regular worshipers. Use this time as an opportunity to meet and invite new families to your church before the rush of fall and the start of the new school year.

Many of the lectionary texts for the summer months focus on faith and Jesus as healer, provider, and savior. Throughout the summer months, we are confronted with stories of Jesus' miracles of healing and feeding. Through these miracles, Jesus demonstrates that faith creates the context in which God acts with power to change lives.

Ideas for Summer

- Use the more relaxed and informal time of summer to incorporate child-friendly songs into your worship. Songs like "Jesus loves me!" (ELW 595, LS 160) and "I've got the joy, joy, joy" (LS 181) are not only kid-friendly but may also prompt adults to reminisce about other songs they learned in their childhood.
- Create a Bible challenge to memorize scripture. Begin on Trinity Sunday with the gospel reading for the day, John 3:16. Each week, challenge children to memorize a verse by passing out small printed cards or slips of paper that have the Bible verse on it from one of the day's readings. Recruit a couple of volunteers who will hear the children say the verse the following week before or after worship and provide a piece of candy or a sticker as a prize.
- During a children's message, talk about faith as putting our trust in God even though we are not able to see or touch God. How do we know who to trust? Sometimes we can follow the evidence of where others have been on the same journey we're now taking. They leave behind their footprints or a trail. The same is

true of God. We cannot see God, but we can see God's footprints everywhere in the world. Provide paper and markers for children to trace their foot, and write in each one a way that they have seen God's footprint in the world.

- Healing stories are also found in the summer lectionary readings. Pass out plastic adhesive bandages to worshipers and encourage them to write on it the name of someone they know who is in need of healing. Have them wrap it around their finger so that each time they see it they will be reminded to pray for the person.
- The series of gospel readings from John 6 (beginning July 26) focus on Jesus as the Bread of life. If possible on these Sundays, bake bread in your church building before worship so that the aroma of bread is in the air. Purchasing prepared dough makes this an easy project, and the loaves are always delicious! Use the loaves for the communion that day.
- For the story of the feeding of the 5,000 (July 26), place loaves of bread around the worship space. Pass them around during the reading and invite people to tear off a piece. At the end there will be bread left over. Or take it one step further by inviting worshipers to close their eyes as you tell the story. When you get to the part where the disciples distribute the bread to the people, have the children pass out the bread to the assembly.
- If your church offers vacation Bible school over the summer, find ways to incorporate elements from the program into your Sunday worship. Have children sing songs they learned or display their artwork somewhere in the church building. Many children who participate in VBS may not be members of your congregation. Be sure to make these families feel welcome, and invite them to worship.
- Include children and teens in the prayers of intercession as they travel to camps or participate in service trips. Invite them to share their experiences with the congregation by displaying pictures, artwork, and videos. Young people appreciate being remembered as they embark on summer faith experiences.

Worship Helps for Summer

Summer Checklist

- If the worship schedule changes, notify local newspapers, update your Web site, and change listings on exterior signs and church answering machines.
- If your space is not air conditioned, consider ways to help worshipers stay cool during warm weather (fans, open windows, inviting people to dress comfortably).
- If outdoor services are held, make sure that the details for the service are covered thoroughly.
- Look ahead to the checklists on pp. 259 and 299 as you plan for the rest of the time after Pentecost.

Shape of the Communion Liturgy

- See the seasonal worship texts for the summer months on p. 210.
- Omit the Kyrie (except on the festival of Holy Trinity).
- Omit or use the hymn of praise (but use on the festival of Holy Trinity).
- Use the Nicene Creed for Holy Trinity; use the Apostles' Creed for remaining Sundays in this season.

- See the prayers of intercession for each Sunday.
- Use the preface for Sundays or Holy Trinity, as appropriate (*Evangelical Lutheran Worship* Leaders Edition, pp. 180, 190).
- Thanksgiving at the table: see options in *Evangelical Lutheran Worship* (Leaders Edition, pp. 198–205); *WOV*, Prayer G (Leaders Edition, p. 71).

Other Helps

- See the suggestions for music and worship space in the essay "Preparing for Summer," pp. 206–207.
- Use one of the blessings for travelers in the seasonal rites section (p. 211) for groups participating in congregational mission trips, youth gatherings, etc.
- Use the farewell and godspeed in the seasonal rites section when people are transferring out of the congregation or moving to a new community, or to bid farewell to graduates leaving for college, other study, or other opportunities.

SEASONAL WORSHIP TEXTS FOR SUMMER

Confession and Forgiveness

All may make the sign of the cross, the sign that is marked at baptism, as the presiding minister begins.

Blessed be the holy Trinity:
the Father, the + Son,
and the Holy Spirit.
Amen.

Sisters and brothers,
bear with one another in love,
maintain the unity of the Spirit in the bond of peace,
and take no part in the unfruitful works of darkness,
but instead expose them.
Let us confess our sin
in the presence of God and of one another.

Silence is kept for reflection.

Holy and gracious God,
**we confess that we have not led a life
worthy of the calling to which we have been called.
We have not loved you with our whole heart;
we have not loved our neighbors as ourselves.
We have not acted according to your will.
We have grieved your Holy Spirit.
Have mercy on us.
Forgive us according to the riches of your grace.
Make us holy and blameless before you in love,
so that we might live to the praise of your glory. Amen.**

In the mercy of almighty God,
Jesus Christ was given to die for you,
and for his sake God forgives you all your sins.
You who once were far off
have been brought near by the blood of Christ.
Amen.

Greeting

The blessing of the Father of our Lord Jesus Christ,
the glorious grace freely bestowed in the Son,
and the power of the promised Holy Spirit be with you all.
And also with you.

Offering Prayer

Holy God, you open the doors of heaven,
giving us every generous and perfect gift from above.
Lift our eyes from the food that perishes,
and nourish us now with the food that endures for eternal life,
Jesus Christ our Lord.
Amen.

Invitation to Communion

Jesus said, "I am the bread of life.
Whoever comes to me will never be hungry,
and whoever believes in me will never be thirsty."

Prayer after Communion

Gracious God, in this meal
you have rained down the true bread from heaven,
the body and blood of your beloved Son.
So by his promise bring us to abide in him, and he in us;
through Jesus Christ our Lord.
Amen.

Sending of Communion

Holy God,
as Moses lifted up the serpent in the wilderness,
so your Son was lifted up,
that whoever believes in him may have eternal life.
Bless those who now carry your word and sacrament
to our sisters and brothers who are absent,
that all the world might be saved through him,
Jesus Christ our Lord.
Amen.

Blessing

Know the love of Christ that surpasses knowledge,
so that you may be filled with all the fullness of God.

Almighty God, Father, + Son, and Holy Spirit,
bless you now and forever.
Amen.

Dismissal

Go in peace. Serve the Lord.
Thanks be to God.

SEASONAL RITES FOR SUMMER

Blessing of Fathers

Gracious God,
pour out your Spirit on all fathers.
Grant to them keen insight into their children's needs.
Help them to be faithful examples of truth and love.
Soften their hearts
so that they might hear their children's cries.
Strengthen their resolve
to be men of commitment and faith.
In times of sorrow and disappointment
let them know that you are by their side.
In times of doubt and confusion
show them the way.
In times of happiness and joy
let them see your face in all that is good and right and true.
In all times sustain them with the knowledge
that they are your beloved children.
We ask this in Jesus' name.
Amen.

Farewell and Godspeed

*This prayer may be used after the prayers of intercession or
following the prayer after communion.*
Eternal God,
we thank you for *name/s* and for our life together
in this congregation and community.
As *they have* been a blessing to us,
so now send *them* forth to be a blessing to others;
through Jesus Christ, our Savior and Lord.
Amen.

Blessings for Travelers

O God, whose glory fills the whole creation,
and whose presence we find wherever we go:
Preserve *us/those* who travel:
surround *us/them* with your loving care;
protect *us/them* from every danger;
and bring *us/them* in safety to *our/their* journey's end;
through Jesus Christ our Lord.
Amen.

Adapted from the prayer for travelers in Prayers and Thanksgivings, *The Book of Common Prayer* (1979 edition).

O God,
our beginning and our end,
you kept Abraham and Sarah in safety
throughout the days of their pilgrimage,
you led the children of Israel through the midst of the sea,
and by a star you led the magi to the infant Jesus.
Protect and guide us now as we *[or substitute the names
of travelers]* set out to travel.
Make our ways safe and our homecomings joyful,
and bring us at last to our heavenly home,
where you dwell in glory with our Lord Jesus Christ
and the life-giving Holy Spirit,
one God, now and forever.
Amen.

Adapted from *Evangelical Lutheran Worship*, p. 331.

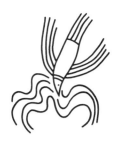

June 7, 2009
The Holy Trinity
First Sunday after Pentecost

When we say God is the triune God, we are saying something about who God is beyond, before, and after the universe: that there is community within God. Our experience of this is reflected in Paul's words today. When we pray to God as Jesus prayed to his Abba (an everyday, intimate parental address), the Spirit prays within us, creating between us and God the same relationship Jesus has with the one who sent him.

Today the church commemorates Chief Seattle of the Duwamish Confederacy, who died in 1866.

Prayer of the Day

Almighty Creator and ever-living God: we worship your glory, eternal Three-in-One, and we praise your power, majestic One-in-Three. Keep us steadfast in this faith, defend us in all adversity, and bring us at last into your presence, where you live in endless joy and love, Father, Son, and Holy Spirit, one God, now and forever.

or

God of heaven and earth, before the foundation of the universe and the beginning of time you are the triune God: Author of creation, eternal Word of salvation, life-giving Spirit of wisdom. Guide us to all truth by your Spirit, that we may proclaim all that Christ has revealed and rejoice in the glory he shares with us. Glory and praise to you, Father, Son, and Holy Spirit, now and forever.

Gospel Acclamation

Alleluia. Holy, holy, holy is the [|] LORD of hosts;* God's glory fills [|] the whole earth. *Alleluia.* (Isa. 6:3)

Readings and Psalm
Isaiah 6:1-8

This reading narrates Isaiah's vision of the Lord surrounded by angels. They sing "Holy, holy, holy," a song the church sings at the beginning of the great thanksgiving. This liturgical text invites the church and all creation to sing in praise of God's glory. That glory is God's mercy toward sinners.

Psalm 29

Worship the LORD in the beauty of holiness. (Ps. 29:2)

Romans 8:12-17

In describing the new life of faith, Paul refers to all three persons of the Trinity: the Spirit leads us to recognize that we are children of God the Father and sisters and brothers with Christ the Son.

John 3:1-17

Jesus' miracles prompt Nicodemus to visit him in secrecy. Jesus tells him about being born of the Spirit and about the Son who has been sent by God to save.

Color   White

CD-ROM Images

Icon Three: 1HolyTrinity_B
Icon Two: HolyTrinity_B
Icon: 038, 099, 168, 169, 267

Prayers of Intercession

With the whole people of God in Christ Jesus, let us pray for the church, those in need, and all of God's creation.

A brief silence.

God of power and mystery, you breathe into our lives the winds of hope and renewal. Open the church to the challenges you place before us, and help us be your presence in the world. God of mercy,

hear our prayer.

You have created a world of breathtaking beauty and rich and abundant resources. Guide us in our search to find ways to be careful stewards of all your creation.

God of mercy,
hear our prayer.
Your mercy is wide, spilling far beyond the borders of the church. Breathe into us a passion for justice, that we might love and serve all people in Jesus' name. God of mercy,
hear our prayer.
Your gentle touch comforts and heals us. Bless all who suffer and those who stand with them (*especially*). In your good time, bring an end to all pain. God of mercy,
hear our prayer.
You challenge us to look beyond the boundaries of the communities that support us. Strengthen the bonds among peoples of all faiths, nations, and ethnic backgrounds for the sake of all the world. God of mercy,
hear our prayer.
Here other intercessions may be offered.
You send us saints and prophets (*like Chief Seattle*) to remind us of promise and possibilities, of failure and faith. Help us to hear their voices this day on behalf of those whose voices have been weakened or silenced. God of mercy,
hear our prayer.
Loving God, you are near to us when we cry out to you. Into your embrace we commend all for whom we pray, through Christ and by the power of your Spirit.
Amen.

Ideas and Images for the Day

Christians call God by a triune name—Father, Son, and Holy Spirit—in prayer, proclamation, and ritual. It is a mystery of our faith that the Holy Trinity is one God in three persons. On Holy Trinity Sunday we celebrate and ponder that mystery. God's three persons correspond to three great theological categories, representing three aspects of God's work in the world: creation, redemption, and sanctification. All three persons participate in all three activities. Today's gospel reading weaves these three strands together into a theology of baptism. Therefore, though some believers, and even whole denominations, may experience God in one person more than another, the church baptizes in the name of all three.

1. John's gospel uses the images of light and darkness frequently to symbolize good and evil, understanding and ignorance, hope and fear. In this Sunday's gospel reading, Nicodemus comes to Jesus at night, in the dark, and encounters the light of the world in him. Jesus uses baptismal imagery to enlighten Nicodemus. In baptism, each Christian is called upon to embody the light of Christ and let his or her light shine to the glory of God (Holy Baptism, *Evangelical Lutheran Worship*, p. 231).

2. In his film *The Apostle* (October Films, 1997), Robert Duvall plays Sonny Dewey, an evangelical preacher on the run from the law. During his escape, in a pivotal scene deeply suggestive of the baptismal rite, he immerses himself in a river and rises to begin a new life with a new identity. Ultimately, Dewey must pay for his crime, but the movie never calls his faith, or his affirmation of baptism, into question.

3. Some characters in the Harry Potter series are so terrified of the villain Voldemort that they will not mention his name, referring to him only as "you-know-who" (J. K. Rowling, *Harry Potter and the Sorcerer's Stone*, Scholastic Press, 1997, p. 11). Others, like Harry, know that to fight evil we must be willing to name it. Christian prophetic tradition agrees and teaches us further that the triune name of God has the power to protect us from any evil, no matter what its name.

4. Artists of all ages have used their imaginative gifts to give us visual images of the Holy Trinity. Some of these visual images can be found at www.textweek.com/art/trinity.htm. Compare also more contemporary approaches at www.weirdload.com/gallery.html.

5. Lutheran theologian Dietrich Bonhoeffer focused almost exclusively on the second person of the Trinity as the essence of our encounter with God (see, for example, *Christ the Center*, Harper and Row, 1978). Bonhoeffer has been criticized by some theologians who say he neglects the other persons of the Trinity. How important is it for us as theologians to work for balance in our understanding of the triune God?

Hymns for Worship
Gathering
Come, join the dance of Trinity   ELW 412
Come, thou almighty King   ELW 408, LBW 522
Come, all you people   ELW 819, WOV 717

Hymn of the Day
Mothering God, you gave me birth   ELW 735, WOV 769
NORWICH
Holy, holy, holy, Lord God Almighty!   ELW 413, LBW 165
NICAEA
All glory be to God on high   ELW 410, LBW 166
ALLEIN GOTT IN DER HÖH

Communion
When long before time   ELW 861, WOV 799
O living Breath of God   ELW 407

Sending

Holy God, we praise your name   ELW 414, LBW 535
My Lord of light   ELW 832, WOV 796
Rise, O church, like Christ arisen   ELW 548

Additional Hymns and Songs

The play of the Godhead   GC 484
O God, almighty Father   GC 485
How wonderful the Three-in-One   GC 488
Alone and filled with fear   HG 143

Music for the Day
Psalmody and Acclamations

Miller, Aaron David. *Gospel Acclamations for Lent–Holy Trinity.* AFP 9780800635589.

Mummert, Mark. "Psalm 29" from *Psalm Settings for the Church Year.* AFP 9780800678562.

Psalter for Worship Year B, Evangelical Lutheran Worship Edition. AFP 9780806683839.

Choral

Bach, J. S./arr. K. Lee Scott. "Come Holy, Quickening Spirit." SAB, kybd. CPH 98-2838.

Distler, Hugo. "For God So Loved the World" from *Chantry Choirbook.* SAB. AFP 9780800657772.

Hopp, Roy. "Come, Join the Dance of Trinity." SATB, kybd, opt C inst. AFP 9780800678296.

▫ Smith, Byron J. "Worthy to Be Praised" (with Nicaea). SATB, pno. LG 52654.

Williams, David McK. "In the Year that King Uzziah Died." SATB, org. HWG GCMR01356.

Children's Choir

Christopherson, Dorothy. "God of the Universe." UE. 2 pt, pno, fl, perc, xyls. CG A821.

Hughes, Howard. "You Have Put On Christ." UE. U, opt canon, org, 2 C inst, fc, drm, orch, hb. GIA G-2283.

Pennycuff, Mary. "Carol of Beauty." LE. U, kybd, rec/fl. CG A251.

Keyboard / Instrumental

Manz, Paul O. "Allein Gott in der Höh" from *Improvisations for Pentecost and Trinity Sunday.* Org. MSM 10-500.

Maynard, Lynette. "Allein Gott in der Höh" from *Let It Rip! at the Piano,* vol. 2. Pno. AFP 9780800675806.

Organ, Ann Krentz/John Helgen. "Nicaea" from *Let It Rip! at the Piano,* vol. 1. Pno. AFP 9780800659066.

Wold, Wayne L. "Norwich" from *Child of the Light.* Org. AFP 9780800657994.

Handbell

McFadden, Jane. "Our Father's World." 3-5 oct, L3. BP HB120A. Full Score: BP HB120.

Moklebust, Cathy. "Nicaea" from *Hymn Stanzas for Handbells.* 4-5 oct, L3. AFP 9780800655761.

Wagner, H. Dean. "Carillon." 4-5 oct, L3. AG 1846.

Praise Ensemble

- ■ Brown, Brenton. "Holy" from www.praisecharts.com. VIN.
- ■ Giglio, Louie/Chris Tomlin. "Holy Is the Lord" from WT. WT/Sixsteps Music.

  Hanson, Handt. "Go, Make Disciples." ELW 540, W&P 47.
- ■ Tomlin, Chris/Ed Cash/Jesse Reeves. "How Great Is Our God" from www.praisecharts.com.

Global

Hawkins, Walter. "I'm Goin' Up a Yonder." SATB, pno. HAL 48004366.

Smallwood, Richard. "Great Day." SATB, cant, pno. ALF BSCM00064.

Sunday, June 7

Seattle, chief of the Duwamish Confederacy, 1866

Noah Seattle was chief of the Suquamish tribe and later became chief of the Duwamish Confederacy, a tribal alliance. When the tribes were faced with an increasing number of white settlers, Seattle chose to live and work peacefully with them rather than engage in wars. After Seattle became a Roman Catholic, he began the practice of morning and evening prayer in the tribe, a practice that continued after his death. On the centennial of his birth, the city of Seattle—named for him against his wishes—erected a monument over his grave.

When parish groups gather today, remember Chief Seattle and his work as a peacemaker. Consider beginning or ending parish events with a simple form of morning or evening prayer, not only today, but also as a regular part of the parish life.

Tuesday, June 9

Columba, 597; Aidan, 651; Bede, 735; renewers of the church

These three monks from the British Isles were pillars among those who kept alive the light of learning and devotion during the Middle Ages. Columba founded three monasteries,

▫ denotes choral suggestions that relate to the hymn of the day.
■ denotes songs that are available on iTunes®.

including one on the island of Iona, off the coast of Scotland. That monastery was left in ruins after the Reformation but today is home to an ecumenical religious community. Aidan, who helped bring Christianity to the Northumbria area of England, was known for his pastoral style and ability to stir people to charity and good works. Bede was a Bible translator and scripture scholar. He wrote a history of the English church and was the first historian to date events anno Domini (A.D.), "year of our Lord." Bede is also known for his hymns, including "A hymn of glory let us sing!" (ELW 393).

Thursday, June 11
Barnabas, Apostle

The Eastern church commemorates Barnabas as one of the Seventy commissioned by Jesus. Though he was not among the Twelve mentioned in the gospels, the book of Acts gives him the title of apostle. His name means "son of encouragement." When Paul came to Jerusalem after his conversion, Barnabas took him in over the fears of the other apostles, who doubted Paul's discipleship. Later, Paul and Barnabas traveled together on missions.

At the Council of Jerusalem, Barnabas defended the claims of Gentile Christians in relation to the Mosaic law. How can his work on behalf of others and his support of other Christians serve as a model for contemporary Christians and churches?

June 14, 2009
Time after Pentecost — Lectionary 11

The mustard seed becomes a shrub that shelters the birds, recalling ancient images of the tree of life. We'd expect a cedar or a sequoia, but Jesus finds the power of God better imaged in a tiny, no-account seed. It's not the way we expect divine activity to look. Yet the tree of life is here, in the cross around which we gather, the tree into which we are grafted through baptism, the true vine that nourishes us with its fruit in the cup we share. It may not appear all that impressive, but while nobody's looking it grows with a power beyond our understanding.

Today the church commemorates four influential fourth-century theologians: Basil the Great, Gregory of Nyssa, and Gregory of Nazianzus (known as the Cappadocian fathers); and Macrina, a teacher who was also the older sister of Basil and Gregory of Nyssa.

Prayer of the Day

O God, you are the tree of life, offering shelter to all the world. Graft us into yourself and nurture our growth, that we may bear your truth and love to those in need, through Jesus Christ, our Savior and Lord.

Gospel Acclamation

Alleluia. Welcome with meekness the im- | planted word* that has the power to | save your souls. *Alleluia.* (James 1:21)

Readings and Psalm
Ezekiel 17:22-24

Tree imagery is used in a messianic prophecy to tell how the Lord will choose someone from Judah's royal family (the

cedar tree) to reign over all creation. This tree will be planted on Mount Zion, the location of the holy temple.

Psalm 92:1-4, 12-15

The righteous shall spread abroad like a cedar of Lebanon. (Ps. 92:12)

2 Corinthians 5:6-10 [11-13] 14-17

Paul encourages believers to live by faith and not by sight. We do not consider Jesus from a human perspective but through the eyes of faith, believing he died for all and was raised. All who are in Christ are now in God's new creation.

Mark 4:26-34

Jesus frequently uses parables to teach ordinary people as they are able to hear and understand. Images of sowing and growing show the vitality of God's kingdom.

Semicontinuous reading and psalm

I Samuel 15:34—16:13

Saul, anointed by the prophet Samuel as the first king of Israel, displeases the Lord. The Lord therefore sends Samuel to Bethlehem, where he anoints David, the youngest of the sons of Jesse, to succeed Saul as king.

Psalm 20

The LORD gives victory to the anointed one. (Ps. 20:6)

Color   Green

CD-ROM Images

Icon Three: 0612-0618_Lect11_B
Icon Two: Proper06_Sun11_B
Icon: 102

Prayers of Intercession

With the whole people of God in Christ Jesus, let us pray for the church, those in need, and all of God's creation.

A brief silence.

O God, let your church be like a great tree, giving shade and shelter to all who seek respite. Under its branches let the world rest in your grace. God of mercy,
hear our prayer.

You have made us caretakers of the land, air, and water you created. Turn us from our patterns of careless and neglectful stewardship of your creation, and make us wise and mindful caretakers. God of mercy,
hear our prayer.

You sow seeds for faith like a careful gardener. Just as sown seeds take root and grow, sow seeds of justice and peace in our troubled world. God of mercy,
hear our prayer.

Your word nourishes like bread. Help us to hear the stories of faith, to make them our own and to share them with others. God of mercy,
hear our prayer.

You are the source of life and health. We pray for those who are ill this day *(especially)*. Surround them with care and bring them to wholeness and healing. God of mercy,
hear our prayer.

Here other intercessions may be offered.

We give you thanks for faithful witnesses who have prepared the way *(especially Basil the Great, Gregory of Nyssa, Gregory of Nazianzus, and Macrina, whom we commemorate today)*. God of mercy,
hear our prayer.

Loving God, you are near to us when we cry out to you. Into your embrace we commend all for whom we pray, through Christ and by the power of your Spirit.
Amen.

Ideas and Images for the Day

What inspiring texts about the inevitability of the coming of the kingdom and of the confidence and hope available to us! Both of the seed parables remind us that the "earth produces of itself" (Mark 4:28)—we have our jobs to do in this world, certainly, but in the end, it's not up to us. The farmer can't physically make the seed grow; he or she can only prepare the soil and plant at the right time. And the reading from 2 Corinthians declares that our confidence is not a vague or misplaced "positive attitude"—it rests on Christ. "We regard no one [and nothing!] from a human point of view" (2 Cor. 5:16). Just as the farmer in the gospel doesn't know exactly how the seed grows, we don't know how forgiveness happens, or how people get sober, or how families reconcile. But we do know that God is in charge and that in the end "everything has become new!" (2 Cor. 5:17).

1. A quote from Mother Teresa expresses well the attitude we should have in regard to our endeavors: "I do not pray for success, I ask for faithfulness" (www.quoteworld.org/quotes/11151). Indeed, we can be confident that in Christ we have all the success we need, and so in life we need only be faithful.

2. What child has not been tempted, after planting seeds in a paper cup on the windowsill, to dig them up and see if they are indeed growing? It is so hard to trust that the seeds are doing exactly what they should be, deep in the dirt and out of our eyesight (or control!).

3. A wonderful song of trust in the newness of God's salvation and redemption is *Evangelical Lutheran Worship* #721, "Goodness is stronger than evil" (text by Desmond Tutu). It is often hard to believe this when climate change, terrorism, and wars are daily realities. But we believe that ultimately victory is ours—the seed will sprout out of the ground and there will be new life.

4. The movie *The Pursuit of Happyness* (Sony Pictures, 2006) is a powerful story of hope, confidence, and perseverance. The main character, played by Will Smith,

eventually becomes quite successful, but it's not until after a long road of faithfully taking the next step and doing his best for his son.

Hymns for Worship
Gathering
For the fruit of all creation   ELW 679, LBW 563
What is this place   ELW 524

Hymn of the Day
Build us up, Lord   ELW 670   *BUILD US UP*
We raise our hands to you, O Lord   ELW 690
   VI REKKER VÅRE HENDER FREM
Lord, your hands have formed   ELW 554, WOV 727
   GAYOM NI HIGAMI

Communion
We walk by faith   ELW 635, WOV 675
Seed that in earth is dying   ELW 330
Lord, let my heart be good soil   ELW 512, WOV 713

Sending
Sent forth by God's blessing   ELW 547, LBW 221
The Spirit sends us forth to serve   ELW 551, WOV 723

Additional Hymns and Songs
What shall we say God's realm is like   HG 91
Awesome God   W&P 13
Open Our Lives to the Word   DH 8
The Word of God is source and seed   ELW 506, WOV 658

Music for the Day
Psalmody and Acclamations
Organ, Anne Krentz. *Gospel Acclamations for Summer.* AFP 9780800678579.

Psalter for Worship Year B, Evangelical Lutheran Worship Edition. AFP 9780806683839.

Weber, Paul. "Psalm 92" from *Psalm Settings for the Church Year.* AFP 9780800678562.

Choral
Cool, Jayne Southwick. "As Trees by the Waters." SAB, assembly, kybd, opt hb. AFP 97808006675073.

Jennings, Carolyn. "Blessed Are They." SATB, org, opt fl. CG A896.

Keesecker, Thomas. "What Is This Place?" SATB, vc, hb, pno. AFP 9780800678845.

Poston, Elizabeth. "Jesus Christ, the Apple Tree." SATB/SA/U, opt kybd. HAL ECS141.

Scott, K. Lee. "Christ the Way of Life Possess Me." SATB, org. OXF 9780193868618.

Children's Choir
Larson, Lloyd. "Ezekiel." UE. 2/3 pt, pno. Fred Bock Music 08739271.

Ramseth, Betty Ann. "Make Times Forgiven." UE. U/2 pt, kybd, fl. CG A289. OP

Tucker, Margaret R. "Jesus Loves Me." UE. 2 pt, opt assembly, org, fl. CG A1065.

Keyboard / Instrumental
Helman, Michael. "Fanfare" from *Organ Music for the Seasons*, vol. 1. Org. AFP 9780800657239.

Sedio, Mark. "Gayom ni higami" from *A Global Piano Tour.* Pno. AFP 9780800658199.

Wold, Wayne L. "Gayom ni higami" from *Organ Music for the Seasons*, vol. 3. Org. AFP 9780800675646.

Handbell
Afdahl, Lee J. "Thaxted." 3-5 oct, opt br, timp, L3. AFP 9780800658144.

Helman, Michael, arr. "Built on a Rock." 3-5 oct hb/hc, L3. AG 19006.

Wagner, H. Dean. "Te Deum." 4-7 oct, L4+. RR BL5027.

Praise Ensemble
■ Brumley, Albert E. "I'll Fly Away" from *Jars of Clay: Redemption Songs.* BBM 1598020021.

■ Hansen, Michael/Christina Peppin. "Fill Me Now" from www.ccli.com. Mercy/VIN.

■ Smith, Martin. "I Could Sing of Your Love Forever" from *I Could Sing of Your Love Forever 2.* WT 0000809251.

■ Walker, Tommy. "That's Why We Praise Him" from www.praisecharts.com. Doulos Publishing/WeMobile Music/MAR.

Global
Haugen, Marty. "The Peace of the Earth/La Paz de la Tierra." Mxd vcs, kybd, gtr, str. GIA G-7109.

Hesla, Bret. "Sing with Creation" from *Justice, Like a Base of Stone.* U, pno, gtr. AFP 9780800623562.

Sunday, June 14

Basil the Great, Bishop of Caesarea, 379; Gregory, Bishop of Nyssa, c. 385; Gregory of Nazianzus, Bishop of Constantinople, c. 389; Macrina, teacher, c. 379

The three men in this group are known as the Cappadocian fathers; all three explored the mystery of the Holy Trinity. Basil was influenced by his sister Macrina to live a monastic life, and he settled near the family estate in Caesarea. Basil's Longer Rule and Shorter Rule for monastic life are the basis for Eastern monasticism to this day, and express a

■ denotes songs that are available on iTunes®.

preference for communal monastic life over that of hermits. Gregory of Nazianzus (nah-zee-AN-zus) was sent to preach on behalf of the Orthodox faith against the Arians in Constantinople, though the Orthodox did not have a church there at the time. He defended Orthodox trinitarian and christological doctrine, and his preaching won over the city. Gregory of Nyssa (NISS-uh) was the younger brother of Basil the Great. He is remembered as a writer on spiritual life and the contemplation of God in worship and sacraments.

Macrina (muh-CREE-nuh) was the older sister of Basil and Gregory of Nyssa. She received an excellent education centered on the Bible, and when her fiancé died, she devoted herself to the pursuit of Christian perfection. She was a leader of a community, based at the family estate, dedicated to asceticism, meditation, and prayer. Macrina's teaching was influential within the early church.

June 21, 2009
Time after Pentecost — Lectionary 12

Now is the acceptable time; now is the day of salvation! Now we are in the storm, the boat almost swamped; but Jesus is here now, and when we call him he will calm the storm. Even the wind and waves listen to him as they would to their creator. We also listen to him and are called to believe in the power of God's word in him, a power greater than all that we fear.

Today the church commemorates Onesimos Nesib, a translator and evangelist who died in 1931.

Prayer of the Day

O God of creation, eternal majesty, you preside over land and sea, sunshine and storm. By your strength pilot us, by your power preserve us, by your wisdom instruct us, and by your hand protect us, through Jesus Christ, our Savior and Lord.

Gospel Acclamation

Alleluia. Now is the accept- | able time;* now is the day | of salvation. *Alleluia.* (2 Cor. 6:2)

Readings and Psalm

Job 38:1-11

At the end of the book of Job, after Job and his companions have argued about the cause of the great suffering Job endures, God finally speaks. These verses begin that speech, which is a grand vision of creation, describing God's ordering of the cosmos and inviting Job to marvel at its beauty.

Psalm 107:1-3, 23-32

You stilled the storm and silenced the waves of the sea. (Ps. 107:29)

2 Corinthians 6:1-13

Paul and his fellow workers experience great hardships and even rejection while carrying out their missionary work. Nevertheless, Paul continuously proclaims that God has not rejected us but is graciously working for our salvation.

Mark 4:35-41

Jesus' calming of the storm on the sea reveals his power over evil, since the sea represents evil and chaos. The boat on the sea is a symbol of the church and invites us to trust God amid life's turbulence.

Semicontinuous reading and psalm

I Samuel 17:[1a, 4-11, 19-23] 32-49

In this passage, the description of the soldier Goliath vividly depicts the superiority of Philistine military might. In contrast, young David is armed with a slingshot and faith in God. David's victory witnesses to the whole earth that "there is a God in Israel."

Psalm 9:9-20

You, O LORD, will be a refuge in time of trouble. (Ps. 9:9)

Color   Green

CD-ROM Images

Icon Three: 0619-0625_Lect12_B

Icon Two: Proper07_Sun12_B

Icon: 103

Prayers of Intercession

With the whole people of God in Christ Jesus, let us pray for the church, those in need, and all of God's creation.

A brief silence.

We pray for the church. Still its storms, calm its fears, and make it an evangelizing witness to your power and justice. God of mercy,

hear our prayer.

We give you thanks for the blessings of your creation. Help us find ways to reverse the damage we have done through carelessness and inattentiveness. God of mercy,

hear our prayer.

We pray for all who desire peace but experience conflict, and for those who hope for faith in the middle of the whirlwind. God of mercy,

hear our prayer.

We give you thanks for fathers and for all who provide fatherly care and love. Bless and keep them, now and always. God of mercy,

hear our prayer.

We pray for all those in need: the hungry, the homeless, those in prison, the oppressed, victims of war, and the sick and dying (*especially*). God of mercy,

hear our prayer.

We pray for this assembly, its presence in this community, and its connections to the world. God of mercy,

hear our prayer.

Here other intercessions may be offered.

We give you thanks for all who have shared the gospel and cared for its language (*especially Onesimus Nesib, translator and evangelist, whom we commemorate today*). Strengthened by their witness, help us to share your saving story. God of mercy,

hear our prayer.

Loving God, you are near to us when we cry out to you. Into your embrace we commend all for whom we pray, through Christ and by the power of your Spirit.

Amen.

Ideas and Images for the Day

The wind plays a dramatic role in today's readings. Is God in the wind? God speaks to Job out of the whirlwind. But in the gospel reading, Jesus, the Son of God, is oblivious to the dangerous wind that surrounds the boat he sleeps in. Waves were swamping the boat, surely getting Jesus wet; and yet he slept! Should we be afraid of the wind? Was Jesus mentoring faith behavior by sleeping and then by demanding the winds cease their fury? At the end of the story the disciples were filled with awe by the power Jesus showed by commanding the wind to stop its howling. Their awe, however, seemed to be inspired by their amazement that even nature (the wind) obeyed this man, Jesus. When the storms of life attack us, does the power of Jesus' word serve to push back life's storms?

1. In the third stage of the 2007 Tour de France, a great wind arose. To prevail against the wind, each team picked a front-runner whom they shielded from the wind by using other team members to ride between the wind and the head cyclist. As a church we can shield each other from the tempests of life through Christ's peace and through our care and support of one another.

2. Did the disciples feel that if they hung with Jesus nothing bad would happen to them? Windstorms, including the storms of life, can be terrible experiences with their ferocity as well as their devastation. Fear can grip the strongest of hearts and incapacitate the power to trust in God. Could such fear rob us of our faith?

3. Some years after the events of September 11, 2001, Hollywood produced movies such as *United 93* (Universal Studios, 2006) and *World Trade Center* (Paramount, 2006) that told the story of what unfolded on that day. Many people found it difficult to go to see these films. The pain and trauma of that day were still too fresh to face again. When life's pain is too much to face, Jesus is there with peace and healing grace.

4. Wind has always played a role in scripture, revealing the power of God to act. The church was born in the power of the wind as the Holy Spirit came upon the disciples gathered together in the upper room. It was like the "rush of a violent wind" (Acts 2:2).

5. "Peace! Be still!" The wind ceased and there was a "dead calm" (Mark 4:39). Elijah heard the word of the Lord as a still small voice in the "sheer silence" following the wind that surrounded him in the cave (1 Kings 19:12). Job heard the voice of God after the calamity of life's storms affected him (Job 38). Jesus' words brought a calm that could be felt; a stillness after the ferocity of the wind. This dead calm suggests a void, emptiness. In that emptiness comes Jesus' question: "Why are you afraid?"

Hymns for Worship

Gathering

We praise you, O God   ELW 870, LBW 241

O God, our help in ages past   ELW 632, LBW 320

Hymn of the Day

My life flows on in endless song   ELW 763, WOV 781
HOW CAN I KEEP FROM SINGING

Jesus, Savior, pilot me   ELW 755, LBW 334   PILOT

Praise, praise! You are my rock   ELW 862   ZACHARY WOODS
ROCK

Communion

Calm to the waves   ELW 794

God the sculptor of the mountains   ELW 736

Precious Lord, take my hand   ELW 773, WOV 731

Sending

God of tempest, God of whirlwind   ELW 400

Praise, praise! You are my rock   ELW 862

Eternal Father, strong to save   ELW 756, LBW 467

Additional Hymns and Songs

The sails were spilling wind   HG 63

Be my home   W&P 16

You have come down to the lakeshore   ELW 817, WOV 784

I sought the Lord   H82 689

When the storms of life are raging   TFF 198

Music for the Day

Psalmody and Acclamations

Organ, Anne Krentz. *Gospel Acclamations for Summer*. AFP
9780800678579.

Psalter for Worship Year B, Evangelical Lutheran Worship Edition.
AFP 9780806683839.

Wold, Wayne L. "Psalm 107" from *Psalm Settings for the Church
Year*. AFP 9780800678562.

Choral

▫ Cherwien, David. "How Can I Keep from Singing?" U/SA/SSA, pno.
AFP 9780800658335.

▫ Ellingboe, Bradley. "How Can I Keep From Singing?" TBB, pno, ob.
KJO 5572.

Ferguson, John. "When the Morning Stars Together." SATB, opt
assembly, org, opt hb. MSM 50-6051.

▫ Roesch, Robert A. "Jesus, Savior, Pilot Me." SATB, kybd. AFP
9780800676223.

Children's Choir

Patterson, Mark. "Let All God's Children Sing" from *Children
Sing with Instruments*. UE. U/2 pt, pno, opt tamb, drm. AFP
9780800620349.

▫ denotes choral suggestions that relate to the hymn of the day.
■ denotes songs that are available on iTunes®.

Patterson, Mark. "With One Heart." UE. U, kybd, opt fl. CG A804.

Sleeth, Natalie. "The Lord Be with You." UE. 2 pt, kybd. HIN
HMC1208.

Keyboard / Instrumental

Bisbee, B. Wayne. "Pilot" from *From the Serene to the Whimsical*.
Org. AFP 9780800654412.

Hassell, Michael. "Pilot" from *Traveling Tunes*. Pno, C/B-flat inst/
vla. AFP 9780800656195.

Organ, Anne Krentz. "How Can I Keep from Singing" from *Eight for
Eighty-Eight*, vol. 3. Pno, C/B-flat inst. AFP 9780800623494.

Young, Jeremy. "How Can I Keep from Singing" from *At the Foot of
the Cross*. Pno. AFP 9780800655396.

Handbell

Dobrinski, Cynthia, arr. "What a Friend We Have in Jesus." 3-5 oct,
L3. AG 1872.

McFadden, Jane. "How Can I Keep from Singing?" 3-5 oct, L3. AFP
9780800658120.

McKlveen, Paul A. "Exuberant Joy." 3-5 oct, L2+. JEF MJHS9028.

Praise Ensemble

■ Agnew, Todd/Chris Collins/Edwin O. Excell/John Newton. "Grace
like Rain" from www.praisecharts.com. Ardent/Koala Music.

DeShazo, Lynn/Gary Sadler. "For the Lord Is Good" from *Outrageous Joy*. INT 000768140567.

■ Story, Laura. "Indescribable" from WT. WT/Sixsteps Music.

■ Tomlin, Chris. "Forever" from *I Could Sing of Your Love Forever 2*.
WT 0000809251.

Global

Haugen, Marty. "Bambelela/Never Give Up." SATB/SAB. GIA
G-6309.

Henke, Christopher. "When the Storms of Life Are Raging." SATB,
sop solo. AFP 9780800678258.

Sunday, June 21

Onesimos Nesib, translator, evangelist, 1931

Onesimos Nesib (oh-NESS-ee-mus neh-SEEB) was born in
Ethiopia. He was captured by slave traders and taken from
his Galla homeland to Eritrea, where he was bought, freed,
and educated by Swedish missionaries. He translated the
Bible into Galla and returned to his homeland to preach the
gospel. His tombstone includes a verse from Jeremiah 22:29,
"O land, land, land, hear the word of the Lord!"

Does your congregation support mission work through
synod or churchwide offerings, or do you have a specific
missionary whom you support? Let the commemoration of
Onesimos Nesib be a way for congregations to focus on missions during the summer months.

Wednesday, June 24

John the Baptist

We are now on the far side of the sun from Christmas and the celebration of Jesus' birth. In the Northern Hemisphere the days now begin to grow shorter as we celebrate the birth of John the Baptist, the forerunner of Messiah. In comparing himself to Jesus, John once said, "He must increase, but I must decrease" (John 3:30). Though John was eager to see his own ministry eclipsed, Jesus honored John as being the greatest prophet.

Thursday, June 25

Presentation of the Augsburg Confession, 1530

On this day in 1530 the German and Latin editions of the Augsburg Confession were presented to Emperor Charles of the Holy Roman Empire. The Augsburg Confession was written by Philipp Melanchthon and endorsed by Martin Luther and consists of a brief summary of points in which the reformers saw their teaching as either agreeing with or differing from that of the Roman Catholic Church of the time. In 1580 when the *Book of Concord* was drawn up, the unaltered Augsburg Confession was included as the principal Lutheran confession.

Philipp Melanchthon, renewer of the church, 1560

Though he died on April 19, Philipp Melanchthon (meh-LAHNK-ton) is commemorated today because of his connection with the Augsburg Confession. Colleague and co-reformer with Martin Luther, Melanchthon was a brilliant scholar, known as "the teacher of Germany." The University of Wittenberg hired him as its first professor of Greek, and there he became a friend of Luther. Melanchthon was a popular professor—even his classes at six in the morning had as many as six hundred students. As a reformer he was known for his conciliatory spirit and for finding areas of agreement with fellow Christians. He was never ordained.

In the spirit of Melanchthon's work, consider a summer ecumenical study group with a nearby Roman Catholic parish. Use the Augsburg Confession and the Joint Declaration on the Doctrine of Justification as study documents.

Saturday, June 27

Cyril, Bishop of Alexandria, 444

Remembered as an outstanding theologian as well as a contentious personality, Cyril defended the orthodox teachings about the person of Christ against Nestorius, bishop of Constantinople. Nestorius taught that the divine and human natures of Christ were entirely distinct, and therefore Mary could not be referred to as the *theotokos*, or bearer of God. This conflict, which also had roots in a rivalry for preeminence between Alexandria and Constantinople, involved all of the major Christian leaders of the time, including the patriarchs of Rome, Antioch, and Jerusalem, and finally also the emperor. In the end it was decided that Cyril's interpretation, that Christ's person included both divine and human natures, was correct.

June 28, 2009
Time after Pentecost — Lectionary 13

A woman finds healing by touching Jesus' cloak, and a girl is restored to life when he takes her by the hand. In both cases a boundary is crossed: in Jesus' time the hemorrhaging woman was considered ritually unclean, polluting others by her touch, and anyone who touched a corpse also became unclean. In Mark's gospel Jesus breaks down barriers, from his first meal at a tax collector's house to his last breath on the cross as the temple curtain is torn in two. We dare to touch Jesus in our "uncleanness" and to live as a community that defines no one as an outsider.

Today the church commemorates Irenaeus, Bishop of Lyons.

Prayer of the Day

Almighty and merciful God, we implore you to hear the prayers of your people. Be our strong defense against all harm and danger, that we may live and grow in faith and hope, through Jesus Christ, our Savior and Lord.

Gospel Acclamation

Alleluia. Our Savior Jesus Christ has a-ǀbolished death* and brought life and immortality to light ǀ through the gospel. *Alleluia.* (2 Tim. 1:10)

Readings and Psalm

Lamentations 3:22-33

The book of Lamentations is one of our most important sources of information about the fall of Jerusalem to the Babylonians in 587 B.C. Though the people admit that God's judgment was just, today's reading declares a fervent trust that God will not leave them forever.

or Wisdom 1:13-15; 2:23-24

Dating from shortly before the time of Christ, the Wisdom of Solomon is a Jewish work influenced by Greek thought. In it, wisdom is personified and is depicted as a gift of God to Israel. In this reading, God is emphatically shown to be the creator and preserver of life.

Psalm 30

I will exalt you, O LORD, because you have lifted me up. (Ps. 30:1)

2 Corinthians 8:7-15

Paul encourages the Corinthians to honor their commitment to participate in the collection his churches are organizing for the Christians in Jerusalem. He presents Jesus as an example of selfless stewardship and reminds them that Christians have received abundantly so that they can share abundantly.

Mark 5:21-43

Jairus, a respected leader, begs Jesus to heal his daughter. A woman with a hemorrhage is ritually unclean, treated as an outcast in Jewish society. Both Jairus and the unnamed woman come to Jesus in faith, believing in his power to heal and bring life out of death.

Semicontinuous reading and psalm

2 Samuel 1:1, 17-27

David laments over the deaths of King Saul and his son Jonathan, who was a beloved friend of David's. David mourns for Saul, the first king of Israel, even though Saul tried to kill him on a number of occasions. Though deeply flawed, Saul was still the Lord's anointed.

Psalm 130

Out of the depths I cry to you, O LORD. (Ps. 130:1)

Color   Green

CD-ROM Images

Icon Three: 0626-0702_Lect13_B
Icon Two: Proper08_Sun13_B
Icon: 104

Prayers of Intercession

With the whole people of God in Christ Jesus, let us pray for the church, those in need, and all of God's creation.
A brief silence.

Let us pray for the church, that we may offer the hand and the healing of Christ to stranger and foe. God of mercy, **hear our prayer.**

Let us pray for clean air and water, an abundant harvest, and generosity to share the gifts of God's creation with those who have little. God of mercy, **hear our prayer.**

Let us pray for a conviction and faith (*like the bishop Irenaeus*) to sustain us in every hour, that we might persevere and be grateful, regardless of circumstance. God of mercy, **hear our prayer.**

Let us pray for songs of faith and for musicians, poets, and composers who put the gospel of Christ on our lips. God of mercy, **hear our prayer.**

Let us pray that the wounds of Christ connect us to the wounds of the world, and that in those wounds we will see, hear, and feel your abiding presence with us. God of mercy, **hear our prayer.**

Let us pray for those whose health or circumstances test their faith and their spirits. Comfort and strengthen those who are ill (*especially*) and give to all a measure of your power. God of mercy, **hear our prayer.**

Here other intercessions may be offered.

Every morning your mercy is new, like the dew upon the grass. Like the faithful who have gone before us, may we wait for your presence with confidence and in stillness. God of mercy, **hear our prayer.**

Loving God, you are near to us when we cry out to you. Into your embrace we commend all for whom we pray, through Christ and by the power of your Spirit. **Amen.**

Ideas and Images for the Day

This reading from Mark includes three stories: the great crowd that gathered around Jesus and pressed in upon him; the healing of the hemorrhaging woman who reached out in faith to touch the hem of Jesus' garment; and the healing and raising of Jairus's twelve-year-old daughter. The response of this town to Jesus' arrival indicates that they saw him as a healer. Little did they know that Jesus could also restore all kinds of life! Not only did he physically bring back to life a twelve-year-old girl, he also made it possible for the hemorrhaging woman to participate fully in the community again. Restoring these two to life, the community was made whole.

1. The crowd is a witness to Jesus' presence and healing power. It is from the crowd's vantage point that we hear the story. We become part of the crowd witnessing the drama unfold. We become the woman—simultaneously terrified and joyful as she is healed. We are the desperate parents of the daughter who lies dying. We are astounded when she is restored to life and to us. We are the friends and neighbors standing around wondering what to do. These encounters are the stories of everyday lives touched by the power of God. These stories are the stuff of amazing grace as individuals are healed and restored to their communities.

2. Refugees have fled many war-torn countries. Caught in refugee camps, sometimes for years, many are separated from family members. Some are relocated to countries such as the United States and Canada, where they become part of the community in which they are placed. These refugees need resources and support as they build a new life in a new country and a new community.

3. Text messaging and Internet blogs have become the new communities for today's young people. How can the realness of persons and the power of God be experienced in cyberspace? A teenage girl died of cancer in a small community. Word of her death spread quickly among the teens as text messages were sent and forwarded, one after another. The parents of the girl who died were startled when friends and acquaintances began showing up at their house to share in their grief. The young people were full of spiritual questions. Their impromptu gathering, made possible by technology, provided an opportunity to express the gospel.

Hymns for Worship
Gathering
Listen, God is calling   ELW 513, WOV 712
I'm so glad Jesus lifted me   ELW 860, WOV 673

Hymn of the Day
If you but trust in God to guide you   ELW 769, LBW 453
  WER NUR DEN LIEBEN GOTT
O Christ, the healer, we have come   ELW 610, LBW 360
  DISTRESS
We come to you for healing, Lord   ELW 617   MARTYRDOM

Communion
Healer of our every ill   ELW 612, WOV 738
Lord, take my hand and lead me   ELW 767, LBW 333
Come, ye disconsolate   ELW 607

Sending

Abide, O dearest Jesus   ELW 539, LBW 263
God, whose giving knows no ending   ELW 678, LBW 408

Additional Hymns and Songs

God's word throughout the ages   HG 43
Great is the Lord   W&P 53
Great is thy faithfulness   ELW 733, WOV 771   √
Give thanks   W&P 41, TFF 292

Music for the Day
Psalmody and Acclamations

Haugen, Marty. "Psalm 30" from *Psalm Settings for the Church Year*.
   AFP 9780800678562.
Organ, Anne Krentz. *Gospel Acclamations for Summer*. AFP
   9780800678579.
Psalter for Worship Year B, Evangelical Lutheran Worship Edition.
   AFP 9780806683839.

Choral

▫ Cherwien, David. "If You But Trust in God to Guide You." SATB,
   solo, assembly, org, opt fl, opt cello. MSM 60-9027.
Ferguson, John. "A Song of Thanksgiving." SATB, org. AFP
   9780800653859. *The Augsburg Choirbook*. AFP 9780800656782.
Sateren, Leland B. "His Compassions Fail Not." SAATBB. LOR
   AM416.
Weber, Paul D. "I Will Sing the Story of Your Love." SATB/U, opt
   assembly, kybd. AFP 9780800657000.

Children's Choir

Horman, John D. "Tell All the World." UE. 2 pt, kybd, opt Orff/hb.
   CG A681.
Melby, James. "In Thee Is Gladness." UE. U, 2 fl, drm. CPH 98-2658.
Sleeth, Natalie. "Make Music for the Lord." UE. 2 pt, kybd. CG A469.

Keyboard / Instrumental

Bach, J. S. "Wer nur den lieben Gott" from *Orgelbüchlein*. Org. CPH
   97-5774U1.
Manz, Paul O. "Wer nur den lieben Gott" from *Improvisations on
   Classic Chorales*. Org. MSM 10-843.
Powell, Robert J. "Distress" from *Early American Hymn Tune Pre-
   ludes*, set 2. Org. CPH 97-6679U1.
Sowash, Bradley. "Wer nur den lieben Gott" from *Great German
   Hymns in Contemporary Style*. Pno. AFP 9780800637446.

Handbell

Buckwalter, Karen Lakey. "Prayer for Healing." 4-6 oct, L4. AG
   46017.
Hanna, Donna, arr. "If You But Trust in God to Guide You." 3-5 oct,
   L2. GIA G-6166.
McKlveen, Paul A. "Faith." 3-5 oct, L2+. JEF MJHS9396.

Praise Ensemble

Dane, Mitch/Bebo Norman. "Nothing without You" from music
   notes.com. New Spring Publishing, Inc./Appstreet Music/Rot-
   ten Banana Music.
■ Park, Andy. "The River Is Here" from *Breakforth Worship Songbook*.
   New Creation Ministries. www.new-creation.net.
■ Smith, Michael W./Martin Smith. "Healing Rain" from *WOW Hits
   2006 Songbook*. WM 080689509285.
■ Zschech, Darlene. "Know You More" from www.praisecharts.com.
   Hillsong Publishing/INT.

Global

Hopson, Hal H. "When We Are Living/Pues si vivimos." SATB,
   kybd. AFP 9780800658304.
Smallwood, Richard. "I Will Sing Praises." SAB, pno. ALF
   BSCM00063.

Sunday, June 28
Irenaeus, Bishop of Lyons, c. 202

Irenaeus (ee-ren-AY-us) believed that the way to remain
steadfast to the truth was to hold fast to the faith handed
down from the apostles. He believed that only Matthew,
Mark, Luke, and John were trustworthy gospels. Irenaeus
was an opponent of gnosticism and its emphasis on dual-
ism. As a result of his battles with the gnostics, he was
one of the first to speak of the church as "catholic." By
catholic he meant that local congregations did not exist
by themselves but were linked to one another in the whole
church. He also maintained that this church was not contained within any national boundaries. He argued that the
church's message was for all people, in contrast to the gnostics and their emphasis on "secret knowledge."

What do we mean when we say that the church is
catholic and apostolic? What are the ways that the apostolic
faith is passed down through the generations?

Monday, June 29
Peter and Paul, Apostles

Today we celebrate two great figures of the early church,
Peter and Paul, who represent the spread of the gospel to
both Jews and Gentiles and, according to tradition, were
martyred on this date. The witness of Peter and Paul
inspires us as we seek ways to faithfully proclaim the gospel
in our contemporary context.

▫ denotes choral suggestions that relate to the hymn of the day.
■ denotes songs that are available on iTunes®.
224

Wednesday, July 1

Catherine Winkworth, 1878; John Mason Neale, 1866; hymn translators

Neale was an English priest associated with the movement for church renewal at Cambridge. Winkworth lived most of her life in Manchester, where she was involved in promoting women's rights. These two hymnwriters translated many hymn texts into English. Catherine Winkworth devoted herself to the translation of German hymns, and John Mason Neale specialized in ancient Latin and Greek hymns.

Many of the most beloved hymns in the English language are the work of these gifted poets.

Friday, July 3

Thomas, Apostle

Thomas is perhaps best remembered as "Doubting Thomas." But alongside this doubt, the Gospel of John shows Thomas as fiercely loyal: "Let us also go, that we may die with him" (John 11:16). And John's gospel shows Thomas moving from doubt to deep faith. Thomas makes one of the strongest confessions of faith in the New Testament, "My Lord and my God!" (John 20:28). From this confession of faith, ancient stories tell of Thomas's missionary work to India, where Christian communities were flourishing a thousand years before the arrival of sixteenth-century missionaries.

The feast of St. Thomas is observed on various dates, and a long tradition in the West placed it on December 21. In 1969, however, the Roman Catholic calendar moved it to July 3 in agreement with the Syrian Church. *Evangelical Lutheran Worship* follows this ecumenical trend.

July 5, 2009
Time after Pentecost — Lectionary 14

Jesus does great deeds of power and gives his disciples authority over demons. Yet none of this power is unilateral; it all must be received by faith. Jesus asks his disciples to go out without money or supplies, so that they will be dependent on how others receive them. When we are sent from the assembly to witness and to heal, we are asked to be vulnerable, to be dependent on the reception of others. The Spirit always operates in the between: between Jesus and his Abba, between Jesus and us, between you and me, between us and those to whom we are sent.

Prayer of the Day

God of the covenant, in our baptism you call us to proclaim the coming of your kingdom. Give us the courage you gave the apostles, that we may faithfully witness to your love and peace in every circumstance of life, in the name of Jesus Christ, our Savior and Lord.

Gospel Acclamation

Alleluia. I will boast gladly ˈ of my weaknesses,* so that the power of Christ may ˈ dwell in me. *Alleluia.* (2 Cor. 12:9)

Readings and Psalm

Ezekiel 2:1-5

In 597 B.C. the priest Ezekiel was removed into exile in Babylon. While there he received a vision of God appearing majestically on a chariot throne. Today's reading recounts God's commissioning of Ezekiel during this vision. The prophet is to speak God's word to a people unwilling to hear.

Psalm 123

Our eyes look to you, O God, until you show us your mercy. (Ps. 123:2)

2 Corinthians 12:2-10

Christians do not boast of their own accomplishments. Rather, Christian boasting focuses attention on how the power of Christ is present in our lives, especially in times of weakness and vulnerability. No matter what our circumstances in life, Christ's grace is sufficient for us.

Mark 6:1-13

At home and abroad, Jesus and his disciples encounter resistance as they seek to proclaim God's word and relieve affliction.

Semicontinuous reading and psalm

2 Samuel 5:1-5, 9-10

Already king over Judah, the southern kingdom, David here is anointed king over Israel, the northern kingdom, as well. Captured by David, Jerusalem is chosen as the political and religious center for the new combined territory. It is known ever after as "the city of David."

Psalm 48

Great is the LORD, and highly to be praised, in the city of our God. (Ps. 48:1)

Color Green

CD-ROM Images

Icon Three: 0703-0709_Lect14_B

Icon Two: Proper09_Sun14_B

Icon: 105

Prayers of Intercession

With the whole people of God in Christ Jesus, let us pray for the church, those in need, and all of God's creation.

A brief silence.

We ask your blessing upon the proclamation and hearing of your word. Sustain those who preach and those who receive it. God of mercy,

hear our prayer.

We pray for those who work to protect and conserve our rich and plentiful resources. Give them insight and innovation as they deal with the vast challenges of caring for your creation. God of mercy,

hear our prayer.

We pray for all nations, for their interdependence, and for the good of humankind. Keep us mindful of the blessings of our country and its freedoms. God of mercy,

hear our prayer.

We pray for all who are ill or in the hospital (*especially*). Surround them with the care of their family and friends, and grant them your healing. God of mercy,

hear our prayer.

We pray for all who long for welcome and hospitality but find only rejection and exclusion. Lead us into a ministry of hospitality in our workplaces, schools, neighborhoods, and homes. God of mercy,

hear our prayer.

Here other intercessions may be offered.

We give you thanks for all the saints and those who rest in you, and pray that the example of their lives might strengthen us in our own witness and service. God of mercy,

hear our prayer.

Loving God, you are near to us when we cry out to you. Into your embrace we commend all for whom we pray, through Christ and by the power of your Spirit.

Amen.

Ideas and Images for the Day

"An expert is someone who comes from more than a hundred miles away and carries an attaché case," the saying goes. The effectiveness of church consultants and intentional interims is based in part on this idea. An itinerant spiritual leader with no personal stake in a congregation's mission can bring a powerful new perspective to a faith community struggling with the demons of "how we've always done it." In today's gospel reading, Jesus himself encounters skepticism from people in his hometown who "knew him when." Later, the apostles are sent out to be traveling ministers and are given the authority by Jesus himself to heal, drive out demons, and call people to repentance in the communities in which they serve. The results are good.

1. In an imaginative scene from the film *The Gospel of John* (Buena Vista Home Entertainment, 2003), we see Jesus in his hometown, working as a carpenter alongside his brothers in the family business. The brothers challenge Jesus to make his prophetic work known more openly, but not because they wish to honor him. John's text assures us that "not even his brothers believed in him" (John 7:3-5). It is not until after his resurrection and ascension that they, like the apostles, develop a fuller sense of Jesus' true nature (Acts 1:14).

2. Dr. Murray Bowen's family systems theory is the basis for much work today in the area of pastoral care and congregational health. Bowen's research has led a generation of church leaders to conclude that defining ourselves in our families of origin is key to the process of developing a clear sense of mission as individuals and as leaders in the church. See Edwin Friedman, *Generation to Generation* (New York: The Guilford Press, 1985), and the work of the Lombard Mennonite Peace Center (www.lmpeacecenter.org; click on "Healthy Congregations").

3. ELCA missionaries today undergo rigorous training before they are sent into the world as teachers, engineers, pastors, and in countless other roles. Whatever the role, each missionary is called upon to witness to Christ in word and deed through his or her vocation. Go to www.elca.org/globalmission to find links that provide more information about missionary work today.

4. The ELCA's vision statement reminds us that we are claimed, gathered and sent by God for the sake of the world; our Sunday liturgy reflects this vision. *Evangelical Lutheran Worship* contains hymns and songs for sending (#534–551). They remind us that like the twelve apostles in today's passage, we are sent forth from an encounter with the living word of God to bring healing to a broken world.

Hymns for Worship
Gathering
In Christ called to baptize   ELW 575
Lord, you give the great commission   ELW 579, WOV 756

Hymn of the Day
The Son of God, our Christ   ELW 584, LBW 434
SURSUM CORDA
O Christ, our light, O Radiance true   ELW 675, LBW 380
O JESU CHRISTE, WAHRES LICHT
Open your ears, O faithful people   ELW 519, WOV 715
YISRAEL V'ORAITA

Communion
We all are one in mission   ELW 576, WOV 755
Draw us in the Spirit's tether   ELW 470, WOV 703
Strengthen for service, Lord   ELW 497, LBW 218

Sending
To be your presence   ELW 546
Rise up, O saints of God!   ELW 669, LBW 383
Build us up, Lord   ELW 670

Additional Hymns and Songs
O carpenter, why leave the bench   HG 118
O Christ, who called the Twelve   HG 55
God of love, have mercy   DH 10
Give thanks   W&P 41, TFF 292
Go in peace and serve the Lord   W&P 46

Music for the Day
Psalmody and Acclamations
Jennings, Carolyn. "Psalm 123" from *Psalm Settings for the Church Year.* AFP 9780800678562.

Organ, Anne Krentz. *Gospel Acclamations for Summer.* AFP 9780800678579.

Psalter for Worship Year B, Evangelical Lutheran Worship Edition. AFP 9780806683839.

Choral
Bender, Jan/arr. John A. Behnke. "O God, O Lord of Heaven and Earth." SATB, opt assembly, org, opt 2 tpt. AFP 9780800652500. *The Augsburg Choirbook.* AFP 9780800656782.

▫ Hobby, Robert A. "O Christ Our Light, O Radiance True." 2 pt mxd, ob, kybd. CPH 98-2891.

▫ Hobby, Robert A. "Open Your Ears, O Faithful People." U/2 pt mxd, hb, fl, fc. AFP 9780800656102.

Thompson, Randall. "My Grace Is Sufficient" from *12 Canticles.* SATB. ECS 4102.

Children's Choir
Brazzeal, David. "Now Paul, He Was a Servant." UE. 2 pt, kybd. CG A782.

Jennings, Carolyn. "America the Beautiful." UE. U/2/3 pt, pno. KJO 6210.

Sleeth, Natalie. "Praise the Lord" from *Sunday Songbook.* LE. U, opt canon, kybd, opt C inst. HIN HMB102.

Keyboard / Instrumental
Albrecht, Mark. "Yisrael v'oraita" from *Three for Piano and Sax.* Pno, inst. AFP 9780800657970.

Behnke, John A. "O Jesu Christe, wahres Licht" from *European Connection*, vol. 1. Org. CPH 97-6782U1.

Phillips, Craig. "Yisrael v'oraita" from *Augsburg Organ Library: Autumn.* Org. AFP 9780800675790.

Sedio, Mark. "O Jesu Christe, wahres Licht" from *Come and Praise.* Org, inst. AFP 9780800678500.

Handbell
Lamb, Linda R., arr. "Freedom Rings." 3-5 oct hb/hc, L3+. GIA G-6589.

Nelson, Susan T. "Give Me Jesus." 3 oct hb/hc, L3. AFP 9780800658137.

Warren, G./Kevin McChesney, arr. "National Hymn." 3-5 oct, L3-. JEF MJHS9298. Brass Ensemble: JEF MJHS9298B. Full Score: JEF MJHS9298FS.

▫ denotes choral suggestions that relate to the hymn of the day.
■ denotes songs that are available on iTunes®.

Praise Ensemble

- Byrd, Marc/Steve Hindalong. "God of Wonders" from *God of Wonders Songbook*. INT 0000768205679.

  Hersch, James. "Send Us Out" from *Dakota Road Music Keyboard/Guitar Edition 1.5*. Dakota Road Music. www.dakotaroadmusic.com.

- Smith, Martin. "Shout to the North" from www.praisecharts.com. Curious? Music UK.

- Thompson, John W./Randy Scruggs. "Sanctuary" from *More Songs for Praise & Worship*. WM 080689310188.

Global

Hassell, Michael. "Jesus Loves Me." SATB, pno, sop/alto sax. AFP 9780800656515.

Haugen, Marty. "This Is My Song." SATB, solo, kybd, gtr, str qrt. GIA G-7104.

Monday, July 6

Jan Hus, martyr, 1415

Jan Hus was a Bohemian priest who spoke against abuses in the church of his day in many of the same ways Luther would a century later. He spoke against the withholding of the cup at the eucharist and because of this stance was excommunicated, not for heresy but for insubordination toward his archbishop. He preached against the selling of indulgences and was particularly mortified by the indulgence trade of two rival claimants to the papacy who were raising money for war against each other. He was found guilty of heresy by the Council of Constance and burned at the stake.

The followers of Jan Hus became known as the Czech Brethren and later became the Moravian Church, an ecumenical partner with the Evangelical Lutheran Church in America.

Saturday, July 11

Benedict of Nursia, Abbot of Monte Cassino, c. 540

Benedict is known as the father of Western monasticism. He was educated in Rome but was appalled by the decline of life around him. He went to live as a hermit, and a community of monks came to gather around him. In the prologue of his rule for monasteries he wrote that his intent in drawing up his regulations was "to set down nothing harsh, nothing burdensome." It is that moderate spirit that characterizes his rule and the monastic communities that are formed by it. Benedict still encourages a generous spirit of hospitality in that visitors to Benedictine communities are to be welcomed as Christ himself.

July 12, 2009
Time after Pentecost — Lectionary 15

When Amos told what he saw when God held up the plumb line of justice next to Israel—that the poor were being trampled—he was a threat to the power of priests and king. John the Baptist also spoke truth to power, and Herod had him beheaded. In Herod's fear that Jesus is John returned from the dead, we may hear hope for the oppressed: that all the prophets killed through the ages are alive in Jesus. We are called to witness to justice in company with them.

Today the church commemorates Nathan Söderblom, Bishop of Uppsala, who died in 1931.

Prayer of the Day

O God, from you come all holy desires, all good counsels, and all just works. Give to us, your servants, that peace which the world cannot give, that our hearts may be set to obey your commandments; and also that we, being defended from the fear of our enemies, may live in peace and quietness, through Jesus Christ, our Savior and Lord.

Gospel Acclamation

Alleluia. May the God of our Lord Jesus Christ enlighten the eyes | of our hearts,* that we may know the hope to which | God has called us. *Alleluia.* (Eph. 1:17-18)

Readings and Psalm
Amos 7:7-15

Amos was not the kind of prophet attached to temples or royal courts. Rather, he was an ordinary farmer from Judah (the southern kingdom) called by God to speak to Israel (the northern kingdom). God's word of judgment through Amos conflicted with the king's court prophet Amaziah, whom Amos encountered at Bethel.

Psalm 85:8-13

I will listen to what the LORD God is saying. (Ps. 85:8)

Ephesians 1:3-14

In Jesus, all of God's plans and purposes have been made known as heaven and earth are united in Christ. Through Jesus, we have been chosen as God's children and have been promised eternal salvation.

Mark 6:14-29

As Jesus and his disciples begin to attract attention, Mark recalls the story of John the Baptist's martyrdom. Like John, Jesus and his disciples will also suffer at the hands of those opposed to the gospel of salvation.

Semicontinuous reading and psalm
2 Samuel 6:1-5, 12b-19

The ark of the covenant, long a symbol of God's presence with Israel, is brought into Jerusalem by David. The entrance of the ark into this new capital city is marked by great rejoicing, and David himself is the chief dancer. His wife Michal, King Saul's daughter, considers such behavior undignified.

Psalm 24

Lift up your heads, O gates, that the King of glory may come in. (Ps. 24:7)

Color   Green

CD-ROM Images

Icon Three: 0710-0716_Lect15_B
Icon Two: Proper10_Sun15_B
Icon: 106

Prayers of Intercession

With the whole people of God in Christ Jesus, let us pray for the church, those in need, and all of God's creation.
A brief silence.
God of truth, grant to your church the gift of speaking truth to power, love to hate, hope to despair. God of mercy,
hear our prayer.
Creator God, you made the world full of glory and mystery, full of creatures beyond number and name. Make us careful stewards of the beauty and diversity of your creation. God of mercy,
hear our prayer.

Gracious God, we give you thanks for prophets like John the Baptist who call us to be disciples of Jesus, who remind us to live in mercy, with justice. God of mercy,
hear our prayer.
God of all mercy, strengthen the baptized in this congregation and throughout the world. Help us to live secure in the promise of life with you. God of mercy,
hear our prayer.
God of all healing, we pray for all who are sick, those who are homebound, and those with special needs (*especially*). Comfort them with your presence and promise. God of mercy,
hear our prayer.
Here other intercessions may be offered.
God of every time and place, we give you thanks for witnesses (*like Bishop Nathan Söderblom*) who point us to you. May their example fill your church with unending hope. God of mercy,
hear our prayer.
Loving God, you are near to us when we cry out to you. Into your embrace we commend all for whom we pray, through Christ and by the power of your Spirit.
Amen.

Ideas and Images for the Day

World leaders need people they can trust to tell them the truth, even it if is difficult for them to hear. King Herod, though he was perplexed by John the Baptist's challenge to his immoral lifestyle, knew John was "a righteous and holy man." Herod tolerated and even protected John. Herodias was not so understanding, and John's integrity cost him his head. Later, Herod, recognizing the truth in the person of Jesus, mistook him for a resurrected John. The church, like John, is called to speak the truth to power. We know this carries risks—if not of death (still a real threat for Christians in some parts of the world), then alienation and hostility from the powers that be. The church's integrity, however, can lead the world to recognize the resurrected Christ in us.

1. In Shakespeare's *King Lear* it is the Fool's job to tell the truth to the king when no one else dares to. To do his job, the Fool must use his ability to make the king laugh, and so earn his trust and affection. Failure to mix humor with hard truths could result in the loss of job and/or head. As "fools for the sake of Christ" (1 Cor. 4:10), can the church use humility and humor to earn the world's trust in our efforts to do the job of speaking the truth from a scriptural perspective?

2. In his book *The Powers That Be* (Doubleday, 1998), Walter Wink asserts that all institutions, including corporations, governments, and churches, embrace cosmic "powers" that define their values. Wink believes that the powers that drive many nations and corporations are violent and domineering, and that their values are therefore idolatrous. Jesus' path of practical nonviolence, he says, is the way God has chosen to confront the powers that be and overthrow evil in the world.

3. Herod Antipas wielded substantial power in his time, even power over life and death. Yet if it were not for his role in the life and mission of Christ, the world would scarcely remember him. Percy Bysshe Shelley's poem "Ozymandias" reflects on the fleeting nature of earthly power, like that of King Herod. "Look on my works, ye mighty, and despair!" is the inscription on the statue of a proud and cruel ruler, found by a traveler among the desolate ruins of a once-mighty kingdom. Read the poem at http://en.wikipedia.org/wiki/Ozymandias.

4. The singer Bono has used his fame and personal charm to establish himself among world leaders as a credible advocate for the poor. He has also used his background in scripture to speak with church leaders about AIDS and other urgent social issues. See, for example, the end of Jann S. Wenner's interview with Bono for the November 3, 2005, issue of *Rolling Stone*. Excerpts at www.rollingstone.com/news/story/8651280/bono.

Hymns for Worship
Gathering
Let us go now to the banquet   ELW 523
Let streams of living justice   ELW 710
O God of light   ELW 507, LBW 237

Hymn of the Day
Let justice flow like streams   ELW 717, WOV 763, TFF 48
ST. THOMAS
Faith of our fathers   ELW 812/813, LBW 500
ST. CATHERINE
Lead on, O King eternal!   ELW 805, LBW 495   *LANCASHIRE*

Communion
We come to the hungry feast   ELW 479, WOV 766
The church of Christ, in every age   ELW 729, LBW 433

Sending
God of tempest, God of whirlwind   ELW 400
The right hand of God   ELW 889 (omit st. 5 except in the Caribbean)

Additional Hymns and Songs

Dancing at the harvest   DH 40
O Lord, let us see your kindness   TFF 8
Open our eyes, Lord   W&P 113
All who would valiant be   LBW 498

Music for the Day
Psalmody and Acclamations

Erickson, Rick. *Gospel Acclamations for Summer.* AFP 9780800678579.

Mummert, Mark. "Psalm 85" from *Psalm Settings for the Church Year.* AFP 9780800678562.

Psalter for Worship Year B, Evangelical Lutheran Worship Edition. AFP 9780806683839.

Choral

Handel, G. F. "All My Spirit Longs to Savor" from *Chantry Choirbook.* SATB, kybd. AFP 9780800657772.

Mendelssohn, Felix/arr. Carl F. Schalk. "Grant Peace, We Pray." SATB, org. CPH 98-2212.

Rorem, Ned. "Mercy and Truth Are Met." SATB, kybd. B&H 6101.

Vulpius, Melchior/arr. Marie Pooler. "Abide with Us, Our Savior" from *Unison and Two-Part Anthems.* U/SA, kybd. AFP 9780800648916.

Children's Choir

Burkhardt, Michael. "Rejoice." UE. 2 pt, kybd. MSM 50-9507.

Christopherson, Dorothy. "The Lord Is My Salvation." LE. U, pno, fl, opt fc. AFP 11-10254. OP

Sleeth, Natalie. "It Is Good" from *Laudamus.* UE. 2 pt, kybd. HIN HMB126.

Keyboard / Instrumental

Carlson, J. Bert. "St. Catherine" from *Let It Rip! at the Piano,* vol. 2. Pno. AFP 9780800675806.

Culli, Benjamin. "St. Thomas" from *Fount of Every Blessing.* Org. CPH 97-7082U1.

Curnow, James. "Lancashire" from *More Great Hymns: Instrumental Solos for Worship.* Org/pno, inst. Org/pno score HAL CMP 9033.04. Six inst scores HAL CMP 0927.04-0932.04.

Helman, Michael. "Lancashire" from *Augsburg Organ Library: Autumn.* Org. AFP 9780800675790.

Handbell

Ingram, Bill. "Festival Piece on 'Lancashire'." 4-5 oct, L2. National Music Publisher HB-349.

Moklebust, Cathy, arr. "Lancashire" from *Hymn Stanzas for Handbells.* 4-5 oct, L3. AFP 9780800655761. 2-3 oct, L3. AFP 9780800657338.

Page, Anna Laura. "Rejoice, Ye Pure in Heart." 3-5 oct, L2. ALF 19648.

Praise Ensemble

Crowder, David, arr. "Doxology" from WT.

■ Furler, Peter/Steve Taylor. "He Reigns" from www.praisecharts.com. Ariose Music/Soylent Tunes.

■ Redman, Matt/Beth Redman. "Blessed Be Your Name" from www.praisecharts.com.

■ Reeves, Jesse/Chris Tomlin. "Not to Us" from WT. WT/Sixsteps Music.

Global

Bayawi, Nabil Wasfi/John Campbell/Maggie Hamilon. "Nasibi/My Portion" from *Pave the Way: Global Songs 3.* SATB, kybd, gtr. AFP 9780800676896.

Makeever, Ray. "Dancing at the Harvest/Psalm 85" from *Dancing at the Harvest.* U, pno, gtr. AFP 9780800655938.

Sunday, July 12
Nathan Söderblom, Bishop of Uppsala, 1931

In 1930, this Swedish theologian, ecumenist, and social activist received the Nobel Prize for peace. Söderblom (ZAY-der-blom) saw the value of the ancient worship of the church catholic and encouraged the liturgical movement. He also valued the work of liberal Protestant scholars and believed social action was a first step on the path toward a united Christianity. He organized the Universal Christian Council on Life and Work, one of the organizations that in 1948 came together to form the World Council of Churches.

Friday, July 17
Bartolomé de Las Casas, missionary to the Indies, 1566

Bartolomé de Las Casas was a Spanish priest and a missionary in the Western Hemisphere. He first came to the West while serving in the military, and he was granted a large estate that included a number of indigenous slaves. When he was ordained in 1513, he granted freedom to his servants. This act characterized much of the rest of Las Casas's ministry. Throughout the Caribbean and Central America, he worked to stop the enslavement of native people, to halt the brutal treatment of women by military forces, and to promote laws that humanized the process of colonization.

In a time when churches continue to work for the rights of all people, we can recall the words of Las Casas: "The Indians are our brothers, and Christ has given his life for them. Why, then, do we persecute them with such inhuman savagery when they do not deserve such treatment?"

■ denotes songs that are available on iTunes®.

July 19, 2009

Time after Pentecost — Lectionary 16

Mark's gospel makes clear how great was the press of the crowd, with its countless needs to be met, on Jesus and his disciples. Yet in today's gospel Jesus advises his disciples to get away and rest, to take care of themselves. Sometimes we think that when others are in great need we shouldn't think of ourselves at all; but Jesus also honors the caregivers' need. We are sent from Christ's table to care for others and for ourselves.

Prayer of the Day

O God, powerful and compassionate, you shepherd your people, faithfully feeding and protecting us. Heal each of us, and make us a whole people, that we may embody the justice and peace of your Son, Jesus Christ, our Savior and Lord.

Gospel Acclamation

Alleluia. My sheep ˡ hear my voice.* I know them, and they ˡ follow me. *Alleluia.* (John 10:27)

Readings and Psalm

Jeremiah 23:1-6

Jeremiah prophesied before the exile in 587 B.C. In this passage, he uses the metaphor of a shepherd to describe the bad kings who have scattered the "flock" of Israel. God promises to gather the flock and to raise up a new king from David's line to save Israel and Judah.

Psalm 23

The LORD is my shepherd; I shall not be in want. (Ps. 23:1)

Ephesians 2:11-22

The author of this letter is reminding his audience that originally they were not part of God's chosen people. Through Jesus' death, however, they are included in God's household of faith, whose cornerstone is Jesus Christ.

Mark 6:30-34, 53-56

When Jesus sent his disciples out to teach and heal, they ministered among large numbers of people. Their work was motivated by Christ's desire to be among those in need.

Semicontinuous reading and psalm

2 Samuel 7:1-14a

Instead of David building a house (temple) for the Lord, the Lord promises to establish David's house (dynasty) forever. Centuries later, after the Babylonian exile, no king sat on the throne. Even then, however, the Israelites remembered this promise and continued to hope for a king, the messiah, the Lord's anointed.

Psalm 89:20-37

Your love, O LORD, forever will I sing. (Ps. 89:1)

Color   Green

CD-ROM Images

Icon Three: 0717-0723_Lect16_B
Icon Two: Proper11_Sun16_B
Icon: 107

Prayers of Intercession

With the whole people of God in Christ Jesus, let us pray for the church, those in need, and all of God's creation.

A brief silence.

Gracious God, send us out into the world as messengers of your gospel. Help us to hear your voice and obey your commands. God of mercy,

hear our prayer.

Eternal God, in the beginning you spoke and a world was created. Renew what we have misused and neglected and make us worthy stewards of the world you have entrusted to our care and tending. God of mercy,

hear our prayer.

Righteous Judge, guide those who serve in governments throughout the world. Give them wisdom to administer justice and to strive for peace in our troubled world. God of mercy,

hear our prayer.

Merciful God, we pray for all your children, for the innocent who suffer, and for all who find themselves the valley of the shadow of death. God of mercy,

hear our prayer.

Loving God, hear our prayers for all who are sick, hospitalized, or who have special needs this day (*especially*). Grant rest to the weary. Hold them close to you and give them respite. God of mercy,

hear our prayer.

Here other intercessions may be offered.

Great Shepherd, in your time gather all your peoples together, so that with one voice we may give you praise. God of mercy,

hear our prayer.

Loving God, you are near to us when we cry out to you. Into your embrace we commend all for whom we pray, through Christ and by the power of your Spirit.

Amen.

Ideas and Images for the Day

Shepherd is both a common noun and an action verb. The noun denotes a role: a tender of sheep, an ancient king, a spiritual guide. The verb tells us more. It means to lead, to protect, to watch over. Shepherding requires great responsibility, care, and even love for the flock. Since the days of the patriarchs the people of Israel have seen God as their great shepherd. Jesus, who is one being with the Father, takes both the role and the activity upon himself. In today's gospel reading he sacrifices for the flock, looking upon his people with compassion and tending their need for nourishment and rest. Later, he will sacrifice much more. He will lay down his life for the world, so that all people may become his flock, and so that his Spirit may guide and care for all the sheep forever.

1. The image of the Good Shepherd is prominent in church stained glass window art throughout the world. This image of Jesus as the shepherd carries implications for Christians of our own "sheep-ness." For a short, contemporary drama on the power of this image and our ambivalence toward it, see "Windows on God" in David Kehret's *Can These Bones Live?* (Augsburg Fortress, 1999, pp. 57-60).

2. Brian Howard's children's song "I Just Wanna Be a Sheep" (www.butterflysong.com) expresses a childlike acceptance of Christ as our shepherd. Howard's list of alternatives to being sheep—Pharisee, Sadducee, hypocrite, Canaanite—provokes glee among children. On deeper consideration, the humorous attributes identified in Howard's verses might provide playful ideas for a sermon or children's message.

3. The Spanish noun for shepherd is *pastor*. Many pastors in today's church struggle with overwork and burnout in their attempts to fill the role of shepherd following Christ's example of self-sacrifice. And frequently the congregational flock has a mind of its own. Is the connotation of shepherding in the pastor's title a helpful one for congregations and clergy today?

4. Historian Paul Johnson, in his *A History of Christianity* (Simon and Schuster, 1976), documents centuries of abuse of power by the church and its leaders. See also 1 and 2 Kings for accounts of shepherds who failed to serve faithfully. Christian evangelists and church leaders rely heavily on God's grace in their ongoing efforts to be servant leaders. In baptism we all receive the promise of that grace.

5. Emma Lazarus's words "Give me your tired, your poor, your huddled masses yearning to breathe free," from her poem "The New Colossus" (1883), are on a plaque inside the pedestal of the Statue of Liberty. Biblical in proportion, the aspirations that the poem ascribes to a nation-state may be even more applicable to a church seeking to bring all God's children safely into the fold of God's embrace.

Hymns for Worship

Gathering

O Christ, your heart, compassionate   ELW 722
Christ, Be Our Light   ELW 715
Gather Us In   ELW 532, WOV 718

Hymn of the Day

I heard the voice of Jesus say   ELW 611   *KINGSFOLD*
    ELW 332, LBW 497   *THIRD MODE MELODY*
How sweet the name of Jesus sounds   ELW 620, LBW 345
    ST. PETER
Jesus, still lead on   ELW 624, LBW 341   *SEELENBRÄUTIGAM*

Communion

Shepherd me, O God   ELW 780
We come to you for healing, Lord   ELW 617

Sending

Praise the Lord, rise up rejoicing   ELW 544, LBW 196
Christ is made the sure foundation   ELW 645, WOV 747

Additional Hymns and Songs

They came, a milling crowd   HG 146
No longer strangers   W&P 102
I Am the Good Shepherd   BC 130
Come, bring them to the table   DH 19

Music for the Day
Psalmody and Acclamations

Erickson, Richard. *Gospel Acclamations for Summer.* AFP 9780800678579.

Farlee, Robert Buckley. "Psalm 23" from *Psalm Settings for the Church Year.* AFP 9780800678562.

Psalter for Worship Year B, Evangelical Lutheran Worship Edition. AFP 9780806683839.

Choral

Farnell, Laura/Russell Farnell. "The King of Love My Shepherd Is." SATB, pno, opt cello. KJO 9059.

◻ Frahm, Frederick. "How Sweet the Name of Jesus Sounds." SAB, kybd. AFP 9780800676209.

Wagner, Douglas E. "Shepherd Me." SA/2 pt mxd, kybd, opt hb. LOR 10/2492K.

Zimmermann, Heinz Werner. "Psalm 23." SATB, org, DB. AFP 9780800645380. *The Augsburg Choirbook.* AFP 9780800656782.

Children's Choir

Carter, John. "The Shepherd Psalm." UE. 2 pt, kybd. HOP A555.

Jothen, Michael. "We Are Children of Our God." UE. U/2 pt, kybd, fl/vln, opt hb, opt assembly. CG A731.

Tallis, Thomas. "Come, Lord Jesus" from *LifeSongs.* LE. U, pno. AFP 9780806642710.

Keyboard / Instrumental

Cherwien, David. "Kingsfold" from *Eight for Eighty-Eight,* vol. 2. Pno. AFP 9780800659059.

Manz, Paul O. "Seelenbräutigam" from *Augsburg Organ Library: Lent.* Org. AFP 9780800658977.

Maynard, Lynette. "St. Peter" from *Songs for All Seasons,* vol. 2. Pno. AFP 9780800677862.

Powell, Robert J. "Kingsfold" from *Augsburg Organ Library: Summer.* Org. AFP 9780800676872.

Sowash, Bradley. "Kingsfold" from *Great English Hymns Arranged in Contemporary Styles.* Pno. AFP 9780800678791.

Handbell

Helman, Michael, arr. "Leaning on the Everlasting Arms." 3-5 oct, L3+. LOR 20/1112L.

McChesney, Kevin. "How Firm a Foundation." 3-5 oct, L4. CPH 97-7225.

Roberts, Philip L., arr. "Kingsfold" from *Hymns for Handbells.* 3-5 oct. GIA G-5770.

Praise Ensemble

■ Beeching, Vicky. "All That I Need" from www.ccli.com. VIN.

■ Paris, Twila. "The Joy of the Lord" from www.musicnotes.com. Ariose Music/Mountain Spring Music.

■ Park, Andy. "In the Secret" from *Best of the Best, The Other Songbook 2.* FEL 1891062034.

■ Redman, Matt. "The Heart of Worship" from *I Could Sing of Your Love Forever 2.* WT 0000809251.

Global

Dexter, Noel. "The Lord Is My Shepherd." SATB, kybd. AFP 9780800638832.

Helgen, John. "That Priceless Grace." SATB, pno. AFP 9780800658595.

Wednesday, July 22
Mary Magdalene, Apostle

The gospels report Mary Magdalene was one of the women of Galilee who followed Jesus. She was present at Jesus' crucifixion and his burial. When she went to the tomb on the first day of the week to anoint Jesus' body, she was the first person to whom the risen Lord appeared. She returned to the disciples with the news and has been called "the apostle to the apostles" for her proclamation of the resurrection. Because John's gospel describes Mary as weeping at the tomb, she is often portrayed in art with red eyes. Icons depict her standing by the tomb and holding a bright red egg.

Thursday, July 23
Birgitta of Sweden, renewer of the church, 1373

Birgitta (beer-GEET-uh) was married at age thirteen and had four daughters with her husband. She was a woman of some standing who, in her early thirties, served as the chief lady-in-waiting to the queen of Sweden. She was widowed at the age of thirty-eight, shortly after she and her husband had made a religious pilgrimage. Following the death of her husband the religious dreams and visions that had begun in her youth occurred more regularly. Her devotional commitments led her to give to the poor and needy all that she owned, and she began to live a more ascetic life. She founded an order of monks and nuns, the Order of the Holy Savior (Brigittines), whose superior was a woman. Today the Society of St. Birgitta is a laypersons' society that continues her work of prayer and charity.

Saturday, July 25
James, Apostle

James is one of the sons of Zebedee and is counted as one of the twelve disciples. Together with his brother John they

◻ denotes choral suggestions that relate to the hymn of the day.
■ denotes songs that are available on iTunes®.

234

had the nickname "sons of thunder." One of the stories in the New Testament tells of their request for Jesus to grant them places of honor in the kingdom. They are also reported to have asked Jesus for permission to send down fire on a Samaritan village that had not welcomed them. James was the first of the Twelve to suffer martyrdom and is the only apostle whose martyrdom is recorded in scripture. He is sometimes called James the Elder to distinguish him from James the Less, commemorated with Philip on May 1, and James of Jerusalem, commemorated on October 23.

James is frequently pictured with a scallop shell. It recalls his life as a fisherman, his call to fish for people, and the gift of our baptism into Christ.

July 26, 2009
Time after Pentecost — Lectionary 17

Today is the first of five Sundays with gospel readings from John 6, the first four of which focus on Jesus as bread of life. Today Jesus feeds thousands of people with five loaves and two fish. What we have, what we bring to Jesus' table seems like it is not nearly enough to meet all the needs we see around us. But it is not the adequacy of our supplies or our skills that finally makes the difference: it is the power of Jesus working in the littlest and least to transform this world into the world God desires, a world where all the hungry are satisfied.

Prayer of the Day

Gracious God, you have placed within the hearts of all your children a longing for your word and a hunger for your truth. Grant that we may know your Son to be the true bread of heaven and share this bread with all the world, through Jesus Christ, our Savior and Lord.

Gospel Acclamation

Alleluia. A great prophet has ris- | en among us!* God has looked favora- | bly on us! *Alleluia.* (Luke 7:16)

Readings and Psalm

2 Kings 4:42-44

Today's reading is part of a larger section of 2 Kings that describes the miracles of Elisha, the successor to Elijah. Here the prophet gives food to a hungry crowd. Though there is not enough food to go around, Elisha trusts God, who provides enough and even more to satisfy the need.

Psalm 145:10-18

You open wide your hand and satisfy the desire of every living thing. (Ps. 145:16)

Ephesians 3:14-21

We have been rooted and grounded in the love of Christ, which surpasses all human knowledge. Because Christ dwells in our hearts, our lives are continuously strengthened and empowered by the ongoing presence of the Spirit.

John 6:1-21

In John's gospel, the miracles of Jesus are called "signs," because they reveal the true character of God. As such, they remain within the mystery of God and cannot be brought under human control.

Semicontinuous reading and psalm

2 Samuel 11:1-15

King David takes Bathsheba, the wife of Uriah, then eventually has her husband murdered. The king, who should be at the battle but stays home, is contrasted in this story with the loyal and upright soldier Uriah.

Psalm 14

God is in the company of the righteous. (Ps. 14:5)

Color Green

CD-ROM Images

Icon Three: 0724-0730_Lect17_B

Icon Two: Proper12_Sun17_B

Icon: 108

Prayers of Intercession

With the whole people of God in Christ Jesus, let us pray for the church, those in need, and all of God's creation.

A brief silence.

Righteous God, you teach your people the way of life. Inspire your church, that all Christian people may be doers of your word. God of mercy,

hear our prayer.

You breathe life into all creation. Infuse this earth with newness of life, especially where it has been devastated and polluted. God of mercy,

hear our prayer.

You promise justice and peace. Enable understanding among people, bring an end to religious violence, and soften hearts hardened by hate. God of mercy,

hear our prayer.

In your compassion supply care to all who suffer from disaster, war, or abuse; from persecution or imprisonment; from depression, illness, and grief (*especially*). God of mercy,

hear our prayer.

With your tenderness attend to the ailments of our community. Strengthen our neighborhoods, schools, and workplaces, that they may be places of caring and support. God of mercy,

hear our prayer.

Here other intercessions may be offered.

We give thanks for those whose earthly journey has ended and now rest in your love (*especially*). Keep us faithful in our journey and confident that nothing can separate us from your love. God of mercy,

hear our prayer.

Loving God, you are near to us when we cry out to you. Into your embrace we commend all for whom we pray, through Christ and by the power of your Spirit.

Amen.

Ideas and Images for the Day

Today's gospel addresses our physical needs and God's physical salvation. Because John doesn't have a last-supper discourse as the other gospels do, scholars believe that this narrative (and the discourse that follows) is in its stead. This story differs from that of the last supper, of course. The feeding is of a multitude of people, certainly not all of whom were disciples or even devoted followers. But even as curious bystanders, they were all hungry and all are fed.

Jesus multiplied the initial offering from one of the crowd, suggesting that any of us might have small offerings that when blessed and multiplied by God could end up doing much more than we imagine. The writer of today's epistle exhorts us to remember that we trust in a God who is able to do more than we can ask or imagine, and whose depths of love are difficult, if not impossible, for us to grasp.

1. Today's texts speak of the abundance of God's love—the 5,000 weren't just given a few cheese cubes on toothpicks. They ate "as much as they wanted" (John 6:11). As Jeff Smith says in *The Frugal Gourmet Keeps the Feast*, "Biblical talk about bread is not about bread at all, but about our total dependence upon the Creator and upon one another" (New York: William Morrow and Company, Inc. 1995, p. 10).

2. The curious detail that Jesus asked the disciples to "gather up the fragments left over, so that nothing may be lost" (John 6:12) hints at Jesus' concern that no one is lost, no one is left out. How many of us feel like fragments or leftovers—not quite whole people leading not quite whole lives? The words to a common offering song speak of this gathering up: "Gather the hopes and dreams of all; unite them with the prayers we offer. Grace our table with your presence, and give us a foretaste of the feast to come" (ELW 181–184). Another hymn that speaks of us as fragments needing gathering is "Gather Us In" (ELW 532, WOV 718).

3. *Cool Hand Luke* (Warner Brothers, 1967), an old Paul Newman film, gives us a twist on the communal aspects of the Lord's supper. This time, however, his chain gang eats his rice when he can't, to prevent him from being punished. By together taking on Luke's burden, they share in his salvation.

4. *Extending the Table*, a cookbook put out by the Mennonite Central Committee, is full of stories, prayers, and recipes from people all around the world and is helpful in understanding the roles that food and hunger play in many people's lives. One story in particular, at the beginning of the "Bread" chapter, is of political prisoners in South Africa who, like the boy who offered his lunch to Jesus, used the little power they had and were eventually able to change their situation (Joetta Handrich Schlabach, Scottsdale, PA: Herald Press, 1991. p. 44). Read this brief story online at www.tsjc .org/tsjc/newsletter/a-place-at-the-table-feb-2004.pdf, "Lenten Story from Lesotho."

Hymns for Worship

Gathering

All who hunger, gather gladly   ELW 461
Let us go now to the banquet   ELW 523
Praise and thanksgiving   ELW 689, LBW 409

Hymn of the Day

All who hunger, gather gladly   ELW 461   HOLY MANNA
Break now the bread of life   ELW 515, LBW 235
　　BREAD OF LIFE
Let us talents and tongues employ   ELW 674, WOV 754,
　　TFF 232   LINSTEAD

Communion

Bread of life, our host and meal   ELW 464
Jesus, priceless treasure   ELW 775, LBW 457, 458

Sending

Sent forth by God's blessing   ELW 547, LBW 221
Let us talents and tongues employ   ELW 674, WOV 754,
　　TFF 232

Additional Hymns and Songs

Blessed Jesus, living Bread   HG 133 (st. 2 & 3 A)
Now in this banquet   W&P 104
The hand of God   GC 828

Music for the Day

Psalmody and Acclamations

Erickson, Richard. *Gospel Acclamations for Summer*. AFP
　　9780800678579.
Mummert, Mark. "Psalm 145" from *Psalm Settings for the Church
　　Year*. AFP 9780800678562.
Psalter for Worship Year B, Evangelical Lutheran Worship Edition.
　　AFP 9780806683839.

Choral

Berger, Jean. "The Eyes of All Wait Upon Thee." SATB. AFP
　　9780800645595. *The Augsburg Choirbook*. AFP 9780800656782.
Ferguson, John. "Gift of Finest Wheat (You Satisfy the Hungry
　　Heart)." SATB, assembly, org. GIA G-3089.
Haugen, Marty. "Bread to Share." SATB, solo, assembly, kybd, opt
　　gtr. GIA G-4279.
Proulx, Richard. "The Eyes of All." SATB. AFP 9780800656461.

Children's Choir

Folkening, John. "Feed Us, Jesus" from *LifeSongs*. LE. U, pno, opt
　　tamb. AFP 9780806642710.
Hubert, Royce. "You Are the Rain" from *Two Rainstick Pieces*. UE.
　　U, pno, rainsticks. CG A685.
Sleeth, Natalie. "Praise the Lord." UE. 2 pt, kybd. HIN HMC207.

Keyboard / Instrumental

Cherwien, David. "Holy Manna" from *Groundings*. Org. AFP
　　9780800659806.
Maynard, Lynette. "Holy Manna" from *Let It Shine*. Pno. AFP
　　9780800677640.
Organ, Anne Krentz. "Linstead" from *Global Piano Reflections*. Pno,
　　xyl, perc. AFP 9780800658014.
Wood, Dale. "Holy Manna" from *Augsburg Organ Library: Autumn*.
　　Org. AFP 9780800675790.

Handbell

Eithun, Sandra, arr. "Break Thou the Bread of Life." 3-5 oct, L2+.
　　SoundForth 249029.
Helman, Michael, arr. "Gift of Finest Wheat." 3-5 hb/hc, L3. AFP
　　9780800657369.
Roberts, Philip L., arr. "Holy Manna" from *Hymns for Handbells*,
　　vol. 2. 3-5 oct. GIA G-5899.

Praise Ensemble

Baloche, Paul. "Taste and See" from www.leadworship.com.
■ Byrd, Marc/Steve Hindalong. "God of Wonders" from www.praise
　　charts.com. New Spring Publishing, Inc./Storm Boy Music/
　　Meaux Mercy.
■ Hall, Mark. "Who Am I" from www.praisecharts.com. SWECS
　　Music/Club Zoo Music.
■ Redman, Matt. "Let Everything That Has Breath" from
　　praisecharts.com.

Global

Cuéllar, Guillermo/Bread for the Journey. "Come, the Ban-
　　quet Hall Is Ready" from *Global Songs 2*. U, pno, gtr. AFP
　　9780800656744.
Haugen, Marty. "Bread of Life from Heaven/Pan de vida eternal."
　　SATB, pno, gtr. GIA G-5652.

Tuesday, July 28

Johann Sebastian Bach, 1750; Heinrich Schütz, 1672; George Frederick Handel, 1759; musicians

These three composers have done much to enrich the worship life of the church. Johann Sebastian Bach drew on the Lutheran tradition of hymnody and wrote about two hundred cantatas, including at least two for each Sunday and festival day in the Lutheran calendar of his day. He has been called "the fifth evangelist" for the ways he proclaimed the gospel through his music. George Frederick Handel was not primarily a church musician, but his great work *Messiah* is a musical proclamation of the scriptures. Heinrich Schütz wrote choral settings of biblical texts and paid special

■ denotes songs that are available on iTunes®.

attention to ways his composition would underscore the meaning of the words.

A musical gathering might be planned to commemorate these and other great church composers. Remember to include a prayer of thanksgiving for organists, choir directors, composers, and all who make music in worship.

Wednesday, July 29

Mary, Martha, and Lazarus of Bethany

Mary and Martha are remembered for the hospitality and refreshment they offered Jesus in their home. Following the characterization drawn by Luke, Martha represents the active life, Mary the contemplative. Mary is identified in the fourth gospel as the one who anointed Jesus before his passion and who was criticized for her act of devotion. Lazarus, Mary's and Martha's brother, was raised from the dead by Jesus as a sign of the eternal life offered to all believers. It was over Lazarus's tomb that Jesus wept for love of his friend.

Olaf, King of Norway, martyr, 1030

Olaf is considered the patron saint of Norway. In his early career he engaged in war and piracy in the Baltic and in Normandy. In Rouen, though, he was baptized and became a Christian. He returned to Norway, succeeded his father as king, and from then on Christianity was the dominant religion of the realm. He revised the laws of the nation and enforced them with strict impartiality, eliminating the possibility of bribes. He thereby alienated much of the aristocracy. The harshness that he sometimes resorted to in order to establish Christianity and his own law led to a rebellion. After being driven from the country and into exile, he enlisted support from Sweden to try to regain his kingdom, but he died in battle.

August 2, 2009
Time after Pentecost — Lectionary 18

Apparently not satisfied by Jesus' feeding of thousands, some who were there press him for a sign of his power; perhaps it is daily manna they want. As always in John's gospel when people want a sign, Jesus offers himself. He is the bread come from heaven to give life to the world. He calls us to come to him and believe in him, and through that relationship to know the one who sent him.

Prayer of the Day

O God, eternal goodness, immeasurable love, you place your gifts before us; we eat and are satisfied. Fill us and this world in all its need with the life that comes only from you, through Jesus Christ, our Savior and Lord.

Gospel Acclamation

Alleluia. One does not live by | bread alone,* but by every word that comes from the | mouth of God. *Alleluia.* (Matt. 4:4)

Readings and Psalm
Exodus 16:2-4, 9-15

A food crisis becomes a faith crisis for the Israelites in the wilderness. The hungry people forget God's saving work in the exodus, and they wish for the food they had in Egypt. Nevertheless, God miraculously meets their needs, with manna for bread and quail for meat.

Psalm 78:23-29

God rained down manna from heaven; so mortals ate the bread of angels. (Ps. 78:24, 25)

Ephesians 4:1-16

Christians share fundamental unity and diversity. Our unity consists in the one body, one Spirit, one Lord, one faith, one baptism, and one God. Our diversity is expressed in various forms of ministry, whose goal is equipping the saints and building up Christ's one body.

John 6:24-35

Many of the five thousand people Jesus fed in the wilderness continued to follow him throughout the countryside. Jesus challenges them to consider the real nature of their quest.

Semicontinuous reading and psalm

2 Samuel 11:26—12:13a

God sends the prophet Nathan to rebuke King David for his abuse of power in taking Bathsheba and killing her husband, Uriah. Confronted with his sin, David repents. This sin, however, marks the beginning of troubled times in David's family.

Psalm 51:1-12

Have mercy on me, O God, according to your steadfast love. (Ps. 51:1)

Color Green

CD-ROM Images

Icon Three: 0731-0806_Lect18_B

Icon Two: Proper13_Sun18_B

Icon: 109

Prayers of Intercession

With the whole people of God in Christ Jesus, let us pray for the church, those in need, and all of God's creation.

A brief silence.

Merciful God, you have revealed your might with compassionate healing. Strengthen your church, that the healing power of Christ may be known throughout the world. God of mercy,

hear our prayer.

We pray for the mending of all creation: for the health of waterways and soil, for the cleansing of the air, and for renewed commitment to care for your creation. God of mercy,

hear our prayer.

We pray for the health of the nations, for peace, for just governments, and for healing in those sick with greed or hate. God of mercy,

hear our prayer.

We pray for healing for the sick, especially for sick children and their parents; for nurses and doctors; for those without healthcare; and for all who suffer alone. God of mercy,

hear our prayer.

We pray for health in our relationships at home, work, and school, and for the health of our congregation. God of mercy,

hear our prayer.

Here other intercessions may be offered.

We give thanks for the lives of those who have died (*especially*). Lift up those who grieve, and bring us all to your eternal rest. God of mercy,

hear our prayer.

Loving God, you are near to us when we cry out to you. Into your embrace we commend all for whom we pray, through Christ and by the power of your Spirit.

Amen.

Ideas and Images for the Day

What gives us satisfaction? After all God had done for the Hebrews escaping Egypt, they were still unsatisfied and complained to Moses. The crowds that had been present to witness Jesus' sign of feeding thousands with five loaves and two fish were still unsatisfied and came chasing after him for more signs. But manna and magic are not lasting. Jesus himself is the bread of life, the food that gives satisfaction. This Sunday is the first of three where Jesus specifically describes himself as the bread of life. Worship leaders might feel challenged trying to plan three (or more) different Sundays around the bread of life theme. Remember that those who come to worship are inundated all week long with the message that they need more of everything to be satisfied. The bread of life Sundays are an opportunity to lift up the message that God's abundance is enough.

1. In the late 1960s the Rolling Stones released their single "(I Can't Get No) Satisfaction." The rock song had an anticommercial theme and suggested that satisfaction couldn't be achieved by what was sold on television or radio, but from the pleasures of being with a girl. In our consumer-driven society we are constantly being told that if we buy this or do that we will be satisfied.

2. When illusionists such as David Blaine or Criss Angel levitate or escape from being tied up and buried alive we ask, "How did they do that?" Jesus doesn't do tricks or magic. John doesn't call what Jesus does miracles, but *signs*. When Jesus performs a sign it is to prompt us to ask, "*Why* did he do that?" The answer is to point us to God.

3. Can we be satisfied and challenged to ministry at the same time? Yes! We are fed so that we can do the work of God in the world. Jesus fed the hungry not just with spiritual food but with actual food, because we need both for life. In what ways does your congregation participate in the fight against hunger?

4. What kind of bread does your congregation use for communion? Just as God promises to adopt us in baptism regardless of how much water is used, Jesus promises to be present in the bite of bread we eat, even if it is gluten-free.

Hymns for Worship

Gathering

All who hunger, gather gladly   ELW 461

What feast of love   ELW 487, WOV 701

Hymn of the Day

O bread of life from heaven   ELW 480, LBW 222

O WELT, ICH MUSS DICH LASSEN

Bread of life from heaven   ELW 474

ARGENTINE SANTO/BREAK NOW THE BREAD

All who hunger, gather gladly   ELW 461   HOLY MANNA

Communion

Eat this bread   ELW 472, WOV 709

I am the Bread of life   ELW 485, WOV 702

We are all one in Christ   ELW 643

Sending

Guide me ever, great Redeemer   ELW 618, LBW 343

By your hand you feed your people   ELW 469

Additional Hymns and Songs

Blessed Jesus, living Bread   HG 133 (sts. 2-3 B)

What is this bread   LSB 629

Bread for the journey   GS2 40

Come and taste   W&P 30

Music for the Day

Psalmody and Acclamations

Erickson, Richard. *Gospel Acclamations for Summer.* AFP 9780800678579.

Nicholson, Paul. "Psalm 78" from *Psalm Settings for the Church Year.* AFP 9780800678562.

Psalter for Worship Year B, Evangelical Lutheran Worship Edition. AFP 9780806683839.

Choral

Carnahan, Craig. "Come, Let Us Eat." SATB, org, hb, fc, ch. AMSI 385.

◻ Isaac, Heinrich. "O Bread of Life from Heaven" from *Chantry Choirbook.* SATB. AFP 9780800657772.

Lovelace, Austin C. "We Come as Guests Invited." SATB, kybd. GIA G-5033.

Young, Carlton R. "Bread of the World, in Mercy Broken" (Rendez à Dieu). 2 pt mxd, kybd. AFP 9780800675592.

◻ denotes choral suggestions that relate to the hymn of the day.
■ denotes songs that are available on iTunes®.

Children's Choir

Anonymous. "I Received the Living God" from *LifeSongs.* LE. U, pno. AFP 9780806642710.

Brazzeal, David. "Now Paul, He Was a Servant." UE. 2 pt, kybd. CG A782.

Hopson, Hal H. "Lord, Lead Us Day by Day." UE. U, kybd. AG HH3908.

Keyboard / Instrumental

Brahms, Johannes. "O Welt, ich muss dich lassen." Org. Various ed.

Diemer, Emma Lou. "O Welt, ich muss dich lassen" from *A New Liturgical Year.* Org. AFP 9780800656713.

Organ, Anne Krentz. "Holy Manna" from *Let It Rip! at the Piano*, vol. 1. Pno. AFP 9780800659066.

Young, Carlton R. "Argentine Santo/Break Now the Bread" from *Organ Music for the Seasons*, vol. 4. Org. AFP 9780800637507.

Handbell

Eithun, Sandra, arr. "All Creatures of Our God and King." 3-5 oct, L3. RR SM7002A.

Moklebust, Cathy. "Bwana Asifiwe!" 3-5 oct, L3+. CG B367. Full score, perc. CG B366.

Morris, Hart, arr. "Holy Manna." 3-5 oct, L3. Fred Bock BG0921.

Praise Ensemble

Anderson, Tai/Brad Avery/David Carr/Mark D. Lee/Johnny Mac Powell. "Communion" from www.ccli.com. Consuming Fire Music.

■ Brown, Brenton/Brian Doerksen. "Hallelujah, Your Love Is Amazing" from *Come, Now Is the Time to Worship.* VIN VMB9367.

■ Cash, Ed/Stephen Sharp/Chris Tomlin. "Made to Worship" from WT. WT/Sixsteps Music/Alletrop Music/Stephan Sharp Publishing.

■ Davis, Holland. "Let It Rise" from *iWorship Songbook 1.* INT 23366.

Global

Hesla, Bret/Bread for the Journey. "Bread for the Journey" from *Global Songs 2.* U, pno, gtr. AFP 9780800656744.

Murray, Shirley Erena. "In the Singing" from *Global Praise 2.* U, pno, gtr. General Board of Global Ministries, GBGMusik 1890569224 . (ELW 466)

Saturday, August 8

Dominic, founder of the Order of Preachers (Dominicans), 1221

Dominic was a Spanish priest who preached against the Albigensians, a heretical sect that held gnostic and dualistic beliefs. Dominic believed that a stumbling block to restoring heretics to the church was the wealth of clergy, so he formed an itinerant religious order, the Order of Preachers

Order Now for 2010—Year C

sundays and Seasons 2010—Year C

Save time and preparation with this comprehensive worship planning guide based on the Revised Common Lectionary. Provides all you need to prepare worship for the whole church year as presented in *Evangelical Lutheran Worship*.

ISBN 978-0-8066-7130-7 $36.00 (3 or more $29.00 ea.)

Worship Planning Calendar 2010—Year C

The perfect complement to *Sundays and Seasons*. This planning guide serves as an appointment calendar and workbook for preparing worship. Contains daily lectionary readings from the Consultation on Common Texts (CCT).

ISBN 978-0-8066-7131-4 $20.00

SAVE 10%—2010 Combo Pack
Sundays and Seasons & Worship Planning Calendar

Sundays and Seasons and the *Worship Planning Calendar* work together to save time and provide all you need to prepare engaging worship.

ISBN 978-0-8066-7132-1 $49.00 ($56.00 if purchased separately)

Bread for the Day 2010

Daily Bible readings and prayers for the full year follows the daily lectionary. Quantity discounts available.

ISBN 978-0-8066-7137-6 $8.95

STANDING ORDERS AVAILABLE!

Standing orders allow you to receive new product each year without reordering. You will be billed after your product is mailed and you can easily change your order one month prior to shipping. Order once and you're done! Convenient and flexible. Order below.

sundays and seasons.com

Sundays and Seasons.com

Sundays and Seasons.com saves you time and effort by providing content and tools to plan worship flexibly and easily for your weekly bulletin or projection. Includes content from all ELCA worship volumes, clip-art, NRSV Bible, children's bulletins, and more!

Visit **sundaysandseasons.com** for more information.

2010 ORDER FORM →

Complete this order card, affix postage, and drop it in the mail.

You can also order by:
Phone: 1-800-328-4648
Fax: 1-800-722-7766
Online: augsburgfortress.org

Augsburg Fortress

31946-0108
Keycode: AO6193

ORDER FORM   Worship Planning Resources 2010—Year C

Prices do not include shipping. Prices valid through April 1, 2009.

Send to: _____
Address: _____
City: _____
State: _____ Zip: _____
Phone: _____
E-mail: _____

Bill to: _____
Address: _____
City: _____
State: _____ Zip: _____
Phone: _____

Method of Payment *(select one)*
AF Account # _____
Credit Card # _____
Exp. Date _____ *(Card must be valid through Sept. 2009. Products ship Aug. 2009)*
Signature _____
(Signature required on all credit card orders.)
Thank you for your order.

Qty.	Title	Price
	Sundays and Seasons 2010	
_____	ISBN 978-0-8066-7130-7	$36.00
_____	ISBN 978-6-0001-7434-7	**Standing Order**
	Worship Planning Calendar 2010	
_____	ISBN 978-0-8066-7131-4	$20.00
_____	ISBN 978-6-0001-7435-4	**Standing Order**
	Sundays and Seasons / Worship Planning Calendar Combo Pack 2010	
_____	ISBN 978-0-8066-7132-1	$49.00
_____	ISBN 978-6-0001-7436-1	**Standing Order**
	Ritual Lectionary	
_____	ISBN 978-0-8066-5615-1	$115.00
	Study Edition Lectionary	
_____	ISBN 978-0-8066-5616-8	$27.50
	Calendar of Word & Season 2010 (w/o imprinting)	
_____	ISBN 978-0-8066-7135-2	$9.95
_____	ISBN 978-6-0001-7439-2	**Standing Order**
	Church Year Calendar 2010	
_____	ISBN 978-0-8066-7133-8	$1.95
	Words for Worship 2010	
_____	ISBN 978-0-8066-7136-9	$199.00
	Bread for the Day	
_____	ISBN 978-0-8066-7137-6	$8.95

Order Now for 2010—Year C

Great gifts and useful resources for living the liturgical year!

Ritual Lectionary—Year C
Includes the complete Revised Common Lectionary for Year C with full texts for all of the readings, art, and a hard cover binding. Elegant and suitable for use in procession.

ISBN 978-0-8066-5615-1
$115.00 ea.

Study Edition Lectionary—Year C
Contains the same texts as the Ritual Lectionary with pronunciation aides and background summaries to help readers prepare with confidence.

ISBN 978-0-8066-5616-8 $27.50 ea.

Words for Worship 2010—Year C
This CD-ROM contains texts and graphical files with content from *Evangelical Lutheran Worship.* Also includes week-to-week elements from *Lectionary for Worship Year C,* Revised Common Lectionary; *Sundays and Seasons 2010*; and the *Psalter for Worship Year C.*

ISBN 978-0-8066-7136-9 $199.00 ea.

Calendar of Word & Season 2010—Year C
Full-color wall calendar with room for adding family and church activities. Features beautiful art each month and identifies church festivals, national holidays, the color of the day, and Revised Common Lectionary citations. 8⅜" x10⅞". Spiral-bound and punched for hanging. Call for custom imprinting.

ISBN 978-0-8066-7135-2

| 1–11 | $9.95 ea. | 12–49 | $4.25 ea. | 500+ | $2.00 ea. |
| 50–99 | $3.25 ea. | 100–499 | $3.00 ea. | | |

ISBN 978-6-0001-7439-2 **Standing Order**

Church Year Calendar 2010—Year C
Provides dates, lectionary readings, hymn of the day, and the liturgical color for each Sunday and festival. The ideal time-saver for pastors, worship and music directors, choir members, altar guilds, and all who live by the liturgical year. Two-sided. 11" x 8½"

ISBN 978-0-8066-7133-8

| 1–12 | $1.95 ea. |
| 12+ | $0.83 ea. |

Place Stamp Here

Augsburg Fortress
Attn: Mailing Center
P.O. Box 1209
Minneapolis, MN 55440-1209

SHIPPING AND HANDLING

Prices and Product Availability are subject to change without notice.

Sales Tax: Exempt customers must provide Augsburg Fortress with a copy of their state issue exemption certificate. Customers without tax-exempt status must add applicable state (province) and local sales tax for their jurisdiction. Canadian customers will be charged GST.

Shipping Charges are additional on all orders. US and Canadian orders (except US cash orders) are assessed actual shipping charges based on standard group rates. Additional shipping charges are accessed for expedited service requests and international shipments. US cash orders are shipped at the following rates: $0.01-$25.00, add $5.25; $25.01-$75.00, add $6.25; $75.01-$100.00, add $9.25; $100.01-150.00, add $11.95; $150.01-$200.01 or more add 6.75% or call Customer Service for a quote. Actual shipping charges are applied to US cash order weighing more than 250 pounds.

Return Policy: With proof of purchase, non-dated, in print product in saleable condition may be returned for credit. Please call customer service at 1-800-328-4648 (U.S.) or 1-800-265-6397 (Canada) for assistance you receive items that are damaged, defective, or were shipped in error. Specific return restrictions apply to some product lines. Please contact us prior to returning a special order item or item shipped directly from the manufacturer. Send US order returns by a secure, prepaid, traceable method to the Augsburg Fortress Distribution Center, 4001 Gantz Road, Suite Grove City, Ohio 43123-1891. Canadian orders may be returned to Augsburg Fortress Canadian Distribution Center 500 Trillium Drive, Box 9940, Kitchener, Ontario N2G 4Y4

(Dominicans), who lived in poverty, studied philosophy and theology, and preached against heresy. The method of this order was to use kindness and gentle argument, rather than harsh judgment, to bring unorthodox Christians back to the fold. Dominic was opposed to burning Christians at the stake. Three times Dominic was offered the office of bishop, which he refused so that he could continue in his work of preaching.

August 9, 2009
Time after Pentecost — Lectionary 19

Jesus says that the bread he gives for the life of the world is his flesh, and whoever eats this bread has eternal life now and will be raised on the last day. In Ephesians Paul tells us what this life Jesus gives us looks like, this life we live as those marked with the seal of the Holy Spirit in baptism. We live in love, as Christ loved us and gave himself up for us. The whole purpose of life is giving yourself for the other.

Prayer of the Day

Gracious God, your blessed Son came down from heaven to be the true bread that gives life to the world. Give us this bread always, that he may live in us and we in him, and that, strengthened by this food, we may live as his body in the world, through Jesus Christ, our Savior and Lord.

Gospel Acclamation

Alleluia. I am the living bread that came | down from heaven.* Whoever eats this bread will | live forever. *Alleluia.* (John 6:51)

Readings and Psalm
I Kings 19:4-8

First Kings chapter 18 describes the contest between Elijah and the prophets of Baal. The contest proves that the Lord is God; and afterwards Elijah orders the killing of the Baal prophets. Angered by the deaths of her prophets, Queen Jezebel threatens to kill Elijah. This reading finds Elijah fleeing, fatigued, and in utter despair.

Psalm 34:1-8

Taste and see that the LORD is good. (Ps. 34:8)

Ephesians 4:25—5:2

Christians are called to be imitators of God. This does not mean Christians are perfect. Rather, the Spirit is at work in our lives so that our actions and attitudes genuinely reflect the love and forgiveness we have received through Christ and his death.

John 6:35, 41-51

After feeding more than five thousand people in the wilderness, Jesus teaches them regarding the true significance of this remarkable sign.

Semicontinuous reading and psalm
2 Samuel 18:5-9, 15, 31-33

This reading describes some of the troubles in King David's family. His son Absalom has amassed an army and seized David's throne. Those loyal to David fight Absalom's forces and defeat them. David himself is chiefly concerned about the well-being of his son, even though that son has betrayed him.

Psalm 130

Out of the depths I cry to you, O LORD. (Ps. 130:1)

Color   Green

CD-ROM Images

Icon Three: 0807-0813_Lect19_B
Icon Two: Proper14_Sun19_B
Icon: 110

Prayers of Intercession

With the whole people of God in Christ Jesus, let us pray for the church, those in need, and all of God's creation.

A brief silence.

Let us pray for God's anointed people, especially for members of the church throughout the world, and for all who make great sacrifice for the sake of the gospel. (*silence*) God of mercy,

hear our prayer.

Let us pray for all of creation: for animals and plants, for prairies, mountains, and wetlands, for farmland and for city streets. (*silence*) God of mercy,

hear our prayer.

Let us pray for the human community throughout the world: for those who teach or heal or feed; those who clean, fix, or build; for those who invent, beautify, or delight. (*silence*) God of mercy,

hear our prayer.

Let us pray for those who suffer disaster, violence, or abuse; those who suffer with addictions, disorders, or depression; those who suffer from grief, despair, or illness (*especially*). (*silence*) God of mercy,

hear our prayer.

Let us pray for the concerns of our own hearts, for the needs of our congregation, friends, and families (*especially*). (*silence*) God of mercy,

hear our prayer.

Here other intercessions may be offered.

Let us give thanks for all who have died (*especially*), entrusting them to God's love. (*silence*) God of mercy,

hear our prayer.

Loving God, you are near to us when we cry out to you. Into your embrace we commend all for whom we pray, through Christ and by the power of your Spirit.

Amen.

Ideas and Images for the Day

Word and sacrament structure both Christian worship and John's bread of life discourse. This week focuses on Jesus as the word; next week, on Jesus as the meal. It takes both to fully appreciate each one. Here, the human from heaven, Jesus of Nazareth, is a comfort and/or obstacle *before* passion-resurrection precisely because his way is not the world's way. Jesus' revelation of grace either draws one anew to God or does not; but human reasoning alone can't determine whether it's true or not. One either recognizes this truth of grace or does not. Those who do find a "spring of water gushing up to eternal life" (John 4:14). Jesus has words that self-generate that which makes life good and worthwhile—even in the face of death.

1. For Paul, the obedience of faith involves attitudes, dispositions, and behaviors of redeeming value in the church. There are models to follow, imitations to master, ways of being to copy. The faith journey is so transforming that even anger, when rightly experienced, builds up rather than tears down. A well-faithed life is an endearing fragrance. Any number of magazines carry perfume and cologne rub-and-sniff ads. What's the smell of believing?

2. Waiting while in affliction is a spiritual gift available to all the faithful. How should our waiting be qualified? What characteristics mark it as faithfulness? When is waiting only despair of God?

3. Be imitators of God! Who are our models? Where do we take our clues for growing up, for responding to the world, for desiring and acting? We should push such questions. "This neglect of imitation is difficult to justify in view of the fact that not only the Gospels but Paul himself, whose importance for Protestant theology is paramount, insists on the positive role of imitation in Christian life" (from *Violence Renounced: René Girard, Biblical Studies, and Peacemaking*, Willard M. Swartley, ed., Telford, PA: Pandora Press, 2000, p. 310, or http://girardianlectionary.net/res/girard_imitatio .htm). Imitating Christ teaches us to avoid rivalry, which makes peace with others possible.

4. Elijah's exhaustion (complementary Old Testament reading) arises from unfulfilled expectations that God will finish the slaughter of Baal prophets that Elijah began. Are our disappointments in ministry tied to expecting God to finish our works? (Think about who is doing what.)

5. Like father, like son? Absalom's death (semicontinuous Old Testament reading) makes David wish for his own instead. Nathan's prophecy rings true—a family dynamics has been born. Would that David could die to his taking of Bathsheba and his conspiring murder of Uriah! When we speak of God's wrath, are we pointing to the unfolding impact of our own negative behavior? See William Faulkner's classic *Absalom! Absalom!* as an illustration.

Hymns for Worship
Gathering

As we gather at your table   ELW 522
You are holy   ELW 525
O living Bread from heaven   ELW 542, LBW 197

Hymn of the Day

I am the Bread of life   ELW 485, WOV 702   *I AM THE BREAD*
O living Bread from heaven   ELW 542, LBW 197   *AURELIA*
Bread of life from heaven   ELW 474
ARGENTINE SANTO/BREAK NOW THE BREAD

Communion

Taste and see   ELW 493, TFF 126
O Bread of life from heaven   ELW 480, LBW 222
You satisfy the hungry heart   ELW 484, WOV 711

Sending

Hallelujah! We sing your praises   ELW 535, WOV 722
O Jesus, joy of loving hearts   ELW 658, LBW 356

Additional Hymns and Songs

Blessed Jesus, living Bread   HG 133 (sts. 2-3 C)
Seed, scattered and sown   W&P 121
Gather in Your Name   GC 823
God is so good   TFF 275

Music for the Day
Psalmody and Acclamations

Cherwien, David. "Psalm 34" from *Psalm Settings for the Church Year*. AFP 9780800678562.
Erickson, Richard. *Gospel Acclamations for Summer*. AFP 9780800678579.
Psalter for Worship Year B, Evangelical Lutheran Worship Edition. AFP 9780806683839.

Choral

Helgen, John. "In God's Presence" (Schmücke dich, O liebe Seele). SATB, pno. KJO 8941.
Hopp, Roy. "Bread of Heaven." SATB, kybd. AFP 9780800678203.
Mathews, Peter. "O Sacrum Convivium." SATB, div. Southern Music Company SC 326.
Music, David W. "O Lord, Have Mercy on Me" (Break Bread Together). SATB, org. AFP 9780800638689.
Wold, Wayne L. "As This Broken Bread" from *Augsburg Easy Choirbook*, vol. 1. 2 pt mxd, org. AFP 9780800676025.

Children's Choir

Jothen, Michael. "I Will Give Thanks." LE. U, pno, opt fl. BP 1101.
Pearson, Brian/Sherry Pearson. "Life Together" from *LifeSongs*. UE. U, pno. AFP 9780806642710.
Sleeth, Natalie. "Make Music for the Lord." UE. 2 pt, kybd. CG A469.

Keyboard / Instrumental

Callahan, Charles. "Prelude in C." Org. MSM 10-913.
Hildebrand, Kevin. "Aurelia" from *Easy Hymn Preludes for Organ*, set III. Org. CPH 97-7052U1.

Manz, Paul. "Aurelia" from *Three Hymn Settings for Organ*, set 2. Org. MSM 10-525.
Organ, Anne Krentz. "Aurelia" from *Piano Reflections for the Church Year*. Pno. AFP 9780800674748.

Handbell

Helman, Michael. "Let Us Talents and Tongues Employ." 2-3 oct, opt perc, L2. AFP 9780800659936.
Helman, Michael. "Variations on 'Gather Us In'." 3-5 oct hb/hc, L4. AFP 9780800674922.
McChesney, Kevin. "The Church's One Foundation." 3-5 oct, opt perc, L2. AFP 9780800658076. OP

Praise Ensemble

■ Founds, Rick. "Lord, I Lift Your Name on High." ELW 857, W&P 90.
Kendrick, Graham. "Here Is Bread, Here Is Wine" from www.ccli.com. Make Way Music. ELW 483, W&P 58.
■ Redman, Matt. "Better Is One Day" from *More Songs for Praise & Worship 2*. WM 080689412875
■ Schultz, Mark. "I Am" from www.musicnotes.com. Crazy Romaine Music/The Loving Company.

Global

Hesla, Bret. "As God Provides" from *Justice, Like a Base of Stone*. SATB. AFP 9780800623562.
Young, Jeremy. "Taste and See." U/2 pt, kybd, opt assembly. AFP 9780800657604.

Monday, August 10
Lawrence, deacon, martyr, 258

Lawrence was one of seven deacons of the congregation at Rome and, like the deacons appointed in Acts, was responsible for financial matters in the church and for the care of the poor. Lawrence lived during a time of persecution under the emperor Valerian. The emperor demanded that Lawrence surrender the treasures of the church. Lawrence gathered lepers, orphans, the blind and lame. He brought them to the emperor and said, "Here is the treasure of the church." This act enraged the emperor, and Lawrence was sentenced to death. Lawrence's martyrdom was one of the first to be observed by the church.

Tuesday, August 11
Clare, Abbess of San Damiano, 1253

At age eighteen, Clare of Assisi heard Francis preach a sermon in a church in town. From that time, she determined to follow in his example of Christian living. With Francis's help (and against the wishes of her father) she and

■ denotes songs that are available on iTunes®.

a growing number of companions established a women's Franciscan community, called the Order of Poor Ladies, or Poor Clares. She became a confidante and advisor to Francis, and in standing up against the wishes of popes for the sake of maintaining complete poverty, she helped inspire other women to pursue spiritual goals.

Thursday, August 13

Florence Nightingale, 1910; Clara Maass, 1901; renewers of society

When Florence Nightingale decided she would be a nurse, her family was horrified. In the early 1800s nursing was done by people with no training and no other way to earn a living. Florence trained at Kaiserswerth, Germany, with a Lutheran order of deaconesses. She returned home and worked to reform hospitals in England. Nightingale led a group of thirty-eight nurses to serve in the Crimean War, where they worked in appalling conditions. She returned to London as a hero and resumed her work there for hospital reform.

Clara Maass was born in New Jersey and served as a nurse in the Spanish-American War, where she encountered the horrors of yellow fever. She later responded to a call for subjects in research on yellow fever. During the experiments, which included receiving bites from mosquitoes, she contracted the disease and died. The commemoration of these women invites the church to give thanks for all who practice the arts of healing.

Friday, August 14

Maximilian Kolbe, 1941; Kaj Munk, 1944, martyrs

Father Kolbe was a Franciscan priest, born Raymond Kolbe. After spending some time working in Asia, he returned in 1936 to his native Poland, where he supervised a friary that came to house thousands of Polish war refugees, mostly Jews. The Nazis were watching, however, and he was arrested. Confined in Auschwitz, Kolbe gave generously of his meager resources, and finally volunteered to be starved to death in place of another man who was a husband and father. After two weeks, he was executed by a lethal injection.

Kaj (pronounced KYE) Munk, a Danish Lutheran pastor and playwright, was an outspoken critic of the Nazis, who occupied Denmark during the Second World War. His plays frequently highlighted the eventual victory of the Christian faith despite the church's weak and ineffective witness. The Nazis feared Munk because his sermons and articles helped to strengthen the Danish resistance movement. He was executed by the Gestapo on January 5, 1944.

Saturday, August 15

Mary, Mother of Our Lord

The church honors Mary with the Greek title *theotokos*, meaning "God-bearer." Origen first used this title in the early church, and the councils of Ephesus and Chalcedon upheld it. Luther upheld this same title in his writings. The honor paid to Mary as *theotokos* and mother of our Lord goes back to biblical times, when Mary herself sang, "from now on all generations will call me blessed" (Luke 1:48). Mary's life revealed the presence of God incarnate, and it revealed God's presence among the humble and poor. Mary's song, the Magnificat, speaks of reversals in the reign of God: the mighty are cast down, the lowly are lifted up, the hungry are fed, and the rich are sent away empty-handed.

Hymns to commemorate Mary as *theotokos* might include "Sing of Mary, pure and lowly" (WOV 634) or a paraphrase of the Magnificat, such as "Canticle of the Turning" (ELW 723).

August 16, 2009
Time after Pentecost — Lectionary 20

Wisdom prepares a feast, sets her table, and invites all to come and eat her bread and drink her wine. The first chapter of John's gospel owes much to the biblical tradition that imagined Wisdom as existing before anything was created and having a role in the work of creation. Christ, the wisdom of God (1 Cor. 1:24), today invites us to eat his flesh and drink his blood. John's gospel includes no account of the institution of the Lord's supper, but here we can't help hearing Jesus' words as an invitation to the meal of bread and wine we share.

Prayer of the Day

Ever-loving God, your Son gives himself as living bread for the life of the world. Fill us with such a knowledge of his presence that we may be strengthened and sustained by his risen life to serve you continually, through Jesus Christ, our Savior and Lord.

Gospel Acclamation

Alleluia. Those who eat my flesh and drink my blood a-│bide in me,* and I a-│bide in them. *Alleluia.* (John 6:56)

Readings and Psalm
Proverbs 9:1-6

Wisdom is portrayed as a woman who invites people to partake of her banquet. Just as ordinary food is necessary for physical life, Wisdom's food—insight and understanding—is necessary for fullness of life with God. Partaking of Wisdom's banquet is the way to life.

Psalm 34:9-14

Those who seek the LORD lack nothing that is good. (Ps. 34:10)

Ephesians 5:15-20

True wisdom integrates our new reality in Christ with our Christian fellowship and daily conduct. Because we are filled with the Spirit, Christians regularly rejoice together, give thanks to God for one another, and care for one another. In this way we revere our Lord Jesus Christ.

John 6:51-58

In John's gospel, the feeding of the five thousand leads to extended teaching in which Jesus identifies himself as the true "bread of life." Finally, in these verses, he makes a connection that would not be understood until after his death, in light of the church's celebration of holy communion.

Semicontinuous reading and psalm
1 Kings 2:10-12; 3:3-14

Solomon, son of David and Bathsheba, becomes king over Israel when his father dies. He asks the Lord for wisdom in order to govern the people. The Lord grants his request, and Solomon becomes known far and wide for his great wisdom.

Psalm 111

The fear of the LORD is the beginning of wisdom. (Ps. 111:10)

Color   Green

CD-ROM Images

Icon Three: 0814-0820_Lect20_B
Icon Two: Proper15_Sun20_B
Icon: 111

Prayers of Intercession

With the whole people of God in Christ Jesus, let us pray for the church, those in need, and all of God's creation.
A brief silence.
Let us pray for all who welcome God's word into their lives, especially for the Christian people, and for churches torn apart by dissension. (*silence*) God of mercy,
hear our prayer.
Let us pray for all lands and waterways, especially where they are polluted, and for courage to live as faithful stewards of God's creation. (*silence*) God of mercy,
hear our prayer.
Let us pray for all nations, especially those that are oppressed, devastated, or impoverished, and for governments and leaders committed to peace and justice. (*silence*) God of mercy,
hear our prayer.

Let us pray for all who suffer: for the excluded, the homeless, refugees, prisoners; for those who grieve, who face death, who are sick (*especially*). (*silence*) God of mercy,
hear our prayer.

Let us pray for all who serve: for nurses and hospice workers, for custodians and housekeepers, for public servants, all who protect and rescue, and all whose service goes unnoticed. (*silence*) God of mercy,
hear our prayer.

Let us pray for children and for young people, and for all who care for them, especially new parents, daycare workers, foster parents, teachers, and counselors. (*silence*)
God of mercy,
hear our prayer.

Here other intercessions may be offered.

Let us give thanks for the saints who have gone before us in the faith and now rest in the arms of God. (*silence*)
God of mercy,
hear our prayer.

Loving God, you are near to us when we cry out to you. Into your embrace we commend all for whom we pray, through Christ and by the power of your Spirit.
Amen.

Ideas and Images for the Day

"To eat flesh" is a Hebraic war metaphor of savage conquest; "to drink blood" describes vicious slaughter. The abhorrent images stun Jesus' audience. Yet such will be his Passion—a Passover that turns the images inside out. His flesh and blood become bread and wine to strengthen our walk in justice and grace. The Son of Man's flesh, in Pauline terms, involves how we are implicated and interconnected with this worldly life. For us, flesh means our minds, hearts, and imagination are caught up in the middle of things. We start from our own needs and desires. Jesus' "flesh" comes from heaven. He thinks from, feels with, and witnesses to God's way of making all life whole. When we break bread and lift the cup, we invoke his life so that it might always shape our lives.

1. From the table to the world, as we are fed, so we feed others, with both bread for sustenance and the Bread of life. Find ways to extend the church's table service to a hungry world at Bread for the World: www.bread.org.

2. Ours is the first generation that has all the tools needed to end the poverty that kills; we lack the collective will-power. The Millennium Development Goals, adopted by the United Nations in 2000, seek to cut extreme poverty in half by 2015. Coupled with the ONE campaign, the church would add its voice to create the willpower needed. See www.millenniumcampaign.org and www.elca.org/ONE.

3. At 3:30 P.M. every Friday, San Francisco's St. Gregory of Nyssa Episcopal Church opens its doors for a food pantry that is set up around the altar in the sanctuary. "The pantry did not become a 'service project' of the church," writes St. Gregory member Sara Miles in her short article "Opening the Table." "It's simply church: a liturgy of acts, modeled directly on the liturgy of the word. It's as necessary and as intimate as breaking bread together: daily bread, the bread of heaven, and the bread that we become. We are bringing each other into communion." Read the article on St. Gregory's Web site: www.saintgregorys.org/Resources_pdfs /Opening_the_Table.pdf. PBS featured a story on St. Gregory's food pantry in May 2007. Watch the report and read more at www.pbs.org/wnet/religionandethics /week1039/profile.html.

4. For many, eucharist is the heart of faith—taking in Jesus' faithful life-giving thanksgiving to God—described in some liturgies as a sacrifice of praise. One of the challenges for incorporating contemporary music in liturgical worship is in marrying the emotions of the music with the rhythm of faith in a way that has theological integrity. How can praise music be used to prepare hearts that have heard the word to come joyfully to receive Christ at the table?

Hymns for Worship
Gathering
Come, let us eat   ELW 491, LBW 214
United at the table   ELW 498

Hymn of the Day
Bread of life from heaven   ELW 474
ARGENTINE SANTO/BREAK NOW THE BREAD
We eat the bread of teaching   ELW 518   *WISDOM'S FEAST*
I am the Bread of life   ELW 485, WOV 702   *I AM THE BREAD*

Communion
By your hand you feed your people   ELW 469
We who once were dead   ELW 495, LBW 207
Soul, adorn yourself with gladness   ELW 488/489, LBW 224

Sending
Praise and thanksgiving   ELW 689, LBW 409
God be with you till we meet again   ELW 536

Additional Hymns and Songs
Blessed Jesus, living Bread   HG 133 (sts. 2-3 D)
Let us be bread   GC 808
I will bless you, O Lord   DH 34
Give thanks   W&P 41, TFF 292

Music for the Day
Psalmody and Acclamations

Cherwien, David. "Psalm 34" from *Psalm Settings for the Church Year*. AFP 9780800678562.

Erickson, Richard. *Gospel Acclamations for Summer*. AFP 9780800678579.

Psalter for Worship Year B, Evangelical Lutheran Worship Edition. AFP 9780806683839.

Choral

Holst, Gustav. "Let All Mortal Flesh Keep Silence." SATB, kybd/orch. ECS 1.5019.

Steffani, Agostino. "Come, Ye Children, and Hearken to Me." SA, kybd. CPH 98-1593.

Thompson, J. Michael. "Taste and See the Lord Is Good." SATB, org, ob. AFP 9780800657031. OP

Young, Jeremy. "Taste and See." U/SA, opt assembly, kybd. AFP 9780800657604.

Children's Choir

Medema, Ken/Jack Schrader/Cora Scholz. "Lord, Listen to Your Children Praying." UE. 3 pt, pno. MFS YS500.

Miller, Aaron David. "Somebody's Knocking at Your Door." UE. U, pno. AFP 9780800677442.

Sleeth, Natalie. "Seek and You Will Find." UE. 2 pt, kybd. HIN HMC589.

Keyboard / Instrumental

Kerr, J. Wayne. "Carillon Cortege" from *Organ Music for the Seasons*, vol. 4. Org. AFP 9780800637507.

Kolander, Keith. "Argentine Santo" from *When Our Song Says Peace*. Pno. AFP 9780800623456.

Roberts, Anne. "I Am the Bread" from *As One Unknown: A Collection of Hymn Adaptations*. Org. AFP 9780800676964.

Schmoltze, Ron. "I Am the Bread" from *Augsburg Organ Library: Baptism and Communion*. Org. AFP 9780800623555.

Handbell

Lamb, Linda R., arr. "When in Our Music God Is Glorified." 3-5 oct, L3. Ring Out Press 3261.

McFadden, Jane. "Our Father's World." 3-5 oct, L3. JEF MJHSH-B120A. Full Score: JEF MJHSHB120.

Wagner, Douglas E. "Make Me a Channel of Your Peace." 3-5 oct, L2. AG 2063.

Praise Ensemble

■ Doerksen, Brian. "You Shine" from *Sing for Joy*. Hosanna! Music 000768213773.

■ Hall, Mark. "Lifesong" from www.praisecharts.com. SWECS Music/Club Zoo Music.

Hunnicutt, Judy. "This Do in Remembrance of Me" from www.ccli .com. The Sacred Music Press.

■ Smith, Henry. "Give Thanks." W&P 41.

Global

Farrell, Bernadette. "Bread for the World." SATB, kybd, gtr. OCP 11727.

Moore, James. "Taste and See." SATB, cant, pno, gtr. GIA G-5338.

Thursday, August 20
Bernard, Abbot of Clairvaux, 1153

Bernard was a Cistercian monk who became an abbot of great spiritual depth. He was a mystical writer deeply devoted to the humanity of Christ and consequently to the affective dimension of spirituality. He was critical of one of the foremost theologians of the day, Peter Abelard, because he believed Abelard's approach to faith was too rational and did not provide sufficient room for mystery. Bernard's devotional writings are still read today. His sermon on the Song of Solomon treats that Old Testament book as an allegory of Christ's love for humanity. Bernard wrote several hymns that are still sung today in translation. His hymn "Jesus, the very thought of you" (ELW 754) could be a way to commemorate this monk at worship.

■ denotes songs that are available on iTunes®.

August 23, 2009
Time after Pentecost — Lectionary 21

In today's gospel many people take offense at Jesus' invitation to eat his flesh and drink his blood; even many of Jesus' disciples peel off. This is the backdrop in John's gospel for Peter's confession of faith. "To whom can we go?" asks Peter, in words we sometimes sing just before the gospel is read. "You have the words of eternal life." In order to take such a stand, as Peter and Joshua did, Paul tells us to arm ourselves with the word of God. We pray in the Spirit that we might be bold ambassadors of the gospel.

Prayer of the Day

Holy God, your word feeds your people with life that is eternal. Direct our choices and preserve us in your truth, that, renouncing what is false and evil, we may live in you, through your Son, Jesus Christ, our Savior and Lord.

Gospel Acclamation

Alleluia. Lord, to whom [|] shall we go?* You have the words of e- [|] ternal life. *Alleluia.* (John 6:68)

Readings and Psalm
Joshua 24:1-2a, 14-18

In the Near East, covenant means agreement or alliance. It describes relationships and is the primary word used to characterize the relationship between God and Israel. By delivering Israel, God has already begun the relationship. Joshua calls upon the people to respond.

Psalm 34:15-22

The eyes of the LORD are upon the righteous. (Ps. 34:15)

Ephesians 6:10-20

Like a general giving a rousing speech to troops before battle, this letter closes by calling on Christians to be equipped for spiritual warfare against evil. The full armor of God includes truth, righteousness, peace, faith, the gift of salvation, and the word of God inspired by the Spirit.

John 6:56-69

The "hard saying" that offends Jesus' disciples is his claim that his followers must eat his flesh and drink his blood. The followers who return to their old lives know something about how odd this sounds. Simon Peter, on the other hand, knows something about the scarcity of living, gracious words. He asks the most important question: "To whom shall we go?"

Semicontinuous reading and psalm
1 Kings 8:[1, 6, 10-11] 22-30, 41-43

Solomon built the temple in Jerusalem and put the ark of the covenant there. This passage includes part of the prayer Solomon prays at the dedication of the temple. He prays for the fulfillment of God's promises to David and for God to hear the prayers of all the faithful.

Psalm 84

How dear to me is your dwelling, O LORD. (Ps. 84:1)

Color   Green

CD-ROM Images
Icon Three: 0821-0827_Lect21_B
Icon Two: Proper16_Sun21_B
Icon: 112

Prayers of Intercession

With the whole people of God in Christ Jesus, let us pray for the church, those in need, and all of God's creation.
A brief silence.
Holy One, you grace your people with powerful gifts. Call many leaders for your church, and strengthen those who serve you, that your love may be felt at all times and places. God of mercy,
hear our prayer.
You created the earth and all that is in it. Provide water for thirsty ground, clean air for troubled lungs, and protection for endangered plants and animals. God of mercy,
hear our prayer.
You breathed life into the first human creatures. By your spirit, renew the whole human family, that all nations may be at peace with one another. God of mercy,
hear our prayer.

Clothe with your love all those in need: the poor, malnourished, or exhausted; the injured or disabled; those in need of constant care; the dying and the sick (*especially*).
God of mercy,
hear our prayer.
You dedicate yourself to your people. Come to the aid of our community (*especially*). Listen to the aching of our hearts and stimulate our faith. God of mercy,
hear our prayer.
Here other intercessions may be offered.
Your light shines through the saints of all ages (*especially*). Comfort the grieving, and gather us all at your feast that has no end. God of mercy,
hear our prayer.
Loving God, you are near to us when we cry out to you. Into your embrace we commend all for whom we pray, through Christ and by the power of your Spirit.
Amen.

Ideas and Images for the Day

In John 6:56-69 we hear Christ draw the comparison between manna, which was not able to sustain life forever, and the bread from heaven, Jesus' body, which brings life for eternity. The readings today address the idea that physical life on this earth is not all there is. The spiritual component of life has its challenges and battles too. As we acknowledge the struggles and rewards of integrating both the spiritual and physical in our faith lives, we open ourselves to the resources of friendship and community.

1. Metaphor and allegory have been used by many writers to illustrate spiritual truths through comparisons and symbols. John Bunyan's classic Christian allegory, *Pilgrim's Progress*, tells the story of one man's search for heaven, using names and places that illustrate the struggles he encounters. The book *Hinds' Feet on High Places* by Hannah Hurnard (Tyndale House, 1975) also describes the faith journey in allegory that casts more than one meaning on the protagonist's adventures. A reading from either of these books could be used for a children's talk or a sermon illustration to aid in understanding Christ's metaphorical teaching on communion.

2. The idea of "blood brothers" occurs in many cultures; blood once mingled with another's is thought to forge a relationship as close as kin from that time on. Jesus may be using this same binding image to foster the belief that as the Father and Jesus are one, so the believers are one with Jesus forever. What other rituals do we observe that underscore our connectedness with others?

3. Meals—family, festive, holiday—all speak to the love, unity, and connection we feel with friends and family. The Lord's supper is a meal to which Christ invites us and at which he serves as host. Binding love characterizes this meal. Images of food and celebration that evoke memories and emotions are powerful ways to explore the meaning of communion as event and relationship.

4. In John 6:56, Jesus uses the Greek word *meno*, which means to abide or remain with. Young people hang out, many of us go to coffee, some athletes rehydrate at a pub; all examples of abiding with one another. As we spend time with God through prayer, meditation, and worship, we grow closer to understanding God's heart and emulating Christ's life.

Hymns for Worship
Gathering
You are the way   ELW 758, LBW 464
Soli Deo Gloria   ELW 878
Rejoice, ye pure in heart!   ELW 873, 874, LBW 553

Hymn of the Day
O Jesus, I have promised   ELW 810, LBW 503   MUNICH
Around you, O Lord Jesus   ELW 468, LBW 496
    O JESU, ÄN DE DINA
O Savior, precious Savior   ELW 820, LBW 514
    ANGEL'S STORY

Communion
Blessed assurance   ELW 638, WOV 699
Eat this bread, drink this cup   ELW 492, WOV 706

Sending
He comes to us as one unknown   ELW 737, WOV 768
On our way rejoicing   ELW 537, LBW 260
O Jesus, blessed Lord   ELW 541, LBW 220

Additional Hymns and Songs
Blessed Jesus, living Bread   HG 133 (sts. 2–3 E)
Hope of the world   LBW 493
Holy One, in you alone   DH 83
All to Jesus I surrender   TFF 235

Music for the Day
Psalmody and Acclamations
Cherwien, David. "Psalm 34" from *Psalm Settings for the Church Year.* AFP 9780800678562.
Erickson, Richard. *Gospel Acclamations for Summer.* AFP 9780800678579.
Psalter for Worship Year B, Evangelical Lutheran Worship Edition. AFP 9780806683839.

Choral

Britten, Benjamin. "Jubilate Deo." SATB, org. OXF 9780193515772.

Fleming, Larry L. "Give Me Jesus." SATB. AFP 9780800645274. *The Augsburg Choirbook.* AFP 9780800656782.

Handel, G. F. "All My Spirit Longs to Savor." SATB, kybd. AFP 9780800638863.

Haydn, F. J./arr. Robert Scholz. "God of Life." SATB, kybd, opt orch. AFP 9780800655990.

Vaughan Williams, Ralph. "O Taste and See." SATB, sop solo. OXF 43-909.

Children's Choir

Hughes, Howard. "You Have Put On Christ." UE. U, opt canon, org, 2 C inst, fc, drm, orch, hb. GIA G-2283.

Jothen, Michael. "Joshua (He Was a Man of God)." UE. 2 pt, kybd. BP 1156.

Kemp, Helen. "Prayer Litany." UE. 2 pt, kybd, opt ob. CG A747.

Keyboard / Instrumental

Cherwien, David. "Munich" from *Evening and Morning.* Org. AFP 9780800675721.

Moore, Bob. "Soliloquy: My Prayers Rise Like Incense" from *Music for Contemporary Ensemble*, vol. 1. Kybd, C inst, gtr, bass. GIA G-4787.

Reuss, Jonathan. "O Jesu, än de dina" from *Organ Music for the Seasons*, vol. 3. Org. AFP 9780800675646.

Willan, Healey. "Angel's Story" from *Organ Works of Healey Willan.* Org. CPH 97-6676U1.

Handbell

Dobrinski, Cynthia, arr. "He Leadeth Me." 3-5 oct, L2+. AG 1461.

Helman, Michael, arr. "Gather Us In." 3-5 oct, L2. CPH 97-6556.

McFadden, Jane. "Our Father's World." 3-5 oct, L3. JEF MJHSHB120A. Full Score: JEF MJHSHB120.

Praise Ensemble

- DeShazo, Lynn. "Ancient Words" from *iWorship Songbook #2.* INT 27516.

- Egan, Jon. "I Am Free" from www.praisecharts.com. Vertical Worship Songs.

- Grant, Amy/Michael W. Smith. "Thy Word" from www.music notes.com. Meadowgreen Music/WM. W&P 144.

- Nelson, Marc. "I Believe in Jesus" from *Breakforth Worship Songbook.* New Creation Ministries. www.new-creation.net.

Global

Haas, David. "Song of the Body of Christ." SATB, cant, kybd, gtr. GIA G-3360.

Westendorf, Omer. "We Eat the Bread of Teaching." Pno, gtr. ELW 518.

- denotes songs that are available on iTunes®.

Monday, August 24

Bartholomew, Apostle

Bartholomew is mentioned as one of Jesus' disciples in Matthew, Mark, and Luke. The list in John does not include him but rather Nathanael. These two are often assumed to be the same person. Except for his name on these lists of the Twelve, little is known. Some traditions say Bartholomew preached in India or Armenia following the resurrection. In art, Bartholomew is pictured holding a flaying knife to indicate the manner in which he was killed.

Friday, August 28

Augustine, Bishop of Hippo, 430

Augustine was one of the greatest theologians of the Western church. Born in North Africa, he was a philosophy student in Carthage, where he later became a teacher of rhetoric. Much of his young life was a debauched one. As an adult he came under the influence of Ambrose, the bishop of Milan, and through him came to see Christianity as a religion appropriate for a philosopher. Augustine was baptized by Ambrose at the Easter Vigil in 387. He was ordained four years later and made bishop of Hippo in 396. Augustine was a defender of the Christian faith and argued, against the Donatists, that the holiness of the church did not depend on the holiness of its members, particularly the clergy, but that holiness comes from Christ, the head of the church. Augustine's autobiography, *Confessions*, tells of his slow move toward faith and includes the line "Late have I loved thee."

Moses the Black, monk, martyr, c. 400

A man of great strength and rough character, Moses the Black was converted to Christian faith toward the close of the fourth century. Prior to his conversion he had been a thief and a leader of a gang of robbers. The story of his conversion is unknown, but eventually he became a desert monk at Skete. The habit of his monastic community was white, though Moses is reported to have said, "God knows I am black within." The change in his heart and life had a profound impact on his native Ethiopia. He was murdered when Berbers attacked his monastery.

August 30, 2009

Time after Pentecost — Lectionary 22

Jesus protests against human customs being given the weight of divine law, while the essence of God's law is ignored. True uncleanness comes not from external things, but from the intentions of the human heart. Last week Jesus told us "the words that I have spoken to you are spirit and life." Now James says God has given us birth by the word of truth. We, having been washed in the word when we were born in the font, return to it every Sunday to ask God to create in us clean hearts.

Prayer of the Day

O God our strength, without you we are weak and wayward creatures. Protect us from all dangers that attack us from the outside, and cleanse us from all evil that arises from within ourselves, that we may be preserved through your Son, Jesus Christ, our Savior and Lord.

Gospel Acclamation

Alleluia. God gave us birth by the | word of truth * so that we would become a kind of first fruits | of creation. *Alleluia.* (James 1:18)

Readings and Psalm

Deuteronomy 4:1-2, 6-9

The Israelites believed the law was a divine gift that provided guidelines for living out the covenant. Moses commands the people to obey the law and neither to add to nor subtract from it. The Israelites are also to teach the law to their children and their children's children.

Psalm 15

LORD, who may dwell in your tabernacle? (Ps. 15:1)

James 1:17-27

The letter of James was intended to provide first-century Christians with instruction in godly behavior. Here, Christians are encouraged to listen carefully and to act on what they hear, especially by caring for those least able to care for themselves.

Mark 7:1-8, 14-15, 21-23

Mark's gospel depicts Jesus as challenging traditional ways in which religious people determine what is pure or impure. For Jesus, the observance of religious practices cannot become a substitute for godly words or deeds that spring from a faithful heart.

Semicontinuous reading and psalm

Song of Solomon 2:8-13

Though using language and images of a love story, the Song of Solomon has long been interpreted allegorically. Jewish lore sees it as a description of the love between the Lord and Israel. Christians have often interpreted the Song as a description of the love between Christ and his church.

Psalm 45:1-2, 6-9

God has anointed you with the oil of gladness. (Ps. 45:7)

Color   Green

CD-ROM Images

Icon Three: 0828-0903_Lect22_B
Icon Two: Proper17_Sun22_B
Icon: 113

Prayers of Intercession

With the whole people of God in Christ Jesus, let us pray for the church, those in need, and all of God's creation.
A brief silence.
Let us pray for the unity of the church of Christ, and for all who struggle to understand God's word. (*silence*)
God of mercy,
hear our prayer.
Let us pray for the earth and all its wonders, for good harvests and favorable weather. (*silence*) God of mercy,
hear our prayer.
Let us pray for the whole human family, for little children, for the aging, for all nations and cultures, and also for our enemies. (*silence*) God of mercy,
hear our prayer.

Let us pray for all who suffer with HIV/AIDS or other diseases, with injuries or with ailments, with addictions or anxieties, joblessness or loneliness, despair or grief (*especially*). (*silence*) God of mercy,
hear our prayer.

Let us pray for families, especially those enduring divorce; for struggling families and abusive families; also for newly formed families, for pregnant women and those in labor. (*silence*) God of mercy,
hear our prayer.

Here other intercessions may be offered.

Let us give thanks for those who have died (*especially*), entrusting them to God's love. (*silence*) God of mercy,
hear our prayer.

Loving God, you are near to us when we cry out to you. Into your embrace we commend all for whom we pray, through Christ and by the power of your Spirit.
Amen.

Ideas and Images for the Day

Using the issue of ritual cleanliness, Jesus tries to teach the Pharisees the difference between the observance of the letter of the law versus living the spirit of the law. Our litigious society is aware of the pharisaical adherence to rules where justice can be overlooked. Yet the law is a gift from God that shows us how to live, and also reveals our sinful ways. Christ would have us live by both the letter and the spirit of the law, with hearts cleansed from sin by God's grace and lives that are at the service of all in need.

1. The contemporary song "Ancient Words" by Lynn DeShazo is suitable for singing in conjunction with the reading of scripture (Integrity's Hosanna! Music, 2001; available online). Contemporary versions of the Bible such as Eugene Peterson's *The Message* provide an accessible perspective on timeless truths (Colorado Springs: NavPress Publishing Group, 2002). Reading the gospel from this paraphrase could help forge a connection with God's ancient words that continue to have life and power in the present.

2. The word *adiaphora*—meaning nonessential—is used to distinguish between what is necessary and that which is a matter of choice. Many rituals have become law in our minds, but an examination of our own particular traditions and observances could be useful to reveal the purpose and function of the things we do in worship.

3. Addressing the Pharisees in Matthew 12:34b, Jesus says "Out of the abundance of the heart the mouth speaks." Jesus contends that what defiles a person comes from within, not without. In the James passage we hear that we should bridle our tongues (1:26). But the tongue only speaks what is in the mind and the heart. How can we cleanse our hearts, transform our egocentric selves to be "theocentric"?

4. Martin Luther's Small Catechism illuminates the ten commandments with Luther's answers to the question "What does this mean?" The explanation of the Eighth Commandment helps us see that in our attempts to obey the law we should also be proactive in helping the neighbor: "We are to fear and love God, so that we do not tell lies about our neighbors, betray or slander them, or destroy their reputations. Instead we are to come to their defense, speak well of them, and interpret everything they do in the best possible light." This transformation of the believer's heart and mind is a result of the Holy Spirit's activity. The entire Small Catechism is printed in *Evangelical Lutheran Worship*, pp. 1160–1167.

Hymns for Worship
Gathering

Awake, my soul, and with the sun   ELW 557, LBW 269
Dearest Jesus, at your word   ELW 520, LBW 248

Hymn of the Day

O God, my faithful God   ELW 806, LBW 504
     WAS FRAG ICH NACH DER WELT
Restore in us, O God   ELW 328   BAYLOR
     WOV 662   CATECHUMEN
Oh, that the Lord would guide my ways   ELW 772,
     LBW 480   EVAN

Communion

Lord, let my heart be good soil   ELW 512, WOV 713
Change my heart, O God   ELW 801
Take, oh, take me as I am   ELW 814

Sending

Strengthen for service, Lord   ELW 497, LBW 218
Savior, again to your dear name   ELW 534, LBW 262

Additional Hymns and Songs

As a chalice cast of gold   HG 62
Stand in the congregation   W&P 131
Our God, to whom we turn   H82 681
Teach me, O Lord, your holy way   NCH 465

Music for the Day
Psalmody and Acclamations

Erickson, Richard. *Gospel Acclamations for Summer.* AFP 9780800678579.

Jennings, Carolyn. "Psalm 15" from *Psalm Settings for the Church Year.* AFP 9780800678562.

Psalter for Worship Year B, Evangelical Lutheran Worship Edition. AFP 9780806683839.

Choral

Bisbee, B. Wayne. "Teach Me Your Way, O Lord." 2 pt mxd, kybd. AFP 9780800654795.

Moyer, J. Harold. "O Thou in Whose Presence." TTBB, tenor solo, ob, opt gtr. MFS MF-1015.

Parker, Alice/Robert Shaw. "His Voice as the Sound." SATB. LG 00915.

Pelz, Walter L. "Show Me Thy Ways." SATB, gtr, ob/fl. AFP 9780800645427. *The Augsburg Choirbook.* AFP 9780800656782.

Children's Choir

Carley, Isabel. "Simple Gifts." UE. Orff, cello, fc/tri, opt hb. AFP 9786000105679. OP

Olson, Howard S. "Listen, God Is Calling" from *LifeSongs.* LE. U, pno, opt drm. AFP 9780806642710.

Sleeth, Natalie. "It's All in the Hands of God." UE. 2 pt, kybd. AMSI 421.

Keyboard / Instrumental

Beck, Theodore. "Was frag ich nach der Welt" from *Basic Hymn Accompaniments*, vol. IV. Pno/org. CPH 97-6636U1.

Bender, Jan. "Evan" from *Master Organ Works of Jan Bender*, vol. 2. Org. CPH 97-7099U1.

Johnson, David N. "Was frag ich nach der Welt" from *Wedding Music*, book 3. Org. AFP 9780800648947.

Manz, Paul. "Aria." Org. MSM 10-906.

Handbell

Hopson, Hal H. "Siyahamba." 3-5 oct, opt perc, L3. HOP 1869.

McChesney, Kevin. "Jubilance." 3-5 oct, L3. CG B234.

McFadden, Jane. "Londonderry Air/O Christ the Same." 2-3 oct hb/hc, opt C/B-flat inst, L2. AFP 9780800656294.

Praise Ensemble

■ Bullock, Geoff. "I Will Never Be" from www.musicnotes.com. WM/MAR.

■ Ewing, Paul. "Dwell in Your House" from www.praisecharts.com. Hillsong Publishing/INT.

■ Redman, Matt. "The Heart of Worship" from *I Could Sing of Your Love Forever 2.* WT 0000809251.

■ Tomlin, Chris. "Forever" from *I Could Sing of Your Love Forever 2.* WT 0000809251.

Global

Glover, Robert. "Stand Firm." SATB, cant, kybd, gtr, perc. GIA G-4593.

Haugen, Marty. "Within the Reign of God." SATB, cant, assembly, kybd, gtr, C inst. GIA G-4963.

Wednesday, September 2
Nikolai Frederik Severin Grundtvig, bishop, renewer of the church, 1872

Grundtvig was one of two principal Danish theologians of the nineteenth century; the other was Søren Kierkegaard. Grundtvig's ministry as a parish pastor had a difficult start. He was officially censured after his first sermon, though he did receive approval a year later to be ordained. He served with his father for two years but was unable to receive a call for seven years after that. In 1826 he was forced to resign after he attacked the notion that Christianity was merely a philosophical idea rather than God's revelation made known to us in Christ and through word and sacrament. This belief would be a hallmark of Grundtvig's writing. He spent his last thirty-three years as a chaplain at a home for elderly women. From his university days he was convinced that poetry spoke to the human spirit better than prose. He wrote more than a thousand hymns, including "God's word is our great heritage" (ELW 509).

■ denotes songs that are available on iTunes®.

Time after Pentecost
Autumn

Preparing for Autumn

Summer reading lists, swimming pools, outdoor festivals, and fairs all have conspired to turn summer vacation from truly lazy days into busy days ordered differently. As a result, many congregations that celebrate a version of "Rally Day" in early September may find necessary a rally for rest, right worship, and the reordering of work centered in God's word and sustained by the Spirit, rather than a rally for yet again more vigorous (if different) activity. Indeed, it may be most important to heed this word of Isaiah:

The Lord GOD has given me
    the tongue of a teacher,
that I may know how to sustain
    the weary with a word. (Isa. 50:4)

There is much joy intrinsic to seasons of return and renewal, and there is little reason to put a damper on the natural impulse of many churches to match the rhythm of school registration and garden harvest—but there is need to ensure that the schooling sustains the weary and the harvest feeds the soul. In a recent survey of formerly churched adults in America, LifeWay Research (www.lifewayresearch.com) discovered that the number-one life change that prompted people to leave the church was that they simply are too busy. The top motivating reason for people to *return* to church is also simple—they want to be closer to God (*Outreach*, July/August 2007, pp. 92–96). Could it be that these two are related? As Rob Bell asks in his nooma video, *Noise*: "Do you wish God's voice would be louder in your life? Does all the noise in our lives make it hard to hear God? If I'm not still, and if I don't listen, how is Jesus going to give me rest?" The length of the time after Pentecost may well invite us to practice more deeply the discipline of silence.

Yet, allow a little music to interpret the silence. Consider spending time listening to Jonathan Rundman's album *Sound Theology* in this late time of the church year. Track 13, "No Time to Breathe," includes this line: "There was no time for me to do nothing / there was no time to think and no time to breathe."

Lectionary

John Chrysostom, whom we commemorate on September 13, was given the name *Chrysostom*—which means golden-mouth—in recognition of his eloquence as a preacher and speaker. The *Divine Liturgy of Saint John Chrysostom*, used on most days of the year by the Eastern Orthodox Church, reminds us that liturgy and proclamation are integrally related. Those responsible for preaching and reading scripture may follow the example of John Chrysostom and gild their words with gold: take time to carefully train lectors to proclaim the word clearly and gracefully. Preachers might renew their own practice of preaching during this time, focusing anew on their craft with study, careful preparation, solicitation of feedback, and consultation with colleagues. Watch video or listen to audio of previous sermons and contemplate whether and how they are eloquent treatments of the word.

In the readings from the Gospel of Mark appointed for September and October, two themes emerge. The bookends, September 6 and October 25, are stories of healing—the healings of the daughter of a Syrophoenician woman, a deaf man, and blind Bartimaeus. In the other readings we hear the proclamation of Jesus as Messiah, and the preparation of the disciples for suffering. Along the way, disputes concerning greatness, the use and authority of Jesus' name, marriage, and wealth all indicate the extent to which Jesus was proclaiming God's vision of a new way. As Pheme Perkins writes, "Jesus is warning the disciples that they must give up the normal human calculations of greatness if they are to participate in the rule of God" (*New Interpreter's Bible Commentary*, vol. 8, p. 647).

Mark's record of Jesus' healing ministry provides a context for congregations to introduce, renew, or continue their use of a service of healing (see pp. 276–278 in *Evangelical Lutheran Worship*). The order for healing can take place within Holy Communion or the Service of the Word, usually following the hymn of the day. The letter of James, read continuously throughout much of the autumn season, also encourages an order of healing during corporate worship. James writes, "Are any among you sick? They should call for the elders of the church and have them pray over them, anointing them with oil in the name of the Lord" (5:14).

James draws a connection between forgiveness and physical healing. Corporate worship that offers opportunity for confession and forgiveness and the anointing of the sick is in keeping with the ministry of Jesus and his first followers.

The early chapters of Hebrews are also read continuously during this season. If any letter of the New Testament bears comparison to Chrysostom's golden mouth, it is this golden-penned letter. The reading for October 4 may be particularly memorable; it contains a sentence used in the daily prayer of the church, at Morning Prayer (Matins) and Evening Prayer (Vespers). At the conclusion of the scripture readings appointed for morning or evening prayer, the leader says or sings, "Long ago God spoke to our ancestors in many and various ways by the prophets," and the assembly responds, "but in these last days God has spoken to us by the Son" (Heb. 1:1). This sentence is an apt introduction to Hebrews, which considers the doctrine of Jesus Christ and his role as mediator.

Music

If hospitality and the invitation of new and returning worshipers is an emphasis in this season, it will be important to sing familiar hymns and songs. In advance of this season, consider recording in a hymnal or elsewhere the dates on which hymns were sung in worship. Then revisit ones that are especially appropriate for the transition to fall.

You could also experiment with the repetition of hymns or refrains throughout the season. During the distribution of communion, consider selecting hymns that are repeatable and easy to memorize, such as those from the Taizé community (ELW 406, 472, 616, or 642). Take time with them, sing them over and over, and rest into them.

If healing is an emphasis during the season, make use of special acclamations designated for this service (ELW 218–221). Or consider making use of more contemporary hymns of healing, including Marty Haugen's "Healer of our every ill" (ELW 612) or Fred Pratt Green's hymn, "O Christ, the healer, we have come" (ELW 610). Green's "Rejoice in God's saints" (ELW 418) would also be appropriate in the commemorations of John Chrysostom and Francis of Assisi.

One hymn not to overlook this season is "We plow the fields and scatter." *Evangelical Lutheran Worship* provides an opportunity to sing this hymn in English only (#681) or as a bilingual hymn in Spanish and English (#680). This hymn can serve as both a celebration of harvest and a musical proclamation of offering as worship. Consider using this hymn during the collection and presentation of the offering.

Space

Recent reflection on stewardship has helped the church understand that our offering is not about paying the bills or meeting the budget; rather, it is a response to a gracious and generous God. Autumn may be the perfect time to breathe new life into the use of space and actions that surround the offering.

While singing "We plow the fields and scatter," consider bringing more than the offering plates up to the table. Train presenters to bring up other gifts as well, especially the bread and wine for the meal. Gather gifts from the congregation, maybe especially products of the fall harvest. Gather produce, canned goods, or other necessities that can be distributed to the poor. Some congregations sponsor an exchange of produce in the fall: bless such a ministry. Set up a table with a sign indicating "free produce," and invite worshipers to set out their extra tomatoes, potatoes, eggplants, and squash for anyone who has a need. Emphasizing the glory of locally produced food, and the joy of cooking and eating it slowly and with care, together with others, is another way to celebrate this season of harvest, rest, and renewal.

One of the most famous events in the life of St. Francis occurred while he was praying in an out-of-the-way chapel, St. Damian's. Looking at the crucifix in the chapel, he heard the Christ figure say to him, "Go, Francis, and repair my house." Francis took the command literally and started at once to try and repair St. Damian's. After various difficulties, and after his vow of poverty, he rebuilt St. Damian's, as well as a few other churches in the area.

Following the example of Francis, this season is a good time to get back to the basics of space. Take time to look at the walls, the ceiling, the floor. What is in ill repair? What needs the care of a contractor or custodian? What needs to be replaced? Contemplate especially the gift that has been given to your congregation by the saints who built and financed the original building. Or if you are in a church that is newly built, take time to celebrate what God has brought forth so recently in the midst of your community.

Finally, consider using your space to bless and celebrate not only the congregation and the building but all of God's creation. Many churches now have a fall blessing of animals (a form is provided in the seasonal rites section, pp. 263–265). One Franciscan prayer for such blessings is: "Blessed are you, Lord God, maker of all living creatures. You called forth fish in the sea, birds in the air, and animals on the land. You inspired St. Francis to call all of them his brothers and sisters. We ask you to bless this animal. By the power of your love, enable it to live according to your plan. May we always praise you for all your beauty in creation. Blessed are you, Lord our God, in all your creatures! Amen."

Celebrating Autumn with Children

Autumn is a time of new beginnings, a return to routines and schedules, and back to school. It may be a time of transition and unfamiliar experiences for young children. Careful planning is important to intentionally include children in the worship experience. Many children will be participating in worship or church educational programs for the first time. Positive and successful experiences will shape children's attitudes, and perhaps also those of adults accompanying children. Be sensitive to children for whom the return to school represents challenges, frustrations, and feelings of failure. Help them feel valued by God no matter what their academic abilities, emphasizing that faith formation is also a matter of the heart.

Ideas for Autumn

- Autumn includes Reformation Sunday. Worship planners and those responsible for Christian education may wish to coordinate a Reformation festival on Reformation Sunday for the Sunday school children, or plan an intergenerational event.

- Highlight the idea of growing and deepening in faith and knowledge of Jesus during the time after Pentecost by distributing leaves in deepening shades of green—this season's liturgical color—each week as children attend worship. Suggest that the children create a tree at home (a drawing hung on the bedroom wall, door, or family refrigerator; a tree branch stuck into a pail of sand or dirt) to display their leaves. If desired, key words from the weekly theme for worship could be printed on the leaves (for example, *follow* or *service*).

- Consider a movable Children's Time, rotating through the four portions of the worship service: gathering, word, meal, and sending. Use the time to acquaint the children with that portion of the service. For example, during the gathering, teach the children to gesture (arms outstretched) in response to the greeting: "The Lord be with you. And also with you." At the sending, the children may clap the rhythm of the response: "Thanks be to God."

- Regardless of which setting your assembly uses, assist those who worship with children in recognizing child-friendly worship elements: repeated phrases such as the Kyrie ("Lord, have mercy"), the refrain for the canticle of praise ("Glory to God" or "This is the feast"), the assembly responses to the great thanksgiving; physical responses, such as standing, sitting, kneeling, and praying. Adults worshiping with children may appreciate the brief, annotated pattern for worship on pages 92–93 of *Evangelical Lutheran Worship*.

- Use spoken or printed announcements to remind all worshipers of the importance of welcoming children in worship. All worshipers can participate in embracing children with the arms of God, providing guidance, creating loving community, affirming the gifts of all ages in God's family. Draw attention to the mention of children in the prayer of the day for both September 20 and October 4 (see pp. 272 and 278).

- Encourage families to read the Gospel of Mark, chapters 7–10; James 2–5; or Hebrews 1–7 for devotions at home during autumn, because they are the continuous readings in the Sunday lectionary.

- Several of the gospel texts refer to Jesus turning things upside down (the first shall be last, the last shall be first; greatness is found in service; using a little child as an example of faith). Jesus lifts up children as models of faith; children will begin to recognize that their faith response is accepted and valued by God.

- September 6: Children enjoy alliteration. Focus on the P words used in the prayer of the day and psalm: *power, presence, people, proclaim, promises, praise*. Because the readings from Isaiah and Mark mention blindness and deafness, demonstrate the ASL sign for P, or punch P from the Braille alphabet.

- September 13: Many congregations appoint a Rally Day. Monday, September 14, is Holy Cross Day. Perhaps that suggests a Rally Day theme around the cross? Teach the children the use of the sign of the cross during worship. *Follow* is a key word in the gospel; use feet (footprints available in foam glow-in-the-dark cutouts at craft stores; trace children's feet; colored paper cutouts) as a tangible reminder of walking with and following Jesus.

Worship Helps for Autumn

Autumn Checklist

- If the worship schedule changes, notify local newspapers, update your Web site, and change listings on exterior signs and church answering machines.
- If a healing service will be held on or near the festival of Luke, Evangelist (October 18), review the form provided in *Evangelical Lutheran Worship* (Pew Edition, pp. 276–278; Leaders Edition, pp. 660–665).
- If a blessing of animals will be held on or near October 4 (Francis of Assisi, renewer of the church, 1226), see a possible order for this celebration in the seasonal rites section, pp. 263–265.
- Look ahead to the checklist on p. 299 as you plan for the rest of the time after Pentecost.
- Begin planning for Advent 2009.

Shape of the Communion Liturgy

- See the seasonal worship texts for the autumn months on pp. 260–261.
- Omit the Kyrie (except, perhaps, for Reformation Sunday).
- Omit or use the hymn of praise ("Glory to God" or hymn equivalent for Reformation Sunday).
- Use the Nicene Creed for Reformation Sunday; use the Apostles' Creed for other Sundays in these months.

- See the prayers of intercession for each Sunday and the Day of Thanksgiving (Canada).
- Use the preface for Sundays; use the preface for weekdays for the Day of Thanksgiving (*Evangelical Lutheran Worship* Leaders Edition, pp. 180, 191).
- Thanksgiving at the table: see options in *Evangelical Lutheran Worship* (Leaders Edition, pp. 198–205); *WOV*, Prayer H (Leaders Edition, p. 72).

Other Helps

- See the suggestions for music and worship space in the essay "Preparing for Autumn," pp. 256–257.
- Consider using the Affirmation of Christian Vocation in *Evangelical Lutheran Worship* (Pew Edition, p. 84) near Labor Day as a way to recognize the various kinds of daily work in which the assembly is engaged.
- Use one of the blessings for teachers and students provided in the seasonal rites section (pp. 262–263) at the beginning of a new Sunday school or academic year.
- If Bibles will be distributed to young readers, consider having their parents or baptismal sponsors involved in physically handing over the Bibles as a way to honor promises made at baptism. Words to accompany this action are provided in the seasonal rites section (p. 263).

SEASONAL WORSHIP TEXTS FOR AUTUMN

Confession and Forgiveness

All may make the sign of the cross, the sign that is marked at baptism, as the presiding minister begins.
Blessed be the Holy Trinity, + one God,
who forgives all our sin, whose mercy endures forever.
Amen.

Let us approach the throne of grace with boldness,
confessing our sin and trusting in God's mercy.

Silence is kept for reflection.

God of truth,
we have all sinned and fallen short of your glory.
We have turned away from you.
We have not kept your commandments.
We have not loved our neighbors as ourselves.
We have neglected the poor,
and we have not welcomed all people in your name.
You know the fullness of our sin.
Forgive us, and turn us again to you,
so that we may receive the fullness of your mercy.
Amen.

Our great high priest, Jesus Christ,
sacrificed himself for us and for our sins.
In Christ, you are freed from your sins
and given a place in God's household forever.
Amen.

Greeting

The grace of our Lord Jesus Christ, the love of God,
and the communion of the Holy Spirit be with you all.
And also with you.

Offering Prayer

God of majesty,
in your might you have created all things,
and you entrust to our care what you have made.
Receive our offerings,
and make them a sign of our dedication
to provide for the needs of all people and creatures,
in the name of the one who sustains all things by his word,
Jesus Christ our Lord.
Amen.

Invitation to Communion

Receive the Lord and live.

Prayer after Communion

Loving God,
in this meal you sustain the weary and heal the broken.
May the gift of your word made flesh,
the body and blood of Christ,
inspire our tongues to praise you
and proclaim to the entire world
the Savior, Jesus Christ our Lord.
Amen.

Sending of Communion

Holy God,
as Moses lifted up the serpent in the wilderness,
so your Son was lifted up,
that whoever believes in him may have eternal life.
Bless those who now carry your word and sacrament
to our sisters and brothers who are absent,
that all the world might be saved through him,
Jesus Christ our Lord.
Amen.

Blessing

The life-giving God, who sets us free in Christ,
encourage you with the presence of the Holy Spirit
and ✛ bless you now and forever.
Amen.

Dismissal

Go in peace. Remember the poor.
Thanks be to God.

SEASONAL RITES FOR AUTUMN

Commissioning and Blessing of Teachers

The following order may be used within the congregation's primary service as a way to recognize those responsible for ministry to and with children and youth. It may be used with as much flexibility as necessary or desired. The leader role may be shared among several people, as suggested.

Those being commissioned for ministry with children and youth gather with the leaders. The first leader addresses the assembly.

A reading from First Corinthians. Now there are varieties of gifts, but the same Spirit; and there are varieties of services, but the same Lord; and there are varieties of activities, but it is the same God who activates all of them in everyone. To each is given the manifestation of the Spirit for the common good. (1 Cor. 12:4-7)

The first leader addresses those being commissioned.

Brothers and sisters, you have volunteered your time, your energy, and your gifts to the children, youth, and family ministries of this congregation. Will you offer your gifted-ness to this ministry in the confidence that it comes from God?
Response: I will, and I ask God to help and guide me.

The second leader addresses the assembly.

A reading from Proverbs. Trust in the LORD with all your heart, and do not rely on your own insight. In all your ways acknowledge him, and he will make straight your paths. (Prov. 3:5-6)

The second leader addresses those being commissioned.

Will you carry out this ministry centered in Christ's call, striving to trust God as your guide and inspiration?
Response: I will, and I ask God to help and guide me.

The third leader addresses the assembly.

A reading from Ephesians. I pray that you may be strengthened in your inner being with power through God's Spirit, and that Christ may dwell in your hearts through faith, as you are being rooted and grounded in love. I pray that you may have the power to comprehend, with all the saints, what is the breadth and length and height and depth, and to know the love of Christ that surpasses knowledge, so that you may be filled with all the fullness of God. (Eph. 3:16-19)

The third leader addresses those being commissioned.

Will you trust in God's care, seek to grow in love for those you serve, strive for excellence in your skills, and honor the gospel with a faithful life?
Response: I will, and I ask God to help and guide me.

The assembly stands. The first leader addresses the assembly.

I now ask you, members of *name of congregation*: Will you today renew your commitment to our youngest brothers and sisters, our children and youth who look to you for guidance, support, and examples of righteous living?
We will, and we ask God to help and guide us.

Those being commissioned face the assembly. The second leader addresses the assembly.

Members of *name of congregation*, will you claim these gifted people as those called by God to help carry out our congregation's ministry to children, youth, and families? Will you support them and enthusiastically celebrate the work they do?
We will, and we ask God to help and guide us.

The third leader addresses the assembly.

Will you pray for these leaders and the young people they serve, celebrating our children and youth as the ones Jesus blessed and welcomed?
We will, and we ask God to help and guide us.

The presiding minister continues:

Let us pray. Gracious God, for Jesus' sake, empower these ministers to care for the young ones in our family of faith. Help them to teach faithfully, lead patiently, and guide confidently. Stir up in these servants the gift of your Holy Spirit: the spirit of wisdom and understanding, the spirit of counsel and might, the spirit of knowledge and fear of the Lord, the spirit of joy in your presence, both now and forever.
Amen.

People in the assembly may raise their hands in blessing as the presiding minister continues.

Almighty God, who has given you the gifts and the will to do these things, graciously give you the strength and compassion to perform them.
Amen.

The first leader concludes with these or similar words.

On behalf of *name of congregation*, we now commission you for ministry, grateful for your gifts and your willingness to serve.

The assembly may offer acclamation with applause.

Blessings for Teachers and Students

For the marvels of your creation,
we praise you, O God.
For the opportunity to explore and study,
we praise you, O God.
For those who guide us, teachers and mentors,
we praise you, O God.
Teach us your ways and guide us in your path,
for you are the creator of all that is seen and unseen.
Amen.
or
Let us pray for all who are beginning a new school year,
that both students and teachers
will be blessed in their academic endeavors.

Almighty God, you give wisdom and knowledge.
Grant teachers the gift of joy and insight,
and students the gift of diligence and openness,
that all may grow in what is good and honest and true.
Support all who teach and all who learn,
that together we may know and follow your ways;
through Jesus Christ our Lord.
Amen.

Presentation of the Bible

A representative of the congregation may present a Bible to each person. These or similar words may be spoken:
Receive this Bible.
Hear God's word with us.
Learn and tell its stories.
Discover its mysteries.
Honor its commandments.
Rejoice in its good news.
May God's life-giving word
inspire you and make you wise.

Blessing of Animals

This service may be used on or near the commemoration of Francis of Assisi, renewer of the church, 1182–1226 (October 4). For practical reasons, an outdoor setting for the service may be preferred. If the service is held indoors, an artful tablescape at the entrance might include feathers, antlers, an abandoned nest or chrysalis, a birdhouse, small cages, fishbowl, leashes, bridles, and the like. A photo display of members with their pets or working animals might enhance informal conversation after the service.

Greeting and Prayer

The joy of our Lord Jesus Christ, the compassion of God, and the creative power of the Holy Spirit be with you all.
And also with you.

Let us pray.
Source and sustainer of life, we cherish the myriad works of your hands. Water, earth, and sky are yours, as are all their inhabitants, wild and tame. We thank you for creatures that nourish and serve us, befriend, enrich, entertain, and protect us. May we, who are made in your image, care for them well. And may your groaning yet wondrous creation rally and thrive, revealing to all who come after us your wise, redemptive, transfiguring love; through Jesus Christ, our Savior and Lord.
Amen.

Reading

Psalm 84:1-4

Hymn

Morning has broken   ELW 556
Oh, that I had a thousand voices   ELW 833, LBW 560

Reading

Genesis 1:1, 20-28

Hymn

This is my Father's world   ELW 824, LBW 554
Many and great, O God   ELW 837, WOV 794

Reading

Matthew 21:1-5

Meditation

Hymn

All creatures, worship God most high!   ELW 835, [LBW 527]
O day of peace   ELW 711, WOV 762

Prayers of Intercession

Let us pray.
Gracious Lord of love, we affirm our vital connection with all living creatures. Empower us to seek their welfare, intervening where needed, defending and tending your world with grace, compassion, and dignity. Lord, in your mercy,
hear our prayer.
Patient Lord of life, guide our choices so that we might safeguard habitats, ensuring, by your grace, that the mysteries and beauties of nature unfold for future generations. Lord, in your mercy,
hear our prayer.
Saving Lord of lords, your word foretells a day when the wolf will lie down with the lamb. Renew our vision for the peaceable kingdom. Lord, in your mercy,
hear our prayer.
Hear our prayers, gracious God, for the sake of Jesus, our Savior and Lord.
Amen.

The minister invites the assembly into one or more of the following options using these or similar words.
People of God, let us live gently alongside other living creatures and with the whole creation.

Option 1: Blessing of Animals

In an outdoor setting, the minister may individually bless companion/working animals. Indoors, the minister might mention them by name (slips of paper with names may be placed in a small "ark" or aquarium near the altar before the service), or may invite worshipers to speak the name and breed aloud during the following prayer.
Let us pray. Maker and master of all that lives, your animals provide us with sources of food and clothing, guidance and rescue, income, companionship, research and medicine, recreation, and so much more. We ask your blessing on these entrusted to us (*names may be spoken here*), and we again pledge ourselves to their comfort and care.
Amen.

Option 2: In Praise of God's Creatures

Preselected worshipers share a three-to-four-minute story of what God has taught them through an animal (see Notes on the service). It is a good idea to have someone help them rehearse beforehand to keep the stories focused, compelling, and brief.

Option 3: Children's Circle

The minister or another leader invites the children to come up as an ensemble sings "All God's critters got a place in the choir" by Bill Staines (from his album The First Million Miles, 1989; it may be downloaded at various online sites). The leader tells the story of Noah and his children being chosen by God to care for the animals in the ark (use Genesis 6:17-22 for reference). Two dog or cat treats per child may be passed out, and each child is then invited to place them in a prepared "ark" as a promise to be kind to the animals they know. As the song is re-sung, four animal cookies are "multiplied back" to each child in a sealed snack bag as they return to their seats.

The service continues with the following dialogue.

God is the source and loving sustainer of all that lives— of species endangered as well as those newly discovered and named. Called as we are to wisely care for this diverse and imperiled web of life, let us again offer ourselves as advocates, donors, and active stewards, being reverent and mindful toward all creation.

Water, earth, and sky are home to us all. We accept God's call, in the name of the Good Shepherd who taught us to pray:

The Lord's Prayer

Blessing

Compassion, creativity, and joy are ours
through Jesus Christ.
May the Holy Spirit
move us to preserve and enhance life on Earth,
giving clear witness to our loving Creator.
Amen.

Sending

Go out into God's world. Live in peace with one another and with all God's creatures.
Thanks be to God.

Sending Song

God of the sparrow   ELW 740
Bless the Beasts and Children by The Carpenters (sheet music available at wwws.sheetmusicplus.com/sheetmusic/detail/HL.353395.html).

Notes on the service

- About a month before the service, worship planners could invite several pet owners and/or members who volunteer at a local animal shelter, zoo, or veterinarian clinic to each prepare a three-to-four-minute story on what God has taught them through the experience.

- Sermon-meditation illustrations are easily found online by entering the keywords "animal sermon illustrations" into a search engine.
- A Kibbles 'n Bits® (appetizers) potluck after the service would allow the congregation to share more animal stories or collect pre-copied recipes for homemade animal treats. New members especially may find this a wonderful icebreaker.

Follow-up activities

- A local animal shelter representative or ecology advocate could briefly address the members.
- Prepared handouts with opportunities to volunteer in the community might spur a church project, or further dialogue.

Other resources

- Anderson, Niki. *What My Cat Has Taught Me About Life*. Colorado Springs: Honor Books, 2007. ISBN 9781562929428.
- Brokering, Herb. *Cat Psalms: Prayers My Cats Have Taught Me*. AFP 9780806644981.
- ———. *Dog Psalms: Prayers My Dogs Have Taught Me*. AFP 9780806651606.
- ———. *More Cat Psalms*. AFP 9780806680354.
- ———. *More Dog Psalms*. AFP 9780806680422.
- Canfield, Jack. *Chicken Soup for the Pet Lover's Soul*. Vermilion, 1999. ISBN 0091819466.
- Caruso, Lynn L., ed. *Blessing the Animals: Prayers and Ceremonies to Celebrate God's Creatures, Wild and Tame*. Skylight Paths Publishing, 2006. ISBN 1594731454.
- www.nature.org
- www.sierraclub.org (Sierra Club)
- www.nwf.org (National Wildlife Federation)
- www.hsus.org (Humane Society)
- www.worldwildlife.org (World Wildlife)

September 6, 2009
Time after Pentecost — Lectionary 23

James tells us to stop showing favoritism in the assembly, treating the rich visitor with more honor than the poor one. Jesus himself seems to show partiality in his first response to the Syrophoenician woman in today's gospel. Was he testing her faith in saying Gentiles don't deserve the goods meant for God's children? Or was he speaking out of his human worldview, but transcended those limits when she took him by surprise with her reply? Either way, the story tells us that God shows no partiality. Everyone who brings her or his need to Jesus is received with equal honor as a child and heir.

Prayer of the Day

Gracious God, throughout the ages you transform sickness into health and death into life. Open us to the power of your presence, and make us a people ready to proclaim your promises to the whole world, through Jesus Christ, our healer and Lord.

Gospel Acclamation

Alleluia. Rejoice in the ^l Lord always;* again I will ^l say, Rejoice. *Alleluia.* (Phil. 4:4)

Readings and Psalm

Isaiah 35:4-7a

These verses are a word of hope to the exiles in Babylon. Chapter 34 portrays God's vengeance on Edom, Israel's age-old enemy, which makes the path from Babylon to Zion safe for the exiles' return. The desert itself will flow with water to give drink to the returning exiles.

Psalm 146

I will praise the LORD as long as I live. (Ps. 146:2)

James 2:1-10 [11-13] 14-17

Faithful Christians do not show partiality to the rich and powerful of the world, especially at the expense of the poor and weak. Likewise, faith does not pay mere lip-service to God's will. Instead, a living Christian faith expresses itself in acts of compassion and mercy for those in need.

Mark 7:24-37

In Mark's gospel, encounters with women usually signify turning points in Jesus' ministry. Here, a conversation with a Syrophoenician woman marks the beginning of his mission to the Gentiles.

Semicontinuous reading and psalm
Proverbs 22:1-2, 8-9, 22-23

The sayings in the book of Proverbs impart the collective wisdom of centuries. Speaking of wealth and poverty, these particular verses teach that those who are blessed by God should honor the poor, for they are within God's special care.

Psalm 125

Those who trust in the LORD stand fast forever. (Ps. 125:1)

Color   Green

CD-ROM Images

Icon Three: 0904-0910_Lect23_B
Icon Two: Proper18_Sun23_B
Icon: 114

Prayers of Intercession

Lord of creation, with confidence in your abiding care, we are bold to pray for the world, the church, and all in need.
A brief silence.
We pray for courage in the church, that we may take your love into places where healing is desperately needed, into lives where hope falters. Hear us, O God.
Your mercy is great.
We pray for unity of purpose and for your guidance as we strive to be better stewards of your good world, for our sake and for those who follow us. Hear us, O God.
Your mercy is great.
We pray that all who labor receive just compensation, that the unemployed find meaningful work, and that all employers create workplaces where justice, fairness, and equity thrive. Hear us, O God.
Your mercy is great.

We pray for those who give their lives for peace, for international organizations bringing medicine, food, shelter, and comfort into forsaken places and into refugees' shattered lives. Hear us, O God.

Your mercy is great.

We pray for competence in exercising the ministry of healing you place into our hands for all who need your presence. Hear us, O God.

Your mercy is great.

Here other intercessions may be offered.

We give thanks for those whose lives have pointed us to you. Keep us in union with them through faith until we celebrate together at your heavenly feast. Hear us, O God.

Your mercy is great.

Lord of creation, into your hands we commend all for whom we pray, trusting in your mercy, through Jesus Christ, our Savior.

Amen.

Ideas and Images for the Day

The bottom line of today's gospel is that Jesus journeyed into Gentile territory and healed a child. Beyond all the trappings of the story or the woman's clever reasoning with Jesus, we ultimately see healing because of faith. The story of the Syrophoenician woman reveals that our God indeed shows no partiality. Christ comes to all humankind; those who believe have access to God's healing and wholeness. Restoration and healing are signs of the kingdom of God. In the reading from James we are reminded that God has "chosen the poor in the world to be rich in faith and to be heirs of the kingdom" (2:5). In our weakness, poverty, or sickness, we are most able to see God's power at work.

1. The Syrophoenician woman stands with others in scripture who argued (Moses), wrestled (Jacob), and matched wits with God (Abraham). To confront and dialogue with God one must at least acknowledge the possibility that God exists. Perhaps we as contemporary believers ought to explore the pharisaical tradition of holy debate and conversation with God and one another. Only in close and trusting relationships are we able to be ourselves, to say what we really think. Through those times of intense interaction we are able to grow in both knowledge and in intimacy with God and others.

2. The Syrophoenician woman kneels humbly before Christ, who is in a position of dominance. What do the postures of dialogue, prayer, and communion that we use in worship communicate about our relationship with God? Explore the reasons behind our liturgical movements and gestures, using those postures to inform our growth in intimacy with the living God.

3. Although God shows no partiality, we do see variances in power and privilege in our churches. Remembering segregation, denial of suffrage, and the lack of opportunity to live out our gifts for ministry, we understand the necessity to revisit this gospel story. Churches, governments, and cultures that allow prejudice against anyone stand in opposition to God's word. Would an examination of our own church reveal ways that we set ourselves against the gospel of inclusion?

Hymns for Worship
Gathering
Let streams of living justice   ELW 710
We come to you for healing, Lord   ELW 617
Open your ears, O faithful people   ELW 519, WOV 715

Hymn of the Day
Lord, whose love in humble service   ELW 712, LBW 423
BEACH SPRING
O Christ, your heart, compassionate   ELW 722
ELLACOMBE
The church of Christ, in every age   ELW 729, LBW 433
WAREHAM

Communion
Jesus loves me!   ELW 595
Light dawns on a weary world   ELW 726
Lord of all nations, grant me grace   ELW 716, LBW 419

Sending
The Spirit sends us forth to serve   ELW 551, WOV 723
Oh, for a thousand tongues to sing   ELW 886, LBW 559

Additional Hymns and Songs
O Son of God, in Galilee   LBW 426
Open our eyes, Lord   W&P 113
We give God thanks for those who knew   HG 128
Lord, I lift your name on high   ELW 857
Come and taste   W&P 30

Music for the Day
Psalmody and Acclamations
Haugen, Marty. "Psalm 146" from *Psalm Settings for the Church Year.* AFP 9780800678562.
Psalter for Worship Year B, Evangelical Lutheran Worship Edition. AFP 9780806683839.
Schalk, Carl F. *Gospel Acclamations for Autumn.* AFP 9780800678623.

Choral

Brahms, Johannes. "Let Grief Not Overwhelm You" from *Chantry Choirbook*. SATB. AFP 9780800657772.

Diemer, Emma Lou. "Praise Ye the Lord." SATB, 1 or 2 pianos. FLA A5021.

□ Fleming, Larry L. "Humble Service." SATB. AFP 9780800646226.

Mendelssohn, Felix/arr. Ronald A. Nelson. "Then Shall the Eyes of the Blind." SAB, pno. CG A927.

Children's Choir

Nagel, Robert. "In Bread and Wine." UE. 2 pt, pno/org, synth, drm set. KJO ED6158.

Patterson, Mark. "Let All the World in Every Corner Sing" from *ChildrenSing: Seven Anthems for Elementary Age Singers*. UE. U, pno, opt tamb. AFP 9780800677695.

Ramseth, Betty Ann/Melissa Ramseth Hoiland. "Stand Up, Stand Up for Jesus" from *Take a Hymn*. UE. U, picc/fl, snare drm, kybd. AFP 9786000106461. OP

Keyboard / Instrumental

Carlson, J. Bert. "Wareham" from *Augsburg Organ Library: Summer*. Org. AFP 9780800676872.

Henkelmann, Brian. "Beach Spring" from *Chorale Preludes for the Liturgical Year*, vol. 1. Kybd, fl. CPH 97-7227.

Proulx, Richard. "Wareham" from *Hymn Intonation, Harmonization, and Free Prelude Series*, vol. VIII. Org. SEL 160-728.

Sedio, Mark. "Beach Spring" from *Dancing In the Light of God*. Pno. AFP 9780800656546.

Handbell

McChesney, Kevin. "Beach Spring." 2-3 oct, L2. AFP 9780800658854. OP

Sherman, Arnold B. "Ovation of Praise." 3-6 oct, L3. AG 2349.

Watanabe, Kiyo. "Beach Spring." 3-5 oct hb/hc, L2. GIA G-6965.

Praise Ensemble

■ Baloche, Paul/Brenton Brown. "Because of Your Love" from www.praisecharts.com. INT/Thankyou Music.

■ Millard, Bart. "I Can Only Imagine" from *iWorship Songbook*. INT 23366.

■ Morgan, Reuben/Darlene Zschech. "Blessed" from www.praise charts.com. Hillsong Publishing/INT.

■ Mullins, Rich. "Awesome God" from *Breakforth Worship Songbook*. New Creation Ministries. www.new-creation.net.

Global

Benson, Robert A. "There Is a Balm in Gilead." SATB, pno. AFP 9780800678159.

Smallwood, Richard. "Total Praise." SAB, pno. ALF BSCM00062.

Wednesday, September 9

Peter Claver, priest, missionary to Colombia, 1654

Peter Claver was born into Spanish nobility and was persuaded to become a Jesuit missionary. He served in Cartagena (in what is now Colombia) by teaching and caring for the slaves. The slaves arrived in ships, where they had been confined in dehumanizing conditions. Claver met and supplied them with medicine, food, clothing, and brandy. He learned their dialects and taught them Christianity. He called himself "the slave of the slaves forever." Claver also ministered to the locals of Cartagena who were in prison and facing death.

Claver's advocacy on behalf of the rights of slaves is a witness to a gospel that is for all people. Pray for contemporary ministries and for persons who offer care and compassion to people living in substandard living conditions.

□ denotes choral suggestions that relate to the hymn of the day.
■ denotes songs that are available on iTunes®.

268

September 13, 2009
Time after Pentecost — Lectionary 24

Three weeks ago we heard John's gospel's version of Peter's confession of faith. This week we hear Mark's version, when Peter says, "You are the Messiah." In John, the stumbling block is Jesus' invitation to eat his flesh, given for the life of the world. In Mark too the scandal has to do with Jesus' words about his own coming death, and here Peter himself stumbles over Jesus' words. But Jesus is anointed (the meaning of "messiah") in Mark only on the way to the cross (14:3); so we are anointed in baptism with the sign of the cross.

Today the church commemorates the famous preacher John Chrysostom, Bishop of Constantinople.

Prayer of the Day

O God, through suffering and rejection you bring forth our salvation, and by the glory of the cross you transform our lives. Grant that for the sake of the gospel we may turn from the lure of evil, take up our cross, and follow your Son, Jesus Christ, our Savior and Lord.

Gospel Acclamation

Alleluia. Christ suffered for sins once for all, the righteous for **|** the unrighteous,* in order to bring **|** you to God. *Alleluia.* (1 Pet. 3:18)

Readings and Psalm
Isaiah 50:4-9a

The image of the servant of the Lord is one of the notable motifs in the book of Isaiah. Today's reading describes the mission of the servant, whom early Christians associated with Jesus. Like Jesus, the servant does not strike back at his detractors but trusts in God's steadfast love.

Psalm 116:1-9

I will walk in the presence of the LORD. (Ps. 116:9)

James 3:1-12

This text uses various images to illustrate how damaging and hurtful the way we speak to and about others can be. Not only are we to control our speech, but what we say and how we say it is to reflect our faith.

Mark 8:27-38

This story provides the turning point in Mark's gospel. Peter is the first human being in the narrative to acknowledge Jesus as the Messiah, but he cannot accept that as the Messiah Jesus will have to suffer. Moreover, Jesus issues a strong challenge to all by connecting discipleship and the cross.

Semicontinuous reading and psalm
Proverbs 1:20-33

In these verses Wisdom is personified as a woman who invites all who will listen to follow her. Though Wisdom offers her hand to those who scoff at her, they spurn all such counsel. That they come to ruin is predictable. Those who find Wisdom, however, find life.

Psalm 19

The teaching of the LORD is perfect and revives the soul. (Ps. 19:7)

or Wisdom 7:26—8:1

God loves nothing so much as the person who lives with wisdom. (Wis. 7:28)

Color   Green

CD-ROM Images

Icon Three: 0911-0917_Lect24_B
Icon Two: Proper19_Sun24_B
Icon: 115

Prayers of Intercession

Lord of creation, with confidence in your abiding care, we are bold to pray for the world, the church, and all in need.
A brief silence.
For the whole church, that it continue to walk in your presence, holding high the cross, transforming lives by serving all in need. Hear us, O God.
Your mercy is great.

For a renewed awareness of the value you placed on creation in the beginning, that we may recover that holy goodness, and practice good stewardship of land, earth, and ocean. Hear us, O God.
Your mercy is great.

For every land shattered by warfare, famine, injustice, and political oppression, that you raise up leaders who seek peace above personal gain and exercise authority in love. Hear us, O God.
Your mercy is great.

For all who need compassion, that our ministry can provide decent shelter, fulfilling work, nutritious food, suitable medicine, and hope for all children. Hear us, O God.
Your mercy is great.

For our congregation, that our service in your name transform neighborhoods and touch those who live around us. Hear us, O God.
Your mercy is great.

Here other intercessions may be offered.

In thanksgiving for church leaders whose faithful lives offer us a vision of service (*especially John Chrysostom, whom we commemorate today*). Hear us, O God.
Your mercy is great.

Lord of creation, into your hands we commend all for whom we pray, trusting in your mercy, through Jesus Christ, our Savior.
Amen.

Ideas and Images for the Day

Peter's confession and denial both come from the same tongue, the same heart, the same man. Cephas, the Rock, becomes both a stepping-stone and a stumbling stone: he confesses his belief in Christ, then denies the way of the cross that Jesus must walk. The gospel reading draws attention to the many choices and perspectives available to all of us. The theology of the cross is lifted high as we see Jesus walking the road to Jerusalem, the place of his ignominious death and his glorification. Though Christ will pray for release from his suffering, he will humbly bow to God's will for the sake of all humanity. In Peter and Jesus we clearly see the duality of our own natures and find strength to bear the cross of obedience.

1. Jesus asks the disciples, "Who do you say that I am?" Our answer to that question will ultimately inform all our actions, speech, and behavior. Though individuals, we are part of a greater body of Christ, the church. We celebrate this individuality in unity when we corporately confess our faith through the Apostles' Creed during worship. Together we say, "I believe." Other examples are reciting the Pledge of Allegiance or singing the words of a national hymn. How do these corporate-personal confessions form bonds between people?

2. For centuries scholars have debated what it means to "take up our cross and follow" Christ. Reflect on various cross designs and what each expresses about service, sacrifice, and selflessness. Find pictures and examples, especially of the Tau cross, Saint Bridget's cross, Mariner's cross, and Jerusalem cross at www.applefielddirect.com/adj_catalog.cgi?dct=on&tt=124. What do the crosses in your worship space look like and what do they "say"?

3. A concept made famous by Martin Luther is *simul iustus et peccator* (saint and sinner at the same time). We are simultaneously completely justified and completely sinful. Luther also wrote: "A Christian is a perfectly free lord of all, subject to none. A Christian is a perfectly dutiful servant of all, subject to all"/("The Freedom of a Christian" in *Martin Luther's Basic Theological Writings*, ed. Timothy Lull, Augsburg Fortress, 1989, p. 596). Explore the promise of justification through Christ that gives us hope in the midst of sin and despair.

Hymns for Worship

Gathering

Lift high the cross   ELW 660, LBW 377
Let us ever walk with Jesus   ELW 802, LBW 487

Hymn of the Day

Take up your cross, the Savior said   ELW 667   *BOURBON*
    LBW 398   *NUN LASST UNS DEN LEIB BEGRABEN*
When pain of the world surrounds us   ELW 704
    CALLED TO FOLLOW
Will you come and follow me   ELW 798   *KELINGROVE*

Communion

How clear is our vocation, Lord   ELW 580
Lord Jesus, you shall be my song   ELW 808
Praise and thanks and adoration   ELW 783, LBW 470

Sending

God of tempest, God of whirlwind   ELW 400
Lead on, O King eternal!   ELW 805, LBW 495

Additional Hymns and Songs

Broken in love   W&P 24
Make our church one joyful choir   HG 1
I will call upon the name of the Lord   TFF 14

Music for the Day
Psalmody and Acclamations

Mummert, Mark. "Psalm 116" from *Psalm Settings for the Church Year*. AFP 9780800678562.

Psalter for Worship Year B, Evangelical Lutheran Worship Edition. AFP 9780806683839.

Schalk, Carl F. *Gospel Acclamations for Autumn*. AFP 9780800678623.

Choral

Busarow, Donald. "Lift High the Cross." SATB/2 pt mxd, opt assembly, org, opt tpt. AFP 9780800645892.

Giamanco, Anthony. "Take Up Your Cross." 2 pt mxd, kybd. AFP 9780800678968.

▢ Hopson, Hal H. "Take Up Your Cross" (Bourbon). 2 pt mxd, kybd. AFP 9780800654504.

Scott, K. Lee. "Open My Eyes." SATB, org. CPH 98-2904.

Tiefenbach, Peter. "What Shall I Render to the Lord?" SATB. AFP 9786000176006. *The Augsburg Choirbook*. AFP 9780800656782.

Children's Choir

Brighton, James. "Tune My Heart." UE. U, pno, opt fl. CG A1101.

Hoiland, Melissa Ramseth. "My Heart Is Longing" from *Take a Hymn*. UE. U, autoharp/gtr, rec/fl. AFP 9786000106461. OP

Kosche, Kenneth T. "Bless God's Holy Name." UE. 2 pt, kybd, opt 6 hb. CG A766.

Keyboard / Instrumental

Dahl, David P. "An English Suite for Organ." Org. AFP 9780800674953.

Honoré, Jeffrey. "Kelvingrove" from *Contemporary Hymn Settings for Organ*. Org. AFP 9780800674786.

Moore, Bob. "Air" from *Five Liturgical Meditations*. Pno, fl/vln/ob. GIA G-4289.

Powell, Robert J. "Bourbon" from *Sent Forth*. Org. AFP 9780800654887.

Handbell

Dobrinski, Cynthia, arr. "Lift High the Cross." 3-5 oct, L3. AG 1491.

Page, Anna Laura. "Somebody's Knocking at Your Door." 3-5 oct, L2. AG 16479.

Roberts, Philip L., arr. "Kelvingrove" from *Hymns for Handbells*, vol. 2. 3-5 oct. GIA G-5899.

Praise Ensemble

■ Houston, Joel. "Everyday" from www.praisecharts.com. Hillsong Publishing/INT.

■ Morgan, Reuben. "With All I Am" from www.praisecharts.com. Hillsong Publishing/INT.

Olson, Larry/Karol Baer. "Take Up Your Cross" from *Work of the People, Volume 1.5*. Dakota Road Music. www.dakotaroadmusic.com.

■ Ruis, David. "You're Worthy of My Praise" from *Maranatha! Music Praise Chorus Book*. WM/MAR 3010101368.

▢ denotes choral suggestions that relate to the hymn of the day.
■ denotes songs that are available on iTunes®.

Global

Dittberner, Larry/Bread for the Journey. "I Shall Walk" from *Global Songs 2*. U, pno, gtr. AFP 9780800656744.

Hampton, Keith. "He's Got the Whole World." SATB. AFP 9780800659608.

Sunday, September 13

John Chrysostom, Bishop of Constantinople, 407

John was a priest in Antioch and an outstanding preacher. His eloquence earned him the nickname "Chrysostom" ("golden mouth"), but it also got him into trouble. As bishop of Constantinople he preached against corruption among the royal court. The empress, who had been his supporter, sent him into exile. His preaching style emphasized the literal meaning of scripture and its practical application. This interpretation stood in contrast to the common style at the time, which emphasized the allegorical meaning of the text Chrysostom's skill in the pulpit resulted in the description of him as the patron of preachers. This week at gatherings of parish groups, include prayers for pastors and all who proclaim the gospel.

Monday, September 14

Holy Cross Day

Helena, the mother of Constantine, made a pilgrimage to Israel to look for Christian holy sites. She found what she believed were the sites of the crucifixion and burial of Jesus, sites that modern archaeologists believe may be correct. Here Constantine built two churches. The celebration of Holy Cross Day commemorates the dedication of the Church of the Resurrection in 335.

Wednesday, September 16

Cyprian, Bishop of Carthage, martyr, c. 258

Cyprian worked for the unity of the church and cared for his flock in North Africa during a time of great persecution. During Cyprian's time as bishop many people had denied the faith under duress. In contrast to some who held the belief that the church should not receive these people back, Cyprian believed they should be welcomed into full communion after a period of penance. He insisted on the need for compassion in order to preserve the unity of the church. His essay *On the Unity of the Catholic Church* stressed the role of bishops in guaranteeing the visible, concrete unity of the church. Cyprian was also concerned for the physical well-being of the people under his care. He organized a program of medical care for the sick during a severe epidemic in Carthage.

Thursday, September 17

Hildegard, Abbess of Bingen, 1179

Hildegard lived virtually her entire life in convents, yet was widely influential within the church. After an uneventful time as a nun, she was chosen as abbess of her community. She reformed her community as well as other convents. Around the same time, she began having visions and compiled them, as instructed, in a book she called *Scivias*. Hildegard's importance went beyond mysticism. She also advised and reproved kings and popes, wrote poems and hymns, and produced treatises in medicine, theology, and natural history. She was also a musician and an artist.

Friday, September 18

Dag Hammarskjöld, renewer of society, 1961

Dag Hammarskjöld (HAH-mar-sheld) was a Swedish diplomat and humanitarian who served as secretary general of the United Nations. He was killed in a plane crash on this day in 1961 in what is now Zambia while he was on his way to negotiate a cease-fire between the United Nations and the Katanga forces. For years Hammarskjöld had kept a private journal, and it was not until that journal was published as *Markings* that the depth of his Christian faith was known. The book revealed that his life was a combination of diplomatic service and personal spirituality, and of contemplation on the meaning of Christ in his life and action in the world.

To commemorate Hammarskjöld, pray for the work of the United Nations and for all peacemakers. Here is an example of a person whose quiet contemplation led to visible action in the world.

September 20, 2009
Time after Pentecost — Lectionary 25

Today we hear James warn against selfish ambition, while the disciples quarrel over which one of them is the greatest. Jesus tells them the way to be great is to serve. Then, to make it concrete, he puts in front of them an actual flesh-and-blood child. We are called to welcome the particular children God puts in front of us, to make room for them in daily interaction, and to give them a place of honor in the assembly.

Prayer of the Day

O God, our teacher and guide, you draw us to yourself and welcome us as beloved children. Help us to lay aside all envy and selfish ambition, that we may walk in your ways of wisdom and understanding as servants of your Son, Jesus Christ, our Savior and Lord.

Gospel Acclamation

Alleluia. God has called us through the proclamation of | the good news,* that we may obtain the glory of our Lord | Jesus Christ. *Alleluia.* (2 Thess. 2:14)

Readings and Psalm
Jeremiah 11:18-20

Today's reading tells of the suffering of the prophet Jeremiah, who announced God's word to Judah but was met with intense opposition and persecution. Jeremiah continues to trust in God in the midst of his suffering.

or Wisdom 1:16—2:1, 12-22

Dating from shortly before the time of Christ, the Wisdom of Solomon is a piece of Jewish wisdom literature. This reading portrays the ungodly planning the downfall of the righteous person. The ungodly are allied with death, and they do not know that God gives eternal life to the righteous.

Psalm 54

God is my helper; it is the LORD who sustains my life.
(Ps. 54:4)

James 3:13—4:3, 7-8a

The wisdom God gives unites our hearts and minds. Instead of living to satisfy our own wants and desires, we manifest this wisdom in peace, gentleness, mercy, and impartiality toward others.

Mark 9:30-37

Jesus' teaching and action in this text are directed to the church whenever it is seduced by the world's definition of greatness: prestige, power, influence, and money. The antidote to such a concern for greatness is servanthood.

Semicontinuous reading and psalm

Proverbs 31:10-31

This passage, which ends the book of Proverbs, describes the good wife. She is a supremely capable and hard-working person, who runs the household and also engages in commercial ventures. She cares both for her family and for the poor, and she fears the Lord.

Psalm 1

They are like trees planted by streams of water. (Ps. 1:3)

Color   Green

CD-ROM Images

Icon Three: 0918-0924_Lect25_B

Icon Two: Proper20_Sun25_B

Icon: 116

Prayers of Intercession

Lord of creation, with confidence in your abiding care, we are bold to pray for the world, the church, and all in need.
A brief silence.
We pray for your church in the world to rejoice in the gift of word and sacrament, that we use our talents and resources wisely to bring good news to all. Hear us, O God.
Your mercy is great.
We pray for the will to create good conversations about how to live well in our communities, to fully enjoy the peoples and landscapes you give us. Hear us, O God.
Your mercy is great.
We pray that those who exercise authority over others do so with mercy and kindness, and that all who govern seek your will to do it on behalf of those they serve. Hear us, O God.
Your mercy is great.

We pray today for children who are hungry and thirsty, who desperately need loving homes, medical care, and futures that lead to life, not death. Hear us, O God.
Your mercy is great.
We pray for the lives we will touch as this family of faith takes the peace of the Lord with us into humble service in our daily lives. Hear us, O God.
Your mercy is great.
Here other intercessions may be offered.
We pray for the courage to proclaim your grace, mercy, and forgiveness until we sing around your throne with all your saints for eternity. Hear us, O God.
Your mercy is great.
Lord of creation, into your hands we commend all for whom we pray, trusting in your mercy, through Jesus Christ, our Savior.
Amen.

Ideas and Images for the Day

Journeying toward Jerusalem, Jesus avoids the crowd-gathering of his initial ministry. He's teaching the way of the cross. Here, the cross illumines the classic motif of juxtaposing intrigue and insignificance. When position jockeying appears in the shadows of Passion predictions, Jesus uses object lessons to refocus attention on mission. So an insignificant, vulnerable child becomes the disciple's model. Wrangling for position, manipulating, and maneuvering fail to evoke or present God; they are the symptoms of fear, collective misunderstanding, and conspiracies of silence. Jesus is betrayed into humanity (*anthropoi*). The disciples are part of that betrayal until they become like "children"— until their desires for the kingdom become childlike, without pretense to power. Then they may indeed welcome the very ones, the "little ones," that God welcomes.

1. The politics of fear, some argue, have seized the imagination of many in the United States. Fear is both a motivator and a curtain—it can move us to act precipitously, and it can hide from our eyes alternative actions we might take. How does the cross help us face fear with strengthened imagination?

2. C.H.A.N.G.E.—Creating Healthy, Active, and Nurturing Growing-up Environments—an initiative of Save the Children, is addressing the growing concern of malnourished children in the United States. Along with hunger, poor diet leads to multiple health and educational issues. How can congregations "welcome" neighborhood children into better nutrition? Read more about this initiative at www.savethechildren.org /programs/us-literacy-and-nutrition/physical.html.

3. *The Story of Us* is a 1999 movie (Castle Rock Entertainment) that chronicles not having the perfect spouse but getting relationship right. While the divorce rate remains high, there is a marriage renaissance underway. See www.smartmarriages.com/index.html for marriage resources.

4. Conflict seems an unavoidable event in human affairs. We respond in different ways. The five identified approaches for dealing with conflict are collaborating, compromising, accommodating, avoiding, and forcing. Knowing how to approach conflict can help in transforming it into something positive. The Peace and Justice Support Network of the Mennonite Church U.S.A. has a useful adult personal-conflict-style inventory on its Web site: http://peace.mennolink.org/resources/conflictstyle/index.html.

Hymns for Worship
Gathering
All Are Welcome   ELW 641
Lord, whose love in humble service   ELW 712, LBW 423
Let us go now to the banquet   ELW 523

Hymn of the Day
We eat the bread of teaching   ELW 518   *WISDOM'S FEAST*
Loving Spirit   ELW 397   *RESTORATION*   WOV 683   *BETH*
Lord, whose love in humble service   ELW 712, LBW 423
    BEACH SPRING

Communion
Bread of life, our host and meal   ELW 464
Children of the heavenly Father   ELW 781, LBW 474
We eat the bread of teaching   ELW 518

Sending
As we gather at your table   ELW 522
Praise the One who breaks the darkness   ELW 843
Lord of light   ELW 688, LBW 405

Additional Hymns and Songs
Beauty for brokenness   W&P 17
For God so loved the world   W&P 39

Music for the Day
Psalmody and Acclamations
Anderson, Mark. "Psalm 54" from *Psalm Settings for the Church Year*. AFP 9780800678562.
Psalter for Worship Year B, Evangelical Lutheran Worship Edition. AFP 9780806683839.
Schalk, Carl F. *Gospel Acclamations for Autumn*. AFP 9780800678623.

Choral
Cherwien, David. "Prayer for Peace" (O God of Love, O King of Peace). 2 pt mxd, opt assembly, org. MSM 50-9209.
Ferguson, John. "Be Thou My Vision." SATB, org. AFP 9780800657932.
Johnson, Ralph M. "Be Thou a Smooth Way." SATB, pno. AFP 9780800659325.
□ Parker, Alice/arr. Robert Shaw. "I Will Arise" (Restoration). SATB. LG 00905.

Children's Choir
Christopherson, Dorothy. "Still Small Voice." UE. U/2 pt, pno, fl, perc. AFP 9780800652425. OP
Dietterich, Philip R. "Come One, Come All, Come Follow." LE. U, opt antiphonal, kybd. CG A553.
Sleeth, Natalie. "Seek and You Will Find." UE. 2 pt, kybd. HIN HMC589.

Keyboard / Instrumental
Albrecht, Timothy. "Restoration" from *Grace Notes V for Organ*. Org. AFP 9780800656249.
Dahl, David. "Restoration" from *Hymn Interpretations for Organ*. Org. AFP 9780800658243.
Linker, Janet. "Beach Spring" from *Augsburg Organ Library: Baptism and Communion*. Org. AFP 9780800623555.
Organ, Anne Krentz. "Beach Spring" from *Woven Together*, vol. 1. Pno, C/B-flat inst. AFP 9780800658168.

Handbell
McChesney, Kevin. "Children of the Heavenly Father." 3-5 oct, opt fl, rec, str, L3. CPH 97-7236.
Moklebust, Cathy. "Thy Holy Wings." 3-4 oct, L3. CPH 97-6518.
Roberts, Philip L., arr. "Beach Spring" from *Hymns for Handbells*, vol. 2. 3-5 oct. GIA G-5899.

Praise Ensemble
■ Baloche, Paul. "Offering" from leadworship.com.
■ Oakley, Paul. "Jesus, Lover of My Soul (It's All About You)" from *Breakforth Worship Songbook*. New Creation Ministries. www.new-creation.net.
■ Paris, Twila. "We Bow Down" from www.musicnotes.com. Singspiration Music. W&P 149.
■ Rice, Chris. "Untitled Hymn (Come to Jesus)" from www.musicnotes.com. Clumsy Fly Music.

Global
Chambi, Zoilo/Bread for the Journey. "Sarantañani/Make the Journey Together" from *Global Songs 2*. U, pno, gtr. AFP 9780800656744.
Hawn, C. Michael. "Um Menino/A Child" from *Halle, Halle: We Sing the World Round*. U, pno, gtr, perc. CG C41.

□ denotes choral suggestions that relate to the hymn of the day.
■ denotes songs that are available on iTunes®.

Monday, September 21

Matthew, Apostle and Evangelist

Matthew was a tax collector for the Roman government in Capernaum. Tax collectors were distrusted because they were dishonest and worked as agents for a foreign ruler, the occupying Romans. In the gospels, tax collectors are mentioned as sinful and despised outcasts, but it was these outcasts to whom Jesus showed his love. Matthew's name means "gift of the Lord." Since the second century, tradition has attributed the first gospel to him.

In the gospels Jesus tells his disciples to act toward notorious sinners as they would Gentiles and tax collectors. That has often been taken as a mandate for the church to avoid such people. But because Jesus brought his ministry to these very people, in what ways might the church not shun "tax collectors" and sinners but extend its ministry to them and see them as gifts of the Lord?

September 27, 2009
Time after Pentecost — Lectionary 26

Someone is casting out demons in Jesus' name who isn't part of Jesus' own circle, and the disciples want him stopped. They appeal to Jesus, as Joshua did to Moses about the elders who prophesied without official authorization. Like Moses, Jesus refuses to see this as a threat. Jesus welcomes good being done in his name, even when it is not under his control. The circle we form around Jesus' word must be able to value good being done in ways we wouldn't do it, by people we can't keep tabs on.

Prayer of the Day

Generous God, your Son gave his life that we might come to peace with you. Give us a share of your Spirit, and in all we do empower us to bear the name of Jesus Christ, our Savior and Lord.

Gospel Acclamation

Alleluia. Your word, O | Lord, is truth;* sanctify us | in the truth. *Alleluia.* (John 17:7)

Readings and Psalm
Numbers 11:4-6, 10-16, 24-29

What constitutes legitimate need and legitimate leadership is the focus of this reading. God provides manna in the wilderness, yet the people crave meat. What is truly needful? God bestows the spirit on seventy elders, yet two men not designated as leaders prophesy in the power of God's spirit. What constitutes real leadership?

Psalm 19:7-14

The commandment of the LORD gives light to the eyes. (Ps. 19:8)

James 5:13-20

Marks of the Christian community include praying for those who are sick and in need, celebrating with those in good health, restoring those who have strayed, confessing sins to one another, and offering forgiveness to each other.

Mark 9:38-50

On the way to Jerusalem, Jesus teaches his disciples about ministry that involves service and sacrifice. His disciples are slow to realize that these words apply to them as well as to others.

Semicontinuous reading and psalm
Esther 7:1-6, 9-10; 9:20-22

This book tells the story of Queen Esther, who saves her people, the Jews, from the murderous schemes of Haman, advisor to the Persian king, her husband. Haman is hanged on the gallows he constructed for Esther's cousin Mordecai, and the Jews celebrate the feast of Purim to commemorate this victory over their enemies.

Psalm 124

We have escaped like a bird from the snare of the fowler. (Ps. 124:7)

Color   Green

CD-ROM Images

Icon Three: 0925-1001_Lect26_B

Icon Two: Proper21_Sun26_B

Icon: 117

Prayers of Intercession

Lord of creation, with confidence in your abiding care, we are bold to pray for the world, the church, and all in need.

A brief silence.

For the church, given peace with God through Christ, that we never tire in our efforts to fill this world with that peace. Hear us, O God.

Your mercy is great.

For our care of this one earth, that we make wise and sustainable use of its bounty, learning to share its riches in ways that bring abundance. Hear us, O God.

Your mercy is great.

For those who govern, that they exercise compassion for the least and the smallest in their societies, their decisions guided by your wisdom. Hear us, O God.

Your mercy is great.

For those imprisoned for placing their trust openly in you, for those unjustly oppressed because of race or clan, that you raise up strong advocates who work tirelessly for justice and freedom. Hear us, O God.

Your mercy is great.

For this family of faith, nourished in prayer, praise, and thanksgiving, that we welcome all to your table, rejoicing in the gifts strangers and guests bring to the fellowship. Hear us, O God.

Your mercy is great.

Here other intercessions may be offered.

In thanksgiving for the faithful who now rest in your love, that we live in joyful expectation of our promised resurrection. Hear us, O God.

Your mercy is great.

Lord of creation, into your hands we commend all for whom we pray, trusting in your mercy, through Jesus Christ, our Savior.

Amen.

Ideas and Images for the Day

The church strives against letting its identity as the body of Christ turn it into a private fraternity. Our baptismal identity helps us differentiate between God's intentions and the world's presumptions so that we can find peace with all people. With Jesus we transcend exclusiveness. The one thing we are to avoid is giving the "little ones" cause not to believe. This is the trap of faith; the scandal that challenges us—that in making claims about Christ's uniqueness, we make false claims about our uniqueness—that God has chosen us against others. Rather, God has chosen the world in Christ. That's the message that preserves and flavors everything around us. When we lose it, we have lost everything. We can embrace the good *wherever* it appears; our task is to say repeatedly, "That's what Jesus is all about!"

1. In *They Like Jesus But Not the Church: Insights from Emerging Generations*, Dan Kimball traces the disjunction between organized churches and emergent communities (Zondervan, 2007). More and more people are looking outside organized religion to find spiritual nurture. Has the salt lost its flavor for denominations? Should Jesus and church be coterminous? What can we do to make it more so?

2. René Girard in his evangelical anthropology finds scandal to be a major New Testament theme ("stumbling block" in Mark's gospel). "Scandals, we found, are permanently conflictual relationships in our individual lives" (*The Girard Reader*, ed. James G. Williams, New York: Crossroad, 1996, p. 199). Explore how the church is a stumbling block or scandal that prevents faith today. See http://girardianlectionary.net/res/skandalon.htm for more leads.

3. "The prayer of faith will save the sick" (James 5:15). Western medicine is undergoing a quiet reform through incorporating spirituality and healing in medical practice. More physicians are praying with patients. Quality of life is becoming important in its own regard, alongside disease control. Explore the research and practices of millennial medicine. See www.massgeneral.org/cancer/crr/topics/wellbeing/info.asp for a list of resources. The wholeness wheel available through the ELCA Board of Pensions Web site maps out a balance of life and health with baptismal grace (www.elcabop.org/LiveWell/Wholeness_wheel.aspx).

Hymns for Worship
Gathering

Soli Deo Gloria   ELW 878

In thee is gladness   ELW 867, LBW 552

When morning gilds the skies   ELW 853, LBW 545, 546

Hymn of the Day

O God, my faithful God   ELW 806, LBW 504
WAS FRAG ICH NACH DER WELT

O Christ, our light, O Radiance true   ELW 675, LBW 380
O JESU CHRISTE, WAHRES LICHT

How clear is our vocation, Lord   ELW 580   REPTON

Communion

Let us break bread together   ELW 471, LBW 212
Spirit of gentleness   ELW 396, WOV 684

Sending

Where cross the crowded ways of life   ELW 719, LBW 429
Go, make disciples   ELW 540
We Are Called   ELW 720

Additional Hymns and Songs

You are the seed   WOV 753
Spirit Song   W&P 130
Make me a servant   W&P 96

Music for the Day
Psalmody and Acclamations

Haugen, Marty. "Psalm 19" from *Psalm Settings for the Church Year*.
AFP 9780800678562.

Psalter for Worship Year B, Evangelical Lutheran Worship Edition.
AFP 9780806683839.

Schalk, Carl F. *Gospel Acclamations for Autumn*. AFP
9780800678623.

Choral

Ashdown, Franklin D. "Jesus, the Very Thought of Thee." SATB,
org, opt C inst. AFP 9780800657505.

Bloch, Ernest. "Silent Devotion and Response." SATB, pno. BRB 179.

Jennings, Carolyn. "The Kingdom of God." SATB, org, opt fl. AMSI
439.

Kemp, Helen. "Praise, O Praise the Lord!" SA, kybd, opt hb. AFP
9780800676339.

Children's Choir

Carter, John. "Sing to the Lord with Joy." UE. 2 pt, kybd. HOP
JC286.

Sleeth, Natalie. "The Holy Book" from *Sunday Songbook*. LE. U,
kybd. HIN HMB102.

Tucker, Margaret R. "Song of Celebration." UE. U, kybd, fl, hb, fc,
drm. CG A512.

Keyboard / Instrumental

Manz, Paul O. "O Jesu Christe, wahres Licht" from *Improvisations
on General Hymns*. Org. MSM 10-830.

Organ, Anne Krentz. "Repton" from *Come to Us, Creative Spirit*.
Pno. AFP 9780800659042.

Powell, Robert J. "Repton" from *Augsburg Organ Library: Autumn*.
Org. AFP 9780800675790.

Sedio, Mark. "Repton" from *How Blessed This Place*. Org. AFP
9780800658038.

Handbell

Dobrinski, Cynthia, arr. "Praise, My Soul, the King of Heaven." 3-5
oct, L3. AG 1974.

Helman, Michael, arr. "My Faith Looks Up to Thee." 3-5 oct, L2.
CPH 97-7240.

Leavitt, John. "Be Thou My Vision." 3-4 oct, L3. CPH 97-7210.

Praise Ensemble

- Barnett, Maria. "Breathe" from *WOW Worship Green Songbook*. INT
000768195567.

- Byrd, Marc/Steve Hindalong. "God of Wonders" from *God of Wonders Songbook*. INT 0000768205679.

- Excell, Edwin O./Louie Giglio/John Newton/John P. Rees/Chris
Tomlin. "Amazing Grace (My Chains Are Gone)" from WT.
WT/Sixsteps Music/Alletrop Music/Stephan Sharp Publishing.

McPherson, Stephen. "Shelter House" from www.ccli.com. Hillsong
Publishing/INT.

Global

Berthier, Jacques. "Come and Pray in Us/Veni, Spirito creatore"
from *Songs and Prayers from Taizé*. U, kybd, gtr, tpt, ob, cl, bsn,
tbn. GIA G-3719-A.

Tuesday, September 29
Michael and All Angels

On this festival day the church ponders the richness and
variety of God's created order and the limits of human
knowledge of it. The scriptures speak of angels who worship God in heaven, and in both testaments angels are God's
messengers on earth. They are remembered most vividly as
they appear to the shepherds and announce the birth of the
Savior. Michael is an angel whose name appears in Daniel
as the heavenly being who leads the faithful dead to God's
throne on the day of resurrection. In Revelation, Michael
fights in a cosmic battle against Satan.

■ denotes songs that are available on iTunes®.

Wednesday, September 30

Jerome, translator, teacher, 420

Jerome is remembered as a biblical scholar and translator. Rather than choosing classical Latin as the basis of his work, he translated the scriptures into the Latin that was spoken and written by the majority of the persons in his day. His translation is known as the Vulgate, from the Latin word for common. While Jerome is remembered as a saint, he could be anything but saintly. He was well known for his short temper and his arrogance, although he was also quick to admit to his personal faults. Thanks to the work of Jerome, many people received the word in their own language and lived a life of faith and service to those in need.

October 4, 2009
Time after Pentecost — Lectionary 27

Today's gospel combines a saying that makes many of us uncomfortable with a story we find comforting. Jesus' saying on divorce is another of his rejections of human legislation in favor of the original intent of God's law. Jesus' rebuke of the disciples who are fending off the children should challenge us as well. What does it mean to receive the kingdom of God as a child does?

Today the church commemorates Francis of Assisi and Theodor Fliedner, renewers of church and society.

Prayer of the Day

Sovereign God, you have created us to live in loving community with one another. Form us for life that is faithful and steadfast, and teach us to trust like little children, that we may reflect the image of your Son, Jesus Christ, our Savior and Lord.

Gospel Acclamation

Alleluia. If we love one another, God | lives in us * and God's love is perfect- | ed in us. *Alleluia.* (1 John 4:12)

Readings and Psalm

Genesis 2:18-24

Genesis 2 stresses that people are not meant to live in isolation but in relationship. Out of love for humanity, God creates them male and female, to provide companionship for each other and to become with each other "one flesh." The Hebrew words used here are *ish* (man) and *ishshah* (woman).

Psalm 8

You crown us with glory and honor. (Ps. 8:5)

Hebrews 1:1-4; 2:5-12

Quoting from the psalms, this passage from Hebrews emphasizes that Jesus, the one through whom God created everything and who sits at God's right hand, is also the one who experienced human suffering and death in order to blaze the path of salvation for us.

Mark 10:2-16

Jesus announced and enacted in history the new reality of God's surprising activity. These two stories demonstrate this new reality: Women and children are accepted and valued, not dismissed as inferior to adult men.

Semicontinuous reading and psalm

Job 1:1; 2:1-10

This passage is part of the prologue of Job. The righteous man Job is severely afflicted as the result of a wager between God and the satan (here not the devil, but "the accuser"). Job responds at first with great patience, but the rest of the book will show him lamenting and protesting.

Psalm 26

Your steadfast love is before my eyes; I have walked faithfully with you. (Ps. 26:3)

Color   Green

CD-ROM Images

Icon Three: 1002-1008_Lect27_B

Icon Two: Proper22_Sun27_B

Icon: 118

Prayers of Intercession

Lord of creation, with confidence in your abiding care, we are bold to pray for the world, the church, and all in need.

A brief silence.

For your holy catholic church, calling the baptized into service for the kingdom's sake. Protect and nourish it with faithful leaders who trust in you. Hear us, O God.

Your mercy is great.

For commitment to planting trees, renewing forests, and sowing seeds for plentiful harvests, that there will be enough for all. Hear us, O God.

Your mercy is great.

For all who represent us in church agencies and international organizations, that you bless their work of carrying life to broken people in broken lands. Hear us, O God.

Your mercy is great.

For the poor, the homeless, the lonely, those who are refugees from their own families as well as those forced to leave their homelands, that your love in our hands will help bring restoration. Hear us, O God.

Your mercy is great.

For grace to live with childlike wonder, offering our ministry to our community, that all may see how we can live together in love. Hear us, O God.

Your mercy is great.

Here other intercessions may be offered.

In thanksgiving for renewers of church and society (*especially Francis of Assisi and Theodor Fliedner*) and all our loved ones who live in the Lord, that their witness lead us to hope. Hear us, O God.

Your mercy is great.

Lord of creation, into your hands we commend all for whom we pray, trusting in your mercy, through Jesus Christ, our Savior.

Amen.

Ideas and Images for the Day

This week Jesus closes loopholes in an ancient interpretation of the law and opens wide the door to those who seek him as a child would. Jesus often sets out a high expectation for obedience to the law, asking his followers to exceed the minimum standard; in this case he speaks of the law against divorce. Yet the context for all Jesus' teaching is grace and forgiveness. He shows us the way to the kingdom as a child would find it, not because a child is innocent of sin but because every child needs and should receive forgiveness and love.

1. In *Under the Tuscan Sun* (Blue Gardenia Productions, 2003) Frances's life is turned upside down when her husband has an affair with another woman. After divorce and a time of sadness in a depressing short-term apartment building, she treats herself to a vacation in Italy. Not quite sure why, Frances becomes involved in restoring an old stone house and its ruined garden. The story is about being brave, patient, and supple following heartbreak, being open to the unknown, and cultivating a hopeful future. What might we learn about being open to possibilities and God's promises of new life? Can we begin to notice people we have overlooked? Does it take a leap into the unknown to find spiritual renewal?

2. One of the pastoral options for introducing the marriage service in *Evangelical Lutheran Worship* reminds the assembly that "Because of sin, our age-old rebellion, the gladness of marriage can be overcast and the gift of a family can become a burden." How true. The passage continues, "But because God, who established marriage, continues still to bless it with abundant and ever-present support, we can be sustained in our weariness and have our joy restored" (Leaders Edition, p. 676). We can trust God to grant this. How can we bring to mind the promises of God when we are overworked or betrayed? Where might we find endurance for the daily struggle in the meantime?

3. The ELCA's Evangelical Outreach and Congregational Mission unit offers a resource on separation and divorce through its Christian Education program. The resource offers this counsel: "We need to acknowledge that divorce rips through the layers of trust, community and security to reshape the very core of a person's faith and identity. During this critical time many people shy away from the church. With a growing insecurity about their sense of belonging, it often becomes difficult to deal with the dynamics of a faith community" ("Nurturing Faith Through Life Transitions," www.elca.org/christianeducation/lifetransitions/pdf/separationdivorce.pdf). How can we be sure separated and divorcing members feel welcome and loved in our congregations?

4. In the story of *Peter Pan*, children who shout "Christmas!" can fly, and they do—zooming off to Neverland, the world of the imagination and everlasting childhood. They encounter danger and the fear of death as well. Jesus tells us the kingdom of God belongs to children. Do children have a unique intuition about God's

love and acceptance? Do some of us understand the promises of God's kingdom with the faith and imagination of a child?

Hymns for Worship

Gathering

God is here!   ELW 526, WOV 719

Our Father, by whose name   ELW 640, LBW 357

Hymn of the Day

God, when human bonds are broken   ELW 603, WOV 735
  MERTON

All Are Welcome   ELW 641   TWO OAKS

Our Father, by whose name   ELW 640, LBW 357
  RHOSYMEDRE

Communion

Jesus loves me!   ELW 595

Loving Spirit   ELW 397, WOV 683

Blest be the tie that binds   ELW 656, LBW 370

Sending

Now thank we all our God   ELW 839, 840, LBW 533, 534

When in our music God is glorified   ELW 850/851,
  LBW 555, WOV 802

Additional Hymns and Songs

As man and woman we were made   WOV 751

Enter in the realm of God   HG 9

How majestic is your name   W&P 66

Who are we   DH 33

Music for the Day

Psalmody and Acclamations

Mummert, Mark. "Psalm 8" from *Psalm Settings for the Church Year*. AFP 9780800678562.

Psalter for Worship Year B, Evangelical Lutheran Worship Edition. AFP 9780806683839.

Schalk, Carl F. *Gospel Acclamations for Autumn*. AFP 9780800678623.

Choral

Andrews, Doug. "How Great Thou Art." S(S)ATB, pno. AFP 9780800678890.

Butler, Eugene. "How Excellent Is Thy Name." SAB, kybd. BRN B205765-356.

Hayes, Mark. "Day by Day." SATB, pno. AFP 9780800658342.

Helgen, John. "In the Singing." SATB, pno. AFP 9780800678289.

Hillert, Richard. "How Great Is Your Name." SATB/U, br qrt, timp. GIA G-3187.

Rutter, John. "For the Beauty of the Earth." SATB, kybd. HIN HMC-550.

Children's Choir

Jothen, Michael. "We Are Children of Our God." UE. U/2 pt, kybd, fl/vln, opt hb, opt assembly. CG A731.

Sleeth, Natalie. "Children of the Lord" from *Sunday Songbook*. LE. U, kybd. HIN HMB102.

Wilson, Mark. "Come as a Child." UE. 2 pt, pno. HIN HNC427.

Keyboard / Instrumental

Benson, Robert A. "Merton" from *A Lovely Rose*. Org. AFP 9780800675714.

Callahan, Charles. "Merton" from *Advent Music for Manuals*, set 2. Kybd. MSM 10-011.

Carlson, J. Bert. "Rhosymedre" from *Let It Rip! at the Piano*, vol. 1. Pno. AFP 9780800659066.

Miller, Aaron David. "Two Oaks" from *Pull Out the Stops*, vol. 2. Org. AFP 9780800677688.

Handbell

Endean, Judy. "Spirit of God, Descend upon My Heart." 2-3 oct, L1+. SoundForth 249045.

McAninch, Diane. "Prelude on 'All Are Welcome'." 3-5 oct hb/hc, fl/C inst, L3. GIA G-7083.

Moklebust, Cathy. "My Song Is Love Unknown" (Rhosymedre). 3-5 oct, L3. CG B203.

Praise Ensemble

■ LeBlanc, Lenny. "Come and See." W&P 29.

Mann, Robin. "Father Welcomes" from www.ccli.com. KV/Robin Mann.

■ Morgan, Reuben. "Hear Our Praises" from www.praisecharts.com. Hillsong Publishing/INT.

■ Zschech, Darlene. "Shout to the Lord." ELW 821, W&P 124.

Global

Bell, John L. "Sing Out Gladly/Munezero" from *Two Gathering Chants*. SATB, cant. GIA G-5287.

Burleigh, Glenn. "Order My Steps." SAB, pno. Glenn Burleigh Music Workshop. www.glenmusik.com/bookorders.html.

Sunday, October 4

Francis of Assisi, renewer of the church, 1226

Francis, the son of a wealthy cloth merchant, renounced his wealth and future inheritance and devoted himself to serving the poor. Francis described this act as being "wedded to Lady Poverty." Under his leadership the Order of Friars Minor (Franciscans) was formed, and they took literally Jesus' words to his disciples that they should take nothing on their journey and receive no payment for their work. Their task in preaching was to "use words if necessary."

■ denotes songs that are available on iTunes®

This commemoration has been a traditional time to bless pets and animals, creatures Francis called his brothers and sisters. A prayer attributed to St. Francis is included in *Evangelical Lutheran Worship* (p. 87) and could be used at worship today.

Theodor Fliedner, renewer of society, 1864

Fliedner's (FLEED-ner) work was instrumental in the revival of the ministry of deaconesses among Lutherans. While a pastor in Kaiserswerth, Germany, he also ministered to prisoners in Düsseldorf. Through his ministry to prisoners, he came in contact with Moravian deaconesses, and it was through this Moravian influence that he was convinced that the ministry of deaconesses had a place among Lutherans. His work and writing encouraged women to care for those who were sick, poor, or imprisoned. Fliedner's deaconess motherhouse in Kaiserswerth inspired Lutherans all over the world to commission deaconesses to serve in parishes, schools, prisons, and hospitals.

Tuesday, October 6

William Tyndale, translator, martyr, 1536

William Tyndale was ordained in 1521, and his life's desire was to translate the scriptures into English. When his plan met opposition from Henry VIII, Tyndale fled to Germany, where he traveled from city to city, living in poverty and constant danger. He was able to produce a New Testament in 1525. Nine years later he revised it and began work on the Old Testament, which he was unable to complete. He was tried for heresy and burned at the stake. Miles Coverdale completed Tyndale's work, and the Tyndale-Coverdale version was published as the "Matthew Bible" in 1537. The style of this translation has influenced English versions of the Bible such as the King James (Authorized Version) and the New Revised Standard Version for four centuries.

Wednesday, October 7

Henry Melchior Muhlenberg, pastor in North America, 1787

Muhlenberg (MYOO-len-berg) was prominent in setting the course for Lutheranism in this country. He helped Lutheran churches make the transition from the state churches of Europe to independent churches of America. Among other things, he established the first Lutheran synod in America and developed an American Lutheran liturgy. His liturgical principles became the basis for the Common Service of 1888, used in many North American service books for a majority of the past century. That Muhlenberg and his work are remembered today was anticipated at his death. The inscription on his grave reads in Latin, "Who and what he was, future ages will know without a stone."

The commemoration of Muhlenberg invites congregations to look back on what shaped their identity, worship, and mission in the past and to look ahead to what might shape it in the future.

October 11, 2009
Time after Pentecost — Lectionary 28

The rich man who comes to ask Jesus what he should do to inherit eternal life is a good man, sincere in his asking. Mark's gospel is alone in saying that Jesus looked on him and loved him. Out of love, not as judgment, Jesus offers him an open door to life: sell all you own and give it to the poor. Our culture bombards us with the message that we will find life by consuming. Our assemblies counter this message with the invitation to find life by divesting for the sake of the other.

Prayer of the Day

Almighty and ever-living God, increase in us your gift of faith, that, forsaking what lies behind and reaching out to what lies ahead, we may follow the way of your commandments and receive the crown of everlasting joy, through Jesus Christ, our Savior and Lord.

Gospel Acclamation

Alleluia. Blessed are the ˡ poor in spirit,* for theirs is the king- ˡ dom of heaven. *Alleluia.* (Matt. 5:3)

Readings and Psalm
Amos 5:6-7, 10-15

Amos was a herdsman by profession and a prophet by God's call. During a time of great prosperity in the northern kingdom of Israel, the prophet speaks to the wealthy upper class. He warns his listeners that fulfilling God's demand for justice brings blessing, while corruption and oppression incur God's wrath.

Psalm 90:12-17

So teach us to number our days that we may apply our hearts to wisdom. (Ps. 90:12)

Hebrews 4:12-16

We cannot hide our thoughts, desires, and actions from God, to whom we are completely accountable. Nevertheless, Jesus understands our human weakness and temptations, because he also experienced them. Therefore we can approach the throne of grace to receive divine mercy from Christ.

Mark 10:17-31

Jesus has been teaching his disciples about what is most valued in God's eyes. Now, a conversation with a rich man brings his message home to the disciples in a way that is surprising but unforgettable.

Semicontinuous reading and psalm
Job 23:1-9, 16-17

Having experienced much loss, Job longs to come into God's presence, where he can defend his own righteousness. Job cannot find God, but he never doubts that God exists and is in relationship with him. Job knows that he will come out of this time of testing refined like pure gold.

Psalm 22:1-15

My God, my God, why have you forsaken me? (Ps. 22:1)

Color   Green

CD-ROM Images

Icon Three: 1009-1015_Lect28_B
Icon Two: Proper23_Sun28_B
Icon: 119

Prayers of Intercession

Lord of creation, with confidence in your abiding care, we are bold to pray for the world, the church, and all in need.
A brief silence.
We pray for a servant church that continues to follow where your commandments lead, loving you above all, loving our neighbors as ourselves. Hear us, O God.
Your mercy is great.
We pray for strength to discover, encourage, and celebrate those among us whose passions to nurture creation run deeply, that they lead us to new ways and new hopes for tending our world. Hear us, O God.
Your mercy is great.
We pray for the gift of wisdom as we count our days, wisdom that helps us live well in communities of blessing where all people are valued. Hear us, O God.
Your mercy is great.

We pray for those who live in fear, for those afraid of dying, for those facing disability and constant pain (*especially*). May we offer them compassion, understanding, and the constancy of your presence through us. Hear us, O God.

Your mercy is great.

We pray that our congregation would refuse to accept worldly limitations, choosing to live instead with great expectations, knowing that all things are possible with you. Hear us, O God.

Your mercy is great.

Here other intercessions may be offered.

In grateful thanksgiving we remember those who have offered us a vision of the kingdom of God at work in the world. Hear us, O God.

Your mercy is great.

Lord of creation, into your hands we commend all for whom we pray, trusting in your mercy, through Jesus Christ, our Savior.

Amen.

Ideas and Images for the Day

Jesus' encounter with the rich man personifies our Lord for many people: the gentle, loving teacher who is also stern and demanding of those who would follow him. The same Jesus who sets a high standard for the seeker who claimed to have kept all the commandments also looks upon this seeker with love. In that shining love we glimpse the heart of Christ. No matter what Jesus asked of him, we wonder how the man could turn away from that love. In the next moment Jesus explains to the disciples just how hard it is to enter the kingdom of God.

1. Jay Gatsby, the title character in F. Scott Fitzgerald's novel *The Great Gatsby*, has not followed the rules but still has a profound sense of entitlement to all his riches—and to true love. Gatsby has fulfilled many of the world's expectations. He has amassed a fortune and built a mansion to live in. He entertains lavishly. But he cannot find happiness with Daisy, the love of his youth. For all his wealth, Gatsby is little more than a gangster and cannot gain the true respect of society. Do you hear a note of entitlement from the rich man in today's gospel text?

2. The rich man in the gospel reading does not appear to be asking for healing. He does not seem to be sick, but perhaps he is. John de Graaf's 1997 documentary *Affluenza*, which aired on public television, is humorous yet hard-hitting. National Public Radio personality Scott Simon narrates as the film helps us look at our culture's bottomless appetite for more of everything. Affluenza (a combination of *affluence* and *influenza*) is making

us and our whole world sick. Do you think the rich man in our text is in need of healing?

3. *A Little Princess*, Frances Hodgson Burnett's 1905 novel, is the story of Sara, a rich little girl, heiress to diamond mines. Her place of privilege is lost when her father dies penniless, turning Sara into an impoverished servant at an elite girls' school. One wet, muddy winter day, she finds a coin that will buy some hot rolls at the bakery. Crouched on the bakery stoop is a barefoot girl in rags. Sara is cold and hungry, but this child is starving. Sara gives her five of her six rolls. How would we respond to Jesus' command to sell everything and give to the poor?

4. In the classic 1980s film *Wall Street* (20th Century Fox, 1987), Gordon Gekko (a role for which Michael Douglas won an Academy Award) speaks to the shareholders at the annual meeting of a corporation he is taking over: "There's a new law of evolution in corporate America. Greed is good." Is this the world's general view? How does this view contrast with the view Jesus expressed?

Hymns for Worship

Gathering

We Are Called   ELW 720
God of grace and God of glory   ELW 705, LBW 415
Come, we that love the Lord   ELW 625, WOV 742

Hymn of the Day

Take my life, that I may be   ELW 583   *TOMA MI VOLUNTAD*
    ELW 685, LBW 406   *PATMOS*
God of grace and God of glory   ELW 705, LBW 415
    CWM RHONDDA
The church of Christ, in every age   ELW 729, LBW 433
    WAREHAM

Communion

Take my life, that I may be   ELW 583/685, LBW 406
We come to the hungry feast   ELW 479, WOV 766
O Jesus, blessed Lord   ELW 541, LBW 220

Sending

God, whose giving knows no ending   ELW 678, LBW 408
The Spirit sends us forth to serve   ELW 551, WOV 723

Additional Hymns and Songs

Spirit of Jesus, if I love my neighbor   HG 32
God of Love, Have Mercy   DH 10
Only by grace   W&P 112
We bring the sacrifice of praise   W&P 150

Music for the Day
Psalmody and Acclamations

Cherwien, David. "Psalm 90" from *Psalm Settings for the Church Year*. AFP 9780800678562.

Psalter for Worship Year B, Evangelical Lutheran Worship Edition. AFP 9780806683839.

Schalk, Carl F. *Gospel Acclamations for Autumn*. AFP 9780800678623.

Choral

Buxtehude, Dietrich. "Everything You Do." from *Chantry Choirbook*. SATB, org. AFP 9780800657772.

Luboff, Norman. "All My Trials." SATB, solo. WAL W3065.

▫ Sedio, Mark. "Take My Life That I May Be" (Toma mi voluntad). SATB, pno, fl, opt gtr. AFP 9780800658298. *Augsburg Easy Choirbook*, vol. 2. AFP 9780800677510.

Vaughan Williams, Ralph. "O How Amiable." SATB, org. OXF 42.056.

Children's Choir

Helgen, John. "This Little Light of Mine." UE. 2 pt, kybd. AFP 9780800675936.

Patterson, Mark. "Sing, Rejoice, Clap Your Hands" from *Young Children* Sing. LE. U, kybd. AFP 9780800676803.

Sleeth, Natalie. "If You Love Me" from *Laudamus*. UE. 2/3 pt, kybd. HIN HMB126.

Keyboard / Instrumental

Blair, Dallas. "Cwm Rhondda" from *Hymn Introductions and Descants for Trumpet and Organ*, set 2. Org, tpt. MSM 20-702.

Cherwien, David. "Patmos" from *Organ Plus*, vol. 2. Org, inst. AFP 9780800678548.

Manz, Paul O. "Cwm Rhondda" from *A New Liturgical Year*. Org. AFP 9780800656713.

Maynard, Lynette. "Toma mi voluntad" from *Let It Shine*. Pno. AFP 9780800677640.

Handbell

Geschke, Susan E. " 'Tis So Sweet to Trust in Jesus." 3-5 oct hb/hc, L2. HOP 2409.

Keller, Michael R. "Guide Us, O God of Grace." 3-5 oct, L3. AG 35257. Full Score, br parts. AG 35258.

Thompson, Martha Lynn. "Great Is Thy Faithfulness." 3-5 oct, L2+. HOP 2268.

Praise Ensemble

■ Hiebert, Lamont. "Sing for Joy" from *Sing for Joy*. Hosanna! Music 000768213773.

■ Morgan, Reuben. "Faith" from www.praisecharts.com. Hillsong Publishing/INT.

■ Zschech, Darlene. "All Things Are Possible" from www.praise charts.com. Hillsong Publishing/INT.

Global

Haas, David. "Prayer for Peace." 2 mxd vcs, pno, gtr. GIA G-3505.

Haugen, Marty. "Seek Truth, Make Peace, Reverence Life." SATB, kybd. GIA G-7102.

Monday, October 12
Day of Thanksgiving (Canada)
See Day of Thanksgiving (U.S.A.), pp. 321–323.

Thursday, October 15
Teresa of Avila, teacher, renewer of the church, 1582

Teresa of Ávila (AH-vee-la) chose the life of a Carmelite nun after reading the letters of Jerome. Frequently sick during her early years as a nun, she found that when she was sick her prayer life flowered, but when she was well it withered. Steadily her life of faith and prayer deepened, as did her sense of God's presence. She worked to reform her monastic community in Ávila, which she believed had strayed from its original purpose. Her reforms asked nuns to live without leaving the monastic enclosure and to identify with the poor by not wearing shoes. Teresa's writings on devotional life are widely read by members of various denominations.

Saturday, October 17
Ignatius, Bishop of Antioch, martyr, c. 115

Ignatius was the second bishop of Antioch in Syria. It was there that the name "Christian" was first used to describe the followers of Jesus. Ignatius is known to us through his letters. In them he encouraged Christians to live in unity sustained with love while standing firm on sound doctrine. Ignatius believed Christian martyrdom was a privilege. When his own martyrdom approached, he wrote in one of his letters, "I prefer death in Christ Jesus to power over the farthest limits of the earth. . . . Do not stand in the way of my birth to real life." Ignatius and all martyrs are a reminder that even today Christians face death because of their faith in Jesus.

▫ denotes choral suggestions that relate to the hymn of the day.
■ denotes songs that are available on iTunes®.

October 18, 2009
Time after Pentecost — Lectionary 29

Today's gospel starts with disciples obsessing over who's number one, which leads Jesus to say something about God's take on importance and power. Here Jesus makes it explicit that the reversal of values in God's community is a direct challenge to the values of the dominant culture, where wielding power over others is what makes you great. When we pray "your kingdom come" we are praying for an end to tyranny and oppression. We pray this gathered around the cross, a sign of great shame transformed to be the sign of great honor and service.

The observance of the festival of Luke, Evangelist, is transferred this year to October 19. St. Luke is remembered in today's prayers, and congregations may wish to include an order for healing in the service.

Prayer of the Day

Sovereign God, you turn your greatness into goodness for all the peoples on earth. Shape us into willing servants of your kingdom, and make us desire always and only your will, through Jesus Christ, our Savior and Lord.

Gospel Acclamation

Alleluia. The Son of Man came not to be served | but to serve,* and to give his life as a ran- | som for many. *Alleluia.* (Mark 10:45)

Readings and Psalm

Isaiah 53:4-12

This reading is from the last of four passages in Isaiah that are often called "servant songs." Christians are probably most familiar with this servant song. In light of Christian faith, the servant's healing ministry and redemptive suffering are understood to be fulfilled in the life and death of Christ.

Psalm 91:9-16

You have made the LORD your refuge, and the Most High your habitation. (Ps. 91:9)

Hebrews 5:1-10

Using imagery from scripture and from Jewish worship practices, Jesus is presented as the great high priest who was obedient to God's saving plan. Through his suffering and death he has become the source of eternal salvation.

Mark 10:35-45

On the way to Jerusalem the disciples ask Jesus to grant them seats of honor. Jesus responds by announcing that he and his followers will "rule" through self-giving service.

Semicontinuous reading and psalm
Job 38:1-7 [34-41]

At the end of the book of Job, after Job and his companions have argued about the cause of the great suffering Job endures, God finally speaks. These verses begin that speech, which is a grand vision of creation, describing God's ordering of the cosmos and inviting Job to marvel at its beauty.

Psalm 104:1-9, 24, 35b

O LORD, how manifold are your works! In wisdom you have made them all. (Ps. 104:24)

Color   Green

CD-ROM Images

Icon Three: 1016-1022_Lect29_B
Icon Two: Proper24_Sun29_B
Icon: 120

Prayers of Intercession

Lord of creation, with confidence in your abiding care, we are bold to pray for the world, the church, and all in need.
A brief silence.
We pray for the church, called into servanthood, that it remain faithful in its mission for the world's sake, even as it works for the unity of all Christians. Hear us, O God.
Your mercy is great.

We pray for wisdom and willing advocates to lead us toward a fuller understanding of how to better care for this good creation given into our hands. Hear us, O God.
Your mercy is great.

We pray for leaders who will lead by following your servant example, who seek your will when making decisions for the welfare of their people, and who work to shape their societies in your image, not their own. Hear us, O God.
Your mercy is great.

We pray (*as we remember Luke, evangelist and physician*) for the sick, the desperate, those who mourn, those in treatment for addiction or disease, and the dying (*especially*). Hear us, O God.
Your mercy is great.

We pray for our family gathered today in worship, that our praise and thanksgiving gives us renewed momentum to enter our daily lives filled with energy, enthusiasm, and great love for those around us. Hear us, O God.
Your mercy is great.

Here other intercessions may be offered.

We give thanks for all those we have loved who now rest from their labors, that as we follow their examples we joyfully serve you, until that day comes when we sit down with them at the endless feast of victory. Hear us, O God.
Your mercy is great.

Lord of creation, into your hands we commend all for whom we pray, trusting in your mercy, through Jesus Christ, our Savior.
Amen.

Ideas and Images for the Day

Two of Jesus' disciples get a rude awakening today as they try to manipulate the Lord into elevating them to positions of power in the kingdom. Jesus brings their ambitions to a screeching halt when he explains the real implications of following him and what it means to drink the cup that he will drink. When squabbling breaks out among the disciples, Jesus explains the difference between earthly tyranny and the reign of God, turning their understanding upside down. Like the disciples, we begin to get the picture as Jesus explains the meaning of real greatness and what is required of us when we follow his example of servanthood. We begin to see the shape of the sacrifice Jesus will undertake for us.

1. "Servant leadership" is an approach to leadership development put forth by management gurus such as Robert Greenleaf and Stephen Covey, emphasizing collaboration and stewarding of resources. While this approach contributes some helpful ideas, it can be criticized as a management fad when applied indiscriminately. When Jesus tells the disciples that to be great they must become servants, even slaves, he is not employing a technique or gimmick. What does Jesus do to our concepts of leadership when he tells us that he will serve unto his very death, and that to follow him means we will do the same?

2. A child wandered to an unreachable spot on a high cliff and became trapped there. While emergency crews scrambled and summoned experts and helicopters, and news reporters declared the situation impossibly dangerous, a woman started climbing toward the child. She slipped and struggled in her quest, but she did not hesitate; she was the child's mother. Does anyone love us enough to risk her life for us?

3. In the movie *Pay It Forward* (Bel Air Entertainment, 2000), a sensitive and insightful teacher inspires one of his students to create a formula for compassion that sets in motion a wave of human goodness. Nothing about Trevor's life would seem to foster greatness, yet he becomes the servant of all, and the world is changed. What does it look like when followers of Jesus take servanthood seriously? Jesus changed the world. What does he ask of us, and what might be the outcome if we listen and understand?

4. The words and sweet music of "The Servant Song" put the joy of servanthood within reach for everyone: "Will you let me be your servant, let me be as Christ to you?" Read the full song text at *Evangelical Lutheran Worship* #659.

Hymns for Worship
Gathering

Many and great, O God   ELW 837, WOV 794
Lord our God, with praise we come   ELW 730, LBW 244
How firm a foundation   ELW 796, LBW 507

Hymn of the Day

O Christ, what can it mean for us   ELW 431   ALL SAINTS NEW
Rise, O church, like Christ arisen   ELW 548
   SURGE ECCLESIA
Let us ever walk with Jesus   ELW 802, LBW 487
   LASSET UNS MIT JESU ZIEHEN

Communion

Will you let me be your servant   ELW 659
Lord, whose love in humble service   ELW 712, LBW 423
When we are living   ELW 639

Sending

To be your presence   ELW 546
The Lord now sends us forth   ELW 538

Additional Hymns and Songs

Lord, help us walk your servant way   HG 150

Make me a servant   W&P 96

On Eagle's Wings   ELW 787, WOV 779

Music for the Day
Psalmody and Acclamations

Psalter for Worship Year B, Evangelical Lutheran Worship Edition.
AFP 9780806683839.

Schalk, Carl F. *Gospel Acclamations for Autumn*. AFP 9780800678623.

Shute, Linda Cable. "Psalm 91" from *Psalm Settings for the Church
Year*. AFP 9780800678562.

Choral

Copley, R. Evan. "Surely He Hath Borne Our Griefs." SATB. AFP
9780800646189.

Handel, G. F. "Surely He Hath Borne Our Griefs." SATB, pno. GS 27123.

Mendelssohn, Felix. "For God Commanded Angels to Watch Over
You." SATB, div. KJO 8798.

Nelson, Ronald A. "Whoever Would Be Great Among Us." SAB,
gtr/kybd. AFP 9780800645809. *The Augsburg Choirbook*. AFP
9780800656782.

Children's Choir

Christopherson, Dorothy. "The Lord Is My Salvation." LE. U, pno,
fl, opt fc. AFP 11-10254. OP

Lindh, Jody W. "Praise the Lord Who Reigns Above." UE. U, pno,
opt hb, tamb, 2 xyl. CG A583.

Sleeth, Natalie. "Hymn of Promise." UE. 2 pt, kybd. HOP A580.

Keyboard / Instrumental

Barber, Samuel/arr. William Strickland. "Adagio for Strings, Opus
11." Org. GS S0024176000.

Boyce, William/arr. S. Drummond Wolff. "Voluntary" from
Baroque Music for Solo Instrument and Keyboard, set V. Kybd,
C/B-flat inst. MSM 20-954.

Gehring, Philip. "Take Me As I Am" from *Five Hymn Preludes for
Organ*. Org. AFP 9780800678777.

Kerr, J. Wayne. "Lasset uns mit Jesu ziehen" from *Let Us Walk with
Jesus*. Org. AFP 9780800677831.

Manz, Paul O. "Lasset uns mit Jesu ziehen" from *Five Hymn Improvisations for Weddings and General Use*. Org. MSM 10-850.

Handbell

Behnke, John A. "When Peace, like a River." 3-5 oct, L2. CPH 97-7220.

Larson, Lloyd. "Simple Gifts." 3 oct, L2. BP HB297.

Page, Anna Laura. "Praise the Father." 2-3 oct, L1. ALF 19647.

Praise Ensemble

- Baloche, Paul. "Rising" from www.praisecharts.com.
- Del Hierro, Jude. "More Love, More Power" from *Breakforth Worship
  Songbook*. New Creation Ministries. www.new-creation.net.

■ denotes songs that are available on iTunes®.

- Fragar, Russell/Darlene Zschech. "God Is in the House" from
  www.praisecharts.com. Hillsong Publishing/INT.
- Pasley, Ben/Robin Pasley. "I Will Not Forget You" from www.ccli
  .com. Corinthian Music.

Global

Bell, John L./Bread for the Journey. "Whoever Lives Beside the
Lord" from *Pave the Way, Global Songs 3*. SATB.
AFP 9780800676896.

Fleming, Larry L. "Every Time I Think About Jesus" SATB. AFP
9780800652616.

Monday, October 19
Luke, Evangelist (transferred)

St. Luke is identified as the author of both Luke and Acts.
Luke is careful to place the events of Jesus' life in both
their social and religious contexts. Some of the most loved
parables, including the good Samaritan and the prodigal son,
are found only in this gospel. Luke's gospel has also given the
church some of its most beautiful songs: the Benedictus sung
at morning prayer, the Magnificat sung at evening prayer, and
the Nunc dimittis sung at the close of the day. These songs
are powerful witnesses to the message of Jesus Christ.

Paul calls Luke the "beloved physician," and some congregations use the day of St. Luke to remember and pray for
those in healing professions. The order of Healing in *Evangelical Lutheran Worship* (pp. 276, 278) may be used. Prayer
for healing in this service would include the emotional,
spiritual, and physical dimensions of our lives.

Friday, October 23
James of Jerusalem, martyr, c. 62

James became an early leader of the church in Jerusalem. He
is described in the New Testament as the brother of Jesus,
and secular historian Josephus calls James the brother of
Jesus, "the so-called Christ." Little is known about James,
but Josephus reported that the Pharisees respected James for
his piety and observance of the law. His enemies had him
put to death.

Was James a blood brother of the Lord? It is difficult
to answer that question, because the Aramaic word for
brother can also mean cousin. Jesus also said, "Whoever
does the will of God is my brother and sister and mother."
The commemoration of James and his connection to Jesus
as "brother" can spark further discussion about how we all
share Christ as our brother through baptism into his death
and resurrection.

October 25, 2009
Reformation Sunday

On this day we celebrate the heart of our faith: the gospel of Christ—the good news—that makes us free! We pray that the Holy Spirit would continue to unite the church today in its proclamation and witness to the world. In the waters of baptism we are made one body; we pray for the day that all Christians will also be one at the Lord's table.

Prayer of the Day

Almighty God, gracious Lord, we thank you that your Holy Spirit renews the church in every age. Pour out your Holy Spirit on your faithful people. Keep them steadfast in your word, protect and comfort them in times of trial, defend them against all enemies of the gospel, and bestow on the church your saving peace, through Jesus Christ, our Savior and Lord, who lives and reigns with you and the Holy Spirit, one God, now and forever.

or

Gracious Father, we pray for your holy catholic church. Fill it with all truth and peace. Where it is corrupt, purify it; where it is in error, direct it; where in anything it is amiss, reform it; where it is right, strengthen it; where it is in need, provide for it; where it is divided, reunite it; for the sake of your Son, Jesus Christ, our Savior, who lives and reigns with you and the Holy Spirit, one God, now and forever.

Gospel Acclamation

Alleluia. If you continue in my word, you are truly [|] my disciples,* and you will know the truth, and the truth will [|] make you free. *Alleluia*. (John 8:31-32)

Readings and Psalm

Jeremiah 31:31-34

The renewed covenant will not be breakable, but like the old covenant it will expect the people to live upright lives. To know the Lord means that one will defend the cause of the poor and needy (Jer. 22:16). The renewed covenant is possible only because the Lord will forgive iniquity and not remember sin. Our hope lies in a God who forgets.

Psalm 46

The Lord of hosts is with us; the God of Jacob is our stronghold. (Ps. 46:7)

Romans 3:19-28

Paul's words stand at the heart of the preaching of Martin Luther and the other Reformation leaders. No human beings make themselves right with God through works of the law. We are brought into a right relationship with God through the divine activity centered in Christ's death. This act is a gift of grace that liberates us from sin and empowers our faith in Jesus Christ.

John 8:31-36

Jesus speaks of truth and freedom as spiritual realities known through his word. He reveals the truth that sets people free from sin.

Color   Red

CD-ROM Images

Icon Three: Reformation01, Reformation02, Reformation03
Icon Two: Reformation01, Reformation02, Reformation03, Reformation04
Icon: 061, 191

Prayers of Intercession

Lord of creation, with confidence in your abiding care, we are bold to pray for the world, the church, and all in need.
A brief silence.
We pray for the whole church, gathered in word and sacrament, in prayer and praise, in loving deeds building up the body, forgiving and reconciling others to Christ.
Hear us, O God.
Your mercy is great.
We pray for renewed commitment to the care and nurture of your creation, that the wonders you have made will be available for generations that follow. Hear us, O God.
Your mercy is great.

We pray for our bishops (*name and name*) and for all who serve the church, that their commitment to justice and peace may be an example for the leaders of our world. Hear us, O God.

Your mercy is great.

We pray for all who struggle with addictions and for those who love and work with them, that they find healing, forgiveness, and hope. Hear us, O God.

Your mercy is great.

We pray for all in any need, those we name now in your presence, surrounded by our brothers and sisters in Christ's love. Hear us, O God.

Your mercy is great.

Here other intercessions may be offered.

We give thanks for all reformers of the church, whose faithful and loving service remains a powerful witness for us to follow. Hear us, O God.

Your mercy is great.

Lord of creation, into your hands we commend all for whom we pray, trusting in your mercy, through Jesus Christ, our Savior.

Amen.

Ideas and Images for the Day

Today Jesus calls us all slaves to sin (John 8:34). The sure knowledge that Jesus saved us from slavery to sin became the foundation of the Reformation, and Martin Luther used this imagery in a great deal of his writing. Like the disciples and the sixteenth-century reformers, we seek to continue faithfully in the word. We remember and honor the Reformation today and keep in mind the continual need for discernment and fresh ideas in the church of Christ.

1. Film critic Roger Ebert had some problems with *Luther*, the movie (Eikon Film, 2003). In his review, he found the cinematic Luther "weak, neurotic, filled with self-doubt." Perhaps Ebert would have cast an action hero to portray a Martin Luther filled with zeal and conviction. Nonetheless, the film provides good insight and opportunity to talk together about the reformer's struggle to reconcile his desire for sanctification with his abhorrence of the corruption pervading the church of his day. We might also consider ways that we long for assurance of God's love today. For more about the movie, see www.lutherthemovie.com. For Ebert's review, see http://rogerebert.suntimes.com and search "Luther."

2. Jesus says, "If you continue in my word, you are truly my disciples; and you will know the truth, and the truth will make you free." Pastor Michael Cooper-White, at the 2003 Luther Colloquium hosted by the Lutheran Theological Seminary at Gettysburg, Pennsylvania, pointed out that some of us might ask, "When? When will we be made free?" Cooper-White asks, "Why couldn't he have uttered his promises in the past or present tense?" Do we believe in the immediate, present fulfillment of Jesus' words? Cooper-White assures us that Jesus' promises are not tenuous. Jesus is coming back, and he is with us today. Jesus himself is the truth. Does this knowledge make the Reformation more relevant in our time? Read Cooper-White's sermon at www.ltsg.edu; use search terms "Cooper-White" and "Luther Colloquium."

3. Many church groups went to the movies together in 2006 to see *Amazing Grace* (Walden Media, 2006). William Wilberforce, a member of the British Parliament in the eighteenth century, converted to Christianity and became a reformer of the brutal penal code and prison system of the day. Wilberforce is known primarily for leading the effort to abolish the British slave trade. The people who were listening to Jesus said they could not be any kind of slave because they were descended from Abraham. Was Jesus telling them that their sins could make them the most unhappy kind of slaves and prisoners?

4. "Lord, keep us steadfast in your word" (ELW 517, LBW 230) supports Jesus' statement, "If you continue in my word, you are truly my disciples." Can we find inspiration in the promises of the word as presented in this hymn text by Martin Luther?

Hymns for Worship

Gathering

A mighty fortress is our God   ELW 503–505, LBW 228, 229
Oh, praise the gracious power   ELW 651, WOV 750

Hymn of the Day

Salvation unto us has come   ELW 590, LBW 297
　　　ES IST DAS HEIL
The church's one foundation   ELW 654, LBW 369   AURELIA
For by grace you have been saved   ELW 598   ARMOLAULU

Communion

Blest be the tie that binds   ELW 656, LBW 370
That priceless grace   ELW 591
For by grace you have been saved   ELW 598

Sending

A mighty fortress is our God   ELW 503–505, LBW 228, 229
The church of Christ, in every age   ELW 729, LBW 433

Additional Hymns and Songs

By grace we have been saved   W&P 25

For by grace   W&P 38

Write your law upon our hearts   DH 91

What a mighty God we serve!   TFF 295

What a mighty Word God gives!   W&P 155

You are the rock of my salvation   W&P 161

Music for the Day
Psalmody and Acclamations

Erickson, Richard. "Psalm 46" from *Psalm Settings for the Church Year*. AFP 9780800678562.

Helgen, John. *Gospel Acclamations for Autumn*. AFP 9780800678623.

Psalter for Worship Year B, Evangelical Lutheran Worship Edition. AFP 9780806683839.

Choral

□   Bach, J. S. "Salvation unto Us Has Come" from *Bach for All Seasons*. SATB. AFP 9780800658540.

Grieg, Edvard/arr. Oscar R. Overby. "God's Son Has Made Me Free." SATB. AFP 9780800645564. *The Augsburg Choirbook*. AFP 9780800656782.

Sarsany, Tim. "God Is Our Strength." TTBB, tenor solo, pno, hrn. LG 52646.

Voth, Ellen Gilson. "There Is a River." SATB, org, opt ob. ECS 6425.

Children's Choir

Ferguson, John. "Jesus, My Lord and God." UE. U/2 pt, org. AFP 9780800646196.

Hopson, Hal H. "The Lord Is My Strength and My Song." LE. U, pno, hb, tamb, fc, drm. CG A101.

Sleeth, Natalie. "Go into the World." UE. 2 pt, kybd. CG A209.

Keyboard / Instrumental

Behnke, John A. "Es ist das Heil" from *Variations for Seven Familiar Hymns*. Org. AFP 9780800655600.

Blair, Dallas. "Aurelia" from *Hymn Introductions and Descants for Trumpet and Organ*, set 4. Org, tpt. MSM 20-703.

Callahan, Charles. "Gospel Fanfare" from *Three Liturgical Fanfares*. Org, tpt. CPH 97-5907U1.

Linker, Janet. "Variations on 'Aurelia'." Org. AFP 9780800637491.

Handbell

McChesney, Kevin. "A Simple Celebration." 3 oct, L1+. AG 3073.

McChesney, Kevin. "The Church's One Foundation." 3-5 oct, opt perc, L2. AFP 9780800658076. OP

Sherman, Arnold B., arr. "A Mighty Fortress." 4-6 oct, L4. AG 2112.

Praise Ensemble

■   Baloche, Paul. "Open the Eyes of My Heart" from www.leadworship.com.

■   Chapman, Steven Curtis/Mark Hall. "Voice of Truth" from www.praisecharts.com. SWECS Music/Club Zoo Music/Sparrow Song/Peach Hill Songs.

■   Crowder, David. "Wholly Yours" from WT. WT/Sixsteps Music.

■   LeBlanc, Lenny. "There Is None Like You" from *Best of the Best, The Other Songbook 2*. FEL 1891062034.

Global

Engelhardt, Michael. "Freedom Is Coming." SATB, pno. www.willowcreek.com/.

Halley, Paul. "Laudate Dominum." SATB/SSA, pno, perc, bass, opt org. Pelago PEL2048. www.pelagosmusic.com.

□ denotes choral suggestions that relate to the hymn of the day.
■ denotes songs that are available on iTunes®.
290

October 25, 2009
Time after Pentecost — Lectionary 30

Can we pray the way Bartimaeus prays? People try to hush him up because by addressing Jesus as "Son of David" he is making a polit-
ically dangerous claim that Jesus is the rightful king. Could our prayers ever be heard as a threat to unjust powers-that-be? Bartimaeus
won't give up or go away quietly, but repeats his call for help more loudly. Do we ask so boldly? And are our prayers an honest answer
to Jesus' question, "What do you want me to do for you?"

Prayer of the Day

Eternal light, shine in our hearts. Eternal wisdom, scatter the darkness of our ignorance. Eternal compassion, have mercy on us. Turn us to seek your face, and enable us to reflect your goodness, through Jesus Christ, our Savior and Lord.

Gospel Acclamation

Alleluia. The Lord will rescue me from every e- ˡ vil attack*
and save me for the heav- ˡ enly kingdom. *Alleluia.*
(2 Tim. 4:18)

Readings and Psalm

Jeremiah 31:7-9

This passage speaks not only of the southern kingdom, Judah, and its homecoming from exile in Babylon, but also of the northern kingdom ("Israel" or "Ephraim") and its restoration. The northern tribes of Israel had been lost in exile to Assyria more than a century before Jeremiah prophesied.

Psalm 126

Those who sowed with tears will reap with songs of joy. (Ps. 126:5)

Hebrews 7:23-28

Human priests of old offered sacrifice for their own sins and served only until their death. In contrast, Jesus is God's Son, the holy, sinless, resurrected high priest. Death did not terminate his priestly service, but through his death he has interceded for our sins.

Mark 10:46-52

Bartimaeus comes to Jesus with faith, asking that he might see again. Recognizing Jesus' identity, Bartimaeus is the first person to call him "Son of David" in the Gospel of Mark.

Semicontinuous reading and psalm

Job 42:1-6, 10-17

After the glorious vision of creation contained in God's speeches at the end of Job, the righteous sufferer proclaims that he has seen God and is humbled. The Lord restores Job's fortunes, and Job dares to live again, fathering more children and giving his daughters an inheritance along with their brothers.

Psalm 34:1-8 [19-22]

Taste and see that the LORD is good. (Ps. 34:8)

Color   Green

CD-ROM Images

Icon Three: 1023-1029_Lect30_B
Icon Two: Proper25_Sun30_B
Icon: 122

Prayers of Intercession

Lord of creation, with confidence in your abiding care, we are bold to pray for the world, the church, and all in need.
A brief silence.
We pray that your church may continue to bring light into this world's darkness, showing compassion to those for whom there is little love and less regard. Hear us, O God.
Your mercy is great.
We pray for the restoration of wonder and joy in the world around us, that we see not only natural resources to be used but also the promise of beauty in creation's well-being for us and for all who follow. Hear us, O God.
Your mercy is great.
We pray for those in positions of power, that their actions turn sorrow into joy, helplessness into hope, and despair into peace. Hear us, O God.
Your mercy is great.

We pray that your Spirit in us may touch the broken and helpless, that all who turn to you find your presence, your blessings, and your healing. Hear us, O God.

Your mercy is great.

We pray for our congregation's musicians that, inspired by the examples of faithful church musicians through the ages, they continue their joyful ministries leading us in praise. Hear us, O God.

Your mercy is great.

Here other intercessions may be offered.

Celebrating our Reformation heritage, we give thanks for all reformers of the church, whose faithful and loving service remains an abundant witness for us to follow. Hear us, O God.

Your mercy is great.

Lord of creation, into your hands we commend all for whom we pray, trusting in your mercy, through Jesus Christ, our Savior.

Amen.

Ideas and Images for the Day

In today's gospel, the encounter with a blind man by the road in Jericho is not coincidental. Mark's gospel is tightly written; no words are wasted. The story of Bartimaeus provides one more opportunity for the followers of Jesus to witness his power and come to faith. Jesus and his followers are on the road to Jerusalem. Jesus sees what will happen there. The disciples see less clearly. They are a rather spiritually sightless bunch in general in this gospel. Jesus has tried three times to help them see his fate. They appear blind to his messiahship. Bartimaeus twice addresses Jesus as "Son of David." It is the sightless one who seems to see, and has faith enough to be made whole and well.

1. Expand the narrative beyond Mark's use of lean language. Fill in the spaces in the story. Bartimaeus follows Jesus to Jerusalem. What does he hope to see there? What does he actually see? Are his hopes fulfilled? Does he return to Jericho? How is his life changed now that he has received his sight?

2. The American twentieth-century novelist Flannery O'Connor once said, "You shall know the truth and the truth shall make you odd." The gospel writer of Mark uses paradox to display Jesus' role as a subversive agent in a world of chaos caused in part by Roman occupation. In today's gospel, the blind see. How odd! In the gospel readings for the next several weeks, paradox is used repeatedly to demonstrate how Jesus' ministry and message turn the world upside down with a new

truth. A focus on the paradoxical nature of the good news, begun today, will be apparent in the gospel readings through the end of the church year.

3. The story of the blind man may broaden the understanding of how the holy is perceived. What senses, other than sight, might be awakened in worship? We taste the holy at the table. We touch the holy in the baptismal font. Some Christians use incense to stimulate an olfactory response in worship. A universally pleasant odor is that of baking bread. Prepare a bread machine to begin a baking cycle in the space about an hour before worship.

4. Today's gospel provides a good opportunity to review how a congregation provides for those with physical challenges. How might a person who is blind be assisted in following the order of worship? Is the worship space fully accessible to all? Are large-print worship aids available? Is the sound system adequate, and does it provide for those who are hearing impaired? How is communion received by those who are not able to come physically to the table?

Hymns for Worship

Gathering

Be thou my vision   ELW 793, WOV 776

Dearest Jesus, at your word   ELW 520, LBW 248

Hymn of the Day

Amazing grace, how sweet the sound   ELW 779, LBW 448
NEW BRITAIN

Rise, shine, you people!   ELW 665, LBW 393
WOJTKIEWIECZ

Praise the One who breaks the darkness   ELW 843
NETTLETON

Communion

We have seen the Lord   ELW 869

Light dawns on a weary world   ELW 726

Sending

Praise the One who breaks the darkness   ELW 843

O Christ, your heart, compassionate   ELW 722

The Spirit sends us forth to serve   ELW 551, WOV 723

Additional Hymns and Songs

Open our eyes, Lord   W&P 113, TFF 98

A blind man sat beside the road   HG 57

Mourning into dancing   W&P 99

O Lord, open my eyes   TFF 134

Music for the Day
Psalmody and Acclamations

Psalter for Worship Year B, Evangelical Lutheran Worship Edition. AFP 9780806683839.

Roberts, William Bradley. "Psalm 126" from *Psalm Settings for the Church Year*. AFP 9780800678562.

Schalk, Carl F. *Gospel Acclamations for Autumn*. AFP 9780800678623.

Choral

Bertalot, John. "Amazing Grace." SATB, org. AFP 9780800649142. *The Augsburg Choirbook*. AFP 9780800656782.

Haugen, Marty. "Healer of Our Every Ill." 2 pt mxd, pno, C inst. GIA G-3478.

Proulx, Richard. "Weary of All Trumpeting" from *The Augsburg Choirbook*. SAB, org. AFP 9780800656782.

Schein, Johann Hermann. "Who With Grieving Soweth." SSATB. PRE 352-00019.

Children's Choir

Exner, Max, V. "Wade in the Water." UE. U, kybd. CG A572.

Hopson, Hal H. "Antiphonal Psalm." UE. 2 pt, pno. HOP HH3901.

Sleeth, Natalie. "Praise the Lord" from *Sunday Songbook*. LE. U, opt canon, kybd, opt C inst. HIN HMB102.

Keyboard / Instrumental

Hobby, Robert A. "New Britain" from *For All the Saints*. Org. AFP 9780800675370.

Keesecker, Thomas. "New Britain" from *Piano Impressions for Communion*. Pno. CPH 97-6742U1.

Manz, Paul O. "Nettleton" from *Improvisations on General Hymns*. Org. MSM 10-830.

Sowash, Bradley. "New Britain" from *Augsburg Jazz: Amazing Grace*. Pno, sax, tpt, bass gtr, drm. AFP 9780800677909.

Handbell

Helman, Michael. "Built on a Rock." 3-5 oct, L3. ALF 19006.

McChesney, Kevin. "Come, Thou Fount of Every Blessing." 3-5 oct, L3. SoundForth 249110.

Moklebust, Cathy. "Amazing Grace." 3-5 oct, opt org, L3. CG B201. Full score: CG B200.

Praise Ensemble

- Collins, Chris/Edwin O. Excell/John Newton/Todd Agnew. "Grace Like Rain" from www.praisecharts.com

- Doerksen, Brian. "Come, Now Is the Time to Worship" from www.praisecharts.com. VIN.

- Evans, Darrel. "Let the River Flow" from *Breakforth Worship Songbook*. New Creation Ministries. www.new-creation.net.

- Millard, Bart. "I Can Only Imagine" from www.praisecharts.com. Simpleville Music.

■ denotes songs that are available on iTunes®.

Global

Mora, Edwin G./Bread for the Journey. "Canto de esperanza/Song of Hope" from *Global Songs, Local Voices*. U, kybd, gtr. AFP 9780806650227.

Ellingboe, Bradley. "Glory, Glory, Hallelujah." SATB. AFP 9780800659561.

Monday, October 26
Philipp Nicolai, 1608; Johann Heermann, 1647; Paul Gerhardt, 1676; hymnwriters

These three outstanding hymnwriters all worked in Germany during times of war and plague. When Philipp Nicolai was a pastor in Westphalia, the plague killed thirteen hundred of his parishioners. One hundred seventy people died in one week. His hymns "Wake, awake for night is flying" and "O Morning Star, how fair and bright" were included in a series of meditations he wrote to comfort his parishioners during the plague. The style of Johann Heermann's hymns moved away from the more objective style of Reformation hymnody toward expressing the emotions of faith. Among his hymns is the plaintive text "Ah, holy Jesus." Paul Gerhardt lost a preaching position at St. Nicholas Church in Berlin because he refused to sign a document stating he would not make theological arguments in his sermons. Some have called him the greatest of Lutheran hymnwriters.

Wednesday, October 28
Simon and Jude, Apostles

Little is known about Simon and Jude. In New Testament lists of the apostles, Simon the "zealot" or Cananaean is mentioned, but he is never mentioned apart from these lists. Jude, sometimes called Thaddeus, is also mentioned in lists of the Twelve. At the last supper Jude asked Jesus why he had chosen to reveal himself to the disciples but not to the world. A traditional story about Simon and Jude says that they traveled together on a missionary journey to Persia and were both martyred there.

The prayer of the day for this lesser festival asks that as Simon and Jude "were faithful and zealous in your mission, so we may with ardent devotion make known the love and mercy of our Savior Jesus Christ."

Saturday, October 31

Reformation Day

By the end of the seventeenth century, many Lutheran churches celebrated a festival commemorating Martin Luther's posting of the Ninety-five Theses, a summary of the abuses in the church of his time. At the heart of the reform movement was the gospel, the good news that it is by grace through faith that we are justified and set free.

With the 1999 signing of the Joint Declaration on the Doctrine of Justification on this date, the question of how the Reformation might be celebrated appropriately is a lively question. If Lutherans and Roman Catholics agree on the basic nature of the gospel, now what? This commemoration is less a victory day for Lutherans than it is an opportunity to be reminded of the reformers' belief that the church would always stand in need of reformation.

TIME AFTER PENTECOST
NOVEMBER

Preparing for November

Lectionary

The time after Pentecost begins to draw to a close on All Saints Day. "The birthday of the church, Pentecost, has its parallel in the birthday of the saints—their martyrdom," writes Philip Pfatteicher. The Holy Spirit continues to call, gather, enlighten, sanctify, and keep us in true faith until the day when Christ returns to raise believers to eternal life. The end of the church year begins with a demonstration of Jesus' power over death, and culminates in the vision of God's everlasting dominion.

The truth to which Jesus testifies is a brilliant beacon of hope and promise. As the northern hemisphere grows darker, the seasonal dying of the earth reminds us of our mortal nature. We ask "Who shall be saved?" and "What *is* God's will for us?" The Thanksgiving readings nicely summarize the November lectionary theme: God will provide, generously, for God's faithful people. The source of our Christian hope is proclaimed in 1 Timothy: "For . . . there is also one mediator between God and humankind, Christ Jesus, himself human, who gave himself a ransom for all" (1 Tim. 2:3-6).

The Readings

Like a shepherd leading his sheep, Jesus calls Lazarus to new life, ordering bystanders to "unbind him, and let him go." The response of believers becomes the November gospel theme. From Mark we hear Jesus' call for a sacrificial giving of love to God and neighbor, and watchful anticipation for the birth of a new creation. Our propensity to worry is addressed by both Mark and Matthew. We want to believe we can control our destiny, participate in our salvation. But sacrificing animals and giving grain offerings for the restoration of our relationship with God are no longer called for. We are justified by grace through faith.

In our merit- and competition-driven society, Chris-
~le to understand grace, unearned mercy, and
Old Testament readings remind us that
needs, now and at the last day. The
alvation. Revelation and Hebrews
that God's home is among mortals
as, is, and shall be "making all things

new" (Rev. 21:5). Christ "who loves us and freed us from our sins by his blood, and made us to be a kingdom, priests serving his God and Father" (Rev. 1:5-6), is the one final, perfect sacrifice for the forgiveness of our sins. He has freely given the ultimate sacrifice to grant us entry to the presence *and* service of God. His sacrifice brings "eternal redemption" (Heb. 9:12) to all who believe. We are asked to respond with faith and trust based on this gift of grace.

November preaching might reflect on faith characteristics suggested in the gospels: listening to Jesus; setting others free in Christ; nurturing a love of God in heart, soul, and mind, not just hands; attentiveness to God's ways and promises in the midst of chaos, fear, and want; striving first for the kingdom of God. What faith habits might we learn and practice this month when it comes to intercessory prayer, Bible reading, praise and adoration, and trust in God's unfailing promises?

Worship
Liturgy

For All Saints Day and Christ the King, the gathering rite might begin with thanksgiving for baptism from *Evangelical Lutheran Worship*—a reminder of our being joined to Christ who makes us heirs of his promise of salvation and servants of all.

Drawn heavily from Revelation, and echoing the New Testament readings, "This is the feast" is an appropriate hymn of praise for November. "All glory be to God on high" (ELW 410) or "Rejoice, for Christ is king!" (ELW 430) can serve as an alternate hymn of praise.

The inclusion of Martin Luther's Small Catechism in *Evangelical Lutheran Worship* (pp. 1160–1167) makes it easier to use this timeless resource in worship. Luther's explanation of the First Article echoes the November Old Testament readings' theme of God providing for God's people. November's New Testament theme—Christ's sacrificial work for our redemption—is explained in Luther's discourse on the Second Article. The explanation of the Third Article picks up the theme of new life woven through the gospel readings. Luther's three explanations can be used over three consecutive Sundays. Consider involving confirmation students and teachers or persons preparing for baptism or membership. Or, might someone learn the explanations by heart and recite them?

Music

On All Saints Day, if worshipers light candles in remembrance of the faithful departed, that is a good time to sing our hope born of faith. Beloved hymns like "Guide me ever, great Redeemer" (ELW 618) can be especially comforting to those who have long sung them. Newer songs of hope from *Worship & Praise* speak to many generations; see the suggestions for salvation, assurance, and trust in the topical index. *This Far by Faith* offers a wealth of stirring songs in the "Struggle, Faith" and "Hope, Comfort" sections. If the rhythms and styles of unfamiliar pieces are too challenging for the congregation, a soloist or ensemble of singers skilled in these styles of music could sing them as anthems. This less-familiar music might be presented as offertory music throughout November. Seasonal songs from Martin Luther's chants to recent praise music are in the new End Time hymn section of *Evangelical Lutheran Worship*.

Space

From rural roadside crosses to urban doorways, we are now familiar with the sight of impromptu shrines in memory of those whose lives have been cut short. Flowers, candles, and notes abound; and often there is a picture of the one who has died.

The November lectionary begins with the reminder that our lives are finite. We remember our forbears in the faith on All Saints Day. Whether they died peacefully or tragically, recently or long ago, these Christians are worthy of remembrance and part of the reason we have come this far by faith. Called by the Holy Spirit through the gospel, they made Christ known to us. Gathered around the Lord's supper as the "church on earth," they are the "host of heaven" we join while praising God's name in unending song.

With the Host of Heaven

As we anticipate the coming kingdom of God, and being reunited with those we love, we keep photos of our loved ones in our homes, portray martyrs and apostles in church windows, display confirmation-class pictures and photo albums from earlier generations in fellowship and entry spaces. Let All Saints Day be set aside for worshipers to bring photographs and other images of family, friends, saints, and martyrs of all ages who have revealed Christ to them. Bring pictures and photo directories out of the church archives. Encourage weekly additions to the display as today's saints journey to Christ the King Sunday.

Remembering that host of heaven as we come to holy communion, photos could be displayed in the worship space on tables, easels, or walls, taking care not to hinder the usual movement of people during worship. Alternatively, this gallery of saints could be set up in areas people pass through on their way to worship as a reminder of the generations of faithful who have gone before them.

With All the Saints

If most of the stained glass windows feature men or people from the biblical era, let the calendar of festivals and commemorations in *Evangelical Lutheran Worship* guide you to women and men of many lands and centuries who proclaimed Christ crucified. Worshipers of all ages and artistic abilities could be commissioned to create pictures, or prints from outside artists could be purchased, all for display in the worship space. With each new image, include the saint's name and a brief biography that helps tell her or his story.

Light in the Darkness

Images and the tolling of bells help us remember with our eyes and ears. One candle lighted in remembrance and the warmth of many candles aid our remembrance through sight and touch. Many worshipers value the ritual action of lighting a candle in remembrance and thanksgiving for a loved one and for Jesus Christ, the Light of the world. Whether candles are lighted before or on the way to communion, provide candles and space for lighted candles at a child-friendly height.

Colors and Symbols

Seasonal decorations can remind us of the cycles of living, dying, resting, and rising anew. In northern climates the earth rests beneath mist, frost, or snow. Simple sprays of evergreen or branches still holding red berries or other colorful growth can witness to life continuing under God's care. Pinecones, which become an immediate food source for some creatures and a long-term source of nutrients for future plants, can remind us of God's providing for us in all times and places. In warmer climates, November may mean a new growing season is under way. Fruits of the recent harvest and signs of the coming harvest can be brought in to recall the unchanging grace of Jesus Christ and his promise that he is making all things new.

Additional colors, brought into the worship space on processional banners, could reflect the local soil—rich black, brown, red, or sandy—as a reminder that we are rooted in Christ. The liturgical color of white, appointed for All Saints Day and Christ the King, could be used throughout November, reflecting the crisp white frost and snow outside, and recalling the baptismal garment and funeral pall that marks our journey into new life with Christ.

Celebrating November with Children

November is an active month in the church year. The color of the paraments and vestments change from white for All Saints, green for two Sundays in the time after Pentecost, white again for Christ the King, and then to blue for the first Sunday of Advent and the beginning of a new church year. Children can be encouraged to notice the changing colors on the altar and the ministers' vestments.

Encourage children to explore the meaning of these changes. Perhaps a confirmation class could act as "color guards" and provide a short worship note as a part of a children's message to explain the meaning of the colors and what it means in our church year. These color guards could wear the seasonal color, carry a banner of the appropriate color, and introduce worship with brief explanations. Consider "Why White?" "Grow with Green," or "Blue for Who?" as slogans.

November also reminds us of the faithful who have died, as well as those who have been baptized, during the past year.

Ideas for November

- Make it Seasoned Saints month. Pair up the older people in your congregation with younger members. Ask them to sit together in worship, and then to share in a fellowship gathering of some sort. Provide some interview questions or talking points for discussion starters and perhaps do an easy craft together, one for each home. For example, decorate salt and pepper shakers for each home, with the families' names on each one. Invite pairs to pray for each other at mealtime.

- Create a Walking Wet wall of baptismal blessings, filled with ways in which baptismal promises are kept by young and old. Each week, feature a different aspect of the baptismal promise (see *Evangelical Lutheran Worship*, p. 228). Invite families to share how they've lived out that aspect of the baptismal promise. Keep paper and markers handy so families can illustrate or write how they live their faith.

- Designate November 8 Noisy Offering Sunday. The gospel reading that day, Mark 12:38-44, tells the story of the widow's offering. Ask people several weeks ahead of time to bring their coins to worship on this day. Collect the coins in metal cans or pails after the regular offering is taken. Transfer the contents into one or two cans that can be brought forward with the regular offering. Designate your Noisy Offerings for community, church, or global charities.

- In November, thoughts turn toward the end of the year, a great opportunity to create awareness of the church year. The terms *Alpha* and *Omega* could be used to introduce Jesus as the beginning and the end. Use a circle to illustrate. Ask the older children to write a few sentences about what it means that Jesus is the beginning and the end. Share some of these statements in your weekly worship bulletin.

- Distribute slips of paper and ask people to write things they are thankful for. Collect these slips with the offering and ask children to share some of these prayers at each worship service in November. Alternatively, these prayers can also form the basis for the Thanksgiving worship prayers.

- Talk to your local grocer to acquire some paper sacks and attach a food-bank need list on the bag. Have children give the bags away during worship, and encourage the congregation to bring back full bags on a designated day. Children could also receive the bags and bring them forward during the offering.

- Create a Harvest of Gratitude display in the sanctuary: Children and families bring in everyday items they're grateful for (school supplies, soap, shampoo, food items, paper products, and others). Share those items with a local shelter or charity.

- Help people to "think thanks" by creating a Thankful Tree, using either of these options:
  Draw or trace a big tree on craft paper. Provide leaf cutouts and ask children to write things they are thankful for. Glue them on the tree.
  Create a Garland of Gratitude to adorn an indoor tree. Use the leaf cutouts, write on them, and string them together for a garland.

Worship Helps for November

November Checklist

- If the worship schedule changes, notify local newspapers, update your Web site, and change listings on exterior signs and church answering machines.
- Consider using harvest decorations during November, from All Saints Day through Thanksgiving.
- Publicize any special food collections and arrange for delivery to the appropriate agency within a day or two after the collection.
- Provide a book of remembrance for All Saints Day and the month of November in which names of loved ones may be written and perhaps remembered aloud in prayers.
- If All Saints is to be observed as a baptismal festival, see the suggestions for the Baptism of Our Lord in the Time after Epiphany checklist, p. 71.
- Continue planning for Advent 2009.

Shape of the Communion Liturgy

- See the seasonal worship texts for November on pp. 300–301.
- Omit the Kyrie (except for the festivals of All Saints and Christ the King).
- Use the hymn of praise (or use "This is the feast" just for the festivals of All Saints and Christ the King).
- Use the Nicene Creed for the festivals of All Saints and Christ the King; use the Apostles' Creed for other Sundays in November.
- See the prayers of intercession for each Sunday and the Day of Thanksgiving (U.S.A.).
- Use the preface for All Saints on All Saints Day; Ascension or Sundays for Christ the King; weekdays for Day of Thanksgiving; and Sundays for other Sundays in November (*Evangelical Lutheran Worship* Leaders Edition, pp. 180, 188, 191, 193).
- Thanksgiving at the table: see options in *Evangelical Lutheran Worship* (Leaders Edition, pp. 198–205); *WOV*, Prayer I (Leaders Edition, p. 73).

Other Helps

- See the suggestions for music and worship space in the essay "Preparing for November," pp. 296–297.
- Incorporate the names of those who have died into a baptismal remembrance or into the prayers of intercession on All Saints Day.
- A possible order for the gathering rite on All Saints Day (which falls on a Sunday this year) is provided in the seasonal rites section (pp. 302–303).

SEASONAL WORSHIP TEXTS FOR NOVEMBER

Confession and Forgiveness

All may make the sign of the cross, the sign that is marked at baptism, as the presiding minister begins.
Trusting in the word of life given in baptism,
we are gathered in the name of the Father,
and of the ☩ Son, and of the Holy Spirit.
Amen.

Before God, our rock and our refuge,
let us keep silence, and then confess our sin.

Silence is kept for reflection.

Most merciful God,
you know our failings better than we do;
our sins are revealed in the light of your face.
Our days and years pass by;
the things we trust fade like grass.
Be gracious to us, O God.
Guide us again to the water of life,
and renew in us the grace of holy baptism;
through Jesus Christ, our Lord. Amen.

You are all children of the light and of the day;
you are God's children now.
In the mercy of God,
Jesus Christ was given to die for you,
and for his sake, God forgives you all your sin.
With all the faithful in heaven and on earth,
rejoice and be glad!
Amen.

Greeting

May the hope to which God has called you,
the power of God at work in Christ,
and the Spirit of wisdom and revelation be with you all.
And also with you.

Offering Prayer

Creator God,
the earth and all that is in it belong to you.
Inspire us to use what you have made
to give justice to the oppressed,
food to the hungry, and freedom to the captives.
May our offerings, given in your name,
lift up those who are bowed down;
through Jesus Christ, our Lord.
Amen.

Invitation to Communion

Feast with the Lord, who has swallowed up death forever.

Prayer after Communion

At your table, O God, we have been made new.
Our mourning and crying and pain pass away,
and we see the glory of your presence among us.
Unite us with this vision,
and make us into your holy people,
one in the body of Christ, our Lord.
Amen.

Sending of Communion

Holy God,
as Moses lifted up the serpent in the wilderness,
so your Son was lifted up,
that whoever believes in him may have eternal life.
Bless those who now carry your word and sacrament
to our sisters and brothers who are absent,
that all the world might be saved through him,
Jesus Christ our Lord.
Amen.

Blessing

God the Alpha and Omega,
Jesus Christ the faithful witness,
God the Holy Spirit of truth,
+ bless you now and forever.
Amen.

Dismissal

Go in peace. Christ is with you.
Thanks be to God.

SEASONAL RITES FOR NOVEMBER

Gathering Rite for All Saints Day

The festival of All Saints occurs just as the landscape in the northern hemisphere heralds the dying of plants and the quiet of winter rest. In like manner, the readings and liturgy of this day call us to rejoice in all the saints: those who have died and now rest in Christ, those who live now, and those yet to come.

As the church year draws to a close, we hear warnings about the end of time, stories of crisis and judgment, and parables of loss and death. The Christian community speaks honestly about human frailty and mortality.

At the same time, we confess our faith in the risen Lord, in the communion of saints, the resurrection of the body, and life everlasting. While both life and death may bring us fear and uncertainty, the liturgy calls us to hear the Lord's promise that he is with us in life and in death. Christ has claimed us in baptism and nourishes us in the communion of his body and blood. He leads us to the new Jerusalem. There we shall join all the saints in praise of God, who has turned our graves into the doorway to eternal life.

Confession and Forgiveness

The presiding minister may lead this order at the baptismal font. All may make the sign of the cross, the sign that is marked at baptism, as the presiding minister begins.
Trusting in the word of life given in baptism,
we are gathered in the name of the Father,
and of the ☩ Son, and of the Holy Spirit.
Amen.

Before God, our rock and our refuge,
let us keep silence, and then confess our sin.

Silence is kept for reflection.

Most merciful God,
you know our failings better than we do;
our sins are revealed in the light of your face.
Our days and years pass by;
the things we trust fade like grass.
Be gracious to us, O God.
Guide us again to the water of life,
and renew in us the grace of holy baptism;
through Jesus Christ, our Lord. Amen.

You are all children of the light and of the day;
you are God's children now.
In the mercy of God,
Jesus Christ was given to die for you,
and for his sake, God forgives you all your sin.
With all the faithful in heaven and on earth,
rejoice and be glad!
Amen.

Remembrance of All Saints

The presiding minister leads the remembrance in these or similar words.
Let us remember all the saints before God.
We praise and bless you, O holy Trinity. You have taught your church that it is an ageless communion of saints. We thank you for gathering those who faithfully waited in hope for the redemption you promised, and now for adding us who celebrate the love of your Christ for the redemption of the world. Prepare a place for us among those who are already with you. Help us remember them as an encouragement to saintly living, exciting us to love, in anticipation of an eternal reunion.

Christ says, Take my yoke upon you, and learn from me;
for I am gentle and humble in heart,
and you will find rest for your souls.
For my yoke is easy, and my burden is light.
And you will find rest for your souls.

Gathering Hymn

Greeting

May the hope to which God has called you,
the power of God at work in Christ,
and the Spirit of wisdom and revelation be with you all.
And also with you.

Hymn of Praise

"This is the feast of victory," *or another suitable hymn*

The service continues with the prayer of the day.

Notes and Ideas

- As they enter the worship space, or just prior to the prayer of remembrance, worshipers may be invited to light a candle of remembrance for loved ones. Votive candles for that purpose may be arranged on a table or stand near the baptismal font.
- To make the connection between baptism and those who have died in Christ more obvious, votive candles for each person baptized since the previous All Saints Day may also be lit.

- If your font is movable, placing it near the entrance to the worship space may provide another dimension for this rite. Baptism marks our entry into the life of Christ, just as death, by virtue of the baptismal promise, becomes the gate and doorway to the eternal union promised in the sacrament.
- Some worshipers might confuse this rite of remembrance and promise with offering prayers to the dead, or invoking the memories of the dead on our behalf. It may be helpful for the pastor or another worship leader to explain that while we revere those who have gone before us in faith and remember them in love, this rite reminds us that in holy baptism God unites *all* the faithful into the one holy catholic and apostolic church: the church on earth *and* the church in heaven. A note to this effect may also be placed in the worship folder.

November 1, 2009
All Saints Day

Of all three years of the lectionary cycle, this year's All Saints readings have the most tears. Isaiah and Revelation look forward to the day when God will wipe away all tears; in John's gospel, Jesus weeps along with Mary and all the gathered mourners before he demonstrates his power over death. On All Saints Day we celebrate the victory won for all the faithful dead, but we grieve for our beloved dead as well, knowing that God honors our tears. We bring our grief to the table and find there a foretaste of Isaiah's feast to come.

Prayer of the Day

Almighty God, you have knit your people together in one communion in the mystical body of your Son, Jesus Christ our Lord. Grant us grace to follow your blessed saints in lives of faith and commitment, and to know the inexpressible joys you have prepared for those who love you, through Jesus Christ, our Savior and Lord, who lives and reigns with you and the Holy Spirit, one God, now and forever.

Gospel Acclamation

Alleluia. They are before the **׀** throne of God,* and the one who is seated on the throne will **׀** shelter them. *Alleluia.* (Rev. 7:15)

Readings and Psalm

Isaiah 25:6-9

Isaiah sees a vision of the end of days, when the Lord will gather all God's people on God's holy mountain and will prepare for them a rich feast. At this banquet the Lord will wipe the tears from all eyes. And there will be no more sorrow, for God will destroy death itself.

or Wisdom 3:1-9

Writing shortly before the time of Jesus, the author of this highly respected wisdom book offers a glorious vision of the righteous resting and at peace in the hand of God.

Psalm 24

They shall receive blessing from the God of their salvation. (Ps. 24:5)

Revelation 21:1-6a

Here is a vision of the new heaven and new earth in which God resides fully with God's people so that mourning, despair, and pain have been eradicated. These renewing words from the God who spans all of time are trustworthy and true.

John 11:32-44

Through the raising of Lazarus, Jesus offers the world a vision of the life to come, when death and weeping will be no more.

Color   White

CD-ROM Images

Icon Three: AllSaints_B
Icon Two: AllSaints_B, AllSaintsABC
Icon: 023, 123, 193

Prayers of Intercession

Gathered together with all the saints, let us pray for the church, the world, and all those in any need.
A brief silence.

God of all compassion, you weep with those who mourn, and you rejoice with those who celebrate. Teach us all to embrace one another with your love, that the bonds of community might be strengthened. God of mercy,
hear our prayer.

God of all nations, we ask you to guide the leaders of our nation and all world leaders, that they might work together for peace and the well-being of all your children. God of mercy,
hear our prayer.

God of all hope, we pray for those who are struggling with situations that appear overwhelming and hopeless. Bless and strengthen all your servants (*especially*), that they might feel your presence in the midst of their trials. God of mercy,
hear our prayer.

God of all creation, we praise you for the gift of this planet. Sustain us in our efforts to care for your creation, that we might preserve it as a gift for those who come after us. God of mercy,
hear our prayer.
God of all wisdom, teach us to walk with humility and compassion, that we might bear witness to your redeeming love by all that we say and do. God of mercy,
hear our prayer.
Here other intercessions may be offered.
God of all life, we thank and praise you for the faithful witness of all your saints. (*Those who have died during the past year may be named.*) Help us also to be faithful to you, that we might live out our baptismal identity in the world. God of mercy,
hear our prayer.
Into your hands, gracious God, we commend all for whom we pray, trusting in your mercy, through Christ, our Lord.
Amen.

Ideas and Images for the Day

Dating back to the third century, the church in all her wisdom has celebrated All Saints Day. This Sunday we honor that tradition as we remember and give thanks for all the beloved baptized into Christ, those among us and those who have gone before us. Today our tender hearts remember loved ones who have died. In our worship we reach out across time to hold hands with Mary and Martha in their encounter with death, and at the same time we grasp the hands of one another as God continues to knit us together into the one beautiful body of Christ Jesus. With clasped hands, we, like Lazarus and his sisters, are called out from the shadow of death and tears into resurrection life.

1. In John's gospel, little time is spent detailing the miraculous works of Jesus. Emphasis is placed on dialogue and discourse, not the intricacies of the miracles themselves. To stimulate the imagination regarding the resurrection of Lazarus, view Rembrandt's *The Raising of Lazarus* in tandem with Vincent Van Gogh's *The Raising of Lazarus (after Rembrandt)*. Both may be seen at www.textweek.com/art/raising_lazarus.htm.

2. If possible in your congregational setting, remember the saints who have died by beginning worship in the parish cemetery or at the columbarium. Following some words of remembrance and a litany of hope rooted in the resurrection, allow the processional cross to lead the assembly in silence to the sanctuary, where the gathering song will loudly and boldly proclaim the promise of the risen Christ.

3. Annual celebrations of the sacrament of baptism on All Saints Sunday practice the theological truth that all the baptized are part of the company of God's saints. If a baptism is not possible, use a thanksgiving for baptism as part of the gathering rite. Consider using the form of the thanksgiving provided in the funeral service in *Evangelical Lutheran Worship* (p. 280).

4. Who in the congregation has experienced the death of a loved one in the past year? How are they being cared for by the congregation? Empower a congregational-care task force of lay leaders to check in with these families. Offer prayers, ongoing support, meals, and personal invitations to All Saints Day worship as ways to acknowledge and care for them in their grief.

5. Are funerals going the way of weddings? That is, are people beginning to make outlandish requests based on individual preferences and desires rather than the promises of God? Schedule adult Sunday school classes or forums to study the liturgy of funerals and consider how funerals proclaim the resurrection and make the communion of saints real. An excellent resource for such a study is Melinda Quivik's book *A Christian Funeral: Witness to the Resurrection* (Augsburg Fortress, 2005). Each short chapter includes questions for reflection and discussion. As a project for the participants, have each person create their own funeral service rooted and grounded in Christian faith and life.

Hymns for Worship
Gathering
For all the saints   ELW 422, LBW 174
Shall we gather at the river   ELW 423
Behold the host arrayed in white   ELW 425, LBW 314

Hymn of the Day
Rejoice in God's saints   ELW 418, WOV 689
    LAUDATE DOMINUM
Sing with all the saints in glory   ELW 426, WOV 691
    MISSISSIPPI
In our day of thanksgiving   ELW 429   *ST. CATHERINE'S COURT*

Communion
Give thanks for saints   ELW 428
Blest are they   ELW 728, WOV 764
Eat this bread, drink this cup   ELW 492, WOV 706

Sending

Holy God, we praise your name ELW 414, LBW 535
For all the saints ELW 422, LBW 174
Rejoice, ye pure in heart! ELW 873, 874, LBW 553

Additional Hymns and Songs

On the mountaintop BC 75
Mourning into dancing W&P 99
No longer strangers W&P 102
Oh, when the saints go marching in TFF 180

Music for the Day
Psalmody and Acclamations

Helgen, John. *Gospel Acclamations for Autumn*. AFP 9780800678623.
Mummert, Mark. "Psalm 24" from *Psalm Settings for the Church Year*. AFP 9780800678562.
Psalter for Worship Year B, Evangelical Lutheran Worship Edition. AFP 9780806683839.

Choral

Lang, Rupert. "The Kontakion." SSAATTBB, org, assembly. B&H 9790051471423.
Miller, Aaron David. "We Will Shine." SATB, pno. AFP 9780800678111.
Nelson, Ronald A. "Jesus at the Door." 2 pt mxd, pno. GIA G-6764.
Roberts, William Bradley. "Sing with All the Saints in Glory" from *Augsburg Easy Choirbook*, vol. 2. U mxd/U trbl, opt solo, org, opt inst. AFP 9780800677510.
Schalk, Carl F. "I Saw a New Heaven and a New Earth" from *The Augsburg Choirbook*. SATB. AFP 9780800656782.

Children's Choir

Jennings, Carolyn. "God Made the Song." UE. 2 pt, pno, opt assembly. CG A888.
Ramseth, Betty Ann/Melissa Ramseth Hoiland. "O Christ, the Healer, We Have Come" from *Hand-Me-Down Hymns*. UE. U, sop glock, vc. AFP 9786000101398. OP
Sleeth, Natalie. "Promised Land." UE. 3 pt, pno. Heritage Music Press HV405.

Keyboard / Instrumental

Cherwien, David. "Laudate Dominum" from *Augsburg Organ Library: Autumn*. Org. AFP 9780800675790.
Hassell, Michael. "Mississippi" from *More Folkways*. Pno, C/B-flat inst/vla. AFP 9780800657307.
Kolander, Keith. "Mississippi" from *Organ Music for the Seasons*, vol. 3. Org. AFP 9780800675646.
Organ, Anne Krentz. "St. Catherine's Court" from *Eight for Eighty-Eight*, vol. 3. Pno, C/B-flat inst. AFP 9780800623494.

Handbell

Buckwalter, Karen Lakey. "Valse Les Adieux." 3-6 oct, L4+. AG 36013.
Page, Anna Laura. "Promised Land." 3-5 oct, L3. AG 13416.
Page, Anna Laura. "The River." 3-5 oct, L4. ALF 8655.

Praise Ensemble

■ Davis, Holland. "Let it Rise" from *iWorship Songbook 1*. INT 23366.
■ Redman, Matt. "The Prayers of the Saints" from www.ccli.com. Thankyou Music.
■ Ruis, David. "You're Worthy of My Praise" from *WOW Worship Green Songbook*. INT 000768195567.
■ Smith, Martin. "Did You Feel the Mountains Tremble?" from www.praisecharts.com. Curious? Music UK.

Global

Makeever, Ray. "Death Be Never Last" from *Dancing at the Harvest*. U, pno, gtr. AFP 9780800655938.
Schultz, Donna Gartman. "Shall We Gather at the River." SATB, kybd. AFP 9780800659370.

■ denotes songs that are available on iTunes®.

November 1, 2009
Time after Pentecost — Lectionary 31

Jesus states the core of God's law: love God with all you are and have, and love your neighbor as yourself. The scribe agrees that Jesus has rightly identified the most important commandments, much more important than sacrifices. It's easy for us to say with the writer of the letter to the Hebrews that sacrifices aren't needed anymore; harder, though, to acknowledge that all our worship, all our community service, all our social action, all our family caregiving is worthless if it is done without love.

Prayer of the Day

Almighty God, you have taught us in your Son that love fulfills the law. Inspire us to love you with all our heart, our soul, our mind, and our strength, and teach us how to love our neighbor as ourselves, through Jesus Christ, our Savior and Lord.

Gospel Acclamation

Alleluia. Beloved, since God loved | us so much,* we also ought to love | one another. *Alleluia.* (1 John 4:11)

Readings and Psalm
Deuteronomy 6:1-9

As the children of Israel enter the promised land, Moses instructs them to love the Lord and to teach God's law to future generations. Verses 4-5 are called the Shema (Hebrew for "hear"), which is still used in Jewish daily prayer and which forms the basis for the "greatest commandment" in today's gospel reading.

Psalm 119:1-8

Happy are they who seek the LORD with all their hearts. (Ps. 119:2)

Hebrews 9:11-14

In ancient systems of worship, temporary forgiveness and purity came through rituals using the blood of sacrificial animals. Now, however, our forgiveness and purity comes eternally through the death of Jesus.

Mark 12:28-34

When a scribe asks Jesus which commandment is first of all, Jesus answers that love of God and love of neighbor are interconnected and define the heart of the kingdom of God.

Semicontinuous reading and psalm
Ruth 1:1-18

In this reading, Ruth, a Moabite woman, goes above and beyond the call of duty to accompany Naomi, her Israelite mother-in-law, to a new life back in Israel. In loving and tender words, Ruth pledges to stay with Naomi and to adopt Naomi's land and God as her own.

Psalm 146

The LORD lifts up those who are bowed down. (Ps. 146:8)

Color   Green

CD-ROM Images

Icon Three: 1030-1105_Lect31_B
Icon Two: Proper26_Sun31_B
Icon: 060

Prayers of Intercession

Gathered together with all the saints, let us pray for the church, the world, and all those in any need.
A brief silence.
God of love, help us to hear your voice above the discord of false gods crying out for our allegiance, that we might serve and love you alone. God of mercy,
hear our prayer.
God of all creation, we praise you for the gift of this planet. Sustain us in our efforts to care for your creation, that we might preserve it as a gift for those who come after us. God of mercy,
hear our prayer.
God of peace, bless all nations as we seek to build safe and peaceful communities in which all people can live and thrive. God of mercy,
hear our prayer.

God of wisdom, we thank you for the many opportunities we have to learn and grow in your word. Bless all teachers, students, and other educational leaders, that they might be enriched in their walk with you. God of mercy,
hear our prayer.

God of healing, we ask you to grant us strength and hope in our times of need. Be with all your children who are struggling in body, mind, or spirit (*especially*). God of mercy,
hear our prayer.

God of hope, help us to bring your light wherever darkness, fear, and confusion reign, that all might be drawn to you. God of mercy,
hear our prayer.

Here other intercessions may be offered.

God of mercy, we praise you for the communion of all the saints, the living expression of your church in all times and places. Help us to be faithful to you all the days of our lives. God of mercy,
hear our prayer.

Into your hands, gracious God, we commend all for whom we pray, trusting in your mercy, through Christ, our Lord.
Amen.

Ideas and Images for the Day

The scribes and Pharisees, temple leaders who collaborate with the Roman government, challenge Jesus with questions throughout Mark's gospel. Today's interaction between Jesus and a scribe, easily viewed as just another one of the Jewish leaders who opposed Jesus, the writer casts differently. Here Mark reveals a scribe who admires Jesus' responses, his wisdom, his knowledge of God. In a post-Holocaust world, it serves Christians well to downplay any apparent anti-Semitism found in the New Testament, including writings in Hebrews that describe how Christ's sacrifice supercedes for all people in all times and places, the Jewish practice of blood sacrifice. Although this interpretation may be drawn from Hebrews, it risks creating a climate of intolerance toward Jews that throughout history has not lent itself to love of neighbor.

1. The scribe in today's story is a flat character in Mark. Speculation that develops this character could result in thoughtful story. Why is *this* scribe willing to be favorably impressed with Jesus' remarks? Is he a high-ranking official who does not need to fear his colleagues? Is he a low-ranking official, courageous enough to be honest in his assessment, despite the outcome? How might listeners connect with this character?

2. It is popular for churches to send groups of youth and adults to Mexico to build a house for what is often designated a deserving family. Although this action is a practical application of love of neighbor, it is at least as important to provide opportunities for people to accompany and hear the stories of those who live in poverty on both sides of the border. Loving relationship results in sacrifices of love. Opportunities with focus on learning and listening allow for the growth of loving relationship. Details of such opportunities may be found at www.rmselca.org (see "Border Immersion" under "Selected Topics"), and www.elca.org/mexico.

3. Mark's Jesus brings paradoxical solutions to the chaos of communities living under Roman oppression. In today's story, a commandment (law) reveals love (gospel). Last Sunday, those who are blind are the ones who see. Today, the law brings the good news of God's love for all people. These odd perspectives on how the world works reveal the kingdom of God. How are Christians called to live out paradox in their daily lives? How are congregations called to live out paradox in their life as a community, within local and global communities?

4. Many children's books are available that promote loving relationship in families, among friends, in congregations, and communities; some with secular themes, some with sacred themes. A lending library of children's books might include titles such as *Amazing Grace* by Mary Hoffman and Caroline Binch (New York: Dial Books, 1991). A congregation with a library, or one without, might consider a library cart for children's books that can be moved and placed in a high traffic area near the worship space, easily seen and accessed by children and families.

Hymns for Worship
Gathering

All Are Welcome   ELW 641
Great God, your love has called us   ELW 358, WOV 666

Hymn of the Day

O Christ, your heart, compassionate   ELW 722
ELLACOMBE
Lord of all nations, grant me grace   ELW 716, LBW 419
BEATUS VIR
Love divine, all loves excelling   ELW 631, LBW 315
HYFRYDOL

Communion

Oh, that the Lord would guide my ways   ELW 772, LBW 480
Jesu, Jesu, fill us with your love   ELW 708, WOV 765, TFF 83

Sending

Lord, whose love in humble service   ELW 712, LBW 423

Son of God, eternal Savior   ELW 655, LBW 364

Additional Hymns and Songs

The call is clear and simple   HG 58

Open Our Lives to the Word   DH 8

Seek ye first the kingdom of God   WOV 783, W&P 122,
    TFF 149

I love you, Lord   W&P 67

Music for the Day
Psalmody and Acclamations

Mummert, Mark. "Psalm 119" from *Psalm Settings for the Church
    Year*. AFP 9780800678562.

Psalter for Worship Year B, Evangelical Lutheran Worship Edition.
    AFP 9780806683839.

Schalk, Carl F. *Gospel Acclamations for Autumn*. AFP
    9780800678623.

Choral

Music, David W. "Do Not I Love Thee." SAB, kybd. CPH 98-2808.

Pelz, Walter L. "Show Me Thy Ways." SATB, gtr, ob/fl. AFP
    9780800645427. *The Augsburg Choirbook*. AFP 9780800656782.

Stanford, Charles Villiers. "Beati Quorum Via." SSATBB. B&H
    OCTB 5318.

White, David Ashley. "O Bread of Life from Heaven." 2 pt mxd,
    org. AFP 9780800650919. *The Augsburg Choirbook*. AFP
    9780800656782.

Children's Choir

Leaf, Robert. "Come with Rejoicing." LE. U/2 pt, pno/org. AFP
    9780800645755.

Sleeth, Natalie. "If You Love Me" from *Laudamus*. UE. 2/3 pt, kybd.
    HIN HMB126.

Ziegenhals, Harriet. "You Shall Have a Song." UE. 2/3 pt, kybd, opt
    fl. HOP A577.

Keyboard / Instrumental

Blair, Dallas. "Hyfrydol" from *Hymn Introductions and Descants for
    Trumpet and Organ*, set 3. Org, tpt. MSM 20-141.

Kolander, Keith. "Beatus vir" from *All Things Are Thine*. Org. AFP
    9780800658007.

Sadowski, Kevin. "Beatus vir" from *Eleven Hymn Preludes*. Org.
    CPH 97-6883U1.

Shehi, Christina. "Ellacombe" from *Songs for All Seasons*, vol. 2.
    Pno. AFP 9780800677862.

Handbell

Hanna, Donna. "Prelude on 'Hyfrydol'." 3-5 oct, L2+. GIA G-7210.

Morris, Hart. "Beyond All Praising." 3-5 oct, opt 3 oct hc, L2+. CPH
    97-7117.

Payne, William. "O God, Beneath Your Guiding Hand." 3-5 oct, L3.
    NMP 118.

Praise Ensemble

- Baloche, Paul/Gary Sadler. "Rise Up and Praise Him" from *WOW
    Worship Green Songbook*. INT 000768195567.
- Doerksen, Brian. "Come, Now Is the Time to Worship" from *Come,
    Now Is the Time to Worship*. VIN VMB9367.
    Park, Andy. "Holy Love" from www.praisecharts.com. Mercy/VIN.
- Smith, Martin. "I Could Sing of Your Love Forever" from
    www.praisecharts.com. Curious? Music UK.

Global

O'Brien, Francis. "The Servant Song." SAB. GIA G-5451.

Hayes, Mark. "Welcome Table." SATB, pno. AFP 9780800676032.

Sunday, November 1
All Saints Day

The custom of commemorating all of the saints of the
church on a single day goes back at least to the third century. All Saints celebrates the baptized people of God, living
and dead, who make up the body of Christ. Today many
congregations will remember the faithful who have died
during the past year.

Our liturgy abounds with references to the saints and
to our continual relationship with them. Today and this
week invite people to reflect on others—living and dead—
who have moved and supported others by their lives of
faith.

Tuesday, November 3
Martín de Porres, renewer of society, 1639

Martín was the son of a Spanish knight and Ana Velázquez,
a freed black slave from Panama. Martín apprenticed himself to a barber-surgeon in Lima, Peru, and was known for
his work as a healer. Martín was a lay brother in the Order
of Preachers (Dominicans) and engaged in many charitable works. He was a gardener as well as a counselor to
those who sought him out. He was noted for his care of all
the poor, regardless of race. His own religious community
described him as the "father of charity." His work included
the founding of an orphanage, a hospital, and a clinic for
dogs and cats. He is recognized as an advocate for Christian
charity and interracial justice.

■ denotes songs that are available on iTunes®.

Saturday, November 7

John Christian Frederick Heyer, 1873;
Bartholomaeus Ziegenbalg, 1719;
Ludwig Nommensen, 1918; missionaries

Three missionaries are commemorated on this date. Heyer was the first missionary sent out by American Lutherans. Ordained in 1820, he established Sunday schools and taught at Gettysburg College and Seminary. Heyer became a missionary in the Andhra region of India. During a break in his mission work he received the M.D. degree from what would later be Johns Hopkins University.

Bartholomaeus Ziegenbalg (ZEEG-en-balg) was a missionary to the Tamils of Tranquebar on the southeast coast of India. The first convert to Christianity was baptized about ten months after Ziegenbalg began preaching. His missionary work was opposed by the local Hindus and also by Danish authorities in that area. Ziegenbalg was imprisoned for his work on a charge of converting the natives. Today, the Tamil Evangelical Lutheran Church carries on his work.

Ludwig Ingwer Nommensen was born in Schleswig-Holstein, Germany. In the early 1860s he went to Sumatra to serve as a Lutheran missionary. His work was among the Batak people, who had previously not seen Christian missionaries. Though he encountered some initial difficulties, the missions began to succeed following the conversion of several tribal chiefs. Nommensen translated the scriptures into Batak while honoring much of the native culture.

November 8, 2009
Time after Pentecost — Lectionary 32

Widows are visible everywhere in today's readings. Jesus denounces those scribes who pray impressive prayers but devour widows' houses. He commends the poor widow who in his view gave far more than the major donors. Jesus doesn't see her simply as an object of compassion or charity. She, like the widow of Zarephath who shares her last bit of food with Elijah, does something of great importance.

Prayer of the Day

O God, you show forth your almighty power chiefly by reaching out to us in mercy. Grant us the fullness of your grace, strengthen our trust in your promises, and bring all the world to share in the treasures that come through your Son, Jesus Christ, our Savior and Lord.

Gospel Acclamation

Alleluia. The LORD raises up the poor | from the dust,* to make them inherit a | seat of honor. *Alleluia.* (1 Sam. 2:8)

Readings and Psalm

1 Kings 17:8-16

This chapter begins the story of Elijah. God sends a drought on Israel because of the sins of King Ahab. This passage depicts God's saving acts not only on behalf of Elijah, but also on behalf of those who are associated with the prophet, even a foreigner, the widow of Zarephath.

Psalm 146

The LORD lifts up those who are bowed down. (Ps. 146:8)

Hebrews 9:24-28

The letter to the Hebrews describes Christ as a high priest who offers himself as a sacrifice for our sin. Christ does not die again and again each year. He died once, is alive with God, and will reveal himself on the last day.

Mark 12:38-44

After engaging in a series of public arguments with religious leaders in the temple, Jesus contrasts the proud and oppressive ways of those leaders with the sacrificial humility and poverty of the widow.

Semicontinuous reading and psalm

Ruth 3:1-5; 4:13-17

Naomi has lost her husband and sons, but is blessed by the love and support of her widowed daughter-in-law Ruth. Naomi is resourceful in arranging the marriage of Ruth to her wealthy kinsman, Boaz; and Ruth, the Moabite, becomes the great-grandmother to that greatest of Israelite kings, David.

Psalm 127

Children are a heritage from the LORD. (Ps. 127:3)

Color Green

CD-ROM Images

Icon Three: 1106-1112_Lect32_B
Icon Two: Proper27_Sun32_B
Icon: 125

Prayers of Intercession

Gathered together with all the saints, let us pray for the church, the world, and all those in any need.

A brief silence.

Wise and compassionate God, you call us out of isolation into community, out of fear into hope. Strengthen the work of your church throughout the world, that we might be your living witnesses. God of mercy,

hear our prayer.

Creating and sustaining God, you have blessed the world with all we need to sustain and enrich life. Inspire us to rededicate our lives to the careful stewardship of the earth's resources. God of mercy,

hear our prayer.

Holy and righteous God, you have given us a vision of life in which justice and peace are not distant dreams, but a present reality. Sustain the efforts of all who seek to create a more just society here and now. God of mercy,

hear our prayer.

Renewing and forgiving God, you offer us grace whenever we fall short and fail to live out our callings in the world. Help us to be patient with ourselves and with each other as we seek to grow in grace. God of mercy,

hear our prayer.

Healing and loving God, you provide strength to the weary, hope to the despairing, and comfort to the bereaved (*especially*). Bless and strengthen the work of all doctors, nurses, and other healing professionals. God of mercy,

hear our prayer.

Here other intercessions may be offered.

Faithful and eternal God, we give you thanks for the lives of the saints, whose pilgrimage on earth is completed. Keep us secure in the faith, until we feast with you at the eternal banquet. God of mercy,

hear our prayer.

Into your hands, gracious God, we commend all for whom we pray, trusting in your mercy, through Christ, our Lord. **Amen.**

Ideas and Images for the Day

Mark's Jesus uses the plight of widows to lift up the systemic ills of his time. He identifies the scribes as the oppressors. His purpose in pointing out the widow's small contribution may well have been not so much to highlight her faithfulness but to expose the oppression and the oppressors under which she lived. The Roman government and the temple leaders collude to devour widows' households—in Greek, their *oikas*, one of this gospel writer's favorite images. Another of this writer's favorite words, *and* (in Greek, *kai*), is used four times in this passage as an indicator of the urgency of the situation he describes. He is about to speak in apocalyptic ways in the next chapter. Revealing the despicable oppression present in society sets up the warnings soon to follow.

1. In her book *Sowing the Gospel: Mark's World in Literary-Historical Perspective* (Fortress Press, 1989), Mary Ann Tolbert suggests that the parable of the soils from Mark 4 is crucial to the overall interpretation of this gospel. The characters in Mark may be categorized as a kind of soil from the parable. What kinds of soil are the scribes, the widow, the disciples? What kind of soil are we?

2. Again, paradox permeates this text from Mark. Widows are wealthy; scribes are poor in the kingdom of God. Who is apparently wealthy in our society? Who is truly poor in our society? There is a difference between material wealth and spiritual wealth. It is easy to romanticize those who are poor but spiritually rich. How do we, as Christians, balance material and spiritual riches in our lives? How possible is it to be rich in material and spiritual matters simultaneously?

3. Christians are called to provide direct aid to those in need. We are also called to address systemic changes that reduce the need for charity. In this gospel text, the writer reveals the systemic problem of oppression. We are called to reveal systemic problems in our society, and we are called to work to solve those problems. We

generally understand how to help others with our charitable giving and acts of compassion, individually and corporately. Understanding, exposing, and correcting systemic oppression is more difficult and best undertaken in community. Go to www.elca.org/advocacy/ for additional information.

4. Mark's use of the Greek word *oikas* to describe a widow's dwelling was probably counterintuitive in that time and place. Widows, not usually considered heads of households, were generally poor and dependent on charity for their livelihood. What constitutes a household—a dwelling for a family group—has changed in our society over the last several decades. Mark's Jesus broadens the concept of household with his use of the word in his time and place. How broad is our understanding of household? How well do we consider single-parent households, alternative families, and foster children in our planning of congregational life?

Hymns for Worship

Gathering
Day by day   ELW 790, WOV 746
Lord, whose love in humble service   ELW 712, LBW 423
Lord, I lift your name on high   ELW 857

Hymn of the Day
Take my life, that I may be   ELW 583   *TOMA MI VOLUNTAD*
    ELW 685, LBW 406   *PATMOS*
We Are an Offering   ELW 692, W&P 146   *OFFERING*
As saints of old   ELW 695   *FOREST GREEN*

Communion
When the poor ones   ELW 725
All who hunger, gather gladly   ELW 461
We come to the hungry feast   ELW 479, WOV 766

Sending
The Lord now sends us forth   ELW 538
For the fruit of all creation   ELW 679, WOV 760, LBW 563
Oh, happy day when we shall stand   ELW 441, LBW 351

Additional Hymns and Songs
The temple rang with golden coins   HG 154
Awesome God   W&P 13
Blest are the pure in heart   H82 656
I'd rather have Jesus   TFF 233

Music for the Day
Psalmody and Acclamations
Haugen, Marty. "Psalm 146" from *Psalm Settings for the Church Year*. AFP 9780800678562.
Psalter for Worship Year B, Evangelical Lutheran Worship Edition. AFP 9780806683839.
Schalk, Carl F. *Gospel Acclamations for Autumn*. AFP 9780800678623.

Choral
Ashdown, Franklin D. "Jesus, the Very Thought of Thee." SATB, org, opt C inst. AFP 9780800657505.
Diemer, Emma Lou. "Praise Ye the Lord." SATB, 1 or 2 pianos. FLA A5021.
Schalk, Carl F. "Lord, It Belongs Not to My Care." SATB, org. AFP 9780800645908.
❑ Sedio, Mark. "Take My Life That I May Be" (Toma mi voluntad). SATB, pno, fl, opt gtr. AFP 9780800658298. *Augsburg Easy Choirbook*, vol. 2. AFP 9780800677510.

Children's Choir
Artman, Ruth. "Prayer of the Norwegian Child." UE. 2 pt, pno, opt fl, hb. HAL 08596454.
Carter, John. "Lamb of God." UE. 3 pt, kybd. HOP A631.
Kemp, Helen. "A Mountain Psalm: A Meditation on Psalm 121." UE. 2 pt, opt assembly, pno. CG A1061.
Ramseth, Betty Ann/Melissa Ramseth Hoiland. "Have No Fear, Little Flock" from *Take a Hymn*. UE. U, kybd, fl, fc, wood blocks, opt cello. AFP 9786000106461. OP

Keyboard / Instrumental
Blair, Dallas. "Forest Green" from *Hymn Introductions and Descants for Trumpet and Organ*, set 3. Org, tpt. MSM 20-141.
Mahnke, Allan. "Patmos" from *Thirteen Pieces for Treble Instrument and Organ*. Org, C/B-flat inst. CPH 97-6030U1.
Manz, Paul O. "Forest Green" from *Improvisations for the Christmas Season*, set 2. Org. MSM 10-101.
Sedio, Mark. "Forest Green" from *Dancing in the Light of God*. Pno. AFP 9780800656546.

Handbell
Dobrinski, Cynthia. "Scherzando." 3-5 oct, L4. FLA HP 5287.
Muschick, John, arr. "Offertory." 4-5 oct, L4-. BP HB166.
Waugh, Timothy. "Shades of Forest Green." 3-5 oct, L3. Ring Out Press 2115.

❑ denotes choral suggestions that relate to the hymn of the day.
■ denotes songs that are available on iTunes®.

Praise Ensemble

Founds, Rick. "Lord, I Lift Your Name on High." ELW 857, W&P 90.

■ Mullins, Rich. "Awesome God" from *Breakforth Worship Songbook*. New Creation Ministries. www.new-creation.net.

■ Redman, Beth/Matt Redman . "Blessed Be Your Name" from www.praisecharts.com. Thankyou Music.

■ Zschech, Darlene. "It Is You" from www.praisecharts.com. Hillsong Publishing/INT.

Global

Hesla, Bret/Tom Witt. "Everything That We Have" from *Pave the Way: Global Songs 3*. U/SATB, pno, gtr. AFP 9780800676896.

Olivar, José Antonio. "When the Poor Ones/Cuando el Pobre." U, pno, gtr. ELW 725.

Wednesday, November 11

Martin, Bishop of Tours, 397

Martin's pagan father enlisted him in the army at age fifteen. One winter day, a beggar approached Martin for aid, and he cut his cloak in half and gave a portion to the beggar. Later, Martin understood that he had seen the presence of Christ in that beggar, and this ended his uncertainty about Christianity. He soon asked for his release from his military duties, but he was imprisoned instead. After his release from prison he began preaching, particularly against the Arians. In 371 he was elected bishop of Tours. As bishop he developed a reputation for intervening on behalf of prisoners and heretics who had been sentenced to death.

Today, as we remember this soldier turned peacemaker, we also remember the end of World War I and veterans of all U.S. wars. Let these commemorations together move us to pray and work for peace in our families, congregations, nation, and world.

Søren Aabye Kierkegaard, teacher, 1855

Kierkegaard (KEER-keh-gore), a nineteenth-century Danish theologian whose writings reflect his Lutheran heritage, was the founder of modern existentialism. Though he was engaged to a woman he deeply loved, he ended the relationship because he believed he was called to search the hidden side of life. Many of his works were published under a variety of names, so that he could reply to arguments from his own previous works. Kierkegaard's work attacked the established church of his day—its complacency, its tendency to intellectualize faith, and its desire to be accepted by polite society. Kierkegaard's work makes room for doubt in the life of faith. He also served as a prophetic challenge to churches that may want to set aside paradox for an easy faith and the gospel for cultural acceptability.

November 15, 2009
Time after Pentecost — Lectionary 33

November begins with All Saints Day and ends in or near Advent, when we anticipate Christ's coming again. So the readings today tell of the final resurrection and the end time. In the turmoil of hope, fear, and disbelief that these predictions provoke in us, Hebrews sounds a note of confident trust. Christ makes a way for us where there is no way, and we walk it confidently, our hearts and bodies washed in baptismal water, trusting the one who has promised. The more we see the last day approaching, the more important it is to meet together to provoke one another to love.

Prayer of the Day

Almighty God, your sovereign purpose brings salvation to birth. Give us faith to be steadfast amid the tumults of this world, trusting that your kingdom comes and your will is done through your Son, Jesus Christ, our Savior and Lord.

Gospel Acclamation

Alleluia. Be alert | at all times,* praying that you may have the strength to stand before the | Son of Man. *Alleluia.* (Luke 23:36)

Readings and Psalm
Daniel 12:1-3

The book of Daniel is an example of apocalyptic literature, which is full of strange visions and symbolism. Arising during times of great persecution, apocalyptic literature is concerned with God's revelation about the end time and the coming kingdom of God, when God will vindicate the righteous who have been persecuted.

Psalm 16

My heart is glad and my spirit rejoices; my body shall rest in hope. (Ps. 16:9)

Hebrews 10:11-14 [15-18] 19-25

Images of worship and sacrifice are used throughout Hebrews to highlight what Christ has uniquely accomplished through his death. Because we have received forgiveness through Christ's death, we live with sincere hearts by trusting in God's promises and encouraging love and good works from each other.

Mark 13:1-8

In the last week of his life, Jesus warned his disciples concerning trials that were to come upon them and upon the world. He exhorts the listener: Do not be alarmed.

Semicontinuous reading and psalm
1 Samuel 1:4-20

This story introduces us to Elkanah, a devout Israelite, and his wife, Hannah, who is barren. God grants Hannah's prayer and she bears a son, Samuel, who will be an important figure in Israel's history. Samuel, the last of Israel's judges, anoints the first two kings of Israel, Saul and David.

1 Samuel 2:1-10

My heart exults in the LORD; my strength is exalted in my God. (1 Sam. 2:1)

Color   Green

CD-ROM Images

Icon Three: 1113-1119_Lect33_B
Icon Two: Proper28_Sun33_B
Icon: 126

Prayers of Intercession

Gathered together with all the saints, let us pray for the church, the world, and all those in any need.
A brief silence.
You call us, Lord God, to trust in you when chaos surrounds us. Grant us the faith we need to walk where you lead us. God of mercy,
hear our prayer.

You call us, Lord God, to be faithful stewards of your creation. Cure our complacency, and give us the knowledge and commitment to restore that which has been harmed through our neglect. God of mercy,
hear our prayer.

You call us, Lord God, to work for peace and hope in our troubled world. Help us to hear the needs of all who suffer throughout the world, that we might respond in compassionate action. God of mercy,
hear our prayer.

You call us, Lord God, to visit the sick and care for the hurting. Lead us as we open our hearts to the poor, the lonely, the outcast, and all those in any need this day (*especially*). God of mercy,
hear our prayer.

You call us, Lord God, to be agents of reconciliation in a divided world. Teach us how to love all people, even those most different from us. God of mercy,
hear our prayer.

You call us, Lord God, to cherish and celebrate the gift of life. Guide us as we seek to make all families safe and loving. God of mercy,
hear our prayer.

Here other intercessions may be offered.

You call us, Lord God, as you called the saints who have gone before us. Strengthen us to be your living witnesses, that the world might know your love. God of mercy,
hear our prayer.

Into your hands, gracious God, we commend all for whom we pray, trusting in your mercy, through Christ, our Lord.
Amen.

Ideas and Images for the Day

These verses from Mark are better understood in the context of what comes before and after. Mark's Jesus, in chapter 12, has pointed out the systemic ills of the time and place in which he lives. The Roman government and temple leaders oppress the people. Widows are robbed of their living; their households are devoured. Now, in chapter 13, when the disciples remark on the enormity of the temple, Jesus teaches that the buildings will be destroyed. He goes on to speak of evil times of hardship. Then, in verses 9-13, Jesus teaches the people how to live in times of persecution: "The good news must first be proclaimed to all nations" (13:10). These words of Jesus, the prophet, are not fortune-telling but teachings on how to live in ways that bring about the kingdom of God.

1. Jesus' insistence that the disciples not be led astray, that the good news be proclaimed, is a call to evangelism. These words provide an opportunity to remind ourselves that the primary goal of evangelism is not to increase the number of members or the giving in our congregation; the primary goal is to share the good news of God's love for all people. The goal, God's goal, is not membership but discipleship. Although we may be certain we will never face the sort of persecution described here, we can teach and learn, through role-playing and storytelling, to share our faith in simple, practical ways in ordinary conversation.

2. The gospel writer of Mark uses the Greek word *kai* ("and") ten times in the first eight verses of chapter 13. There is a clear sense of urgency reflected by this repetition, and by the presence of another of the writer's favorite words, *dei* ("it is necessary for"). What do we as twenty-first-century Christians feel urgent about? What can we learn from a first-century prophet about how to manage our sense of urgency? A discussion group following worship could provide an opportunity for worshipers to voice their urgencies in a safe, accepting environment.

3. These verses in Mark have been inappropriately strung together by some fundamentalist Christian writers with verses from the Hebrew prophets and from Revelation to teach an understanding of the future of our world that does not reflect God's love for God's creation. In *The Rapture Exposed: The Message of Hope in the Book of Revelation* (New York: Westview Press, 2004), Barbara Rossing offers a hopeful view of the future of God's world that stands in bright contrast to the dire predictions offered by other writers.

4. An understanding of how our anxiety and sense of urgency can influence our decision making and escalate into unnecessary difficulties in our relationships with self and others is humorously illustrated in a series of children's books by Laura Numeroff that includes *If You Give a Moose a Muffin* (Harper Collins, 1991).

Hymns for Worship
Gathering

Canticle of the Turning   ELW 723
Jesus shall reign   ELW 434, LBW 530

Hymn of the Day

Through the night of doubt and sorrow   ELW 327, LBW 355   *EBENEZER*
Bring Peace to Earth Again   ELW 700   *PACE MIO DIO*
By gracious powers   ELW 626   *TELOS*   WOV 736   *BERLIN*

Communion

My Lord, what a morning   ELW 438, WOV 627
Wait for the Lord   ELW 262

Sending

Lead on, O King eternal!   ELW 805, LBW 495
Jesus, still lead on   ELW 624, LBW 341

Additional Hymns and Songs

Once he came in blessing   LBW 312
O Day of God, draw nigh   HG 95
The Lord Is My Portion   BC 47
For he alone is worthy   TFF 284

Music for the Day
Psalmody and Acclamations

Miller, Aaron David. "Psalm 16" from *Psalm Settings for the Church Year*. AFP 9780800678562.

Psalter for Worship Year B, Evangelical Lutheran Worship Edition. AFP 9780806683839.

Schalk, Carl F. *Gospel Acclamations for Autumn*. AFP 9780800678623.

Choral

▫ Ferguson, John. "By Gracious Powers." SATB, opt assembly, org, fl. AFP 9780800675493.

Parker, Alice/Robert Shaw. "My God Is a Rock." SATB, bar solo. LG 51107.

▫ Roberts, William Bradley. "By Gracious Powers." U/SATB, org. AFP 9780800678210.

Sirett, Mark G. "Thou Shalt Know Him When He Comes." SATB. AFP 9780800655204. *The Augsburg Choirbook*. AFP 9780800656782.

Willan, Healey. "Lo, in the Time Appointed." SATB. OXF 9780193851788.

Children's Choir

Besig, Don. "Clap Your Hands and Sing Hallelujah!" UE. 2 pt, pno. SHW EA155.

Eggert, John. "Is There Anybody Here." LE. U, solo, opt desc, pno. AFP 9780800651992. OP

Hoiland, Melissa Ramseth. "Lord, Whose Love in Humble Service" from *Take a Hymn*. UE. U, autoharp/gtr, rec/fl. AFP 9786000106461. OP

Keyboard / Instrumental

Foote, Arthur/arr. Susan Marchant. "Cantilena in G, Opus 71." Org, vln. CPH 97-5735.

Hildebrand, Kevin. "Ebenezer" from *Easy Hymn Preludes for Organ*, set III. Org. CPH 97-7052U1.

Manz, Paul. "Ebenezer" from *Improvisations on Great Hymns of Faith*. Org. MSM 10-839.

Oquin, Wayne. "Ebenezer" from *All Things New*. Pno. CPH 97-7205U1.

Handbell

Hanna, Donna, arr. "If You But Trust in God to Guide You." 3-5 oct, L2. GIA G-6166.

McChesney, Kevin. "God of Grace and God of Glory." 3-5 oct, L3. CPH 97-6584.

Rogers, Sharon Elery, arr. "Once to Every Man and Nation." 3-5 oct, L3. JEF MJHS9206.

Praise Ensemble

■ Baloche, Paul. "Offering" from www.leadworship.com.

■ Hall, Mark/Bernie Herms. "East to West" from www.musicnotes.com. SWECS Music/Club Zoo Music/Sparrow Song/Peach Hill Songs.

■ Redman, Matt. "Better Is One Day" from www.praisecharts.com. Thankyou Music.

■ Scott, Kathryn. "Hungry" from *More Songs for Praise & Worship 3*. WM 080689452871.

Global

Burleigh, Glenn. "Study War No More." SATB, pno. Glenn Burleigh Music Workshop. www.glenmusik.com/bookorders.html.

Cambodian traditional/Bread for the Journey. "Now I Know" from *Pave the Way: Global Songs 3*. Cant, assembly. AFP 9780800676896.

Tuesday, November 17

Elizabeth of Hungary, renewer of society, 1231

This Hungarian princess gave large sums of money, including her dowry, for relief of the poor and sick. She founded hospitals, cared for orphans, and used the royal food supplies to feed the hungry. Though she had the support of her husband, her generosity and charity did not earn her friends within the royal court. At the death of her husband, she was driven out. She joined a Franciscan order and continued her charitable work, though she suffered abuse at the hands of her confessor and spiritual guide. Her lifetime of charity is particularly remarkable when one remembers that she died at the age of twenty-four. She founded two hospitals, and many more are named for her.

▫ denotes choral suggestions that relate to the hymn of the day.
■ denotes songs that are available on iTunes®.
316

November 22, 2009

Christ the King
Last Sunday after Pentecost — Lectionary 34

Even after Israel had experienced the vagaries of kings, they still longed for a true king to set things right. He would have the king's title of Anointed One (Messiah); he would be the "one like a human being" (Son of Man) given dominion in Daniel's vision. Jesus is given these titles, even though he is nothing like an earthly king. His authority comes from the truth to which he bears witness, and those who recognize the truth voluntarily listen to him. We look forward to the day he is given dominion, knowing his victory will be the nonviolent victory of love.

Prayer of the Day

Almighty and ever-living God, you anointed your beloved Son to be priest and sovereign forever. Grant that all the people of the earth, now divided by the power of sin, may be united by the glorious and gentle rule of Jesus Christ, our Savior and Lord, who lives and reigns with you and the Holy Spirit, one God, now and forever.

Gospel Acclamation

Alleluia. Blessed is the one who comes in the name ˡ of the Lord.* Blessed is the coming kingdom of our an- ˡ cestor David. *Alleluia.* (Mark 11:9)

Readings and Psalm

Daniel 7:9-10, 13-14

To the community for whom this passage was written, it seemed as though the oppression they were experiencing would never end. Daniel's message is: It shall end. The Ancient One who is judge will call all nations to account and will give dominion to "one like a human being," the Messiah.

Psalm 93

Ever since the world began, your throne has been established. (Ps. 93:2)

Revelation 1:4b-8

The book of Revelation begins by celebrating the Almighty God, who spans all of time. Similarly, Jesus is celebrated as the firstborn from the dead who rules over the world's rulers. He is the one whose return we eagerly await.

John 18:33-37

In John's gospel, the story of Jesus and Pilate presents two different ways of exercising power: through force or with love.

Semicontinuous reading and psalm

2 Samuel 23:1-7

This song attributed to David speaks of a promise: God will establish David's house (dynasty) forever. Indeed, David's dynasty endured over four hundred years, until the exile in 587 B.C. When there was no longer a Davidic king on the throne, this promise was understood to refer to the Messiah.

Psalm 132:1-12 [13-18]

Let your faithful people sing with joy. (Ps. 132:9)

Color   White *or* Green

CD-ROM Images

Icon Three: 1120-1126_Lect34_ChrKing_B
Icon Two: Proper29_Sun34_ChrKing_B
Icon: 091, 127

Prayers of Intercession

Gathered together with all the saints, let us pray for the church, the world, and all those in any need.
A brief silence.
God of all, unite your church throughout the world, that we might bear witness to the power of your redeeming word. God of mercy,
hear our prayer.

God of life, you have blessed us with land, air, and water to sustain us and all living creatures. Do not allow us to neglect and waste your creation, but make us careful guardians of all that you have made. God of mercy,
hear our prayer.

God of peace, our world is too often torn by bloodshed and violence. Grant wisdom and humility to all nations of the world, that we might know and do the things that make for peace. God of mercy,
hear our prayer.

God of mercy, look with kindness upon all who struggle on this day (*especially*). Grant hope and guidance to all who seek your grace. God of mercy,
hear our prayer.

God of truth, you shine your light into our hearts and our minds, revealing to us the glory of your Son. Strengthen us as we seek to follow you amid all the conflicting voices that surround us. God of mercy,
hear our prayer.

Here other intercessions may be offered.

God of eternal life, as you supported our ancestors in the faith, so guide and support us, that when our earthly journey is complete, we may rest eternally with you. God of mercy,
hear our prayer.

Into your hands, gracious God, we commend all for whom we pray, trusting in your mercy, through Christ, our Lord. **Amen.**

Ideas and Images for the Day

In John's unique account of Jesus before Pilate, he calls the crucified "King." John's Jesus makes clear that his kingdom is otherworldly, odd, paradoxical. He announces that for this he was born—to be king, to be crucified. On this last Sunday of the church year, John recalls for us how Jesus came into the world and how he will leave the world. Placing these verses in the context of those that precede and follow allows a full appreciation of how the character of Pilate is developed. Pilate's ambivalence and uncertainty reflect the struggles of all followers of Jesus across time and place. Struggles with faith, doubt, and denial are illustrated by Peter in the courtyard of the high priest, earlier in this chapter. As twenty-first-century Christians we face these same struggles. But faith without doubt would not require any faith at all. This may be the ultimate paradox for followers of Jesus, then and now.

1. Pilate's character is fully developed in John's gospel. A review of his responses and actions throughout John 18 reveals his full humanity and may help us understand our own in new ways. Paint a word portrait of this very human ruler that contrasts with the divine ruler he questions.

2. The movie *The Queen* (Miramax, 2006) provides a fictional glimpse of the life of a contemporary monarch. Although the accuracy of the account of Queen Elizabeth's response to the death of Princess Diana is debatable, the portrayal of the princess as saint and sinner, alternately loved and despised by the royal family, offers insight into the human condition and human relationships common to all people, monarch or commoner.

3. Isaac Watts, hymnwriter, died on November 25, 1748. As the commemoration approaches in the week following this Christ the King Sunday, the hymn text "Jesus shall reign" (ELW 434, LBW 530) may be used to describe the kingdom of God this monarch seeks to bring to the world. The hymn stanzas could be sung, interspersed throughout a sermon that reflects on Watts's images of the kingship of Jesus.

4. In a post-holocaust world, it is important to avoid emphasizing the anti-Semitism found in this typical Johannine text. An opportunity arises to teach people about Martin Luther's anti-Semitic writings. The Evangelical Lutheran Church in America condemned Luther's "Writings against the Jews" at its Churchwide Assembly in 1991. We are all, it seems, saint and sinner.

Hymns for Worship

Gathering

The head that once was crowned   ELW 432, LBW 173
Crown him with many crowns   ELW 855, LBW 170
Beautiful Savior   ELW 838, LBW 518

Hymn of the Day

O Christ, what can it mean for us   ELW 431
    ALL SAINTS NEW
Lo! he comes with clouds descending   ELW 435, LBW 27
    HELMSLEY
Jesus shall reign   ELW 434, LBW 530   DUKE STREET

Communion

What feast of love   ELW 487, WOV 701
O Christ the same   ELW 760, WOV 778
Jesus, remember me   ELW 616, WOV 740

Sending

Thine the amen   ELW 826, WOV 801
Lift high the cross   ELW 660, LBW 377

Additional Hymns and Songs

The King of glory   RWSB 105, W&P 136
Majesty   W&P 94
To God be the glory   TFF 272

Music for the Day
Psalmody and Acclamations

Anderson, Mark. "Psalm 93" from *Psalm Settings for the Church Year*. AFP 9780800678562.
Psalter for Worship Year B, Evangelical Lutheran Worship Edition. AFP 9780806683839.
Schalk, Carl F. *Gospel Acclamations for Autumn*. AFP 9780800678623.

Choral

Clausen, René. "All That Hath Life and Breath Praise Ye the Lord!" SATB, div, sop solo. MFS MF-223.
Manz, Paul. "E'en So, Lord Jesus, Quickly Come." SATB. MSM 50-0001.
Mechem, Kirke. "Blow Ye the Trumpet." SATB, kybd/orch. GS HL50481534.
Schalk, Carl F. "O Christ the Same." SATB, org. AFP 9780800678272.
Wood, Dale. "Jubilate Deo/Psalm 100" from *Augsburg Easy Choirbook*, vol. 1. 2 pt mxd, org. AFP 9780800676025. *The Augsburg Choirbook*. AFP 9780800656782.

Children's Choir

Leaf, Robert. "To the Glory of Our King." LE. U, pno/org. CG A173.
Nelson, Ronald A. "I Know Not How." UE. 2 pt, org/pno. Celebrations Unlimited 228.
Paradowski, John R. "Forever We Shall Sing." UE. U/2 pt, pno, opt fl, hand perc. CG A1096.

Keyboard / Instrumental

Albrecht, Mark. "Duke Street" from *Timeless Tunes for Piano and Solo Instrument*, vol. 2. Pno, C/B-flat inst. AFP 9780800659851.
Bender, Jan. "Duke Street" from *Five Festive Preludes on Easter Hymns*. Org. CPH 97-5495U1.
Helman, Michael. "Diademata" from *Trumpet Tunes on Hymns for Organ*. Org. AFP 9780800678753.
Osterland, Karl. "Helmsley" from *Augsburg Organ Library: Advent*. Org. AFP 9780800658953.
Stanley, John. "Solo I" from *John Stanley Complete Works for Solo Instrument and Keyboard*, Opus 1. Org/pno, fl/vln/ob, cello/bsn. CPH 97-5267.

Handbell

McFadden, Jane, arr. "Londonderry Air/O Christ the Same." 2-3 oct hb/hc, C/B-flat inst, L2. AFP 9780800656294.
Page, Anna Laura, arr. "Rejoice, the Lord Is King." 3-5 oct, L2. ALF 16460.
Roth, Karen, arr. "Jesus Shall Reign." 3-5 oct, L3. Ringing Word 8194.

Praise Ensemble

■ Furler, Peter. "It Is You" from More Songs for Praise & Worship 3. WM 080689318184.
■ Getty, Keith/Stuart Townend. "In Christ Alone" from www.praisecharts.com. Thankyou Music.
■ Smith, Martin. "I Could Sing of Your Love Forever" from *I Could Sing of Your Love Forever 2*. WT 0000809251.
■ Zschech, Darlene. "Free to Dance" from www.ccli.com. Hillsong Publishing/INT.

Global

Corbitt, Nathan J. "Mwamba ni Yesu/The Rock Is Jesus" from *Four African Hymns*. SATB, perc. CG A686.
Haugen, Marty. "Within the Reign of God." SATB, cant, assembly, kybd, gtr, C inst. GIA G-4963.

Monday, November 23

Clement, Bishop of Rome, c. 100

Clement was the third bishop of Rome and served at the end of the first century. He is best remembered for a letter he wrote to the Corinthian congregation, still having difficulty with divisions despite Paul's canonical letters. Clement's writing echoes Paul's. "Love . . . has no limits to its endurance, bears everything patiently. Love is neither servile nor arrogant. It does not provoke schisms or form cliques, but always acts in harmony with others." Clement's letter is also a witness to early understandings of church government and the way each office in the church works for the good of the whole.

Clement's letter reminds us that divisions within the church are a sad part of our history and that pastoral love for people must be present amid our differing views of authority, scripture, and ministry.

Miguel Agustín Pro, martyr, 1927

Miguel Agustín Pro grew up among oppression in Mexico, where revolutionaries accused the church of siding with the rich. He was a Jesuit priest who served during a time of intense anticlericalism, and therefore he carried out much of his ministry in private settings. He worked on behalf of the poor and homeless. Miguel and his two brothers were arrested, falsely accused of throwing a bomb at the car of a government official, and executed by a firing squad. Just before the guns fired, he yelled, "¡Viva Cristo Rey!" which means "Long live Christ the king!"

As we celebrate the abundance of Thanksgiving Day (in the U.S.) and are preparing for holiday shopping, make plans for work that can be done on behalf of the poor in the upcoming weeks. Raise questions of what long-term solutions may bridge the gap between rich and poor.

Tuesday, November 24

Justus Falckner, 1723; Jehu Jones, 1852; William Passavant, 1894; pastors in North America

A native of Saxony, Falckner was the son of a Lutheran pastor and, seeing the stresses his father endured, did not plan on becoming a pastor himself, though he studied theology in Halle. Instead, he joined with his brother in the real estate business in Pennsylvania. Through this business he became acquainted with a Swedish pastor in America, and finally he decided to become ordained. He served congregations in New York and New Jersey. Not only was he the first Lutheran ordained in North America, but he published a catechism that was the first Lutheran book published on the continent.

A native of Charleston, South Carolina, Jones was ordained by the New York Ministerium in 1832, and was the Lutheran church's first African American pastor. Upon returning to South Carolina he was arrested under a law prohibiting free blacks from reentering the state, so he was unable to join the group of Charlestonians he had been commissioned to accompany to Liberia. For nearly twenty years Jones carried out missionary work in Philadelphia in the face of many difficulties. There he led in the formation of the first African American Lutheran congregation, St. Paul's, and the construction of its church building.

William Passavant created and nurtured a new level of organized social ministry in western Pennsylvania. It was the seed of the system of social services that is now known as Lutheran Services in America. Passavant and his legacy sought to serve the poorest of the poor, providing shelter, medical, and living assistance.

Wednesday, November 25

Isaac Watts, hymnwriter, 1748

Isaac Watts was born in England to a family of nonconformists, people who thought the Church of England had not carried its reforms far enough. As a youth, Watts complained to his father about the quality of hymnody in the metrical psalter of his day. That was the start of his hymnwriting career. He wrote about six hundred hymns, many in a two-year period beginning when he was twenty years old. Some of Watts's hymns are based on psalms, a nonconformist tradition. When criticized for writing hymns not taken from scripture, he responded that if we can pray prayers that are not from scripture but written by us, then surely we can sing hymns that we have made up ourselves. Ten of Watts's hymn texts are in *Evangelical Lutheran Worship*.

November 26, 2009
Day of Thanksgiving (U.S.A.)

Today's readings reflect two of the strains that go into the celebration of a national day of thanksgiving: gratitude for abundant harvest (Joel) and civic prayer for a peaceable common life (1 Timothy). The core meaning of Thanksgiving for many of us—a home feast for extended family and friends—is not reflected in the readings; but it is reflected weekly in the church's meal of thanksgiving (eucharist). What we wish for both these thanksgiving meals is that they will go deeper than celebration of one another and our own blessings, to recognize in our true Host one who wants everyone brought to the table.

Prayer of the Day

Almighty God our Father, your generous goodness comes to us new every day. By the work of your Spirit lead us to acknowledge your goodness, give thanks for your benefits, and serve you in willing obedience, through Jesus Christ, our Savior and Lord.

Gospel Acclamation

Alleluia. God is able to provide you with every blessing [|] in abundance,* so that by always having enough of everything, you may share abundantly in ev- [|] 'ry good work. *Alleluia*. (2 Cor. 9:8)

Readings and Psalm

Joel 2:21-27

The prophet Joel understood that a locust plague that ravaged the land of Judah was God's judgment on the people, whom he then called to repentance. Today's reading points beyond the judgment to a time when the Lord will bless the land and cause it to produce food in abundance.

Psalm 126

The LORD has done great things for us, and we are glad indeed. (Ps. 126:3)

1 Timothy 2:1-7

Christians are encouraged to offer prayers and thanks for all people, including rulers (who were pagans rather than Christians). We offer such inclusive, far-reaching prayers because God desires to save all people.

Matthew 6:25-33

In the Sermon on the Mount, Jesus taught his disciples about the providence of God so that they would regard life with thanksgiving and trust rather than anxiety.

Color Green

CD-ROM Images

Icon Three: Thanksgiving
Icon Two: Thanksgiving01, Thanksgiving02
Icon: 208

Prayers of Intercession

Gathered together with all the saints, let us pray for the church, the world, and all those in any need.
A brief silence.
We give you thanks, O God, for the blessings of this church. Guide and strengthen all the leaders of our congregations throughout the world, that together we might bless the world with your love. God of mercy,
hear our prayer.
We give you thanks, O God, for your abundant blessings to us and for the bounty of the world's resources. Help us to exercise care in the use of natural resources and to share our plenty with those in need. God of mercy,
hear our prayer.
We give you thanks, O God, for the freedoms we enjoy. Guide us and all our leaders, that we may use our freedom and power to make the world a place of peace and prosperity for all. God of mercy,
hear our prayer.
We give you thanks, O God, for the gift of family, friends, and loved ones. Bless our gatherings in the days and weeks to come, that our homes might be places of peace and joy in a world of conflict and stress. God of mercy,
hear our prayer.
We give you thanks, O God, for the gift of healing, and we ask that you might use us all to bring comfort and peace to those who are ill (*especially*). God of mercy,
hear our prayer.

Here other intercessions may be offered.

We give you thanks, O God, for the saints of every time and place who now sing your praises in your eternal kingdom. Keep us faithful to the end of our journey. God of mercy, **hear our prayer.**

Into your hands, gracious God, we commend all for whom we pray, trusting in your mercy, through Christ, our Lord. **Amen.**

Ideas and Images for the Day

In God's world good things happen each and every day. Without seeking our permission, the rain pours down and waters the fields; the sun bathes the soil with warmth and causes the seeds to germinate and grow. It's a good world that God has created, and today we celebrate the Lord's handiwork by reflecting on just how blessed we truly are. Whether we are farmers rejoicing over a field of abundant crops or are counted among those who work in offices and shops, many of us have good reason to give thanks for all God has given. But what of those less fortunate? What of those who toil in vain? Does God care for them? Actually, God does. God's plan of caring is quite simple: those with much should give to those with less. But how willing are we to do our part? As scripture says, "The earth is the LORD's and all that is in it" (Ps. 24:1). The earth is a gift from God to all. It's a world, however, that is dependent upon cooperating with God in making true justice happen.

1. Demonstrate how serious your congregation is about becoming a vehicle for justice by parking a truck outside your church this week and expecting it to be filled with food for your local food shelf. Give your plan time to work by handing out grocery bags after worship for three or four weeks and making it clear you expect them to come back filled.

2. There are many people out there without any significant human contact. Some appear in our local newspapers as victims of crime, accidents, or tragic health issues. Send a card to them (you can probably get an address out of the phone book), letting them know that someone out there is thinking about them.

3. Turn your Thanksgiving Day into a day of decision by picking out a local, national, or international project and giving 1 percent of your income to that cause. The ELCA's Web site (www.elca.org) can give you ideas for causes you might consider.

4. Be a "buddy" to someone in your church who has some special need. Perhaps there is someone who is without transportation and could use a ride to the doctor. You could, perhaps, organize a job bank to address the needs of those who are unemployed and commit yourself to maintaining the bank for at least a year to give it time to establish itself.

Hymns for Worship
Gathering
For the beauty of the earth   ELW 879, LBW 561
We plow the fields and scatter   ELW 680/681, LBW 362
Come, ye thankful people, come   ELW 693, LBW 407

Hymn of the Day
For the fruit of all creation   ELW 679, WOV 760
AR HYD Y NOS   LBW 563   *SANTA BARBARA*
Praise and thanksgiving   ELW 689, LBW 409   *BUNESSAN*
Let all things now living   ELW 881, LBW 557
THE ASH GROVE

Communion
The numberless gifts of God's mercies   ELW 683
Bread of life, our host and meal   ELW 464
Now the silence   ELW 460, LBW 205

Sending
Now thank we all our God   ELW 839/840, LBW 533/534
How Great Thou Art   ELW 856, LBW 532
Praise to the Lord, the Almighty   ELW 858/859, LBW 543

Additional Hymns and Songs
Seek ye first the kingdom of God   WOV 783, W&P 122, TFF 149
Give thanks   W&P 41, TFF 292
Seek for the kingdom with all of your powers   HG 36

Music for the Day
Psalmody and Acclamations
Psalter for Worship Year B, Evangelical Lutheran Worship Edition. AFP 9780806683839.
Roberts, William Bradley. "Psalm 126" from *Psalm Settings for the Church Year*. AFP 9780800678562.
Schalk, Carl F. *Gospel Acclamations for Autumn*. AFP 9780800678623.

Choral
Bach, J. S. "Now Thank We All Our God" from *Bach for All Seasons*. SATB, kybd. AFP 9780800658540.
Copland, Aaron. "The Promise of Living." SATBB, 4 hands pno/orch. B&H M-051-45020-6.

Mozart, W. A. "Laudate Dominum." SATB, sop solo, kybd/orch. ECS 2280.

Patterson, Mark. "When in Our Music God Is Glorified." U, opt desc, pno, opt hb. AFP 9780800638108.

Rosewall, Michael. "Now Thank We All Our God." SB, kybd. AFP 9780800623852.

Children's Choir

Arenson, Carole Lea. "Now Thank We All Our God and O Loving God." LE. U, SATB, 2 kybd. AFP 9786000103248. OP

Patterson, Mark. "Lord, We Give Thanks." U, kybd. AFP 9780800678401.

Sleeth, Natalie. "For These Blessings" from *Sunday Songbook*. LE. U/2 pt, kybd. HIN HMB102.

Taylor, Terry D. "Come, Sing Your Thanks to the Lord." UE. U, pno, opt fl, maracas, claves. CG A1097.

Keyboard / Instrumental

Hassell, Michael. "Bunessan" from *Jazz Pastorale*. Pno. AFP 9780800658052.

Manz, Paul. "Ar hyd y nos" from *Three Hymn Improvisations*. Org. MSM 10-867.

Powell, Robert J. "Rustington" from *Organ Tunes from the British Isles*. Org. AFP 9780800678746.

Powell, Robert J. "The Ash Grove" from *Three for Thanksgiving*. Inst trio. CPH 97-5976.

Vivaldi, Antonio. "Allegro" from *Vivaldi for Instrument and Keyboard*. Org/pno, C inst. CPH 97-6283.

Handbell

Linker, Janet/Jane McFadden, arr. "Morning Has Broken." 3-5 oct, L2. AFP 9780800654320.

McChesney, Kevin, arr. "Now Thank We All Our God." 3-5 oct, L3. LOR 20/1034.

McChesney, Kevin, arr. "We Gather Together." 3 oct, L3. Lake State Publications 95040.

Praise Ensemble

■ Baloche, Paul/Don Moen. "Thank You Lord" from www.praisecharts.com. INT.

■ Cash, Ed/Jesse Reeves/Chris Tomlin. "How Great Is Our God" from *WT*. WT/Sixsteps Music/Alletrop Music.

■ Evans, Darrell. "Trading My Sorrows" from *WOW Worship Green Songbook*. INT 000768195567.

Lafferty, Karen. "Seek Ye First the Kingdom of God." WOV 783, W&P 122.

■ Paris, Twila. "We Bow Down" from *Best of the Best, The Other Songbook 2*. FEL 1891062034.

Smith, Henry. "Give Thanks." W&P 41.

Global

Botswanan traditional/Bread for the Journey. "Reamo Leboga/To God Our Thanks We Give" from *Global Songs 2*. SATB. AFP 9780800656744.

Haugen, Marty. "O Be Joyful in God" from *Two Simple Songs for Gathering*. SATB. GIA G-6937.

Haugen, Marty. "Thanks Be to God." SATB, children, kybd, gtr. GIA G-3994.

Sedio, Mark. "Be Thankful to God/Al Dios creador." U, opt desc, kybd. AFP 9780800658700.

■ denotes songs that are available on iTunes®.

Resources

* denotes new or newer print resource

∞ denotes electronic or Web resource

Lectionaries

* *Lectionary for Worship Year B.* Minneapolis: Augsburg Fortress, 2008. The Revised Common Lectionary. Includes first reading, psalm citation, second reading, and gospel for each Sunday and lesser festival. Each reading is "sense-lined" for clearer proclamation of the scriptural texts. New Revised Standard Version. Available in study (includes reader helps) and ritual editions.

Revised Common Lectionary Daily Readings. Consultation on Common Texts. Minneapolis: Fortress Press, 2005.

Readings for the Assembly (B). Gordon Lathrop and Gail Ramshaw, eds. Minneapolis: Augsburg Fortress, 1996. The Revised Common Lectionary. Emended NRSV with inclusive language.

Worship Books

* *Evangelical Lutheran Worship.* Minneapolis: Augsburg Fortress, 2006. Ten holy communion settings, more than 650 hymns, complete psalter, daily prayer resources, and more. Available in pew, leaders ritual, leaders desk, gift, pocket, and enlarged print editions.

Evangelical Lutheran Worship Accompaniment Edition: Liturgies. Minneapolis: Augsburg Fortress, 2006. Complete keyboard accompaniments for all ten holy communion settings and additional music within liturgies.

Evangelical Lutheran Worship Accompaniment Edition: Service Music and Hymns (2 vols). Minneapolis: Augsburg Fortress, 2006. Full accompaniments to all hymns and songs in the pew edition, #151–893. Simplified Keyboard and Guitar editions also available.

* *Evangelical Lutheran Worship Pastoral Care:* Readings, Prayers, and Occasional Services. Minneapolis: Augsburg Fortress, 2008. An essential tool for caregivers conducing the church's ministry of care outside the worshiping assembly.

Libro de Liturgia y Cántico. Minneapolis: Augsburg Fortress, 1998. A complete Spanish-language worship resource including liturgies and hymns, some with English translations. Leader edition (2001) with additional psalms and indexes.

Lutheran Book of Worship. Minneapolis: Augsburg Publishing House; Philadelphia: Board of Publication, Lutheran Church in America, 1978.

Occasional Services: A Companion to Lutheran Book of Worship. Minneapolis: Augsburg Publishing House; Philadelphia: Board of Publication, Lutheran Church in America, 1982.

Ritos Ocasionales. Minneapolis: Augsburg Fortress, 2000. Spanish language translation of rites from *Occasional Services.*

This Far by Faith: An African American Resource for Worship. Minneapolis: Augsburg Fortress, 1999. A supplement of worship orders, psalms, service music, and hymns representing African American traditions and developed by African American Lutherans.

With One Voice: A Lutheran Resource for Worship. Minneapolis: Augsburg Fortress, 1995. Pew, leader, and accompaniment editions; instrumental parts, organ accompaniment for the liturgy, cassette/CD (selections).

Worship Planning Tools, Indexes, Calendars

∞ *Evangelical Lutheran Worship* Liturgies CD-ROM. Minneapolis: Augsburg Fortress, 2006. Liturgical material from Pew Edition in editable text files; assembly singing lines provided as graphics. For use in desktop publishing.

∞ www.sundaysandseasons.com. A subscription-based online worship planning tool. Select and download content for worship folder preparation. Complements *Sundays and Seasons.*

Indexes to Evangelical Lutheran Worship. Minneapolis: Augsburg Fortress, 2007. Indexes the hymns and songs in *Evangelical Lutheran Worship.* Includes extensive lectionary, scripture, and topical indexes.

Choral Literature for Sundays and Seasons. Bradley Ellingboe, ed. Minneapolis: Augsburg Fortress, 2004. A comprehensive listing of time-tested choral works, indexed to the lessons for each Sunday and principal festival of the three-year lectionary. Includes information on voicing, instrumentation, composers, and publishers.

Choosing Contemporary Music: Seasonal, Topical, Lectionary Indexes. Minneapolis: Augsburg Fortress, 2000. Provides references to multiple collections of contemporary praise and liturgical songs. Includes extensive scripture and topic indexes.

* ∞ *Words for Worship: 2009, Year B.* Minneapolis: Augsburg Fortress, 2008. CD-ROM includes lectionary readings, worship texts, seasonal rites, and more for use in worship folders and other self-published materials.

* *Calendar of Word and Season 2009: Liturgical Wall Calendar.* Minneapolis: Augsburg Fortress, 2008. Features art from *Sundays and Seasons* by Julie Lonneman. Date blocks identify seasonal or festival color. Includes Revised Common Lectionary readings for Sundays and festivals. A reference tool for home, sacristy, office.

* *Church Year Calendar 2009.* Minneapolis: Augsburg Fortress, 2008. A one-sheet calendar of lectionary citations and liturgical colors for each Sunday and festival of the liturgical year. Appropriate for bulk purchase and distribution.

* *Worship Planning Calendar 2009.* Minneapolis: Augsburg Fortress, 2008. A two-page per week calendar helpful for worship planners, with space to record appointments and notes for each day. Specially designed to complement *Sundays and Seasons.* Features daily readings from the daily lectionary developed by the Consultation on Common Texts.

Leading Worship

* Brugh, Lorraine, and Gordon Lathrop. *The Sunday Assembly.* Minneapolis: Augsburg Fortress, 2008. A resource to guide leaders in their understanding and interpretation of the *Evangelical Lutheran Worship* resources. The first of three volumes in a series of pastoral guides, Using *Evangelical Lutheran Worship*, focusing on holy communion.

* Bushkofsky, Dennis, and Craig Satterlee. *The Christian Life: Baptism and Life Passages.* Minneapolis: Augsburg Fortress, 2008. A resource to guide leaders in their understanding and interpretation of the *Evangelical Lutheran Worship* resources. The second of three volumes in a series of pastoral guides, Using *Evangelical Lutheran Worship*, containing detailed information on holy baptism and its related rites, as well as marriage, healing, and funeral.

* Ramshaw, Gail, and Mons Teig. *Keeping Time: The Church's Years.* Minneapolis: Augsburg Fortress, 2008. A resource to guide leaders in their understanding and interpretation of the *Evangelical Lutheran Worship* resources. The third of three volumes in a series of pastoral guides, Using *Evangelical Lutheran Worship*, containing detailed information on Sundays, seasons, festivals, and commemorations, as well as daily prayer.

Adams, William Seth. *Shaped by Images: One Who Presides.* New York: Church Hymnal Corporation, 1995. An excellent review of the ministry of presiding at worship.

Huck, Gabe, and Gerald T. Chinchar. *Liturgy with Style and Grace,* 3rd. ed. Chicago: Liturgy Training Publications, 1998. The first three chapters offer a practical, well-written overview of the purpose of worship, the elements of worship, and liturgical leadership.

Huffman, Walter C. *Prayer of the Faithful: Understanding and Creatively Leading Corporate Intercessory Prayer,* rev. ed. Minneapolis: Augsburg Fortress, 1992. A helpful treatment of communal prayer, the Lord's Prayer, and the prayers of the people.

Worship Handbook Series. Minneapolis: Augsburg Fortress, 2001–. Brief guides to liturgical ministries and celebrations for those who lead and participate in worship.
Acolytes and Servers. Gerald Spice.
Assisting Ministers and Readers. Gerald Spice.
Christian Burial. Karen Bockelman.
Marriage. Karen Bockelman.
Ministers of Communion from the Assembly. Donald Luther.
Musicians in the Assembly. Robert Buckley Farlee.
Preparing the Assembly's Worship. Craig Mueller.
Presiding in the Assembly. Craig Satterlee.
Sponsors and Baptism. Elaine Ramshaw.
The Pastor: A Spirituality. Gordon Lathrop
Ushers and Greeters. Gerald Spice.
Welcome to Worship. Karen Bockelman.

Choirbooks

Augsburg Choirbook, The. Minneapolis: Augsburg Fortress, 1998. Kenneth Jennings, ed. Sixty-seven anthems primarily from twentieth-century North American composers.

* *Augsburg Choirbook for Advent, Christmas, and Epiphany.* Minneapolis: Augsburg Fortress, 2007. Thirty-three anthems, mostly easy-to-medium difficulty, for the Christmas cycle.

Augsburg Choirbook for Men. Minneapolis: Augsburg Fortress, 2004. Fourteen anthems for two- to four-part male chorus.

* *Augsburg Choirbook for Women.* Minneapolis: Augsburg Fortress, 2006. Diverse selections for choirs of all ages and abilities from high school through adult.

Augsburg Easy Choirbook, vol. 1. Minneapolis: Augsburg Fortress, 2003. Fourteen unison and two-part mixed anthems for the church year.

Augsburg Easy Choirbook, vol. 2. Minneapolis: Augsburg Fortress, 2005. Sixteen anthems for the church year; accessible, quality music for the smaller, less-experienced choir.

Bach for All Seasons. Minneapolis: Augsburg Fortress, 1999. Richard Erickson and Mark Bighley, eds. Offers movements from cantatas and oratorios presented with carefully reconstructed keyboard parts and fresh English texts. Instrumental parts available.

Chantry Choirbook. Minneapolis: Augsburg Fortress, 2000. Choral masterworks of European composers spanning five centuries, many with new English translations, and indexed for use in the liturgical assembly throughout the year.

GladSong Choirbook. Minneapolis: Augsburg Fortress, 2005. Eleven titles for fall, Advent, and Christmas use, plus Reformation, Thanksgiving, All Saints, Christ the King, Epiphany, and communion.

* *Hear Our Prayer.* Minneapolis: Augsburg Fortress, 2007. A collection of sung prayer responses to be used between the petitions of the prayers of intercession or as a call or closing to prayer.

Let the Peoples Sing, vol. 1: Sacred Choral Music from the Caribbean. Minneapolis: Augsburg Fortress, 2002. Marian Dolan, ed. Nine texts and tunes.

Let the Peoples Sing, vol. 2: Sacred Choral Music of the Baltics. Minneapolis: Augsburg Fortress, 2003. Marian Dolan, ed. Twelve choral pieces from Estonia, Latvia, and Lithuania.

Let the Peoples Sing, vol. 3: An International Christmas. Minneapolis: Augsburg Fortress, 2005. Marian Dolan, ed. A collection of Advent, Christmas, and Epiphany choral music representing countries as diverse as India, Korea, Palestine, Venezuela, and Sweden.

* *Wade in the Water: Easy Choral Music for All Ages.* Minneapolis: Augsburg Fortress, 2007. A collection of two- and three-part choral music for the less-experienced singer.

Hymn and Song Collections

As Sunshine to a Garden: Hymns and Songs. Rusty Edwards. Minneapolis: Augsburg Fortress, 1999. Forty-six collected hymns from the author of "We all are one in mission."

Bread of Life: Mass and Songs for the Assembly. Minneapolis: Augsburg Fortress, 2000. Jeremy Young's complete eucharistic music based on *With One Voice* Setting 5 and twelve of his worship songs.

Dancing at the Harvest: Songs by Ray Makeever. Minneapolis: Augsburg Fortress, 1997. More than 100 songs and service music items.

Earth and All Stars: Hymns and Songs for Young and Old. Herbert F. Brokering. Minneapolis: Augsburg Fortress, 2003. A collection of hymn texts by the popular writer.

Justice Like a Base of Stone. Bret Hesla. Minneapolis: Augsburg Fortress, 2006. A new collection of peace and justice songs in a variety of styles, easily taught to the congregation. Also audio CD.

O Blessed Spring: Hymns of Susan Palo Cherwien. Minneapolis: Augsburg Fortress, 1997. New hymn texts set to both new and familiar hymn tunes.

Pave the Way: Global Songs 3. Bread for the Journey. Minneapolis: Augsburg Fortress, 2004. Eighteen songs from around the world, with performance notes.

Worship & Praise. Minneapolis: Augsburg Fortress, 1999. A collection of songs in various contemporary and popular styles, with helps for using them in Lutheran worship.

Psalm Collections

* ∞ *Psalter for Worship Year B,* Evangelical Lutheran Worship Edition. Minneapolis: Augsburg Fortress, 2008. Settings of psalm antiphons by various composers with *Evangelical Lutheran Worship* psalm tones. Coordinate with *Celebrate* and *Today's Readings* inserts. Revised Common Lectionary. Includes a CD-ROM with psalm texts, refrains, and tones.

* ∞ *Psalm Settings for the Church Year.* Mark Mummert, ed. Minneapolis: Augsburg Fortress, 2008. A new collection of psalm settings in a wide variety of styles and structures. Contains all psalms used in the Revised Common Lectionary.

* ∞ Bruxvoort Colligan, Richard. *The Psalm Project: Sharing the Road, Songs for Lent.* Minneapolis: Augsburg Fortress, 2007. Fifteen comtemporary worship songs that bring the Psalms to life. Songbook and audio CD.

Anglican Chant Psalter, The. Alec Wyton, ed. New York: Church Hymnal Corporation, 1987.

Daw, Carl P., and Kevin R. Hackett. *A Hymn Tune Psalter.* New York: Church Publishing, 1999.

Grail Gelineau Psalter, The. Chicago: GIA Publications, Inc., 1972. 150 psalms and eighteen canticles.

Guimont, Michel. *Lectionary Psalms.* Chicago: GIA Publications, Inc., 1998. Responsorial psalm settings for the three-year Roman Catholic lectionary.

Plainsong Psalter, The. James Litton, ed. New York: Church Hymnal Corporation, 1988.

Portland Psalter, The. Robert A. Hawthorne. 2 vols. New York: Church Publishing. Book One contains settings for RCL psalms; Book Two contains settings for lesser festivals and the Easter Vigil.

Psalter, The. International Commission on English in the Liturgy (ICEL). Chicago: Liturgy Training Publications, 1995.

Psalter: Psalms and Canticles for Singing, The. Louisville, KY: Westminster John Knox Press, 1993. Various composers.

St. Martin's Psalter, Year B. Thomas Pavlechko, arr. Hopkinsville, KY: St. James Music Press, 2005. Revised Common Lectionary. Matches refrains with hymn-based psalm tones.

Selah Psalter, The. Richard Leach and David P. Schaap, eds. Kingston, NY: Selah Publishing Co., 2001. Sixty-six psalms in a variety of styles.

Preparing Music for Worship

Cherwien, David. *Let the People Sing! A Keyboardist's Creative and Practical Guide to Engaging God's People in Meaningful Song.* St. Louis: Concordia Publishing House, 1997. Emphasis on the organ.

* ∞ *Evangelical Lutheran Worship* Liturgies Audio CD, vol. 1. Minneapolis: Augsburg Fortress, 2006. Complete recordings of Holy Communion Settings One, Two, and Eight.

* ∞ *Evangelical Lutheran Worship* Liturgies Audio CD, vol. 2. Minneapolis: Augsburg Fortress, 2006. Complete recordings of Holy Communion Settings Five, Six, and Seven.

* ∞ *Evangelical Lutheran Worship* Hymns Audio CD, vols. 1 and 2. Minneapolis: Augsburg Fortress, 2006, 2007. Recordings of four dozen hymns and songs from *Evangelical Lutheran Worship,* both new and familiar. Performed by choirs from St. Olaf and Lenoir Rhyne colleges.

* *Evangelical Lutheran Worship* Simplified Keyboard Accompaniment Edition: Service Music and Hymns. Minneapolis: Augsburg Fortress, 2007.

* *Evangelical Lutheran Worship* Guitar Accompaniment Edition (2 vols). Minneapolis: Augsburg Fortress, 2007. "Lead sheet"-style accompaniments for every piece in the service music section and every hymn in the pew edition.

Farlee, Robert Buckley, gen. ed. *Leading the Church's Song.* Minneapolis: Augsburg Fortress, 1998. Articles by various contributors, with musical examples and audio CD, giving guidance on the interpretation and leadership of various genres of congregational song.

∞ *Favorite Hymns Accompanied.* John Ferguson, organist. Minneapolis: Augsburg Fortress, 2005. A 2-CD set of 52 hymns from all seasons of the year, most widely known, played without singing.

Handbells in the Liturgy: A Practical Guide for the Use of Handbells in Liturgical Worship Traditions. St. Louis: Concordia Publishing House, 1996.

Haugen, Marty. *Instrumentation and the Liturgical Ensemble.* Chicago: GIA Publications, Inc., 1991.

* Highben, Zebulon M., and Kristina M. Langlois, eds. *With a Voice of Singing: Essays on Children, Choirs, and Music in the Church.* Minneapolis: Kirk House Publishers, 2007.

Hopson, Hal H. *The Creative Use of Handbells in Worship; The Creative Use of Choir in Worship; The Creative Use of Instruments in Worship; The Creative Use of Descants in Worship; The Creative Use of Organ in Worship.* Carol Stream, IL: Hope Publishing Co.

* *Introductions and Alternate Accompaniments* to hymns and songs in *Evangelical Lutheran Worship.* Minneapolis: Augsburg Fortress, 2007–. Two 10-volume series, one for organ and one for piano, covering every *Evangelical Lutheran Worship* hymn and song. Various composers.

Let It Rip! at the Piano (vol. 1 & 2) and *Pull Out the Stops* (vol. 1 & 2). Minneapolis: Augsburg Fortress, 2000–2005. Collections for piano and organ respectively, each containing introductions and varied musical accompaniments by various composers for more than 100 widely used hymns and songs. Emphasis on current musical styles including blues, gospel, new age, jazz, and rolling contemporary.

* *Musicians Guide to Evangelical Lutheran Worship.* Minneapolis: Augsburg Fortress, 2007. An introduction to the music, including specific suggestions for each liturgical music item, service music item, and hymn.

* *Piano Plus: Hymns for Piano and Treble Instrument, Advent/Christmas.* Minneapolis: Augsburg Fortress, 2006. Fifty-one arrangements by various composers that range in difficulty from simple cradle songs to jazz, and span numerous world cultures and several centuries.

Weidler, Scott, and Dori Collins. *Sound Decisions.* Chicago: Evangelical Lutheran Church in America, 1997. Theological principles for the evaluation of contemporary worship music.

Westermeyer, Paul. *The Church Musician,* rev. ed. Minneapolis: Augsburg Fortress, 1997. Foundational introduction to the role and task of the church musician as the leader of the people's song.

————. *Te Deum: The Church and Music.* Minneapolis: Fortress Press, 1998. A historical and theological introduction to the music of the church.

Wold, Wayne. *Preaching to the Choir: The Care and Nurture of the Church Choir.* Minneapolis: Augsburg Fortress, 2003. Practical helps for the choir director.

————. *Tune My Heart to Sing.* Minneapolis: Augsburg Fortress, 1997. Devotions for choirs based on the lectionary.

Visual and Media Ministry Resources

* ∞ *Icon Three: Visual Images for Every Sunday.* Minneapolis: Augsburg Fortress, 2007. 260 images by artist Julie Lonneman presented in both black-and-white and colorized versions on CD-ROM. Suitable for use in self-published materials or for projection using presentation software.

∞ *Icon Two for Projection.* Minneapolis: Augsburg Fortress, 2005. 250 colorized images based on the Revised Common Lectionary by liturgical artist Lucinda Naylor suitable for projection using presentation software.

∞ *Icon Two: Visual Images for Every Sunday.* Minneapolis: Augsburg Fortress, 2004. 250 images by liturgical artist Lucinda Naylor based on the church year and lectionary gospel readings for use in self-published materials.

∞ Graphics for Worship 2.0. Minneapolis: Augsburg Fortress. A collection of 358 graphics by Tanja Butler, Steve Erspamer, Jane Pitz, Nicholas Markell, Barbara Zuber, and others.

Crowley, Eileen D. *A Moving Word: Media Art in Worship.* Minneapolis: Augsburg Fortress, 2006. An exploration of how visual elements in worship can enhance the assembly's understanding of the gospel.

∞ Jensen, Richard. *Envisioning the Word: The Use of Visual Images in Preaching, with CD-ROM.* Minneapolis: Fortress Press, 2005. A discussion of how vital, if controversial, image making has always been in Christian tradition, followed by a demonstration of how preaching with images is both profoundly traditional and necessary to contemporary proclamation.

* ∞ Wilson, Kent V. *For the Sake of the Gospel: A Media Ministry Primer* (with DVD). Minneapolis: Augsburg Fortress, 2006. A case for the *why*, *how*, and *what* of media ministry with practical helps and examples.

∞ Wilson, Len, and Jason Moore. *Digital Storytellers: The Art of Communicating the Gospel in Worship (with DVD).* Nashville, Abingdon Press, 2002. Representing the word of God as image and art in a digital culture.

Preparing Environment and Art

Chinn, Nancy. *Spaces for Spirit: Adorning the Church.* Chicago: Liturgy Training Publications, 1998. Imaginative thinking about ways to treat visual elements in the worship space.

Christopherson, D. Foy. *A Place of Encounter: Renewing Worship Spaces.* Minneapolis: Augsburg Fortress, 2004. An exploration of principles for planning and renewing worship spaces.

Clothed in Glory: Vesting the Church. David Philippart, ed. Chicago: Liturgy Training Publications, 1997. Photos and essays about liturgical paraments and vestments.

Giles, Richard. *Re-Pitching the Tent: Reordering the Church Building for Worship and Mission.* Collegeville, MN: The Liturgical Press, 1999.

Huffman, Walter C., S. Anita Stauffer, and Ralph R. Van Loon. *Where We Worship.* Minneapolis: Augsburg Publishing House, 1987. Written by three Lutheran worship leaders, this volume sets forth the central principles for understanding and organizing space for worship. Study book and leader guide.

Mazar, Peter. *To Crown the Year: Decorating the Church through the Seasons.* Chicago: Liturgy Training Publications, 1995. A contemporary guide for decorating the worship space throughout the seasons of the year.

Stauffer, S. Anita. *Altar Guild and Sacristy Handbook.* Minneapolis: Augsburg Fortress, 2000. Revised and expanded edition of this classic on preparing the table and the worship environment.

Seasons and Liturgical Year

* *Keeping Time: The Church's Years.* Minneapolis: Augsburg Fortress, 2008. A resource to guide leaders in their understanding and interpretation of the *Evangelical Lutheran Worship* resources. The third of three volumes in a series of pastoral guides, Using *Evangelical Lutheran Worship*, containing detailed information on Sundays, seasons, festivals, and commemorations, as well as daily prayer.

Prayer in the Paschal Triduum, rev. ed. Chicago: Liturgy Training Publications, 1992. For worship committees, an excellent introduction to worship during the Three Days.

Hynes, Mary Ellen. *Companion to the Calendar.* Chicago: Liturgy Training Publications, 1993. An excellent overview of the seasons, festivals and lesser festivals, and many commemorations Written from an ecumenical/Roman Catholic perspective, including commemorations unique to the Lutheran calendar.

Ramshaw, Gail. *The Three-Day Feast: Maundy Thursday, Good Friday, Easter.* Minneapolis: Augsburg Fortress, 2004. A little history and a lot of suggestions about how these services can enrich the assembly's worship life.

Children

* Kids Celebrate Worship Series. Minneapolis: Augsburg Fortress, 2006–. A series of seasonal and topical 8-page booklets that introduce children and their families to worship and *Evangelical Lutheran Worship.* Pre-reader and young reader versions. Includes ideas and helps for parents, pastors, educators, and children's choir directors. For use in worship, Sunday school, or home.

Our Worship Book (2006). A kid-friendly introduction to *Evangelical Lutheran Worship.*

Sunday Worship (2006). Focuses on the gathering, word, meal, sending pattern of Holy Communion.

Advent & Christmas (2006). Introduction to the Advent-Christmas season with activities.

Lent & Easter (2006). Introduction to the seasons of Lent and Easter with activities.

Three Amazing Days (2006). Introduction to Maundy Thursday, Good Friday, and the Easter Vigil.

* *Holy Communion* (2007). Introduction to the sacrament of Holy Communion.

* *Baptism* (2007). Introduction to the sacrament of Holy Baptism and baptismal living.

* *Our Prayers* (2007). Focuses on how and when the assembly prays in worship, and prayer in the home.

* *The Bible* (2007). Introduction to the ways in which scripture is used in worship.

∞ *Kids Celebrate: Worship Bulletins for Children, Lectionary Year B.* Minneapolis: Augsburg Fortress, 2002. A full year's worth of reproducible bulletins that engage children in the weekly gathering of God's people. Includes CD-ROM.

LifeSongs (children's songbook, leader book, and audio CDs). Minneapolis: Augsburg Fortress, 1999. A well-rounded selection of age-appropriate songs, hymns, and liturgical music that builds a foundation for a lifetime of singing the faith.

Patterson, Mark. *Young ChildrenSing, ChildrenSing,* and *ChildrenSing with Instruments.* Minneapolis: Augsburg Fortress, 2004–2006. Short anthems for young singers.

Ramshaw, Gail. *Every Day and Sunday, Too.* Minneapolis: Augsburg Fortress, 1996. An illustrated book for parents and children. Daily life is related to the central actions of the liturgy.

———. *Sunday Morning.* Chicago: Liturgy Training Publications, 1993. A book for children and adults on the primary words of Sunday worship.

∞ Vandermeer, Harriet; illustrated by Elizabeth Steele Halstead. *Rings, Kings, and Butterflies: Lessons on Christian Symbols for Children (with CD-ROM).* Minneapolis: Augsburg Fortress, 2006. An illustrated explanation of Christian seasons and symbols. Ideas for children's messages, and activities for teachers and parents.

Daily Prayer Resources

Book of Common Worship: Daily Prayer. Louisville, KY: Westminster John Knox Press, 1993. Presbyterian.

* *Bread for the Day 2009: Daily Bible Readings and Prayers.* Minneapolis: Augsburg Fortress, 2009. Daily scripture texts for individual or group prayer based on the daily lectionary in *Evangelical Lutheran Worship.*

Cherwien, David. *Stay with Us, Lord: Liturgies for Evening.* Minneapolis: Augsburg Fortress, 2001. Settings for Evening Prayer and Holy Communion, available in full music and congregational editions.

Haugen, Marty. *Holden Evening Prayer.* Chicago: GIA Publications, Inc., 1990.

Haugen, Marty and Susan Briehl. *Unfailing Light.* Chicago: GIA Publications, Inc., 2004.

Makeever, Ray. *Joyous Light Evening Prayer.* Minneapolis: Augsburg Fortress, 2000.

Revised Common Lectionary Daily Readings. Consultation on Common Texts. Minneapolis: Fortress Press, 2005.

Ramshaw, Gail. *Between Sundays: Daily Bible Readings Based on the Revised Common Lectionary.* Minneapolis: Augsburg Fortress, 1997. Readings, indexes, and other helps for daily prayer.

Worship Studies, series

* Worship Matters Series. Minneapolis: Augsburg Fortress, 2004–. The series explores worship-related topics growing out of the ELCA's Renewing Worship initiative.

Christopherson, D. Foy. *A Place of Encounter: Renewing Worship Spaces* (2004).

Crowley, Eileen D. *A Moving Word: Media Art in Worship* (2006).

Dahill, Lisa. *Truly Present: Practicing Prayer in the Liturgy* (2005).

Lathrop, Gordon. *Central Things: Worship in Word and Sacrament* (2005).

Quivik, Melinda. *A Christian Funeral: Witness to the Resurrection* (2005).

Ramshaw, Gail. *A Three-Year Banquet: The Lectionary for the Assembly* (2004).

———. *The Three-Day Feast: Maundy Thursday, Good Friday, Easter* (2004).

Rimbo, Robert A. *Why Worship Matters* (2004). Foreword by Mark S. Hanson.

Torvend, Samuel. *Daily Bread, Holy Meal: Opening the Gifts of Holy Communion* (2004).

* Wengert, Timothy, ed. *Centripetal Worship: The Evangelical Heart of Lutheran Worship* (2007). With contributions from Mark Mummert, Dirk Lange, Melinda Quivik, and Russell Mitman.

Ylvisaker, John. *What Song Shall We Sing?* (2005).

Welcome to Christ. Minneapolis: Augsburg Fortress, 1997–2003. A Lutheran approach to incorporating adult catechumens.

A Lutheran Catechetical Guide.

A Lutheran Introduction to the Catechumenate.

Lutheran Rites for the Catechumenate.

Sponsors Guide.

Worship Studies, individual titles

* *The Sunday Assembly.* Minneapolis: Augsburg Fortress, 2007. The first of three volumes in a series of pastoral guides to *Evangelical Lutheran Worship.*

* *The Christian Life: Baptism and Life Passages.* Minneapolis: Augsburg Fortress, 2008. The second of three volumes in a series of pastoral guides, Using *Evangelical Lutheran Worship,* containing detailed information on Holy Baptism and its related rites, as well as marriage, healing, and funeral.

Gathered and Sent: An Introduction to Worship. Participant book by Karen Bockelman. Leader guide by Roger Prehn. Minneapolis: Augsburg Fortress, 1999. Basic worship study course for inquirers and general adult instruction in congregations.

Inside Out: Worship in an Age of Mission. Thomas Schattauer, gen. ed. Minneapolis: Fortress Press, 1999. Lutheran seminary teachers address the mission of the church as it pertains to various aspects of worship.

Lathrop, Gordon. *Holy Ground: A Liturgical Cosmology.* Minneapolis: Fortress Press, 2003. Explores how the symbols and interactions of the liturgy lead to a new understanding and experience of the world.

———. *Holy People: A Liturgical Ecclesiology.* Minneapolis: Fortress Press, 1999. The concept of "church" is defined using the activities of worship.

———. *Holy Things: A Liturgical Theology.* Minneapolis: Fortress Press, 1998. A call for worship leaders to discern what is central in the liturgy and to lift those up through liturgical reform.

Senn, Frank. *Christian Liturgy: Catholic and Evangelical.* Minneapolis: Fortress Press, 1997. A comprehensive historical introduction to the liturgy of the Western church with particular emphasis on Lutheran traditions.

* ———. *The People's Work: A Social History of the Liturgy.* Minneapolis: Fortress Press, 2006. The first book to document the full history of ordinary Christians' liturgical expression.

Use of the Means of Grace: A Statement on the Practice of Word and Sacrament, The. Chicago: Evangelical Lutheran Church in America, 1997. Also available in Spanish and Mandarin versions.

What Do You Seek? Welcoming the Adult Inquirer. Minneapolis: Augsburg Fortress, 2000. An introduction to a congregational process for welcoming Christians through affirmation of their baptism.

Web Sites

∞ www.alcm.org. Association of Lutheran Church Musicians. Links to conferences and resources available through this pan-Lutheran musicians' organization. Also a bulletin board and placement service.

∞ www.elca.org/worship. The worship Web site of the Evangelical Lutheran Church in America. Contains links to articles and essays on a variety of worship-related topics. Includes a section on frequently asked questions about church year, language, lectionary, liturgy, worship planning, worship space, and many other topics. Also an online Worship News newsletter.

∞ www.newproclamation.com An online sermon preparation resource that combines in-depth exegesis with homiletic advice from practicing preachers.

∞ www.sundaysandseasons.com. A subscription-based online worship planning tool. Select and download content for worship folder preparation. Complements *Sundays and Seasons.*

∞ www.worship.ca. Lift Up Your Hearts: The worship and spirituality site of the Evangelical Lutheran Church in Canada. Contains a variety of resources and news about events related to Lutheran worship.

Preaching Resources

Brueggemann, Walter, et al. *Texts for Preaching: A Lectionary Commentary Based on the NRSV.* Cycles A, B, C. Louisville, KY: Westminster John Knox Press, 1993–95.

Craddock, Fred, et al. *Preaching through the Christian Year.* Three volumes for Cycles A, B, C. Valley Forge, PA: Trinity Press International, 1992, 1993. In three volumes, various authors comment on the Sunday readings and psalms as well as various festival readings.

Hedahl, Susan K. *Who Do You Say that I Am? 21st Century Preaching.* Minneapolis: Augsburg Fortress, 2003. An exploration of Lutheran preaching. A Lutheran Voices title.

Homily Service: An Ecumenical Resource for Sharing the Word. Silver Spring, MD: The Liturgical Conference. A quarterly/seasonal publication with commentary on the Sunday readings, ideas, and illustrations for preaching. customerservice@taylorandfrancis.com. 800/354-1420, ext. 216.

* *New Proclamation, Year B.* Minneapolis: Augsburg Fortress, 2008–2009. Various authors. A sound and useful series of commentaries on year B readings. In two volumes, Advent–Holy Week and Easter–Christ the King. www.newproclamation.com.

Ramshaw, Gail. *Treasures Old and New: Images in the Lectionary.* Minneapolis: Fortress Press, 2002. A creative unfolding of forty images drawn from the lectionary readings.

∞ Sloyan, Gerard. *Preaching from the Lectionary: An Exegetical Commentary with CD-ROM.* Minneapolis: Fortress Press, 2003. Exegetical analysis of each text from the three-year Revised Common Lectionary.

Stiller, Brian. *Preaching Parables to Postmoderns.* Minneapolis: Fortress Press, 2005. An introduction to postmodern sensibilities and how it informs preaching the parables.

∞ www.homileticsonline.com. An online sermon preparation resource including illustrations and visuals.

Periodicals

Assembly. Notre Dame Center for Pastoral Liturgy. Chicago: Liturgy Training Publications. Published six times a year. Each issue examines a particular aspect of worship. 800/933-1800.

Catechumenate: A Journal of Christian Initiation. Chicago: Liturgy Training Publications. Published six times a year with articles on congregational preparation of older children and adults for the celebration of baptism and eucharist. 800/933-1800.

CrossAccent. Journal of the Association of Lutheran Church Musicians. Publication for church musicians and worship leaders in North America. 800/624-ALCM.

Faith & Form. Journal of the Interfaith Forum on Religion, Art and Architecture. www.faithandform.com.

Liturgy. Quarterly journal of The Liturgical Conference. Each issue explores a worship-related issue from an ecumenical perspective. customerservice@taylorandfrancis.com. 800/354-1420, ext. 216.

Pastoral Liturgy. Published six times a year by Liturgy Training Publications. A liturgy magazine for the whole parish. 800/933-1800.

Worship. Collegeville, MN: The Order of St. Benedict, published through The Liturgical Press six times a year. One of the primary journals of liturgical renewal among the churches. 800/858-5450.

Key to Music Publishers

ABP	Abingdon	CC	Changing Church/	HOP	Hope	NOV	Novello (Shawnee)
AFP	Augsburg Fortress		Prince of Peace	HWG	H. W. Gray (Warner)	OCP	Oregon Catholic
AG	Agape (Hope)	CG	Choristers Guild	INT	Integrity (Word)		Press
ALF	Alfred		(Lorenz)	JEF	Jeffers	OXF	Oxford University
AMC	Arista	CPH	Concordia	KJO	Kjos		Press
AMSI	Arts Masters Studio	DUR	Durand (Presser)	KV	Kevin Mayhew	PRE	Presser
	Inc. (Lorenz)	EAR	EarthSongs	LAK	Lake State	RR	Red River Music
AUR	Aureole	ECS	E. C. Schirmer	LG	Lawson Gould	SEL	Selah
B&H	Boosey & Hawkes	FEL	Fellowship Ministries		(Hal Leonard)	SHW	Shawnee
BAR	Bärenreiter	FLA	Flammer (Shawnee)	LOR	Lorenz	SMP	Sacred Music Press
BBM	Brentwood-Benson	GAL	Galaxy	LP	The Liturgical Press		(Lorenz)
	Music	GIA	GIA Publications	MAR	Maranatha	VIN	Vineyard Music
BP	Beckenhorst Press	GS	G. Schirmer (Hal	MCF	McAfee Music Corp	WAL	Walton
BRB	Broude Brothers		Leonard)		(Warner)	WRD	Word Music
BRD	Broadman	HAL	Hal Leonard	MFS	Mark Foster	WT	WorshipTogether.com
BRN	Bourne	HIN	Hinshaw Music Co.	MSM	MorningStar Music		

Music for Worship Key

acc	accompaniment	tc	finger cymbals	ob	oboe	tba	tuba
bar	baritone	fl	flute	oct	octave	tbn	trombone
bng	bongos	glock	glockenspiel	opt	optional	tpt	trumpet
br	brass	gtr	guitar	orch	orchestra	timp	timpani
bsn	bassoon	hb	handbells	org	organ	trbl	treble
cant	cantor	hc	handchimes	perc	percussion	tri	triangle
ch	chimes	hp	harp	picc	piccolo	U	unison
cl	clarinet	hpd	harpsichord	pno	piano	UE	upper elementary
cont	continuo	hrn	horn	pt	part	vc	violoncello
cym	cymbal	inst	instrument	qnt	quintet	vcs	voices
DB	double or string	kybd	keyboard	qrt	quartet	vla	viola
	bass	LE	lower elementary	rec	recorder	vln	violin
dbl	double	M	medium	sax	saxophone	ww	woodwind
desc	descant	MH	medium high	sop	soprano	xyl	xylophone
div	divisi	ML	medium low	str	strings		
drm	drum	mxd	mixed	synth	synthesizer		
eng hrn	English horn	narr	narrator	tamb	tambourine		

Key to Hymn and Psalm Collections

* Indicates resources whose hymns are, at least in part, included in the online worship planning tool Sundays and Seasons.com.

BC   Borning Cry. Second ed. New Generation Publishers.

DH *   Dancing at the Harvest. Augsburg Fortress.

ELW *   Evangelical Lutheran Worship. Augsburg Fortress.

GC   Gather Comprehensive. GIA Publications.

GS2 *   Global Songs 2: Bread for the Journey. Augsburg Fortress.

H82   The Hymnal 1982 (Episcopal). The Church Pension Fund.

HFG   Hymns for the Gospels. GIA Publications.

LBW *   Lutheran Book of Worship. Augsburg Fortress.

LLC   Libro de Liturgia y Cántico. Augsburg Fortress.

LS *   LifeSongs. Augsburg Fortress.

LSB   Lutheran Service Book (Lutheran Church – Missouri Synod). Concordia Publishing House.

MBW   Moravian Book of Worship (Moravian Church in America). Interprovincial Board of Publications and Communications.

NCH   The New Century Hymnal (United Church of Christ). The Pilgrim Press.

OBS *   O Blessed Spring: Hymns of Susan Palo Cherwien. Augsburg Fortress.

RWSB *   Renewing Worship Songbook. Augsburg Fortress.

TFF *   This Far by Faith. Augsburg Fortress.

UMH   The United Methodist Hymnal. The United Methodist Publishing House.

W&P *   Worship & Praise. Augsburg Fortress.

WOV *   With One Voice. Augsburg Fortress.

A Note on Music Listings

Please note that some choral and instrumental music in the day listings may be out of print. We are unable to research whether musical pieces form other publishers are still available.

Why do we still list music if it is out of print? Primarily because many music planners may have that piece in their files, and can consider it for use. If a planner wishes to use a piece that has gone out of print, that may still be possible. For Augsburg Fortress resources, call 800/421-0239 or e-mail copyright@augsburgfortress.org to inquire about onetime reprint rights or to see whether a piece may be available by print on demand.

Selected Publishers

Arts Masters Studio, Inc.
Contact the Lorenz Corp.

Abingdon Press
201 Eighth Avenue South
PO Box 801
Nashville TN 37202-0801
800/251-3320 Customer Service
800/836-7802 Fax
www.abingdonpress.com

Alfred Publishing Co., Inc.
PO Box 10003
Van Nuys CA 91410-0003
818/892-2452
818/830-6252 Fax
www.alfred.com

American Lutheran Publicity Bureau
PO Box 327
Delhi NY 13753-0327
607/746-7511
www.alpb.org

Augsburg Fortress
PO Box 1209
Minneapolis MN 55440-1209
800/328-4648 Ordering
800/421-0239 Permissions
612/330-3300 General
www.augsburgfortress.org

Beckenhorst Press
PO Box 14273
Columbus OH 43214
614/451-6461 General
614/451-6627 Fax
www.beckenhorstpress.com

Brentwood-Benson Music
960 East Mark St.
Winona MN 55987
www.brentwood-benson.com

Broadman Holman Genevox
See LifeWay Christian Resources

Boosey & Hawkes, Inc
35 East 21st Street
New York NY 10010-6212
212/358-5300
212/358-5305 Fax
www.boosey.com

Changing Church Forum, Inc.
13901 Fairview Drive
Burnsville MN 55337
800/874-2044
952/435-8065 Fax
www.changingchurch.org

Chester Music
Contact Hal Leonard Corp.—Music Dispatch

Concordia Publishing House
3558 South Jefferson
Saint Louis MO 63118
800/325-3040 Customer Service
800/490-9889 Fax
www.cph.org

E.C. Schirmer Music Co.
138 Ipswich Street
Boston MA 02215-3534
617/236-1935 General
617/236-0261 Fax
www.ecspublishing.com

Dakota Road Music
29225 468th Avenue
Beresford SD 57004
605/957-2333
www.dakotaroadmusic.com

GIA Publications, Inc.
7404 South Mason Avenue
Chicago IL 60638
800/442-1358 General
708/496-3828 Fax
www.giamusic.com

Hinshaw Music, Inc.
PO Box 470
Chapel Hill NC 27514-0470
919/933-1691 General
919/967-3399 Fax
www.hinshawmusic.com

Hal Leonard Corp.
PO Box 13819
7777 West Bluemound Road
Milwaukee WI 53213
414/774-3630 General
414/774-3259 Fax
www.halleonard.com

Hope Publishing Co.
380 South Main Place
Carol Stream IL 60188
800/323-1049 General
630/665-2552 Fax
www.hopepublishing.com

Hosanna! Music
See Integrity Music

Integrity Music
1000 Cody Road
Mobile, AL 36695
800/533-6912 Customer Service
www.integritymusic.com
www.integritydirect.com

Kevin Mayhew Ltd.
Buxhall, Stowmarket
Suffolk IP14 3BW
England
01449-737978 General
01449-737834 Fax
sales@kevinmayhewltd.com

Lead Worship
P.O. Box 2101
Lindale TX 75771
903/882-5755
903/882-5059 Fax
www.leadworship.com

LifeWay Christian Resources
One LifeWay Plaza
Nashville TN 37234
800/251-3225 Broadman & Holman
800/884-7712 Genevox
customerservice@lifeway.com

The Liturgical Conference
PO Box 31
Evanston IL 60204
847/866-3875
www.liturgicalconference.org

The Liturgical Press
St. John's Abbey
PO Box 7500
Collegeville MN 56321-7500
800/858-5450 General
320/363-2213 General
320/363-3299 Fax
sales@litpress.org

Liturgy Training Publications
1800 North Hermitage Avenue
Chicago IL 60622-1101
800/933-4779 Customer Service
800/933-7094 Fax
orders@ltp.org

The Lorenz Corporation
501 East Third Street
Dayton OH 45402
800/444-1144 General
937/223-2042 Fax
www.lorenz.com

Ludwig Music Publishing Co.
557 East 140th Street
Cleveland OH 44110-1999
800/851-1150 General
216/851-1958 Fax
info@ludwigmusic.com

Maranatha!
PO Box 1077
Dana Point CA 92629
800/245-7664

MorningStar Music Publishers
1727 Larkin Williams Road
Fenton MO 63026
800/647-2117 Ordering
636/305-0121 Fax
morningstar@morningstarmusic.com

musicnotes.com
800/944-4667
www.musicnotes.com

New Creation Ministries
P.O. Box 80010
Broadmoor Postal Outlet
Sherwood Park AB T8A 5T4
Canada
info@new-creation.net
www.new-creation.net

Oregon Catholic Press
OCP Publications
PO Box 18030
Portland OR 97218-0030
800/548-8749 General
800/462-7329 Fax
liturgy@ocp.org

Oxford University Press
2001 Evans Road
Cary NC 27513
800/445-9714 Customer Service
919/677-1303 Fax
custserv@oup-usa.org

Praise Charts
Suite 123
#505-8840 210th St.
Langley BC V1M 2Y2
Canada
800/695-6293 Customer Service
www.praisecharts.com

Red River Music
316 Dublin
Tyler TX 75703
877/547-4837
903/839-0809 Fax

Selah Publishing Co.
PO Box 98066
Pittsburgh PA 15227
800/852-6172 Ordering
412/886-1022 Fax
www.selahpub.com

Shawnee Press
PO Box 690
49 Waring Drive
Delaware Water Gap PA 18327-1690
570/476-0550 General
570/476-5247 Fax
shawnee-info@shawneepress.com

Thankyou Music
26-28 Lottbridge Drive
Eastbourne BN23 6NT
UK
01440-1323437712
01440-1323411970 Fax
www.thankyoumusic.co.uk

Theodore Presser Co.
588 North Gulph Road
King of Prussia PA 19406
610/525-3636
610/527-7841 Fax
www.presser.com

Vineyard Music
12650 Directors Drive
Suite 500
Stafford TX 77477
281/565-8463
281/565-8467 Fax

Word Music Inc.
3319 West End Avenue
Suite 200
Nashville TN 37203
888/324-9673
888/324-4329 Fax
questions@wordmusic.com

WorshipTogether.com
101 Winners Circle
Brentwood TN 37027
888/711-0198
www.worshiptogether.com

About the Artist

This engaging art library was created by Julie Lonneman exclusively for Augsburg Fortress Publishers. In their simple humanity, these expressive images touch the heart with a fresh proclamation of the good news.

Cincinnati artist Julie Lonneman has employed her talents in service to the church since 1978, first as an art director and graphic designer, and currently as a freelance illustrator. She is the author of *Clip Art for Sundays and Solemnities*, published in 2003 by Liturgy Training Publications of Chicago. Her work has appeared in magazines such as *America*, *Sojourners*, *St. Anthony Messenger,* and *Weavings*, and graced the covers of many books and newsletters. Her work was featured in the 2006 *Calendar of Word and Season* published by Augsburg Fortress, and she contributed the frontispiece art for the "Lent and the Three Days" section of *Evangelical Lutheran Worship*.